SEMANTICS OF BELIEF CHANGE OPERATORS
FOR INTELLIGENT AGENTS:
ITERATION, POSTULATES, AND REALIZABILITY

Dissertations in Artificial Intelligence

Artificial Intelligence (AI) is one of the fastest growing research areas in computer science with a strong impact on various fields of science, industry, and society. This series publishes excellent doctoral dissertations in all sub-fields of AI, ranging from foundational work on AI methods and theories to application-oriented theses.

Editor-in-Chief:
Professor Dr. Ralph Bergmann
Department of Business Information Systems II, University of Trier,
54286 Trier, Germany

Volume 352

Previously published in this series:

ISSN 0941-5769 (print)
ISSN 2666-2175 (online)

Semantics of Belief Change Operators for Intelligent Agents: Iteration, Postulates, and Realizability

Kai Sauerwald

FernUniversität in Hagen, Germany

IOS Press

ISBN 978-3-89838-768-2 (AKA, print)
ISBN 978-1-64368-324-9 (IOS Press, print)
ISBN 978-1-64368-325-6 (IOS Press, online)
doi: 10.3233/DAI352

Bibliographic information available from the Katalog der Deutschen Nationalbibliothek (German National Library Catalogue) at https://www.dnb.de

Dissertation, approved by the Faculty of Mathematics and Computer Science, FernUniversität in Hagen
Date of the defense: 05.07.2022
1. Reviewer: Prof. Dr. Christoph Beierle
2. Reviewer: Prof. Dr. Gabriele Kern-Isberner

ORCID page of the author: https://orcid.org/0000-0002-1551-7016

Publisher
Akademische Verlagsgesellschaft AKA GmbH, Berlin

Represented by Co-Publisher IOS Press
IOS Press BV
Nieuwe Hemweg 6B
1013 BG Amsterdam
The Netherlands
Tel: +31 20 688 3355
Fax: +31 20 687 0019
email: order@iospress.nl

Preface

In Artificial Intelligence, a core problem is the modelling of human reasoning and intelligent behaviour, and the representation of knowledge and reasoning about it are of fundamental importance for this. In particular, the agent paradigma makes this observation evident. An intelligent agent must be able to built up a complete epistemic state from her knowledge and beliefs in order to reason plausibly, to draw inferences, and for planning her actions. Normally, an autonomous intelligent agent does not live in a static, but in a changing and dynamically evolving environment. Such an agent must adapt her beliefs and epistemic state to new information she receives. The theory of belief change deals with these kinds of changes, and Kai Sauerwald's dissertation addresses several important and significant research questions in belief change theory.

A fundamental result of revision theory is that plausibility orderings, given by total preorders over possible worlds, characterize belief revision. Kai Sauerwald analyzes this connection for general classical logics and characterizes precisely those conditions in which the relationship between total preorders and belief revision still holds. Moreover, he investigates a relaxation of the principle of minimal change for non-prioritized revision, yielding revision operators in complex epistemic settings where classical revision theory provides no operators. For iterated belief changes, Kai Sauerwald analyzes a whole landscape of different iteration principles for contraction. For each principle, he identifies characterizations from the viewpoint of changing plain beliefs, from the viewpoint of changing conditional beliefs, and from the viewpoint of changing plausibility orderings.

Throughout the whole thesis, Kai Sauerwald convincingly presents his ideas, refines and advances existing proposals of belief change, developes novel concepts and approaches, rigorously defines the introduced concepts, and formally proves all technical claims, propositions, and theorems. Given the numerous remarkable results to belief change theory, with his thesis, Kai Sauerwald significantly advances the state of the art in this field.

Hagen, August 2022   Christoph Beierle

Abstract

The ability to change their beliefs is a central characteristic of intelligent agents. In Knowledge Representation and Reasoning, the subarea of belief change deals with the different aspects of how an agent may change her beliefs. State-of-the-art belief change theory is rooted in the work by Alchourrón, Gärdenfors, and Makinson (AGM) which assumes that beliefs are given as statements of some underlying classical logic. The approach by AGM makes use of the underlying logic and considers mainly two kinds of belief changes: revision, the process of incorporation of new beliefs, while maintaining consistency, and contraction, the process of removal of beliefs, such that afterwards the removed belief can not be inferred. While the AGM approach is very successful, it has potential for further extensions and generalizations with respect to several aspects. This includes the generalizations to other logics and the conceptual expansion by relaxing some idealizations about how agents treat beliefs. Such extensions should be made to apply the theory of belief change in domains like intentional forgetting or cognitive logics.

We study AGM belief revision and AGM belief contraction from a semantic perspective. Due to Katsuno and Mendelzon, it is known that for propositional logic AGM belief revision and AGM belief contraction operators are characterized by total preorders over the interpretations assigned to belief states. The characterizations show that when the beliefs of the agent are changed according to new information, the posterior beliefs are characterized semantically as minimal elements (with respect to the new information) of the given total preorder that is assigned to the prior belief state.

This thesis provides four major contributions. Our first major contribution is a characterization of those logics for which the correspondence between AGM revision and total preorder holds, as in the result by Katsuno and Mendelzon for propositional logic. Moreover, we consider AGM revision in the Darwiche-Pearl framework for belief change over arbitrary sets of epistemic states. We demonstrate that for some sets of epistemic states no AGM revision operator exists, and, as our second major contribution, we characterize exactly those sets of epistemic states for which AGM revision operators do exist. Third, we introduce and characterize dynamic-limited revision operators, a relaxation of (non-prioritized) AGM revision operators that allows partial prioritization of the initial beliefs. We consider specifications for the acceptance behaviour of these belief change operators and characterize those specifications that are realizable by dynamic-limited revision operators. Moreover, we consider the iteration of AGM contraction in the Darwiche-Pearl framework in much detail and, as our fourth major contribution, we characterize several known and novel iteration postulates for contraction and show how these are related.

Zusammenfassung

Eine zentrale Eigenschaft intelligenter Agenten ist deren Fähigkeit, ihr Wissen anhand von neuen Informationen anzupassen. Im Kontext der Wissensrepräsentation und Künstlichen Intelligenz beschäftigt sich insbesondere das Forschungsgebiet der Wissensänderungen mit den verschiedenen Aspekten, wie ein Agent sein Wissen ändern kann. Aktuelle Forschung zur Wissensänderungen beruht auf den Arbeiten von Alchourrón, Gärdenfors und Makinson (AGM), die Wissen eines Agenten als Aussagen einer klassischen Logik verstehen. Der Ansatz von AGM nutzt die zugrundeliegende Logik und betrachtet hauptsächlich zwei Arten von Wissensänderungen: Die Revision, der Prozess der Aufnahme neuer Überzeugungen unter Beibehaltung der Konsistenz, und die Kontraktion, der Prozess der Entfernung von Wissen, so dass dieses nicht mehr abgeleitet werden kann. Die AGM-Theorie ist sehr erfolgreich und bietet Raum für Erweiterungen, zum Beispiel durch Ausweitung der Theorie auf andere Logiken oder durch abschwächen von Idealisierungen darüber, wie Agenten mit Wissen umgehen. Solche Erweiterungen sind auch hilfreich, um die Theorie der Wissensänderungen zum Beispiel in den Bereichen des intentionalen Vergessens und der kognitiven Logiken anzuwenden.

Wir betrachten AGM-Revision und AGM-Kontraktion aus einer semantischen Perspektive. Basierend auf der Arbeit von Katsuno und Mendelzon wurde gezeigt, dass in der Aussagenlogik sowohl AGM-Revision als auch AGM-Kontraktion zu totalen Präordnungen über Interpretationen korrespondieren. Danach ist das Ergebnis einer Wissensänderung semantisch charakterisiert durch die bezüglich der neuen Informationen minimalen Elemente der gegebenen totalen Präordnung.

Diese Arbeit liefert vier wichtige Beiträge zum Gebiet der Wissensänderungen. Der erster Beitrag ist eine Charakterisierung derjenigen Tarski-Logiken, für die die Korrespondenz zwischen AGM-Revision und totalen Präordnungen gilt, wie in der Charakterisierung von Katsuno und Mendelzon für propositionale Logik. Wir betrachten AGM-Revision ebenso im Darwiche-Pearl Framework und demonstrieren, dass es für gewisse Mengen epistemischer Zustände keine AGM-Revisionsoperatoren gibt. Der zweite Hauptbeitrag ist eine Charakterisierung genau derjenigen Mengen von epistemischen Zuständen, für die es AGM-Revisions-Operatoren gibt. Als dritten Beitrag führen wir dynamisch begrenzte Revision ein, die es erlaubt, das initiale Wissen eines Agenten partiell zu priorisieren. Wir betrachten Spezifikationen für das Akzeptanzverhalten von Operatoren und charakterisieren diejenigen Spezifikationen, die durch dynamisch begrenzte Revisions-Operatoren realisierbar sind. Außerdem betrachten wir die Iteration der AGM-Kontraktion im Darwiche-Pearl Framework. Unser vierter Beitrag ist die Charakterisierung von bekannten und neuen Iterations-Postulaten für die AGM-Kontraktion, und wie diese Postulate zusammenhängen.

Acknowledgements

The last couple of years were a joy for me due to the excellent working environment, and I want to thank everyone who was part of it.

First of all, Christoph Beierle, who was there for me as *Doktorvater* in the broadest sense over all these years. He always found the right words, had always the time for feedback, the time to discuss new ideas with me, and the time for carefully listening and pointing to the right literature or the right direction. I cannot say how much I learned from him about scientific writing, how to conduct and present research, and the values of carefulness and responsibility. He provided for me a platform for taking the detours I had to take and provided what it needed to give me the opportunity to head in new directions. This includes providing a productive research environment and writing that many papers together with me. Thank you, Christoph!

I want to thank Gabriele Kern-Isberner for introducing me to the area and community of belief change, the many exciting discussions and extensive explanations, the many papers we wrote together and for the always valuable feedback. Sebastian Rudolph and Faiq Miftakhul Falakh for inviting me to work together, the fascinating problems and the joint digging into the depths of logic. Again any time. My colleagues in Hagen, Steven Kutsch, Jonas Haldimann, and Martin van Berg for being so supportive and always having time for wonderful and insightful discussions, which were often the deal-breaker. Last but not least thank you for compensating my insufficient coffee-cooking skills. I like to thank all people from chair 1 at Dortmund, especially for the journal club meetings (including the food) and the great discussions. The folks from Freiburg, in particular, Marco Ragni and Hannah Dames; it was always fun to work with you all, and still today, I enjoy every meeting with you. I also want to thank the German Research Foundation (DFG) for funding me via the grants BE 1700/9-1 and BE 1700/10-1 awarded to Christoph Beierle. Moreover, I want to thank all from the DFG priority program 1921 "Intentional Forgetting in Organizations" and the belief change community for providing such a friendly and productive research environment, conferences and meetings.

Thanks to all my friends and my family – You all make every day of my life better, and I'm grateful for your understanding and support over the period I wrote this thesis. Special thanks go to Christine, Juliane, and Katharina for proofreading and the support during the writing period.

Contents

Part II. Non-Prioritized Revision over Epistemic States

Chapter 1

Introduction

This chapter presents the research context and overall motivation of this thesis. The organization of the thesis, the addressed research questions, and the main contributions of the thesis will be outlined. In the last section of this chapter, publications are presented that are related to this thesis, authored or co-authored by myself and that have already been published or are currently under review.

1.1. Motivation and Research Context

This thesis is located in the area of *Knowledge Representation and Reasoning*, a major subarea of Artificial Intelligence [128] that deals with the fundamental issue of how to represent and process symbolic knowledge and beliefs [34]. On the one hand, this research area is committed to the aspects of representations and reasoning of knowledge as a medium of human expression [42]; on the other hand, it deals with efficiency with respect to the size of representations and the ability to process the knowledge and beliefs efficient with respect to the representation. Knowledge Representation and Reasoning makes mainly use of logics as representation languages for knowledge and beliefs.

Research in Artificial Intelligence makes use of the idea of having an intelligent agent [128], which could be a human, an animal, an electronic, a mechanical [34], or a pure virtual system, or an organization. Agents are often confronted with a dynamic and evolving environment, and an important property of successful agents is the ability to adapt according to the changing environment. If a car is approaching an agent very fast, it could be beneficial to move out of the way. A spontaneous visit of a friend may require the adaption of the meal plan for the day. Computer networks adapt the routing tables when new hosts enter the network or a host is temporarily unavailable. When new insights about the environmental impact of an industry are available, a government may revoke the subsidies of this industry. Medical doctors may have to change therapeutical treatment because the patient shows a new serious symptom.

Treatment of changes in the world is an important aspect of agents, and thus, it is in the concern of Artificial Intelligence to understand the phenomenon of change to make these available for intelligent systems. Especially the ability to change their own *beliefs* according to new information is significant for intelligent agents, as, e.g, the change of beliefs is a precursor for behavioural change or initiation of new actions [35]. When new insights about the environmental impact of an industry are available, a precursor of a governmental revocation of subsidies is a change of mind about this industry. A medical doctor draws conclusions about the disease from new symptoms before she changes the therapeutical treatment.

Change of beliefs is a non-trivial task, as beliefs have extended meaning and do not only stand for their own. A red light is more than just a red light when it is emitted by a traffic signal. This semantic entanglement makes especially the withdrawal of beliefs difficult, as the process of contraction has to consider the semantic connections among beliefs. Changing beliefs sometimes involves performing non-trivial reorganizations of the beliefs of an agent. The reorganization of beliefs is actually a desirable operation for agents, as otherwise, the growing amount of information could make feasible reasoning impossible. In the digital society, humans, systems and organizations are confronted with a heavily increasing amount of information that creates a demand of techniques for *intentional forgetting* [21, 151], and from a theoretical point of view, forgetting can be viewed as a kind of belief change [16, 50]. Thus, research on belief change provides also foundations for approaches to intentional forgetting. The priority program SPP 1921 "Intentional Forgetting in Organizations"[1] of the German Research

---

[1]   www.spp1921.de

Foundation (*Deutsche Forschungsgemeinschaft*, DFG) provided an environment for developing this thesis.

Theory of Belief Change. The *theory of belief change* (often also just denoted as *belief dynamics* or *belief revision.*) is a subfield of Knowledge Representation and Reasoning that treats the question of how symbolic knowledge of an agent should and could evolve under given new information. Examples of early approaches to belief change are *truth maintenance systems* [47] and approaches from database theory [52, 51]. A precursor is also the indispensable work from philosophy, e.g., by Levi [102]. The root of today's most prominent approaches to belief change is the work by Alchourrón, Gärdenfors, and Makinson [2] (AGM), which captures the *principle of minimal change*, i.e., when new information arrives, then the process of belief change should change the prior beliefs of the agent as minimally as possible. Formally, the AGM approach models the change of beliefs operationally [64] by *belief change operators*. A set of prior beliefs of an agent is changed under a given new belief to the new posterior set of beliefs of the agent. The AGM theory acknowledges that they are *multiple* reasonable ways of changing the beliefs of an agent; families of belief change operators are the main object of the approach. AGM theory considers mainly two families of belief change operators. The first is *revision*, the process of incorporating new beliefs while maintaining consistency. The second is *contraction*, the process of removal of beliefs, such that afterwards the removed belief can not be inferred.

The AGM approach favours axiomatic descriptions of families of belief change operators. Research in belief change follows this tradition and considers new meaningful families of belief change operators at first axiomatically. Besides of that, a major objective of the research is about providing representation theorems and characterizations theorems that connect axiomatic descriptions with alternative viewpoints, e.g.:

Constructive Approaches using Subsets of the Initial Beliefs. In this research, families of belief change operators are identified with constructive approaches that yield the same results as operators of the family of belief change operators. Basic techniques are approaches based on the intersection of selected remainders [2],

which are maximal subsets of the initial beliefs that do not imply
the new beliefs, or based on the incision over kernels [75], which
are minimal subsets of the initial beliefs that do imply the new
belief. The former leads to partial meet contraction, the latter
to kernel contraction. An in-depth textbook on these subjects
is due to Hansson [73].

Semantic Approaches Employing Possible Worlds. These approaches
characterize belief change operators semantically by employing
semantic structures. An important concept for these approaches
is the idea of *possible worlds*, which stand for scenarios an agent
is able to imagine. Typically, possible worlds are identified with
the interpretations of the underling logic. System of spheres [67]
or relations over possible worlds [84] are typical formalisms used
in several approaches.

Extensions of the AGM Theory. The (AGM) theory of belief
change has been extended by various aspects and extended into various
directions that are not covered by the original approach by Alchourrón,
Gärdenfors, and Makinson [57]. This led to a rich body of research
on extensions and generalizations of the approach by AGM to deal
with different aspects of belief change [72, 56] or to apply them to
new domains [124]. Such extensions are also connected with applying
belief change in research approaches like intentional forgetting [16] or
cognitive logics [119, 129]. We consider briefly some research directions
that are relevant for this thesis:

Extension to other Logics. The original approach by AGM has been
designed with propositional logic in mind [76], implying in particular that the underlying logic is a monotonic logic that is closed
under standard connectives and satisfies compactness [61]. In a
very generic way, the relationship among the AGM postulates,
the construction of change operators from remainder sets and
kernels, and the underlying logic has been studied in-depth [124].
Semantic characterizations of AGM-like belief change in general
logics settings have been investigated by, e.g., Delgrande et al.
[43, 46] and Aiguier et al. [1]. More specific approaches are
dealing with specific logics like first-order logic [158], description
logics [118] or Horn-logic [45].

Treatment of Iterative Belief Change and Epistemic States. How
agents treat new information is influenced by previous expe-

riences. Priorly given information might influence how agents treat new beliefs. For instance, if it was just announced that some person is an active skydiver, it is more likely that an agent accepts that this person jumped from a skyscraper and survived. The original AGM approach does not constrain the process of iterated change. This has been widely criticized for being insufficient [32, 41, 126, 127]. In the context of research on iteration, it was demonstrated [41] that iteration processes require the usage of richer representations as beliefs states instead of the deductively closed sets of beliefs used in the AGM approach. This led to the Darwiche-Pearl framework [41], which does not make use of concrete beliefs states but instead makes use of an abstract notion of *epistemic states*.

Non-Prioritized Belief Change. How an intelligent agent deals with newly arriving information is a complex and subjective matter. For different agents, the same information has different meanings and importance. Symptoms of a patient could be an important sign for a medical doctor to identify the right treatment, while for a non-expert certain signs seem to be unimportant and get just ignored. Such a differentiated treatment of new beliefs is not covered by the original AGM approach, mainly because of the success condition associated with different kinds of belief change operations. Approaches that relax the success condition are denoted as *non-prioritized* belief changes [72], as they do not prioritize the success condition.

1.2. Research Questions and Contributions

The objective of this thesis is to advance the fundamental understanding of how the change of beliefs is related to the semantics of the underlying logic. Our investigations here are guided by the following motto:

Investigation of belief change through a careful extension of existing approaches, while keeping their original spirit.

The results in the thesis can be considered as contributions to three topics which we will consider in the following. We present four research questions for which this thesis provides novel contributions.

Semantics of AGM Revision in General Logics

We consider the semantics of AGM revision operators in general Tarskian logics. Tarskian logics are a large group of monotonic logics, which encompass many classical logics like first-order predicate logic, second-order predicate logic, propositional logic and description logics. Note that Tarskian logics not necessarily satisfy the AGM assumptions like compactness or closure under standard connectives [124]. In recent joint work [54], the family of all belief change operators that satisfy the AGM revision postulates over an arbitrary Tarskian logic has been semantically characterized. This characterization shows that each AGM revision operator over a Tarskian logic corresponds to a family of total relations (that satisfies further conditions). Surprisingly, our result on AGM revision in Tarskian logics differs from the well-established characterization of AGM revision in propositional logic by Katsuno and Mendelzon [84], which states that each AGM revision operator in propositional logics corresponds to a family of total preorders. The consequence of this difference is that several Tarskian logics have a different structure than propositional logic, such that some AGM revision operators do not correspond to a family of total preorders. We denote AGM revision operators that are representable by a family of total preorders as *total-preorder-representable*. This gives rise to the following research questions:

> *In which Tarskian logics is every AGM revision operator total-preorder-representable?*

Clearly, this question asks implicitly for the identification of a structural property of Tarskian logics where every AGM revision operator is total-preorder-representable. In the course of this thesis we will consider this question in detail.

The first major contribution of this thesis is the notion of *critical loop*, which is a structural property of a Tarskian logic that describes a situation where sets of statements can be arranged circularly. We will show that this is indeed the desired property in the following sense: every AGM revision operator of a Tarskian logic is total-preorder-representable if and only if this logic has no critical loop.

Relationship between Sets of Epistemic States, Non-Prioritized Revision and Acceptance

Today's most established approach for considering iterated belief change is the framework by Darwiche and Pearl [41]. In this framework, in order to abstract from concrete representations, it is assumed that belief change happens on an abstract set of epistemic states. This abstraction leads to infinitely many possible instantiations of the framework, each given by choosing a particular set of epistemic states. In the first place, this could be understood as a formalization mistake – an abstraction into arbitrariness. However, we propose to understand this variability as a means that expresses the heterogeneity of "epistemic capabilities" of different agents, and that the consequences of different choices of the set of epistemic states deserve exploration.

The choice of the set of epistemic states explicitly highlights a dimension of belief change operators. In the Darwiche-Pearl framework, belief change operators are functions that map an epistemic state and new information to another epistemic state. Consequently, when considering a certain set of postulates, e.g. the AGM revision postulates, then for each set of epistemic states $\mathcal{E}$ there is a unique family of belief change operators for $\mathcal{E}$ that satisfies the postulates.

We consider several aspects in this thesis that deal with the choice of the set of epistemic states. A main question we consider is the following one:

> *What are the requirements for a set of epistemic states $\mathcal{E}$ such that a belief change operator for $\mathcal{E}$ of a certain type exists?*

The second major contribution of this thesis is to answer this question for AGM revision operators and AGM contraction operators. Beyond that, we extend our investigation to non-prioritized revision operators. More specifically, we take inspiration from *credibility-limited revision* [77], which distinguishes between beliefs that are credible and those that are not credible. If new information α arrives that is credible, then the belief of the agent is revised by α; if α is not credible, then α is neglected (and the beliefs of the agent are not altered). In the first case, we say that α got *accepted for revision*.

For our research, we assume that real agents show a wide variety of different patterns of acceptance for revision. Our investigations demonstrate that for several patterns of acceptance for revision and for several sets of epistemic states no credibility-limited revision operator in the Darwiche-Pearl framework [27] exists. This leads to the goal of identifying a generalization of credibility-limited revision that deals with various patterns of acceptance for revision:

> *Which generalization of credibility-limited revision operators is able to reproduce arbitrary patterns of the acceptance for revision for arbitrary sets of epistemic states, while keeping the original spirit of credibility-limited revision?*

We will identify that one reason for the failure of credibility-limited revision is that credibility-limited revision prioritizes the initial beliefs of an agent. Next, we discuss postulates that allow partial prioritization of the initial beliefs, which is different from how credibility-limited revision and AGM revision operators treat initial beliefs.

As the third main contribution of this thesis, we introduce the family of *dynamic-limited revision operators* for epistemic states. Our characterization shows that dynamic-limited revision operators are (roughly) characterized by families of sets of total preorders over subsets of the interpretations of the underlying logic.

Principles for Iterated Contraction

Iteration of AGM contraction is the third realm on which this thesis provides contributions. Principles for the iteration of AGM revision are a well-studied topic in belief change [56]. The situation is different for AGM contraction, as there is a much smaller body of literature specially devoted to the topic of principles for iterated contraction [81, 40, 111, 98, 122]. Our investigations on iterated contraction take inspiration from research on iterated revision and provide counterparts for contraction to principles for iterated revision.

> *What are natural analogues for contraction to iteration principles for revision?*

Our main source of inspiration are the principles by Darwiche and

Pearl [41] for revision. Contraction analogues for the Darwiche-Pearl postulates are object of multiple investigations [111, 98, 122].

Our fourth main contribution are several new postulates for iterated contraction and the coherent picture we provide overall these principles of iterated contraction. In particular, for all considered contraction principles we provide corresponding postulates from the viewpoint of changing beliefs, from the viewpoint of changing conditional beliefs, and from the viewpoint of changing relations over possible worlds. Especially the description of how conditional beliefs are affected by contraction counterparts of the Darwiche-Pearl postulates is a novelty. We consider further revision-inspired principles for iteration of contraction given by Nayak et al. [112, 111, 123]. As another novelty, we consider contraction analogues for the independence principle for revision [82].

1.3. Organization of the Thesis

This work is divided into 12 chapters, where some chapters depend on other chapters. The overall outline of the thesis is illustrated in Figure 1.1; the arrows in Figure 1.1 represent the dependencies among the chapters.

This thesis starts with presenting the preliminaries and giving a basic introduction to the area of belief change. The preliminaries are presented in Chapter 2 and provide the mathematical notion used in this thesis and give an introduction to propositional logic. In Chapter 3, we introduce the postulates for revision and contraction as given by Alchourrón, Gärdenfors, and Makinson [2] (AGM). Furthermore, we consider the semantic characterizations of AGM revision by Katsuno and Mendelzon [84] for propositional logic and the characterizations of AGM contraction by Caridroit, Konieczny, and Marquis [38] for propositional logic.

The main body of this thesis is organized into three parts. Every part starts with an introduction and an overview of the content of the part.

Part I. This part considers AGM revision for Tarskian logics and consists of Chapter 4 and Chapter 5. The notion of critical loop is introduced in this part, which is the first major contributions of this thesis. Chapter 4 gives an introduction to Tarskian logics and the notion of a *base logic*. We present a semantic characterization of AGM revision, given in recent joint work with Faiq Miftakhul Falakh and Sebastian Rudolph [54], that shows that each AGM revision operators corresponds to a family of total relations. Chapter 5 introduces the notion of *critical loop*. In the course of Chapter 5 we show that for a Tarskian logic, the existence of a critical loop is one and only cause for the existence of an AGM revision operator that is not total-preorder-representable.

Part II. This part considers (non-prioritized) revision operators for epistemic states. Chapter 6 introduces the Darwiche-Pearl framework and AGM revision operators for epistemic states. We characterize the relation between sets of epistemic states and the existence of AGM revision operators for sets of epistemic states, which we consider as the second main contribution of this thesis. Chapter 7 introduces the problem of acceptance of revision. We introduce credibility-limited revision operators for epistemic states as given by Booth et al. [27] in a slightly generalized version that can deal with inconsistent beliefs. We describe those sets of epistemic states for which generalized credibility-limited revision operators exist. Moreover, we characterize those patterns of acceptance for revision that are realizable by generalized credibility-limited revision operators. In Chapter 8 we introduce dynamic-limited revision operators, the third main contribution of this thesis. We characterize dynamic-limited revision operators semantically and consider the postulates of dynamic-limited revision operators in detail. The remaining parts of Chapter 8 investigate properties of dynamic-limited revision operators. In particular, we characterize those patterns of acceptance for revision that are realizable by dynamic-limited revision operators.

Part III. This part provides the fourth main contribution of this work: we consider and characterize several old and novel iteration principles for AGM contraction and provide a coherent picture thereof. Chapter 9 recalls the Darwiche-Pearl framework and introduces AGM contraction operators for epistemic states. We characterize the relation between sets of epistemic states and the existence of AGM contraction operators for sets of epistemic states. Moreover, we introduce contractionals, special conditionals proposed by Bochman [24]

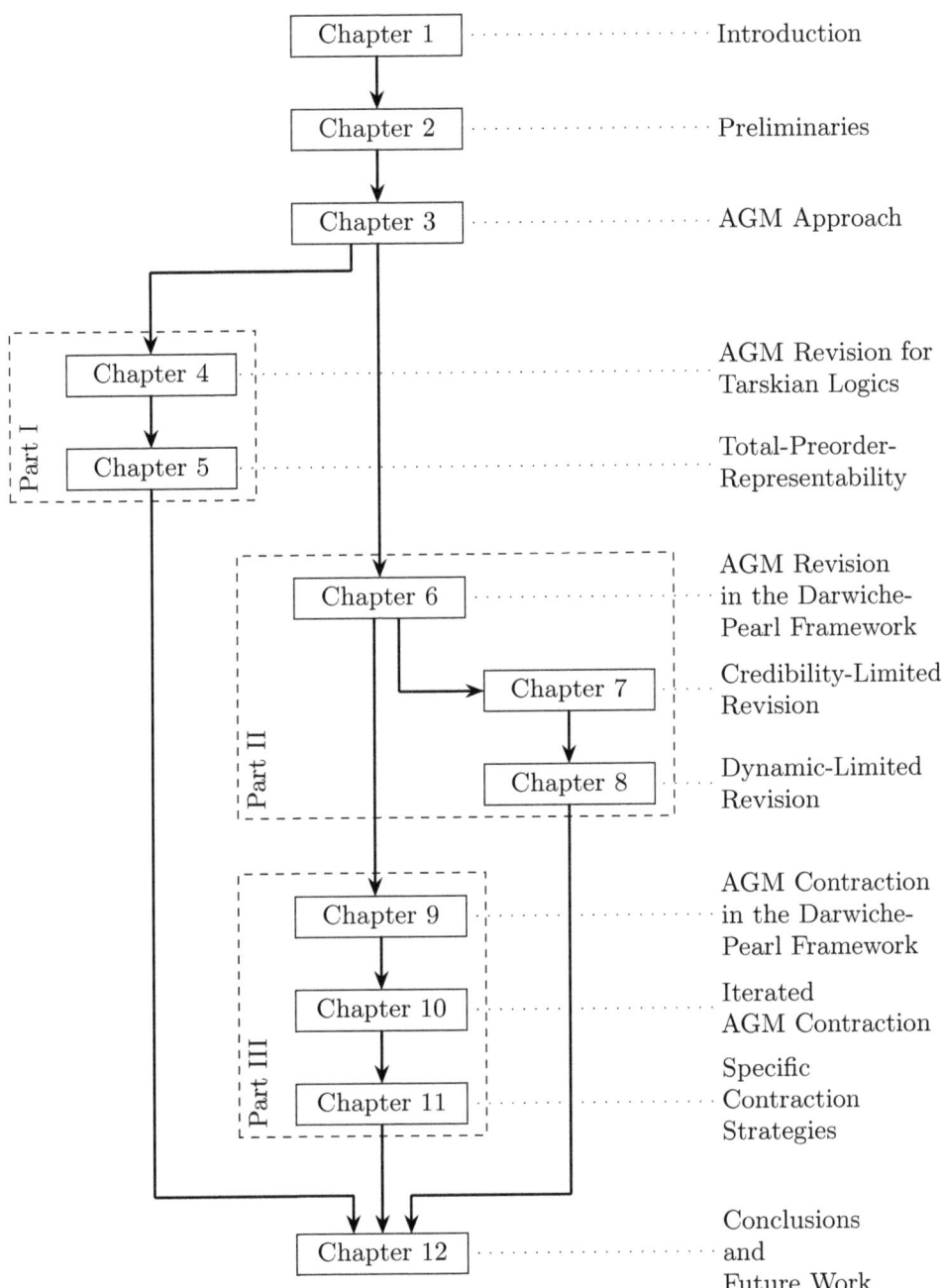

Figure 1.1: Organization of the thesis.

that encode contraction operators. In Chapter 10 several iteration principles for contraction are considered in detail which are inspired by iteration principles for contraction from Darwiche and Pearl [41]. We characterize iteration principles by postulates having the viewpoint of change of beliefs, the viewpoint of change of conditional beliefs, and the viewpoint of changing relations over possible worlds. Chapter 11 considered specific strategies for contraction. We characterize these strategies by postulates having the viewpoint of change of beliefs, change of conditional beliefs, and change of relations over possible worlds. Finally, we present a map of relationships among different principles for contraction.

This thesis closes with conclusions and discussion of future work in Chapter 12.

1.4. Previous Publications

During the last five years, the period when this thesis was written, I was involved in multiple research activities and worked jointly together with various colleagues. This includes participation in two research projects, the project

> Intentional Forgetting Through Cognitive-Computational Methods of Priorization, Knowledge Compression and Contraction (FADE),

and the project

> Intentional Forgetting and Changes in Work Processes: A Process-Conditional Approach in the Administrative and IT Context (FADEp).

Both are funded by the German Research Foundation (Deutsche Forschungsgemeinschaft, DFG) as part of the priority program 1921 "Intentional Forgetting in Organizations". I gratefully acknowledge the financial support by the DFG grants BE 1700/9-1 and BE 1700/10-1, both awarded to Christoph Beierle.

In the context of these research activities, I authored multiple publications jointly with colleagues.

1.4.1. Publications Containing Results of this Thesis

In the following, I give an overview of those previous publications that contain results also presented in this thesis and point out what are my contributions to these publications.

Part I. Together with Faiq Miftakhul Falakh and Sebastian Rudolph, I investigated AGM revision in Tarskian logics, leading to the publication

> [54] Faiq Miftakhul Falakh, Sebastian Rudolph, and Kai Sauerwald. *Semantic Characterizations of General Belief Base Revision.* A preprint is available, 62 pp., arXiv: 2104.14512. Submitted for publication (2021),

which is now submitted for publication to a journal. A preliminary report of this joint work was published as

> [53] Faiq Miftakhul Falakh, Sebastian Rudolph, and Kai Sauerwald. "A Katsuno-Mendelzon-Style Characterization of AGM Belief Base Revision for Arbitrary Monotonic Logics (Preliminary Report)". In: *Proceedings of the 7th Workshop on Formal and Cognitive Reasoning (FCR 2021) co-located with the 44th German Conference on Artificial Intelligence (KI 2021)*. Ed. by Christoph Beierle, Marco Ragni, Frieder Stolzenburg, and Matthias Thimm. Vol. 2961. CEUR Workshop Proceedings. CEUR-WS.org, 2021, pp. 48–59.

The framework of base change operators presented in Chapter 4 was developed in this joint work. My specific contribution to all those results of Chapter 4 that are also presented in [54] was to provide expertise in the field of belief change, propose enhancements and provide support in developing the ideas and the proofs. For all those results of Chapter 5 that are also presented in [54], excluding Table 5.1, I developed, in particular, the notions introduced there, e.g., critical loop, and conceptualized and conducted the proofs of the propositions.

Part II. Together with Christoph Beierle and Gabriele Kern-Isberner, I investigated non-prioritized revision, leading to the following published draft:

> [138] Kai Sauerwald, Gabriele Kern-Isberner, and Christoph Beierle. "On Limited Non-Prioritised Belief Revision Operators with Dynamic Scope". In: *CoRR* abs/2108.07769 (2021). arXiv: 2108.07769.

I developed the concept and the outline of the paper [138]. Furthermore, my contributions to [138] encompass also the draft and design of the postulates, propositions and theorems, and the draft, design and elaboration of the proofs for the propositions and theorems given in this paper. Part II contains results and texts that were also presented in [138].

Part III. Together with Christoph Beierle and Gabriele Kern-Isberner, I investigated iteration principles for AGM contraction, leading to the publication

> [136] Kai Sauerwald, Gabriele Kern-Isberner, and Christoph Beierle. "A Conditional Perspective for Iterated Belief Contraction". In: *Proceedings of the 24nd European Conference on Artificial Intelligence (ECAI 2020)*. Ed. by Giuseppe De Giacomo, Alejandro Catalá, Bistra Dilkina, Michela Milano, Senén Barro, Alberto Bugarín, and Jérôme Lang. IOS Press, 2020, pp. 889–896.

A largely extended version of this conference paper is now submitted for publication to a journal, a preprint is available:

> [137] Kai Sauerwald, Gabriele Kern-Isberner, and Christoph Beierle. *A Conditional Perspective on the Logic of Iterated Belief Contraction.* A preprint is available, 37 pp., arXiv: 2202.03196. Submitted for publication (2022),

I developed the concept and the outline of the papers [136] and [137]. Furthermore, my contributions to [136, 137] encompass also the draft and design of the postulates, propositions and theorems, and the draft, design and elaboration of the proofs for the propositions and theorems given in these papers. Part III contains results and texts that were also presented in [136] and [137].

1.4.2. Further Publications

Besides of publications mentioned in the previous section, I authored and co-authored several publications on research topics related to the results given in this thesis. In the following these publications are listed and ordered by topic. Working on these publications had an indirect influence on this thesis — the discussions with my co-authors gave me the inspiration to investigate certain topics considered in this thesis.

Decrement Operators. AGM contraction is very drastic in the sense that it directly discards any belief presented for contraction. Real agents however sometimes show a more cautious behaviour and might withdraw a belief only if multiple occasions give reason to discard a belief. Jointly with Christoph Beierle, I developed *decrement operators* as a gradual approach of (non-prioritized) contraction. Decrementation is the process of (potentially) gradually decreasing the plausibility of a belief. The axiomatization and the overall approach is inspired by *improvement operators* [97], and decrement operators could be understood as a natural counter-part to improvement operators. Our joint research has been published as follows:

> [130] Kai Sauerwald and Christoph Beierle. "Decrement Operators in Belief Change". In: *Proceedings of the 15th European Conference Symbolic and Quantitative Approaches to Reasoning with Uncertainty (ECSQARU 2019)*. Ed. by Gabriele Kern-Isberner and Zoran Ognjanovic. Vol. 11726. Lecture Notes in Computer Science. Springer, 2019, pp. 251–262,

The Principle of Conditional Preservation. The *principle of conditional preservation* from Kern-Isberner [87] is a powerful change paradigm that implies several well-established principles for iterated belief change, e.g., the Darwiche and Pearl postulates (see Section 10.1) or iteration postulates for contraction [92] (see Chapter 10). At the same time, the principle of conditional preservation is agnostic about the specific form of change. In joint work, we make use of this principle for different approaches to belief change and reasoning.

Iterated Contraction and the Principle of Conditional Preservation. In joint work with Gabriele Kern-Isberner, Tanja Bock and Christoph Beierle, we showed that several principles for iterated contraction, e.g., those mentioned in Theorem 10.23, are satisfied when the principle of conditional preservation holds:

> [92] Gabriele Kern-Isberner, Tanja Bock, Kai Sauerwald, and Christoph Beierle. "Iterated contraction of propositions and conditionals under the principle of conditional preservation". In: *Proceedings of the 3rd Global Conference on Artificial Intelligence (GCAI 2017)*. Ed. by Christoph Benzmüller, Christine Lisetti, and Martin Theobald. Vol. 50. EPiC Series in Computing. EasyChair, 2017, pp. 78–92

Conditional Descriptor Revision. Belief change in the AGM approach focuses on postulates for specific kinds of belief changes like revision and contraction. Hansson introduced *descriptor revision* as a framework that addresses belief change in a uniform way [74, 78]. The central means in this framework are *descriptors*, which are truth-functional connections of statements of the form $\mathfrak{B}\varphi$. A descriptor is meant to describe the success condition of a change on a belief representation, i.e., $\mathfrak{B}\varphi$ has the intended meaning that φ should be believed after the change.

In joint work with Jonas Haldimann, Martin van Berg, Christoph Beierle and Gabriele Kern-Isberner, I connected descriptor revision with the principle of conditional preservation to *conditional descriptor revision*. The approach uses ranking functions by Spohn [146] as belief representations (see Chapter 6). Conditional descriptor revision can be characterized by a constraint satisfaction problem. This joint research led to several joint publications:

[133] Kai Sauerwald, Jonas Haldimann, Martin von Berg, and Christoph Beierle. "Descriptor Revision for Conditionals: Literal Descriptors and Conditional Preservation". In: *Proceedings of the 43rd German Conference on Artificial Intelligence (KI 2020)*. Ed. by Ute Schmid, Franziska Klügl, and Diedrich Wolter. Vol. 12325. Lecture Notes in Computer Science. Springer, 2020, pp. 204–218

[68] Joans Haldimann, Kai Sauerwald, Martin von Berg, Gabriele Kern-Isberner, and Christoph Beierle. "Towards a Framework of Hansson's Descriptor Revision for Conditionals". In: *Proceedings of the 36th ACM/SIGAPP Symposium on Applied Computing (SAC 2021)*. Ed. by Chih-Cheng Hung, Jiman Hong, Alessio Bechini, and Eunjee Song. New York, NY, USA: ACM, 2021, pp. 889–891

[69] Jonas Haldimann, Kai Sauerwald, Martin von Berg, Gabriele Kern-Isberner, and Christoph Beierle. "Conditional Descriptor Revision and Its Modelling by a CSP". in: *Proceedings of the 17th European Conference on Logics in Artificial Intelligence (JELIA 2021)*. Ed. by Wolfgang Faber, Gerhard Friedrich, Martin Gebser, and Michael Morak. Vol. 12678. Lecture Notes in Computer Science. Springer, 2021, pp. 35–49

C-Inference. Employing the *principle of conditional preservation* led to the concept of *c-representations*, and model-based inference induced by single c-representations [87, 86]. C-Inference as the skeptical inference taking all c-representations into account was introduced by Beierle, Eichhorn, Kern-Isberner, and Kutsch [10, 12]. Further inference relations based on c-representations have been developed [13, 18, 17, 100, 11]. In joint work with Christoph Beierle and Steven Kutsch, we considered compilation to optimize querying answering for c-inference relations:

[19] Christoph Beierle, Steven Kutsch, and Kai Sauerwald. "Compilation of Conditional Knowledge Bases for Computing C-Inference Relations". In: *Foundations of Information and Knowledge Systems - 10th International Symposium (FoIKS 2018)*. Ed. by Flavio Ferrarotti and Stefan Woltran. Vol. 10833. Lecture Notes in Computer Science. Springer, 2018, pp. 34–54

[20] Christoph Beierle, Steven Kutsch, and Kai Sauerwald. "Compilation of static and evolving conditional knowledge bases for computing induced nonmonotonic inference relations". In: *Annals of Mathematics and Artificial Intelligence* 87.1-2 (2019), pp. 5–41

Computational Universality of Belief Change over Epistemic States. The computational complexity for particular problems for belief revision operators over epistemic states was investigated for specific setups [105, 140]; however, investigations on the general computability are missing. Together with Christoph Beierle, I closed this gap and demonstrated that iterated belief change (and especially belief revision) is Turing complete. The behaviour of a Turing machines can be encoded in a belief change operator. A construction is presented which makes use of ranking functions, where certain ranking functions represent configurations of a Turing machine. Our result holds even, for instance, when the Darwiche and Pearl postulates are required to hold. This work will be published as follows:

[131] Kai Sauerwald and Christoph Beierle. "Iterated Belief Change, Computationally". In: *Proceedings of the 19th International Conference on Principles of Knowledge Representation and Reasoning (KR 2022)*. Ed. by Gabriele Kern-Isberner and Thomas Meyer. 2022. To appear

Forgetting in KR. So far forgetting has been considered mainly as *variable elimination* or as removal of syntactic elements [106] in Knowledge Representation and Reasoning (see Eiter and Kern-Isberner [50] or Delgrande [44] for a summary). Together with Christoph Beierle, Tanja Bock, Hanna Dames, Diana Howey, Gabriele Kern-Isberner, Marco Ragni and others, we worked on a more common sense understanding and formalization of forgetting. We developed an ontology of different types of forgetting operators, and analysed instantiations of this approach. This led to several publications:

[151] Ingo J. Timm et al. "Intentional Forgetting in Artificial Intelligence Systems: Perspectives and Challenges". In: *Proceedings of the 41st German Conference on Artificial Intelligence (KI 2018)*. Ed. by Frank Trollmann and Anni-Yasmin Turhan. 2018, pp. 357–365

[9] Christoph Beierle, Tanja Bock, Gabriele Kern-Isberner, Marco Ragni, and Kai Sauerwald. "Kinds and Aspects of Forgetting in Common-Sense Knowledge and Belief Management". In: *Proceedings of the 41st German Conference on Artificial Intelligence (KI 2018)*. Ed. by Frank Trollmann and Anni-Yasmin Turhan. 2018, pp. 366–373

[91] Gabriele Kern-Isberner, Tanja Bock, Kai Sauerwald, and Christoph Beierle. "Belief Change Properties of Forgetting Operations over Ranking Functions". In: *Proceedings of the 16th Pacific Rim International Conference on Artificial Intelligence (PRICAI 2019)*. Ed. by Abhaya C. Nayak and Alok Sharma. 2019, pp. 459–472

[90] Gabriele Kern-Isberner, Tanja Bock, Christoph Beierle, and Kai Sauerwald. "Axiomatic Evaluation of Epistemic Forgetting Operators". In: *Proceedings of the 32nd International Florida Artificial Intelligence Research Society Conference (FLAIRS-32)*. Ed. by Roman Barták and Keith W. Brawner. 2019, pp. 470–475

[16] Christoph Beierle, Gabriele Kern-Isberner, Kai Sauerwald, Tanja Bock, and Marco Ragni. "Towards a General Framework for Kinds of Forgetting in Common-Sense Belief Management". In: *Künstliche Intelligenz* 33.1 (2019), pp. 57–68

[129] Kai Sauerwald. "Modelling the dynamics of forgetting and remembering by a system of belief changes: student research abstract". In: *Proceedings of the 34th ACM/SIGAPP Symposium on Applied Computing (SAC 2019)*. Ed. by Chih-Cheng Hung and George A. Papadopoulos. ACM, 2019, pp. 1168–1171

[8] Alexander Becker, Gabriele Kern-Isberner, Kai Sauerwald, and Christoph Beierle. "Forgetting Formulas and Signature Elements in Epistemic States". In: *Proceedings of the 19th International Workshop on Non-Monotonic Reasoning (NMR 2021)*. Ed. by Leila Amgoud and Richard Booth. 2021, pp. 233–242

Implementation of Iterative Belief Change Operators. Together with Jonas Haldimann, Philip Heltweg and Christoph Beierle, I developed and implemented tools for the execution of iterative belief change operators and for checking of satisfaction of postulates. Work on this subject has been published as follows:

[132] Kai Sauerwald and Jonas Haldimann. "WHIWAP: Checking Iterative Belief Changes". In: *Proceedings of the 8th Workshop on Dynamics of Knowledge and Belief (DKB-2019) and the 7th Workshop KI & Kognition (KIK-2019) co-located with the 42rd German Conference*

on Artificial Intelligence (KI 2019). Ed. by Christoph Beierle, Marco Ragni, Frieder Stolzenburg, and Matthias Thimm. Vol. 2445. CEUR Workshop Proceedings. CEUR-WS.org, 2019, pp. 14–23

[134] Kai Sauerwald and Philip Heltweg. "On Using Model Checking for the Certification of Iterated Belief Changes". In: *Proceedings of the 7th Workshop on Formal and Cognitive Reasoning (FCR 2021) co-located with the 44th German Conference on Artificial Intelligence (KI 2021).* Ed. by Christoph Beierle, Marco Ragni, Frieder Stolzenburg, and Matthias Thimm. Vol. 2961. CEUR Workshop Proceedings. CEUR-WS.org, 2021, pp. 23–33

[135] Kai Sauerwald, Philip Heltweg, and Christoph Beierle. "Certification of Iterated Belief Changes via Model Checking and its Implementation". In: *Proceedings of the 19th International Workshop on Non-Monotonic Reasoning (NMR 2021).* Ed. by Leila Amgoud and Richard Booth. 2021, pp. 250–253

Cognitive Aspects. Jointly with colleagues, we considered cognitive aspects of Knowledge Representation and Reasoning (see also the work on forgetting in KR).

Cognitive Logics. Humans are highly successful agents with excellent capabilities to deal with knowledge and beliefs. The cognitive logics approach aims at bringing together logics from Artificial Intelligence and cognitive theories and cognitive models of human reasoning for the mutual benefit of both areas[2]. We presented ideas related to cognitive logics to a broader audience in several talks[2] and in the following publication:

[119] Marco Ragni, Gabriele Kern-Isberner, Christoph Beierle, and Kai Sauerwald. "Cognitive Logics - Features, Formalisms, and Challenges". In: *Proceedings of the 24nd European Conference on Artificial Intelligence (ECAI 2020).* Ed. by Giuseppe De Giacomo, Alejandro Catalá, Bistra Dilkina, Michela Milano, Senén Barro, Alberto Bugarín, and Jérôme Lang. Vol. 325. Frontiers in Artificial Intelligence and Applications. IOS Press, 2020, pp. 2931–2932

Cognitive Architectures. Cognitive architectures are a means of cognitive psychology to represent knowledge on how humans process information principally. Many cognitive architectures are software platforms in which cognitive psychologists can program models. In joint work with Marco Ragni, Tanja Bock, Gabriele Kern-Isberner,

---

[2]   www.cognitive-logics.org

Paulina Friemann, and Christoph Beierle I worked on a common formal framework that captures the features of human-like computations
which many cognitive architectures like ACT-R [4] and SOAR [101]
have in common. This led to the following publication:

[120] Marco Ragni, Kai Sauerwald, Tanja Bock, Gabriele Kern-Isberner,
Paulina Friemann, and Christoph Beierle. "Towards a Formal Founda-
tion of Cognitive Architectures". In: *Proceedings of the 40th Annual
Meeting of the Cognitive Science Society (CogSci 2018)*. Ed. by Chuck
Kalish, Martina A. Rau, Xiaojin (Jerry) Zhu, and Timothy T. Rogers.
2018

In joint work with Marco Wilhelm, Diana Howey, Gabriele Kern-
Isberner, and Christoph Beierle, we combined ideas from the cognitive
architecture ACT-R with focussed inference by Marco Wilhelm and
Gabriele Kern-Isberner [155]. This led to the following publications:

[153] Marco Wilhelm, Diana Howey, Gabriele Kern-Isberner, Kai Sauerwald, and Christoph Beierle. "A Brief Introduction Into Activation-
Based Conditional Inference". In: *Proceedings of the 7th Workshop
on Formal and Cognitive Reasoning (FCR 2021) co-located with the
44th German Conference on Artificial Intelligence (KI 2021)*. Ed. by
Christoph Beierle, Marco Ragni, Frieder Stolzenburg, and Matthias
Thimm. Vol. 2961. CEUR Workshop Proceedings. CEUR-WS.org,
2021, pp. 4–8

[154] Marco Wilhelm, Diana Howey, Gabriele Kern-Isberner, Kai Sauer-
wald, and Christoph Beierle. "Integrating Cognitive Principles From
ACT-R Into Probabilistic Conditional Reasoning by Taking the Ex-
ample of Maximum Entropy Reasoning". In: *Proceedings of the 35th
International Florida Artificial Intelligence Research Society Conference
(FLAIRS-35)*. 2022. To appear

Chapter 2

Preliminaries and Propositional Logic

In this chapter, we introduce the basic notions used in this thesis.

Set Theory and Numbers. We rely on the basic set theory. With $X \times Y$ we denote the Cartesian product of two sets X and Y, likewise we use $X \cup Y$ for the union of X and Y, and $X \cap Y$ for intersection of X and Y, and $X \setminus Y$ for set difference of Y to X. With $\subseteq$ we denote the subset relation (including equality) and with $\subsetneq$ we denote the strict subset relation. $\mathcal{P}(X)$ denotes the power set of X, i.e., the set of all subsets of X, and $\mathcal{P}_{\text{fin}}(X)$ denotes the set of all finite subsets of X. With $\mathbb{N} = \{1, 2, 3, \dots\}$ we denote all natural numbers and with $\mathbb{N}_0 = \mathbb{N} \cup \{0\}$ we denote all natural numbers with zero.

Notions from Order Theory. Let X be a set and let $R \subseteq X \times X$ be a binary relation on X (or over X). We write binary relations as usually infix. In the following we define several properties for R:

for all $a \in X$	$a \, R \, a$	(Reflexivity)
for all $a, b \in X$	not $a \, R \, b$	(Irreflexivity)
for all $a, b \in X$	$a \, R \, b$ or $b \, R \, a$	(Totality)
for all $a, b \in X$	$a \, R \, b$ and $b \, R \, c$ implies aRc	(Transitivity)
for all $a, b \in X$	$a \, R \, b$ and $b \, R \, a$ implies $a = b$	(Antisymmetry)
for all $a, b \in X$	$a \, R \, b$ if and only if $b \, R \, a$	(Symmetry)
for all $a, b, c \in X$	$a \, R \, b$ implies $c \, R \, a$ or $b \, R \, c$	(Modularity)

The relation R is called a *partial order* over X if R is reflexive, antisymmetric and transitive. We say R is a *linear order* over X if R is a total partial order. Moreover, we say the relation R is a *preorder* over X if R is reflexive and transitive. The *strict part* of R is the relation $R \setminus \{(a, b) \in R \mid a\,R\,b$ and $b\,R\,a\}$, i.e., all pairs of R that not equivalent according to R, and the *equivalent part* of R is the relation $\{(a, b) \in R \mid a\,R\,b$ and $b\,R\,a\}$, i.e., all pairs of R that equivalent according to R. For an element $x \in X$ we say x is minimal with respect to R if there exists no $y \in X$ such that $y\,R\,x$. For a subset $X' \subseteq X$ let $\min(X', R)$ denote the minimal elements of X' with respect to R, i.e.:

$$\min(X', R) = \{x \in X' \mid \text{there is no } y \in X' \text{ with } y\,R\,x\}$$

If X' is not a subset of X, then let $\min(X', R)$ denote the set $\min(X' \cap X, R)$. Especially *total preorders* will occur in multiple situations in this thesis, and we will make use of the following property of total preorders.

Lemma 2.1. *Let R be a total preorder over a set X. For each $A, B \subseteq X$ it holds:*

$$\min(A \cup B, R) = \begin{cases} \min(A, R) & or \\ \min(B, R) & or \\ \min(A, R) \cup \min(B, R) \end{cases}$$

Proof. Let $x_1, x_2 \in \min(X, R)$. By totality of the order R, we have $x_1\,R\,x_2$. Observe now that by transitivity of the order R, we have $x_1 \in \min(X \cup Y, R)$ if and only if $x_2 \in \min(X \cup Y, R)$. This implies the claim. $\square$

Functions as Relations. Moreover, we will deal with functions, which are, as usual, special relations. Consider the following properties for a relation $f \subseteq X \times Y$ over sets X and Y:

$$\text{for all } a \in X \text{ exists } b \in Y \text{ with } afb \qquad \text{(Left-total)}$$
$$afb \text{ and } afc \text{ implies } b = c \qquad \text{(Right-unqiue)}$$

A relation $f \subseteq X \times Y$ over sets X and Y is called a *function* if f is *left-total* and *right-unique*. For a function f we denote for every $a \in X$ with $f(a)$ the unique element $b \in Y$ with $(a, b) \in f$, i.e., $a\,f\,b$ holds. We also say f has the *type* $X \to Y$, often denoted as $f : X \to Y$. For a binary function $\circ : X_1 \times X_2 \to Y$, we may also use infix notation, i.e., for $(x_1, x_2) \in X_1 \times X_2$ we write $x_1 \circ x_2$ as shorthand for $\circ((x_1, x_2))$, i.e., the unique element $b \in Y$ such that $(x_1, x_2) f b$ holds. If it is clear by the context that x, respectively y, is an elements from a set X, respectively Y, we use $x \mapsto f(y)$ as shorthand for a function $f : X \to Y$ that maps each $x \in X$ to the element $f(y) \in Y$.

Propositional Logic. A propositional signature $\Sigma = \{a, b, c, \ldots\}$ is non-empty set of *propositional variables*, also denoted as *atoms*. The set of formulas $\mathcal{L}_\Sigma^{\text{prop}}$ of the propositional logic over Σ is the smallest set obeying the following:

- Every atom in Σ is a formula (the atomic formulas), i.e., $a, b,$ $c, \ldots \in \Sigma$ are formulas of $\mathcal{L}_\Sigma^{\text{prop}}$.
- If $\varphi, \psi \in \mathcal{L}_\Sigma^{\text{prop}}$, then $\varphi \vee \psi, \varphi \wedge \psi$ and $\neg\varphi$ are formulas of $\mathcal{L}_\Sigma^{\text{prop}}$.

Our approach to propositional logic is model-theoretic. The interpretations (also denoted as *possible worlds*) of propositional logic over Σ are all valuation functions of type $\omega : \Sigma \to \{0, 1\}$, where 0 denotes *false* and 1 denotes *true*. With Ω we denote the set of all valuation functions. An evaluation function $[\![\cdot]\!] . : \mathcal{L}_\Sigma^{\text{prop}} \times (\Sigma \to \{0, 1\}) \to \{0, 1\}$ of Σ is defined for all $\varphi, \varphi_1, \varphi_2 \in \mathcal{L}_\Sigma^{\text{prop}}$ and $\omega \in \Omega$:

- For each $a \in \Sigma$ it holds that $[\![a]\!]_\omega = \omega(a)$,
- $[\![\neg\varphi]\!]_\omega = 1$ if and only if $[\![\varphi]\!]_\omega = 0$,
- $[\![\varphi_1 \vee \varphi_2]\!]_\omega = 1$ if and only if $[\![\varphi_1]\!]_\omega = 1$ or $[\![\varphi_2]\!]_\omega = 1$, and
- $[\![\varphi_1 \wedge \varphi_2]\!]_\omega = 1$ if and only if $[\![\varphi_1]\!]_\omega = 1$ and $[\![\varphi_2]\!]_\omega = 1$.

We write $\omega \models \varphi$ if $[\![\varphi]\!]_\omega = 1$. A valuation function ω is a *model* of φ if $\omega \models \varphi$, and with $[\![\varphi]\!]$ we denote the set of all models of φ. For two formulas φ, ψ we say ψ is a logical consequence of φ, written $\varphi \models \psi$, if $[\![\varphi]\!] \subseteq [\![\psi]\!]$. With $\mathrm{Cn}(\varphi)$ we denote the set of all logical consequences of φ, i.e., $\mathrm{Cn}(\varphi) = \{\psi \mid \varphi \models \psi\}$. These notions lift naturally to sets of formulas $L \subseteq \mathcal{L}_\Sigma^{\text{prop}}$, i.e., $\mathrm{Cn}(L) = \bigcap_{\varphi \in L} \mathrm{Cn}(\varphi)$ and $[\![L]\!] = \bigcap_{\varphi \in L}[\![\varphi]\!]$. We say that a set of formulas L is *deductively closed* if L is closed under logical consequences, i.e., $\mathrm{Cn}(L) = L$. We often write elements from Ω as sequences of all propositional variables, where overlining denotes assignment to false, e.g., given $\Sigma = \{a, b, c\}$, the sequence $\overline{a}bc$ denotes the valuation where the variable a is evaluated to false (and b, c to true).

We use $\varphi \to \psi$ as shorthand for $\neg\varphi \vee \psi$ and $\varphi \leftrightarrow \psi$ as shorthand for $(\varphi \to \psi) \wedge (\psi \to \varphi)$. Each of the symbols $\bot$ (*falsum*) and $\top$ (*verum*)

is used as a synonymy for an arbitrary (unique) formula such that
$[\![\bot]\!] = \emptyset$ and $[\![\top]\!] = \Omega$ holds. If $M \subseteq \Omega$ is a set of interpretations
and $\omega_1, \ldots, \omega_n \in \Omega$ are interpretations, then φ_M and $\varphi_{\omega_1,\ldots,\omega_n}$ denote arbitrary (but uniquely chosen) propositional formulas such that
$[\![\varphi_M]\!] = M$ and $\varphi_{\omega_1,\ldots,\omega_n} = \{\omega_1, \ldots, \omega_n\}$ holds. If not stated otherwise,
we will assume that the set of atoms is finite, i.e., that Σ is finite,
and we write $\mathcal{L}$ instead of $\mathcal{L}_{\Sigma}^{\mathrm{prop}}$ when Σ is clear form the context or
consideration of a particular Σ is not of any importance. This applies
to all parts of this thesis except for Part I. In Part I, we will deal
with many more logics than just propositional logic and use specific
notion to describe logics in a general and abstract way, introduced
in that part. This will also cover propositional logics with infinitely
many atoms.

Chapter 3

Background on Belief Change

The most prominent paradigm of belief change theory is due to Al-chourrón, Gärdenfors, and Makinson (AGM), and the work in this thesis is rooted in their approach to belief change and the theory built upon their foundational work. In the original approach, beliefs of an agent are represented by deductively closed sets of formulas (belief sets) and change happens when new information arrives, leading then to a new belief set. The fundamental principle which the AGM approach identified (and axiomatized) is the *principle of minimal change*, stating that changing should affect the previously given beliefs of an agent as little as possible.

The theoretical framework developed around AGM theory has become very rich, and reasons for this are the clear axiomatization and various characterizations [56]. However, the original approach left some points unclear. For instance, as Segerberg points outs, there are essentially two readings of the change-setting which AGM change considers [142]:

One-Shot Change. In this reading, change happens on one specific (but generic) belief set, and after the prior belief set is modified according to the new information, the change is done and everything that happens afterwards is not in the concern of the theory ("And this is the entire scenario." [142]).

Iterative Change. In this reading, change can happen iteratively. Thus, after a change happened on a belief set, the resulting belief set could be again the subject of a new change, and so on.

In this thesis, we will follow the second reading of AGM, the iterative reading. However, the "one-shot" reading is considered as the setup which is more close to the original "spirit" of the AGM approach. Therefore, in the following we will start by introducing AGM revision and AGM contraction as change operators of the one-shot setting. We will then switch to an iterative interpretation of the AGM approach given by Katsuno and Mendelzon [84].

3.1. One-Shot AGM Belief Change

The AGM approach models the beliefs of an agent as a deductively closed set of formulas, called a belief set. This is an idealization which especially implements logical omniscience[1] [149].

Definition 3.1. *A* belief set *K (over a logical language $\mathcal{L}$) is a deductively closed set of formulas.*

In this approach, the process of change is modelled input-driven and abstracts from aspects like the cause and source of the new information and other aspects like time. Given a belief set K and new information α, a change process leads to a new belief set $K \circ \alpha$. The mathematical object $\circ$ is — in the one-shot reading — a function of type $\mathcal{L} \to \mathcal{P}(\mathcal{L})$, simply called a *change operator* in the following, given for the one specific individual belief set K.

Three classes of change operators are considered in the AGM approach: expansion, revision and contraction. In the following, we consider these three of different kinds of belief changes.

Expansion. This is the kind of belief change where new beliefs are simply added to the prior beliefs of an agent. This has been characterized by the unique function $+$, given by

$$K + \alpha = Cn(K \cup \{\alpha\}).$$

Note that the original approach to expansion is axiomatic [63], but we will not consider this axiomatization here. One reason is that in the Darwiche and Pearl framework for iterative belief change we introduce in Part II, there exists no common accepted notion for expansion [59].

---

[1]   The assumption that agents have unlimited deductive power, i.e., if an agent knows A, then the agents knows also all logical consequences of A.

Nevertheless, we will make extensive use of the expansion operator $+$, but always on belief sets.

AGM Revision. Revision is the kind of change which incorporates new beliefs into the prior beliefs while obtaining a consistent belief set, whenever that is possible. AGM revision is given axiomatically, by axioms (postulates) which respect the principle of minimal change.

Definition 3.2 (AGM Revision [2]). *Let K be a belief set and $*$ be a change operator for K. Then $*$ is an AGM revision operator if the following postulates are satisfied:*

(AGM$*$1) $\alpha \in K * \alpha$.   (*Success (of revision)*)
(AGM$*$2) $K * \alpha \subseteq K + \alpha$.   (*Inclusion*)
(AGM$*$3) *If $K + \alpha$ is consistent, then $K * \alpha = K + \alpha$.*   (*Vacuity*)
(AGM$*$4) *If α is consistent, then $K * \alpha$ is consistent.* (*Consistency*)
(AGM$*$5) *If $\alpha \equiv \beta$, then $K * \alpha = K * \beta$.*   (*Extensionality*)
(AGM$*$6) $K * (\alpha \wedge \beta) \subseteq (K * \alpha) + \beta$.   (*Superexpansion*)
(AGM$*$7) *If $\neg\beta \notin K*\alpha$, then $(K*\alpha)+\beta \subseteq K*(\alpha\wedge\beta)$.* (*Subexpansion*)

The postulates (AGM$*$1)–(AGM$*$5) are typically denoted as the *basic postulates* for revision, sometimes also denoted as the *basic Gärdenfors postulates* for revision. The first postulate (AGM$*$1) describes that revision always successfully incorporates a new incoming belief. Due to inclusion (AGM$*$2), an AGM revision operator does never yield more beliefs than an expansion would do. If the initial beliefs K are consistent with α, then, due to vacuity (AGM$*$4), it is ensured that revision by α of K is nothing more than an expansion of K by α. Consistency (AGM$*$4) ensures that consistent new information leads to a new consistent belief set. In reverse, due to (AGM$*$1), revision of K by an inconsistent belief α yields an inconsistent belief set[2], regardless whether K is consistent or not. The postulate of extensionality (AGM$*$5), also known as *syntax independence* postulate, ensures that syntactic differences in the representation of beliefs does not have an impact on the revision process.

The remaining postulates (AGM$*$6) and (AGM$*$7) are often denoted as *extended postulates* for revision; another name is *supplementary Gärdenfors postulates* for revision. The superexpansion postulate

---

[2]   At least in classical logics like propositional logic.

(AGM∗6) is typically motivated as extension of the inclusion postulate (AGM∗2) to conjunctive beliefs. For a conjunction $\alpha \wedge \beta$ one should obtain $K * (\alpha \wedge \beta) \subseteq (K * \alpha) + \beta$ in addition to $K * (\alpha \wedge \beta) \subseteq K + (\alpha \wedge \beta)$ [73]. In the same way the subexpansion postulate (AGM∗6) is an extension of the vacuity postulate (AGM∗3) to conjunctive beliefs.

AGM Contraction. Contraction is the kind of belief change which removes a belief α from the prior beliefs, such that afterwards, α can not be obtained any more from the posterior belief set. AGM contraction is also given by set of postulates, which again implement the principle of minimal change.

Definition 3.3 (AGM Contraction [2]). *Let K be a belief set and $\div$ be a change operator for K. Then $\div$ is an AGM contraction operator if the following postulates are satisfied:*

(AGM÷1) $K \div \alpha \subseteq K$.   *(Inclusion)*
(AGM÷2) $\alpha \notin K \div \alpha$.   *(Success (of contraction))*
(AGM÷3) *If $\alpha \notin K$, then $K \div \alpha = K$.*   *(Vacuity)*
(AGM÷4) *If $\alpha \equiv \beta$, then $K \div \alpha = K \div \beta$.*   *(Extensionality)*
(AGM÷5) $K \subseteq (K \div \alpha) + \alpha$.   *(Recovery)*
(AGM÷6) $(K \div \alpha) \cap (K \div \beta) \subseteq K \div (\alpha \wedge \beta)$. *(Conjunctive overlap)*
(AGM÷7) *If $\alpha \notin K \div (\alpha \wedge \beta)$, then $K \div (\alpha \wedge \beta) \subseteq K \div \alpha$. (Conjunctive inclusion)*

As for revision, the first postulates (AGM÷1)–(AGM÷5) are typically denoted as the *basic postulates* for contribution, sometimes also denoted as the *basic Gärdenfors postulates* for contraction. Considering postulate (AGM÷1) reveals that an AGM contraction never introduces new beliefs; a contraction of α from K only revokes beliefs. Postulate (AGM÷2) states that contraction successfully removes the contracted belief. By the vacuity postulate (AGM÷3) it is ensured that for cases when α is not believed initially, the beliefs are not altered. The extensionality postulate (AGM÷4), also known as *syntax independence* postulate, ensures, like for revision, that syntactic differences in the representation of beliefs does not have an impact on the contraction process. Due to the recovery postulate (AGM÷5) (and (AGM÷1)), the contraction of α and subsequent addition of α by expansion restores the initial beliefs.

The remaining postulates (AGM÷6) and (AGM÷7) are also denoted as *extended postulates* for contraction, another name is *supplementary Gärdenfors postulates* for contraction. The postulate (AGM÷6) is an extension of the inclusion postulate (AGM÷1) to conjunctive beliefs. Likewise, the postulate (AGM÷7) is an extension of vacuity (AGM÷3) to conjunctions.

Connection of AGM Revision and AGM Connection. There is an apparent duality between the postulates for revision and the postulates for contraction which is not a random coincidence. It is known, for instance for propositional logic, that AGM revision and AGM contraction are interdefinable by two identities [63]:

$$K * \alpha = (K \div \neg \alpha) + \alpha \qquad \text{(Levi-Identity [102])}$$
$$K \div \alpha = K \cap (K * \neg \alpha) \qquad \text{(Harper-Identity [80])}$$

In the settings we will consider in the course of this thesis, we can not rely on these identities, as we leave the safe ground of the underlying logical assumptions of the original approach; the correspondence between AGM revision and AGM contraction in more general logics is more involved than in propositional logic [98].

3.2. Iterable AGM Change in Propositional Logic

An iterable approach to belief change is due to Katsuno and Mendelzon [84] (KM). Their approach concentrates on propositional logic as introduced in Chapter 2 over finitely many atoms.

To simplify matters Katsuno and Mendelzon (KM) consider belief change on formulas instead of belief sets; belief change operators in their framework are functions ∘ with type $\mathcal{L} \times \mathcal{L} \to \mathcal{L}$, which we call in the following *KM-belief change operators*. The mathematical object ∘ describes — in this iterative reading — for all belief sets at once how to revise each of them. Consequently, we can use ∘ for iteration, e.g., $((\mathcal{K} \circ \alpha_1) \circ \alpha_2) \ldots \circ \alpha_n$. The rationale for considering propositional formulas instead of belief sets is that a feature of propositional logic is that for every set of formulas $H \subseteq \mathcal{L}$ there exists a formula φ equivalent to H, i.e. $H \equiv \varphi$. Consequently, considering AGM belief change on formulas, is, for propositional logic, no limitation. Within this setup, there are operators that correspond to AGM revision operators and there are operators that correspond to AGM contraction operators.

AGM Revision. KM-belief change operators do not match the intended pattern of the AGM revision postulates (AGM∗1)–(AGM∗7), as these postulates are designed for changes on belief sets. The following is an auxiliary construction to connect KM-belief change operators with the AGM postulates.

Definition 3.4. *Let* $\circ : \mathcal{L} \times \mathcal{L} \to \mathcal{L}$ *be a KM-belief change operator. We say* $\circ$ *is an AGM revision operator if the function* $* : (\mathrm{Cn}(\varphi), \alpha) \mapsto \mathrm{Cn}(\varphi \circ \alpha)$, *defined for each* $\varphi, \alpha \in \mathcal{L}$, *satisfies for each belief set* $\mathcal{K} \subseteq \mathcal{L}$ *and* $\alpha, \beta \in \mathcal{L}$ *the postulates* (AGM∗1)–(AGM∗7).

Given this notion, we will present in the following the Katsuno and Mendelzon adaption of the AGM revision postulates for propositional logic, which exactly capture AGM revision operators.

Proposition 3.5 ([84, Lem. 3.1/3.2] and [37, Thm. 3]). *A KM-belief change operator* $\circ : \mathcal{L} \times \mathcal{L} \to \mathcal{L}$ *is an AGM revision operator if and only if the following holds[3]:*

     (KM1) $\varphi \circ \alpha \models \alpha$.
     (KM2)   *If* $\varphi \wedge \alpha$ *is consistent, then* $\varphi \circ \alpha \equiv \varphi \wedge \alpha$.
     (KM3)   *If* α *is consistent, then* $\varphi \circ \alpha$ *is consistent.*
     (KM4)   *If* $\varphi_1 \equiv \varphi_2$ *and* $\alpha \equiv \beta$, *then* $\varphi_1 \circ \alpha \equiv \varphi_2 \circ \beta$.
     (KM5) $(\varphi \circ \alpha) \wedge \beta \models \varphi \circ (\alpha \wedge \beta)$.
     (KM6)   *If* $(\varphi \circ \alpha) \wedge \beta$ *is consistent, then* $\varphi \circ (\alpha \wedge \beta) \models (\varphi \circ \alpha) \wedge \beta$.

The relation between (KM1)–(KM6) and (AGM∗1)–(AGM∗7) is evident. The only salient difference is between (KM2) and (AGM∗2) and (AGM∗3). However, one can obtain (KM2) by fusion of (AGM∗2) and (AGM∗3).

AGM Contraction. Similar to revision, a set of postulates for KM-belief change operators is known for AGM contraction [37]. In the following, we proceed as for revision.

Definition 3.6. *Let* $\circ : \mathcal{L} \times \mathcal{L} \to \mathcal{L}$ *be a KM-belief change operator. We say* $\circ$ *is an AGM contraction operator if the function* $\div : (\mathrm{Cn}(\varphi), \alpha) \mapsto$

---

[3]   The abbreviation *KM* stands for *Katsuno and Mendelzon*.

$\mathrm{Cn}(\varphi \circ \alpha)$, *defined for each* $\varphi, \alpha \in \mathcal{L}$, *satisfies for each belief set* $\mathcal{K} \subseteq \mathcal{L}$ *and* $\alpha, \beta \in \mathcal{L}$ *the postulates* (AGM÷1)–(AGM÷7).

In the following, we present the adaption of the AGM contraction postulates for propositional logic by Caridroit, Konieczny, and Marquis, which exactly capture AGM contraction operators.

Proposition 3.7 ([37, Prop. 8]). *A KM-belief change operator* ÷ : $\mathcal{L} \times \mathcal{L} \to \mathcal{L}$ *is an AGM contraction operator if and only if the following holds*[4]:

(CKM1) $\varphi \models \varphi \div \alpha$.
(CKM2) *If* $\varphi \not\models \alpha$, *then* $\varphi \div \alpha \models \varphi$.
(CKM3) *If* $\varphi \div \alpha \models \alpha$, *then* $\alpha \equiv \top$.
(CKM4) $(\varphi \div \alpha) \wedge \alpha \models \varphi$.
(CKM5) *If* $\varphi \equiv \psi$ *and* $\alpha \equiv \beta$, *then* $\varphi \div \alpha \equiv \psi \div \beta$.
(CKM6) $\varphi \div (\alpha \wedge \beta) \models (\varphi \div \alpha) \vee (\varphi \div \beta)$.
(CKM7) *If* $\varphi \div (\alpha \wedge \beta) \not\models \alpha$, *then* $\varphi \div \alpha \models \varphi \div (\alpha \wedge \beta)$.

The relation between (CKM1)–(CKM7) and (AGM÷1)–(AGM÷7) is evident, and given by a straightforward reformulation.

3.3. Semantic Characterizations in Propositional Logic

In this thesis, we consider change operators from a semantic point of view via characterization theorems. This section presents the overall style of how we will address belief change semantically in this thesis. We start by briefly introducing Grove's [67] semantic characterization of one-shot AGM revision. Afterwards, we introduce Katsuno and Mendelzon's [84] characterization of AGM revision, and then, we introduce how AGM contraction could be characterized analogously.

Revision and System of Spheres. Grove showed [67], having the one-shot reading of the AGM approach in mind, that an AGM revision operator $* : \mathcal{L} \to \mathcal{P}(\mathcal{L})$ for a belief set K is semantically representable by two components:

---

[4]   The abbreviation *CKM* stands for *Caridroit, Konieczny, and Marquis*.

- a *system of spheres*[5] $\mathcal{S}$ of the possible worlds (arranging the elements of Ω in layers, like in an onion), which is centred around K, i.e., the models of K are the innermost layer of $\mathcal{S}$, and
- a function $f : \alpha \mapsto \min(\llbracket \alpha \rrbracket, \mathcal{S})$, which yields all models of α contained in the innermost layer of $\mathcal{S}$ which contains a model of α.

Given these two components, one can reconstruct the behaviour of $*$ semantically, as the following holds:

$$\llbracket K * \alpha \rrbracket = \min(\llbracket \alpha \rrbracket, \mathcal{S}).$$

Characterization of AGM Revision. Katsuno and Mendelzon approach AGM revision in a way similar to Grove's system of spheres. The main means for their approach are assignments, which are functions that map each belief set $\mathcal{K}$ to a total preorder $\leq_K$ over Ω, such that the models of K are respected by $\leq_K$.

Definition 3.8 (Faithfulness [84]). *A function $\varphi \mapsto \leq_\varphi$, which maps every formula φ to a total preorder $\leq_\varphi$ over Ω, is called a* faithful KM-assignment *if for each φ it holds that*

$$\llbracket \varphi \rrbracket = \min(\Omega, \leq_\varphi).$$

Here, faithfulness serves the same purpose as centring around K for a system of spheres $\mathcal{S}$. Katsuno and Mendelzon proof the following representation theorem.

Theorem 3.9 ([84, Thm 3.3]). *A KM-belief change operator $*$ is an AGM revision operator if and only if there exists a faithful KM-assignment $\varphi \mapsto \leq_\varphi$ such that the following holds*

$$\llbracket \varphi * \alpha \rrbracket = \min(\llbracket \alpha \rrbracket, \leq_\varphi).$$

The typical interpretation of Theorem 3.9 is that each $\leq_\Psi$ represents an ordering of possible worlds by plausibility, whereby smaller means

---

[5]   We will not introduce this formally and refer the interested reader to [67] or [57] for an overview and the formal definitions. For the setting considered in this thesis, a system of spheres $\mathcal{S}$ with center K could be identified with a total preorder $\leq_\mathcal{S}$ on Ω with $\min(\Omega, \leq_\mathcal{S}) = \llbracket K \rrbracket$.

more plausible. Consequently, by this interpretation, the prior beliefs are the most plausible worlds and AGM revision by α is selection of the most plausible α worlds.

Characterization of AGM Contraction. In an analogue way to Theorem 3.9, AGM contraction has been characterized by Caridroit et al. [38].

Proposition 3.10 ([38, Thm. 14]). *A KM-belief change operator $\div$ is an AGM contraction operator if and only if there exists a faithful KM-assignment $\varphi \mapsto \leq_\varphi$ such that the following holds*

$$[\![\varphi \div \alpha]\!] = [\![\varphi]\!] \cup \min([\![\neg\alpha]\!], \leq_\varphi).$$

By the characterization given in Proposition 3.10, the main characteristic of a contraction with α is that the worlds of the previous state remain plausible and that the most plausible counter-models of α become plausible.

In course of this thesis, we will encounter different classes of belief change operators. We will characterize them semantically in a similar way as Katsuno and Mendelzon did for revision, and as Caridroit et al. did for contraction, respectively. However, we will consider these various classes of belief change operators in more powerful frameworks.

3.4. Further remarks

Just for the sake of completeness we want to remark that standard set theory provides a means to connect both views the one-shot and the iterative point of view, on AGM belief change. Every iterative change operator can be decomposed into a family of "one-shot"-change operators, which provides for every belief set K exactly one belief change operator for K. Clearly, every such family of "one-shot"-change operators yields bijectively an iterable change operator.

All postulates we consider in this chapter are just "talking" about one-step changes, and thus, the iterative viewpoints yielded no benefit so far. However, when considering iterated belief change, and in particular postulates for iterated change, which consider two or more subsequent changes, the one-shot viewpoint is not sufficient any more.

We will consider such postulates in Part III. Note that iterated change is also connected to *conditionals*, and when considering conditionals in the context of belief revision it is only reasonable that a "full" belief change operator [88] is an operator of the iterative type.

In the following part, Part I, we reconsider the characterization of AGM revision by Katsuno and Mendelzon in much more detail. We will generalize their theorem to a more general setup of base changes, and present an adaption of their characterization-result for the large class of Tarskian logics. In contrast to the propositional case (cf. Theorem 3.9), it will turn out that, in Tarskian logics, total preorders are not the class of relations corresponding to AGM revision. The main contribution of Part I is a full characterization of those Tarskian logics, where AGM revision corresponds to total preorders.

Part I

Base Revision in Tarskian Logics

Introduction to Part I

A popular semantic characterization of AGM revision (see Chapter 3) is due to Katsuno and Mendelzon [84] characterizing AGM revision in propositional logic in terms of relations over possible worlds (the interpretations). Therefore, instead of representing belief states by belief sets, Katsuno and Mendelzon represent each belief state by a propositional formula φ. This is no principal restriction, as in propositional logic for every set of interpretations there exists a formula having exactly this set of interpretations as set of models. As already mentioned before (see Chapter 3), Katsuno and Mendelzon showed that AGM revision is characterized as follows: an operator $\circ$ is an AGM revision operator if and only if it can be represented semantically by assigning to each formula φ a *total preorder* $\leq_\varphi$ such that especially

$$\llbracket \varphi \circ \alpha \rrbracket = \min(\llbracket \alpha \rrbracket, \leq_\varphi),$$

is satisfied, i.e., the result of revision by α is given, semantically, by the minimal models of α with respect to $\leq_\varphi$. Like many characterizations of AGM revision [125] the approach by Katsuno and Mendelzon generalizes to various other logics [46, 1]; in particular, when compactness, closure under standard connectives, deduction, or supra-classicality are given [67]. However, the characterization by Katsuno and Mendelzon does not carry over to all arbitrary logics, e.g., the result does not hold for Horn logic [45].

This leads to the question of the characteristics of those logics for which every AGM revision operator is total-preorder-representable. This question is of particular importance, as the connection between (AGM) revision and total preorders became a de facto standard, and many results rely on this connection, e.g., in the area of iterated belief change.

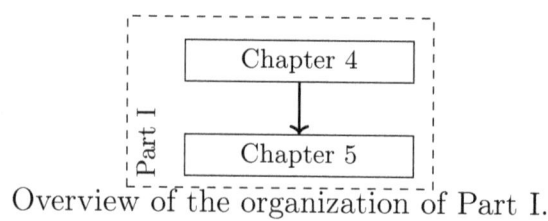

Overview of the organization of Part I.

In the course of this part, we will focus on Tarskian logics, i.e., monotonic logics exhibiting a classically defined model theory. Tarskian logics encompass first-order predicate logic, propositional logic over finitely and infinitely many atoms, descriptions logics and many more. Moreover, instead of considering revision for belief sets, we will consider multiple belief revision for the more general setting of *base logics*, recently introduced in joint work with Faiq Miftakhul Falakh and Sebastian Rudolph [54]. The notion of base logic combines two concepts:

- a Tarskian logic, given in a model-theoretic manner, and
- a set of subsets of formulas over that given logic (closed under conjunction), which are considered as the representation for the belief state (thus, generalizing belief sets).

Multiple revision refers to revision operators taking more than one formula as input for revision at once. Consequently, the setting we consider is an abstraction of the original AGM setting.

A core contribution of this part will be the notion of *critical loops*. A critical loop is a circular situation found in a (base) logic, which will turn out as a "forbidden minor" in the following sense: if a base logic $\mathbb{B}$ exhibits no critical loop, then each (multiple) belief revision operator for $\mathbb{B}$ can be represented by total preorders (as in the result by Katsuno and Mendelzon).

We present the results of this part in two chapters, whereby the second chapter depends on the first chapter. The chapters consider the following topics:

Chapter 4. The chapter introduces the setting of belief change in base logics and revisits Katsuno and Mendelzon's key contributions in characterizing AGM revision operators in finite-signature propositional logic. We consider the suitability of Katsuno and Mendelzon's approach for our generalized setting and introduce the necessary adjustments. The main result of this chapter will be various characterizations of AGM revision operators over base logics. We consider relaxations regarding the dependence of operators on the syntax.

Chapter 5. The chapter presents the main result of this part. We introduce the notion of critical loop and give some intuition for this notion. Next, we show in two steps that critical loops characterize those Tarksian logics where some AGM revisions are not total-preorder-representable. We continue with examples and consequences of the main theorem. The chapter closes with a discussion and conclusion of this part.

Remark. The contents of Chapter 4 and Chapter 5 is based on joint work with Faiq Miftakhul Falakh and Sebastian Rudolph [54] (see Section 1.4). To stay close to this joint work, we sometimes use notions different from the one given in Chapter 2.

Chapter 4

Revision in Base Logics

Original AGM theory assumes that an agent's belief state is given by a deductively closed set of sentences, referred to as a *belief set* (see Chapter 3). However, *belief sets* has been often criticized as a too idealistic representation for real agents. As an alternative, sets of formulas (called *belief bases*) are frequently considered [73]. Moreover, the AGM approach has been criticized for only dealing with singleton inputs, i.e., it provides no information on how to deal with situations where multiple new information arrives at once.

Katsuno and Mendelzon deal with the issues of belief bases and multiple inputs elegantly [84]: as in propositional logic, every set of sentences (including an infinite one) is equivalent to one single sentence, belief states and multiple inputs are considered as such single sentences. In this setting, Katsuno and Mendelzon provide the following set of postulates, derived from the AGM revision postulates, where $\varphi, \varphi_1, \varphi_2, \alpha,$ and β are propositional sentences, and $\circ$ is a base change operator:

(KM1) $\varphi \circ \alpha \models \alpha.$
(KM2) If $\varphi \wedge \alpha$ is consistent, then $\varphi \circ \alpha \equiv \varphi \wedge \alpha.$
(KM3) If α is consistent, then $\varphi \circ \alpha$ is consistent.
(KM4) If $\varphi_1 \equiv \varphi_2$ and $\alpha \equiv \beta$, then $\varphi_1 \circ \alpha \equiv \varphi_2 \circ \beta.$
(KM5) $(\varphi \circ \alpha) \wedge \beta \models \varphi \circ (\alpha \wedge \beta).$
(KM6) If $(\varphi \circ \alpha) \wedge \beta$ is consistent, then $\varphi \circ (\alpha \wedge \beta) \models (\varphi \circ \alpha) \wedge \beta.$

The postulates (KM1)–(KM6) together are equivalent to the AGM revision postulates when considering propositional logic [84] (see also

Section 3.2), thus they also yield minimal change with respect to the initial beliefs.

In this chapter, we introduce the setting of (multiple) base change over arbitrary Tarskian logics and will semantically characterize AGM revision operators in this framework. The framework and characterization result we will present here generalizes a result by Katsuno and Mendelzon [84], assigning to each belief base a total preorder on the interpretations, which expresses – intuitively speaking – a degree of "modelishness". The models of the result of any AGM revision then coincide with the preferred (i.e., preorder-minimal) models of the new belief.

Our approach generalizes this idea of preferences over interpretations to the general setting of base logics, which necessitates adjusting the nature of the "modelishness-indicating" assignments: We have to explicitly require that minimal models always exist (*min-completeness*) and that they can be described in the logic (*min-expressibility*). Moreover, we show that demanding preference relations to be preorders is infeasible in our setting; we have to waive transitivity and retain only a weaker property (*min-retractivity*).

The next section introduces a general model-theoretic point of view on monotonic logics. Moreover, we introduce base logics and change for them.

Remark. The contents of this chapter, the Chapter 4, is based on joint work with Faiq Miftakhul Falakh and Sebastian Rudolph [54] (see also Section 1.4).

4.1. Preliminaries

In this section, we introduce the logical and algebraic notions used in this part.

4.1.1. Logics with Classical Model-Theoretic Semantics

We consider logics endowed with a classical model-theoretic semantics. The syntax of such a logic $\mathbb{L}$ is given syntactically by a (possibly infinite) set $\mathcal{L}$ of *sentences*, while its model theory is provided by specifying a (potentially infinite) class Ω of *interpretations* (also called *worlds*) and a binary relation $\models$ between Ω and $\mathcal{L}$ where $w \models \varphi$ indicates that w is a model of φ. Hence, a logic $\mathbb{L}$ is identified by the triple $(\mathcal{L}, \Omega, \models)$. We let $[\![\varphi]\!] = \{w \in \Omega \mid w \models \varphi\}$ denote the set of all models of $\varphi \in \mathcal{L}$. Logical entailment is defined as usual (overloading "$\models$") via models: for two sentences φ and ψ we say φ *entails* ψ (written $\varphi \models \psi$) if $[\![\varphi]\!] \subseteq [\![\psi]\!]$.

Notions of modelhood and entailment can be easily lifted from single sentences to sets. We obtain the models of a set $\mathcal{K} \subseteq \mathcal{L}$ of sentences via $[\![\mathcal{K}]\!] = \bigcap_{\varphi \in \mathcal{K}} [\![\varphi]\!]$. For $\mathcal{K} \subseteq \mathcal{L}$ and $\mathcal{K}' \subseteq \mathcal{L}$ we say $\mathcal{K}$ *entails* $\mathcal{K}'$ (written $\mathcal{K} \models \mathcal{K}'$) if $[\![\mathcal{K}]\!] \subseteq [\![\mathcal{K}']\!]$. We write $\mathcal{K} \equiv \mathcal{K}'$ to express $[\![\mathcal{K}]\!] = [\![\mathcal{K}']\!]$. A (set of) sentence(s) is called *consistent with* another (set of) sentence(s) if the two have models in common. Unlike many other belief revision frameworks, we impose no further requirements on $\mathcal{L}$ (like closure under certain operators or compactness).

The existence of a classical model-theoretic semantics as above is equivalent to the logic being *Tarskian* [150, 143]. Among others properties, this means that all logics considered here are monotonic, i.e., they satisfy the following condition:

$$\text{If } \mathcal{K}_1 \models \varphi \text{ and } \mathcal{K}_1 \subseteq \mathcal{K}_2, \text{ then } \mathcal{K}_2 \models \varphi. \qquad \text{(monotonicity)}$$

The notion of Tarskian logic captures many well-known classical logical formalisms and before we will give some examples, we will state precisely in the following how model-theoretic logics as sketched here are related to Tarskian logics.

4.1.2. Equivalence of Tarskian and Model Theoretic Logics

In the following, we show that the class of logics defined model-theoretically and the class of Tarskian logics coincide (as asserted in Section 4.1.1). We start by providing the definition of Tarskian logics.

Definition 4.1. *Let $\mathcal{L}$ be a set. A function $Cn : \mathcal{P}(\mathcal{L}) \to \mathcal{P}(\mathcal{L})$ is a called a* Tarskian *consequence operator (on $\mathcal{L}$) if it is a closure operator, i.e., it satisfies the following properties for all subsets $\mathcal{K}, \mathcal{K}_1, \mathcal{K}_2 \subseteq \mathcal{L}$:*

$$\mathcal{K} \subseteq Cn(\mathcal{K}) \qquad \text{(extensive)}$$
$$\text{if } \mathcal{K}_1 \subseteq \mathcal{K}_2, \text{ then } Cn(\mathcal{K}_1) \subseteq Cn(\mathcal{K}_2) \qquad \text{(monotone)}$$
$$Cn(\mathcal{K}) = Cn(Cn(\mathcal{K})) \qquad \text{(idempotent)}$$

Any Tarskian consequence operator $Cn : \mathcal{P}(\mathcal{L}) \to \mathcal{P}(\mathcal{L})$ gives rise to a Tarskian consequence relation $\models\ \subseteq \mathcal{P}(\mathcal{L}) \times \mathcal{L}$ *defined by* $\mathcal{K} \models \varphi$ *if* $\varphi \in Cn(\mathcal{K})$. *Each* $(\mathcal{L}, \models)$ *obtained from a Tarskian consequence operator* $Cn : \mathcal{P}(\mathcal{L}) \to \mathcal{P}(\mathcal{L})$ *will be called a* Tarskian logic *here.*

We proceed to show that the existence of a model-theoretically defined semantics is sufficient and necessary for a logic being Tarskian.

Proposition 4.2. *For every model theory* $(\mathcal{L}, \Omega, \models)$ *there exists a Tarskian logic* $(\mathcal{L}, \models)$ *with* $\mathcal{K} \models \varphi$ *if and only if* $\mathcal{K} \models \varphi$ *for all* $\varphi \in \mathcal{L}$ *and* $\mathcal{K} \in \mathcal{P}(\mathcal{L})$.

Proof. Given $(\mathcal{L}, \Omega, \models)$, let $Cn : \mathcal{P}(\mathcal{L}) \to \mathcal{P}(\mathcal{L})$ be defined by $\mathcal{K} \mapsto \{\varphi \in \mathcal{L} \mid [\![\mathcal{K}]\!] \subseteq [\![\varphi]\!]\}$. For the course of this proof, we identify the empty intersection with Ω. We will show that Cn is a Tarskian consequence operator:

(Extensivity) Consider some arbitrary $\psi \in \mathcal{K}$. Then we obtain $[\![\mathcal{K}]\!] = \bigcap_{\varphi \in \mathcal{K}}[\![\varphi]\!] \subseteq [\![\psi]\!]$ and hence $\psi \in Cn(\mathcal{K})$. Hence, since ψ was chosen arbitrarily, we obtain $\mathcal{K} \subseteq Cn(\mathcal{K})$.

(Monotonicity) Suppose $\mathcal{K}_1 \subseteq \mathcal{K}_2$. Then $[\![\mathcal{K}_2]\!] = \bigcap_{\varphi \in \mathcal{K}_2}[\![\varphi]\!] \subseteq \bigcap_{\varphi \in \mathcal{K}_1}[\![\varphi]\!] = [\![\mathcal{K}_1]\!]$. Therefore, we obtain $Cn(\mathcal{K}_1) = \{\varphi \in \mathcal{L} \mid [\![\mathcal{K}_1]\!] \subseteq [\![\varphi]\!]\} \subseteq \{\varphi \in \mathcal{L} \mid [\![\mathcal{K}_1]\!] \subseteq [\![\varphi]\!]\} = Cn(\mathcal{K}_2)$.

(Idempotency) We show bidirectional inclusion. $Cn(\mathcal{K}) \subseteq Cn(Cn(\mathcal{K}))$ is an immediate consequence of extensivity already shown. For the other direction, consider an arbitrary $\psi \in Cn(Cn(\mathcal{K}))$. Then, we obtain $[\![Cn(\mathcal{K})]\!] \subseteq [\![\psi]\!]$. On the other hand, we have

$$[\![Cn(\mathcal{K})]\!] = \bigcap_{\substack{\varphi \in \mathcal{L} \\ [\![\mathcal{K}]\!] \subseteq [\![\varphi]\!]}} [\![\varphi]\!] = \left(\bigcap_{\substack{\varphi \in \mathcal{L} \setminus \mathcal{K} \\ [\![\mathcal{K}]\!] \subseteq [\![\varphi]\!]}} [\![\varphi]\!] \right) \cap \left(\bigcap_{\varphi \in \mathcal{K}} [\![\varphi]\!] \right) = \bigcap_{\varphi \in \mathcal{K}} [\![\varphi]\!] = [\![\mathcal{K}]\!],$$

and therefore, we obtain $[\![\mathcal{K}]\!] \subseteq [\![\psi]\!]$ and finally $\psi \in Cn(\mathcal{K})$. Hence, since ψ was chosen arbitrarily, we obtain $Cn(Cn(\mathcal{K})) \subseteq Cn(\mathcal{K})$.

Let now $\models$ denote the Tarskian consequence relation induced by Cn. Then we obtain for all $\mathcal{K} \subseteq \mathcal{L}$ and $\varphi \in \mathcal{L}$ the following:

$$\mathcal{K} \models \varphi \iff \varphi \in Cn(\mathcal{K}) \iff [\![\mathcal{K}]\!] \subseteq [\![\varphi]\!] \iff \mathcal{K} \models \varphi. \qquad \square$$

As last step, we show that for each Tarskian logic there is a canonical model-theoretic semantics for this Tarskian logic.

Proposition 4.3. *For every Tarskian logic $(\mathcal{L}, \models)$ there exists a model theory $(\mathcal{L}, \Omega, \models)$ such that $\mathcal{K} \models \varphi$ if and only if $\mathcal{K} \models \varphi$ holds for all $\varphi \in \mathcal{L}$ and $\mathcal{K} \in \mathcal{P}(\mathcal{L})$.*

Proof. Let $(\mathcal{L}, \models)$ be a Tarskian logic and let $Cn : \mathcal{P}(\mathcal{L}) \to \mathcal{P}(\mathcal{L})$ be the corresponding Tarskian consequence operator. We now define an appropriate $(\mathcal{L}, \Omega, \models)$ as follows: Let $\Omega = \{Cn(T) \mid T \subseteq \mathcal{L}\}$. For the course of this proof, we identify the empty intersection with Ω. Define the models relation $\models \subseteq \Omega \times \mathcal{L}$ such that some $Cn(T) \in \Omega$ is a model of some $\varphi \in \mathcal{L}$ whenever $\varphi \in Cn(T)$.

Then we obtain for all $\mathcal{K} \subseteq \mathcal{L}$ and $\varphi \in \mathcal{L}$ the following:

$$\mathcal{K} \models \varphi \Longleftrightarrow [\![\mathcal{K}]\!] \subseteq [\![\varphi]\!]$$
$$\Longleftrightarrow \bigcap_{\psi \in \mathcal{K}}[\![\psi]\!] \subseteq [\![\varphi]\!]$$
$$\Longleftrightarrow \{Cn(T) \mid T \subseteq \mathcal{L}, \ \mathcal{K} \subseteq Cn(T)\}$$
$$\subseteq \{Cn(T) \mid T \subseteq \mathcal{L}, \ \varphi \in Cn(T)\}$$
$$\Longleftrightarrow \forall T \subseteq \mathcal{L} : \mathcal{K} \subseteq Cn(T) \Rightarrow \varphi \in Cn(T) \qquad (*)$$

Moreover, we obtain

$$(*) \Longrightarrow \mathcal{K} \subseteq Cn(\mathcal{K}) \Rightarrow \varphi \in Cn(\mathcal{K}) \text{ (instantiate } T = \mathcal{K})$$
$$\Longrightarrow \varphi \in Cn(\mathcal{K}) \qquad \text{(extensivity of } Cn)$$
$$\Longrightarrow \mathcal{K} \models \varphi,$$

and on the other hand:

$$\mathcal{K} \models \varphi \Longrightarrow \varphi \in Cn(\mathcal{K})$$
$$\Longrightarrow \forall S \subseteq \mathcal{L} : Cn(\mathcal{K}) \subseteq S \Rightarrow \varphi \in S$$
$$\Longrightarrow \forall T \subseteq \mathcal{L} : Cn(\mathcal{K}) \subseteq Cn(T) \Rightarrow \varphi \in Cn(T)$$
$$\text{(restriction to closed sets)}$$
$$\Longrightarrow \forall T \subseteq \mathcal{L} : Cn(\mathcal{K}) \subseteq Cn(Cn(T)) \Rightarrow \varphi \in Cn(T)$$
$$\text{(idempotency of } Cn)$$
$$\Longrightarrow (*) \qquad \text{(monotonicity of } Cn)$$

Concluding, we have established that for all $\mathcal{K} \subseteq \mathcal{L}$ and $\varphi \in \mathcal{L}$ the following holds:

$$\mathcal{K} \models \varphi \Longleftrightarrow (*) \Longleftrightarrow \mathcal{K} \models \varphi. \qquad \square$$

As next step, we consider examples for Tarskian logics.

4.1.3. Tarskian Logics: Examples

We start by providing an example where sentences and interpretations are finite sets, which allows us to specify them (as well as the model relation) explicitly. We note that this is an extension of an example given by Delgrande et al. [46], which will serve as a running example throughout this part.

Example 4.4 (based on [46]). *Let* $\mathbb{L}_{Ex} = (\mathcal{L}_{Ex}, \Omega_{Ex}, \models_{Ex})$ *be the logic defined by* $\mathcal{L}_{Ex} = \{\psi_0, \ldots, \psi_5, \varphi_0, \varphi_1, \varphi_2, \chi, \chi'\}$ *and* $\Omega_{Ex} = \{\omega_0, \ldots, \omega_5\}$, *with the models relation* $\models_{Ex}$ *implicitly given by:*

$$\llbracket \psi_i \rrbracket = \{\omega_i\} \qquad\qquad \llbracket \varphi_0 \rrbracket = \{\omega_0, \omega_1\}$$
$$\llbracket \chi \rrbracket = \{\omega_0, \ldots, \omega_5\} \qquad\qquad \llbracket \varphi_1 \rrbracket = \{\omega_1, \omega_2\}$$
$$\llbracket \chi' \rrbracket = \{\omega_0, \omega_1, \omega_2, \omega_4, \omega_5\} \qquad\qquad \llbracket \varphi_2 \rrbracket = \{\omega_2, \omega_0\}$$

Since $\mathbb{L}_{Ex}$ *is defined in the classical model-theoretic way,* $\mathbb{L}_{Ex}$ *is a Tarskian logic. Note that logic* $\mathbb{L}_{Ex}$ *has no connectives. Figure 4.1 illustrates the logic setting* $\mathbb{L}_{Ex}$.

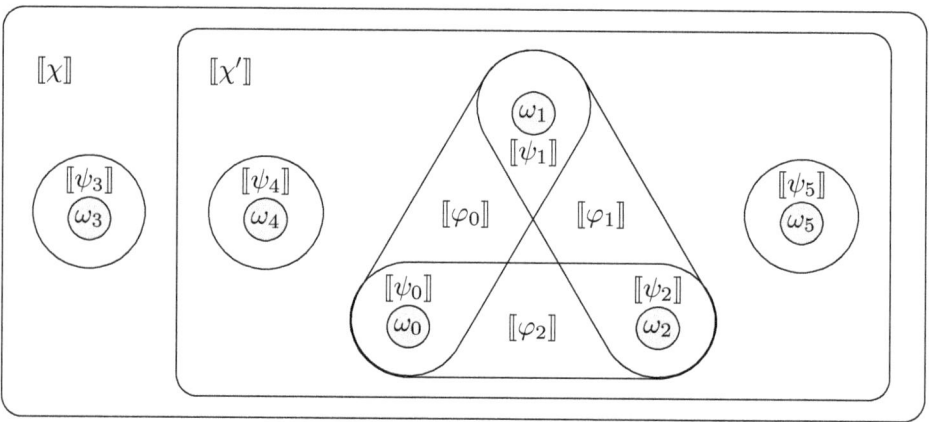

Figure 4.1: Illustration of the logic $\mathbb{L}_{Ex}$, including the modelhood relations where the solid borders represent the set of models.

Next we turn to propositional logic, observing that the distinction between a finite or infinite set of propositional atoms leads to differences that we will revisit later on. We start with propositional logic with a finite set of propositional atoms.

Example 4.5 ($\mathbb{PL}_n$, propositional logic over n propositional atoms). *The logic is defined by* $\mathbb{PL}_n = (\mathcal{L}_{\mathbb{PL}_n}, \Omega_{\mathbb{PL}_n}, \models_{\mathbb{PL}_n})$ *in the usual way:*

Given a finite set $\Sigma_p = \{p_1, \ldots, p_n\}$ of atomic propositions, we let $\mathcal{L}_{PL_n}$ be the set of Boolean expressions built from $\Sigma_p \cup \{\top, \bot\}$ using the usual set of propositional connectives ($\neg$, $\wedge$, $\vee$, $\rightarrow$, and $\leftrightarrow$). We then let the set Ω_{PL_n} of interpretations contain all functions from Σ_p to $\{\text{true}, \text{false}\}$. The relation $\models_{PL_n}$ is then defined inductively over the structure of sentences in the usual way.

Notably, finiteness of Σ implies finiteness of Ω_{PL_n} (more specifically, $|\Omega_{PL_n}| = 2^n$). This in turn ensures that, despite $\mathcal{L}_{PL_n}$ being infinite, there are only finitely many (namely 2^n) sentences which are pairwise semantically distinct. Even more so: for every (finite or infinite) set $\mathcal{K}$ of PL_n sentences, there exists some sentence $\varphi \in \mathcal{L}_{PL_n}$ with $\varphi \equiv \mathcal{K}$.

Next we consider propositional logic with an infinite set of propositional atoms.

Example 4.6 (PL_∞, propositional logic over infinite signature). *The basic definitions for $PL_\infty = (\mathcal{L}_{PL_\infty}, \Omega_{PL_\infty}, \models_{PL_\infty})$ are just like in the previous example, with the notable difference of $\Sigma_p = \{p_1, p_2, \ldots\}$ being countably infinite. This implies immediately that Ω_{PL_∞} is infinite (in fact, even uncountable), implying that there are infinitely many sentences that are pairwise non-equivalent (e.g., all the atomic ones). Also, there exist infinite sets of sentences for which no single equivalent sentence from $\mathcal{L}_{PL_\infty}$ exists (e.g., $\{p_2, p_4, p_6, \ldots\}$).*

Many more (and more expressive) logics are captured by the model-theoretic framework assumed by us, e.g. first-order and second-order predicate logic, modal logics, and description logics. Our considerations do, however, **not** apply to non-monotonic formalisms, such as default logic, circumscription, or logic programming frameworks using negation as failure.

4.1.4. Relation over Interpretations

For describing belief revision on the semantic level, it is expedient to endow the interpretation space Ω with some structure. In particular, we will employ binary relations $\preceq$ over Ω (formally: $\preceq \subseteq \Omega \times \Omega$), where the intuitive meaning of $\omega_1 \preceq \omega_2$ is that ω_1 is "equally good or better" than ω_2 when it comes to serving as a model. We call $\preceq$ *total* if $\omega_1 \preceq \omega_2$ or $\omega_2 \preceq \omega_1$ for any $\omega_1, \omega_2 \in \Omega$ holds, and we call $\preceq$ a *preorder* if it is transitive and reflexive (as in Chapter 2).

We write $\omega_1 \prec \omega_2$ as a shorthand, whenever $\omega_1 \preceq \omega_2$ and $\omega_2 \not\preceq \omega_1$ (the intuition being that ω_1 is "strictly better" than ω_2). For a selection $\Omega' \subseteq \Omega$ of interpretations, an $\omega \in \Omega'$ is called $\preceq$-*minimal in* Ω' if $\omega \preceq \omega'$ for all $\omega' \in \Omega'$.[1] We let $\min(\Omega', \preceq)$ denote the set of $\preceq$-minimal interpretations in Ω'. Note that there might be no $\preceq$-minimal elements in Ω', and thus, $\min(\Omega', \preceq)$ might be the empty set.

For a relation $R \subseteq \Omega \times \Omega$, the *transitive closure* of R is the relation $TC(R) = \bigcup_{i=0}^{\infty} R^i$, where $R^0 = R$ and $R^{i+1} = R^i \cup \{(\omega_1, \omega_3) \mid \exists \omega_2.(\omega_1, \omega_2) \in R^i$ and $(\omega_2, \omega_3) \in R^i\}$.

4.1.5. Bases

This part addresses the revision of and by *bases*. In the belief revision community, the term of base commonly denotes an arbitrary (possibly infinite) set of sentences. However, in certain scenarios, other assumptions might be more appropriate. Hence, for the sake of generality, we decided to define the notion of a base on an abstract level with minimal requirements (just as we introduced our notion of *logic*), allowing for its instantiation in many ways.

Definition 4.7. *A* base logic *is a quintuple* $\mathbb{B} = (\mathcal{L}, \Omega, \models, \mathfrak{B}, \uplus)$, *where*

- $(\mathcal{L}, \Omega, \models)$ *is a logic,*
- $\mathfrak{B} \subseteq \mathcal{P}(\mathcal{L})$ *is a family of sets of sentences, called* bases, *and*
- $\uplus : \mathfrak{B} \times \mathfrak{B} \to \mathfrak{B}$ *is a binary operator over bases, called the* abstract union, *satisfying* $[\![\mathcal{B}_1 \uplus \mathcal{B}_2]\!] = [\![\mathcal{B}_1]\!] \cap [\![\mathcal{B}_2]\!]$.

Next, we will demonstrate how, for some logic $\mathbb{L} = (\mathcal{L}, \Omega, \models)$, a corresponding base logic can be chosen depending on one's preferences regarding what bases should be.

Arbitrary Sets. If all (finite and infinite) sets of sentences should qualify as bases, one can simply set $\mathfrak{B} = \mathcal{P}(\mathcal{L})$. In that case, $\uplus$ can be instantiated by set union $\cup$, then the claimed behaviour follows by

---

[1]   If $\preceq$ is total, this definition is equivalent to the *absence* of any $\omega'' \in \Omega'$ with $\omega'' \prec \omega$ (as given in Chapter 2). Note that we encounter in Chapter 5 relations that are not total. Moreover, this notion of minimality used here provides a beneficial point of view on minimality for understanding many proofs given in Chapter 4 and in Chapter 5.

definition. This setting is close to the setup of base change used by Hansson [73].

Finite Sets. In some settings, it is more convenient to assume bases to be finite (e.g. when computational properties or implementations are to be investigated). In such cases, one can set $\mathfrak{B} = \mathcal{P}_{\text{fin}}(\mathcal{L})$, i.e., all (and only) the finite sets of sentences are bases. Again, $\uplus$ can be instantiated by set union $\cup$ (as a union of two finite sets will still be finite).

Belief Sets. This setting is closer to the original framework by AGM (see Chapter 3), where the "knowledge states" to be modified were assumed to be deductively closed sets of sentences. We can capture such situations by accordingly letting $\mathfrak{B} = \{\mathcal{B} \subseteq \mathcal{L} \mid \forall \varphi \in \mathcal{L} : \mathcal{B} \models \varphi$ implies $\varphi \in \mathcal{B}\}$. In this case, the abstract union operator needs to be defined via $\mathcal{B}_1 \uplus \mathcal{B}_2 = \{\varphi \in \mathcal{L} \mid \mathcal{B}_1 \cup \mathcal{B}_2 \models \varphi\}$.

Single Sentences. In this popular setting, one prefers to operate on single sentences only (rather than on proper collections of those). For this to work properly, an additional assumption needs to be made about the underlying logic $\mathbb{L} = (\mathcal{L}, \Omega, \models)$: it must be possible to express conjunction on a sentence level, either through the explicit presence of the Boolean operator $\wedge$ or by some other means. Formally, we say that $\mathbb{L} = (\mathcal{L}, \Omega, \models)$ *supports conjunction*, if for any two sentences $\varphi, \psi \in \mathcal{L}$ there exists some sentence $\varphi \otimes \psi \in \mathcal{L}$ satisfying $[\![\varphi \otimes \psi]\!] = [\![\varphi]\!] \cap [\![\psi]\!]$ (if $\wedge$ is available within the logic, we would simply have $\varphi \otimes \psi = \varphi \wedge \psi$). For such a logic, we can "implement" the single-sentence setting by letting $\mathfrak{B} = \{\{\varphi\} \mid \varphi \in \mathcal{L}\}$ and defining $\{\varphi\} \uplus \{\psi\} = \{\varphi \otimes \psi\}$.

For any of the four different notions of bases presented above, one can additionally choose to disallow or allow the empty set as a base, while maintaining the required closure under abstract union.

In the following, we will always operate on the abstract level of "base logics"; our notions, results and proofs will only make use of the few general properties specified for these. This guarantees that our results are generically applicable to any of the four described (and any other) instantiations, and hence, are independent of the question what the right notion of bases ought to be. The cognitive overload caused by this abstraction should be minimal; e.g., readers only interested in the case of arbitrary sets can safely assume $\mathfrak{B} = \mathcal{P}(\mathcal{L})$ and mentally replace any $\uplus$ by $\cup$.

4.1.6. Base Change Operators

In this part we use base change operators to model multiple revision, which is the process of incorporating multiple new beliefs into the present beliefs held by an agent, in a consistent way (whenever that is possible). We define change operators over a base logic as follows.

Definition 4.8. *Let* $\mathbb{B} = (\mathcal{L}, \Omega, \models, \mathfrak{B}, \uplus)$ *be a base logic. A function* $\circ : \mathfrak{B} \times \mathfrak{B} \to \mathfrak{B}$ *is called a* multiple base change operator *over* $\mathbb{B}$.

We will use multiple base change operators in the "standard" way of the belief change community: the first parameter represents the actual beliefs of an agent, the second parameter contains the new beliefs. The operator then yields the agent's revised beliefs. The term "multiple" references the fact that the second input to $\circ$ is not just a single sentence, but a belief base that may consist of several sentences. For convenience, we will henceforth drop the term "multiple" and simply speak of base change operators instead.

So far, the pure notion of base change operator is unconstrained and can be instantiated by an arbitrary binary function over bases. Obviously, this does not reflect the requirements or expectations one might have when speaking of a revision operator. Hence, in line with the traditional approach, we will consider additional constraints ("postulates") for base change operators, in order to capture the gist of revisions.

4.1.7. Postulates for Revision

We consider multiple revision, focusing on package semantics for revision (sometimes also denoted as priority revision [55]), which is that all given sentences have to be incorporated, i.e., given a base $\mathcal{K}$ and new information Γ (also a base here), we demand success of revision, i.e. $\mathcal{K} \circ \Gamma \models \Gamma$.

Besides the success condition, the belief change community has brought up and discussed several further requirements for belief change operators to make them *rational,* for summaries see, e.g., [73, 57]. This has led to the now famous AGM approach of revision [2], originally proposed through a set of rationality postulates, which correspond to the postulates (KM1)–(KM6) presented in the beginning of this chapter. In this part, we will make use of the Katsuno and Mendelzon version of the AGM postulates[2] adjusted to our generic notion of a base logic $\mathbb{B} = (\mathcal{L}, \Omega, \models, \mathfrak{B}, \uplus)$:

(G1) $\mathcal{K} \circ \Gamma \models \Gamma$.
(G2) If $[\![\mathcal{K} \uplus \Gamma]\!] \neq \emptyset$ then $\mathcal{K} \circ \Gamma \equiv \mathcal{K} \uplus \Gamma$.
(G3) If $[\![\Gamma]\!] \neq \emptyset$ then $[\![\mathcal{K} \circ \Gamma]\!] \neq \emptyset$.
(G4) If $\mathcal{K}_1 \equiv \mathcal{K}_2$ and $\Gamma_1 \equiv \Gamma_2$ then $\mathcal{K}_1 \circ \Gamma_1 \equiv \mathcal{K}_2 \circ \Gamma_2$.
(G5) $(\mathcal{K} \circ \Gamma_1) \uplus \Gamma_2 \models \mathcal{K} \circ (\Gamma_1 \uplus \Gamma_2)$.
(G6) If $[\![(\mathcal{K} \circ \Gamma_1) \uplus \Gamma_2]\!] \neq \emptyset$ then $\mathcal{K} \circ (\Gamma_1 \uplus \Gamma_2) \models (\mathcal{K} \circ \Gamma_1) \uplus \Gamma_2$.

Together, the postulates implement the paradigm of minimal change for revision, stating that a rational agent should change her beliefs as little as possible in the process of belief revision. We consider the postulates in more detail: (G1) guarantees that the newly added belief must be a logical consequence of the result of the revision. (G2) says that if the expansion of φ by α is consistent, then the result of the revision is equivalent to the expansion of φ by α. (G3) guarantees the consistency of the revision result if the newly added belief is consistent. (G4) is the principle of the irrelevance of the syntax, stating that the revision operation is independent of the syntactic form of the bases. (G5) and (G6) ensure more careful handling of (abstract) unions of belief bases. In particular, together, they enforce that $\mathcal{K} \circ (\Gamma_1 \uplus \Gamma_2) \equiv (\mathcal{K} \circ \Gamma_1) \uplus \Gamma_2$, unless Γ_2 contradicts $\mathcal{K} \circ \Gamma_1$.

We can see that, item by item, (G1)–(G6) tightly correspond to (KM1)–(KM6) presented in the introduction. Note also that further formulations similar to (G1)–(G6) are given in multiple particular contexts, e.g. in the context of belief base revision specifically for Description Logics [118], for parallel revision [43] and investigations on multiple revision [157, 114, 94]. An advantage of the specific form of the postulates (G1)–(G6) chosen for our presentation is that it does not require $\mathcal{L}$ to support conjunction (while, of course, conjunction on the sentence level is still implicitly supported via (abstract) union of bases).

---

[2] The abbreviation G stands for *generalized*.

4.2. Base Revision in Propositional Logic

A well-known and by now popular characterization of base revision has been described by Katsuno and Mendelzon [84] for the special case of propositional logic. To be more specific and apply our terminology, Katsuno and Mendelzon's approach applies to the base logic

$$\mathbb{PL}_n = (\mathcal{L}_{\mathrm{PL}_n}, \Omega_{\mathrm{PL}_n}, \models_{\mathrm{PL}_n}, \mathcal{P}_{\mathrm{fin}}(\mathcal{L}_{\mathrm{PL}_n}), \cup)$$

for arbitrary, but fixed n (cf. Example 4.5). The assumption of the finiteness on the underlying signature of atomic propositions is not mentioned explicitly in Katsuno and Mendelzon's article, but it becomes apparent upon investigating their arguments and proofs – we will see shortly, their characterization fails as soon as this assumption is dropped. Katsuno and Mendelzon's approach also hinges on other particularities of this setting: As discussed earlier, any propositional belief base $\mathcal{K}$ can be equivalently written as a single propositional sentence. Consequently, in their approach, belief bases are actually represented by single sentences, without loss of expressivity.

One key contribution of Katsuno and Mendelzon is to provide an alternative characterization of the propositional base revision operators satisfying (KM1)–(KM6) by model-theoretic means, i.e. through comparisons between propositional interpretations. In the following, we present their results in a formulation that facilitates later generalization. One central notion for the characterization is the notion of *faithful assignment*.

Definition 4.9 (Assignment, Faithful). *Let* $\mathbb{B} = (\mathcal{L}, \Omega, \models, \mathfrak{B}, \cup)$ *be a base logic. An* assignment *for* $\mathbb{B}$ *is a function* $\preceq_{(.)} \colon \mathfrak{B} \to \mathcal{P}(\Omega \times \Omega)$ *that assigns to each belief base* $\mathcal{K} \in \mathfrak{B}$ *a total binary relation* $\preceq_{\mathcal{K}}$ *over* Ω. *An assignment* $\preceq_{(.)}$ *for* $\mathbb{B}$ *is called* faithful *if it satisfies the following conditions for all* $\omega, \omega' \in \Omega$ *and all* $\mathcal{K}, \mathcal{K}' \in \mathfrak{B}$:

  (F1) *If* $\omega, \omega' \models \mathcal{K}$, *then* $\omega \prec_{\mathcal{K}} \omega'$ *does not hold.*
  (F2) *If* $\omega \models \mathcal{K}$ *and* $\omega' \not\models \mathcal{K}$, *then* $\omega \prec_{\mathcal{K}} \omega'$.
  (F3) *If* $\mathcal{K} \equiv \mathcal{K}'$, *then* $\preceq_{\mathcal{K}} = \preceq_{\mathcal{K}'}$.

An assignment $\preceq_{(.)}$ *is called a* preorder assignment *if* $\preceq_{\mathcal{K}}$ *is a preorder for every* $\mathcal{K} \in \mathfrak{B}$.

Intuitively, faithful assignments provide information about which of two interpretations is "closer to $\mathcal{K}$-modelhood". Consequently, the actual $\mathcal{K}$-models are $\preceq_{\mathcal{K}}$-minimal. The next definition captures the idea of an assignment adequately representing the behaviour of a revision operator.

Definition 4.10 (Compatible). *Let* $\mathbb{B} = (\mathcal{L}, \Omega, \models, \mathfrak{B}, \mathbb{U})$ *a base logic. A base change operator $\circ$ for $\mathbb{B}$ is called* compatible[3] *with some assignment $\preceq_{(.)}$ for $\mathbb{B}$ if it satisfies*

$$[\![\mathcal{K} \circ \Gamma]\!] = \min([\![\Gamma]\!], \preceq_{\mathcal{K}})$$

for all bases $\mathcal{K}$ and Γ from $\mathfrak{B}$.

With these notions in place, Katsuno and Mendelzon's representation result (Theorem 3.9) can be smoothly expressed as follows:

Theorem 4.11 (Adapted, Katsuno and Mendelzon [84]). *A base change operator $\circ$ for $\mathbb{PL}_n$ satisfies (G1)–(G6) if and only if it is compatible with some faithful preorder assignment for $\mathbb{PL}_n$.*

Theorem 4.11 is of particular importance, as for instance, it is the base result for AGM-based belief change in epistemic states by Darwiche and Pearl [41] which we will heavily use in Part II and Part III. As a bibliographic remark, we want to highlight that for revision of belief sets (instead of belief bases) Theorem 4.11 is a special case of a result by Grove [67].

In the next section, we discuss and provide a generalization of the overall approach to the setting of arbitrary base logics.

4.3. Approach for Arbitrary Base Logics

In this section, we prepare our main result by revisiting Katsuno and Mendelzon's concepts for propositional logic and investigating their suitability for our general setting of base logics. The result by Katsuno and Mendelzon established an elegant combination of the notions of preorder assignments, faithfulness, and compatibility in order to semantically characterize AGM base change operators. However, as we mentioned before and will make more precise in the following, Katsuno

---

[3] A name like "revision-compatible" would be more appropriate. However, we use "compatible" here to have the same notion as used in [54].

and Mendelzon's characterization hinges on features of signature-finite propositional logic that do not generally hold for Tarskian logics. So far, attempts to find similar formulations for less restrictive logics have made good progress for understanding the nature of AGM revision [67, 1, 46]. Here we go further, by extending the Katsuno and Mendelzon approach by novel notions to the very general setting of base logics.

4.3.1. First Problem: Non-Existence of Minima

The first issue with Katsuno and Mendelzon's original characterization when generalizing to base logics is the possible absence of $\preceq_{\mathcal{K}}$-minimal elements in $[\![\Gamma]\!]$.

Observation 4.12. *For arbitrary base logics, the minimum from Definition 4.10, required in Theorem 4.11, might be empty.*

One way this might happen is due to infinite descending $\preceq_{\mathcal{K}}$-chains of interpretations. To illustrate this problem (and to show that it arises even for propositional logic, if the signature is infinite but bases are finite), consider the base logic

$$\mathbb{PL}_\infty = (\mathcal{L}_{\mathrm{PL}_\infty}, \Omega_{\mathrm{PL}_\infty}, \models_{\mathrm{PL}_\infty}, \mathcal{P}_{\mathrm{fin}}(\mathcal{L}_{\mathrm{PL}_\infty}), \cup),$$

i.e., propositional logic with finite bases, but countably infinitely many distinct atomic propositions $\Sigma = \{p_1, p_2, \ldots\}$ (cf. Example 4.6). We will exhibit a base change operator that is compatible with a faithful preorder assignment, yet does violate one of the postulates, due to the problem mentioned above.

Example 4.13. *We define $\circ^\cup$ by simply letting $\mathcal{K} \circ^\cup \Gamma = \mathcal{K} \cup \Gamma$. Obviously $\circ^\cup$ violates (G3) as one can see by picking, say $\mathcal{K} = \{p_1\}$ and $\Gamma = \{\neg p_1\}$. Nevertheless, for this operator, a compatible assignment exists, as we will show next. Assume a base $\mathcal{K}$ and two propositional interpretations $\omega_1, \omega_2 : \Sigma \to \{\mathbf{true}, \mathbf{false}\}$. Let $\omega_k^{\mathbf{true}}$ denote $\{p_i \in \Sigma \mid \omega_k(p_i) = \mathbf{true}\}$ for $k \in \{1, 2\}$, i.e., the set of atomic symbols that ω_k maps to $\mathbf{true}$. Then we let $\omega_1 \preceq_{\mathcal{K}}^\cup \omega_2$ if at least one of the following is the case:*

(1) $\omega_1 \models \mathcal{K}$
(2) $\omega_2 \not\models \mathcal{K}$ *and* $\omega_2^{\mathbf{true}}$ *is infinite*
(3) $\omega_1, \omega_2 \not\models \mathcal{K}$, *both* $\omega_1^{\mathbf{true}}$ *and* $\omega_2^{\mathbf{true}}$ *are finite, and* $|\omega_1^{\mathbf{true}}| \geq |\omega_2^{\mathbf{true}}|$

We see that this definition provides a faithful preorder assignment compatible with ∘ (see Proposition 4.14).

Proposition 4.14. *The relation $\preceq_{\mathcal{K}}^{\cup}$ is a faithful preorder assignment and is compatible with the base change operator $\circ^{\cup}$ for $\mathbb{PL}_{\infty}$, yet $\circ^{\cup}$ does not satisfy (G3).*

Proof. We show that $\preceq_{\mathcal{K}}^{\cup}$ is a preorder assignment.

(Totality) For totality, assume the contrary, i.e. there are two interpretations ω_1, ω_2 with $\omega_1 \npreceq_{\mathcal{K}}^{\cup} \omega_2$ and $\omega_2 \npreceq_{\mathcal{K}}^{\cup} \omega_1$. From the definition of $\preceq_{\mathcal{K}}^{\cup}$, we have $\omega_1, \omega_2 \not\models \mathcal{K}$ where both ω_1 and ω_2 are finite with $|\omega_1^{\mathbf{true}}| \not\geq |\omega_2^{\mathbf{true}}|$ and $|\omega_2^{\mathbf{true}}| \not\geq |\omega_1^{\mathbf{true}}|$. Since $\geq$ is total over integers, this is a contradiction. Reflexivity follows from totality.

(Transitivity) For transitivity, suppose $\omega_1 \preceq_{\mathcal{K}}^{\cup} \omega_2$ and $\omega_2 \preceq_{\mathcal{K}}^{\cup} \omega_3$. We make a case distinction by $\omega_1 \preceq_{\mathcal{K}}^{\cup} \omega_2$ and the definition of $\preceq_{\mathcal{K}}^{\cup}$:

   (1) The case of $\omega_1 \models \mathcal{K}$. Then $\omega_1 \preceq_{\mathcal{K}}^{\cup} \omega_3$ follows immediately.
   (2) The case of $\omega_2 \not\models \mathcal{K}$ and $\omega_2^{\mathbf{true}}$ is infinite. As $\omega_2 \preceq_{\mathcal{K}}^{\cup} \omega_3$, we
       consider three subcases:
          (2.1) $\omega_2 \models \mathcal{K}$. This contradicts the prior assumption, and
          hence this case is not possible.
          (2.2) $\omega_3 \not\models \mathcal{K}$ with infinite $\omega_3^{\mathbf{true}}$. Then $\omega_1 \preceq_{\mathcal{K}}^{\cup} \omega_3$ follows.
          (2.3) $\omega_2^{\mathbf{true}}$ and $\omega_3^{\mathbf{true}}$ are finite. This is also impossible due to
          immediate contradiction.
   (3) The case of $\omega_1, \omega_2 \not\models \mathcal{K}$, both $\omega_1^{\mathbf{true}}$ and $\omega_2^{\mathbf{true}}$ are finite and
       $|\omega_1^{\mathbf{true}}| \geq |\omega_2^{\mathbf{true}}|$. From $\omega_2 \preceq_{\mathcal{K}}^{\cup} \omega_3$ we consider three subcases:
          (3.1) $\omega_2 \models \mathcal{K}$. This is not possible, immediate contradiction.
          (3.2) $\omega_3 \not\models \mathcal{K}$ with infinite $\omega_3^{\mathbf{true}}$. This implies $\omega_1 \preceq_{\mathcal{K}}^{\cup} \omega_3$.
          (3.3) $\omega_2, \omega_3 \not\models \mathcal{K}$, both $\omega_2^{\mathbf{true}}$ and $\omega_3^{\mathbf{true}}$ are finite with $|\omega_2^{\mathbf{true}}| \geq$
          $|\omega_3^{\mathbf{true}}|$. Since $|\omega_1^{\mathbf{true}}| \geq |\omega_2^{\mathbf{true}}|$ and $|\omega_2^{\mathbf{true}}| \geq |\omega_3^{\mathbf{true}}|$, from
          transitivity of $\geq$ over integers, we have $|\omega_1^{\mathbf{true}}| \geq |\omega_3^{\mathbf{true}}|$ and
          finally $\omega_1 \preceq_{\mathcal{K}}^{\cup} \omega_3$.

We show that $\preceq_{\mathcal{K}}^{\cup}$ is faithful and that $\preceq_{(.)}^{\cup}$ is compatible with $\circ^{\cup}$.

(Faithfulness) The first condition of faithfulness, the Condition (F1), follows from the assumption $\omega_1, \omega_2 \models \mathcal{K}$ and case (1) of the definition of $\preceq_{\mathcal{K}}^{\cup}$, given in Example 4.13.

For (F2), let $\omega_1 \models \mathcal{K}$ and $\omega_2 \not\models \mathcal{K}$. From the case (1) of the definition, $\omega_1 \preceq_{\mathcal{K}}^{\cup} \omega_2$ holds. Now for contradiction assume that $\omega_2 \preceq_{\mathcal{K}}^{\cup} \omega_1$. Following the definition of $\preceq_{\mathcal{K}}^{\cup}$, we consider three cases. (Case 1) $\omega_2 \models \mathcal{K}$ contradicts our assumption. The (Case 2) and (Case 3) are not applicable because they require $\omega_1 \not\models \mathcal{K}$. Hence, $\omega_2 \not\preceq_{\mathcal{K}}^{\cup} \omega_1$ and therefore $\omega_1 \prec_{\mathcal{K}}^{\cup} \omega_2$ holds.

For (F3), assume $\mathcal{K} \equiv \mathcal{K}'$ (i.e. $[\![\mathcal{K}]\!] = [\![\mathcal{K}']\!]$) and let $\omega_1 \preceq_{\mathcal{K}}^{\cup} \omega_2$. We consider three cases. (Case 1) $\omega_1 \models \mathcal{K}$. Then it also holds $\omega_1 \models \mathcal{K}'$, and hence $\omega_1 \preceq_{\mathcal{K}'} \omega_2$. (Case 2) $\omega_2 \not\models \mathcal{K}$ and $\omega_2^{\mathbf{true}}$ is infinite. Then $\omega_2 \not\models \mathcal{K}'$ and hence $\omega_1 \preceq_{\mathcal{K}'} \omega_2$. (Case 3) where $\omega_1, \omega_2 \not\models \mathcal{K}$ we also have $\omega_1, \omega_2 \not\models \mathcal{K}'$ and consequently $\omega_1 \preceq_{\mathcal{K}'} \omega_2$. Therefore, we have $\preceq_{\mathcal{K}}^{\cup} = \preceq_{\mathcal{K}'}^{\cup}$ (i.e. $\omega_1 \preceq_{\mathcal{K}}^{\cup} \omega_2$ if and only if $\omega_1 \preceq_{\mathcal{K}'} \omega_2$).

(Compatibility with $\circ$) For the compatibility with $\circ^{\cup}$, we show that $[\![\mathcal{K} \circ^{\cup} \Gamma]\!] = \min([\![\Gamma]\!], \preceq_{\mathcal{K}}^{\cup})$. For any inconsistent Γ, we have $[\![\mathcal{K} \circ^{\cup} \Gamma]\!] = \emptyset = \min([\![\Gamma]\!], \preceq_{\mathcal{K}}^{\cup})$. If $\mathcal{K} \cup \Gamma$ is consistent, then we have $[\![\mathcal{K} \circ \Gamma]\!] = [\![\mathcal{K} \cup \Gamma]\!]$. Because $\preceq_{\mathcal{K}}^{\cup}$ is faithful, we directly obtain $[\![\mathcal{K} \circ \Gamma]\!] = \min([\![\Gamma]\!], \preceq_{\mathcal{K}}^{\cup})$. Thus, for the remaining steps of the proof, we assume that $\mathcal{K} \cup \Gamma$ is inconsistent and Γ is consistent.

We show in the following that $\min([\![\Gamma]\!], \preceq_{\mathcal{K}}^{\cup}) = \emptyset$ holds by contradiction, i.e., there exists some $\omega_1 \in \min([\![\Gamma]\!], \preceq_{\mathcal{K}}^{\cup})$. This means, that $\omega_1 \in [\![\Gamma]\!]$ and there is no other $\omega_2 \in [\![\Gamma]\!]$ such that $\omega_2 \prec_{\mathcal{K}}^{\cup} \omega_1$. Note that from the definition of $\circ^{\cup}$ and our case assumption, we have $[\![\mathcal{K} \circ^{\cup} \Gamma]\!] = [\![\mathcal{K} \cup \Gamma]\!] = \emptyset$, and hence $\omega_1, \omega_2 \not\models \mathcal{K}$. Let $\Sigma_\Gamma \subseteq \Sigma$ be a set of atomic symbols occurring in Γ. Because Γ is finite, we have that Σ_Γ contains finitely many atoms. We have two cases: $\omega_1^{\mathbf{true}}$ can be finite or infinite.

$(\omega_1^{\mathbf{true}}$ is finite) Then, there exists an atomic symbol q such that $q \in \Sigma \setminus (\omega_1^{\mathbf{true}} \cup \Sigma_\Gamma)$ (as both $\omega_1^{\mathbf{true}}$ and Σ_Γ are finite and Σ is infinite). Then we could define another interpretation ω_2 such that $\omega_2(q) = \mathbf{true}$ and $\omega_2(p_i) = \omega_1(p_i)$ for all $p_i \in \Sigma \setminus \{q\}$. Since q does not occur in Γ, we have $\omega_2 \in [\![\Gamma]\!]$ and $|\omega_2^{\mathbf{true}}| = |\omega_1^{\mathbf{true}}| + 1$. Hence, $\omega_2 \prec_{\mathcal{K}}^{\cup} \omega_1$, a contradiction to the minimality of ω_1.

$(\omega_1^{\mathbf{true}}$ is infinite) We define another interpretation ω_2 such that for all $p_i \in \Sigma$ we set $\omega_2(p_i) = \mathbf{true}$ if $p_i \in (\Sigma_\Gamma \cap \omega_1^{\mathbf{true}})$ and $\omega_2(p_i) = \mathbf{false}$ otherwise. As ω_1 and ω_2 coincide on Σ_Γ, we obtain $\omega_2 \in [\![\Gamma]\!]$. Since $\omega_2^{\mathbf{true}}$ is finite while $\omega_1^{\mathbf{true}}$ is infinite, we have $\omega_2 \prec_{\mathcal{K}}^{\cup} \omega_1$, which again is a contradiction to the minimality of ω_1. $\qquad\square$

To remedy the problem exposed above, one needs to impose the requirement that minima exist whenever needed, as specified in the notion of *min-completeness*, defined next.

Definition 4.15 (min-complete). *Let* $\mathbb{B} = (\mathcal{L}, \Omega, \models, \mathfrak{B}, \mathbb{U})$ *be a base logic. A binary relation* $\preceq$ *over* Ω *is called* min-complete *(for* $\mathbb{B}$*) if* $\min(\llbracket \Gamma \rrbracket, \preceq) \neq \emptyset$ *holds for every* $\Gamma \in \mathfrak{B}$ *with* $\llbracket \Gamma \rrbracket \neq \emptyset$.

The following example demonstrates that for a binary relation it depends on the base logic whether the relation is min-complete or not.

Example 4.16. *Consider two base logics* $\mathbb{B}_{\mathbb{Z}\leq}$ *and* $\mathbb{B}_{\mathbb{Z}\geq}$ *with*

$$\mathbb{B}_{\mathbb{Z}\leq} = (\mathcal{L}_1, \mathbb{Z}, \models, \mathcal{P}_{\mathrm{fin}}(\mathcal{L}_1) \setminus \{\emptyset\}, \cup), \text{ and}$$
$$\mathbb{B}_{\mathbb{Z}\geq} = (\mathcal{L}_2, \mathbb{Z}, \models, \mathcal{P}_{\mathrm{fin}}(\mathcal{L}_2) \setminus \{\emptyset\}, \cup),$$

where $\mathcal{L}_1 = \{[\leq n] \mid n \in \mathbb{Z}\}$ *and* $\mathcal{L}_2 = \{[\geq n] \mid n \in \mathbb{Z}\}$. *Furthermore let* $m \models [\leq n]$ *if* $m \leq n$ *and* $m \models [\geq n]$ *if* $n \leq m$, *assuming the usual meaning of* $\leq$ *for integers. In words, these logics talk about the domain of integers by means of comparisons with a fixed integer. We now define the relation* $\preceq$ *over* Ω *by letting* $m_1 \preceq m_2$ *if and only if* $m_1 \leq m_2$. *It can be verified that the relation is transitive and for any consistent base* $\Gamma \in \mathcal{P}_{\mathrm{fin}}(\mathcal{L}_1)$, *respectively for* $\Gamma \in \mathcal{P}_{\mathrm{fin}}(\mathcal{L}_2)$, *we have infinitely many models* $\llbracket \Gamma \rrbracket$.

Note that for each set of sentences of the form $[\leq n] \in \mathcal{L}_1$, *there are no minimal models* $\min(\llbracket \Gamma \rrbracket, \preceq)$, *and thus,* $\preceq$ *is not* min-complete *for* $\mathbb{B}_{\mathbb{Z}\leq}$. *However, for* $\mathbb{B}_{\mathbb{Z}\geq}$, *the relation* $\preceq$ *is min-complete.*

In the special case of $\preceq$ being transitive and total, min-completeness trivially holds whenever Ω is finite (as, e.g., in the case of propositional logic over n propositional atoms; cf. Example 4.5). In the infinite case, however, it might need to be explicitly imposed, as already noted in earlier works [46] (cf. also the notion of *limit assumption* by Lewis [103]). Note that min-completeness does not entirely disallow infinite descending chains (as well-foundedness would), it only ensures that minima exist inside all model sets of consistent belief bases.

4.3.2. Second Problem: Transitivity of Preorder

When generalizing from the setting of propositional to arbitrary base logics, the requirement that assignments must produce preorders (and hence transitive relations) turns out to be too restrictive.

Observation 4.17. *Transitivity of the relation produced by the assignment, as required in Theorem 4.11, is a too strict property for characterizing AGM revision in arbitrary Tarskian logics.*

In fact, it has been observed before that the incompatibility between transitivity and Katsuno and Mendelzon's approach already arises for propositional Horn logic [45]. The following example builds on Example 4.4 and provides an operator and a belief base for which no compatible transitive assignment exists.

Example 4.18 (Continuation of Example 4.4). *Consider the base logic* $\mathbb{B}_{\mathrm{Ex}} = (\mathcal{L}_{\mathrm{Ex}}, \Omega_{\mathrm{Ex}}, \models_{\mathrm{Ex}}, \mathcal{P}(\mathcal{L}_{\mathrm{Ex}}), \cup)$. *Let* $\mathcal{K}_{\mathrm{Ex}} = \{\psi_3\}$ *and let* $\circ_{\mathrm{Ex}}$ *be the base change operator defined as follows:*

$$
\mathcal{K}_{\mathrm{Ex}} \circ_{\mathrm{Ex}} \Gamma =
\begin{cases}
\mathcal{K}_{\mathrm{Ex}} \cup \Gamma & \text{if } [\![\mathcal{K}_{\mathrm{Ex}} \cup \Gamma]\!] \neq \emptyset, \\
\Gamma \cup \{\psi_4\} & \text{if } [\![\mathcal{K}_{\mathrm{Ex}} \cup \Gamma]\!] = \emptyset \text{ and } [\![\{\psi_4\} \cup \Gamma]\!] \neq \emptyset, \\
\Gamma \cup \{\psi_0\} & \text{if } [\![\mathcal{K}_{\mathrm{Ex}} \cup \Gamma]\!] = \emptyset \text{ and } [\![\{\psi_0\} \cup \Gamma]\!] \neq \emptyset \\
& \quad\text{and } [\![\{\psi_2\} \cup \Gamma]\!] = \emptyset, \\
\Gamma \cup \{\psi_1\} & \text{if } [\![\mathcal{K}_{\mathrm{Ex}} \cup \Gamma]\!] = \emptyset \text{ and } [\![\{\psi_1\} \cup \Gamma]\!] \neq \emptyset \\
& \quad\text{and } [\![\{\psi_0\} \cup \Gamma]\!] = \emptyset, \\
\Gamma \cup \{\psi_2\} & \text{if } [\![\mathcal{K}_{\mathrm{Ex}} \cup \Gamma]\!] = \emptyset \text{ and } [\![\{\psi_2\} \cup \Gamma]\!] \neq \emptyset \\
& \quad\text{and } [\![\{\psi_1\} \cup \Gamma]\!] = \emptyset, \\
\Gamma & \text{if none of the above applies,}
\end{cases}
$$

Moreover, for all $\mathcal{K}'$ *with* $\mathcal{K}' \equiv \mathcal{K}_{\mathrm{Ex}}$ *we define* $\mathcal{K}' \circ_{\mathrm{Ex}} \Gamma = \mathcal{K}_{\mathrm{Ex}} \circ_{\mathrm{Ex}} \Gamma$ *and for all* $\mathcal{K}'$ *with* $\mathcal{K}' \not\equiv \mathcal{K}_{\mathrm{Ex}}$ *we define*

$$
\mathcal{K}' \circ_{\mathrm{Ex}} \Gamma =
\begin{cases}
\mathcal{K}' \cup \Gamma & \text{if } \mathcal{K}' \cup \Gamma \text{ consistent} \\
\Gamma & \text{otherwise.}
\end{cases}
$$

For all $\mathcal{K}'$ *with* $\mathcal{K}' \not\equiv \mathcal{K}_{\mathrm{Ex}}$, *there is no violation of the postulates (G1)–(G6) since we obtain a trivial revision, which satisfies (G1)–(G6) (cf. Example 4.38). For the case of* $\mathcal{K}' \equiv \mathcal{K}_{\mathrm{Ex}}$, *the satisfaction of (G1)–(G6) can be shown case by case or using Theorem 4.36 in Section 4.5.*

Now assume there were a preorder assignment $\preceq_{(.)}$ *compatible with* $\circ_{\mathrm{Ex}}$. *This means that for all bases* $\mathcal{K}$ *and* Γ *from* $\mathcal{P}(\mathcal{L}_{\mathrm{Ex}})$, *the relation* $\preceq_{\mathcal{K}}$ *is a preorder and* $[\![\mathcal{K} \circ_{\mathrm{Ex}} \Gamma]\!] = \min([\![\Gamma]\!], \preceq_{\mathcal{K}_{\mathrm{Ex}}})$. *Now consider* $\Gamma_0 = \{\varphi_0\}$, $\Gamma_1 = \{\varphi_1\}$, *and* $\Gamma_2 = \{\varphi_2\}$. *From the definition of* $\circ_{\mathrm{Ex}}$

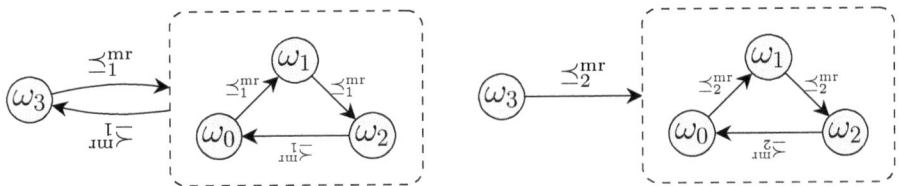

(a) Not min-retractive relation $\preceq_1^{\mathrm{mr}}$ (b) Min-retractive relation $\preceq_2^{\mathrm{mr}}$ for
for $\mathbb{B}_{\mathrm{mr}}$. $\mathbb{B}_{\mathrm{mr}}$.

Figure 4.2: Illustration of the two relations $\preceq_1^{\mathrm{mr}}$ and $\preceq_2^{\mathrm{mr}}$ from Example 4.20.

and compatibility, we obtain $[\![\mathcal{K}_{\mathrm{Ex}} \circ_{\mathrm{Ex}} \Gamma_0]\!] = \{\omega_0\} = \min([\![\Gamma_0]\!], \preceq_{\mathcal{K}_{\mathrm{Ex}}})$,
$[\![\mathcal{K}_{\mathrm{Ex}} \circ_{\mathrm{Ex}} \Gamma_1]\!] = \{\omega_1\} = \min([\![\Gamma_1]\!], \preceq_{\mathcal{K}_{\mathrm{Ex}}})$, and $[\![\mathcal{K}_{\mathrm{Ex}} \circ_{\mathrm{Ex}} \Gamma_2]\!] = \{\omega_2\} =$
$\min([\![\Gamma_2]\!], \preceq_{\mathcal{K}_{\mathrm{Ex}}})$. Recall that $[\![\Gamma_0]\!] = \{\omega_0, \omega_1\}$, $[\![\Gamma_1]\!] = \{\omega_1, \omega_2\}$, and
$[\![\Gamma_2]\!] = \{\omega_2, \omega_0\}$. Yet, this implies $\omega_0 \prec_{\mathcal{K}_{\mathrm{Ex}}} \omega_1$, $\omega_1 \prec_{\mathcal{K}_{\mathrm{Ex}}} \omega_2$, and
$\omega_2 \prec_{\mathcal{K}_{\mathrm{Ex}}} \omega_0$, contradicting the assumption that $\preceq_{\mathcal{K}_{\mathrm{Ex}}}$ is transitive.
Hence, it cannot be a preorder.

As a consequence, we cannot help but waive transitivity (and hence the property of the assignment providing a preorder) if we want our characterization result to hold for all Tarskian logics. However, for our result, we need to retain a new, weaker property (which is implied by transitivity) defined next.

Definition 4.19 (min-retractive). *Let $\mathbb{B} = (\mathcal{L}, \Omega, \models, \mathcal{B}, \mathbb{U})$ be a base logic. A binary relation $\preceq$ over Ω is called* min-retractive *(for $\mathbb{B}$) if, for every $\Gamma \in \mathcal{B}$ and $\omega', \omega \in [\![\Gamma]\!]$ with $\omega' \preceq \omega$, $\omega \in \min([\![\Gamma]\!], \preceq)$ implies $\omega' \in \min([\![\Gamma]\!], \preceq)$.*

Note that min-retractivity prevents minimal elements from being $\preceq$-equivalent to elements with $\prec$-lower neighbours, for instance elements lying on a "$\prec$-cycle" or elements being part of an infinite descending chain. Consider the following illustrative example.

Example 4.20. *Let $\mathbb{B}_{\mathrm{mr}} = (\mathcal{L}, \Omega, \models, \mathcal{B}, \mathbb{U})$ be a base logic with just one base $\mathcal{B} = \{\Gamma_{\mathrm{mr}}\}$ and four interpretations $\Omega = \{\omega_0, \omega_1, \omega_2, \omega_3\}$ such that $[\![\Gamma_{\mathrm{mr}}]\!] = \Omega$. Now consider the following total relation $\preceq_1^{\mathrm{mr}}$ on Ω*

illustrated in Figure 4.2a and given by

$$\omega_i \preceq_{\mathcal{K}_{\mathrm{Ex}}}^{\circ \mathrm{Ex}} \omega_i, \ 0 \leq i \leq 3, \qquad\qquad \omega_0 \prec_{\mathcal{K}_{\mathrm{Ex}}}^{\circ \mathrm{Ex}} \omega_1,$$

$$\omega_3 \prec_{\mathcal{K}_{\mathrm{Ex}}}^{\circ \mathrm{Ex}} \omega_i, \ 0 \leq i \leq 2, \qquad\qquad \omega_1 \prec_{\mathcal{K}_{\mathrm{Ex}}}^{\circ \mathrm{Ex}} \omega_2,$$

$$\omega_i \prec_{\mathcal{K}_{\mathrm{Ex}}}^{\circ \mathrm{Ex}} \omega_3, \ 0 \leq i \leq 2, \qquad\qquad \omega_2 \prec_{\mathcal{K}_{\mathrm{Ex}}}^{\circ \mathrm{Ex}} \omega_0.$$

We show that $\preceq_1^{\mathrm{mr}}$ is not min-retractive for $\mathbb{B}_{\mathrm{mr}}$. The $\preceq_1^{\mathrm{mr}}$-minimal models of Γ_{mr} are given by $\min([\![\Gamma_{\mathrm{mr}}]\!], \preceq_1^{\mathrm{mr}}) = \{\omega_3\}$. Observe that ω_0 is a non-minimal model of Γ_{mr} while being $\preceq_1^{\mathrm{mr}}$-equivalent to ω_3, and in particular $\omega_0 \preceq_1^{\mathrm{mr}} \omega_3$. This is a violation of min-retractivity.

Let $\preceq_2^{\mathrm{mr}}$ be the same relation as $\preceq_1^{\mathrm{mr}}$, except that $\preceq_2^{\mathrm{mr}}$ strictly prefers ω_3 over all other interpretations, i.e., $\preceq_2^{\mathrm{mr}} = \preceq_1^{\mathrm{mr}} \setminus \{(\omega, \omega_3) \mid \omega \neq \omega_3\}$. An illustration of $\preceq_2^{\mathrm{mr}}$ is given in Figure 4.2b. Indeed, we have that $\preceq_2^{\mathrm{mr}}$ is min-retractive for $\mathbb{B}_{\mathrm{mr}}$. In particular, observe that the prior counterexample for $\preceq_1^{\mathrm{mr}}$ does not apply to $\preceq_2^{\mathrm{mr}}$, as we have $\omega_0 \not\preceq_2^{\mathrm{mr}} \omega_3$.

As an aside, let us note that, if $\preceq$ is total but not transitive, min-completeness can be violated even in the setting where Ω is finite, by means of strict cyclic relationships.

Example 4.21. *Let $\mathbb{B}_{\mathrm{rps}} = (\mathcal{L}, \Omega, \models, \mathcal{P}(\mathcal{L}), \cup)$ be the base logic defined by $\mathcal{L} = \{\text{ALL-THREE}\}$ and $\Omega = \{\text{🖐}, \text{✊}, \text{✌}\}$, with the models relation $\models$ given by $[\![\text{ALL-THREE}]\!] = \Omega$. We now define the relation $\preceq^{\mathrm{rps}}$ as the common game "rock-paper-scissors": paper beats rock ($\text{✊} \prec^{\mathrm{rps}} \text{🖐}$), scissors beat paper ($\text{✌} \prec^{\mathrm{rps}} \text{✊}$), and rock beats scissors ($\text{🖐} \prec^{\mathrm{rps}} \text{✌}$). Clearly, the set of interpretations Ω is finite and the relation $\preceq^{\mathrm{rps}}$ is total, but not transitive. It is, however vacuously min-retractive. By considering a consistent base Γ containing the only sentence ALL-THREE, we find that $\min([\![\Gamma]\!], \preceq^{\mathrm{rps}}) = \emptyset$, and hence a violation of min-completeness.*

As a last act in this section, we conveniently unite the two identified properties into one notion.

Definition 4.22 (min-friendly). *Let $\mathbb{B} = (\mathcal{L}, \Omega, \models, \mathfrak{B}, \mathbb{U})$ be a base logic. A binary relation $\preceq$ over Ω is called **min-friendly** (for $\mathbb{B}$) if it is both min-retractive and min-complete. An assignment $\preceq_{(.)} \colon \mathfrak{B} \to \mathcal{P}(\Omega \times \Omega)$ is called **min-friendly** if $\preceq_{\mathcal{K}}$ is min-friendly for all $\mathcal{K} \in \mathfrak{B}$.*

4.4. One-Way Representation Theorem

We are now ready to generalize Katsuno and Mendelzon's representation theorem from propositional to arbitrary Tarskian logics, by employing the notion of compatible min-friendly faithful assignments.

Theorem 4.23. *Let $\circ$ be a base change operator for some base logic $\mathbb{B}$. Then, $\circ$ satisfies (G1)–(G6) if and only if it is compatible with some min-friendly faithful assignment for $\mathbb{B}$.*

We show Theorem 4.23 in three steps. First, we provide a canonical way of obtaining an assignment for a given revision operator. Next, we show that our construction indeed yields a min-friendly faithful assignment that is compatible with the revision operator. Finally, we show that the notion of min-friendly compatible assignment is adequate to capture the class of base revision operators satisfying (G1)–(G6).

4.4.1. From Postulates to Assignments

Very central for the original result by Katsuno and Mendelzon [84] is a constructive way to obtain the assignment from a revision operator. In their proof for Theorem 4.11, they provided the following way of extracting the preference relations from the revision operator:

$$\omega_1 \leq_\mathcal{K} \omega_2 \text{ if } \omega_1 \models \mathcal{K} \text{ or } \omega_1 \models \mathcal{K} \circ form(\omega_1, \omega_2) \qquad (4.1)$$

where $form(\omega_1, \omega_2) \in \mathcal{L}$ denotes a sentence with $[\![form(\omega_1, \omega_2)]\!] = \{\omega_1, \omega_2\}$. Unfortunately, this method for obtaining a canonical encoding of the revision strategy of $\circ$ does not generalize to the general setting here. This is because a belief base Γ satisfying $[\![\Gamma]\!] = \{\omega_1, \omega_2\}$ may not exist.

As a recourse, we suggest the following construction, which we consider one of the core contributions of this approach. It realizes the idea that one should (strictly) prefer ω_1 over ω_2 only if there is a witness belief base Γ that certifies that $\circ$ prefers ω_1 over ω_2. Should no such witness exist, ω_1 and ω_2 will be deemed equally preferable.

Definition 4.24. *Let* $\mathbb{B} = (\mathcal{L}, \Omega, \models, \mathfrak{B}, \mathbb{U})$ *be a base logic, let* $\circ$ *be a base change operator for* $\mathbb{B}$ *and let* $\mathcal{K} \in \mathfrak{B}$ *be a belief base. The relation* $\sqsubseteq_{\mathcal{K}}^{\circ}$ *over* Ω *is defined by*

$$\omega_1 \sqsubseteq_{\mathcal{K}}^{\circ} \omega_2 \;\; \text{if}$$
$$\omega_2 \models \mathcal{K} \circ \Gamma \;\text{implies}\; \omega_1 \models \mathcal{K} \circ \Gamma \;\text{for all}\; \Gamma \in \mathfrak{B} \;\text{with}\; \omega_1, \omega_2 \in \llbracket \Gamma \rrbracket.$$

Definition 4.24 already yields an adequate encoding strategy for many base logics. However, to also properly cope with certain "degenerate" base logics, we have to hard-code that the prior beliefs of an agent are prioritized in all cases, that is, only models of the prior beliefs are minimal. The following relation builds upon the relation $\sqsubseteq_{\mathcal{K}}^{\circ}$, takes explicit care of handling prior beliefs and could be considered as the *canonical assignment* for Theorem 4.23.

Definition 4.25. *Let* $\mathbb{B} = (\mathcal{L}, \Omega, \models, \mathfrak{B}, \mathbb{U})$ *be a base logic, let* $\circ$ *be a base change operator for* $\mathbb{B}$ *and let* $\mathcal{K} \in \mathfrak{B}$ *be a belief base. The relation* $\preceq_{\mathcal{K}}^{\circ}$ *over* Ω *is then defined by*

$$\omega_1 \preceq_{\mathcal{K}}^{\circ} \omega_2 \;\; \text{if}\;\; \omega_1 \models \mathcal{K} \;\text{or}\; (\; \omega_1, \omega_2 \not\models \mathcal{K} \;\text{and}\; \omega_1 \sqsubseteq_{\mathcal{K}}^{\circ} \omega_2 \;).$$

Let $\preceq_{(.)}^{\circ} \colon \mathfrak{B} \to \mathcal{P}(\Omega \times \Omega)$ *denote the mapping* $\mathcal{K} \mapsto \preceq_{\mathcal{K}}^{\circ}$.

In the following, we apply the relation encoding given in Definition 4.25 to our running example and show that the relation is not transitive, yet min-friendly.

Example 4.26 (Continuation of Example 4.18). *Applying Definition 4.25 to* $\mathcal{K}_{\mathrm{Ex}}$ *and* $\circ_{\mathrm{Ex}}$ *yields the following relation* $\preceq_{\mathcal{K}_{\mathrm{Ex}}}^{\circ_{\mathrm{Ex}}}$ *on* Ω_{Ex} *(where* $\omega \prec_{\mathcal{K}_{\mathrm{Ex}}}^{\circ_{\mathrm{Ex}}} \omega'$ *denotes* $\omega \preceq_{\mathcal{K}_{\mathrm{Ex}}}^{\circ_{\mathrm{Ex}}} \omega'$ *and* $\omega' \not\preceq_{\mathcal{K}_{\mathrm{Ex}}}^{\circ_{\mathrm{Ex}}} \omega$):*

$$\omega_i \preceq_{\mathcal{K}_{\mathrm{Ex}}}^{\circ_{\mathrm{Ex}}} \omega_i, 0 \leq i \leq 5 \qquad \omega_0 \prec_{\mathcal{K}_{\mathrm{Ex}}}^{\circ_{\mathrm{Ex}}} \omega_1 \qquad \omega_4 \prec_{\mathcal{K}_{\mathrm{Ex}}}^{\circ_{\mathrm{Ex}}} \omega_i, i \in \{0,1,2,5\}$$
$$\omega_3 \prec_{\mathcal{K}_{\mathrm{Ex}}}^{\circ_{\mathrm{Ex}}} \omega_i, i \in \{0,1,2,4,5\} \qquad \omega_1 \prec_{\mathcal{K}_{\mathrm{Ex}}}^{\circ_{\mathrm{Ex}}} \omega_2 \qquad \omega_i \prec_{\mathcal{K}_{\mathrm{Ex}}}^{\circ_{\mathrm{Ex}}} \omega_5, 0 \leq i < 4$$
$$\omega_2 \prec_{\mathcal{K}_{\mathrm{Ex}}}^{\circ_{\mathrm{Ex}}} \omega_0$$

Observe that $\preceq_{\mathcal{K}_{\mathrm{Ex}}}^{\circ_{\mathrm{Ex}}}$ *is not transitive, since* $\omega_0, \omega_1, \omega_2$ *form a* $\prec_{\mathcal{K}_{\mathrm{Ex}}}^{\circ_{\mathrm{Ex}}}$*-circle (see Figure 4.3). Yet, one can easily verify that* $\preceq_{\mathcal{K}_{\mathrm{Ex}}}^{\circ_{\mathrm{Ex}}}$ *is a total and min-friendly relation. In particular, as* Ω_{Ex} *is finite, min-completeness can be checked by examining minimal model sets of all consistent bases in* $\mathbb{L}_{\mathrm{Ex}}$. *Moreover, there is no belief base* $\Gamma \in \mathcal{P}(\mathcal{L}_{\mathrm{Ex}})$ *such that there is some* $\omega \notin \min(\llbracket \Gamma \rrbracket, \preceq_{\mathcal{K}_{\mathrm{Ex}}}^{\circ_{\mathrm{Ex}}})$ *and* $\omega' \in \min(\llbracket \Gamma \rrbracket, \preceq_{\mathcal{K}_{\mathrm{Ex}}}^{\circ_{\mathrm{Ex}}})$ *with* $\omega \preceq_{\mathcal{K}_{\mathrm{Ex}}}^{\circ_{\mathrm{Ex}}} \omega'$.

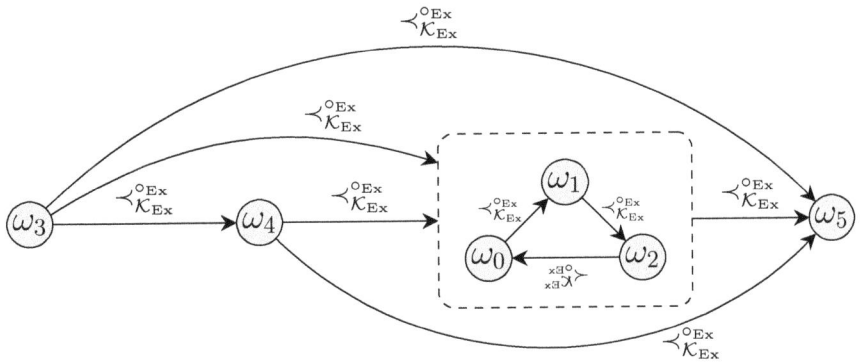

Figure 4.3: The structure of relation $\preceq_{\mathcal{K}}^{\circ\mathrm{Ex}}$ on Ω_{Ex}, where a solid arrow represents $\omega \prec_{\mathcal{K}}^{\circ\mathrm{Ex}} \omega'$ for any $\omega, \omega' \in \Omega_{\mathrm{Ex}}$.

Note that such a situation could appear in $\preceq_{\mathcal{K}_{\mathrm{Ex}}}^{\circ\mathrm{Ex}}$ if an interpretation ω would be $\preceq_{\mathcal{K}_{\mathrm{Ex}}}^{\circ\mathrm{Ex}}$-equivalent to ω_0, ω_1 and ω_2 and there would be a belief base Γ satisfied in all these interpretations, e.g., if $\omega = \omega_5$ would be equal to ω_0, ω_1 and ω_2, and $\llbracket\Gamma\rrbracket = \{\omega_0, \omega_1, \omega_2, \omega_5\}$. However, this is not the case in $\preceq_{\mathcal{K}_{\mathrm{Ex}}}^{\circ\mathrm{Ex}}$ and such a belief base Γ does not exist in $\mathbb{B}_{\mathrm{Ex}}$. Therefore, the relation $\preceq_{\mathcal{K}_{\mathrm{Ex}}}^{\circ\mathrm{Ex}}$ is min-retractive.

As a first insight, we obtain that the construction in Definition 4.25 is strong enough for always obtaining a relation that is total and reflexive.

Lemma 4.27 (Totality). *If $\circ$ satisfies (G5) and (G6), the relations $\preceq_{\mathcal{K}}^{\circ}$ and $\sqsubseteq_{\mathcal{K}}^{\circ}$ are total (and hence reflexive) for every $\mathcal{K} \in \mathfrak{B}$.*

Proof. Note that by construction, totality of $\preceq_{\mathcal{K}}^{\circ}$ is an immediate consequence of totality of $\sqsubseteq_{\mathcal{K}}^{\circ}$. We show the latter by contradiction: Assume the contrary, i.e. there are $\sqsubseteq_{\mathcal{K}}^{\circ}$-incomparable ω_1 and ω_2. Due to Definition 4.24, there must exist $\Gamma_1, \Gamma_2 \in \mathfrak{B}$ with $\omega_1, \omega_2 \models \Gamma_1$ and $\omega_1, \omega_2 \models \Gamma_2$, such that $\omega_1 \models \mathcal{K} \circ \Gamma_1$ and $\omega_2 \not\models \mathcal{K} \circ \Gamma_1$ whereas $\omega_1 \not\models \mathcal{K} \circ \Gamma_2$ and $\omega_2 \models \mathcal{K} \circ \Gamma_2$. Since $\omega_1 \in \llbracket\mathcal{K} \circ \Gamma_1\rrbracket \cap \llbracket\Gamma_2\rrbracket = \llbracket(\mathcal{K} \circ \Gamma_1) \uplus \Gamma_2\rrbracket$ and thus $\llbracket(\mathcal{K} \circ \Gamma_1) \uplus \Gamma_2\rrbracket \neq \emptyset$, (G5) and (G6) jointly entail $\llbracket(\mathcal{K} \circ \Gamma_1) \uplus \Gamma_2\rrbracket = \llbracket\mathcal{K} \circ (\Gamma_1 \uplus \Gamma_2)\rrbracket$. From commutativity of $\uplus$, $\llbracket\mathcal{K} \circ (\Gamma_1 \uplus \Gamma_2)\rrbracket = \llbracket\mathcal{K} \circ (\Gamma_2 \uplus \Gamma_1)\rrbracket$ follows. Now again, since $\omega_2 \in \llbracket\mathcal{K} \circ \Gamma_2\rrbracket \cap \llbracket\Gamma_1\rrbracket = \llbracket(\mathcal{K} \circ \Gamma_2) \uplus \Gamma_1\rrbracket$ and hence $\llbracket(\mathcal{K} \circ \Gamma_2) \uplus \Gamma_1\rrbracket \neq \emptyset$, (G5) and (G6) together entail $\llbracket\mathcal{K} \circ (\Gamma_2 \uplus \Gamma_1)\rrbracket = \llbracket(\mathcal{K} \circ \Gamma_2) \uplus \Gamma_1\rrbracket$. So, together, we obtain $\omega_1 \in \llbracket(\mathcal{K} \circ \Gamma_2) \uplus \Gamma_1\rrbracket = \llbracket\mathcal{K} \circ \Gamma_2\rrbracket \cap \llbracket\Gamma_1\rrbracket$ which directly contradicts our assumption $\omega_1 \notin [\![\mathcal{K} \circ \Gamma_2]\!]$.

Reflexivity follows immediately from totality. □

We proceed with an auxiliary lemma about belief bases and $\preceq_{\mathcal{K}}^{\circ}$.

Lemma 4.28. *Let $\circ$ satisfy (G2), (G5) and (G6) and let $\mathcal{K} \in \mathfrak{B}$. Then the following statements hold:*

(a) *If $\omega_1 \npreceq_{\mathcal{K}}^{\circ} \omega_2$ and $\omega_2 \not\models \mathcal{K}$, then there exists some Γ with $\omega_1, \omega_2 \models \Gamma$ as well as $\omega_2 \models \mathcal{K} \circ \Gamma$ and $\omega_1 \not\models \mathcal{K} \circ \Gamma$.*

(b) *If there is a Γ with $\omega_1, \omega_2 \models \Gamma$ such that $\omega_1 \models \mathcal{K} \circ \Gamma$, then $\omega_1 \preceq_{\mathcal{K}}^{\circ} \omega_2$.*

(c) *If there is a Γ with $\omega_1, \omega_2 \models \Gamma$ such that $\omega_1 \models \mathcal{K} \circ \Gamma$ and $\omega_2 \not\models \mathcal{K} \circ \Gamma$, then $\omega_1 \prec_{\mathcal{K}}^{\circ} \omega_2$.*

Proof. For the proofs of all statements, recall that by Lemma 4.27, the relation $\preceq_{\mathcal{K}}^{\circ}$ is total.

(a) By totality of $\preceq_{\mathcal{K}}^{\circ}$, guaranteed by Lemma 4.27 , we obtain $\omega_2 \preceq_{\mathcal{K}}^{\circ} \omega_1$. By definition of $\preceq_{\mathcal{K}}^{\circ}$, this together with $\omega_2 \not\models \mathcal{K}$ entails $\omega_1 \not\models \mathcal{K}$. Therefore, again by definition, we obtain $\omega_1 \npreceq_{\mathcal{K}}^{\circ} \omega_2$. Consequently, in view of Definition 4.24, there must exist some $\Gamma \in \mathfrak{B}$ with $\omega_1, \omega_2 \models \Gamma$ such that $\omega_2 \models \mathcal{K} \circ \Gamma$ does not imply $\omega_1 \models \mathcal{K} \circ \Gamma$. Yet this can only be the case if $\omega_2 \models \mathcal{K} \circ \Gamma$ and $\omega_1 \not\models \mathcal{K} \circ \Gamma$, as claimed.

(b) Let Γ and ω_1, ω_2 be as assumed. We proceed by case distinction:

$\omega_2 \models \mathcal{K}$. Then $\omega_2 \in [\![\mathcal{K}]\!] \cap [\![\Gamma]\!] = [\![\mathcal{K} \uplus \Gamma]\!]$ and thus $[\![\mathcal{K} \uplus \Gamma]\!] \neq \emptyset$. Therefore, by (G2), we obtain $[\![\mathcal{K} \circ \Gamma]\!] = [\![\mathcal{K} \uplus \Gamma]\!] = [\![\mathcal{K}]\!] \cap [\![\Gamma]\!]$ and consequently $\omega_1 \models \mathcal{K}$. By Definition 4.25, we conclude $\omega_1 \preceq_{\mathcal{K}}^{\circ} \omega_2$.

$\omega_2 \not\models \mathcal{K}$. Toward a contradiction, suppose $\omega_1 \npreceq_{\mathcal{K}}^{\circ} \omega_2$. Then, by part (a) above, there is a Γ' with $\omega_1, \omega_2 \models \Gamma', \omega_1 \not\models \mathcal{K} \circ \Gamma'$ and $\omega_2 \models \mathcal{K} \circ \Gamma'$. Thus ω_1 and ω_2 witness non-emptiness of $[\![(\mathcal{K} \circ \Gamma) \uplus \Gamma']\!]$ and $[\![(\mathcal{K} \circ \Gamma') \uplus \Gamma]\!]$, respectively. Then, using (G5) and (G6) twice, we obtain $(\mathcal{K} \circ \Gamma') \uplus \Gamma \equiv \mathcal{K} \circ (\Gamma \uplus \Gamma') \equiv (\mathcal{K} \circ \Gamma) \uplus \Gamma'$. But this allows to conclude $\omega_1 \in [\![\mathcal{K} \circ \Gamma]\!] \cap [\![\Gamma']\!] = [\![(\mathcal{K} \circ \Gamma) \uplus \Gamma']\!] = [\![(\mathcal{K} \circ \Gamma') \uplus \Gamma]\!] =$

$[\![\mathcal{K} \circ \Gamma']\!] \cap [\![\Gamma]\!] \subseteq [\![\mathcal{K} \circ \Gamma']\!]$, and thus $\omega_1 \models \mathcal{K} \circ \Gamma'$, which contradicts $\omega_1 \not\models \mathcal{K} \circ \Gamma'$ above.

(c) Let Γ and ω_1, ω_2 be as assumed. We already know $\omega_1 \preceq^\circ_\mathcal{K} \omega_2$ due to part (b). It remains to show $\omega_2 \npreceq^\circ_\mathcal{K} \omega_1$. We proceed by case distinction:

> $\omega_1 \models \mathcal{K}$. Then $\omega_1 \in [\![\mathcal{K}]\!] \cap [\![\Gamma]\!] = [\![\mathcal{K} \Cup \Gamma]\!]$ and thus $[\![\mathcal{K} \Cup \Gamma]\!] \neq \emptyset$. Therefore, by (G2), we obtain $[\![\mathcal{K} \circ \Gamma]\!] = [\![\mathcal{K} \Cup \Gamma]\!] = [\![\mathcal{K}]\!] \cap [\![\Gamma]\!]$. Since $\omega_2 \not\models \mathcal{K} \circ \Gamma$ but $\omega_2 \models \Gamma$ we can infer $\omega_2 \not\models \mathcal{K}$. Consequently, by Definition 4.25, we obtain $\omega_2 \npreceq^\circ_\mathcal{K} \omega_1$.
>
> $\omega_1 \not\models \mathcal{K}$. Since we already established $\omega_1 \preceq^\circ_\mathcal{K} \omega_2$, Definition 4.25 ensures $\omega_2 \not\models \mathcal{K}$. Yet, by Definition 4.24, the existence of Γ implies $\omega_2 \not\sqsubseteq^\circ_\mathcal{K} \omega_1$, and thus Definition 4.25 yields $\omega_2 \npreceq^\circ_\mathcal{K} \omega_1$. $\square$

We show that our construction indeed yields a compatible assignment.

Lemma 4.29 (Compatibility). *If $\circ$ satisfies (G1)–(G3), (G5), and (G6), then it is compatible with $\preceq^\circ_{(\cdot)}$.*

Proof. We have to show that $[\![\mathcal{K} \circ \Gamma]\!] = \min([\![\Gamma]\!], \preceq^\circ_\mathcal{K})$. In the following, we show inclusion in both directions.

($\subseteq$) Let $\omega \in [\![\mathcal{K} \circ \Gamma]\!]$. By (G1), we obtain $\omega \in [\![\Gamma]\!]$. But then, using Lemma 4.28(b), we can conclude $\omega \preceq^\circ_\mathcal{K} \omega'$ for any $\omega' \in [\![\Gamma]\!]$, hence $\omega \in \min([\![\Gamma]\!], \preceq^\circ_\mathcal{K})$.

($\supseteq$) Let $\omega \in \min([\![\Gamma]\!], \preceq^\circ_\mathcal{K})$. Due to $[\![\Gamma]\!] \neq \emptyset$ and (G3), there exists an $\omega' \in [\![\mathcal{K} \circ \Gamma]\!]$. From the ($\subseteq$)-proof follows $\omega' \in \min([\![\Gamma]\!], \preceq^\circ_\mathcal{K})$. Then, by (G1) and Lemma 4.28(b), we obtain $\omega' \preceq^\circ_\mathcal{K} \omega$ from $\omega \in [\![\Gamma]\!]$ and $\omega' \in [\![\Gamma]\!]$ and $\omega' \in [\![\mathcal{K} \circ \Gamma]\!]$. From $\omega \in \min([\![\Gamma]\!], \preceq^\circ_\mathcal{K})$ and $\omega' \in [\![\Gamma]\!]$ follows $\omega \preceq^\circ_\mathcal{K} \omega'$. We proceed by case distinction:

> $\omega \models \mathcal{K}$. Then $\omega \in [\![\mathcal{K}]\!] \cap [\![\Gamma]\!] = [\![\mathcal{K} \Cup \Gamma]\!]$ and thus $[\![\mathcal{K} \Cup \Gamma]\!] \neq \emptyset$. Therefore, by (G2), we obtain $[\![\mathcal{K} \circ \Gamma]\!] = [\![\mathcal{K} \Cup \Gamma]\!] = [\![\mathcal{K}]\!] \cap [\![\Gamma]\!]$ and hence $\omega \in [\![\mathcal{K} \circ \Gamma]\!]$.
>
> $\omega \not\models \mathcal{K}$. Then by Definition 4.25, $\omega \preceq^\circ_\mathcal{K} \omega'$ requires $\omega' \not\models \mathcal{K}$ and therefore $\omega \sqsubseteq^\circ_\mathcal{K} \omega'$ must hold. Consequently, by Definition 4.24, $\omega, \omega' \in [\![\Gamma]\!]$ and $\omega' \in [\![\mathcal{K} \circ \Gamma]\!]$ imply $\omega \in [\![\mathcal{K} \circ \Gamma]\!]$. $\square$

For min-friendliness, we have to show that each $\preceq^\circ_\mathcal{K}$ is min-complete and min-retractive.

Lemma 4.30 (Min-Friendliness). *If $\circ$ satisfies (G1)–(G3), (G5), and (G6), then $\preceq^\circ_\mathcal{K}$ is min-friendly for every $\mathcal{K} \in \mathfrak{B}$.*

Proof. Observe that min-completeness is a consequence of (G3) and the compatibility of $\preceq^\circ_{(.)}$ with $\circ$ from Lemma 4.29.

For min-retractivity, suppose towards a contradiction that it does not hold. That means there is a belief base Γ and interpretations $\omega', \omega \models \Gamma$ with $\omega' \preceq^\circ_\mathcal{K} \omega$ and $\omega \in \min(\llbracket\Gamma\rrbracket, \preceq^\circ_\mathcal{K})$ but $\omega' \notin \min(\llbracket\Gamma\rrbracket, \preceq^\circ_\mathcal{K})$. From Lemma 4.29 we obtain $\omega \models \mathcal{K} \circ \Gamma$ and $\omega' \not\models \mathcal{K} \circ \Gamma$. Now, applying Lemma 4.28(c) yields $\omega \prec^\circ_\mathcal{K} \omega'$, contradicting $\omega' \preceq^\circ_\mathcal{K} \omega$. □

We show that $\preceq^\circ_{(.)}$ yields faithful relations for every belief base.

Lemma 4.31 (faithfulness). *If $\circ$ satisfies (G2), (G4), (G5), and (G6), the assignment $\preceq^\circ_{(.)}$ is faithful.*

Proof. We show satisfaction of the three conditions of faithfulness, (F1)–(F3).

    (F1) Let $\omega, \omega' \in \llbracket\mathcal{K}\rrbracket$. Then $\omega' \preceq^\circ_\mathcal{K} \omega$ is an immediate consequence of Definition 4.25. This implies $\omega \not\prec^\circ_\mathcal{K} \omega'$.

    (F2) Let $\omega \in \llbracket\mathcal{K}\rrbracket$ and $\omega' \notin \llbracket\mathcal{K}\rrbracket$. By Definition 4.25 we obtain $\omega \preceq^\circ_\mathcal{K} \omega'$ and $\omega' \not\preceq^\circ_\mathcal{K} \omega$.

    (F3) Let $\mathcal{K} \equiv \mathcal{K}'$ (i.e. $\llbracket\mathcal{K}\rrbracket = \llbracket\mathcal{K}'\rrbracket$). From Definition 4.25 and (G4) follows $\preceq^\circ_\mathcal{K} = \preceq^\circ_{\mathcal{K}'}$, i.e., $\omega_1 \preceq^\circ_\mathcal{K} \omega_2$ if and only if $\omega_1 \preceq^\circ_{\mathcal{K}'} \omega_2$. □

The previous lemmas can finally be used to show that the construction of $\preceq^\circ_{(.)}$ according to Definition 4.25 yields an assignment with the desired properties.

Proposition 4.32. *If $\circ$ satisfies (G1)–(G6), then $\preceq^\circ_{(.)}$ is a min-friendly faithful assignment compatible with $\circ$.*

Proof. Assume (G1)–(G6) are satisfied by $\circ$. Then $\preceq^\circ_{(.)}$ is an assignment since every $\preceq_\mathcal{K}$ is total by Lemma 4.27; it is min-friendly by Lemma 4.30; it is faithful by Lemma 4.31; and it is compatible with $\circ$ by Lemma 4.29. □

4.4.2. From Assignments to Postulates

Now, it remains to show the "if" direction of Theorem 4.23.

Proposition 4.33. *If there exists a min-friendly faithful assignment $\preceq_{(.)}$ compatible with $\circ$, then $\circ$ satisfies (G1)–(G6).*

Proof. Let $\preceq_{(.)} \colon \mathcal{K} \mapsto \preceq_{\mathcal{K}}$ be as described. We now show that $\circ$ satisfies all of (G1)–(G6).

(G1) Let $\omega \in [\![\mathcal{K} \circ \Gamma]\!]$. Since $[\![\mathcal{K} \circ \Gamma]\!] = \min([\![\Gamma]\!], \preceq_{\mathcal{K}})$, we have that $\omega \in \min([\![\Gamma]\!], \preceq_{\mathcal{K}})$. Then, we also have that $\omega \in [\![\Gamma]\!]$. Thus, we have that $[\![\mathcal{K} \circ \Gamma]\!] \subseteq [\![\Gamma]\!]$ as desired.

(G2) Assume $[\![\mathcal{K} \uplus \Gamma]\!] \neq \emptyset$. We prove $[\![\mathcal{K} \circ \Gamma]\!] = [\![\mathcal{K} \uplus \Gamma]\!]$ by showing inclusion in both directions.

    ($\subseteq$) Let $\omega \in [\![\mathcal{K} \circ \Gamma]\!]$. By compatibility, we obtain $\omega \in \min([\![\Gamma]\!], \preceq_{\mathcal{K}})$ and thus trivially also $\omega \in [\![\Gamma]\!]$. Since $[\![\mathcal{K} \uplus \Gamma]\!] \neq \emptyset$, there exists some other $\omega' \in [\![\mathcal{K} \uplus \Gamma]\!] = [\![\mathcal{K}]\!] \cap [\![\Gamma]\!]$, which implies $\omega' \in [\![\mathcal{K}]\!]$ and $\omega' \in [\![\Gamma]\!]$. Therefore, $\omega \in \min([\![\Gamma]\!], \preceq_{\mathcal{K}})$ implies $\omega \preceq_{\mathcal{K}} \omega'$, which means that $\omega' \prec_{\mathcal{K}} \omega$ cannot hold and therefore, by contraposition, (F2) ensures $\omega \in [\![\mathcal{K}]\!]$. Yet then $\omega \in [\![\mathcal{K}]\!] \cap [\![\Gamma]\!] = [\![\mathcal{K} \uplus \Gamma]\!]$ as desired.

    ($\supseteq$) Let $\omega \in [\![\mathcal{K} \uplus \Gamma]\!] = [\![\mathcal{K}]\!] \cap [\![\Gamma]\!]$, i.e. $\omega \in [\![\mathcal{K}]\!]$ and $\omega \in [\![\Gamma]\!]$. Since $\omega \in [\![\mathcal{K}]\!]$, we obtain from (F1) and (F2) that $\omega \preceq_{\mathcal{K}} \omega'$ must hold for all $\omega' \in [\![\Gamma]\!]$. Hence, $\omega \in \min([\![\Gamma]\!], \preceq_{\mathcal{K}})$, and by compatibility $\omega \in [\![\mathcal{K} \circ \Gamma]\!]$.

(G3) Assume $[\![\Gamma]\!] \neq \emptyset$. By min-completeness, we have $\min([\![\Gamma]\!], \preceq_{\mathcal{K}}) \neq \emptyset$. Since $[\![\mathcal{K} \circ \Gamma]\!] = \min([\![\Gamma]\!], \preceq_{\mathcal{K}})$ by compatibility, we obtain $[\![\mathcal{K} \circ \Gamma]\!] \neq \emptyset$.

(G4) Suppose there exist $\mathcal{K}_1, \mathcal{K}_2, \Gamma_1, \Gamma_2 \in \mathfrak{B}$ with $\mathcal{K}_1 \equiv \mathcal{K}_2$ and $\Gamma_1 \equiv \Gamma_2$. Then, $[\![\mathcal{K}_1]\!] = [\![\mathcal{K}_2]\!]$ and $[\![\Gamma_1]\!] = [\![\Gamma_2]\!]$. From (F3), we conclude $\preceq_{\mathcal{K}_1} = \preceq_{\mathcal{K}_2}$. Now assume some $\omega \in [\![\mathcal{K}_1 \circ \Gamma_1]\!]$, then by compatibility $\omega \in \min([\![\Gamma_1]\!], \preceq_{\mathcal{K}_1}) = \min([\![\Gamma_2]\!], \preceq_{\mathcal{K}_2})$. Therefore, again by compatibility, $\omega \in [\![\mathcal{K}_2 \circ \Gamma_2]\!]$. Thus, $[\![\mathcal{K}_1 \circ \Gamma_1]\!] \subseteq [\![\mathcal{K}_2 \circ \Gamma_2]\!]$ holds. Inclusion in the other direction follows by symmetry. Therefore, we have $\mathcal{K}_1 \circ \Gamma_1 \equiv \mathcal{K}_2 \circ \Gamma_2$.

(G5) Let $\omega \in [\![(\mathcal{K} \circ \Gamma_1) \uplus \Gamma_2]\!] = [\![\mathcal{K} \circ \Gamma_1]\!] \cap [\![\Gamma_2]\!]$. This means that $\omega \in [\![\Gamma_2]\!]$ but – since $[\![\mathcal{K} \circ \Gamma_1]\!] = \min([\![\Gamma_1]\!], \preceq_{\mathcal{K}})$ by compatibility – we also obtain $\omega \in \min([\![\Gamma_1]\!], \preceq_{\mathcal{K}})$, meaning that $\omega \preceq_{\mathcal{K}} \omega'$ holds for all $\omega' \in [\![\Gamma_1]\!]$. Yet then $\omega \preceq_{\mathcal{K}} \omega'$ holds particularly for all $\omega' \in [\![\Gamma_1]\!] \cap [\![\Gamma_2]\!]$ and hence $\omega \in \min([\![\Gamma_1]\!] \cap [\![\Gamma_2]\!], \preceq_\mathcal{K}) = \min([\![\Gamma_1 \uplus \Gamma_2]\!], \preceq_\mathcal{K})$. By compatibility follows $\omega \in [\![\mathcal{K} \circ (\Gamma_1 \uplus \Gamma_2)]\!]$. Thus $[\![(\mathcal{K} \circ \Gamma_1) \uplus \Gamma_2]\!] \subseteq [\![\mathcal{K} \circ (\Gamma_1 \uplus \Gamma_2)]\!]$ as desired.

(G6) Let $(\mathcal{K} \circ \Gamma_1) \uplus \Gamma_2 \neq \emptyset$, thus $\omega' \in [\![(\mathcal{K} \circ \Gamma_1) \uplus \Gamma_2]\!] = [\![\mathcal{K} \circ \Gamma_1]\!] \cap [\![\Gamma_2]\!]$ for some ω'. By compatibility, we then obtain $\omega' \in \min([\![\Gamma_1]\!], \preceq_\mathcal{K})$. Now consider an arbitrary ω with $\omega \in [\![\mathcal{K} \circ (\Gamma_1 \uplus \Gamma_2)]\!]$. By compatibility we obtain $\omega \in \min([\![\Gamma_1 \uplus \Gamma_2]\!], \preceq_\mathcal{K})$ and therefore, since $\omega' \in [\![\Gamma_1]\!] \cap [\![\Gamma_2]\!] = [\![\Gamma_1 \uplus \Gamma_2]\!]$, we can conclude $\omega \preceq_\mathcal{K} \omega'$. This and $\omega' \in \min([\![\Gamma_1]\!], \preceq_\mathcal{K})$ imply $\omega \in \min([\![\Gamma_1]\!], \preceq_\mathcal{K})$ by min-retractivity. Hence every $\omega \in [\![\mathcal{K} \circ (\Gamma_1 \uplus \Gamma_2)]\!]$ satisfies $\omega \in \min([\![\Gamma_1]\!], \preceq_\mathcal{K}) = [\![\mathcal{K} \circ \Gamma_1]\!]$ but also $\omega \in [\![\Gamma_2]\!]$, whence $[\![\mathcal{K} \circ (\Gamma_1 \uplus \Gamma_2)]\!] \subseteq [\![\mathcal{K} \circ \Gamma_1]\!] \cap [\![\Gamma_2]\!] = [\![(\mathcal{K} \circ \Gamma_1) \uplus \Gamma_2]\!]$ as desired. □

The proof of Theorem 4.23 follows from Proposition 4.32 and Proposition 4.33.

4.5. Two-Way Representation Theorem

Theorem 4.23 establishes the correspondence between operators and assignments under the assumption that $\circ$ is given and therefore known to exist. What remains unsettled is the question if generally **every** min-friendly faithful assignment is compatible with some base change operator that satisfies (G1)–(G6). It is not hard to see that this is not the case.

Example 4.34. *Consider the base logic $\mathbb{B}_{nb} = (\mathcal{L}, \Omega, \models, \mathcal{P}(\mathcal{L}), \cup)$ with $\mathcal{L} = \{none, both\}$ and $\Omega = \{\omega_1, \omega_2\}$ satisfying $[\![none]\!] = \emptyset$ and $[\![both]\!] = \{\omega_1, \omega_2\} = \Omega$. There are four bases in this logic, satisfying $\{none\} \equiv \{none, both\}$ and $\emptyset \equiv \{both\}$. Let the assignment $\preceq^{nb}_{(.)}$ be such that $\preceq^{nb}_{\{\}} = \preceq^{nb}_{\{both\}} = \Omega \times \Omega$ and $\preceq^{nb}_{\{none\}} = \preceq^{nb}_{\{none, both\}} = \{(\omega_1, \omega_1), (\omega_1, \omega_2), (\omega_2, \omega_2)\}$. It is straightforward to check that $\preceq^{nb}_{(.)}$ is a min-friendly faithful assignment. Note that any $\circ$ compatible with $\preceq^{nb}_{(.)}$ would have to satisfy $[\![\{none\} \circ \{both\}]\!] = \min([\![\{both\}]\!], \preceq^{nb}_{\{none\}}) = \{\omega_1\}$, yet, as we have seen, no base with this model set exists, therefore such an operator $\circ$ is impossible.*

Therefore, toward a full, two-way correspondence, we have to provide an additional condition on assignments, capturing operator existence.

As indicated by the example, for the existence of an operator, it will turn out to be essential that any minimal model set of a belief base obtained from an assignment corresponds to some belief base, a property which is formalized by the following notion.

Definition 4.35 (min-expressible). *Let $\mathbb{B} = (\mathcal{L}, \Omega, \models, \mathfrak{B}, \mathbb{U})$ be a base logic. A binary relation $\preceq$ over Ω is called* min-expressible *if for each $\Gamma \in \mathfrak{B}$ there exists a belief base $\mathcal{B}_{\Gamma,\preceq} \in \mathfrak{B}$ such that $[\![\mathcal{B}_{\Gamma,\preceq}]\!] = \min([\![\Gamma]\!], \preceq)$. An assignment $\preceq_{(.)}$ will be called* min-expressible, *if for each $\mathcal{K} \in \mathfrak{B}$, the relation $\preceq_{\mathcal{K}}$ is min-expressible. Given a min-expressible assignment $\preceq_{(.)}$, let $\circ_{\preceq_{(.)}}$ denote the base change operator defined by $\mathcal{K} \circ_{\preceq_{(.)}} \Gamma = \mathcal{B}_{\Gamma,\preceq_{\mathcal{K}}}$.*

It should be noted that min-expressibility is a straightforward generalization of the notion of *regularity* by Delgrande et al. [46] to base logics. By virtue of this extra notion, we now find the following bidirectional relationship between assignments and operators, amounting to a full characterization.

Theorem 4.36. *Let $\mathbb{B}$ be a base logic. Then the following statements hold:*

- *Every base change operator for $\mathbb{B}$ satisfying (G1)–(G6) is compatible with some min-expressible min-friendly faithful assignment.*
- *Every min-expressible min-friendly faithful assignment for $\mathbb{B}$ is compatible with some base change operator satisfying (G1)–(G6).*

Proof. For the first item, let $\circ$ be the corresponding base change operator. Then, by Proposition 4.32, the assignment $\preceq_{(.)}^{\circ}$ as given in Definition 4.25 is min-friendly, faithful, and compatible with $\circ$. As for min-expressibility, recall that, by compatibility, $[\![\mathcal{K} \circ \Gamma]\!] = \min([\![\Gamma]\!], \preceq_{\mathcal{K}}^{\circ})$ for every Γ. As $\mathcal{K} \circ \Gamma$ is a belief base, min-expressibility follows immediately.

For the second item, let $\preceq_{(.)}$ be the corresponding min-expressible assignment and $\circ_{\preceq_{(.)}}$ as provided in Definition 4.35. By construction, $\circ_{\preceq_{(.)}}$ is compatible with $\preceq_{(.)}$. Proposition 4.33 implies that $\circ_{\preceq_{(.)}}$ satisfies (G1)–(G6). $\square$

As an aside, note that the above theorem also implies that every min-expressible min-friendly faithful assignment is compatible **only** with AGM base change operators. This is due to the fact that, one the one hand, any such assignment fully determines the corresponding compatible base change operator model-theoretically and, on the other hand, (G1)–(G6) are purely model-theoretic conditions.

Continuing our running example, we observe that $\preceq^{\circ_{\mathrm{Ex}}}_{\mathcal{K}_{\mathrm{Ex}}}$ is also a min-expressible relation.

Example 4.37 (Continuation of Example 4.26). *Consider again* $\preceq^{\circ_{\mathrm{Ex}}}_{(.)}$, *and observe that* $\preceq^{\circ_{\mathrm{Ex}}}_{(.)}$ *is compatible with* $\circ_{\mathrm{Ex}}$, *e.g.* $[\![\mathcal{K}_{\mathrm{Ex}} \circ_{\mathrm{Ex}} \Gamma]\!] = \min([\![\Gamma]\!], \preceq^{\circ_{\mathrm{Ex}}}_{\mathcal{K}_{\mathrm{Ex}}})$. *Thus, for every belief base* $\Gamma \in \mathcal{P}(\mathcal{L}_{\mathrm{Ex}})$, *the minimum* $\min(\Gamma, \preceq^{\circ_{\mathrm{Ex}}}_{\mathcal{K}_{\mathrm{Ex}}})$ *yields a set expressible by a belief base. Theorem 4.36 guarantees us that* $\circ_{\mathrm{Ex}}$ *satisfies (G1)–(G6), as* $\preceq^{\circ_{\mathrm{Ex}}}_{(.)}$ *is a faithful min-expressible and min-friendly assignment.*

As a last step of this section, we will apply the theory developed here to demonstrate that the standard operator of trivial revision[4] [73, 57] indeed satisfies (G1)–(G6) in the general setting of base logics.

Example 4.38. *Let* $\mathbb{B} = (\mathcal{L}, \Omega, \models, \mathcal{P}(\mathcal{L}), \mathbb{U})$ *be an arbitrary base logic. We define the* trivial revision operator $\circ^{\mathrm{fm}}$ *for* $\mathbb{B}$ *by*

$$\mathcal{K} \circ^{\mathrm{fm}} \Gamma = \begin{cases} \mathcal{K} \mathbin{\mathbb{U}} \Gamma & \textit{if } [\![\mathcal{K} \mathbin{\mathbb{U}} \Gamma]\!] \textit{ is consistent} \\ \Gamma & \textit{otherwise} \end{cases}$$

To show satisfaction of (G1)–(G6) we construct a min-expressible min-friendly faithful assignment $\preceq^{\mathrm{fm}}_{(.)}$ *compatible with* $\circ^{\mathrm{fm}}$. *For each* $\mathcal{K} \in \mathfrak{B}$ *let* $\omega_1 \preceq^{\mathrm{fm}}_{\mathcal{K}} \omega_2$ *if* $\omega_1 \models \mathcal{K}$ *or* $\omega_2 \not\models \mathcal{K}$. *Obviously, the relation* $\preceq^{\mathrm{fm}}_{\mathcal{K}}$ *is a total preorder where* ω_1, ω_2 *are* $\preceq^{\mathrm{fm}}_{\mathcal{K}}$-*equivalent, if either* $\omega_1, \omega_2 \models \mathcal{K}$ *or* $\omega_1, \omega_2 \not\models \mathcal{K}$ *holds. Moreover, it is not hard to see that the relation* $\preceq^{\mathrm{fm}}_{\mathcal{K}}$ *is min-complete and min-retractive. By construction of* $\preceq^{\mathrm{fm}}_{(.)}$ *we obtain that* $\min([\![\Gamma]\!], \preceq^{\mathrm{fm}}_{\mathcal{K}}) = [\![\Gamma]\!]$ *if* $\mathcal{K} \mathbin{\mathbb{U}} \Gamma$ *is inconsistent. If* $\mathcal{K} \mathbin{\mathbb{U}} \Gamma$ *is consistent, we obtain* $\min([\![\Gamma]\!], \preceq^{\mathrm{fm}}_{\mathcal{K}}) = [\![\mathcal{K}]\!] \cap [\![\Gamma]\!] = [\![\mathcal{K} \mathbin{\mathbb{U}} \Gamma]\!]$. *In summary, the assignment* $\preceq^{\mathrm{fm}}_{(.)}$ *is min-expressible and min-friendly, and the base change operator* $\circ^{\mathrm{fm}}$ *is compatible with it.*

4.6. Base Changes and Syntax Independence

Up to this point, we have been considering base change operators fulfilling the full set of postulates (G1)–(G6). However, one might remark that the AGM postulates were specifically designed for describing the

---

[4]   Note, trivial revision is known to coincide with full meet revision in many logical settings.

change of belief sets, i.e., deductively closed theories, which naturally include all syntactic variants. As opposed to this, approaches to describing the change of (not necessarily deductively closed) bases might take the syntax into account [73]. The research on base changes deals with syntax-dependent changes, and in our approach the postulate (G4) implies that a base change operator yields semantically the same result on all semantically equivalent bases. Under such circumstances, the syntax independence expressed by (G4) might be called into question. As a consequence, one might conclude that the base change operators considered here have only limited freedom when it comes to taking the syntactic structure into account when changing.

However, note that neither the postulates (G1)–(G6) nor our representation results make assumptions about the specific syntactic structure of a base obtained by a base change operator. Thus, for syntactically different bases Γ_1 and Γ_2 that are semantic equivalent, we might obtain syntactically different results after revision, which are semantic equivalent.

Example 4.39. *Consider the logic $\mathbb{PL}_2$ (cf. Example 4.5), e.g. propositional logic over the signature $\{p, q\}$ as follows. Given $\mathcal{K}_1 = \{p, q\}, \mathcal{K}_2 = \{p \wedge q\}, \Gamma_1 = \{p, p \rightarrow \neg q\}$, and $\Gamma_2 = \{p \wedge \neg q\}$. We have $\mathcal{K}_1$ and $\mathcal{K}_2$, as well as Γ_1 and Γ_2, which are two semantic equivalent bases with different syntax. By applying the trivial revision operation $\circ^{\mathrm{fm}}$ (cf. Example 4.38) to $\mathcal{K}_1$ by Γ_1 and to $\mathcal{K}_2$ by Γ_2, we obtain $\mathcal{K}_1 \circ \Gamma_1 = \{p, p \rightarrow \neg q\}$ and $\mathcal{K}_2 \circ \Gamma_2 = \{p \wedge \neg q\}$. The two revision results are different syntactically, yet semantically equivalent (i.e. $[\![\mathcal{K}_1 \circ \Gamma_1]\!] = [\![\mathcal{K}_2 \circ \Gamma_2]\!] = \{\omega : p \mapsto true, q \mapsto false\}$).*

Moreover, the semantic viewpoint developed here in this chapter is flexible and is eligible for further liberation regarding syntax-dependence of a base change operator. In particular, our approach allows us to drop (G4). As an alternative to (G4), consider the following weaker version [73]:

(G4w) If $\Gamma_1 \equiv \Gamma_2$, then $\mathcal{K} \circ \Gamma_1 \equiv \mathcal{K} \circ \Gamma_2$.

The main difference between (G4w) and (G4) is that by (G4w) a base change operator is not restricted to treat semantically equivalent prior belief bases equivalently. When considering the extended AGM postulates (G5) and (G6) it turns out that postulate (G4w) is a baseline of syntax independence, as (G1), (G5) and (G6) together already imply (G4w), which is a generalization of a result by Aiguier et al. 2018, Prop. 3.

Proposition 4.40. *Let $\circ$ be a base change operator for a base logic $\mathbb{B} = (\mathcal{L}, \Omega, \models, \mathfrak{B}, \uplus)$. If $\circ$ satisfies (G1), (G5) and (G6), then $\circ$ satisfies (G4w).*

Proof. Let $\mathcal{K}, \Gamma_1, \Gamma_2 \in \mathfrak{B}$ be belief bases such that $\Gamma_1 \equiv \Gamma_2$. By (G1), the postulate (G4w) holds if Γ_1 is inconsistent. For the remaining parts of the proof, we assume consistency of Γ_1. First observe that $(\mathcal{K} \circ \Gamma_1) \uplus \Gamma_2 \equiv \mathcal{K} \circ \Gamma_1$ by (G1) and analogously $(\mathcal{K} \circ \Gamma_2) \uplus \Gamma_1 \equiv \mathcal{K} \circ \Gamma_2$. By (G5) we obtain $(\mathcal{K} \circ \Gamma_1) \uplus \Gamma_2 \models \mathcal{K} \circ (\Gamma_1 \uplus \Gamma_2)$. Moreover, because $(\mathcal{K} \circ \Gamma_1) \uplus \Gamma_2$ is consistent, we obtain $\mathcal{K} \circ (\Gamma_1 \uplus \Gamma_2) \models (\mathcal{K} \circ \Gamma_1) \uplus \Gamma_2$ by (G6). In summary we obtain $(\mathcal{K} \circ \Gamma_1) \uplus \Gamma_2 \equiv \mathcal{K} \circ (\Gamma_1 \uplus \Gamma_2)$. By an analogous line of arguments we obtain $(\mathcal{K} \circ \Gamma_1) \uplus \Gamma_2 \equiv \mathcal{K} \circ (\Gamma_1 \uplus \Gamma_2) \equiv (\mathcal{K} \circ \Gamma_2) \uplus \Gamma_1$. Using our prior observations this expands to $\mathcal{K} \circ \Gamma_1 \equiv \mathcal{K} \circ \Gamma_2$. $\square$

To obtain a representation theorem for base change operators without (G4), relaxing the constraint on the syntactic side requires the relation of the conditions on the semantic side. For dropping (G4), we weaken the notion of faithfulness to the notion of quasi-faithfulness.

Definition 4.41 (Quasi-Faithful)**.** *An assignment $\preceq_{(.)}$ is called quasi-faithful if it satisfies the following conditions:*

(F1) *If $\omega, \omega' \models \mathcal{K}$, then $\omega \prec_{\mathcal{K}} \omega'$ does not hold.*
(F2) *If $\omega \models \mathcal{K}$ and $\omega' \not\models \mathcal{K}$, then $\omega \prec_{\mathcal{K}} \omega'$.*

Note that quasi-faithful assignments might assign to every belief base a different order, independent from whether they are semantically equivalent or not. Thus, this enables a base change operator to treat bases differently depending on their syntactic structure.

Luckily, our canonical assignment $\preceq_{(.)}^{\circ}$ (cf. Definition 4.25) carries over to the setting where (G4) is not satisfied. The following lemma attests that $\preceq_{(.)}^{\circ}$ yields a quasi-faithful assignment for this cases.

Lemma 4.42. *If $\circ$ satisfies (G2), (G5), and (G6), then the assignment $\preceq_{(.)}^{\circ}$ is quasi-faithful.*

Proof. The proof of the two conditions of quasi-faithfulness, (F1) and (F2), is identical to the proof of (F1) and (F2) in Lemma 4.31. □

Using the notion of quasi-faithfulness and $\preceq^{\circ}_{(.)}$ (cf. Definition 4.25) we obtain the following characterization result, which is similar to a result already provided by Aiguier et al. 2018, Thm. 2.

Proposition 4.43. *Let* ∘ *be a base change operator. The operator* ∘ *satisfies (G1)–(G3), (G5), and (G6) if and only if it is compatible with some min-friendly quasi-faithful assignment.*

Proof (Sketch). The proof is nearly the same as for Theorem 4.23. Note that the proof of Theorem 4.23, which shows correspondence between (G1)–(G6) and compatible min-friendly faithful assignments uses (G4) and (F3) only in special situations. In particular, observe that condition (F3) is only used to show satisfaction of (G4) in the proof of Proposition 4.33. Moreover, note that $\preceq^{\circ}_{\mathcal{K}}$ from Definition 4.25 is a total min-friendly relation due to Lemma 4.27 and Lemma 4.30 for each $\mathcal{K} \in \mathfrak{B}$; compatibility of $\preceq^{\circ}_{(.)}$ with ∘ is ensured by Lemma 4.29 while satisfaction of quasi-faithfulness is ensured by Lemma 4.42. □

In view of this, we can now present the syntax-dependent version of our two-way representation theorem.

Theorem 4.44. *Let* $\mathbb{B}$ *be a base logic. Then the following statements hold:*

- *Every base change operator for* $\mathbb{B}$ *satisfying (G1)–(G3), (G5), and (G6) is compatible with some min-expressible min-friendly quasi-faithful assignment.*
- *Every min-expressible min-friendly quasi-faithful assignment for* $\mathbb{B}$ *is compatible with some base change operator satisfying (G1)– (G3), (G5), and (G6).*

4.7. Interim Conclusion and Remarks

In Section 4.3 to Section 4.5, we presented how Katsuno and Mendelzon's result about semantically characterizing AGM belief revision in finite-signature propositional logic can be generalized to arbitrary base logics. Thereby, we cover all Tarskian logics and support any notion of bases that are closed under "abstract union". We demonstrated certain central aspects by our running example (see Example 4.4, Example 4.18, Example 4.26, Example 4.37), which can be summarized as follows.

Fact 4.45. *The operator $\circ_{\mathrm{Ex}}$ for the base logic $\mathbb{B}_{\mathrm{Ex}}$ satisfies (G1)–(G6) and is compatible with the faithful min-friendly and min-expressible assignment $\preceq^{\circ_{\mathrm{Ex}}}_{(.)}$. That is, for any base $\mathcal{K}$ of $\mathbb{B}_{\mathrm{Ex}}$, the relation $\preceq^{\circ_{\mathrm{Ex}}}_{\mathcal{K}}$ is min-friendly and min-expressible. However, there is a base $\mathcal{K}_{\mathrm{Ex}}$, such that $\preceq^{\circ}_{\mathcal{K}_{\mathrm{Ex}}}$ is not transitive. In fact, no transitive faithful min-friendly and min-expressible assignment compatible with $\circ_{\mathrm{Ex}}$ exists, whatsoever.*

Our rationale has been to cover the most general setting of base logics possible, while sticking to the complete set of the AGM postulates and without adding further conditions. For the sake of generality, we had to replace the stronger requirement of transitivity by the weaker notion of min-retractivity inside the assignments. Waiving transitivity (and hence preorders) might be considered unconventional, as a transitive preference relation is often deemed to be the actual motivation behind the postulates (G1) and (G6). This raises the question for which Tarskian logics the existence of a compatible **preorder** assignment for any AGM revision operator can be guaranteed. In the following chapter we will discuss these aspects in detail.

Remark on the Type of Base Revision. We close this chapter with a remark on the "type" of *base revision* considered here. In the following, we summarize some differences between Hansson's approach [73] and the one by Katsuno and Mendelzon [84].

Katsuno and Mendelzon argue that revision of belief bases should be independent of the syntax of the belief base and the new arriving information [84, p. 264f]. This position on the matter of syntax independence is reflected by the postulate (KM4) (and the generalization (G4) used in this chapter). Hansson understands the change of bases differently, and one might note that work by Hansson is the more prominent one and is often associated with changes of bases. In Hansson's approach, the syntax of the belief base and the syntax of new arriving beliefs may matter, yet not arbitrarily. Hansson considers various special postulates for the revision (and contraction) of bases, e.g., prominently by the *relevance* and *uniformity* postulates [73, p. 240].

Belief change operators in these two approaches are also fundamentally different. As in the AGM approach, Hansson considers belief change operators where the belief state and the newly arriving beliefs are of different types: belief states are arbitrary sets of formulas (the belief base), and the newly arriving information is a statement. For Katsuno and Mendelzon's belief change operators, the belief state and the new beliefs are of the same type: both are statements. In the same manner, base change operators considered here in this thesis represent belief state and newly arriving information as elements of an underlying base logic.

The way how base change operators are characterized is another notable difference between the approach by Hansson and the approach by Katsuno and Mendelzon. As extensively investigated in this chapter, Katsuno and Mendelzon provide semantic representations of belief change operators by relations over interpretations. Hansson mainly investigates satisfaction of postulates by constructive approaches based on partial meet contractions or kernel contractions [73].

Our approach, including the notions of base logic and base change operator given in Section 4.1, is a generalization of Katsuno and Mendelzon's approach and their interpretation of base changes. Consequently, our approach inherits all the characteristics of Katsuno and Mendelzon's approach mentioned above: we consider the semantic characterization of change operators via relations of interpretations, ignore syntactic differences given in the representation of belief bases, and our base change operators assume that the belief state and the newly arriving information are of the same type (bases of a base logic). As discussed in Section 4.6, our generalization is flexible enough to comply (at least partially) with Hansson's understanding of base revision: a base logic can be instantiated such that the bases are arbitrary sets, as in the approach by Hansson. Moreover, dropping the syntax independence postulate (G4), leads to operators where syntactic differences of the initial belief state may matter. However, just dropping (G4) does not provide the same "amount" of syntax dependence as the approach by Hansson. It remains to investigate whether our approach can be relaxed even further such that syntactic differences in the newly arriving beliefs have an impact. Another interesting topic for future work is the adaption of our approach to operators with mixed input types.

Chapter 5

Characterization of Total-Preorder-Representability

As we have shown in the last chapter not every AGM belief revision operator in every Tarskian logic can be described by a (total) preorder assignment. Yet, we also saw that, for some logics (like propositional logic with finitely many atoms), this correspondence does indeed hold. As total preorders are a standard way of representation in belief change [57], the question of the characteristics of those logics for which every AGM revision operator is total-preorder-representable arises.

In the course of this chapter, we will make use of the framework introduced in Chapter 4, and provide a characterization of precisely those logics wherein every AGM base change operator (operators that satisfy (G1)–(G6)) is representable by a total preorder. The characterization we develop in the following will be by providing a "forbidden minor"[1], called *critical loop*. We show that the absence of critical loops is the sufficient and necessary property of a logic for having only total-preorder-representable AGM revision operators. The main theorem will be for the more general setting of AGM revision operators that do not necessarily satisfy syntax independence (G4). In the following, we start this chapter with a remark on syntax independence and total-preorder-representablity.

Remark. The contents of this chapter, the Chapter 5, is based on joint work with Faiq Miftakhul Falakh and Sebastian Rudolph [54] (see also Section 1.4).

---

[1]   This is a reference to forbidden minor-characterizations in graph theory [85].

5.1. Total-Preorder-Representability

The following definition captures the notion of operators that are representable by a total preorder in the framework of base logics, given in Chapter 4.

Definition 5.1 (Total-Preorder-Representable). *A base change operator* ∘ *for some base logic is called* total-preorder-representable *if there is a min-complete quasi-faithful preorder assignment compatible with* ∘.

Recall that in the framework we use here we presume that assignments always yield total relations and thus, a preorder assignment always yields total preorders. Moreover, transitivity implies min-retractivity, and thus, every min-complete preorder is automatically min-friendly.

In Section 4.6 we use the notion of quasi-faithfulness to accommodate the syntax-dependent base change operators. As the following lemma shows, the definition of total-preorder-representability is also adequate in the syntax independent setting.

Lemma 5.2. *For any base change operator* ∘ *that satisfies (G4), total-preorder-representability coincides with the existence of a min-complete* faithful *preorder assignment compatible with* ∘.

Proof. Any compatible min-complete *faithful* preorder assignment is also *quasi-faithful* and the existence of such an assignment implies total-preorder-representability. For the other direction, let $\preceq_{(.)}$ be a min-complete quasi-faithful preorder assignment compatible with ∘. We define $\preceq_{(.)}^{\text{ff}}$ as $\mathcal{K} \mapsto \preceq_{\sigma([\mathcal{K}]_\equiv)}$ where σ is a selection function mapping every $\equiv$-equivalence class of $\mathfrak{B}$ to one of its elements (i.e., $\sigma([\mathcal{K}]_\equiv) \in [\mathcal{K}]_\equiv$). The property of being a min-complete quasi-faithful preorder assignment compatible with ∘ carries over pointwise from $\preceq_{(.)}$ to $\preceq_{(.)}^{\text{ff}}$, while the construction ensures that $\preceq_{(.)}^{\text{ff}}$ also satisfies (F3) from Definition 4.9 and hence is faithful. □

5.2. Critical Loops

The following definition describes the occurrence of a certain relationship between several bases. Such an occurrence will turn out to be the one and only reason to prevent total-preorder-representability.

Definition 5.3 (Critical Loop). *Let* $\mathbb{B} = (\mathcal{L}, \Omega, \models, \mathfrak{B}, \uplus)$ *be a base logic. Three or more bases* $\Gamma_{0,1}, \Gamma_{1,2}, \ldots, \Gamma_{n,0} \in \mathfrak{B}$ *are said to form a critical loop of length* $n + 1$ *for* $\mathbb{B}$ *if there exists a base* $\mathcal{K} \in \mathfrak{B}$ *and consistent bases* $\Gamma_0, \ldots, \Gamma_n \in \mathfrak{B}$ *such that*

(1) $[\![\mathcal{K} \uplus \Gamma_{i,i\oplus 1}]\!] = \emptyset$ *for every* $i \in \{0, \ldots, n\}$, *where* $\oplus$ *is addition* mod $(n+1)$,
(2) $[\![\Gamma_i]\!] \cup [\![\Gamma_{i\oplus 1}]\!] \subseteq [\![\Gamma_{i,i\oplus 1}]\!]$ *and* $[\![\Gamma_j \uplus \Gamma_i]\!] = \emptyset$ *for each* $i, j \in \{0, \ldots, n\}$ *with* $i \neq j$, *and*
(3) *for each* $\Gamma_{\triangledown} \in \mathfrak{B}$ *that is consistent with at least three bases from* $\Gamma_0, \ldots, \Gamma_n$, *there exists some* $\Gamma'_{\triangledown} \in \mathfrak{B}$ *such that* $[\![\Gamma'_{\triangledown}]\!] \neq \emptyset$ *and* $[\![\Gamma'_{\triangledown}]\!] \subseteq [\![\Gamma_{\triangledown}]\!] \setminus ([\![\Gamma_{0,1}]\!] \cup \ldots \cup [\![\Gamma_{n,0}]\!])$.

The three conditions in Definition 5.3 describe the canonic situation brought about by some bases $\Gamma_{0,1}, \ldots, \Gamma_{n,0}$ allowing for the construction of a revision operator that unavoidably gives rise to a circular compatible relation. Note that due to Condition (3), every three of $\Gamma_{0,1}, \Gamma_{1,2}, \ldots, \Gamma_{n,0}$ together are inconsistent, but due to Condition (2) each two of them which have an index in common are consistent, i.e. $\Gamma_{i,i\oplus 1} \uplus \Gamma_{i\oplus 1, i\oplus 2}$ is consistent for each $i \in \{0, \ldots, n\}$.

In the following, we provide some intuition for the notion of critical loop. The bases $\Gamma_0, \ldots, \Gamma_n$ provide model sets that are pairwise disjoint (cf. the second part of Condition (2)) and can be thought of as arranged in a circle, while the bases $\Gamma_{0,1}, \ldots, \Gamma_{n,0}$ overlap any two adjacent model sets as indicated by their indices (cf. the first part of Condition (2)). Exploiting this situation, we now want to define the result of revising $\mathcal{K}$ such that the circular arrangement governs the choice of the "$\mathcal{K}$-preferred" models as follows: the models of $\mathcal{K} \circ \Gamma_{i,i\oplus 1}$, obtained by revising $\mathcal{K}$ with $\Gamma_{i,i\oplus 1}$, encompass all models of Γ_i, but no model of $\Gamma_{i\oplus 1}$. Consequently, for any i, the revision $\mathcal{K} \circ \Gamma_{i,i\oplus 1}$ provides a preference of Γ_i over $\Gamma_{i\oplus 1}$. Thus, a relation compatible to $\circ$ has to contain a "preference-loop" of interpretations. In order to guarantee that this arrangement technique is applicable, Condition (1) and Condition (3) from Definition 5.3 are ruling out all cases, where other bases of $\mathbb{B}$ together with (G1)–(G6) prevent our intended construction from working:

Condition (1) ensures that none of the bases $\Gamma_{0,1}, \ldots, \Gamma_{n,0}$ has models in common with the current belief base $\mathcal{K}$ (c.f. Figure 5.1a).

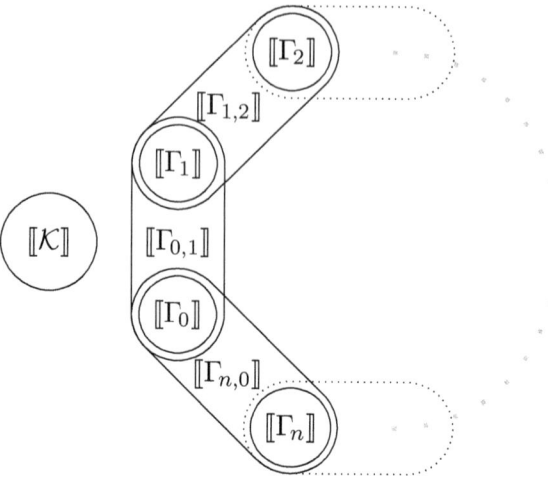

(a) By Condition (2), the models of each base $\Gamma_{i,i\oplus1}$ encompass the models of Γ_i and of $\Gamma_{i\oplus1}$, while by Condition (1), all these model sets are disjoint from the models of $\mathcal{K}$.

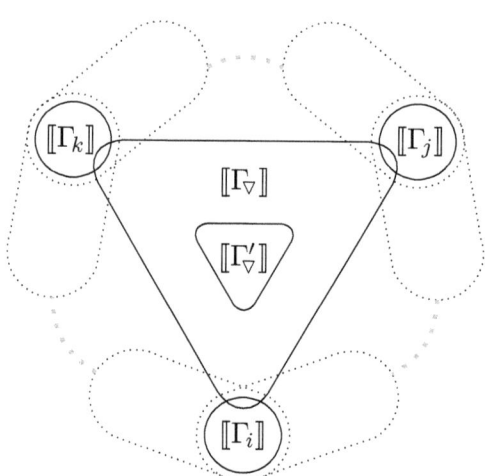

(b) By Condition (3), for each $\Gamma_\triangledown$ that is consistent with at least three distinct elements of the circle (e.g. $\Gamma_i, \Gamma_j, \Gamma_k \in \{\Gamma_0, \ldots, \Gamma_n\}$), there exists a base $\Gamma'_\triangledown$ that is subsumed by $\Gamma_\triangledown$ but inconsistent with all $\Gamma_{0,1}, \ldots, \Gamma_{n-1,n}$, $\Gamma_{n,0}$.

Figure 5.1: Illustrations of the Conditions (1)–(3) of a critical loop given in Definition 5.3.

If one base $\Gamma_{i,i\oplus 1}$ would have a model in common with $\mathcal{K}$, then the postulate (G2) would prevent a circular situation. Thus, this condition is necessary for admitting circular situations.

Condition (3) comes into play if a belief base $\Gamma_\triangledown$ "covers" three or more elements of the circle, meaning that three or more interpretations of a circle are models of this base $\Gamma_\triangledown$. For any such $\Gamma_\triangledown$, there is a consistent belief base $\Gamma'_\triangledown$ which shares all of its models with $\Gamma_\triangledown$ but no model with any of the $\Gamma_{i,i\oplus 1}$ (c.f. Figure 5.1b). This is crucial for the presence of circles: if no such $\Gamma'_\triangledown$ would exist, the operator would (by min-completeness and min-expressibility) choose models of the circle, e.g., the bases $\Gamma_i \uplus \Gamma_\triangledown$, as the result of the revision by $\Gamma_\triangledown$. In the end, this would give one base Γ_i preference over $\Gamma_{i\oplus 1}, \ldots, \Gamma_{i\oplus n}$ and thus, would prevent creation of a circle. Therefore, Condition (3) rules out the cases where min-completeness and min-expressibility and non-existence of such a $\Gamma'_\triangledown$ together would prevent formation of a circle.

Definition 5.3 is inspired by our running example. Before explicating this link, we continue with the presentation of the general results.

The next theorem is the central result of this chapter, stating that the notion of critical loop captures exactly those base logics for which some operator exists that is not total-preorder-representable. By contraposition, this just means that for all base logics $\mathbb{B}$, the absence of critical loops from $\mathbb{B}$ is a necessary and sufficient criterion for universal total-preorder-representability and hence for the existence of a characterization result for $\mathbb{B}$ that is based on total preorders.

This characterization result will be more general by also covering operators that are syntax independent (in the sense of Section 4.6), i.e., the result will not only hold for base change operators that satisfy (G1)–(G6), but also for operators that does not satisfy (G4), but the remaining postulates (G1)–(G3), (G5), and (G6). To provide a result applicable for both groups of postulates, we will show for the necessary and sufficient direction the respectively stronger result, i.e., if our base logic exhibits a critical loop we provide a construction for a non-total-preorder-representable base change operator that satisfies (G1)–(G6), and for the other direction, we show that in the absence of critical loops every operator that satisfies (G1)–(G3), (G5), and (G6) is total-preorder-representable.

Theorem 5.4. *For all base logics* $\mathbb{B}$, *the following statements hold:*

(I) *If* $\mathbb{B}$ *exhibits a critical loop, then there exists a base change operator for* $\mathbb{B}$ *that satisfies (G1)–(G6) and is not total-preorder-representable.*

(II) *If* $\mathbb{B}$ *does not admit a critical loop, then every base change operator for* $\mathbb{B}$ *that satisfies (G1)–(G3), (G5), and (G6) is total-preorder-representable.*

We dedicate Section 5.3 to the first statement of Theorem 5.4 while the second statement is shown in Section 5.4.

5.3. Total-Preorder-Representability Implies Absence of Critical Loops

We proceed to show (by contraposition) that the absence of critical loops is necessary for total-preorder-representability of all AGM change operators. To this end, we will provide a construction which, given a critical loop $\mathfrak{C}$ in some base logic $\mathbb{B}$, yields an AGM change operator $\circ_{\mathfrak{C}}$ for $\mathbb{B}$ that is demonstrably not total-preorder-representable.

Definition 5.5. *Let* $\mathbb{B} = (\mathcal{L}, \Omega, \models, \mathfrak{B}, \uplus)$ *be a base logic with a critical loop* $\mathfrak{C} = (\Gamma_{0,1}, \Gamma_{1,2}, \ldots, \Gamma_{n,0})$ *and let* $\Gamma_0, \ldots, \Gamma_n \in \mathfrak{B}$ *and* $\mathcal{K}$ *as in Definition 5.3.*

Let $\mathcal{C}$ *denote the set of all* Γ'_{∇} *guaranteed by Condition (3) from Definition 5.3, i.e.* $\Gamma'_{\nabla} \in \mathcal{C}$ *if there is some* Γ_{∇} *with* $\emptyset \neq [\![\Gamma'_{\nabla}]\!] \subseteq [\![\Gamma_{\nabla}]\!] \setminus ([\![\Gamma_{0,1}]\!] \cup \ldots \cup [\![\Gamma_{n,0}]\!])$ *and* Γ_{∇} *is consistent with three (or more) bases from* $\{\Gamma_0, \ldots, \Gamma_n\}$. *Now let* $\mathcal{C}' = \{\Gamma'_{\nabla} \in \mathcal{C} \mid [\![\Gamma'_{\nabla} \uplus \mathcal{K}]\!] = \emptyset\}$, *i.e., all belief bases from* $\mathcal{C}$ *that are inconsistent with* $\mathcal{K}$. *Let* $\leqslant_{\mathcal{C}'}$ *be an arbitrary linear order on* $\mathcal{C}'$ *with respect to which every non-empty subset of* $\mathcal{C}'$ *has a minimum.*[2]

We now define $\circ_{\mathfrak{C}}$ *as follows: for every* $\mathcal{K}' \not\equiv \mathcal{K}$ *and any* Γ, *let* $\mathcal{K}' \circ_{\mathfrak{C}} \Gamma = \mathcal{K}' \uplus \Gamma$ *if* $\mathcal{K}' \uplus \Gamma$ *is consistent, otherwise* $\mathcal{K}' \circ_{\mathfrak{C}} \Gamma = \Gamma$. *For* $\mathcal{K}' \equiv \mathcal{K}$, *we*

---

[2]   Such a $\leqslant_{\mathcal{C}'}$ exists due to the well-ordering theorem, by courtesy of the *axiom of choice* [156].

define:

$$
\mathcal{K}' \circ_{\mathfrak{C}} \Gamma = \begin{cases} \Gamma \uplus \mathcal{K}' & \text{if } [\![\mathcal{K}' \uplus \Gamma]\!] \neq \emptyset, \\ \Gamma \uplus \Gamma^{\mathcal{C}'}_{\min} & \text{if } [\![\mathcal{K}' \uplus \Gamma]\!] = \emptyset, \text{ and } [\![\Gamma \uplus \Gamma'_{\triangledown}]\!] \neq \emptyset \text{ for some } \Gamma'_{\triangledown} \in \mathcal{C}', \\ \Gamma \uplus \Gamma_i & \text{if none of the above applies, } [\![\Gamma_i \uplus \Gamma]\!] \neq \emptyset, \\ & \text{and } \bigcup_{j \in \{0,\dots,n\} \setminus \{i, i \oplus 1\}} [\![\Gamma_j \uplus \Gamma]\!] = \emptyset, \\ \Gamma & \text{if none of the cases above applies,} \end{cases}
$$

where $\Gamma^{\mathcal{C}'}_{\min} = \min(\{\Gamma'_{\triangledown} \in \mathcal{C}' \mid [\![\Gamma'_{\triangledown} \uplus \Gamma]\!] \neq \emptyset\}, \leqslant_{\mathcal{C}'})$.

In the following, we show that $\circ_{\mathfrak{C}}$ from Definition 5.5 is indeed an AGM revision, but not total-preorder-representable.

Proposition 5.6. *For a base logic $\mathbb{B}$ with a critical loop $\mathfrak{C}$, the operator $\circ_{\mathfrak{C}}$ for $\mathbb{B}$ satisfies (G1)–(G6) and is not total-preorder-representable.*

Proof. We will first show that $\circ_{\mathfrak{C}}$ satisfies (G1)–(G6). For $\mathcal{K}' \not\equiv \mathcal{K}$ we obtain a trivial revision which satisfies (G1)–(G6) (cf. Example 4.38). Consider the remaining case of $\mathcal{K}$ (and any equivalent base):

Postulates (G1)–(G4). The satisfaction of (G1)–(G3) follows directly from the construction of $\circ_{\mathfrak{C}}$. For (G4) observe that, when computing $\mathcal{K} \circ_{\mathfrak{C}} \Gamma$, the case distinction above only considers the model sets of the participating bases rather than their syntax. Thus, for $\mathcal{K} \equiv \mathcal{K}'$ and $\Gamma_1^* \equiv \Gamma_2^*$ we always obtain $\mathcal{K} \circ_{\mathfrak{C}} \Gamma_1^* \equiv \mathcal{K}' \circ_{\mathfrak{C}} \Gamma_2^*$.

Postulate (G5) and (G6). Consider two belief bases Γ_1^* and Γ_2^*. If Γ_2^* is inconsistent with $\mathcal{K} \circ_{\mathfrak{C}} \Gamma_1^*$, then we obtain satisfaction of (G5) immediately. For the remaining case of (G5) and for (G6) we assume $\mathcal{K} \circ_{\mathfrak{C}} \Gamma_1^*$ to be consistent with Γ_2^*, i.e., $[\![(\mathcal{K} \circ_{\mathfrak{C}} \Gamma_1^*) \uplus \Gamma_2^*]\!] \neq \emptyset$. Consequently, there exists some interpretation ω such that $\omega \in [\![\mathcal{K} \circ_{\mathfrak{C}} \Gamma_1^*]\!]$ and $\omega \in [\![\Gamma_2^*]\!]$. The postulate (G1) implies that $\omega \in [\![\Gamma_1^*]\!]$ and hence $\Gamma_1^* \uplus \Gamma_2^*$ is consistent. We now inspect all different cases from the definition of $\circ_{\mathfrak{C}}$ above that may apply when revising $\mathcal{K}$ by Γ_1^*:

If Γ_1^* is consistent with $\mathcal{K}$, then we obtain from $[\![(\mathcal{K} \circ_{\mathfrak{C}} \Gamma_1^*) \uplus \Gamma_2^*]\!] \neq \emptyset$ and (G2) that $\mathcal{K}$ is consistent with $\Gamma_1^* \uplus \Gamma_2^*$. This implies $(\mathcal{K} \circ_{\mathfrak{C}} \Gamma_1^*) \uplus \Gamma_2^* \equiv (\mathcal{K} \uplus \Gamma_1^*) \uplus \Gamma_2^* \equiv \mathcal{K} \uplus (\Gamma_1^* \uplus \Gamma_2^*) \equiv \mathcal{K} \circ_{\mathfrak{C}} (\Gamma_1^* \uplus \Gamma_2^*)$; yielding satisfaction of (G5) and (G6).
Next, consider the second case of the definition, where Γ_1^* is inconsistent with $\mathcal{K}$, but consistent with some $\Gamma'_{\triangledown} \in \mathcal{C}'$ and assume

$\Gamma'_\triangledown$ is the $\leqslant_{\mathcal{C}'}$-minimal such base, i.e., $\Gamma'_\triangledown = (\Gamma^*_1)^{\mathcal{C}'}_{\min}$. Then, from the construction of $\circ_{\mathfrak{C}}$ and the consistency of $(\mathcal{K} \circ_{\mathfrak{C}} \Gamma^*_1) \uplus \Gamma^*_2$ we obtain $[\![(\mathcal{K} \circ_{\mathfrak{C}} \Gamma^*_1) \uplus \Gamma^*_2]\!] = [\![\Gamma^*_1 \uplus \Gamma'_\triangledown \uplus \Gamma^*_2]\!] \neq \emptyset$. Consequently, the set $\Gamma^*_1 \uplus \Gamma^*_2$ is also consistent with $\Gamma'_\triangledown$, which, together with $\Gamma'_\triangledown = (\Gamma^*_1)^{\mathcal{C}'}_{\min}$, implies $\Gamma'_\triangledown = (\Gamma^*_1 \uplus \Gamma^*_2)^{\mathcal{C}'}_{\min}$. For determining $\mathcal{K} \circ_{\mathfrak{C}} (\Gamma^*_1 \uplus \Gamma^*_2)$, note that from $\mathcal{K}$ being inconsistent with Γ^*_1, it follows that $\mathcal{K}$ must also be inconsistent with $\Gamma^*_1 \uplus \Gamma^*_2$, therefore, due to the existence of $\Gamma'_\triangledown$, the second line of the definition of $\circ_{\mathfrak{C}}$ must apply. We obtain $(\mathcal{K} \circ_{\mathfrak{C}} \Gamma^*_1) \uplus \Gamma^*_2 \equiv ((\Gamma^*_1)^{\mathcal{C}'}_{\min} \uplus \Gamma^*_1) \uplus \Gamma^*_2 \equiv \Gamma'_\triangledown \uplus \Gamma^*_1 \uplus \Gamma^*_2 \equiv (\Gamma^*_1 \uplus \Gamma^*_2)^{\mathcal{C}'}_{\min} \uplus (\Gamma^*_1 \uplus \Gamma^*_2) \equiv \mathcal{K} \circ_{\mathfrak{C}} (\Gamma^*_1 \uplus \Gamma^*_2)$; establishing (G5) and (G6) for this case.

We now inspect the third case from the definition, i.e., we consider some Γ^*_1 that is inconsistent with $\mathcal{K}$ and with all elements from $\mathcal{C}'$. If Γ^*_1 is consistent with Γ_i and inconsistent with all Γ_j, where $j \in \{0, \dots, n\} \setminus \{i, i \oplus 1\}$, then by the construction of $\circ_{\mathfrak{C}}$ and the consistency of $(\mathcal{K} \circ_{\mathfrak{C}} \Gamma^*_1) \uplus \Gamma^*_2$ we have $[\![(\mathcal{K} \circ_{\mathfrak{C}} \Gamma^*_1) \uplus \Gamma^*_2]\!] = [\![\Gamma^*_1 \uplus \Gamma_i \uplus \Gamma^*_2]\!] \neq \emptyset$. Then, likewise $\Gamma^*_1 \uplus \Gamma^*_2$ is consistent with Γ_i and inconsistent with all Γ_j with $j \in \{0, \dots, n\} \setminus \{i, i \oplus 1\}$. Moreover, if Γ^*_1 is inconsistent with $\mathcal{K}$ and with all elements from $\mathcal{C}'$, then so is $\Gamma^*_1 \uplus \Gamma^*_2$, i.e., when determining $\mathcal{K} \circ_{\mathfrak{C}} (\Gamma^*_1 \uplus \Gamma^*_2)$, the third case of the definition applies. Hence, by the definition of $\circ_{\mathfrak{C}}$ we obtain $(\mathcal{K} \circ_{\mathfrak{C}} \Gamma^*_1) \uplus \Gamma^*_2 \equiv \Gamma^*_1 \uplus \Gamma^*_2 \uplus \Gamma_i \equiv \mathcal{K} \circ_{\mathfrak{C}} (\Gamma^*_1 \uplus \Gamma^*_2)$. If none of the conditions above applies to Γ^*_1, then they also do not apply to $\Gamma^*_1 \uplus \Gamma^*_2$. From the construction of $\circ_{\mathfrak{C}}$ we obtain $\mathcal{K} \circ_{\mathfrak{C}} (\Gamma^*_1 \uplus \Gamma^*_2) \equiv (\mathcal{K} \circ_{\mathfrak{C}} \Gamma^*_1) \uplus \Gamma^*_2 \equiv \Gamma^*_1 \uplus \Gamma^*_2$.

In summary, we obtain that $\circ_{\mathfrak{C}}$ satisfies (G5) and (G6) in all cases. It remains to show that $\circ_{\mathfrak{C}}$ is not total-preorder-representable. Towards a contradiction suppose the contrary, i.e., there is a min-complete faithful preorder assignment $\preceq_{(.)}$, such that $\circ_{\mathfrak{C}}$ is compatible with $\preceq_{(.)}$. Transitivity and min-completeness imply that $\preceq_{(.)}$ is min-friendly. As all $\Gamma_0, \dots, \Gamma_n$ are consistent, there are $\omega_i \in [\![\Gamma_i]\!]$ for all $i \in \{0, \dots, n\}$. By construction of $\circ_{\mathfrak{C}}$ and Condition (2) of Definition 5.3, we have $\mathcal{K} \circ_{\mathfrak{C}} \Gamma_{i,i\oplus1} = \Gamma_{i,i\oplus1} \uplus \Gamma_i \equiv \Gamma_i$, and consequently $\omega_i \models \mathcal{K} \circ_{\mathfrak{C}} \Gamma_{i,i\oplus1}$ and $\omega_{i\oplus1} \not\models \mathcal{K} \circ_{\mathfrak{C}} \Gamma_{i,i\oplus1}$ for each $i \in \{0, \dots, n\}$. As $\circ_{\mathfrak{C}}$ is compatible with $\preceq_{(.)}$, we obtain $[\![\mathcal{K} \circ_{\mathfrak{C}} \Gamma_{i,i\oplus1}]\!] = \min([\![\Gamma_{i,i\oplus1}]\!], \preceq_{\mathcal{K}})$. In particular, the definition of $\circ_{\mathfrak{C}}$ yields $\omega_i \in \min([\![\Gamma_{i,i\oplus1}]\!], \preceq_{\mathcal{K}})$ and $\omega_i, \omega_{i\oplus1} \models \Gamma_{i,i\oplus1}$ and $\omega_{i\oplus1} \notin \min([\![\Gamma_{i,i\oplus1}]\!], \preceq_{\mathcal{K}})$. We obtain thereof the strict relationship $\omega_i \prec_{\mathcal{K}} \omega_{i\oplus1}$. In summary, we get $\omega_0 \prec_{\mathcal{K}} \omega_1 \prec_{\mathcal{K}} \dots \prec_{\mathcal{K}} \omega_n \prec_{\mathcal{K}} \omega_0$, which contradicts the presumed transitivity of $\preceq_\mathcal{K}$. □

This establishes that the absence of critical loops is a necessary condition for universal total-preorder-representability in any Tarskian logic, because Theorem 5.4 (I) is an immediate consequence of Proposition 5.6.

5.4. Absence of Critical Loops Implies Total-Preorder-Representability

We will now show that the identified criterion of critical loop (Definition 5.3) is also sufficient, even in the more general, syntax-dependent setting. That is, we will demonstrate in the following that Theorem 5.4 (II) holds. To this end, we need to argue that any base change operator ∘ that satisfies (G1)–(G3), (G5), and (G6) for any critical-loop-free $\mathbb{B}$ gives rise to a compatible min-complete quasi-faithful preorder assignment $\preccurlyeq^\circ_{(.)}$. We will show how to obtain $\preccurlyeq^\circ_{(.)}$ via a step-wise transformation of the assignment $\preceq^\circ_{(.)}$ from Definition 4.25.

The transformation from $\preceq^\circ_{(.)}$ to $\preccurlyeq^\circ_{(.)}$ consists of three steps. For the start, recall that $\preceq^\circ_{(.)}$ is a min-complete quasi-faithful assignment compatible with ∘ by Proposition 4.43. This means that $\preceq^\circ_\mathcal{K}$ is a total relation for each $\mathcal{K}$, whence transitivity is the only condition that $\preceq^\circ_\mathcal{K}$ fails to meet to qualify as a total preorder.

For the first step, we will identify a group of interpretation pairs $\mathfrak{D}^\circ_\mathcal{K} \subseteq \preceq^\circ_\mathcal{K}$ such that at least one pair from $\mathfrak{D}^\circ_\mathcal{K}$ is involved whenever $\preceq^\circ_\mathcal{K}$ violates transitivity. The first step then consists in drastically removing all $\mathfrak{D}^\circ_\mathcal{K}$ from $\preceq^\circ_\mathcal{K}$, resulting in $\preceq^{\circ}_\mathcal{K}{}'$. The relation $\preceq^{\circ}_\mathcal{K}{}'$ will be a non-transitive and non-total relation, but minima of models of bases will be preserved. We will then extend $\preceq^{\circ}_\mathcal{K}{}'$ to a transitive relation $\preceq^{\circ}_\mathcal{K}{}''$ in the second step, by taking the transitive closure. We will show that only elements from $\mathfrak{D}^\circ_\mathcal{K}$ can be added back by the transitive closure, which guarantees that, again, minima of models of bases are preserved. In a last step, we obtain the final result $\preccurlyeq^\circ_{(.)}$ by "linearizing" $\preceq^{\circ}_\mathcal{K}{}'$ to a total preorder in a way that minima of models of bases are again preserved.

Step I: Removing detached pairs

Let $\circ$ be a base change operator that satisfies (G1)–(G3), (G5), and (G6). Then, for any two bases $\mathcal{K}, \Gamma \in \mathfrak{B}$, all quasi-faithful assignments $\preceq_{(.)}$ compatible with $\circ$ yield the same set of minimal interpretations of $[\![\Gamma]\!]$ with respect to $\preceq_\mathcal{K}$. This property already stipulates much of $\preceq_\mathcal{K}$ for each $\mathcal{K}$ (for some base logics, $\preceq_\mathcal{K}$ is even completely determined by that property). Still, in the general case, when forming a compatible assignment, there is certain freedom on relating those interpretations for which the given base change operator gives no hint about how to order them. The following notion formally defines such pairs of interpretations.

Definition 5.7. *Let $\circ$ be a base change operator for $\mathbb{B}$ and $\mathcal{K}$ a base of $\mathbb{B}$. A pair $(\omega, \omega') \in \Omega \times \Omega$ is called* detached *from $\circ$ in $\mathcal{K}$, if $\omega, \omega' \not\models \mathcal{K} \circ \Gamma$ for all $\Gamma \in \mathfrak{B}$ with $\omega, \omega' \models \Gamma$. With $\mathfrak{D}_\mathcal{K}^\circ$ we denote the set of all pairs (ω, ω') which are detached from $\circ$ in $\mathcal{K}$ and satisfy $\omega \neq \omega'$.*

Note that detachment is a symmetric property, i.e., (ω, ω') is detached if and only if (ω', ω) is. It so happens that $\preceq_\mathcal{K}^\circ$ may contain too many of such detached pairs, i.e., in some cases, $\preceq_\mathcal{K}^\circ$ is not a total preorder even if the base change operator $\circ$ is total preorder-representable [54]. In the following, we show that every violation of transitivity in $\preceq_\mathcal{K}^\circ$ involves a detached pair (as illustrated in Figure 5.2).

Lemma 5.8. *Assume $\mathbb{B}$ is a base logic which does not admit a critical loop and $\circ$ a base change operator for $\mathbb{B}$ which satisfies (G1)–(G3), (G5), and (G6). If $\omega_0 \preceq_\mathcal{K}^\circ \omega_1$ and $\omega_1 \preceq_\mathcal{K}^\circ \omega_2$ with $\omega_0 \npreceq_\mathcal{K}^\circ \omega_2$, then (ω_0, ω_1) or (ω_1, ω_2) is detached from $\circ$ in $\mathcal{K}$.*

Proof. Let $\omega_0, \omega_1, \omega_2$ such that a violation of transitivity is obtained as given above, i.e. $\omega_0 \preceq_\mathcal{K}^\circ \omega_1$ and $\omega_1 \preceq_\mathcal{K}^\circ \omega_2$ with $\omega_0 \npreceq_\mathcal{K}^\circ \omega_2$. By Definition 4.25, we have that $\omega_0 \npreceq_\mathcal{K}^\circ \omega_2$ is only possible if $\omega_0 \not\models \mathcal{K}$. From Definition 4.25 and $\omega_0 \preceq_\mathcal{K}^\circ \omega_1$, we obtain $\omega_1 \not\models \mathcal{K}$. By an analogue argument we obtain $\omega_2 \not\models \mathcal{K}$. Thus, for the rest of the proof we have $\omega_0, \omega_1, \omega_2 \not\models \mathcal{K}$.

Towards a contradiction, assume that (ω_0, ω_1) and (ω_1, ω_2) are both not detached from $\circ$ in $\mathcal{K}$. By Lemma 4.27 the relation $\preceq_\mathcal{K}^\circ$ is total, and thus we have that $\omega_2 \prec_\mathcal{K}^\circ \omega_0$. As $\omega_2 \not\models \mathcal{K}$ and $\omega_0 \npreceq_\mathcal{K}^\circ \omega_2$, due to

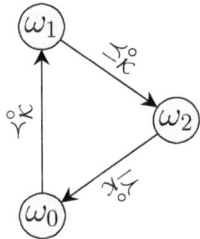

Figure 5.2: Illustration of a critical loop-situation of length 3 on the semantic side. If $\mathbb{B}$ does not exhibit a critical loop, then this situation is, due to Lemma 5.8, only possible when (w_1,w_2) or (w_2,w_0) is a detached pair.

Lemma 4.28(a), there is a base $\Gamma_{2,0} \in \mathfrak{B}$ with $w_0, w_2 \models \Gamma_{2,0}$ such that $w_2 \models \mathcal{K} \circ \Gamma_{2,0}$ and $w_0 \not\models \mathcal{K} \circ \Gamma_{2,0}$. By $w_0, w_1, w_2 \not\models \mathcal{K}$ and Definition 4.25 we obtain $w_0 \sqsubseteq_{\mathcal{K}}^{\circ} w_1$ and $w_1 \sqsubseteq_{\mathcal{K}}^{\circ} w_2$ (cf. Definition 4.24). Because (w_0, w_1) is not detached, there is some $\Gamma_{0,1} \in \mathfrak{B}$ with $w_0, w_1 \models \Gamma_{0,1}$ such that $w_0 \models \mathcal{K} \circ \Gamma_{0,1}$ or $w_1 \models \mathcal{K} \circ \Gamma_{0,1}$. By Definition 4.24 and $w_0 \sqsubseteq_{\mathcal{K}}^{\circ} w_1$ we obtain that $w_0 \models \mathcal{K} \circ \Gamma_{0,1}$. Using an analogue argumentation, there exist $\Gamma_{1,2} \in \mathfrak{B}$ satisfying $w_1, w_2 \models \Gamma_{1,2}$ and $w_1 \models \mathcal{K} \circ \Gamma_{1,2}$.

Recall that $\preceq_{(.)}^{\circ}$ is compatible, min-retractive and quasi-faithful by Lemma 4.29 and by the proof of Lemma 4.42. Let $\Gamma_i = (\mathcal{K} \circ \Gamma_{i,i\oplus 1}) \uplus \Gamma_{i\oplus 2,i}$ for each $i \in \{0, 1, 2\}$. Note that each Γ_i is a consistent base, since we have $w_i \in [\![\Gamma_i]\!]$. We now show that Conditions (1) and Condition (2) from Definition 5.3 are satisfied:

(1) Towards a contradiction, assume that $\mathcal{K}$ is consistent with some $\Gamma_{i,i\oplus 1}$. From (G2) we obtain $[\![\mathcal{K} \circ \Gamma_{i,i\oplus 1}]\!] = [\![\mathcal{K} \uplus \Gamma_{i,i\oplus 1}]\!]$ for some $i \in \{0, 1, 2\}$. Since $w_i \in [\![\Gamma_i]\!]$, by the definition of Γ_i we have $w_i \in [\![(\mathcal{K} \circ \Gamma_{i,i\oplus 1}) \uplus \Gamma_{i\oplus 2,i}]\!] = [\![(\mathcal{K} \uplus \Gamma_{i,i\oplus 1}) \uplus \Gamma_{i\oplus 2,i}]\!]$ and obtain $w_i \in [\![\mathcal{K}]\!]$ for some $i \in \{0, 1, 2\}$, which contradicts $w_0, w_1, w_2 \not\models \mathcal{K}$.

(2) By the postulate (G1) we have $[\![\mathcal{K} \circ \Gamma_{i,i\oplus 1}]\!] \subseteq [\![\Gamma_{i,i\oplus 1}]\!]$ for each $i \in \{0, 1, 2\}$. The definition of Γ_i yields $[\![\Gamma_i]\!] \subseteq [\![\Gamma_{i,i\oplus 1} \uplus \Gamma_{i\oplus 2,i}]\!]$ for each $i \in \{0, 1, 2\}$. Substituting i by $i \oplus 1$ yields $[\![\Gamma_{i\oplus 1}]\!] \subseteq [\![\Gamma_{i\oplus 1,i\oplus 2} \uplus \Gamma_{i,i\oplus 1}]\!]$; showing that $[\![\Gamma_i]\!] \cup [\![\Gamma_{i\oplus 1}]\!] \subseteq [\![\Gamma_{i,i\oplus 1}]\!]$ holds for each $i \in \{0, 1, 2\}$.

We show that each $\Gamma_i \uplus \Gamma_j$ is inconsistent, by assuming the contrary, i.e., there are some $i, j \in \{0, 1, 2\}$ such that $i \neq j$ and $\Gamma_i \uplus \Gamma_j$ is consistent, i.e. there exists some $w^* \in [\![\Gamma_i]\!] \cap [\![\Gamma_j]\!]$.

From the definition of Γ_i and the definition of Γ_j, we obtain $\omega^* \in [\![\mathcal{K} \circ \Gamma_{i,i\oplus 1}]\!] \cap [\![\Gamma_{i\oplus 2,i}]\!] \cap [\![\mathcal{K} \circ \Gamma_{j,j\oplus 1}]\!] \cap [\![\Gamma_{j\oplus 2,j}]\!]$. Hence, we obtain $\omega^* \in [\![\Gamma_{i\oplus 2,i} \uplus \Gamma_{j\oplus 2,j}]\!]$ and from compatibility of $\preceq^\circ_{(.)}$ with $\circ$, we obtain $\omega^* \in \min([\![\Gamma_{i,i\oplus 1}]\!], \preceq^\circ_\mathcal{K})$ and $\omega^* \in \min([\![\Gamma_{j,j\oplus 1}]\!], \preceq^\circ_\mathcal{K})$. Now observe that $\omega_0, \omega_1, \omega_2 \in [\![\Gamma_{i,i\oplus 1}]\!] \cup [\![\Gamma_{j,j\oplus 1}]\!]$ holds; this is because we have $[\![\Gamma_k]\!] \subseteq [\![\Gamma_{k,k\oplus 1}]\!] \cup [\![\Gamma_{k\oplus n,k}]\!]$ for each $k \in \{0, 1, 2\}$. Hence, independent of the specific i and j, we obtain $\omega^* \preceq^\circ_\mathcal{K} \omega_k$ from $\omega^* \in [\![\mathcal{K} \circ \Gamma_{i,i\oplus 1}]\!]$ and Lemma 4.28(b) for each $k \in \{0, 1, 2\}$. Together, $\omega_i \in [\![\mathcal{K} \circ \Gamma_{i,i\oplus 1}]\!]$, $\omega_j \in [\![\mathcal{K} \circ \Gamma_{j,j\oplus 1}]\!]$, and compatibility, imply $\omega_i \preceq^\circ_\mathcal{K} \omega^*$ and $\omega_j \preceq^\circ_\mathcal{K} \omega^*$. Because of $[\![\Gamma_i]\!] \cup [\![\Gamma_{i\oplus 1}]\!] \subseteq [\![\Gamma_{i,i\oplus 1}]\!]$, we have that $\omega_i, \omega_j, \omega^* \in [\![\Gamma_{i,i\oplus 1}]\!]$ or $\omega_i, \omega_j, \omega^* \in [\![\Gamma_{j,j\oplus 1}]\!]$ holds. For the case $\omega_i, \omega_j, \omega^* \in [\![\Gamma_{i,i\oplus 1}]\!]$, since $\omega_j \preceq^\circ_\mathcal{K} \omega^*$ and $\omega^* \in \min([\![\Gamma_{i,i\oplus 1}]\!], \preceq^\circ_\mathcal{K})$, from min-retractivity we obtain $\omega_j \in \min([\![\Gamma_{i,i\oplus 1}]\!], \preceq^\circ_\mathcal{K})$. As $\omega_i \in \min([\![\Gamma_{i,i\oplus 1}]\!], \preceq^\circ_\mathcal{K})$, we obtain $\omega_i \preceq^\circ_\mathcal{K} \omega_j$ and $\omega_j \preceq^\circ_\mathcal{K} \omega_i$. By an analogue argumentation, we obtain for the case of $\omega_i, \omega_j, \omega^* \in [\![\Gamma_{j,j\oplus 1}]\!]$ the same conclusion, i.e., $\omega_i \preceq^\circ_\mathcal{K} \omega_j$ and $\omega_j \preceq^\circ_\mathcal{K} \omega_i$. This shows that $\omega_i \preceq^\circ_\mathcal{K} \omega_j$ and $\omega_j \preceq^\circ_\mathcal{K} \omega_i$ must hold in general.

We consider in the following all possible choices for i and j. For the case of $i = 0$ and $j = 2$, we obtain a contradiction to $\omega_2 \prec^\circ_\mathcal{K} \omega_0$. We next consider the case of $i = 1$ and $j = 2$. Because of $[\![\Gamma_0]\!] = [\![\mathcal{K} \circ \Gamma_{0,1}]\!] \cap [\![\Gamma_{2,0}]\!] = \min([\![\Gamma_{0,1}]\!], \preceq^\circ_\mathcal{K}) \cap [\![\Gamma_{2,0}]\!]$, we have that $\omega_0, \omega_2, \omega^* \in [\![\Gamma_{2,0}]\!]$ holds. As $\omega_0 \preceq^\circ_\mathcal{K} \omega^*$ and $\omega^* \in \min([\![\Gamma_{2,0}]\!], \preceq^\circ_\mathcal{K})$ holds, min-retractivity of $\preceq^\circ_\mathcal{K}$ yields $\omega_0 \in \min([\![\Gamma_{2,0}]\!], \preceq^\circ_\mathcal{K})$. Consequently, we obtain that $\omega_0 \preceq^\circ_\mathcal{K} \omega_2$ holds, which is a contradiction to $\omega_2 \prec^\circ_\mathcal{K} \omega_0$. The proof for the case of $i = 2$ and $j = 1$ is analogous to the case of $i = 1$ and $j = 2$. We obtain that Condition (2) from Definition 5.3 is satisfied.

Recall that by assumption, the base logic $\mathbb{B}$ does not exhibit a critical loop. Yet $\Gamma_{0,1}, \Gamma_{1,2}, \Gamma_{2,0}$ satisfy Conditions (1) and Condition (2) of a a critical loop, hence Condition (3) of Definition 5.3 must be violated. This means that there exists some $\Gamma_\triangledown \in \mathfrak{B}$ such that $[\![\Gamma_i \uplus \Gamma_\triangledown]\!] \neq \emptyset$ for every $i \in \{0, 1, 2\}$, but no required base $\Gamma'_\triangledown \in \mathfrak{B}$ such that Condition (3) is satisfied. Consequently, for all $\Gamma \in \mathfrak{B}$ holds

$$[\![\Gamma]\!] \neq \emptyset \text{ implies } [\![\Gamma]\!] \not\subseteq [\![\Gamma_\triangledown]\!] \setminus ([\![\Gamma_{0,1}]\!] \cup [\![\Gamma_{1,2}]\!] \cup [\![\Gamma_{2,0}]\!]). \qquad (\star 1)$$

For the remaining parts of the proof, let $\omega_i^\triangledown \in \Omega$ be an interpretation with $\omega_i^\triangledown \in [\![\Gamma_i]\!] \cap [\![\Gamma_\triangledown]\!]$ for each $i \in \{0, 1, 2\}$. Because $\circ$ satisfies (G1) and (G3), we obtain $[\![\mathcal{K} \circ \Gamma_\triangledown]\!] \subseteq [\![\Gamma_\triangledown]\!]$ and consistency of $\mathcal{K} \circ \Gamma_\triangledown$. Together with $(\star 1)$ we obtain that there exists $k \in \{0, 1, 2\}$ with $[\![\mathcal{K} \circ \Gamma_\triangledown]\!] \cap [\![\Gamma_{k,k\oplus 1}]\!] \neq \emptyset$. We consider each of the two cases $[\![\mathcal{K} \circ \Gamma_\triangledown]\!] \cap [\![\mathcal{K} \circ \Gamma_{k,k\oplus 1}]\!] \neq \emptyset$ and $[\![\mathcal{K} \circ \Gamma_\triangledown]\!] \cap [\![\mathcal{K} \circ \Gamma_{k,k\oplus 1}]\!] = \emptyset$ independently.

The case of $[\![\mathcal{K} \circ \Gamma_\triangledown]\!] \cap [\![\mathcal{K} \circ \Gamma_{k,k\oplus 1}]\!] \neq \emptyset$. As first step, we show that

$$\omega_0^\triangledown \preceq_\mathcal{K}^\circ \omega_2^\triangledown \text{ and } \omega_2^\triangledown \preceq_\mathcal{K}^\circ \omega_1^\triangledown \text{ and } \omega_1^\triangledown \preceq_\mathcal{K}^\circ \omega_0^\triangledown \qquad (\star 2)$$

holds for this case. Clearly, $[\![\mathcal{K} \circ \Gamma_\triangledown]\!] \cap [\![\mathcal{K} \circ \Gamma_{k,k\oplus 1}]\!] \neq \emptyset$ implies that there exists some $\omega_k^\star \in \Omega$ such that $\omega_k^\star \in [\![\mathcal{K} \circ \Gamma_\triangledown]\!]$ and $\omega_k^\star \in [\![\mathcal{K} \circ \Gamma_{k,k\oplus 1}]\!]$. From the compatibility of $\circ$ with $\preceq_{(.)}^\circ$, we obtain $\omega_k^\star \in \min([\![\Gamma_{k,k\oplus 1}]\!], \preceq_\mathcal{K}^\circ)$, implying that $\omega_k^\triangledown \preceq_\mathcal{K}^\circ \omega_k^\star$ holds. Remember that $\omega_k^\triangledown, \omega_k^\star \in [\![\Gamma_\triangledown]\!]$ and $\omega_k^\star \in \min([\![\Gamma_\triangledown]\!], \preceq_\mathcal{K}^\circ)$, by min-retractivity we obtain $\omega_k^\triangledown \in \min([\![\Gamma_\triangledown]\!], \preceq_\mathcal{K}^\circ)$. From this last observation and from $\omega_{k\oplus 1}^\triangledown, \omega_{k\oplus 2}^\triangledown \in [\![\Gamma_\triangledown]\!]$ we obtain that $\omega_k^\triangledown \preceq_\mathcal{K}^\circ \omega_{k\oplus 1}^\triangledown$ and $\omega_k^\triangledown \preceq_\mathcal{K}^\circ \omega_{k\oplus 2}^\triangledown$ holds. Remember that by Condition (2) we have $\omega_k^\triangledown, \omega_{k\oplus 2}^\triangledown \in [\![\Gamma_{k\oplus 2,k}]\!]$ and by compatibility we obtain $\omega_{k\oplus 2}^\triangledown \in \min([\![\Gamma_{k\oplus 2,k}]\!], \preceq_\mathcal{K}^\circ)$. This last observation, together with $\omega_k^\triangledown \preceq_\mathcal{K}^\circ \omega_{k\oplus 2}^\triangledown$, $\omega_k \models \mathcal{K} \circ \Gamma$ and min-retractivity, yields $\omega_k^\triangledown \in \min([\![\Gamma_{k\oplus 2,k}]\!], \preceq_\mathcal{K}^\circ)$. Thus, we have $\omega_{k\oplus 2}^\triangledown \preceq_\mathcal{K}^\circ \omega_k^\triangledown$. By a symmetric argument, we have $\omega_{k\oplus 1}^\triangledown, \omega_{k\oplus 2}^\triangledown \in [\![\Gamma_{k\oplus 1,k\oplus 2}]\!]$ and $\omega_{k\oplus 1}^\triangledown \in [\![\mathcal{K} \circ \Gamma_{k\oplus 1,k\oplus 2}]\!]$. Thus, we obtain $\omega_{k\oplus 1}^\triangledown \preceq_\mathcal{K}^\circ \omega_{k\oplus 2}^\triangledown$ from Lemma 4.28(b). By combination of these observations with $\omega_{k\oplus 1}^\triangledown, \omega_{k\oplus 2}^\triangledown \in [\![\Gamma_\triangledown]\!]$ and $\omega_k^\triangledown \in \min([\![\Gamma_\triangledown]\!], \preceq_\mathcal{K}^\circ)$, we obtain $\omega_k^\triangledown, \omega_{k\oplus 1}^\triangledown, \omega_{k\oplus 2}^\triangledown \in \min([\![\Gamma_\triangledown]\!], \preceq_\mathcal{K}^\circ)$ from min-retractivity. As direct consequence, we obtain that $(\star 2)$ holds.

We will now show that a contradiction with $\omega_2 \prec_\mathcal{K}^\circ \omega_0$ is unavoidable. Recall that $\omega_0, \omega_2 \in [\![\Gamma_{2,0}]\!]$ and $\omega_2 \models \mathcal{K} \circ \Gamma_{2,0}$, but $\omega_0 \not\models \mathcal{K} \circ \Gamma_{2,0}$. The last observation together with the compatibility of $\preceq_{(.)}^\circ$ with $\circ$ implies that $\omega_2^\triangledown \in \min([\![\Gamma_{2,0}]\!], \preceq_\mathcal{K}^\circ)$ holds. Because $(\star 2)$ holds, we obtain $\omega_0^\triangledown \in \min([\![\Gamma_{2,0}]\!], \preceq_\mathcal{K}^\circ)$ from min-retractivity of $\preceq_{(.)}^\circ$. Similarly, we obtain $\omega_0, \omega_0^\triangledown \in \min([\![\Gamma_{0,1}]\!], \preceq_\mathcal{K}^\circ)$ from compatibility and $\omega_0, \omega_0^\triangledown \in [\![\mathcal{K} \circ \Gamma_{0,1}]\!]$; showing that $\omega_0 \preceq_\mathcal{K}^\circ \omega_0^\triangledown$ holds. Because of $\omega_0^\triangledown, \omega_0, \omega_2 \in [\![\Gamma_{2,0}]\!]$, we obtain $\omega_0 \in \min([\![\Gamma_{2,0}]\!], \preceq_\mathcal{K}^\circ)$ from $\omega_0^\triangledown \in \min([\![\Gamma_{2,0}]\!], \preceq_\mathcal{K}^\circ)$ and min-retractivity, and consequently, we obtain the contradiction $\omega_0 \preceq_\mathcal{K}^\circ \omega_2$.

The case of $[\![\mathcal{K} \circ \Gamma_\triangledown]\!] \cap [\![\mathcal{K} \circ \Gamma_{k,k\oplus 1}]\!] = \emptyset$. Using $[\![\mathcal{K} \circ \Gamma_\triangledown]\!] \cap [\![\Gamma_{k,k\oplus 1}]\!] \neq \emptyset$ yields that there exist some $\omega^* \in [\![\mathcal{K} \circ \Gamma_\triangledown]\!] \cap [\![\Gamma_{k,k\oplus 1}]\!]$. From Lemma 4.28(c) and $\omega^*, \omega_k^\triangledown \in [\![\Gamma_{k,k\oplus 1}]\!]$ and $\omega_k^\triangledown \in [\![\mathcal{K} \circ \Gamma_{k,k\oplus 1}]\!]$ and $\omega^* \notin [\![\mathcal{K} \circ \Gamma_{k,k\oplus 1}]\!]$ we obtain $\omega_k^\triangledown \prec_\mathcal{K}^\circ \omega^*$. Because (G1) is satisfied by $\circ$, we have that $\omega^* \in [\![\mathcal{K} \circ \Gamma_\triangledown]\!]$ implies $\omega^* \in [\![\Gamma_\triangledown]\!]$. We obtain the contradiction $\omega^* \preceq_\mathcal{K}^\circ \omega_k^\triangledown$ from $\omega^*, \omega_k^\triangledown \in [\![\Gamma_\triangledown]\!]$ and $\omega^* \in [\![\mathcal{K} \circ \Gamma_\triangledown]\!]$ by using Lemma 4.28(b).

In summary, this shows that Conditions (1)–(3) from Definition 5.3 are satisfied, i.e., $\Gamma_{0,1}, \Gamma_{1,2}, \Gamma_{2,0}$ form a critical loop. This contradicts the prerequisite that $\mathbb{B}$ does not exhibit a critical loop and consequently, (ω_0, ω_1) or (ω_1, ω_2) is detached from $\circ$ in $\mathcal{K}$. $\square$

Lemma 5.8 provides the rationale for the first transformation step: For every $\mathcal{K} \in \mathfrak{B}$, we obtain $\preceq_\mathcal{K}^{\circ\prime}$ by removing all non-reflexive detached pairs from $\preceq_\mathcal{K}^\circ$, that is, $\preceq_\mathcal{K}^{\circ\prime} = \preceq_\mathcal{K}^\circ \setminus \mathfrak{D}_\mathcal{K}^\circ$. The resulting $\preceq_\mathcal{K}^{\circ\prime}$ is not guaranteed to be total anymore, and it is not necessarily transitive. But we will show that $\preceq_\mathcal{K}^{\circ\prime}$ inherits other important properties from $\preceq_\mathcal{K}^\circ$.

Lemma 5.9. *Let $\mathbb{B} = (\mathcal{L}, \Omega, \models, \mathfrak{B}, \uplus)$ be a base logic which does not admit a critical loop, let $\circ$ be a base change operator satisfying (G1)–(G3), (G5), and (G6) and let $\preceq_\mathcal{K}^\circ$ be a quasi-faithful min-friendly assignment compatible with $\circ$. For each $\mathcal{K}, \Gamma \in \mathfrak{B}$, it holds that $\min([\![\Gamma]\!], \preceq_\mathcal{K}^{\circ\prime}) = \min([\![\Gamma]\!], \preceq_\mathcal{K}^\circ)$ and $\preceq_\mathcal{K}^{\circ\prime}$ is min-complete and reflexive.*

Proof. By definition of $\preceq_\mathcal{K}^{\circ\prime}$ we have $\omega \preceq_\mathcal{K}^{\circ\prime} \omega'$ if and only if $\omega \preceq_\mathcal{K}^\circ \omega'$ for all $(\omega, \omega') \in \Omega \times \Omega$ which are not detached pairs. Because for every $\omega, \omega' \in [\![\Gamma]\!]$ with $\omega \in \min([\![\Gamma]\!], \preceq_\mathcal{K}^\circ)$ we have $\omega \models \mathcal{K} \circ \Gamma$ by compatibility of $\preceq_{(.)}^\circ$ with $\circ$. Consequently, the pair (ω, ω') is not detached and thus $\min([\![\Gamma]\!], \preceq_\mathcal{K}^{\circ\prime}) = \min([\![\Gamma]\!], \preceq_\mathcal{K}^\circ)$. The latter implies that min-completeness of $\preceq_\mathcal{K}^\circ$ carries over to $\preceq_\mathcal{K}^{\circ\prime}$. Reflexivity of $\preceq_\mathcal{K}^{\circ\prime}$ is ontained by construction, the reflexivity of $\preceq_\mathcal{K}^\circ$ and by the definition of $\mathfrak{D}_\mathcal{K}^\circ$. $\square$

Step II: Taking the transitive closure

In this step, for every $\mathcal{K} \in \mathfrak{B}$, we obtain $\preceq_\mathcal{K}^{\circ\prime\prime}$ by taking the transitive closure of $\preceq_\mathcal{K}^{\circ\prime}$, i.e., we have $\preceq_\mathcal{K}^{\circ\prime\prime} = TC(\preceq_\mathcal{K}^{\circ\prime}) = TC(\preceq_\mathcal{K}^\circ \setminus \mathfrak{D}_\mathcal{K}^\circ)$. The resulting $\preceq_\mathcal{K}^{\circ\prime\prime}$ is still not guaranteed to be total, but it is reflexive and transitive by construction, and it inherits further important properties from $\preceq_\mathcal{K}^{\circ\prime}$. It will turn out that the transitive closure will only add pairs to $\preceq_\mathcal{K}^{\circ\prime}$ that are detached pairs. This means that $\preceq_\mathcal{K}^{\circ\prime\prime}$ contains

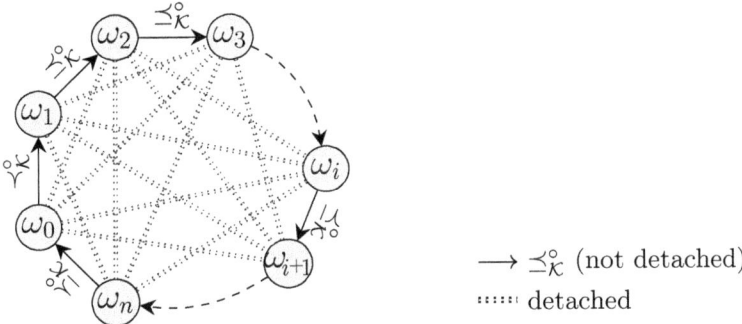

$\longrightarrow \preceq_{\mathcal{K}}^{\circ}$ (not detached)

::::: detached

Figure 5.3: Illustration of a critical loop-situation of length $n+1$ on the semantic side. This situation is due to Lemma 5.12 impossible for $\preceq_{\mathcal{K}}^{\circ}$ if $\mathbb{B}$ does not exhibit a critical loop.

only elements from $\preceq_{\mathcal{K}}^{\circ}{}'$ and from $\mathfrak{D}_{\mathcal{K}}^{\circ}$. Because adding detached pairs does not influence minimal sets of models of a base Γ with respect to $\preceq_{\mathcal{K}}$, we will obtain that these sets are preserved when taking the transitive closure. If the transitive closure would (hypothetically) add non-detached pairs to $\preceq_{\mathcal{K}}^{\circ}{}'$, then the relation $\preceq_{\mathcal{K}}^{\circ}$ would contain a circle of interpretations consisting only of non-detached pairs (such as the circle illustrated in Figure 5.3).

We continue by preparing a lemma which captures this intuition. The lemma will make use of circles of interpretations which are violating the situation given in Figure 5.3. To make such situations easier to handle, we introduce the following notion which make use of $\preceq_{(.)}^{\circ}$, defined in Definition 4.25.

Definition 5.10. *Let* $\mathbb{B} = (\mathcal{L}, \Omega, \models, \mathfrak{B}, \mathbb{U})$ *be a base logic, let* $\mathcal{K} \in \mathfrak{B}$ *be a base, and let* $\circ$ *be a base change operator for* $\mathbb{B}$ *that satisfies (G1)–(G3), (G5), and (G6). A sequence of interpretations* $\circlearrowright = \omega_0, \ldots, \omega_n, \omega_0$ *from* Ω *is said to form a* strict circle *of length* $n+1$ *(with respect to* $\circ$ *and* $\mathcal{K}$*) if*

- $\omega_0, \ldots, \omega_n$ *are satisfying*
  (a) $\omega_0 \prec_{\mathcal{K}}^{\circ} \omega_1$ *and*
  (b) $\omega_i \preceq_{\mathcal{K}}^{\circ} \omega_{i\oplus1}$ *for all* $i \in \{1, \ldots, n\}$*, where* $\oplus$ *is addition* $\mathrm{mod}(n+1)$*, and*
- (ω_i, ω_{i+1}) *is not a detached pair for each* $i \in \{0, \ldots, n\}$*.*

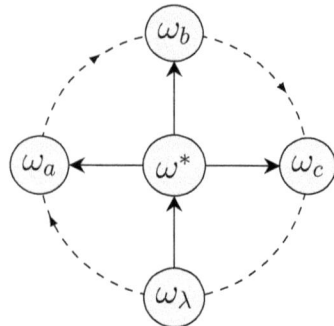

Figure 5.4: Exemplary situation of Lemma 5.11. Four interpretations lying on a strict circle, connected by another interpretation ω^*.

We will also substitute elements in a strict circle $\circlearrowright$ and use therefore the following notion. For a substitution $\sigma = \{\omega_{i_1} \mapsto x_1,\ \omega_{i_2} \mapsto x_2,\ \ldots\}$, we denote by $\circlearrowright[\sigma]$ the simultaneous replacement of ω_{i_j} by x_j in $\circlearrowright$ for all $\omega_{i_j} \mapsto x_j \in \sigma$.

The following lemma will be useful, and describes situations like in Figure 5.4.

Lemma 5.11 (Cross Lemma). *Let $\mathbb{B} = (\mathcal{L}, \Omega, \models, \mathfrak{B}, \mathbb{U})$ be a base logic which does not admit a critical loop, let $\mathcal{K} \in \mathfrak{B}$ be a base, and let $\circ$ be a base change operator for $\mathbb{B}$ that satisfies (G1)–(G3), (G5), and (G6). If there are $\omega_0, \ldots, \omega_n \in \Omega$, with $n > 3$, and pairwise distinct $\lambda, a, b, c \in \{0, \ldots, n\}$, such that*

(a) $\omega_0, \omega_1, \ldots, \omega_n, \omega_0$ is a strict circle of length $n + 1$,
(b) there exists an interpretation ω^* such that

$$\omega^* \preceq_{\mathcal{K}}^{\circ} \omega_a \qquad \omega^* \preceq_{\mathcal{K}}^{\circ} \omega_b \qquad \omega^* \preceq_{\mathcal{K}}^{\circ} \omega_c \qquad \omega_\lambda \preceq_{\mathcal{K}}^{\circ} \omega^* \ , \ and$$

(c) every pair of $\preceq_{\mathcal{K}}^{\circ}$ considered in (b) is not detached from $\circ$ in $\mathcal{K}$,

then there is a strict circle of length m with $3 \leq m \leq n$.

Proof. We assume $a < b < c$, and we assume that the path $\omega_c, \ldots, \omega_\lambda$ does not contain ω_a and ω_b (when seeing $\preceq_{\mathcal{K}}^{\circ}$ as graph). All other cases will follow by symmetry. We continue by consider several cases:

The case of $\omega_\lambda \prec_{\mathcal{K}}^{\circ} \omega^*$. We obtain $\omega_\lambda \prec_{\mathcal{K}}^{\circ} \omega^* \preceq_{\mathcal{K}}^{\circ} \omega_c \preceq_{\mathcal{K}}^{\circ} \ldots \preceq_{\mathcal{K}}^{\circ} \omega_\lambda$, which yields that $\circlearrowright_{\lambda c} = \omega_\lambda, \omega^*, \omega_c, \ldots, \omega_\lambda$ is a strict circle. Note that because $\circlearrowleft_{\lambda c}$ contains ω^* and in addition only elements of $\{\omega_0, \ldots, \omega_n\} \setminus \{\omega_a, \omega_b\}$, we have that $\circlearrowleft_{\lambda c}$ has a length of at most n.

The case of $\omega^* \prec_{\mathcal{K}}^{\circ} \omega_c$ and no prior case applies. If $\omega^* \prec_{\mathcal{K}}^{\circ} \omega_c$, then we obtain $\omega^* \prec_{\mathcal{K}}^{\circ} \omega_c \preceq_{\mathcal{K}}^{\circ} \cdots \preceq_{\mathcal{K}}^{\circ} \omega_\lambda \preceq_{\mathcal{K}}^{\circ} \omega^*$, yielding that $\circlearrowleft_{c\lambda} = \omega^*, \omega_c, \ldots, \omega_\lambda, \omega^*$ is a strict circle. Note that because $\circlearrowleft_{c\lambda}$ contains ω^* and in addition only elements of $\{\omega_0, \ldots, \omega_n\} \setminus \{\omega_a, \omega_b\}$, we have that $\circlearrowleft_{c\lambda}$ has a length of at most n.

The case of $\omega^* \prec_{\mathcal{K}}^{\circ} \omega_b$ and no prior case applies. In this case we have $\omega_c \preceq_{\mathcal{K}}^{\circ} \omega^*$. We obtain $\omega^* \prec_{\mathcal{K}}^{\circ} \omega_b \preceq_{\mathcal{K}}^{\circ} \cdots \preceq_{\mathcal{K}}^{\circ} \omega_c \preceq_{\mathcal{K}}^{\circ} \omega^*$, which yields that $\circlearrowleft_{bc} = \omega^*, \omega_b, \ldots, \omega_c, \omega^*$ is a strict circle. Note that because $\circlearrowleft_{bc}$ contains, beside of ω^*, only elements of $\{\omega_0, \ldots, \omega_n\} \setminus \{\omega_a, \omega_\lambda\}$, we have that $\circlearrowleft_{bc}$ has a length of at most n.

The case of $\omega^* \prec_{\mathcal{K}}^{\circ} \omega_a$ and no prior case applies. In this case we have $\omega_b \preceq_{\mathcal{K}}^{\circ} \omega^*$. We obtain $\omega^* \prec_{\mathcal{K}}^{\circ} \omega_a \preceq_{\mathcal{K}}^{\circ} \cdots \preceq_{\mathcal{K}}^{\circ} \omega_b \preceq_{\mathcal{K}}^{\circ} \omega^*$, which yields that $\circlearrowleft_{ab} = \omega^*, \omega_a, \ldots, \omega_b, \omega^*$ is a strict circle. Note that because $\circlearrowleft_{ab}$ contains, beside of ω^*, only elements of $\{\omega_0, \ldots, \omega_n\} \setminus \{\omega_c, \omega_\lambda\}$, we have that $\circlearrowleft_{ab}$ has a length of at most n.

If none of the cases above applies, then we have that $\omega^* \preceq_{\mathcal{K}}^{\circ} \omega_\lambda$ and $\omega_a \preceq_{\mathcal{K}}^{\circ} \omega^*$ and $\omega_b \preceq_{\mathcal{K}}^{\circ} \omega^*$ and $\omega_c \preceq_{\mathcal{K}}^{\circ} \omega^*$ holds. For the following line of arguments, recall that $a < b < c$ holds. We consider the case of $0 < \lambda < a$; for all other cases (where $0 < \lambda < a$ does not hold), the line of arguments is symmetric to the proof we present here in the following for the case of $0 < \lambda < a$. Because $\omega_0, \omega_1, \ldots, \omega_n, \omega_0$ is a strict circle of length $n+1$, we obtain that $\omega_0 \prec_{\mathcal{K}}^{\circ} \omega_1 \preceq_{\mathcal{K}}^{\circ} \cdots \preceq_{\mathcal{K}}^{\circ} \omega_\lambda \preceq_{\mathcal{K}}^{\circ} \omega^* \preceq_{\mathcal{K}}^{\circ} \omega_c \preceq_{\mathcal{K}}^{\circ} \cdots \preceq_{\mathcal{K}}^{\circ} \omega_0$. This show that $\circlearrowleft_{0\lambda c} = \omega_0, \omega_1, \ldots, \omega_\lambda, \omega^*, \omega_c, \ldots, \omega_0$ is a strict circle. Because $\circlearrowleft_{0\lambda c}$ contains ω^* and additionally only elements from $\omega_0, \ldots, \omega_n$, but not ω_a and ω_b, we obtain that $\circlearrowleft_{0\lambda c}$ has a length of at most n.

In summary, we obtain a strict circle of length m with $3 \leq m \leq n$ for each case. $\qquad\square$

Note that it is not necessary to assume that ω^* is distinct from $\omega_0, \ldots, \omega_n$ in Lemma 5.11. We now present the central Lemma of this step.

Lemma 5.12. *Let* $\mathbb{B} = (\mathcal{L}, \Omega, \models, \mathfrak{B}, \uplus)$ *be a base logic which does not admit a critical loop, let* $\mathcal{K} \in \mathfrak{B}$ *be a base, and let* $\circ$ *be a base change operator for* $\mathbb{B}$ *that satisfies (G1)–(G3), (G5), and (G6). If there are three or more interpretations* $\omega_0, \ldots, \omega_n \in \Omega$, *i.e.* $n \geq 2$, *such that*

(a) $\omega_0 \prec_{\mathcal{K}}^{\circ} \omega_1$,
(b) $\omega_i \preceq_{\mathcal{K}}^{\circ} \omega_{i\oplus1}$ *for all* $i \in \{1, \ldots, n\}$, *where* $\oplus$ *is addition* $\mathrm{mod}(n+1)$,

then there is some $i \in \{1, \ldots, n\}$ *such that* $(\omega_i, \omega_{i\oplus1})$ *is a detached pair.*

Proof. Let $\omega_0, \ldots, \omega_n \in \Omega$ such that Condition (a) and Condition (b) of Lemma 5.12 are satisfied. With $\oplus$ we denote addition $\mathrm{mod}(n+1)$. The proof will be by induction. Note that for $n = 2$ we obtain the result by Lemma 5.8. We proceed the proof for the case of $n > 2$ and assume that Lemma 5.12 already holds for all m with $2 \leq m < n$. A consequence of the induction hypothesis is that there is no strict circle of length c for $3 \leq c \leq n$.

We are striving for a contradiction. Therefore, we assume $\circlearrowleft_{0n} = \omega_0, \ldots, \omega_n, \omega_0$ is a strict circle of length $n+1$, which is, due to Condition (a) and Condition (b) from Lemma 5.12, equivalent to assume that $(\omega_i, \omega_{i\oplus1})$ is not a detached pair for each $i \in \{1, \ldots, n\}$. The remaining parts of the proof show that the existence of the strict circle $\circlearrowleft_{0n}$ implies existence of a critical loop.

As first step, we show that $\omega_0, \ldots, \omega_n \notin [\![\mathcal{K}]\!]$ holds. If $\omega_1 \in [\![\mathcal{K}]\!]$, then due Definition 4.25, we obtain $\omega_1 \preceq_{\mathcal{K}}^{\circ} \omega_0$, which contradicts Condition (a). If $\omega_i \in [\![\mathcal{K}]\!]$ for some $i \in \{0, 2, 3, \ldots, n\}$, then, because of Condition (b), there is some j with $\omega_j \preceq_{\mathcal{K}}^{\circ} \omega_{j\oplus1}$ and $\omega_j \notin [\![\mathcal{K}]\!]$ and $\omega_{j\oplus1} \in [\![\mathcal{K}]\!]$; which is again impossible due to Definition 4.25. Thus, we have $\omega_0, \ldots, \omega_n \notin [\![\mathcal{K}]\!]$ for the remaining parts of the proof.

We continue by showing the existence of several bases, which will form a critical loop. Definition 4.25 and Definition 5.7 together implies that for each $i \in \{1, \ldots, n\}$ exists a base $\Gamma_{i,i\oplus1} \in \mathfrak{B}$ such that

$$\omega_i, \omega_{i\oplus1} \models \Gamma_{i,i\oplus1} \text{ and } \omega_i \models \mathcal{K} \circ \Gamma_{i,i\oplus1} \qquad (\#1)$$

holds. Moreover, by $\omega_0 \prec_{\mathcal{K}}^{\circ} \omega_1$ from Condition (1) and $\omega_1 \not\models \mathcal{K}$ and Lemma 4.28(a), there exists a base $\Gamma_{0,1} \in \mathfrak{B}$ such that the following holds:

$$\omega_0, \omega_1 \models \Gamma_{0,1} \text{ and } \omega_0 \models \mathcal{K} \circ \Gamma_{0,1} \text{ and } \omega_1 \not\models \mathcal{K} \circ \Gamma_{0,1}. \qquad (\#2)$$

We show that $\Gamma_{0,1}, \Gamma_{1,2}, \ldots, \Gamma_{n,0}$ is forming a critical loop. To this end we are setting $\Gamma_i = (\mathcal{K} \circ \Gamma_{i,i\oplus1}) \uplus \Gamma_{i\oplus n,i}$ for each $i \in \{0, \ldots, n\}$. By $(\#1)$ and $(\#2)$ each Γ_i is a consistent base with $\omega_i \in [\![\Gamma_i]\!]$. We continue by verifying that Conditions (1)–(3) from Definition 5.3 are satisfied.

(1) If $\mathcal{K}$ is inconsistent, then Condition (1) is immediately satisfied. We consider the case where $\mathcal{K}$ is consistent and $[\![\mathcal{K} \uplus \Gamma_{i,i\oplus1}]\!] \neq \emptyset$ for some $i \in \{0, \ldots, n\}$. From (G2) we obtain $[\![\mathcal{K} \circ \Gamma_{i,i\oplus1}]\!] = [\![\mathcal{K} \uplus \Gamma_{i,i\oplus1}]\!]$. From $\omega_i \in [\![\Gamma_i]\!]$ and the definition of Γ_i, we obtain $\omega_i \in [\![\mathcal{K} \circ \Gamma_{i,i\oplus1}]\!] \cap [\![\Gamma_{i\oplus n,i}]\!]$. As $[\![\mathcal{K} \circ \Gamma_{i,i\oplus1}]\!] = [\![\mathcal{K} \uplus \Gamma_{i,i\oplus1}]\!]$, we obtain $\omega_i \in [\![\mathcal{K} \uplus \Gamma_{i,i\oplus1}]\!] \cap [\![\Gamma_{i\oplus n,i}]\!]$. Consequently, we there exists some $i \in \{0, \ldots, n\}$ such that $\omega_i \in [\![\mathcal{K}]\!]$, yielding a contradiction to $\omega_0, \ldots, \omega_n \notin [\![\mathcal{K}]\!]$.

(2) By the postulate (G1) we have $[\![\mathcal{K} \circ \Gamma_{i,i\oplus1}]\!] \subseteq [\![\Gamma_{i,i\oplus1}]\!]$ for each $i \in \{0, \ldots, n\}$. The definition of Γ_i yields $[\![\Gamma_i]\!] \subseteq [\![\Gamma_{i,i\oplus1} \uplus \Gamma_{i\oplus n,i}]\!] \subseteq [\![\Gamma_{i,i\oplus1}]\!]$ for each $i \in \{0,1,2\}$. Substitution of i by $i \oplus 1$ yields $[\![\Gamma_{i\oplus1}]\!] \subseteq [\![\Gamma_{i\oplus1,i\oplus2} \uplus \Gamma_{i,i\oplus1}]\!] \subseteq [\![\Gamma_{i,i\oplus1}]\!]$; showing that $[\![\Gamma_i]\!] \cup [\![\Gamma_{i\oplus1}]\!] \subseteq [\![\Gamma_{i,i\oplus1}]\!]$ holds for each $i \in \{0, \ldots, n\}$.

We show that each $\Gamma_i \uplus \Gamma_j$ is inconsistent, by assuming the contrary, i.e. there are some $i, j \in \{0, \ldots, n\}$ such that $i \neq j$ and $\Gamma_i \uplus \Gamma_j$ is consistent. Because of the commutativity of $\uplus$, we assume $i < j$ without loss of generality. By compatibility and definition of Γ_i and by definition of Γ_j, there exists some $\omega^* \in [\![\Gamma_{i\oplus n,i} \uplus \Gamma_{j\oplus n,j}]\!]$ with $\omega^* \in \min([\![\Gamma_{i,i\oplus1}]\!], \preceq_{\mathcal{K}}^{\circ})$ and $\omega^* \in \min([\![\Gamma_{j,j\oplus1}]\!], \preceq_{\mathcal{K}}^{\circ})$. Recall that $\omega_i, \omega_{i\oplus1} \in [\![\Gamma_{i,i\oplus1}]\!]$ and $\omega_j, \omega_{j\oplus1} \in [\![\Gamma_{j,j\oplus1}]\!]$. Consequently, for all $k \in \{i, i \oplus 1, j, j \oplus 1\}$ holds $\omega^* \preceq_{\mathcal{K}}^{\circ} \omega_k$. Moreover, because of $(\#1)$ and $(\#2)$ we obtain $\omega_i \preceq_{\mathcal{K}}^{\circ} \omega^*$ and $\omega_j \preceq_{\mathcal{K}}^{\circ} \omega^*$ from Lemma 4.28(b). From $\omega^* \in [\![\Gamma_{i\oplus n,i} \uplus \Gamma_{j\oplus n,j}]\!]$ we obtain, by an analogue argumentation, that $\omega_{i\oplus n} \preceq_{\mathcal{K}}^{\circ} \omega^*$ and $\omega_{j\oplus n} \preceq_{\mathcal{K}}^{\circ} \omega^*$ holds. In summary, we have:

$$\begin{array}{cccc} \omega^* \preceq_{\mathcal{K}}^{\circ} \omega_i & \omega^* \preceq_{\mathcal{K}}^{\circ} \omega_j & \omega^* \preceq_{\mathcal{K}}^{\circ} \omega_{i\oplus1} & \omega_{i\oplus n} \preceq_{\mathcal{K}}^{\circ} \omega^* \\ \omega_i \preceq_{\mathcal{K}}^{\circ} \omega^* & \omega_j \preceq_{\mathcal{K}}^{\circ} \omega^* & \omega^* \preceq_{\mathcal{K}}^{\circ} \omega_{j\oplus1} & \omega_{j\oplus n} \preceq_{\mathcal{K}}^{\circ} \omega^* \end{array} \qquad (\boxtimes 1)$$

Note that all pairs (ω^*, ω_ξ), $(\omega^*, \omega_{\xi\oplus1})$ and $(\omega_{\xi\oplus n}, \omega^*)$ with $\xi \in \{i, j\}$ are not detached.

We are now striving for a contradiction by showing the existence of a strict circle with a length of at most n. Recall that $\circlearrowleft_{0n} = \omega_0, \ldots, \omega_n, \omega_0$ is a strict circle of length $n + 1$. At first, we consider two particular cases:

($\omega_i = \omega_{j \oplus 1}$) We obtain a strict circle of length of at most n from Lemma 5.11 by using $\circlearrowleft_{0n}$ and setting $\lambda = i$, $a = j$, $b = i \oplus 1$, and $c = j \oplus n$. Note that λ, a, b, c are pairwise distinct indices.

($\omega_j = \omega_{i \oplus 1}$) We obtain a strict circle of length of at most n from Lemma 5.11 by using $\circlearrowleft_{0n}$ and setting $\lambda = i$, $a = j$, $b = j \oplus 1$, and $c = i \oplus n$. Note that λ, a, b, c are pairwise distinct indices.

For all situations not covered by the cases above, we obtain that $i, i \oplus 1, j, j \oplus 1$ are pairwise distinct. Because of ($\boxasterisk 1$), we can apply Lemma 5.11 by using $\circlearrowleft_{0n}$ and setting $\lambda = i$, $a = i \oplus 1$, $b = j$, and $c = j \oplus n$. This yields a strict circle with a length of at most n.

In summary, for every possible case we obtain a contradiction, which shows that Condition (2) of critical loops (cf. Definition 5.3) is satisfied.

(3) We show Condition (3) from Definition 5.3 by contradiction. Therefore, assume there is a base $\Gamma_\triangledown \in \mathfrak{B}$ such that for

$$B = \{\Gamma_i \mid [\![\Gamma_\triangledown \uplus \Gamma]\!] \neq \emptyset\} \subseteq \{\Gamma_0, \ldots, \Gamma_n\} \qquad (\star 1)$$

holds $|B| \geq 3$ and there exists no base $\Gamma'_\triangledown \in \mathfrak{B}$ as required by Condition (3). Consequently, for each base $\Gamma \in \mathfrak{B}$ we have

$$[\![\Gamma]\!] \neq \emptyset \text{ implies } [\![\Gamma]\!] \not\subseteq [\![\Gamma_\triangledown]\!] \setminus ([\![\Gamma_{0,1}]\!] \cup \ldots \cup [\![\Gamma_{n,0}]\!]). \qquad (\star 2)$$

From ($\star 1$) we obtain that $\Gamma_\triangledown$ is consistent, and thus, by (G3), that $\mathcal{K} \circ \Gamma_\triangledown$ is consistent and from satisfaction of (G1) we obtain $[\![\mathcal{K} \circ \Gamma_\triangledown]\!] \subseteq [\![\Gamma_\triangledown]\!]$. Consequently, because of ($\star 2$), we have $[\![\mathcal{K} \circ \Gamma_\triangledown]\!] \not\subseteq [\![\Gamma_\triangledown]\!] \setminus ([\![\Gamma_{0,1}]\!] \cup \ldots \cup [\![\Gamma_{n,0}]\!])$. This implies that $[\![\mathcal{K} \circ \Gamma_\triangledown]\!] \cap [\![\Gamma_{k,k \oplus 1}]\!] \neq \emptyset$ for some $k \in \{0, \ldots, n\}$. Let $\omega_k^\star$ be an interpretation with $\omega_k^\star \in [\![\mathcal{K} \circ \Gamma_\triangledown]\!] \cap [\![\Gamma_{k,k \oplus 1}]\!]$. From (G5) and (G6), $\omega_k^\star \in [\![\mathcal{K} \circ \Gamma_\triangledown]\!] \cap [\![\Gamma_{k,k \oplus 1}]\!]$ and commutativity of $\uplus$ we obtain

$$\omega_k^\star \in \min([\![\Gamma_\triangledown]\!], \preceq_\mathcal{K}^\circ) \cap [\![\Gamma_{k,k \oplus 1}]\!]$$
$$= \min([\![\Gamma_{k,k \oplus 1} \uplus \Gamma_\triangledown]\!], \preceq_\mathcal{K}^\circ) \text{ and } \omega_k \preceq_\mathcal{K}^\circ \omega_k^\star, \qquad (\star 3)$$

whereby the latter is a direct consequence of $\omega_k^\star \in [\![\Gamma_{k,k \oplus 1}]\!]$ and $\omega_k \in \min([\![\Gamma_{k,k \oplus 1}]\!], \preceq_\mathcal{K}^\circ)$. Furthermore, let $\omega_i^\triangledown$ be some interpretation with $\omega_i^\triangledown \in [\![\Gamma_\triangledown \uplus \Gamma_i]\!]$ for each $\Gamma_i \in B$. We show as next for each $\Gamma_\xi \in B$ and for each $\omega^*_{\xi \oplus n} \in [\![\Gamma_{\xi \oplus n}]\!]$ and for each $\omega^*_{\xi \oplus 1} \in [\![\Gamma_{\xi \oplus 1}]\!]$ that we have

$$\omega^*_k \preceq^\circ_\mathcal{K} \omega^\triangledown_\xi \quad \omega^*_{\xi \oplus n} \preceq^\circ_\mathcal{K} \omega^\triangledown_\xi \quad \omega_\xi \preceq^\circ_\mathcal{K} \omega^\triangledown_\xi$$
$$\omega^\triangledown_\xi \preceq^\circ_\mathcal{K} \omega^*_{\xi \oplus 1} \quad \omega^\triangledown_\xi \preceq^\circ_\mathcal{K} \omega_\xi . \tag{$\star$4}$$

We obtain $\omega^*_k \preceq^\circ_\mathcal{K} \omega^\triangledown_\xi$ from Lemma 4.28(b), because $\omega^*_k, \omega^\triangledown_\xi \in [\![\Gamma_\triangledown]\!]$ and $\omega^*_k \in [\![\mathcal{K} \circ \Gamma_\triangledown]\!]$ holds. From $\omega_\xi, \omega^\triangledown_\xi \in \min([\![\Gamma_{\xi,\xi \oplus 1}]\!], \preceq^\circ_\mathcal{K})$ we directly obtain $\omega_\xi \preceq^\circ_\mathcal{K} \omega^\triangledown_\xi$ and $\omega^\triangledown_\xi \preceq^\circ_\mathcal{K} \omega_\xi$. Compatibility of $\preceq^\circ_{(.)}$ with $\circ$, together with the definitions of Γ_ξ and Condition (2), yields the remaining statements of ($\star$4).

Moreover, as next step, we show for each $\Gamma_\xi \in B$ and for each $\omega^*_{\xi \oplus n} \in [\![\Gamma_{\xi \oplus n}]\!]$ and for each $\omega^*_{\xi \oplus 1} \in [\![\Gamma_{\xi \oplus 1}]\!]$ the following holds:

$$\omega^*_{\xi \oplus n} \prec^\circ_\mathcal{K} \omega_\xi \quad \text{if and only if} \quad \omega^*_{\xi \oplus n} \prec^\circ_\mathcal{K} \omega^\triangledown_\xi$$
$$\omega_\xi \prec^\circ_\mathcal{K} \omega^*_{\xi \oplus 1} \quad \text{if and only if} \quad \omega^\triangledown_\xi \prec^\circ_\mathcal{K} \omega^*_{\xi \oplus 1} \tag{$\star$5}$$

Observe that ($\star$5) holds, otherwise, we would obtain a strict circle of length 3. These strict circles are directly obtainable from ($\star$4): if $\omega^*_{\xi \oplus n} \prec^\circ_\mathcal{K} \omega_\xi$ and $\omega^\triangledown_\xi \preceq^\circ_\mathcal{K} \omega^*_{\xi \oplus n}$, obtain the strict circle $\omega^*_{\xi \oplus n} \prec^\circ_\mathcal{K} \omega_\xi \preceq^\circ_\mathcal{K} \omega^\triangledown_\xi \preceq^\circ_\mathcal{K} \omega^*_{\xi \oplus n}$ with a length of 3. For all other cases, we obtain analogously a strict circle of length 3.

Now let $\ell_{\min}, \ell_{\mathrm{med}}, \ell_{\max}$ be integers with $0 \le \ell_{\min} < \ell_{\mathrm{med}} < \ell_{\max} \le n$ such that $\Gamma_{k \oplus \ell_{\min}}, \Gamma_{k \oplus \ell_{\mathrm{med}}}, \Gamma_{k \oplus \max} \in B$ and $\ell_{\min}$ is the smallest number from $\{0, \ldots, n\}$ with $\Gamma_{k \oplus \ell_{\min}} \in B$, and $\ell_{\max}$ is the greatest number from $\{0, \ldots, n\}$ with $\Gamma_{k \oplus \max} \in B$. For convenience, we will sometimes write ℓ_x and ω_x, instead of $\ell_{k \oplus \ell_x}$ and $\omega_{k \oplus \ell_x}$, respectively, for any $x \in \{\min, \mathrm{med}, \max\}$.

We now establish that replacing ω_i in $\circlearrowleft_{0n}$ by $\omega^\triangledown_i$ for some $\Gamma_i \in B$ yields again a strict circle. Remember that each pair given in ($\star$4) and ($\star$5) is a non-detached pair. Because of this and because $\circlearrowleft_{0n}$ is a strict circle of length $n+1$, we obtain from ($\star$4) and ($\star$5) that $\circlearrowleft_{0n}[\sigma]$ is also a strict circle of length $n+1$ for each substitution σ with

$$\sigma \subseteq \{\omega_{\min} \mapsto \omega^\triangledown_{\min}, \ \omega_{\mathrm{med}} \mapsto \omega^\triangledown_{\mathrm{med}}, \ \omega_{\max} \mapsto \omega^\triangledown_{\max}\} ,$$

i.e., substituting each ω_x by $\omega^\triangledown_x$ in $\omega_0, \omega_1, \ldots, \omega_n$, for some of $x \in \{\min, \mathrm{med}, \max\}$, yields a strict circle of length $n+1$.

We consider two cases, the case where $\Gamma_k \uplus \Gamma_\nabla$ is inconsistent and the case where $\Gamma_k \uplus \Gamma_\nabla$ is consistent.

The case of $\Gamma_k \uplus \Gamma_\nabla$ is inconsistent. For this case we have that $\Gamma_k \notin B$ holds. Remember that by $(\star 3)$ and $(\star 4)$ the following holds:

$$\omega_k \preceq_\mathcal{K}^\circ \omega_k^\star \qquad \omega_k^\star \preceq_\mathcal{K}^\circ \omega_{med}^\nabla$$
$$\omega_k^\star \preceq_\mathcal{K}^\circ \omega_{min}^\nabla \qquad \omega_k^\star \preceq_\mathcal{K}^\circ \omega_{max}^\nabla$$

We obtain that there exists a strict circle with a length of at most n by using Lemma 5.11 when setting $\lambda = k$, $a = k \oplus \ell_{min}$, $b = k \oplus \ell_{med}$ and $c = k \oplus \ell_{max}$, using the strict circle $\circlearrowleft_{0n}[\omega_a \mapsto \omega_p^\nabla, \omega_b \mapsto \omega_\tau^\nabla, \omega_c \mapsto \omega_q^\nabla]$.

The case of $\Gamma_k \uplus \Gamma_\nabla$ is consistent. This case is equivalent to having $\ell_{min} = 0$, i.e., $\Gamma_{min} = \Gamma_k \in B$. Consequently, we have that $\omega_k^\nabla \in [\![\Gamma_k \uplus \Gamma_\nabla]\!]$. From the definition of Γ_k, and from $\omega_k^\nabla, \omega_k^\star \in [\![\Gamma_{k,k\oplus1}]\!]$ with $\omega_k^\nabla \in [\![\mathcal{K} \circ \Gamma_{k,k\oplus1}]\!]$, and from compatibility and min-retractivity we also obtain $\omega_k^\star, \omega_k^\nabla \in [\![\mathcal{K} \circ \Gamma_{k,k\oplus1}]\!] \cap [\![\Gamma_\nabla]\!] = \min([\![\Gamma_{k,k\oplus1}]\!], \preceq_\mathcal{K}^\circ) \cap [\![\Gamma_\nabla]\!]$. Consequently, all observations for $\omega_k^\star$ do also hold for ω_k^∇; in particular, this applies to $(\star 3)$–$(\star 5)$. Thus, we assume $\omega_k^\star = \omega_k^\nabla$ in the following.

Together with $(\star 4)$ and $(\star 5)$ we can summarize as follows:

$$\omega_k^\star \preceq_\mathcal{K}^\circ \omega_{max}^\nabla \qquad \omega_k^\star \preceq_\mathcal{K}^\circ \omega_{k\oplus1} \qquad \omega_k^\star \preceq_\mathcal{K}^\circ \omega_k \tag{$\star 6$}$$
$$\omega_k^\star \preceq_\mathcal{K}^\circ \omega_{med}^\nabla \qquad \omega_{k\oplus n} \preceq_\mathcal{K}^\circ \omega_k^\star \qquad \omega_k \preceq_\mathcal{K}^\circ \omega_k^\star$$

We are striving for a contradiction by showing the existence of a strict circle of length that is strictly smaller than $n + 1$. Therefore, we will make use of Lemma 5.11, whenever that is possible. We consider three cases in the following, depending on the values of ℓ_{med} and ℓ_{max}. Recall that $1 \leq \ell_{med} < \ell_{max} \leq n$ holds.

($\ell_{med} \neq 1$) Because of $(\star 6)$, we can directly apply Lemma 5.11 by setting $\lambda = k$, $a = k \oplus 1$, $b = k \oplus \ell_{med}$ and $c = k \oplus \ell_{max}$, and by using the strict circle $\circlearrowleft_{0n}[\omega_\tau \mapsto \omega_\tau^\nabla, \omega_q \mapsto \omega_q^\nabla]$ for Lemma 5.11, which yields a strict circle with a length of at most n.

($\ell_{max} \neq n$) We apply Lemma 5.11 by setting $\lambda = k$, $a = k \oplus \ell_{med}$, $b = k \oplus \ell_{max}$ and $c = k \oplus n$, and by using the strict circle

$\circlearrowright_{0n}[\omega_p \mapsto \omega_p^{\triangledown}, \omega_\tau \mapsto \omega_\tau^{\triangledown}]$, which yields again a strict circle with a length of at most n.

($\ell_{\text{med}} = 1$ and $\ell_{\text{max}} = n$) Because of $\ell_{\text{max}} = n$, we have that $\omega_{\text{max}}^{\triangledown} \in [\![\Gamma_{k \oplus n}]\!]$. Together with $\omega_k^\star \in [\![\Gamma_k]\!]$, we obtain from ($\star 4$) that $\omega_{\text{max}}^{\triangledown} \preceq_{\mathcal{K}}^\circ \omega_k^\star$. From the min-retractivity of $\preceq_{\mathcal{K}}^\circ$ and $\Gamma_{k \oplus n} \in B$, we obtain $\omega_{\text{max}}^{\triangledown} \in \min([\![\Gamma_{\triangledown}]\!], \preceq_{\mathcal{K}}^\circ)$, which implies $\omega_{\text{max}}^{\triangledown} \preceq_{\mathcal{K}}^\circ \omega_{\text{med}}^{\triangledown}$.

If $\omega_{\text{max}}^{\triangledown} \prec_{\mathcal{K}}^\circ \omega_{\text{med}}^{\triangledown}$, then we obtain the strict circle $\omega_{\text{max}}^{\triangledown}$, $\omega_{\text{med}}^{\triangledown}, \omega_{k \oplus (\ell_{\text{med}}+1)}, \ldots, \omega_{k \oplus (\ell_{\text{max}}+n)}, \omega_{\text{max}}^{\triangledown}$ which has a length of at most n. Due to the induction hypothesis there is no such strict circle, and thus, $\omega_{\text{max}}^{\triangledown} \prec_{\mathcal{K}}^\circ \omega_{\text{med}}^{\triangledown}$ is impossible. From totality of $\preceq_{\mathcal{K}}^\circ$ we obtain that $\omega_{\text{med}}^{\triangledown} \preceq_{\mathcal{K}}^\circ \omega_{\text{max}}^{\triangledown}$ holds. If $k \oplus \ell_{\text{max}} = 0$, then we obtain the strict circle $\omega_{\text{max}}^{\triangledown}, \omega_k, \omega_{\text{med}}^{\triangledown}, \omega_{\text{max}}^{\triangledown}$ of length 3. If $k = 0$, then we obtain the strict circle $\omega_k, \omega_{\text{med}}^{\triangledown}, \omega_{\text{max}}^{\triangledown}, \omega_k$ of length 3. If none of the prior cases applies, then $\circlearrowright = \omega_0, \omega_1, \ldots, \omega_{\text{max}}^{\triangledown}, \omega_{\text{med}}^{\triangledown}, \ldots, \omega_0$ is a strict circle. Note that ω_k is not part of the strict circle $\circlearrowright$, and consequently the length of $\circlearrowright$ is bounded by n.

We obtain a contradiction in every case, which shows that Condition (3) of Definition 5.3 is satisfied.

In summary, assuming that each $(\omega_i, \omega_{i \oplus 1})$ is not a detached pair leads to formation of a critical loop by $\Gamma_{0,1}, \Gamma_{1,2}, \ldots, \Gamma_{n,0}$; contradicting the critical loop-freeness of $\mathbb{B}$. Consequently, at least one $(\omega_i, \omega_{i \oplus 1})$ has to be a detached pair. This completes the proof of Lemma 5.12. $\qquad\square$

By employing Lemma 5.12 we show now that transformation of $\preceq_{\mathcal{K}}^{\circ\prime}$ to $\preceq_{\mathcal{K}}^{\circ\prime\prime}$ by taking the transitive closure only adds detached pairs.

Lemma 5.13. *Let $\mathbb{B} = (\mathcal{L}, \Omega, \models, \mathfrak{B}, \mathbb{U})$ be a base logic which does not admit a critical loop, let $\mathcal{K} \in \mathfrak{B}$ be a base, and let $\circ$ be a base change operator for $\mathbb{B}$ that satisfies (G1)–(G3), (G5), and (G6). The following holds:*

$$\preceq_{\mathcal{K}}^{\circ\prime} \subseteq \preceq_{\mathcal{K}}^{\circ\prime\prime} \subseteq \preceq_{\mathcal{K}}^\circ$$

Proof. By construction of $\preceq_{\mathcal{K}}^{\circ\prime\prime}$, we have $\preceq_{\mathcal{K}}^{\circ\prime} \subseteq \preceq_{\mathcal{K}}^{\circ\prime\prime}$, and by construction of $\preceq_{\mathcal{K}}^{\circ\prime}$ we have $\preceq_{\mathcal{K}}^{\circ\prime} \subseteq \preceq_{\mathcal{K}}^\circ$. To show that $\preceq_{\mathcal{K}}^{\circ\prime\prime} \subseteq \preceq_{\mathcal{K}}^\circ$ holds, we assume the contrary, i.e., there exists a pair $(\omega_1, \omega_0) \in \preceq_{\mathcal{K}}^{\circ\prime\prime}$ such that $\omega_1 \npreceq_{\mathcal{K}}^\circ \omega_0$. From $\preceq_{\mathcal{K}}^{\circ\prime} \subseteq \preceq_{\mathcal{K}}^\circ$ we obtain $\omega_1 \npreceq_{\mathcal{K}}^{\circ\prime} \omega_0$ and because $\preceq_{\mathcal{K}}^\circ$ is a total relation, we have that $\omega_0 \prec_{\mathcal{K}}^\circ \omega_1$ holds. By the definition of transitive closure (cf. Section 4.1.4), there exists $\omega_2, \ldots, \omega_n \in \Omega$, for some $n \in \mathbb{N}$, such that $\omega_1 \preceq_{\mathcal{K}}^{\circ\prime} \omega_2$ and $\omega_n \preceq_{\mathcal{K}}^{\circ\prime} \omega_0$ and $\omega_i \preceq_{\mathcal{K}}^{\circ\prime} \omega_{i+1}$ for each $i \in \{2, \ldots, n-1\}$. From $\preceq_{\mathcal{K}}^{\circ\prime} \subseteq \preceq_{\mathcal{K}}^{\circ}$, we obtain $\omega_0 \prec_{\mathcal{K}}^{\circ} \omega_1 \preceq_{\mathcal{K}}^{\circ} \omega_2 \ldots \preceq_{\mathcal{K}}^{\circ} \omega_n \preceq_{\mathcal{K}}^{\circ} \omega_0$. We obtain a contradiction, because $\preceq_{\mathcal{K}}^{\circ\prime}$ does not contain any detached pairs, but due to Lemma 5.12 there is some $i \in \{2, \ldots, n-1\}$ such that (ω_i, ω_{i+1}) is a detached pair. Consequently, we obtain $\preceq_{\mathcal{K}}^{\circ\prime\prime} \subseteq \preceq_{\mathcal{K}}^{\circ}$. $\qquad\square$

Combining Lemma 5.9 and Lemma 5.13 yields that $\preceq_{\mathcal{K}}^{\circ\prime\prime}$ is a (possibly non-total) preorder with useful properties. In particular, the sets of minimal models for every base $\Gamma \in \mathfrak{B}$ coincide for $\preceq_{\mathcal{K}}^{\circ\prime}$ and $\preceq_{\mathcal{K}}^{\circ\prime\prime}$.

Lemma 5.14. *Let* $\mathbb{B} = (\mathcal{L}, \Omega, \models, \mathfrak{B}, \mathbb{U})$ *be a base logic which does not admit a critical loop, let* $\mathcal{K} \in \mathfrak{B}$ *and let* $\circ$ *be a base change operator for* $\mathbb{B}$ *which satisfies (G1)–(G3), (G5), and (G6). Then* $\preceq_{\mathcal{K}}^{\circ\prime\prime}$ *is a min-complete preorder and for any* $\Gamma \in \mathfrak{B}$ *holds* $\min(\llbracket\Gamma\rrbracket, \preceq_{\mathcal{K}}^{\circ\prime\prime}) = \min(\llbracket\Gamma\rrbracket, \preceq_{\mathcal{K}}^{\circ\prime})$.

Proof. Because of Lemma 5.13 we have $\min(\llbracket\Gamma\rrbracket, \preceq_{\mathcal{K}}^{\circ\prime\prime}) = \min(\llbracket\Gamma\rrbracket, \preceq_{\mathcal{K}}^{\circ\prime})$ for any $\Gamma \in \mathfrak{B}$, since $\preceq_{\mathcal{K}}^{\circ\prime\prime} \setminus \mathfrak{D}_{\mathcal{K}}^{\circ} = \preceq_{\mathcal{K}}^{\circ} \setminus \mathfrak{D}_{\mathcal{K}}^{\circ}$. Recall that by Lemma 5.9 we have that $\preceq_{\mathcal{K}}^{\circ\prime}$ is min-complete and reflexive. Consequently, the transitive closure $\preceq_{\mathcal{K}}^{\circ\prime\prime}$ of $\preceq_{\mathcal{K}}^{\circ\prime}$ is a preorder. Moreover, as in the proof of Lemma 5.9, from $\min(\llbracket\Gamma\rrbracket, \preceq_{\mathcal{K}}^{\circ\prime\prime}) = \min(\llbracket\Gamma\rrbracket, \preceq_{\mathcal{K}}^{\circ\prime})$ we obtain that min-completeness carries over from $\preceq_{\mathcal{K}}^{\circ\prime}$ to $\preceq_{\mathcal{K}}^{\circ\prime\prime}$. $\qquad\square$

Step III: Linearizing

As last step, we extend $\preceq_{\mathcal{K}}^{\circ\prime\prime}$ to a total relation without losing transitivity. In order to obtain totality, we make use of the following result. Note that this theorem requires the *axiom of choice*.

Theorem 5.15 (Hansson [71], Lemma 3). *For every preorder* $\leq$ *on a set* X *there exists a total preorder* $\leq^{\text{lin}}$ *on* X *such that*

- *if* $x \leq y$, *then* $x \leq^{\text{lin}} y$, *and*
- *if* $x \leq y$ *and* $y \nleq x$, *then* $x \leq^{\text{lin}} y$ *and* $y \nleq^{\text{lin}} x$.

As stated in Lemma 5.14, the relation $\preceq_{\mathcal{K}}^{\circ\prime\prime}$ is a preorder. Thus, we can safely apply Theorem 5.15 to obtain $\preccurlyeq_{\mathcal{K}}^{\circ}$ from $\preceq_{\mathcal{K}}^{\circ\prime\prime}$ through extension, i.e., $\preccurlyeq_{\mathcal{K}}^{\circ} = (TC(\preceq_{\mathcal{K}}^{\circ} \setminus \mathfrak{D}_{\mathcal{K}}^{\circ}))^{\text{lin}}$. We denote this process *linearization*[3]. The resulting relation $\preceq^{\circ}_{\mathcal{K}}$ is then a total preorder, while it still coincides with $\preceq^{\circ}_{\mathcal{K}}{}''$ regarding the relevant properties. Combining Theorem 5.15, Lemma 5.9 and Lemma 5.14 we obtain the desired result.

Proposition 5.16. *If $\mathbb{B}$ does not admit a critical loop, then, for any given base change operator $\circ$ for $\mathbb{B}$ satisfying (G1)–(G3), (G5), and (G6), the mapping $\preceq^{\circ}_{(\cdot)}: \mathcal{K} \mapsto \preceq^{\circ}_{\mathcal{K}}$ is a min-friendly quasi-faithful preorder assignment compatible with $\circ$.*

Proof. From Lemma 5.14 we obtain that $\preceq^{\circ}_{(\cdot)}{}''$ is a min-complete preorder assigment. Application of Theorem 5.15 yields a total preorder $\preceq^{\circ}_{\mathcal{K}}$. Observe that linearization by Theorem 5.15 retains strict relations, i.e., if $\omega_1 \preceq^{\circ}_{\mathcal{K}}{}'' \omega_2$ and $\omega_2 \npreceq^{\circ}_{\mathcal{K}}{}'' \omega_1$, then $\omega_1 \prec^{\circ}_{\mathcal{K}} \omega_2$ and $\omega_2 \nprec^{\circ}_{\mathcal{K}} \omega_1$. Thus, we have $\omega_1 \in \min(\llbracket\Gamma\rrbracket, \preceq^{\circ}_{\mathcal{K}}{}'')$ and only if $\omega_1 \in \min(\llbracket\Gamma\rrbracket, \preceq^{\circ}_{\mathcal{K}})$, which yields $\min(\llbracket\Gamma\rrbracket, \preceq^{\circ}_{\mathcal{K}}{}'') = \min(\llbracket\Gamma\rrbracket, \preceq^{\circ}_{\mathcal{K}})$ for each base $\Gamma \in \mathbb{B}$. Consequently, min-completeness carries over from $\preceq^{\circ}_{\mathcal{K}}{}''$ to $\preceq^{\circ}_{\mathcal{K}}$. Moreover, by Lemma 5.9 and Lemma 5.14 we obtain $\min(\llbracket\Gamma\rrbracket, \preceq^{\circ}_{\mathcal{K}}) = \min(\llbracket\Gamma\rrbracket, \preceq^{\circ}_{\mathcal{K}})$ for each base Γ of $\mathbb{B}$. As every $\preceq^{\circ}_{\mathcal{K}}$ is transitive and total, we obtain that $\preceq^{\circ}_{\mathcal{K}}$ is min-retractive and thus, $\preceq^{\circ}_{(\cdot)}$ is a min-friendly assignment. Because $\preceq^{\circ}_{(\cdot)}$ is a quasi-faithful assignment which is compatible with $\circ$ and we have $\min(\llbracket\Gamma\rrbracket, \preceq^{\circ}_{\mathcal{K}}) = \min(\llbracket\Gamma\rrbracket, \preceq^{\circ}_{\mathcal{K}})$ for each $\mathcal{K} \in \mathfrak{B}$, we also obtain that $\preceq^{\circ}_{(\cdot)}$ is a quasi-faithful assignment which is compatible with $\circ$. $\qquad\square$

This completes the argument regarding the correspondence between the absence of critical loops and total-preorder-representability, by establishing that the former is also sufficient for the latter. Obviously, Theorem 5.4 (II) is a direct consequence of Proposition 5.16.

5.5. Characterization Theorems and Example

Combining the two arguments presented in Section 5.3 and Section 5.4, we establish that the absence of critical loop coincides with universal total-preorder-representability, i.e., Theorem 5.4 holds.

We will now employ the novel notion of critical loop (cf. Definition 5.3) and our representation theorem for total-preorder-representability

---

[3]   This is a reference to linearization of partial orders to total preorders [109].

(Theorem 5.4), to show that there is no (total) preorder assignment for the operator $\circ_{\mathrm{Ex}}$ from our running example.

Example 5.17 (Continuation of Example 4.26). *We will now see that the base logic $\mathbb{B}_{\mathrm{Ex}} = (\mathcal{L}_{\mathrm{Ex}}, \Omega_{\mathrm{Ex}}, \models_{\mathrm{Ex}}, \mathcal{P}(\mathcal{L}_{\mathrm{Ex}}), \cup)$ from Example 4.18 constructed from $\mathbb{L}_{\mathrm{Ex}}$ exhibits a critical loop.*

For this, choose $\Gamma_{i,i\oplus 1} = \{\varphi_i\}$, and $\mathcal{K} = \mathcal{K}_{\mathrm{Ex}} = \{\psi_3\}$ (as in Example 4.18) and $\Gamma_i = \{\psi_i\}$ for $i \in \{0, 1, 2\}$, where $\oplus$ denotes addition mod 3. We consider each of the three conditions of Definition 5.3 as a separate case:

> Condition (1). *Observe that $\mathcal{K}_{\mathrm{Ex}}$ is inconsistent with $\Gamma_{0,1}$, $\Gamma_{1,2}$ and $\Gamma_{2,0}$. Thus, Condition (1) is satisfied.*
>
> Condition (2). *For each $i \in \{0, 1, 2\}$, the models of bases Γ_i and $\Gamma_{i\oplus 1}$ are contained in $[\![\Gamma_{i,i\oplus 1}]\!]$, but Γ_i is inconsistent with Γ_j with $i \neq j$, e.g. $[\![\{\psi_0\}]\!] \cup [\![\{\psi_1\}]\!] \subseteq [\![\{\varphi_0\}]\!]$ and $\{\psi_0\}$ is not consistent with neither $\{\psi_1\}$ nor $\{\psi_2\}$.*
>
> Condition (3). *The belief base $\Gamma_{\triangledown} = \{\chi'\}$ is the only belief base consistent with Γ_0, Γ_1, and Γ_2. For the satisfaction of Condition (3) observe that $\Gamma'_{\triangledown} = \{\psi_4\}$ fulfils the required condition $\emptyset \neq [\![\Gamma'_{\triangledown}]\!] \subseteq [\![\Gamma_{\triangledown}]\!] \setminus ([\![\Gamma_{0,1}]\!] \cup [\![\Gamma_{1,2}]\!] \cup [\![\Gamma_{2,0}]\!])$.*

In summary $\Gamma_{0,1}$, $\Gamma_{1,2}$, and $\Gamma_{2,0}$ form a critical loop for $\mathbb{B}_{\mathrm{Ex}}$ (see Figure 5.5). As given by Theorem 5.4 (I), every min-complete faithful assignment compatible with $\circ_{\mathrm{Ex}}$ yields, for some bases, a non-transitive relation. To illustrate this, we use here the assignment $\preceq^{\circ_{\mathrm{Ex}}}_{(.)}$ defined in Example 4.26 and sketched in Figure 4.3 for $\mathcal{K}_{\mathrm{Ex}}$ (see also Figure 5.5). Consider the revisions $\mathcal{K}_{\mathrm{Ex}} \circ_{\mathrm{Ex}} \Gamma_{0,1}$, $\mathcal{K}_{\mathrm{Ex}} \circ_{\mathrm{Ex}} \Gamma_{1,2}$, and $\mathcal{K}_{\mathrm{Ex}} \circ_{\mathrm{Ex}} \Gamma_{2,0}$. From the construction of $\circ_{\mathrm{Ex}}$ given in Definition 5.5 and compatibility of $\preceq^{\circ_{\mathrm{Ex}}}_{(.)}$ with $\circ_{\mathrm{Ex}}$, we have

$$\omega_0 \in \min([\![\Gamma_{0,1}]\!], \preceq^{\circ_{\mathrm{Ex}}}_{\mathcal{K}_{\mathrm{Ex}}}), \text{ but } \omega_1 \notin \min([\![\Gamma_{0,1}]\!], \preceq^{\circ_{\mathrm{Ex}}}_{\mathcal{K}_{\mathrm{Ex}}}) ,$$

$$\omega_1 \in \min([\![\Gamma_{1,2}]\!], \preceq^{\circ_{\mathrm{Ex}}}_{\mathcal{K}_{\mathrm{Ex}}}), \text{ but } \omega_2 \notin \min([\![\Gamma_{1,2}]\!], \preceq^{\circ_{\mathrm{Ex}}}_{\mathcal{K}_{\mathrm{Ex}}}) , \text{ and}$$

$$\omega_2 \in \min([\![\Gamma_{2,0}]\!], \preceq^{\circ_{\mathrm{Ex}}}_{\mathcal{K}_{\mathrm{Ex}}}), \text{ but } \omega_0 \notin \min([\![\Gamma_{2,0}]\!], \preceq^{\circ_{\mathrm{Ex}}}_{\mathcal{K}_{\mathrm{Ex}}}) ,$$

showing $\omega_0 \prec^{\circ_{\mathrm{Ex}}}_{\mathcal{K}_{\mathrm{Ex}}} \omega_1 \prec^{\circ_{\mathrm{Ex}}}_{\mathcal{K}_{\mathrm{Ex}}} \omega_2 \prec^{\circ_{\mathrm{Ex}}}_{\mathcal{K}_{\mathrm{Ex}}} \omega_0$, which is impossible for a transitive relation.

Moreover, observe that the construction of $\circ_{\mathrm{Ex}}$ presented in Example 4.18 illustrates the construction given by Definition 5.5 and used in the proof of Proposition 5.6. In particular, for the example presented

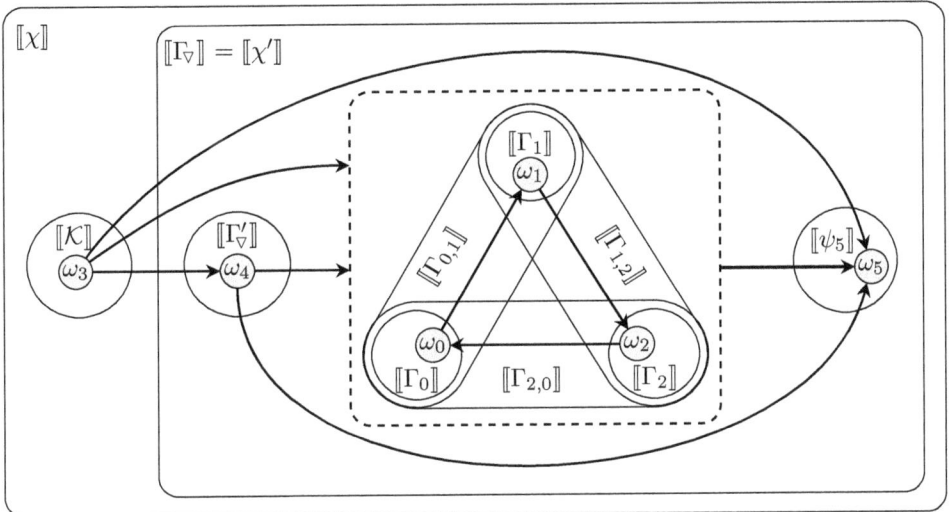

Figure 5.5: Critical loop situation in $\mathbb{B}_{Ex}$ presented in Example 5.17. The solid borders represent the sets of models and each arrow depicts the relation $\prec_{\mathcal{K}_{Ex}}^{\circ Ex}$ between models.

here one would obtain $\mathcal{C}' = \{\Gamma_\nabla'\} = \{\{\psi_4\}\}$ when following the outline of the construction.

Having established the necessary and sufficient criterion for total-preorder-representability, we can now provide two more versions of the two-way representation theorem. The first representation theorem is one where the base change operator satisfies (G4), thus abstracting from the syntactic form of the belief bases. Note that transitivity implies min-retractivity, and thus a transitive min-complete relation is automatically min-friendly.

Theorem 5.18. *Let $\mathbb{B}$ be a base logic which does not admit a critical loop. Then the statements following hold:*

- *Every base change operator for $\mathbb{B}$ satisfying (G1)–(G6) is compatible with some min-expressible min-complete faithful preorder assignment.*
- *Every min-expressible min-complete faithful preorder assignment for $\mathbb{B}$ is compatible with some base change operator satisfying (G1)–(G6).*

Proof. The first statement is a consequence of statement (II) of Theorem 5.4 together with Lemma 5.2. The second statement is an immediate consequence of the second statement of Theorem 4.36.   □

The second representation theorem is for base change operators which do not necessarily satisfy (G4), and thus might be sensitive to the syntax of the prior belief base.

Theorem 5.19. *Let $\mathbb{B}$ be a base logic which does not admit a critical loop. Then the statements following hold:*

- *Every base change operator for $\mathbb{B}$ satisfying (G1)–(G3), (G5), and (G6) is compatible with some min-expressible min-complete quasi-faithful preorder assignment.*
- *Every min-expressible min-complete quasi-faithful preorder assignment for $\mathbb{B}$ is compatible with some base change operator satisfying (G1)–(G3), (G5), and (G6).*

Proof. The first statement is a consequence of statement (II) of Theorem 5.4. The second statement is an immediate consequence of the second statement of Theorem 4.44.   □

We close this section with an implication of Theorem 5.4. A base logic $\mathbb{B} = (\mathcal{L}, \Omega, \models, \mathfrak{B}, \mathbb{U})$ is called *disjunctive*, if for every two bases $\Gamma_1, \Gamma_2 \in \mathfrak{B}$ there is a base $\Gamma_1 \oslash \Gamma_2 \in \mathfrak{B}$ such that $[\![\Gamma_1 \oslash \Gamma_2]\!] = [\![\Gamma_1]\!] \cup [\![\Gamma_2]\!]$. This includes the case of any (base) logic allowing disjunction to be expressed on the sentence level, i.e., when for every $\gamma, \delta \in \mathcal{L}$ there exists some $\gamma \oslash \delta \in \mathcal{L}$ with $[\![\gamma \oslash \delta]\!] = [\![\gamma]\!] \cup [\![\delta]\!]$, such that $\Gamma_1 \oslash \Gamma_2$ can be obtained as $\{\gamma \oslash \delta \mid \gamma \in \Gamma_1, \delta \in \Gamma_2\}$.

Corollary 5.20. *In a disjunctive base logic, every belief change operator satisfying (G1)–(G6) is total-preorder-representable.*

Proof. A disjunctive base logic never exhibits a critical loop; Condition (3) would be violated by picking $\Gamma = ((\Gamma_0 \oslash \Gamma_1) \ldots) \oslash \Gamma_n$.   □

As a consequence, for a vast amount of well-known logics, including all classical logics such as first-order and second order predicate logic, one directly obtains total-preorder-representablility of every AGM base change operator by Corollary 5.20.

5.6. Conclusion and Discussion

In this part we addressed the question of the characteristics of those logics for which every AGM revision operator is total-preorder-representable. This question refers to the fact that in propositional logic AGM revision is characterized by total preorders over interpretations [84], yet this characterization does not carry over to, e.g., Horn logic.

To tackle this question we made use of the framework of belief change over base logics, presented in Chapter 4, which is joint work with Faiq Miftakhul Falakh and Sebastian Rudolph [54]. The framework generalizes (multiple) AGM (base) revision to arbitrary sets of bases in Tarskian logics (as long as the bases are closed under abstraction union). In Chapter 4 we presented several characterization theorems for AGM revision in this setting (which are part of the joint work). The running example given in this part (see Fact 4.45) demonstrates that **not** every AGM revision operator in a Tarskian logic is representable by a total preorder.

The main contribution of this part is presented in Chapter 5: *critical loops*, a notion precisely characterizing those base logics for which an AGM revision operator exists that is not representable by a total preorder. We showed that the absence of a critical loop is indeed the sufficient and necessary condition for *total-preorder-representability*. While the criterion by itself may be somewhat technical and unwieldy, it can be shown to subsume all logics featuring disjunction and therefore all classical logics. This justifies to formulate these findings in two theorems: a syntax independent version (Theorem 5.18) and a syntax-dependent one (Theorem 5.19).

Several other researchers considered the problem of a semantic characterization of AGM revision in a abstract logical setting, as we did in Chapter 5: Grove [67], Delgrande et al. [46], and Aiguier et al. [1]. Table 5.1 summarizes their results and compares them with Katsuno and Mendelzon's result [84] and the approach given in Chapter 5, which comes in 4 variants. For a detailed discussion we refer to [54].

Note that the question of *total-preorder-representability* is novel and was not asked before or avoided in these other approaches:

Grove [67] and Aiguier et al. [1]. One semantic-based approach related to the one of Katsuno and Mendelzon was proposed by Grove

logic setting	belief bases	assignment	postulates	notes
		Katsuno and Mendelzon [84]		
propositional logic over finite signature	$\mathcal{P}(\mathcal{L})$, $\mathcal{P}_{\mathrm{fin}}(\mathcal{L})$, $\mathcal{L}$	preorder, faithful	(G1)-(G6)	logic natively free of critical loops; natively min-friendly; two-way representation theorem
		Grove [67], reformulated by Delgrande et al. [46]		
Boolean-closed logics that are Ω-expressible	$\mathcal{P}(\mathcal{L})$	preorder, faithful, min-complete	(G1)-(G6)	all such logics natively free of critical loops; any assignment min-expressible; two-way representation theorem
		Delgrande et al. [46]		
Tarskian logics with finite Ω, any ω, ω' distinguishable by some sentence	$\mathcal{P}(\mathcal{L})$	preorder, faithful, min-expressible	(G1)-(G6), (Acyc)	extra postulate (Acyc) rules out "non-preorder operators"; two-way representation theorem
		Aiguier et al. [1]		
Tarskian logics	$\mathcal{P}(\mathcal{L})$	quasi-faithful, min-complete	(G1)-(G3), (G5),(G6)	non-standard notion of inconsistency; additional ad-hoc constraint on compatibility; one-way representation theorem
		approach presented in this part		
Tarskian logics	arbitrary, closed under abstract union	faithful, min-complete, min-retractive, min-expressible	(G1)-(G6)	most general (syntax-independent version); two-way representation theorem (Thm. 4.36)
Tarskian logics		quasi-faithful, min-complete, min-retractive, min-expressible	(G1)-(G3), (G5),(G6)	most general (syntax-dependent version); two-way representation theorem (Thm. 4.44)
Tarskian logics without critical loop (e.g., with disjunction)		preorder, faithful, min-complete, min-expressible	(G1)-(G6)	preorder preference (syntax-independent version); two-way representation theorem (Thm. 5.18)
Tarskian logics without critical loop (e.g., with disjunction)		preorder, quasi-faithful, min-complete, min-expressible	(G1)-(G3), (G5),(G6)	preorder preference (syntax-dependent version); two-way representation theorem (Thm. 5.19)

Table 5.1: Characterization results and comparison with related work (adapted [54]).

[67] in the setting of Boolean-closed logics. Consequently, in the logical setting that *Grove* considers all logics are closed under disjunction. As we have shown (Corollary 5.20), in this setup every AGM revision operator is total-preorder presentable and thus, this question does not appear. The work by Aiguier et al. [1] considers revision in a framework closely related to the framework used here; however, Aiguier et al. do not consider the question of total-preorder-representability.

Delgrande et al. [46]. The representation result of Delgrande et al. [46] confines the considered logics to those where the set Ω of interpretations (or possible worlds) is finite[4] and where any two different interpretations $\omega, \omega' \in \Omega$ can be distinguished by some sentence $\varphi \in \mathcal{L}$, i.e., $\omega \in [\![\varphi]\!]$ and $\omega' \notin [\![\varphi]\!]$. Moreover, they extend the AGM postulates by the following extra one:

> For any base $\mathcal{K}$ and all $\Gamma_1, \ldots, \Gamma_n \in \mathcal{P}(\mathcal{L})$ with $[\![\Gamma_i \cup \mathcal{K} \circ \Gamma_{i+1}]\!] \neq \emptyset$ for each $1 \leq i < n$ as well as $[\![\Gamma_n \cup \mathcal{K} \circ \Gamma_1]\!] \neq \emptyset$ (Acyc) holds $[\![\Gamma_1 \cup \mathcal{K} \circ \Gamma_n]\!] \neq \emptyset$.

With these ingredients in place, Delgrande et al. [46] establish that, for the logics they consider, there is a two-way correspondence between those AGM revision operators satisfying (Acyc) and min-expressible faithful preorder assignments. Instead of the term "min-expressible", they use the term *regular*.

The approach of Delgrande et al. can be seen as complementary to the results presented in this part. As we saw before, in logics exhibiting critical loops, one cannot hope for a characterization of all AGM revision operators by means of assignments producing preorders. Our proposal is to relinquish the requirement of using preorders, giving up transitivity and merely retaining min-retractivity. As an alternative to this approach, one might argue that those AGM revision operators **not** corresponding to some preorder assignment are somewhat "unnatural" and should be ruled out from the consideration. The additional postulate (Acyc) serves precisely this purpose: it allows for a preorder characterization even in logics with critical loops, by disallowing some "unnatural" AGM revision operators. In other words, (Acyc) is meant

---

4   Note that this precondition excludes more complex logics such as first-order or modal logics and most of their fragments, but also propositional logic with infinite signature. On the positive side, this choice guarantees min-completeness of any preorder.

to characterize those AGM revision operators that are total-preorder-representable. In the setting considered by Delgrande et al., it has been shown that (Acyc) has precisely this effect [46]. It is an open problem whether (Acyc) characterizes total-preorder-representable AGM revision operators in the general setting of base logics considered here. In contrast, the notion of critical loop characterizes exactly those settings where AGM revision operators exist that are not total-preorder-representable. Thus, only when critical loops appear in a base logic, a property like (Acyc) would be effective. This is because the absence of critical loops already guarantees that every AGM revision operator is total-preorder-representable, as shown in this chapter.

In this part, we focused on characterizations of AGM revision in a general logical setting. The next parts will also consider other types of change operators than AGM revision, and will especially focus on principles for the iterated execution of these change operators. Therefore, we will leave the general setting of base logics (Tarskian logics), will consider only propositional logic (over a finite set of atoms) and make use of the change framework by Darwiche and Pearl. Although the setting of base logics is powerful, the framework by Darwiche and Pearl is tailored for iterated belief change, as they consider epistemic states. The difference to the belief states in the framework of base change operators considered here is that epistemic states may contain more information than just the plain beliefs. This is necessary to treat iteration processes adequately.

Part II

Non-Prioritized Revision over Epistemic States

Introduction to Part II

When considering real agents, like humans, it becomes apparent that agents show a wide variety of different ways in how they treat new beliefs and which beliefs they consider as credible. Moreover, when observing how agents change their beliefs over a long time, one can see that in the course of change the opinion regarding the credibility of certain beliefs may evolve. For instance, consider the following example.

Example. *The little boy Lukas likes to play with bricks a lot and thus believes that "it's funny to play with bricks". He is absolutely willing to accept a new belief which states that Martha (another child) also likes bricks. However, things become different when Lukas gets to know that Martha plays with children whom Lukas does not like. After receiving this information, Lukas does not accept the belief that Martha also likes to play with bricks anymore. Moreover, he might even change his mind about how funny it is to play with bricks.*

In this part, we introduce and study principles meant to *model* agents that may have *varying* and *evolving* attitudes towards new beliefs[5]. As central means for describing "attitudes towards to new beliefs", we make use of the notion of *scope*. Informally, the scope describes those beliefs an agent accepts when presented as information for revision. More formally, for an epistemic state Ψ, with beliefs $\mathrm{Bel}(\Psi)$, and a change operator $\circ$ for epistemic states, the scope of Ψ (and $\circ$) is given

---

[5]   This phrase is intentionally similar to the title of a work by Haret and Woltran [79].

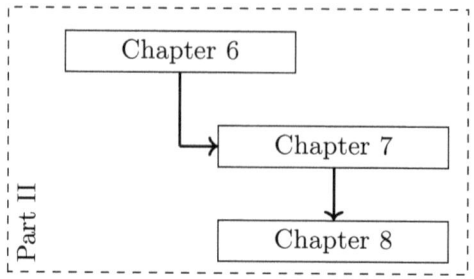

Overview of the organization of Part II.

by:

$$Scp°(\Psi) = \{\alpha \in \mathcal{L} \mid \alpha \in \text{Bel}(\Psi \circ \alpha)\}$$

We will investigate whether for sets of belief change operators an element with a particular scope exists. Moreover, we consider how a certain semantic structure realizes a certain pattern of acceptance for revision.

Towards this end, we will carefully generalize AGM revision operators to *dynamic-limited revision operators*. Note that AGM revision is not meant to model different attitudes, which is also reflected by its formalization (see Section 3); an AGM revision operator accepts every new belief for revision and never alters this policy. Consequently, for every AGM revision operator $*$, we have that the scope encompasses all possible beliefs, i.e., $Scp^*(\Psi) = \mathcal{L}$. Dynamic-limited revision operators will have only a few restrictions with respect to the scope, so that the scope may be different for every epistemic state, and thus provide a platform for studying principles for the evolution of the scope.

The following steps of this part are structured in consecutive organized chapters:

Chapter 6. We introduce the background and formal preliminaries for our studies: we present the framework of belief change operators over epistemic states by Darwiche and Pearl [41], in which dynamic-limited revision operators will be formulated, and we present and study AGM revision operators in general sets of epistemic states.

Chapter 7. We introduce the notion of acceptance descriptions and scope. AGM revision will be identified as insufficient for realizing certain scopes, and we will switch to non-prioritized approaches to revision. Credibility-limited revision [27] is presented, a class of non-prioritized revision operators which will be generalized by dynamic-limited revision operators. We see how credibility-limited revision can be generalized to encompass AGM revision operators, and we characterize the scope of these operators.

Chapter 8. We motivate and introduce dynamic-limited revision operators. The dynamic-limited revision operators will be characterized semantically by relations of subsets of the interpretations. Finally, we see that the typical relational approach fails to capture (non-prioritized) revision operators in arbitrary sets of epistemic states.

Chapter 6

Belief Change over Epistemic States and AGM Revision

In this chapter, we introduce a framework for belief change operators, originated in work by Darwiche and Pearl [41], in which we will formulate *dynamic-limited revision operators*. The setting will make use of epistemic states, a setup which is richer compared to the classical setting of AGM, and different from the setting of change for base logics used in Part I.

The distinctive feature of using epistemic states as belief states is that they do not only consist of plain beliefs, but it is also possible to encode information about the revision history into a belief state. Darwiche and Pearl provide the following example, based on work by Goldszmidt and Pearl [66], which demonstrates the role of epistemic content that is different from plain beliefs for belief revision.

Example 6.1 (From [41, 66], adapted). *Two jurors, Juror 1 and Juror 2, in a murder trial possess different biases; summarized here in the following:*

> Juror 1: *"A is the murderer, B is a remote but unbelievable possibility while C is definitely innocent".*
> Juror 2: *"A is the murderer, C is a remote but unbelievable possibility while B is definitely innocent".*

The two jurors share the same belief set $\mathrm{Bel}(\Psi_1) = \mathrm{Bel}(\Psi_2) \equiv \psi = $ "A *is the only murderer". A surprising evidence now obtains: α = "A is not the murderer". Clearly, revision by α should lead to different results for Juror 1 and Juror 2, i.e., $\text{Bel}(\Psi_1 \circ \alpha)$ and $\text{Bel}(\Psi_2 \circ \alpha)$ should be different. This is only possible if $\Psi_1 \circ \alpha$ and $\Psi_2 \circ \alpha$ do not only depend on $\text{Cn}(\psi)$.*

This is important for our subsequent studies of the evolution of the scope in this part. This will particularly become relevant for those cases where we will consider iteration principles (in Part III) where the state has an influence on the beliefs after two subsequent changes, e.g., when information given for Ψ partially determines $\text{Bel}(\Psi \circ \alpha \circ \beta)$.

6.1. The Darwiche-Pearl Framework

Darwiche and Pearl made the general proposal regarding belief change and belief states that belief states should also encode the change strategy itself [41], leading to the framework we present in the following.

The key difference to the approaches considered in Chapter 3 and Part I is that instead of belief sets the belief changes happen on *epistemic states*. Following Darwiche and Pearl [41], an epistemic state Ψ is an object providing a belief set $\text{Bel}(\Psi)$, which is again a deductively closed set of formulas with respect to some underlying logical language $\mathcal{L}$ (see Chapter 3).

When considering belief change over epistemic states, the history of changes becomes an important aspect, as the richer structure of epistemic states allows to "store" the changes made in history. However, an ontological problem of belief change itself appears here when describing change operators for epistemic states: we have to specify on which epistemic states the changes happen, an aspect which was not explicitly treated by Darwiche and Pearl and rediscovered several times [62, 5, 139]. In this thesis, we deal with this problem by specifying the set of all possible epistemic states explicitly.

Convention. We will use $\mathcal{E}$ to denote a set of epistemic state and assume $\mathcal{E}$ to be always non-empty. As mentioned above, we assume that $\mathcal{E}$ is always implicitly equipped with a function $\text{Bel}(\cdot)$ that yields a deductively closed set of formulas $\text{Bel}(\Psi)$ for every epistemic state $\Psi \in \mathcal{E}$. We use $[\![\Psi]\!]$ as shorthand for $[\![\text{Bel}(\Psi)]\!]$.

Given $\mathcal{E}$, we model belief change operators for a set of epistemic states $\mathcal{E}$ as functions in the mathematical sense, describing globally, on all epistemic states from $\mathcal{E}$, how belief changes happen. The following definition describes this formally.

Definition 6.2. *Let $\mathcal{E}$ be a set of epistemic states. A belief change operator for $\mathcal{E}$ (and $\mathcal{L}$) is a function $\circ : \mathcal{E} \times \mathcal{L} \to \mathcal{E}$.*

If $\mathcal{E}$ is clear by the context (or not of particular importance) we also say $\circ$ is a *belief change operator for epistemic states*.

A belief change operator $\circ$ for $\mathcal{E}$ is called *neutral*, if $\mathrm{Bel}(\Psi) = \mathrm{Bel}(\Psi \circ \alpha)$ for all $\Psi \in \mathcal{E}$ and for all $\alpha \in \mathcal{L}$. Of course, in general, operators as in Definition 6.2 could behave arbitrary, and we will consider constraints (postulates) for operators. But, before considering concrete classes of operators, we state a remark on the logical framework used, and then continue with instantiations for the set of epistemic states $\mathcal{E}$.

Remark on the Underlying Logic. Iterated belief change is mainly considered for propositional logic (over finitely many atoms). We make no exception here and assume for the rest of this thesis that the underlying logical framework is propositional logic as introduced in Chapter 2. Consequently, $\mathcal{L}$ denotes a set of propositional formula over a finite set of atoms Σ. A study of the Darwiche-Pearl framework in the context of other logics remains an open task.

Next, we consider an example for a simple belief change operator.

Example 6.3. *Let $\Sigma = \{a, b\}$ and thus $\Omega = \{ab, \bar{a}b, a\bar{b}, \bar{a}\bar{b}\}$. Consider the following set of epistemic states $\mathcal{E} = \{\Psi_a, \Psi_{a \vee b}, \Psi_{a \vee \neg b}, \Psi_\top\}$ such that:*

$$\llbracket \Psi_a \rrbracket = \{ab, a\bar{b}\} = \llbracket a \rrbracket \qquad \llbracket \Psi_{a \vee b} \rrbracket = \{ab, a\bar{b}, \bar{a}b\} = \llbracket a \vee b \rrbracket$$
$$\llbracket \Psi_\top \rrbracket = \Omega = \llbracket \top \rrbracket \qquad \llbracket \Psi_{a \vee \neg b} \rrbracket = \{ab, a\bar{b}, \bar{a}\bar{b}\} = \llbracket a \vee \neg b \rrbracket$$

The set $\mathcal{E}$ contains only epistemic states where the agent believes in consequences of the formula a, i.e., $\llbracket a \rrbracket \subseteq \llbracket \Psi \rrbracket$ for all $\Psi \in \mathcal{E}$. Let $\circ$ be the belief change operator for $\mathcal{E}$ given as follows for all $\Psi \in \mathcal{E}$ and $\alpha \in \mathcal{L}$:

$$\Psi \circ \alpha = \begin{cases} \Psi_\chi & , \text{if } \alpha \in \mathrm{Bel}(\Psi) \text{ where } \chi \equiv \alpha \\ \Psi & , \text{otherwise} \end{cases}$$

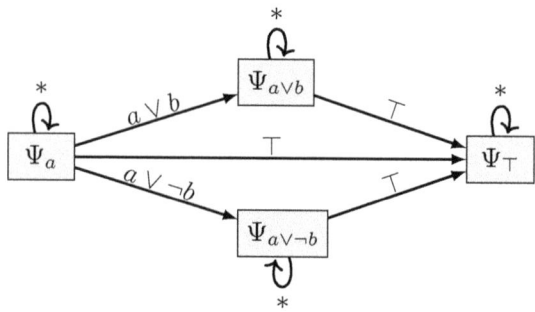

Figure 6.1: Graphical representation of the revision operator ∘ for $\mathcal{E}$ given in Example 6.3. The boxes represent the epistemic states from $\mathcal{E}$. Each edge represents a change from one epistemic state to another by the given formula on the label of the edge. We assume that belief change operators like ∘ respect semantic equivalence, and thus formulas on edges stand for all semantically equivalent formulas. Moreover, ∗ stands for all not explicitly given edges, e.g., the changes $\Psi_a \circ \bot = \Psi_a$ and $\Psi_a \circ (\neg a) = \Psi_a$ are covered by the self loop on Ψ_a labelled with ∗. Sometimes we also write sets of formulas on edges, which is a shorthand for multiple edges labelled with the elements of the set.

Informally, ∘ models an agent which only accepts new beliefs that are already believed, and take the new beliefs as new truth. In this part and the following parts of this thesis we sometimes represent operators graphically. For a graphical representation of ∘ consider Figure 6.1 which also contains an explanation how to read these graphical representations.

6.2. Sets of Epistemic States

In this section, we present instantiations for the set of epistemic states $\mathcal{E}$ commonly used in the area of knowledge representation and reasoning. Afterwards, we introduce some common properties considered for $\mathcal{E}$. Typical instantiations make use of the concept of plausibility ordering on the possible worlds:

Ranking Functions. Spohn introduced a plausibility-based representation which considers ranks [146, 147]. A function κ :

$\Omega \to \mathbb{N}_0$ is called an *ordinal conditional function*, or *ranking function*, if there exists some $\omega \in \Omega$ such that $\kappa(\omega) = 0$. The rank $\kappa(\omega)$ of the interpretation ω is typically understood as rank of (im)plausibility, where 0 stands for maximally plausible. In conformance with this reading, φ is believed by an agent with state κ if φ holds in all most plausible worlds, i.e.,

$$\text{Bel}(\kappa) = \{\varphi \in \mathcal{L} \mid \kappa(\omega) = 0 \text{ implies } \omega \models \varphi \text{ for each } \omega \in \Omega\}.$$

Relations over Possible Worlds. A common representation chosen for iterated belief change are total preorders over possible worlds (interpretations); this is because in the classical AGM setting (where belief states are plain sets of beliefs), AGM revision is characterized in many logical setting by *total preorders* [67, 84] (see also Chapter 3). Several publications consider other kinds of relations as representations [23, 31, 115]. Technically, given a binary relation $\leqslant$ on Ω, the beliefs of $\leqslant$ are typically defined via the minimal worlds of $\leqslant$, i.e.,

$$\text{Bel}(\leqslant) = \{\varphi \in \mathcal{L} \mid \omega \in \min(\Omega, \leqslant) \text{ implies } \omega \models \varphi \text{ for each } \omega \in \Omega\}.$$

Different representations are also connected, for instance, ranking functions are a generalization of total preorders [147]. Besides these representations, many other representations are considered, like *possibility measures* [49, 48] or *probability distributions* [33]. A systematic study of complex non-plausibility based representations, like specific finite structures, could be a fruitful endeavour.

While for many purposes the restriction to one particular representation is handy, we will keep it abstract and leave it open how to represent epistemic states. As an alternative to dealing with concrete instantiations, we will investigate belief change operators in this thesis in abstract sets of epistemic states fulfilling certain reasonable constraints. We will mainly make use of the following criterion on the existence of specific epistemic states.

Unbiased. We ensure that for every belief set there exists an epistemic state with that belief set:

If $L \subseteq \mathcal{L}$ and L is a belief set,
    then there exists $\Psi \in \mathcal{E}$ with $\text{Cn}(L) = \text{Bel}(\Psi)$.   (unbiased)

This property describes that the logic we are using describes only valid statements that in real agents might appear (otherwise there would be belief sets without a corresponding epistemic state). Note that this includes the inconsistent belief set $L = Cn(\bot)$.

Another common assumption made in research on iterated belief change is the following criterion.

Global Consistency. This criterion demands that every belief set considered is consistent:

$$\text{If } \Psi \in \mathcal{E}, \text{ then } \text{Bel}(\Psi) \neq Cn(\bot) \qquad \text{(global consistent)}$$

By global consistentcy, we model agents which always resolve all inconsistencies.

Before we consider AGM revision for epistemic states in the next section, we want to make two remarks on studying belief change on abstract sets of epistemic states. First, many approaches for belief change consider concrete (classes of) representations for epistemic states like ranking functions, (conditional) belief bases or probability functions. This has many advantages, e.g, it allows making use of the structure of the representation for optimization techniques like *syntax-splitting* [93, 70, 6] or employing the structure of the representation for having specific operators [88, 15, 7, 116]. Clearly, considering concrete representations is also helpful for implementing belief change approaches [14, 60, 135]. In contrast, considering belief change in abstract sets of epistemic states is a means for obtaining general conceptual results regarding structural properties of approaches to belief change – which is one aim of this thesis.

Second, we like to remark that a more structured study of belief change operators for epistemic states over different variations of properties for $\mathcal{E}$ might reveal a deep connection to the *types of reasoners* by Smullyan [144] and different axioms for *modal logic* [65].

6.3. Revision for Epistemic States

Revision is the process of incorporating new beliefs into an agent's belief set, in a consistent way, whenever this is possible. The postulates for revision given by Alchourrón, Gärdenfors, and Makinson [2] have counterparts in the framework of epistemic states by Darwiche and Pearl [41], which is inspired by the approach of Katsuno and Mendelzon [84] (see Chapter 3).

Definition 6.4 (AGM Revision Operator for Epistemic States [41]). *Let $\mathcal{E}$ be a set of epistemic states. A belief change operator $*$ for $\mathcal{E}$ is called an AGM revision operator for $\mathcal{E}$ if the following postulates are satisfied[1]:*

(R1) $\alpha \in \mathrm{Bel}(\Psi * \alpha)$.
(R2) *If* $\mathrm{Bel}(\Psi) + \alpha$ *consistent, then* $\mathrm{Bel}(\Psi * \alpha) = \mathrm{Bel}(\Psi) + \alpha$.
(R3) *If* α *is consistent, then* $\mathrm{Bel}(\Psi * \alpha)$ *is consistent.*
(R4) *If* $\alpha \equiv \beta$, *then* $\mathrm{Bel}(\Psi * \alpha) = \mathrm{Bel}(\Psi * \beta)$.
(R5) $\mathrm{Bel}(\Psi * (\alpha \wedge \beta)) \subseteq \mathrm{Bel}(\Psi * \alpha) + \beta$.
(R6) *If* $\mathrm{Bel}(\Psi * \alpha) + \beta$ *is consistent, then* $\mathrm{Bel}(\Psi * \alpha) + \beta \subseteq \mathrm{Bel}(\Psi * (\alpha \wedge \beta))$.

If no specific set of epistemic states $\mathcal{E}$ is considered, or $\mathcal{E}$ is clear from the context, we also use *AGM revision operator for epistemic states* instead of AGM revision operator for $\mathcal{E}$. The revision postulates (R1)–(R6) are clearly inspired by the revision postulates by Katsuno and Mendelzon [84] (see Chapter 3 and Part I). These postulates aim at establishing minimal change on the prior beliefs when revising an epistemic state. Note the specific difference between postulate (R4) and (KM4) (see p. 30), which reflects the intention that additional meta-information in the epistemic state might have influence on the change.

Semantic Characterization. As shown by Katsuno and Mendelzon [84] an AGM revision operator (in the classical AGM setting) is representable by a total preorder over the interpretations (Chapter 3). Darwiche and Pearl [41] adapt this approach to the framework of epistemic states, by equipping each epistemic state Ψ with a total preorder $\leq_\Psi$ over the possible worlds satisfying the faithfulness condition.

---

[1]   The abbreviation R stands for *revision*.

Definition 6.5 (Faithful Assignment, adapted [41]). *Let $\mathcal{E}$ be a set of epistemic states. A function $\Psi \mapsto \leq_\Psi$ that maps each epistemic state from $\mathcal{E}$ to a total preorder on interpretations is said to be a* faithful assignment *(for $\mathcal{E}$) if the following holds:*

(FA1) *If $\omega_1 \in [\![\Psi]\!]$ and $\omega_2 \in [\![\Psi]\!]$, then $\omega_1 \simeq_\Psi \omega_2$.*
(FA2) *If $\omega_1 \in [\![\Psi]\!]$ and $\omega_2 \notin [\![\Psi]\!]$, then $\omega_1 <_\Psi \omega_2$.*

We will encounter faithful assignments as defined in Definition 6.5 often in Part II and Part III. For a faithful assignment $\Psi \mapsto \leq_\Psi$, we denote with $<_\Psi$ the strict part of $\leq_\Psi$ and with $=_\Psi$ the equivalent part of $\leq_\Psi$ (see Chapter 2). Intuitively, the relation $\leq_\Psi$ orders the worlds by plausibility, and the faithfulness condition guarantees that minimal worlds with respect to $\leq_\Psi$ are the most plausible worlds, i.e., conformance of $[\![\Psi]\!]$ and $\min(\Omega, \leq_\Psi)$, i.e., $[\![\Psi]\!] = \min(\Omega, \leq_\Psi)$ if $\mathrm{Bel}(\Psi)$ is consistent. For the case of an inconsistent belief set $\mathrm{Bel}(\Psi)$, faithfulness makes no assumptions about the minimal worlds of $\leq_\Psi$. To link assignments with belief revision operators, we use the following notion of compatibility (compare to Definition 4.10 in Part I).

Definition 6.6 (Revision-Compatible). *Let $\mathcal{E}$ be a set of epistemic states. A faithful assignment $\Psi \mapsto \leq_\Psi$ (for $\mathcal{E}$) is called* revision-compatible *with a belief change operator $*$ (for $\mathcal{E}$) if the following holds:*

$$[\![\Psi * \alpha]\!] = \min([\![\alpha]\!], \leq_\Psi) \qquad \text{(revision-compatible)}$$

As demonstrated by Darwiche and Pearl, faithful assignments are a valid means to characterize AGM revision operators for epistemic states. In the following, we present their characterization result for AGM revision operators for epistemic states adapted to the notion of revision-compatibility.

Proposition 6.7 (Characterization of AGM Revision, adapted [41, Thm. 9]). *Let $\mathcal{E}$ be a set of epistemic states and let $*$ be a belief change operator for $\mathcal{E}$. The operator $*$ is an AGM revision operator for $\mathcal{E}$ if and only if there is a faithful assignment $\Psi \mapsto \leq_\Psi$ for $\mathcal{E}$ which is revision-compatible with $*$.*

Darwiche and Pearl declare no assumptions on $\mathcal{E}$ [41, Thm. 9]. But, Darwiche and Pearl explain that the characterization given in Proposition 6.7 implies that an AGM revision operators for epistemic states is "equivalent to a set of total preorders" [41, Section 5.2]. This statement might give the impression that there are undeclared assumptions on $\mathcal{E}$ in Darwiche and Pearl's formulation of Proposition 6.7. However, a reexamination of their proof makes clear that Proposition 6.7 ([41, Thm. 9]) holds for arbitrary $\mathcal{E}$.

For the sake of clarity, note that AGM revision operators are not "equivalent" to a set of total preorders in a strong sense. In particular, Proposition 6.7 does not imply that epistemic states are equivalent (or isomorphic) to total preorders, i.e., the result $\Psi * \alpha$ of a revision of Ψ by α may not completely be determined by $\leq_\Psi$ and α. Due to Proposition 6.7, for each $\alpha \in \mathcal{L}$ and for each $\Psi_1, \Psi_2 \in \mathcal{E}$ we have that $\leq_{\Psi_1} = \leq_{\Psi_2}$ implies $\mathrm{Bel}(\Psi_1 * \alpha) = \mathrm{Bel}(\Psi_2 * \alpha)$. However, this does not imply that the resulting epistemic states are the same, i.e., we may have $\Psi_1 * \alpha \neq \Psi_2 * \alpha$, and it could be the case[2] that subsequent revisions by some $\alpha_1, \ldots, \alpha_n \in \mathcal{L}$ yield different belief sets, i.e., we could have that $\mathrm{Bel}(\Psi_1 * \alpha * \alpha_1 * \ldots * \alpha_n) \neq \mathrm{Bel}(\Psi_2 * \alpha * \alpha_1 * \ldots * \alpha_n)$ holds. The same observation was already implicitly made in [97].

Existence of Operators. Before considering an example, we show that the existence of an AGM revision operator for $\mathcal{E}$ imposes certain requirements on $\mathcal{E}$.

Theorem 6.8. *Let $\mathcal{E}$ be a set of epistemic states. There exists an AGM revision operator $*$ for $\mathcal{E}$ if and only if the following postulates are satisfied by $\mathcal{E}$:*

(AGM-ES1) *For each $\omega \in \Omega$ there exists some $\Psi_\omega \in \mathcal{E}$ with $[\![\Psi_\omega]\!] = \{\omega\}$.*
(AGM-ES2) *For each $\Psi \in \mathcal{E}$ and for each $M \subseteq [\![\Psi]\!]$ there exists $\Psi_M \in \mathcal{E}$ such that $[\![\Psi_M]\!] = M$.*

Proof. We start by showing that the existence of $*$ implies satisfaction of (AGM-ES1) and (AGM-ES2). From satisfaction of (R1) and (R3) we obtain satisfaction of (AGM-ES1). Therefore, pick an arbitrary epistemic state $\Psi \in \mathcal{E}$ and a formula φ_ω such that $[\![\varphi_\omega]\!] = \{\omega\}$. Because of (R1) and (R3) there exists some epistemic state $\Psi_\omega \in \mathcal{E}$ such that $[\![\Psi_\omega]\!] = \{\omega\}$ and $\Psi * \varphi_\omega = \Psi_\omega$. For satisfaction of (AGM-ES2) consider

---

[2]   In the framework considered by Katsuno and Mendelzon for revision [84], this can not happen because in their framework epistemic states are just belief sets, thus, $\mathrm{Bel}(\Psi_1 * \alpha) = \mathrm{Bel}(\Psi_2 * \alpha)$ implies $\Psi_1 * \alpha = \Psi_2 * \alpha$.

some $\Psi \in \mathcal{E}$. For each $M \subseteq [\![\Psi]\!]$ let φ_M be such that $[\![\varphi_M]\!] = M$. Clearly, because of (R2), revision of Ψ by φ_M yields an epistemic state $\Psi * \varphi_M$ such that $[\![\Psi * \varphi_M]\!] = M$ is satisfied.

For the remaining direction, let $\mathcal{E}$ be a (non-empty) set of epistemic states that satisfies (AGM-ES1) and (AGM-ES2). Let $\ll$ be an arbitrary linear order on Ω and for each $M \subseteq \Omega$ let Ψ_M denote a uniquely chosen epistemic state from $\mathcal{E}$ such that $[\![\Psi_M]\!] = M$ (as far as such an epistemic state Ψ_M exists in $\mathcal{E}$). We construct a revision operator $*$ as follows:

$$\Psi * \alpha = \begin{cases} \Psi_{[\![\Psi]\!] \cap [\![\alpha]\!]} & \text{if } [\![\Psi]\!] \cap [\![\alpha]\!] \neq \emptyset \\ \Psi_{\min([\![\alpha]\!], \ll)} & \text{otherwise} \end{cases}$$

Observe that, because of (AGM-ES2), the epistemic state $\Psi_{[\![\Psi]\!] \cap [\![\alpha]\!]}$ exists whenever $[\![\Psi]\!] \cap [\![\alpha]\!] \neq \emptyset$ holds. Moreover, because $\ll$ is a linear order, we have, for every consistent α, that $\min([\![\alpha]\!], \ll)$ is a singleton set, and thus, by (AGM-ES1) the epistemic state $\Psi_{\min([\![\alpha]\!], \ll)}$ exists. For inconsistent α, the epistemic state $\Psi_{\min([\![\alpha]\!], \ll)}$ exists by (AGM-ES2) (and non-emptiness of $\mathcal{E}$). In summary, for every $\Psi \in \mathcal{E}$ and $\alpha \in \mathcal{L}$ the epistemic state $\Psi * \alpha$ exists.

We show satisfaction of (R1)–(R6) by $*$. The postulates (R1)–(R3) are immediately satisfied due to the construction of $*$. For (R4) observe that the behaviour of $*$ by input α is only defined via models of Ψ and α. Consequently, equivalent input formulas are treated equivalently. If $[\![\Psi * \alpha]\!] \cap [\![\beta]\!]$ is inconsistent, then (R5) and (R6) are immediately satisfied. In the following assume that $[\![\Psi * \alpha]\!] \cap [\![\beta]\!]$ is consistent. For the case of $[\![\Psi * \alpha]\!] \cap [\![\Psi]\!] \neq \emptyset$, we obtain (R5) and (R6) from (R2). For the case of $[\![\Psi * \alpha]\!] \cap [\![\Psi]\!] = \emptyset$, we have by construction that $[\![\Psi * \alpha]\!]$ is a singleton set, i.e., $[\![\Psi * \alpha]\!] = \{\omega\}$. Consequently, from consistence of $[\![\Psi * \alpha]\!] \cap [\![\beta]\!]$ we obtain $\omega \in [\![\beta]\!]$. From minimality of ω with respect to $\ll$, we obtain that $\min([\![\alpha]\!] \cap [\![\beta]\!], \ll) = \{\omega\}$. We obtain satisfaction of (R5) and (R6). □

Example and Further Remarks. In the following example we illustrate AGM revision operators for epistemic states. Moreover, we illustrate the construction used in the proof for Theorem 6.8.

Example 6.9. *Let* $\Sigma = \{a, b\}$ *and let* $\mathcal{E} = \{\Psi_\perp, \Psi_{ab}, \Psi_{\bar{a}b}, \Psi_{a\bar{b}}, \Psi_{\bar{a}\bar{b}}\}$ *be a set of epistemic states with:*

$$\llbracket\Psi_\perp\rrbracket = \emptyset \qquad\qquad \llbracket\Psi_{ab}\rrbracket = \{ab\} \qquad\qquad \llbracket\Psi_{a\bar{b}}\rrbracket = \{a\bar{b}\}$$

$$\llbracket\Psi_{\bar{a}b}\rrbracket = \{\bar{a}b\} \qquad\qquad \llbracket\Psi_{\bar{a}\bar{b}}\rrbracket = \{\bar{a}\bar{b}\}$$

Furthermore, let $\ll$ *be the linear order on* Ω *with:*

$$ab \ll \bar{a}b \ll a\bar{b} \ll \bar{a}\bar{b}$$

We define an AGM revision operator $*$ *for* $\mathcal{E}$ *as follows:*

$$\Psi * \alpha = \begin{cases} \Psi_{\llbracket\Psi\rrbracket\cap\llbracket\alpha\rrbracket} & \text{if } \llbracket\Psi\rrbracket \cap \llbracket\alpha\rrbracket \neq \emptyset \\ \Psi_{\min(\llbracket\alpha\rrbracket, \ll)} & \text{otherwise} \end{cases}$$

When considering the state Ψ_{ab} *the operator* $*$ *behaves, e.g., for all* α *with* $a \wedge b \models \alpha$ *and for all* β *with* $\neg a \wedge b \models \beta$ *and* $\beta \models \neg a \vee \neg b$ *as follows:*

$$\Psi_{ab} \star \alpha = \Psi_{ab} \qquad\qquad\qquad \Psi_{ab} \star \beta = \Psi_{\bar{a}b}$$

We show that $*$ *is an AGM revision operator for* $\mathcal{E}$ *via Proposition 6.7 by providing a faithful assignment. Let* $\Psi \mapsto \leq_\Psi$ *be the mapping for which each* $\leq_\Psi$ *given as*

$$\leq_\Psi = (\ll \setminus (\Omega \times \llbracket\Psi\rrbracket)) \cup (\llbracket\Psi\rrbracket \times \Omega),$$

i.e., the total preorder where the minimal elements are $\llbracket\Psi\rrbracket$*, and all other elements are ordered according to* $\ll$*. Indeed this is a faithful assignment that is revision-compatible. Figure 6.2 illustrates* $*$ *graphically.*

Theorem 6.8 reveals another detail about Proposition 6.7 we want to highlight. The bare existence of a faithful assignment $\Psi \mapsto \preceq_\Psi$ for $\mathcal{E}$ does not guarantee the existence of a belief change operator $*$ for $\mathcal{E}$ that is compatible with $\Psi \mapsto \preceq_\Psi$. This is because faithful assignments do exist for every set of epistemic states $\mathcal{E}$, but not for every set of epistemic states $\mathcal{E}$ there exists an AGM revision operator for $\mathcal{E}$, cf. Theorem 6.8. The formulation of Darwiche and Pearls' characterization theorem we use in Proposition 6.7 was chosen to reflect this observation. Because of the deliberations here, Proposition 6.7 is

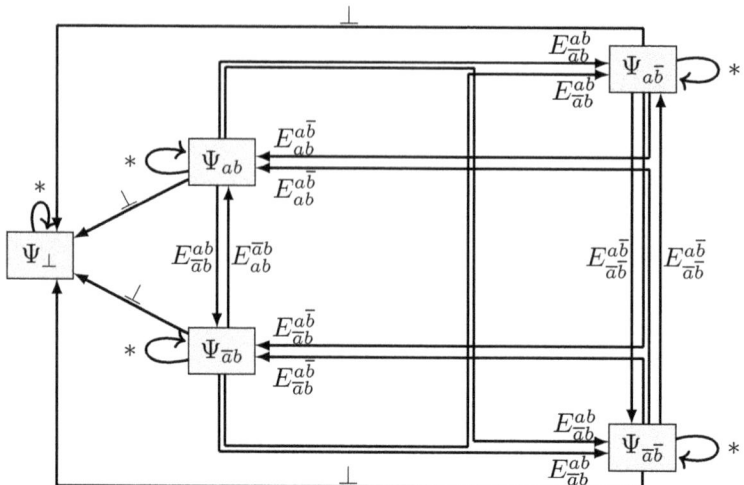

Figure 6.2: Graphical representation of the revision operator given in Example 6.9. E_x^y stands for $\{\alpha \mid y \notin [\![\alpha]\!], \min([\![\alpha]\!], \ll) = \{x\}\}$, i.e., for all formulas α where y is not a model of and x is the minimal model of α with respect to $\ll$. Moreover, $*$ stands for all not explicitly given edges, cf. Figure 6.1.

more a *characterization theorem* and than a representation theorem [41]. Note that, due to the different setup, Theorem 3.9 by Katsuno and Mendelzon is a *representation theorem* in a strong sense [108], and every KM-assignment yields a KM-belief change operator (cf. Section 4.5).

We will now evaluate properties for $\mathcal{E}$ given in Section 6.2 according to Theorem 6.8. First, note that the satisfaction of (AGM-ES1) and (AGM-ES2) by $\mathcal{E}$ due to Theorem 6.8 has the immediate consequence that $\mathcal{E}$ satisfies:

(AGM-ES$_\perp$) There exists some $\Psi_\perp \in \mathcal{E}$ with $[\![\Psi_\perp]\!] = \emptyset$.

Global consistency seems to be a very reasonable principle for $\mathcal{E}$. However, global consistency is incompatible with (AGM-ES$_\perp$), and thus, there is no AGM revision operator for $\mathcal{E}$ which satisfies global consistency. The situation is different for unbiased sets of epistemic states, as an unbiased set of epistemic states $\mathcal{E}$ satisfies (AGM-ES1) and (AGM-ES2).

Statements analogue to Theorem 6.8 are not known for many other classes of change operators, e.g., for many subclasses of AGM revision operators for epistemic states we do not know which are the properties of $\mathcal{E}$, such that an AGM revision operator for epistemic states of this subclass exists for $\mathcal{E}$. To simplify matters, we will sometimes do not consider whether a belief change operator $\circ$ for $\mathcal{E}$ exists, and will simply assume that $\circ$ exists or we will choose $\mathcal{E}$ such that the existence of operators is guaranteed.

Chapter 7

Acceptance and Non-Prioritized Revision

Not every agent accepts all beliefs for revision, as, e.g., agents make distinctions based on the quality and credibility of beliefs, and thus sometimes ignores a new belief. Because of this, it has often been stated, e.g. in [72], that AGM revision operators (for epistemic states) are not an adequate model of how agents treat beliefs for revision, in the sense that agents do not accept all beliefs for revision, whereas AGM revision assumes that every belief is accepted for revision. This gives rise to the question of means for the description of different qualities of the distinction between acceptable beliefs for performing revision and unacceptable beliefs for performing revision for different agents. The area of non-prioritized revision considers such approaches, which have in common that they consider revision-like operations that do not accept all beliefs for revision.

In this and the following chapter, we consider and develop approaches to non-prioritized revision from a viewpoint that makes use of a thought experiment. More specifically, we introduce functions A that are meant to describe which belief an agent accepts for revision and consider then classes of belief change operators R for which it is guaranteed (a property that we will call *realizability*) that there is at least one operator in R that shows the behaviour which A describes, i.e., there is a witness in R that shows that R is able to realize A.

7.1. Introduction to Non-Prioritized Revision

The original approach of AGM revision considers change of belief sets (see Section 3) and it has the following attitude towards new beliefs:

Prioritization of New Beliefs. AGM revision operators consider every new information as undeniable and fully acceptable. This attitude towards new beliefs is mostly realized by the *success condition* of revision (R1):

$$\alpha \in \mathrm{Bel}(\Psi * \alpha)$$

For real agents, this has often been criticized as a too unrealistic simplification of change processes. This leads to approaches to belief revision which relax revision regarding this attitude. They encompass mainly three different ways to cope with the wide variety of how new beliefs could be treated in the process of change:

Limitingly. An underlying revision operation is guarded by a preselection process. Every new incoming belief is evaluated regarding its credibility. If it is considered credible, then it is delegated to the revision operator and a revision happens, otherwise, the belief gets discarded. *Credibility-limited revision* by Hansson, Fermé, Cantwell and Falappa [77] realizes this prototypically, by making use of a set of beliefs denoted as credible, and revision is only performed whenever the new belief is an element of this set.

Selectively. New incoming beliefs may be modified by the agent according to her own needs (the right belief gets selected), before the belief is handed over to an underlying revision operator. A prototypical approach is *selective revision* by Fermé and Hansson [58].

Gradually. Instead of accepting the belief directly, the credibility of the belief is improved. Thus, for such agents believing depends on a degree of credibility, and beliefs with a sufficiently high credibility are believed. As revision by a belief increases its credibility. The prototypical approach to this kind of change are *improvement operators* [97, 96].

All these approaches have in common that, in general, they do not immediately accept every new belief entirely and thus *violate* success of revision. However, as they follow the same intention as revision theory (cf. Chapter 3 in Part I), they are denoted as *non-prioritized revision* operators. Consequently, there exist efforts to unify these approaches (e.g. see [117, 26, 139]). A more fine-grained and complete taxonomy of non-prioritized revision approaches is given by Hansson and Fermé [72, 57].

In the course of this part, we will mainly follow the *limiting* approach to new beliefs and generalize existing approaches to non-prioritized belief revision in epistemic states in a way that they are more flexible regarding the acceptance or rejection of new beliefs (and also exploring the limits of this approach). Nevertheless, note that also the selective and gradual approach could be (even more) appropriate to deal with the problems we consider in this part. However, investigations to follow these lines of research are out of the scope of this thesis.

7.2. Acceptance Descriptions

Suppose we would have conducted experiments on how an agent revises her beliefs according to new information. The agent might not accept every belief α, thus there are beliefs α for which the revision is successful, i.e., α is believed after revision by α, but for other beliefs this does not hold, i.e., those beliefs α that are not believed after revision by α.

Ideally, such experiments would give rise to a function $\mathcal{A} : \mathcal{E} \to \mathcal{P}(\mathcal{L})$ that for each epistemic states Ψ yields those beliefs which the agent accepts for revision. When starting from experimental data, one has to expect that $\mathcal{A}(\Psi)$ contains arbitrary formulas. For example, $\mathcal{A}(\Psi)$ may contain $\alpha \to \beta$ but not $\neg\beta \to \neg\alpha$. The following is debatable, but here we will rule out those cases and say that it is *not* in the concern of the theory of belief change to choose the right underlying logical framework, and an appropriate logic has to be chosen externally[1]. That means especially that we delegate the problem of *logical omniscience* [149] to the underlying logic.

In the following we provide our basic assumptions about how the

---

[1]   It is an open task to adapt the Darwiche-Pearl framework to other logics.

underlying logic, $\mathcal{E}$ and $\mathcal{A}(\Psi)$ are related in the approach we consider here.

Respecting the Underlying Logic. Our investigations presume propositional logic, as introduced in Chapter 2. To describe the beliefs accepted for revision (the sets $\mathcal{A}(\Psi)$), we will make use of the following conditions [77] for a set of formulas X:

If $\alpha \in X$ and $\alpha \equiv \beta$, then $\beta \in X$.

(closure under logical equivalence)

If $\alpha \in X$ and $\alpha \models \beta$, then $\beta \in X$.   (single-sentence closure)

If $\alpha \vee \beta \in X$, then $\alpha \in X$ or $\beta \in X$.

(disjunction completeness)

The property of *closure under logical equivalence* states that semantically equivalent formulas will be either all accepted for revision or none of them. The property of *single-sentence closure* states that consequences of acceptable formulas are also acceptable, and the property of *disjunction completeness* states that when a disjunction is acceptable for revision, then also one of the disjuncts is acceptable for revision. Because single-sentence closure implies closure under logical equivalence, we will not mention closure under logical equivalence any more in the following when single-sentence closure is given.

Compatibility Between $\mathcal{A}(\Psi)$ and $\mathcal{E}$. The intended meaning of $\alpha \in \mathcal{A}(\Psi)$ is that the agents accepts α for revision, which implies that the agent has the epistemic capability for believing in α, i.e., there is an epistemic state $\Psi \in \mathcal{E}$ such that $\alpha \in \mathrm{Bel}(\Psi)$.

We compile these assumptions into the following notion of acceptance descriptions.

Definition 7.1. *Let $\mathcal{E}$ be a set of epistemic states. A function $\mathcal{A} : \mathcal{E} \to \mathcal{P}(\mathcal{L})$ is called an* acceptance description *for $\mathcal{E}$ if the following properties are satisfied:*

(AD-ES1) *$\mathcal{A}(\Psi)$ satisfies single-sentence closure and disjunction completeness.*

(AD-ES2) *If $\alpha \in \mathcal{A}(\Psi)$ for some $\Psi \in \mathcal{E}$, then there exists $\Psi_\alpha \in \mathcal{E}$ with $\alpha \in \mathrm{Bel}(\Psi_\alpha)$.*

In the next section we will discuss the connection between acceptance descriptions and belief revision operators for epistemic states. In the following, we introduce useful properties of $\mathcal{A}(\Psi)$, i.e., properties of sets of formulas X that satisfy single-sentence closure and disjunction completeness. The following theorem is based on work by Hansson, Fermé, Cantwell, and Falappa [77].

Theorem 7.2 (Extension of [77, Thm. 11]). *Let $X \subseteq \mathcal{L}$ be a subset of $\mathcal{L}$. The set X satisfies single-sentence closure and disjunction completeness if and only if $X = \mathcal{L}$ or there is a set of interpretations $M \subseteq \Omega$ with $X = \{\alpha \in \mathcal{L} \mid [\![\alpha]\!] \cap M \neq \emptyset\}$.*

Proof. For the case of $X = \mathcal{L}$, we immanently obtain satisfaction of single-sentence closure and disjunction completeness. If $X = \emptyset$, then by choosing $M = \emptyset$ we obtain $X = \{\alpha \in \mathcal{L} \mid [\![\alpha]\!] \cap M \neq \emptyset\}$. In the following, we show that each $X \subseteq \mathcal{L}$ with $\emptyset \neq X \neq \mathcal{L}$ satisfies single-sentence closure and disjunction completeness if and only if a set M as above exists. We consider both directions of the proof independently:

From M to X. Suppose that we have $M \subseteq \Omega$. In the following, we show that $X = \{\alpha \in \mathcal{L} \mid [\![\alpha]\!] \cap M \neq \emptyset\}$ satisfies single-sentence closure and disjunction completeness. If $M = \emptyset$, then we have $X = \emptyset$. Thus, in this case, we have that single-sentence closure and disjunction completeness are trivially satisfied by X. We consider single-sentence closure and disjunction completeness independently, for the case of $M \neq \emptyset$:

single-sentence closure. Let α be a formula such that $\alpha \in X$, i.e., we have that $[\![\alpha]\!] \cap M \neq \emptyset$ holds. From $\alpha \models \beta$ we obtain $[\![\alpha]\!] \subseteq [\![\beta]\!]$ by definition of $\models$. Consequently, we obtain $[\![\beta]\!] \cap M \neq \emptyset$, and thus we have $\beta \in X$.

disjunction completeness. Let α, β be formulas such that $\alpha \vee \beta \in X$, i.e., we have that $[\![\alpha \vee \beta]\!] \cap M \neq \emptyset$ holds. Next, observe that $[\![\alpha \vee \beta]\!] \cap M \neq \emptyset$ implies that $[\![\alpha]\!] \cap M \neq \emptyset$ or $[\![\beta]\!] \cap M \neq \emptyset$ holds. From this observation we obtain $\alpha \in X$ or $\beta \in X$.

From X to M. In the following, suppose that $X \subseteq \mathcal{L}$ is a set such that we have $\emptyset \neq X \neq \mathcal{L}$ and that X satisfies single-sentence closure and disjunction completeness. First, observe that our assumptions imply $\bot \notin X$, as X satisfies single-sentence closure, and, consequently, $\bot \in X$ would imply $X = \mathcal{L}$. In the following, we assume that X contains only consistent formulas.

The remaining steps of this proof are based on the proof by Hansson et al. [77, Thm. 11]. Let $M \subseteq \Omega$ be the set of models of $S = \{\psi \mid \neg\psi \notin X\}$, i.e., $M = [\![S]\!]$. Because of $\bot \notin X$, we have $\top \in S$ and hence $S \neq \emptyset$ [77]. We show that $X = \{\alpha \in \mathcal{L} \mid [\![\alpha]\!] \cap M \neq \emptyset\}$ holds. This claim is equivalent to the statement $\alpha \in X$ if and only if $M \nsubseteq [\![\neg\alpha]\!]$.

From $M \nsubseteq [\![\neg\alpha]\!]$ to $\alpha \in X$. Towards a contradiction, we assume $\alpha \notin X$. For the next step, recall that single-sentence closure of X implies closure under logical equivalence of X. Since $\psi \in S$ if and only if $\neg\psi \notin X$, we obtain $\neg\alpha \in S$ from $\alpha \notin X$. Now observe that $M \nsubseteq [\![\neg\alpha]\!]$ implies $\psi \nvDash \neg\alpha$ for each $\psi \in S$. This observation contradicts the former conclusion $\neg\alpha \in S$.

From $\alpha \in X$ to $M \nsubseteq [\![\neg\alpha]\!]$. First, we show that there exists an interpretation $\omega \in [\![\alpha]\!]$ such that we have $\varphi_\omega \in X$, where φ_ω is a formula with $[\![\varphi_\omega]\!] = \{\omega\}$. Recall that α is consistent. For the case of $[\![\alpha]\!] = \{\omega\}$ the statement immediately holds. For the case of $|[\![\alpha]\!]| > 1$ let α_1 and α_2 be consistent formulas with $\alpha \equiv \alpha_1 \vee \alpha_2$ and disjoint model sets, i.e., we have $[\![\alpha_1]\!] \cap [\![\alpha_2]\!] = \emptyset$. By using the disjunction completeness of X, we obtain $\alpha_1 \in X$ or $\alpha_2 \in X$. By an inductive argument, we obtain an interpretation ω with $\varphi_\omega \in X$ such that $\omega \in [\![\alpha_1]\!]$ or $\omega \in [\![\alpha_2]\!]$ holds for $|[\![\alpha_1]\!]| < |[\![\alpha]\!]|$ and $|[\![\alpha_2]\!]| < |[\![\alpha]\!]|$. Because of $\alpha_1 \vDash \alpha$ and $\alpha_2 \vDash \alpha$, this shows that there exists an interpretation $\omega \in [\![\alpha]\!]$ such that we have $\varphi_\omega \in X$.

For the next steps recall that we have $\psi \in S$ if and only if $\neg\psi \notin X$. We obtain $\neg\varphi_\omega \notin S$ from $\varphi_\omega \in X$. Moreover, because X satisfies single-sentence closure, we obtain for each formula β, that $\varphi_\omega \vDash \beta$ implies $\beta \in X$ and hence $\neg\beta \notin S$. This observation shows that each $\psi \in S$ is consistent with φ_ω, i.e. we have $[\![\varphi_\omega]\!] \cap [\![\psi]\!] \neq \emptyset$ for each $\psi \in S$. Because of $\omega \in [\![\alpha]\!]$, we obtain $M \nsubseteq [\![\neg\alpha]\!]$ from our last observation. $\square$

The following proposition paraphrases Proposition 7.2 and collects useful consequences of Proposition 7.2. In particular, it points out the difference between the case of $\bot \in X$ and $\bot \notin X$ in Proposition 7.2.

Proposition 7.3. *If* X, X_1, X_2 *are subsets of* $\mathcal{L}$, *then the following statements hold:*

(a) *For* $X = \mathcal{L}$, *we have that* X *satisfies single-sentence closure and disjunction completeness. Moreover, we have* $\mathcal{L} = \{\beta \mid \beta \equiv \perp\} \cup \{\alpha \in \mathcal{L} \mid \llbracket \alpha \rrbracket \cap \Omega \neq \emptyset\}$.

(b) *If* $X \neq \mathcal{L}$, *then* X *satisfies single-sentence closure and disjunction completeness if and only if there exists a set of interpretations* $M \subseteq \Omega$ *with* $X = \{\alpha \in \mathcal{L} \mid \llbracket \alpha \rrbracket \cap M \neq \emptyset\}$.

(c) *If* X *satisfies single-sentence closure and disjunction completeness, then for each consistent* $\alpha \in X$ *there exists an interpretation* $\omega \in \llbracket \alpha \rrbracket$ *with* $\varphi_\omega \in X$.

(d) *If* X *satisfies single-sentence closure and disjunction completeness, then* $\perp \in X$ *if and only if* $X = \mathcal{L}$.

(e) *If* X_1, X_2 *both satisfy single-sentence closure and disjunction completeness, then* $X_1 \cup X_2$ *satisfies single-sentence closure and disjunction completeness.*

(f) *If* X_1, X_2 *both satisfy single-sentence closure and disjunction completeness, then* $X_1 \cap X_2$ *satisfies single-sentence closure and disjunction completeness.*

Proof. The statements (a), (b) and (d) are direct consequences of Proposition 7.2. We consider the remaining statements.

(c) For the statement (c), we use (a) and (b) to obtain $w_\alpha \in M$ with $w_\alpha \models \alpha$ for each $\alpha \in X$. Having this, we obtain $\varphi_{w_\alpha} \in X$ by using (a) and (b) again.

(e) If $X_1 = \mathcal{L}$ or $X_2 = \mathcal{L}$, then we obtain $X_1 \cup X_2 = \mathcal{L}$, which satisfies single-sentence closure and disjunction completeness according to (a). For the case of $X_1 \neq \mathcal{L}$ and $X_1 \neq \mathcal{L}$, we use (b) to obtain two sets $M_1, M_2 \subseteq \Omega$ such that:

$$X_1 = \{\alpha \in \mathcal{L} \mid \llbracket \alpha \rrbracket \cap M_1 \neq \emptyset\}$$
$$X_2 = \{\alpha \in \mathcal{L} \mid \llbracket \alpha \rrbracket \cap M_2 \neq \emptyset\}$$

By applying basic set theory we obtain:

$$X_1 \cup X_2 = \{\alpha \in \mathcal{L} \mid [\![\alpha]\!] \cap M_1 \neq \emptyset\} \cup \{\alpha \in \mathcal{L} \mid [\![\alpha]\!] \cap M_2 \neq \emptyset\}$$
$$= \{\alpha \in \mathcal{L} \mid [\![\alpha]\!] \cap (M_1 \cup M_2) \neq \emptyset\}$$

From (b) we obtain that $X_1 \cup X_2$ satisfies single-sentence closure and disjunction completeness.

(f) If $X_1 = \mathcal{L}$, then we obtain $X_1 \cap X_2 = X_2$, which satisfies single-sentence closure and disjunction completeness. Analogously, if $X_2 = \mathcal{L}$, then we obtain $X_1 \cap X_2 = X_1$, which satisfies single-sentence closure and disjunction completeness. If $X_1 \cap X_2 = \emptyset$ the statement (f) is given according to (b). For the case of $X_1 \cap X_2 \neq \emptyset$ with $X_1 \neq \mathcal{L}$ and $X_1 \neq \mathcal{L}$, we use (b) to obtain two sets $M_1, M_2 \subseteq \Omega$ such that:

$$X_1 = \{\alpha \in \mathcal{L} \mid [\![\alpha]\!] \cap M_1 \neq \emptyset\}$$
$$X_2 = \{\alpha \in \mathcal{L} \mid [\![\alpha]\!] \cap M_2 \neq \emptyset\}$$

By applying basic set theory we obtain:

$$X_1 \cap X_2 = \{\alpha \in \mathcal{L} \mid [\![\alpha]\!] \cap M_1 \neq \emptyset\} \cap \{\alpha \in \mathcal{L} \mid [\![\alpha]\!] \cap M_2 \neq \emptyset\}$$
$$= \{\alpha \in \mathcal{L} \mid [\![\alpha]\!] \cap M_1 \cap M_2 \neq \emptyset\}$$

From (b) we obtain that $X_1 \cap X_2$ satisfies single-sentence closure and disjunction completeness. □

7.3. Scope, Realizability and AGM Revision

In this section we introduce notions for connecting acceptance descriptions with belief change operators. Especially, we define what it means for a belief change operator for epistemic states to *comply* with an acceptance description $\mathcal{A}$.

Scope of Operators. In the following we introduce the notion of the scope of a belief change operator with respect to an epistemic state.

Definition 7.4 (Scope). *Let $\mathcal{E}$ be a set of epistemic states, let $\circ$ be a belief change operator for $\mathcal{E}$ and let $\Psi \in \mathcal{E}$ be an epistemic state. The set*

$$Scp^\circ(\Psi) = \{\alpha \in \mathcal{L} \mid \alpha \in \mathrm{Bel}(\Psi \circ \alpha)\}$$

is called the scope *of $\circ$ with respect to Ψ.*

For AGM revision operators for epistemic states we immediately obtain the following proposition.

Proposition 7.5. *Let $\mathcal{E}$ be a set of epistemic states. For each AGM revision operator $*$ for $\mathcal{E}$ we have $Scp^*(\Psi) = \mathcal{L}$ for each $\Psi \in \mathcal{E}$.*

Proof. We obtain the claim from (R1), which is satisfied by each AGM revision operator $*$ for $\mathcal{E}$ (see Definition 6.4). $\qquad\square$

Clearly, Proposition 7.5 shows that every AGM revision operator for a set of epistemic states $\mathcal{E}$ shows the behaviour given by the unique acceptance description $\mathcal{E}$ that accepts every belief. In the following we introduce the notion of compliance that describes a relationship between a belief change operator and an acceptance description.

Compliance of $\mathcal{A}$ with a Belief Change Operator. Connecting an acceptance description $\mathcal{A}$ with a belief revision operator $\circ$ requires dealing with a non-trivial aspect. The particular problem is that an acceptance description $\mathcal{A}$ does not describe how $\circ$ should deal with those beliefs that get not accepted for revision.

Here, we follow the approach that $\circ$ will fall back to the prior beliefs (which is also the case for all approaches mentioned in Section 7.1, but not all approaches in the literature [141, 57]), i.e., if α is not accepted for revision, then we obtain $\mathrm{Bel}(\Psi \circ \alpha) = \mathrm{Bel}(\Psi)$. However, by this choice, $Scp^\circ(\Psi)$ may contain beliefs that are not accepted for revision in cases where α is an element of $\mathrm{Bel}(\Psi)$. The following notion of compliance deals with this aspect by treating the elements of $\mathrm{Bel}(\Psi)$ explicitly.

Definition 7.6 (Compliance). *Let $\mathcal{E}$ be a set of epistemic states and let $\mathcal{A} : \mathcal{E} \to \mathcal{P}(\mathcal{L})$ be an acceptance description for $\mathcal{E}$. We say a belief change operator $\circ$ for $\mathcal{E}$ complies with $\mathcal{A}$ if for each $\Psi \in \mathcal{E}$ the following holds:*

$$Scp^\circ(\Psi) = \mathrm{Bel}(\Psi) \cup \mathcal{A}(\Psi)$$

We will use the notion of compliance symmetrically, i.e., if $\circ$ complies with $\mathcal{A}$, then we also say that $\mathcal{A}$ complies with $\circ$. For comparing families of acceptance descriptions with families of belief change operators with respect to compliance, we introduce the concept of realizability in the following.

Realizability. A set of acceptance descriptions $\mathbb{A}$ for a set of epistemic states $\mathcal{E}$ is said to be *realized*[2] by a set R of belief change operators for $\mathcal{E}$ if for each $\mathcal{A} \in \mathbb{A}$ there exists some belief change operator in R that complies with $\mathcal{A}$. Furthermore, if this is the case, we say that R *strongly realizes* $\mathbb{A}$ if each belief change operator in R complies with some $\mathcal{A} \in \mathbb{A}$. Figure 7.1 illustrates this notion of *realizability*. The notion of realizability extends naturally to families of acceptance descriptions and families of belief change operators both indexed by sets of epistemic states.

7.4. Credibility-Limited Revision

In this section we consider credibility-limited revision in propositional logic designed for belief changes over epistemic states. We will adapt this approach so that the AGM revision operators for epistemic states are included.

Credibility-Limited Revision in Propositional Logic. Credibility-limited revision was introduced by Hansson et al. [77] and restricts the process of revision to credible beliefs. For the setting of belief change operators for epistemic states, credibility-limited revision was adapted by Booth, Fermé, Konieczny and Pino Pérez to operators obeying the following postulates[3] [27]:

(CL1) $\alpha \in \mathrm{Bel}(\Psi \circledast \alpha)$ or $\mathrm{Bel}(\Psi \circledast \alpha) = \mathrm{Bel}(\Psi)$.

(CL2) If $\mathrm{Bel}(\Psi) + \alpha$ is consistent, then $\mathrm{Bel}(\Psi \circledast \alpha) = \mathrm{Bel}(\Psi) + \alpha$.

(CL3) $\mathrm{Bel}(\Psi \circledast \alpha)$ is consistent.

(CL4) If $\alpha \equiv \beta$, then $\mathrm{Bel}(\Psi \circledast \alpha) = \mathrm{Bel}(\Psi \circledast \beta)$.

(CL5) If $\alpha \in \mathrm{Bel}(\Psi \circledast \alpha)$ and $\alpha \models \beta$, then $\beta \in \mathrm{Bel}(\Psi \circledast \beta)$.

(CL6) $\mathrm{Bel}(\Psi \circledast (\alpha \vee \beta)) = \begin{cases} \mathrm{Bel}(\Psi \circledast \alpha) \text{ or} \\ \mathrm{Bel}(\Psi \circledast \beta) \text{ or} \\ \mathrm{Bel}(\Psi \circledast \alpha) \cap \mathrm{Bel}(\Psi \circledast \beta) \end{cases}$.

---

[2]   Kleene coined the term realizability in the context of proof theory [95]. The notion of realizability used here is inspired by the usage of the notion as "existence of an element with a given specification" used for instance by Vardi [152]. Here, realizability means the following: A family of formally specified objects (the belief change operators in R specified by postulates) is able to realize (in the sense of providing a representative in R for) every possible observation (the acceptance descriptions in $\mathbb{A}$).

[3]   The abbreviation *CL* stands for *credibility-limited* revision.

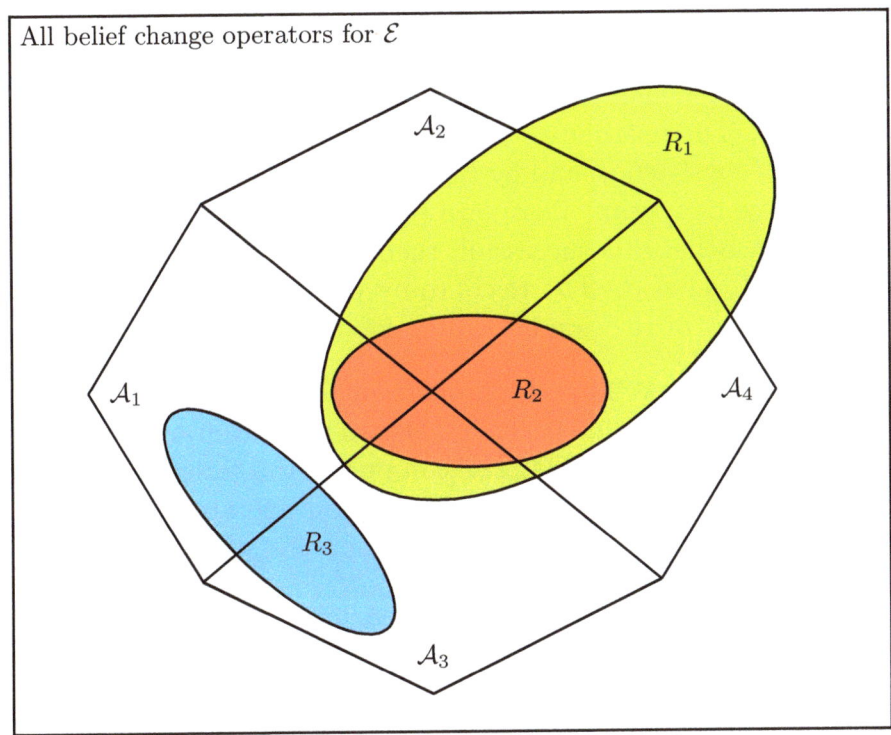

Figure 7.1: This figure illustrates the notion of realizability. Assume that $\mathcal{E}$ is a set of epistemic states, that $\mathbb{A} = \{\mathcal{A}_1, \mathcal{A}_2, \mathcal{A}_3, \mathcal{A}_4\}$ is a set of acceptance descriptions for $\mathcal{E}$, and that R_1, R_2 and R_3 are sets of belief change operators for $\mathcal{E}$. The whole framed area represents the space of all belief change operators for $\mathcal{E}$. Each polygonal area around $\mathcal{A}_i \in \mathbb{A}$ represents the belief change operators for $\mathcal{E}$ that comply with $\mathcal{A}_i$. Each ellipsoid area around some R_i represents the belief change operators in R_i.

The sets R_1 and R_2 realize $\mathbb{A}$, and the set R_3 does not realize $\mathbb{A}$. R_1 and R_2 realize $\mathbb{A}$, as for every $\mathcal{A}_i \in \mathbb{A}$ there is some belief change operator in R_1 and R_2 that complies with $\mathcal{A}_i$. Furthermore, the set R_2 strongly realizes $\mathbb{A}$ as every belief change operator in R_2 complies with some element in $\mathbb{A}$. The set R_3 does not realize $\mathbb{A}$, as there is no belief change operator in R_3 that complies with $\mathcal{A}_2$ and there is no belief change operator in R_3 that complies with $\mathcal{A}_4$.

The postulate (CL1) is known as *relative success* and denotes that either the agents keeps its prior beliefs (falling back to prior beliefs) or the belief change is successful in achieving the success condition of revision (the beliefs get accepted for revision). Through (CL2), known as *vacuity*, new beliefs are just added when they are not in conflict with $\text{Bel}(\Psi)$. The postulate (CL3), also known as *strong consistency* [77], ensures consistency, and by (CL4) the operator has to implement independence of syntax. Postulate (CL5) guarantees that when the revision by a belief α is successful, then it is also successful for every more general belief β. The trichotomy postulate (CL6) guarantees decomposability of revision of disjunctive beliefs.

Note that for each AGM revision operator $*$ for epistemic states $[\![\Psi *\bot]\!] = \emptyset$ holds due to (R1). In the full Darwiche-Pearl framework, which we use in this thesis, no AGM revision operator $*$ for epistemic states satisfies (CL3). Consequently, AGM revision operators for epistemic states are no[4] credibility-limited revision operators for epistemic states in the sense of (CL1)–(CL6).

Generalized Credibility-Limited Revision. In the following, we describe how we adapt the approach by Booth et al. [27] of credibility-limited revision in epistemic states so that AGM revision operators are not excluded. We start by dropping (CL3) on the postulate side[5]. Observe that just taking (CL1)–(CL6), while excluding (CL3), would have drastic consequence, because we would include operators that would yield randomly inconsistent states for certain inputs. The following example contains a fairly simple operator which has such a behaviour.

Example 7.7. *Let* $\Sigma = \{a\}$ *and let* $\mathcal{E} = \{\Psi_\bot, \Psi_a\}$ *be a set of epistemic states with:*

$$[\![\Psi_\bot]\!] = \emptyset \qquad\qquad [\![\Psi_a]\!] = \{ab\}$$

---

[4]   This is not so apparent in [27], because [27] considers a restricted version of the Darwich-Pearl framework, which rules out the cases of inconsistent belief states [27]. A consequence of these restrictions is that (CL3) is a postulate with no effect (in their considerations).

[5]   Note that (CL3) is denoted as a *core postulate* by Hansson et al. [77]. A philosophical judgment on this matter is out of scope of this thesis. However, the rationale for our investigations is to provide a coherent picture.

We define a belief change operator $\circledast$ for $\mathcal{E}$ as follows:

$$\Psi \circledast \alpha = \begin{cases} \Psi_a & \text{if } [\![\alpha]\!] = \{a\} \\ \Psi_\perp & \text{if } [\![\alpha]\!] \subseteq \{\overline{a}\} \\ \Psi & \text{otherwise} \end{cases}$$

Figure 7.2 illustrates $\circledast$ graphically. We make two observations regarding $\circledast$:

Observation I. *There are situations where $\circledast$ yields an inconsistent belief set for a consistent formula (on a consistent belief set), e.g., we have $[\![\Psi_a \circledast \neg a]\!] = \emptyset$.*

Observation II. *There are situations where $\circledast$ yields a consistent belief set for a consistent formula α (on an inconsistent belief set) and yields an inconsistent belief set for some consequences of α, e.g., we have $[\![\Psi_\perp \circledast a]\!] = \{a\}$ and $[\![\Psi_\perp \circledast \top]\!] = \emptyset$.*

By definition of $\circledast$ we directly obtain that $\circledast$ satisfies (CL1), (CL2), and (CL4). We show satisfaction of (CL5) and (CL6):

(CL5) *Note that we have $\alpha \in \mathrm{Bel}(\Psi)$ for each $\Psi \in \mathcal{E}$ and for each $\alpha \in \mathcal{L}$. Consequently, $\circledast$ satisfies (CL5).*

(CL6) *Let $\gamma = \alpha \vee \beta$. For $\alpha \equiv \beta$ we obtain $[\![\Psi \circledast \gamma]\!] = [\![\Psi \circledast \alpha]\!] = [\![\Psi \circledast \beta]\!]$ from (CL4). In the following we assume $[\![\alpha]\!] \neq [\![\beta]\!]$. Observe that this implies $[\![\gamma]\!] \neq \emptyset$. Next, we consider two subcases for $\Psi \in \mathcal{E}$:*

$\Psi = \Psi_\perp$. *Observe that we have $[\![\Psi \circledast \varphi]\!] = [\![\Psi]\!] = \emptyset$ for all φ with $[\![\varphi]\!] \neq \{a\}$. Consequently, if $a \notin [\![\gamma]\!]$, then we obtain $[\![\Psi \circledast \gamma]\!] = [\![\Psi]\!] = [\![\Psi \circledast \alpha]\!] = [\![\Psi \circledast \beta]\!] = \emptyset$. If $[\![\gamma]\!] = \{a\}$, then we have $[\![\Psi \circledast \gamma]\!] = \{a\}$ and we obtain from $[\![\alpha]\!] \neq [\![\beta]\!]$ that either $[\![\alpha]\!] = \{a\}$ or $[\![\beta]\!] = \{a\}$. Thus, we obtain either $[\![\Psi \circledast \gamma]\!] = [\![\Psi \circledast \alpha]\!]$ or $[\![\Psi \circledast \gamma]\!] = [\![\Psi \circledast \beta]\!]$ by (CL4). We consider the remaining case of $\{a\} \subsetneq [\![\gamma]\!]$. Then we have $[\![\Psi \circledast \gamma]\!] = \emptyset$. From $[\![\alpha]\!] \neq [\![\beta]\!]$ we obtain that $[\![\alpha]\!] \neq \{a\}$ or $[\![\beta]\!] \neq \{a\}$ holds. Thus, we obtain either $[\![\Psi \circledast \gamma]\!] = [\![\Psi \circledast \alpha]\!]$ or $[\![\Psi \circledast \gamma]\!] = [\![\Psi \circledast \beta]\!]$.*

$\Psi = \Psi_a$. *Observe that we have $[\![\Psi \circledast \varphi]\!] = [\![\Psi]\!] = \{a\}$ for all φ with $[\![\varphi]\!] \not\subseteq \{\overline{a}\}$. Consequently, if $\overline{a} \notin [\![\gamma]\!]$, then we obtain $[\![\Psi \circledast \gamma]\!] = [\![\Psi]\!] = [\![\Psi \circledast \alpha]\!] = [\![\Psi \circledast \beta]\!] = \emptyset$. If $[\![\gamma]\!] = \{\overline{a}\}$, then we have $[\![\Psi \circledast \gamma]\!] = \emptyset$ and we obtain from $[\![\alpha]\!] \neq [\![\beta]\!]$*

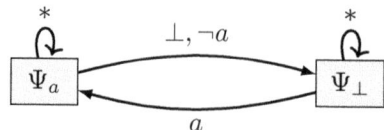

Figure 7.2: Graphical representation of the operator ⊛ given in Example 7.7.

> that either $[\![\alpha]\!] = \{\bar{a}\}$ or $[\![\beta]\!] = \{\bar{a}\}$. Thus, we obtain either $[\![\Psi \circledast \gamma]\!] = [\![\Psi \circledast \alpha]\!]$ or $[\![\Psi \circledast \gamma]\!] = [\![\Psi \circledast \beta]\!]$ by (CL4). We consider the remaining case of $\{\bar{a}\} \subsetneq [\![\gamma]\!]$. Then we have $[\![\Psi \circledast \gamma]\!] = \{a\}$. From $[\![\alpha]\!] \neq [\![\beta]\!]$ we obtain that $[\![\alpha]\!] \neq \{\bar{a}\}$ or $[\![\beta]\!] \neq \{\bar{a}\}$ holds. Thus, we obtain either $[\![\Psi \circledast \gamma]\!] = [\![\Psi \circledast \alpha]\!]$ or $[\![\Psi \circledast \gamma]\!] = [\![\Psi \circledast \beta]\!]$.

In summary, ⊛ satisfies (CL1)–(CL6) *except for* (CL3).

For generalized credibility-limited revision we replace (CL3) by postulates that prevent the behaviour given in Observation I and Observation II in Example 7.7. The first postulate is

(CL3wcp) If $\mathrm{Bel}(\Psi \circledast \alpha)$ is inconsistent, then $\mathrm{Bel}(\Psi)$ or α is inconsistent.

which is already known in its contrapositive formulation,

(WCP) If $\mathrm{Bel}(\Psi)$ and α are consistent, then $\mathrm{Bel}(\Psi \circledast \alpha)$ is consistent.

as *weak consistency preservation* [77, 83]. The postulate (CL3wcp) states that the inconsistency of the result of a change on Ψ by α is rooted in inconsistency of either $\mathrm{Bel}(\Psi)$ or α. Moreover, we will assume satisfaction of the following postulate:

(CL3u) If $\mathrm{Bel}(\Psi \circledast \alpha)$ is consistent and $\alpha \models \beta$, then $\mathrm{Bel}(\Psi \circledast \beta)$ is consistent.

The postulate (CL3u) states that the consistency of a change on Ψ by α is inherited "upward" to all changes on Ψ by consequences of α. Note that (CL3) implies (CL3u) and (CL3wcp), and therefore also (WCP). Regarding our observations in Example 7.7: the postulate

(CL3wcp) prevents situations like in Observation I, and the postulate (CL3u) rules out situations mentioned in Observation II of Example 7.7.

Given these postulates, we define generalized credibility-limited revision operators (for epistemic states) in the following as operators that satisfy (CL1), (CL2), (CL3wcp), (CL3u) and (CL4)–(CL6). For the sake of clarity, we give this set of postulates its own naming.

Definition 7.8 (Generalized Credibility-Limited Revision, inspired by [27]). *Let $\mathcal{E}$ be a set of epistemic states. A belief change operator $\circledast$ for $\mathcal{E}$ is a generalized credibility-limited revision operator for $\mathcal{E}$ if $\circledast$ satisfies[6].:*

(GCL1) $\alpha \in \mathrm{Bel}(\Psi \circledast \alpha)$ *or* $\mathrm{Bel}(\Psi \circledast \alpha) = \mathrm{Bel}(\Psi)$.
(GCL2) *If* $\mathrm{Bel}(\Psi) + \alpha$ *is consistent, then* $\mathrm{Bel}(\Psi \circledast \alpha) = \mathrm{Bel}(\Psi) + \alpha$.
(GCL3) *If* $\mathrm{Bel}(\Psi \circledast \alpha)$ *is inconsistent, then* $\mathrm{Bel}(\Psi)$ *or* α *is inconsistent.*
(GCL4) *If* $\mathrm{Bel}(\Psi \circledast \alpha)$ *is consistent and* $\alpha \models \beta$, *then* $\mathrm{Bel}(\Psi \circledast \beta)$ *is consistent.*
(GCL5) *If* $\alpha \equiv \beta$, *then* $\mathrm{Bel}(\Psi \circledast \alpha) = \mathrm{Bel}(\Psi \circledast \beta)$.
(GCL6) *If* $\alpha \in \mathrm{Bel}(\Psi \circledast \alpha)$ *and* $\alpha \models \beta$, *then* $\beta \in \mathrm{Bel}(\Psi \circledast \beta)$.
(GCL7) $\mathrm{Bel}(\Psi \circledast (\alpha \vee \beta)) = \begin{cases} \mathrm{Bel}(\Psi \circledast \alpha) & or \\ \mathrm{Bel}(\Psi \circledast \beta) & or \\ \mathrm{Bel}(\Psi \circledast \alpha) \cap \mathrm{Bel}(\Psi \circledast \beta) \end{cases}$.

Semantic Characterization. Next, we characterize generalized credibility-limited revision operators semantically. Booth et al. [27] proposed to adapt faithful assignments (see Definition 6.5) to capture the class of credibility-limited revision operators. In the following, we present an extended version of their assignments, which are meant to capture generalized credibility-limited revision operators.

Definition 7.9 (Credibility-Limited Assignment, adapted [27]). *Let $\mathcal{E}$ be a set of epistemic states. A function $\Psi \mapsto (\preceq_\Psi, C_\Psi, b_\Psi)$ is called a credibility-limited assignment for $\mathcal{E}$ if $C_\Psi \subseteq \Omega$ is a set of interpretations with $[\![\Psi]\!] \subseteq C_\Psi$, and $\preceq_\Psi$ is a total preorder over C_Ψ, and $b_\Psi \in \{\top, \bot\}$ for all $\Psi \in \mathcal{E}$ such that the following holds:*

(CLA$_\bot$) *If* $b_\Psi = \bot$, *then* $C_\Psi = \Omega$.

---
[6]   The abbreviation *GCL* stands for *generalized credibility-limited revision*

Credibility-limited assignments carry two kinds of information. First, C_Ψ describes semantically all consistent beliefs denoted as credible and b_Ψ represents whether an inconsistent formula is considered as credible or not. Note that b_Ψ is an extension to the assignments considered in [27]. Second, the total preorder $\preceq_\Psi$ serves the same purpose as for revision; representing the preferences of the agent. Note that $\preceq_\Psi$, in contrast to $\leq_\Psi$ of faithful assignments in Definition 6.5, might be a relation over a strict subset of Ω. In order to highlight the difference, we will always use $\preceq$ for relations over some subsets of Ω, while $\leq$ will always denote a relation over Ω. For a relation $\preceq$ over a subset of Ω, with $\prec$ we denote the strict part of $\preceq$ and with $\simeq$ the equivalent part of $\preceq$ (see Chapter 2).

Definition 7.10 (Faithful Credibility-Limited Assignment, adapted [27]). *Let $\mathcal{E}$ be a set of epistemic states. A credibility-limited assignment $\Psi \mapsto (\preceq_\Psi, C_\Psi, b_\Psi)$ for $\mathcal{E}$ is called* faithful *if the following holds:*

(CLFA1) *If $\omega_1 \in \llbracket \Psi \rrbracket$ and $\omega_2 \in \llbracket \Psi \rrbracket$, then $\omega_1 \simeq_\Psi \omega_2$.*
(CLFA2) *If $\omega_1 \in \llbracket \Psi \rrbracket$ and $\omega_2 \notin \llbracket \Psi \rrbracket$, then $\omega_1 <_\Psi \omega_2$.*

To link credibility-limited assignments with belief change operators, we use the following notion of compatibility.

Definition 7.11 (Credibility-Limited-Compatible). *A credibility-limited assignment $\Psi \mapsto (\preceq_\Psi, C_\Psi, b_\Psi)$ is called (credibility-limited)* revision-compatible *with a belief change operator $\circledast$ if the following holds:*

$$
\llbracket \Psi \circledast \alpha \rrbracket = \begin{cases} \min(\llbracket \alpha \rrbracket, \preceq_\Psi) & , \llbracket \alpha \rrbracket \cap C_\Psi \neq \emptyset \\ \emptyset & , \llbracket \alpha \rrbracket = \emptyset \text{ and } b_\Psi = \bot \\ \llbracket \Psi \rrbracket & , \text{otherwise} \end{cases}
$$

(revision-compatible)

Given the notion of revision-compatible, we will now show that faithful credibility-limited assignments fully capture generalized credible-limited revision operators for epistemic states. The following proposition builds on Theorem 2 in [27], but it extends it, as it holds in the unrestricted Darwiche-Pearl framework as introduced in Section 6.1.

Theorem 7.12. *Let $\mathcal{E}$ be a set of epistemic states and let $\circledast$ be a belief change operator for $\mathcal{E}$. Then $\circledast$ is a generalized credibility-limited revision operator for $\mathcal{E}$ if and only if there is a faithful credibility-limited assignment $\Psi \mapsto (\preceq_\Psi, C_\Psi, b_\Psi)$ that is revision-compatible with $\circledast$.*

Proof. We consider both directions of the claim independently.

The "$\Rightarrow$"-direction. Let $\circledast$ be a credibility-limited revision operator for $\mathcal{E}$. We construct a mapping $\Psi \mapsto (\preceq_\Psi, C_\Psi, b_\Psi)$. We set C_Ψ as follows

$$C_\Psi = \{\omega \mid [\![\varphi_\omega]\!] = [\![\Psi \circledast \varphi_\omega]\!]\}, \qquad \text{(see [27, Remark 1])}$$

for each $\Psi \in \mathcal{E}$, where φ_ω denotes a formula with $[\![\varphi_\omega]\!] = \{\omega\}$. If $[\![\Psi]\!] \neq \emptyset$ and $\bot \in \text{Bel}(\Psi \circledast \bot)$, then we set $b_\Psi = \bot$; otherwise we set $b_\Psi = \top$. For each $\Psi \in \mathcal{E}$ let $\preceq_\Psi \subseteq C_\Psi \times C_\Psi$ be the relation such that

$$\omega_1 \preceq_\Psi \omega_2 \text{ if and only if } \omega_1 \in [\![\Psi \circledast \varphi_{\omega_1, \omega_2}]\!]$$

holds, where $\varphi_{\omega_1, \omega_2}$ denotes a formula with $[\![\varphi_{\omega_1, \omega_2}]\!] = \{\omega_1, \omega_2\}$.

Next, we show that $\Psi \mapsto (\preceq_\Psi, C_\Psi, b_\Psi)$ is a credibility-limited assignment.

$[\![\Psi]\!] \subseteq C_\Psi$. Let $\omega \in [\![\Psi]\!]$ and φ_ω such that $[\![\varphi_\omega]\!] = \{\omega\}$. Clearly, φ_ω is a formula such that $\text{Bel}(\Psi) \cup \{\varphi_\omega\}$ is consistent. From (GCL2) we obtain $[\![\varphi_\omega]\!] = [\![\Psi \circledast \varphi_\omega]\!]$. Consequently, we obtain $\omega \in C_\Psi$ from the definition of C_Ψ. This shows $[\![\Psi]\!] \subseteq C_\Psi$.

$\preceq_\Psi$ *is a total preorder.* Reflexivity is a direct consequence of totality, thus in the following we show only totality and transitivity of $\preceq_\Psi$:

Totality. Let $\omega_1, \omega_2 \in C_\Psi$. We show totality by contradiction. Therefore, assume $\omega_1 \not\preceq_\Psi \omega_2$ and $\omega_2 \not\preceq_\Psi \omega_1$ in the following. From the definition of $\preceq_\Psi$ we obtain $\omega_1, \omega_2 \notin [\![\Psi \circledast \varphi_{\omega_1, \omega_2}]\!]$, where $\varphi_{\omega_1, \omega_2}$ is a formula such that $[\![\Psi \circledast \varphi_{\omega_1, \omega_2}]\!] = \{\omega_1, \omega_2\}$. From (GCL5), we obtain that $[\![\Psi \circledast \varphi_{\omega_1, \omega_2}]\!] = [\![\Psi \circledast (\varphi_{\omega_1} \vee \varphi_{\omega_2})]\!]$ holds. By (GCL7) we have that $[\![\Psi \circledast (\varphi_{\omega_1} \vee \varphi_{\omega_2})]\!]$ is equivalent to either $[\![\Psi \circledast \varphi_{\omega_1}]\!]$ or $[\![\Psi \circledast \varphi_{\omega_2}]\!]$ or $[\![\Psi \circledast \varphi_{\omega_1}]\!] \cup [\![\Psi \circledast \varphi_{\omega_2}]\!]$. From the definition of C_Ψ we obtain $[\![\Psi \circledast \varphi_{\omega_1}]\!] = \{\omega_1\}$ and $[\![\Psi \circledast \varphi_{\omega_2}]\!] = \{\omega_2\}$. Consequently, we obtain that $\omega_1 \in [\![\Psi \circledast \varphi_{\omega_1,\omega_2}]\!]$ or $\omega_2 \in [\![\Psi \circledast \varphi_{\omega_1,\omega_2}]\!]$ holds, which is a contradiction to our prior observation of $\omega_1, \omega_2 \notin [\![\Psi \circledast \varphi_{\omega_1,\omega_2}]\!]$.

Transitivity. Let $\omega_1, \omega_2, \omega_3 \in C_\Psi$. We show transitivity by contradiction. Therefore, we assume $\omega_1 \preceq_\Psi \omega_2$ and $\omega_2 \preceq_\Psi \omega_3$ and $\omega_1 \npreceq_\Psi \omega_3$ in the following. The latter assumption and the definition of $\preceq_\Psi$ yield $\omega_1 \notin [\![\Psi \circledast (\varphi_{\omega_1,\omega_3})]\!]$. By the definition of C_Ψ, and using (GCL5) and (GCL7), we obtain $[\![\Psi \circledast (\varphi_{\omega_1,\omega_3})]\!] = \{\omega_3\}$. In the following, we consider the same cases as in [41, p. 22]:

$\omega_1 \in [\![\Psi]\!]$. Observe that $\circledast$ satisfies (GCL2), and thus we obtain the contradiction $\omega_1 \in [\![\Psi \circledast \varphi_{\omega_1,\omega_3}]\!]$.

$\omega_1 \notin [\![\Psi]\!]$ *and* $\omega_2 \in [\![\Psi]\!]$. Observe that $\circledast$ satisfies (GCL2), and thus we have $\omega_2 \in [\![\Psi \circledast \varphi_{\omega_1,\omega_2}]\!]$ and $\omega_1 \notin [\![\Psi \circledast \varphi_{\omega_1,\omega_2}]\!]$. Thus, by the definition of $\preceq_\Psi$, we obtain the contradiction $\omega_1 \npreceq_\Psi \omega_2$.

$\omega_1 \notin [\![\Psi]\!]$ *and* $\omega_2 \notin [\![\Psi]\!]$. In the following let $\varphi_{\omega_1,\omega_2,\omega_3}$ be a formula such that $[\![\varphi_{\omega_1,\omega_2,\omega_3}]\!] = \{\omega_1, \omega_2, \omega_3\}$. Recall that by the definition of C_Ψ we have $[\![\Psi \circledast \varphi_\omega]\!] = \{\omega\}$ for each $\omega \in \{\omega_1, \omega_2, \omega_3\}$. We consider two subcases:

The case of $[\![\Psi \circledast \varphi_{\omega_1,\omega_2,\omega_3}]\!] = \{\omega_3\}$. Using (GCL5) we obtain $[\![\Psi \circledast \varphi_{\omega_1,\omega_2,\omega_3}]\!] = [\![\Psi \circledast (\varphi_{\omega_1} \vee \varphi_{\omega_2,\omega_3})]\!]$. Because we have $\omega_3 \notin [\![\Psi \circledast \varphi_{\omega_1}]\!]$, we obtain $[\![\Psi \circledast \varphi_{\omega_1,\omega_2,\omega_3}]\!] = [\![\Psi \circledast \varphi_{\omega_2,\omega_3}]\!]$ from (GCL7). Using the definition of $\preceq_\Psi$ and $[\![\Psi \circledast \varphi_{\omega_1,\omega_2,\omega_3}]\!] = \{\omega_3\}$ we obtain the contradiction $\omega_2 \npreceq_\Psi \omega_3$.

The case of $[\![\Psi \circledast \varphi_{\omega_1,\omega_2,\omega_3}]\!] \neq \{\omega_3\}$. By using (GCL5) we obtain $[\![\Psi \circledast \varphi_{\omega_1,\omega_2,\omega_3}]\!] = [\![\Psi \circledast (\varphi_{\omega_1,\omega_2} \vee \varphi_{\omega_1,\omega_3})]\!]$. Because we have $[\![\Psi \circledast \varphi_{\omega_1,\omega_3}]\!] = \{\omega_3\}$ and $[\![\Psi \circledast \varphi_{\omega_1,\omega_2,\omega_3}]\!] \neq \{\omega_3\}$, we obtain $[\![\Psi \circledast \varphi_{\omega_1,\omega_2}]\!] \subseteq [\![\Psi \circledast \varphi_{\omega_1,\omega_2,\omega_3}]\!]$ from (GCL7). By using the definition of $\preceq_\Psi$ and $\omega_1 \preceq_\Psi \omega_2$ we obtain $\omega_1 \in [\![\Psi \circledast \varphi_{\omega_1,\omega_2}]\!]$. Consequently, we have $\omega_1 \in [\![\Psi \circledast \varphi_{\omega_1,\omega_2,\omega_3}]\!]$.

By using (GCL5) again, we obtain $[\![\Psi \circledast \varphi_{\omega_1,\omega_2,\omega_3}]\!] = [\![\Psi \circledast (\varphi_{\omega_2} \vee \varphi_{\omega_1,\omega_3})]\!]$. Because we have $\omega_1 \in [\![\Psi \circledast \varphi_{\omega_1,\omega_2,\omega_3}]\!]$ and $[\![\Psi \circledast \varphi_{\omega_2}]\!] = \{\omega_2\}$, we obtain $[\![\Psi \circledast \varphi_{\omega_1,\omega_2,\omega_3}]\!] \cap \{\omega_1, \omega_3\} = [\![\Psi \circledast \varphi_{\omega_1,\omega_3}]\!]$ from (GCL7). Consequently, we obtain $\omega_1 \in [\![\Psi \circledast \varphi_{\omega_1,\omega_3}]\!]$, which yields the contradiction $\omega_1 \preceq_\Psi \omega_3$.

Satisfaction of (CLA$_\perp$). Suppose that $b_\Psi = \perp$ holds. Then, by the definition of b_Ψ we have $[\![\Psi]\!] \neq \emptyset$ and $\bot \in \mathrm{Bel}(\Psi \circledast \bot)$. We show $C_\Psi = \Omega$ by contradiction and assume therefore the existence of an $\omega \in \Omega$ such that $\omega \notin C_\Psi$. Because $\circledast$ satisfies (GCL6), we obtain $[\![\Psi \circledast \varphi_\omega]\!] \subseteq \{\omega\}$ from $\bot \in \mathrm{Bel}(\Psi \circledast \bot)$ and $\bot \models \varphi_\omega$. From $\omega \notin C_\Psi$ and the definition of C_Ψ we obtain that $[\![\Psi \circledast \varphi_\omega]\!] \neq \{\omega\}$ holds. By these observations, $[\![\Psi \circledast \varphi_\omega]\!] = \emptyset$ remains as the only possibility. From (GCL3) we obtain the contradiction that either $[\![\Psi]\!] = \emptyset$ or $[\![\varphi_\omega]\!] = \emptyset$ holds. Consequently, we have $\omega \in C_\Psi$.

In summary, $\Psi \mapsto (\preceq_\Psi, C_\Psi, b_\Psi)$ is a credibility-limited assignment.

We show that $\Psi \mapsto (\preceq_\Psi, C_\Psi, b_\Psi)$ is faithful. Therefore, suppose $[\![\Psi]\!] \neq \emptyset$.

(CLFA1) Let $\omega_1 \in [\![\Psi]\!]$ and $\omega_2 \in [\![\Psi]\!]$. From the satisfaction of (GCL2) by $\circledast$ we obtain $\omega_1, \omega_2 \in [\![\Psi \circledast \varphi_{\omega_1,\omega_2}]\!]$. Then, applying the definition of $\preceq_\Psi$ yields $\omega_1 \simeq_\Psi \omega_2$, i.e., $\omega_1 \preceq_\Psi \omega_2$ and $\omega_2 \preceq_\Psi \omega_1$.

(CLFA2) Let $\omega_1 \in [\![\Psi]\!]$ and $\omega_2 \notin [\![\Psi]\!]$. Using the satisfaction of (GCL2) by $\circledast$ again, we obtain $\omega_1 \in [\![\Psi \circledast \varphi_{\omega_1,\omega_2}]\!]$ and $\omega_2 \notin [\![\Psi \circledast \varphi_{\omega_1,\omega_2}]\!]$. From the definition of $\preceq_\Psi$ we obtain $\omega_1 <_\Psi \omega_2$.

Next, we show that $\Psi \mapsto (\preceq_\Psi, C_\Psi, b_\Psi)$ is revision-compatible with $\circledast$. Therefore, we consider four cases in the following: the case of $[\![\alpha]\!] \cap C_\Psi \neq \emptyset$, the case of $[\![\alpha]\!] = \emptyset$ and $b_\Psi = \bot$, the case of $[\![\alpha]\!] = \emptyset$ and $b_\Psi = \top$, and the case of $[\![\alpha]\!] \neq \emptyset$ and $[\![\alpha]\!] \cap C_\Psi = \emptyset$.

The case of $[\![\alpha]\!] \cap C_\Psi \neq \emptyset$. In this case, we directly obtain that α is consistent. Moreover, from $[\![\alpha]\!] \cap C_\Psi \neq \emptyset$ we obtain an interpretation $\omega \in [\![\alpha]\!] \cap C_\Psi$. The definition of C_Ψ yields $[\![\Psi \circledast \varphi_\omega]\!] = \{\omega\}$. We obtain $[\![\Psi \circledast \alpha]\!] \neq \emptyset$ from (GCL4) and $\varphi_\omega \models \alpha$, and from (GCL6) that $[\![\Psi \circledast \alpha]\!] \subseteq [\![\alpha]\!]$ holds.

As the next step, we show $\min([\![\alpha]\!], \preceq_\Psi) \subseteq [\![\Psi \circledast \alpha]\!]$ by contradiction. Suppose that there exists some $\omega \in \min([\![\alpha]\!], \preceq_\Psi)$ such that $\omega \notin [\![\Psi \circledast \alpha]\!]$ holds. We consider two subcases.

$\omega \in [\![\Psi]\!]$. Then we obtain $\omega \in [\![\Psi \circledast \alpha]\!]$ from (GCL2).

$\omega \notin [\![\Psi]\!]$. Because of $[\![\Psi \circledast \alpha]\!] \neq \emptyset$ there exists some $\omega' \in [\![\Psi \circledast \alpha]\!]$.

We consider the case of $\omega' \notin C_\Psi$. Consequently, we have $\omega' \notin [\![\Psi]\!]$. Now let γ be a formula with $\alpha \equiv \gamma \vee \varphi_{\omega'}$ and $\omega' \not\models \gamma$. Using (GCL5) we obtain that $[\![\Psi \circledast \alpha]\!] = [\![\Psi \circledast (\gamma \vee \varphi_{\omega'})]\!]$

holds. Note that by (GCL1) we have $[\![\Psi \circledast \gamma]\!] = [\![\Psi]\!]$ or $[\![\Psi \circledast \gamma]\!] \subseteq [\![\gamma]\!]$. This implies that we have $\omega' \notin [\![\Psi \circledast \gamma]\!]$. Consequently, we obtain $\omega' \in [\![\Psi \circledast \varphi_{\omega'}]\!]$ from (GCL7). Using $\omega' \notin [\![\Psi]\!]$, $\omega' \in [\![\Psi \circledast \varphi_{\omega'}]\!]$ and (GCL1), we obtain $[\![\Psi \circledast \varphi_{\omega'}]\!] = \{\omega'\}$, which yields the contradiction $\omega' \in C_\Psi$.

We consider the case of $\omega' \in C_\Psi$. Because of $\omega \in \min([\![\alpha]\!], \preceq_\Psi)$ we have $\omega \preceq_\Psi \omega'$. Moreover, from faithfulness and $\omega \notin [\![\Psi]\!]$, we obtain $\omega' \notin [\![\Psi]\!]$ from $\omega \in \min([\![\alpha]\!], \preceq_\Psi)$. From the definition of $\preceq_\Psi$ we obtain $\omega \in [\![\Psi \circledast \varphi_{\omega,\omega'}]\!]$. Now let γ be a formula such that $\omega, \omega' \notin [\![\gamma]\!]$ and $\alpha \equiv \gamma \vee \varphi_{\omega,\omega'}$. Note that by (GCL1) we have $[\![\Psi \circledast \gamma]\!] = [\![\Psi]\!]$ or $[\![\Psi \circledast \gamma]\!] \subseteq [\![\gamma]\!]$. This together with $\omega, \omega' \notin [\![\Psi]\!]$ implies $\omega' \notin [\![\Psi \circledast \gamma]\!]$. Using (GCL5) we obtain that $[\![\Psi \circledast \alpha]\!] = [\![\Psi \circledast (\gamma \vee \varphi_{\omega,\omega'})]\!]$ holds. Because $\circledast$ satisfies (GCL7) and $\omega' \notin [\![\Psi \circledast \gamma]\!]$ holds, we have $[\![\Psi \circledast \alpha]\!] = [\![\Psi \circledast \varphi_{\omega,\omega'}]\!]$ or $[\![\Psi \circledast \alpha]\!] = [\![\Psi \circledast \gamma]\!] \cup [\![\Psi \circledast \varphi_{\omega,\omega'}]\!]$. In both cases we obtain $\omega \in [\![\Psi \circledast \alpha]\!]$ from $\omega \in [\![\Psi \circledast \varphi_{\omega,\omega'}]\!]$.

In summary, $\min([\![\alpha]\!], \preceq_\Psi) \subseteq [\![\Psi \circledast \alpha]\!]$ holds.

We show in the following by contradiction that $[\![\Psi \circledast \alpha]\!] \subseteq \min([\![\alpha]\!], \preceq_\Psi)$ holds. Therefore, suppose that there exists some $\omega_1 \in [\![\Psi \circledast \alpha]\!]$ such that $\omega_1 \notin \min([\![\alpha]\!], \preceq_\Psi)$. The faithfulness of $\Psi \mapsto (\preceq_\Psi, C_\Psi, b_\Psi)$ and $\omega_1 \in [\![\Psi]\!]$ together imply $\omega_1 \in \min([\![\alpha]\!], \preceq_\Psi)$. In the following we consider the remaining case of $\omega_1 \notin [\![\Psi]\!]$. From $[\![\alpha]\!] \cap C_\Psi \neq \emptyset$ we obtain that there exists some $\omega_2 \in \Omega$ with $\omega_2 \in \min([\![\alpha]\!], \preceq_\Psi)$. As shown before, we have $\omega_2 \in [\![\Psi \circledast \alpha]\!]$. Because $\circledast$ satisfies (GCL2) and $\omega_2 \in [\![\Psi \circledast \alpha]\!]$, we obtain $\omega_2 \notin [\![\Psi]\!]$ from $\omega_1 \notin [\![\Psi]\!]$. Now let γ be a formula such that $\alpha \equiv \gamma \vee \varphi_{\omega_1,\omega_2}$ and $\omega_1, \omega_2 \notin [\![\gamma]\!]$. Note that by (GCL1) we have $[\![\Psi \circledast \gamma]\!] = [\![\Psi]\!]$ or $[\![\Psi \circledast \gamma]\!] \subseteq [\![\gamma]\!]$. This together with $\omega_1, \omega_2 \notin [\![\Psi]\!]$ implies $\omega_1, \omega_2 \notin [\![\Psi \circledast \gamma]\!]$. Using (GCL5) we obtain that $[\![\Psi \circledast \alpha]\!] = [\![\Psi \circledast (\gamma \vee \varphi_{\omega,\omega'})]\!]$ holds. Because $\circledast$ satisfies (GCL7) and $\omega_1, \omega_2 \notin [\![\Psi \circledast \gamma]\!]$ holds, we have $[\![\Psi \circledast \alpha]\!] = [\![\Psi \circledast \varphi_{\omega_1,\omega_2}]\!]$ or $[\![\Psi \circledast \alpha]\!] = [\![\Psi \circledast \gamma]\!] \cup [\![\Psi \circledast \varphi_{\omega_1,\omega_2}]\!]$. We obtain $[\![\Psi \circledast \alpha]\!] \cap \{\omega_1, \omega_2\} = [\![\Psi \circledast \varphi_{\omega_1,\omega_2}]\!] = \{\omega_1, \omega_2\}$. Applying (GCL5) and (GCL7) again yields $[\![\Psi \circledast \varphi_{\omega_1,\omega_2}]\!] = [\![\Psi \circledast \varphi_{\omega_1}]\!] \cup [\![\Psi \circledast \varphi_{\omega_2}]\!]$. This together with $\omega_1 \notin [\![\Psi]\!]$ and (GCL1) yields $[\![\Psi \circledast \varphi_{\omega_1}]\!] = \{\omega_1\}$. By the definition of C_Ψ, we obtain $\omega_1 \in C_\Psi$. Moreover, from $[\![\Psi \circledast \varphi_{\omega_1,\omega_2}]\!] = \{\omega_1, \omega_2\}$ we obtain $\omega_1 \preceq_\Psi \omega_2$ from the definition of $\preceq_\Psi$. This last observation together with $\omega_2 \in \min(\llbracket \alpha \rrbracket, \preceq_\Psi)$ implies the contradiction $\omega_1 \in \min(\llbracket \alpha \rrbracket, \preceq_\Psi)$.

The case of $\llbracket \alpha \rrbracket = \emptyset$ *and* $b_\Psi = \perp$. We show $\alpha \in \text{Bel}(\Psi \circledast \alpha)$, i..e, $\llbracket \Psi \circledast \alpha \rrbracket = \emptyset$. From the definition of b_Ψ we obtain $\perp \in \text{Bel}(\Psi \circledast \perp)$ from $b_\Psi = \perp$. Because $\circledast$ satisfies (GCL5), we obtain $\alpha \in \text{Bel}(\Psi \circledast \alpha)$.

The case of $\llbracket \alpha \rrbracket = \emptyset$ *and* $b_\Psi = \top$. We show $\text{Bel}(\Psi \circledast \alpha) = \text{Bel}(\Psi)$, i.e., $\llbracket \Psi \circledast \alpha \rrbracket = \llbracket \Psi \rrbracket$. Consulting (GCL1) yields that $\alpha \in \text{Bel}(\Psi \circledast \alpha)$ is the only non-trivial case to consider. Because $\circledast$ satisfies (GCL5) we obtain $\perp \in \text{Bel}(\Psi \circledast \perp)$. From the definition of b_Ψ, and from $b_\Psi = \top$ and $\perp \in \text{Bel}(\Psi \circledast \perp)$, we obtain $\llbracket \Psi \rrbracket = \emptyset$. Consequently, we have $\text{Bel}(\Psi \circledast \alpha) = \text{Bel}(\Psi)$.

The case of $\llbracket \alpha \rrbracket \neq \emptyset$ *and* $\llbracket \alpha \rrbracket \cap C_\Psi = \emptyset$. We show $\text{Bel}(\Psi \circledast \alpha) = \text{Bel}(\Psi)$. Note that $\llbracket \Psi \rrbracket \subseteq C_\Psi$ holds, and therefore $\llbracket \alpha \rrbracket \cap C_\Psi = \emptyset$ implies $\llbracket \alpha \rrbracket \cap \llbracket \Psi \rrbracket \neq \emptyset$. From the definition of C_Ψ we obtain $\llbracket \Psi \circledast \varphi_\omega \rrbracket \neq \{\omega\}$ for each $\omega \in \llbracket \alpha \rrbracket$.

If $\llbracket \alpha \rrbracket$ is a singleton set, then we obtain $\llbracket \Psi \circledast \alpha \rrbracket = \emptyset$. From consistency of α and (GCL3) we obtain that $\text{Bel}(\Psi)$ is inconsistent, showing that $\llbracket \Psi \rrbracket = \llbracket \Psi \circledast \alpha \rrbracket$ holds.

We consider the remaining case of $\llbracket \alpha \rrbracket = \{\omega_1, \ldots, \omega_n\}$ for $n > 1$. Towards a contradiction, suppose $\llbracket \Psi \rrbracket \neq \llbracket \Psi \circledast \alpha \rrbracket$. Thus, by (GCL1) we have $\llbracket \Psi \circledast \alpha \rrbracket \subseteq \llbracket \alpha \rrbracket$. We consider two subcases:

$\llbracket \Psi \circledast \alpha \rrbracket = \emptyset$. As before, from consistency of α and (GCL3) we obtain that $\text{Bel}(\Psi)$ is inconsistent, showing that $\llbracket \Psi \rrbracket = \llbracket \Psi \circledast \alpha \rrbracket$ holds.

$\llbracket \Psi \circledast \alpha \rrbracket \neq \emptyset$. Let $\omega \in \llbracket \Psi \circledast \alpha \rrbracket$ and let γ_ω be a formula such that $\alpha \equiv \gamma_\omega \vee \varphi_\omega$ and $\omega \notin \llbracket \gamma_\omega \rrbracket$. Note that by (GCL1) we have $\llbracket \Psi \circledast \gamma_\omega \rrbracket = \llbracket \Psi \rrbracket$ or $\llbracket \Psi \circledast \gamma_\omega \rrbracket \subseteq \llbracket \gamma_\omega \rrbracket$. This together with $\omega \notin \llbracket \Psi \rrbracket$ implies $\omega \notin \llbracket \Psi \circledast \gamma_\omega \rrbracket$. By (GCL5) we obtain $\llbracket \Psi \circledast \alpha \rrbracket = \llbracket \Psi \circledast (\gamma_\omega \vee \varphi_\omega) \rrbracket$. Because $\circledast$ satisfies (GCL7) and $\omega \notin \llbracket \Psi \circledast \gamma_\omega \rrbracket$ holds, we have $\llbracket \Psi \circledast \alpha \rrbracket = \llbracket \Psi \circledast \varphi_\omega \rrbracket$ or $\llbracket \Psi \circledast \alpha \rrbracket = \llbracket \Psi \circledast \gamma_\omega \rrbracket \cup \llbracket \Psi \circledast \varphi_\omega \rrbracket$. From this observation, we obtain $\llbracket \Psi \circledast \alpha \rrbracket \cap \{\omega\} = \llbracket \Psi \circledast \varphi_\omega \rrbracket = \{\omega\}$, a contradiction to $\llbracket \Psi \circledast \varphi_\omega \rrbracket \neq \{\omega\}$.

The "$\Leftarrow$"-direction. In the following, let $\circledast$ be a belief change operator for $\mathcal{E}$ and let $\Psi \mapsto (\preceq_\Psi, C_\Psi, b_\Psi)$ be a faithful credibility-limited assignment that is revision-compatible with $\circledast$. We show satisfaction of (GCL1), (GCL2), (GCL4), (GCL3) and (GCL5)–

(GCL7).

(GCL1) Due to the credibility-limited-compatibility of $\Psi \mapsto (\preceq_\Psi, C_\Psi, b_\Psi)$ with $\circledast$ there are three cases to consider. If $\llbracket \alpha \rrbracket \cap C_\Psi \neq \emptyset$, we obtain $\llbracket \Psi \circledast \alpha \rrbracket \subseteq \llbracket \alpha \rrbracket$. Consequently, we have that $\alpha \in \mathrm{Bel}(\Psi \circledast \alpha)$. If $\llbracket \alpha \rrbracket = \emptyset$ and $b_\Psi = \bot$ holds, we obtain $\llbracket \Psi \circledast \alpha \rrbracket = \emptyset$. Consequently, we have $\mathrm{Bel}(\Psi \circledast \alpha) = \mathrm{Cn}(\bot)$, and thus $\alpha \in \mathrm{Bel}(\Psi \circledast \alpha)$ holds. If none of the cases above applies, we obtain $\llbracket \Psi \circledast \alpha \rrbracket = \llbracket \Psi \rrbracket$, which is equivalent to $\mathrm{Bel}(\Psi \circledast \alpha) = \mathrm{Bel}(\Psi)$.

(GCL2) Suppose that $\mathrm{Bel}(\Psi) + \alpha$ is consistent, i.e., $\llbracket \Psi \rrbracket \cap \llbracket \alpha \rrbracket$ is non-empty. Due to the faithfulness of $\Psi \mapsto (\preceq_\Psi, C_\Psi, b_\Psi)$, we obtain that $\llbracket \Psi \rrbracket \cap \llbracket \alpha \rrbracket = \min(\llbracket \alpha \rrbracket, \preceq_\Psi)$ holds. From the credibility-limited-compatibility of $\Psi \mapsto (\preceq_\Psi, C_\Psi, b_\Psi)$ with $\circledast$ we obtain $\llbracket \Psi \circledast \alpha \rrbracket = \llbracket \Psi \rrbracket \cap \llbracket \alpha \rrbracket$. This is equivalent to $\mathrm{Bel}(\Psi \circledast \alpha) = \mathrm{Bel}(\Psi) + \alpha$.

(GCL5) Let $\alpha \equiv \beta$, i.e., $\llbracket \alpha \rrbracket = \llbracket \beta \rrbracket$. From credibility-limited-compatibility of $\Psi \mapsto (\preceq_\Psi, C_\Psi, b_\Psi)$ with $\circledast$ we immediately obtain $\llbracket \Psi \circledast \alpha \rrbracket = \llbracket \Psi \circledast \beta \rrbracket$.

(GCL4) Suppose that $\mathrm{Bel}(\Psi \circledast \alpha)$ is consistent and $\alpha \models \beta$ holds, i.e., we have $\llbracket \Psi \circledast \alpha \rrbracket \neq \emptyset$ and $\llbracket \alpha \rrbracket \subseteq \llbracket \beta \rrbracket$. We show that $\mathrm{Bel}(\Psi \circledast \beta)$ is consistent. If $\alpha \equiv \beta$, we obtain the claim directly from (GCL5). In the following we assume $\llbracket \alpha \rrbracket \subsetneq \llbracket \beta \rrbracket$. Consequently, we have that $\llbracket \beta \rrbracket \neq \emptyset$. From credibility-limited-compatibility of $\Psi \mapsto (\preceq_\Psi, C_\Psi, b_\Psi)$ with $\circledast$ and consistency of $\llbracket \Psi \circledast \alpha \rrbracket$ we obtain that either $\llbracket \Psi \circledast \alpha \rrbracket = \min(\llbracket \alpha \rrbracket, \preceq_\Psi)$ or $\llbracket \Psi \circledast \alpha \rrbracket = \llbracket \Psi \rrbracket$ holds. We consider three cases:

α *is inconsistent.* In this case, we have $\llbracket \Psi \circledast \alpha \rrbracket = \llbracket \Psi \rrbracket$. As a direct consequence, we obtain from credibility-limited-compatibility that $\llbracket \Psi \rrbracket \neq \emptyset$ holds. Recalling that β is consistent, consultation of credibility-limited-compatibility reveals that $\mathrm{Bel}(\Psi \circledast \beta)$ is consistent in all cases.

α *is consistent and* $\llbracket \Psi \circledast \alpha \rrbracket = \min(\llbracket \alpha \rrbracket, \preceq_\Psi)$. From credibility-limited-compatibility of $\Psi \mapsto (\preceq_\Psi, C_\Psi, b_\Psi)$ with $\circledast$ we obtain $\llbracket \alpha \rrbracket \cap C_\Psi \neq \emptyset$. Consequently, we also have $\llbracket \beta \rrbracket \cap C_\Psi \neq \emptyset$. Consulting credibility-limited-compatibility yields that $\mathrm{Bel}(\Psi \circledast \beta)$ is consistent.

α *is consistent and* $\llbracket \Psi \circledast \alpha \rrbracket = \llbracket \Psi \rrbracket$. From consistency of α we obtain consistency of β. Thus, by credibility-limited-compatibility, we obtain that $\mathrm{Bel}(\Psi \circledast \beta)$ is consistent.

(GCL3) Suppose that $\text{Bel}(\Psi \circledast \alpha)$ is inconsistent. We show that
$\text{Bel}(\Psi)$ is inconsistent or α is inconsistent, by obtaining a contradiction when assuming the contrary, i.e., $\text{Bel}(\Psi)$ is consistent and α is consistent. From credibility-limited-compatibility
of $\Psi \mapsto (\preceq_\Psi, C_\Psi, b_\Psi)$ with $\circledast$ and consistency of α, we obtain
$[\![\Psi \circledast \alpha]\!] = [\![\Psi]\!]$, a contradiction between the inconsistency of
$\text{Bel}(\Psi \circledast \alpha)$ and the consistency of $\text{Bel}(\Psi)$.

(GCL6) Suppose $\alpha \in \text{Bel}(\Psi \circledast \alpha)$ and $\alpha \models \beta$, i.e., $[\![\Psi \circledast \alpha]\!] \subseteq [\![\alpha]\!]$
and $[\![\alpha]\!] \subseteq [\![\beta]\!]$. We show $\beta \in \text{Bel}(\Psi \circledast \beta)$. If $[\![\beta]\!] \cap C_\Psi$ is
non-empty, then we obtain $\beta \in \text{Bel}(\Psi \circledast \beta)$. If $[\![\beta]\!] = \emptyset$, then
$[\![\alpha]\!] = \emptyset$. We obtain from $[\![\Psi \circledast \alpha]\!] \subseteq [\![\alpha]\!]$ that $\beta \in \text{Bel}(\Psi \circledast \beta)$
holds. In the remaining case of $[\![\beta]\!] \cap C_\Psi = \emptyset$ and β is
consistent, we obtain $[\![\alpha]\!] \cap C_\Psi = \emptyset$ from $[\![\alpha]\!] \subseteq [\![\beta]\!]$. From
$[\![\Psi \circledast \alpha]\!] \subseteq [\![\alpha]\!]$ and the credibility-limited-compatibility of
$\Psi \mapsto (\preceq_\Psi, C_\Psi, b_\Psi)$ with $\circledast$ we obtain two cases:

$[\![\Psi \circledast \alpha]\!] = [\![\Psi]\!]$. Using the consistency of β and the credibility-
limited-compatibility of $\Psi \mapsto (\preceq_\Psi, C_\Psi, b_\Psi)$ with $\circledast$ again,
we obtain $[\![\Psi \circledast \beta]\!] = [\![\Psi]\!]$. From $[\![\Psi]\!] = [\![\Psi \circledast \alpha]\!] \subseteq [\![\alpha]\!]$ and
$[\![\alpha]\!] \subseteq [\![\beta]\!]$ we obtain $[\![\Psi \circledast \alpha]\!] = [\![\Psi]\!] = [\![\Psi \circledast \beta]\!] \subseteq [\![\beta]\!]$.

$[\![\alpha]\!] = \emptyset$ and $b_\Psi = \bot$. Because β is consistent and $(\text{CLA}_\bot)$ holds,
we obtain $C_\Psi = \Omega$, which is a contradiction to $[\![\beta]\!] \cap C_\Psi = \emptyset$.

(GCL7) In the following, suppose that α, β, γ are formulas with
$\gamma = \alpha \vee \beta$. We show that $[\![\Psi \circledast \gamma]\!] = [\![\Psi \circledast \alpha]\!]$ or $[\![\Psi \circledast \gamma]\!] =$
$[\![\Psi \circledast \beta]\!]$ or $[\![\Psi \circledast \gamma]\!] = [\![\Psi \circledast \alpha]\!] \cup [\![\Psi \circledast \beta]\!]$ holds. Note that by
credibility-limited-compatibility of $\Psi \mapsto (\preceq_\Psi, C_\Psi, b_\Psi)$ with $\circledast$
there are several cases for each of α and β. In the following, we
consider (potentially overlapping) cases, all other not explicitly
mentioned cases will follow by (GCL5) and symmetry:

The case of $[\![\alpha]\!] \cap C_\Psi \neq \emptyset$ and $[\![\beta]\!] \cap C_\Psi \neq \emptyset$. For this case
observe that $[\![\gamma]\!] \cap C_\Psi = ([\![\alpha]\!] \cap C_\Psi) \cup ([\![\beta]\!] \cap C_\Psi)$ holds. We
obtain satisfaction of (GCL7) by Lemma 2.1.

The case of $[\![\alpha]\!] \cap C_\Psi \neq \emptyset$ and $[\![\beta]\!] \cap C_\Psi = \emptyset$. In this case, we
obtain $[\![\gamma]\!] \cap C_\Psi = [\![\alpha]\!] \cap C_\Psi$ from $[\![\alpha]\!] \cap C_\Psi \neq \emptyset$. Considering
credibility-limited-compatibility yields that $[\![\Psi \circledast \gamma]\!] = [\![\Psi \circledast$
$\alpha]\!]$ holds.

The case of $[\![\alpha]\!] = [\![\beta]\!]$. We obtain that $[\![\gamma]\!] = [\![\alpha]\!] = [\![\beta]\!]$. From
(GCL5) we obtain $[\![\Psi \circledast \gamma]\!] = [\![\Psi \circledast \alpha]\!] = [\![\Psi \circledast \beta]\!]$.

The case of $[\![\alpha]\!] \cap C_\Psi = \emptyset$, and $[\![\beta]\!] \cap C_\Psi = \emptyset$ and $[\![\alpha]\!] \neq [\![\beta]\!]$.
We obtain $[\![\gamma]\!] = [\![\alpha]\!] \cup [\![\beta]\!] \neq \emptyset$ from $[\![\alpha]\!] \neq [\![\beta]\!]$. Because

$[\![\alpha]\!] \cap C_\Psi = \emptyset$ and $[\![\beta]\!] \cap C_\Psi = \emptyset$ hold, we have $[\![\gamma]\!] \cap C_\Psi = \emptyset$. We obtain $[\![\Psi \circledast \gamma]\!] = [\![\Psi]\!]$. Moreover, we have that $[\![\alpha]\!] \neq \emptyset$ or $[\![\beta]\!] \neq \emptyset$ holds. This implies that $[\![\Psi \circledast \alpha]\!] = [\![\Psi]\!]$ or $[\![\Psi \circledast \beta]\!] = [\![\Psi]\!]$ holds. We obtain that at last one of $[\![\Psi \circledast \gamma]\!] = [\![\Psi \circledast \alpha]\!]$ or $[\![\Psi \circledast \gamma]\!] = [\![\Psi \circledast \beta]\!]$ holds.

This completes the proof of Theorem 7.12.   □

In the following, we consider an example for a generalized credibility-limited revision operator and demonstrate the semantic characterization by Theorem 7.12.

Example 7.13. *Let* $\Sigma = \{a, b\}$ *and let* $\mathcal{E} = \{\Psi_\bot, \Psi_{\{ab\}}, \Psi_{\{\overline{a}b\}}, \Psi_{\{a\overline{b}\}}, \Psi_{\{\overline{ab}\}}, \Psi_{\{\overline{ab},a\overline{b}\}}\}$ *be a set of epistemic states with:*

$$[\![\Psi_\bot]\!] = \emptyset \qquad [\![\Psi_{\{ab\}}]\!] = \{ab\} \qquad [\![\Psi_{\{a\overline{b}\}}]\!] = \{a\overline{b}\}$$

$$[\![\Psi_{\{\overline{ab},a\overline{b}\}}]\!] = \{\overline{a}b, a\overline{b}\} \qquad [\![\Psi_{\{\overline{a}b\}}]\!] = \{\overline{a}b\} \qquad [\![\Psi_{\{\overline{ab}\}}]\!] = \{\overline{ab}\}$$

In the following we will obtain a generalized credibility-limited revision operator $\circledast$ *by specifying a faithful credibility-limited assignment that is revision-compatible with* $\circ$*. We use the following linear order* $\ll$ *on* Ω *given by:*

$$ab \quad \ll \quad \overline{a}b \quad \ll \quad a\overline{b} \quad \ll \quad \overline{ab}$$

We specify $\Psi \mapsto (\preceq_\Psi, C_\Psi, b_\Psi)$ *stepwise and start by providing* C_Ψ *for each* $\Psi \in \mathcal{E}$*:*

$$C_{\Psi_\bot} = \emptyset \qquad C_{\Psi_{\{ab\}}} = \Omega \qquad C_{\Psi_{\{a\overline{b}\}}} = \{ab, a\overline{b}\}$$

$$C_{\Psi_{\{\overline{ab},a\overline{b}\}}} = \{\overline{a}b, a\overline{b}, \overline{ab}\} \qquad C_{\Psi_{\{\overline{a}b\}}} = \{\overline{a}b\} \qquad C_{\Psi_{\{\overline{ab}\}}} = \{\overline{a}b, a\overline{b}, \overline{aa}\}$$

We set $b_\Psi = \top$ *for each* $\Psi \in \mathcal{E} \setminus \{\Psi_{\{ab\}}\}$*, and set* $b_{\Psi_{\{ab\}}} = \bot$*. For each* $\Psi \in \mathcal{E} \setminus \{\Psi_{\{\overline{ab}\}}\}$ *we set* $\preceq_\Psi \subseteq (C_\Psi \times C_\Psi)$ *as*

$$\preceq_\Psi = ((\ll \cap (C_\Psi \times C_\Psi)) \setminus (C_\Psi \times [\![\Psi]\!])) \cup ([\![\Psi]\!] \times C_\Psi),$$

i.e., $\preceq_\Psi$ *is the total preorder on* C_Ψ *such that* $\min(C_\Psi, \preceq_\Psi) = [\![\Psi]\!]$ *and the remaining elements in* $C_\Psi \setminus [\![\Psi]\!]$ *are ordered according to* $\ll$*. For* $\Psi_{\{\overline{ab}\}}$ *we specify* $\preceq_{\Psi_{\{\overline{ab}\}}} \subseteq (C_{\Psi_{\{\overline{ab}\}}} \times C_{\Psi_{\{\overline{ab}\}}})$ *as follows:*

$$\overline{ab} \preceq_{\Psi_{\{\overline{ab}\}}} \overline{a}b \qquad \overline{a}b \preceq_{\Psi_{\{\overline{ab}\}}} \overline{a}b \qquad a\overline{b} \preceq_{\Psi_{\{\overline{ab}\}}} \overline{a}b$$

$$\overline{ab} \preceq_{\Psi_{\{\overline{ab}\}}} a\overline{b} \qquad \overline{a}b \preceq_{\Psi_{\{\overline{ab}\}}} a\overline{b} \qquad a\overline{b} \preceq_{\Psi_{\{\overline{ab}\}}} a\overline{b}$$

$$\overline{ab} \preceq_{\Psi_{\{\overline{ab}\}}} \overline{ab}$$

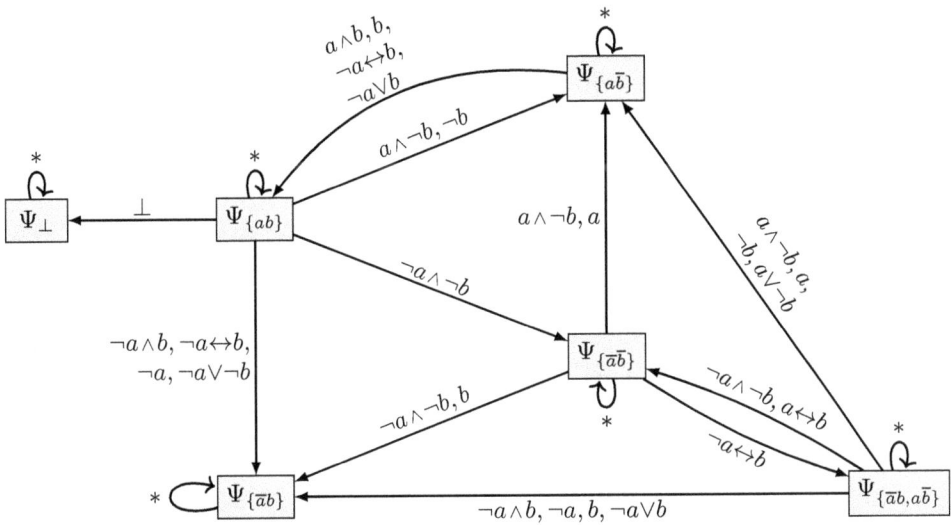

Figure 7.3: Graphical representation of the generalized credibility-limited revision operator ∘ given in Example 6.9.

A belief change operator ⊛ *for* $\mathcal{E}$ *that is compatible with* $\Psi \mapsto (\preceq_\Psi, C_\Psi, b_\Psi)$ *is then:*

$$\Psi \circledast \alpha = \begin{cases} \Psi_{\llbracket\Psi\rrbracket \cap \llbracket\alpha\rrbracket} & \text{if } \llbracket\Psi\rrbracket \cap \llbracket\alpha\rrbracket \neq \emptyset \\ \Psi_\bot & \text{if } \llbracket\Psi\rrbracket = \emptyset \text{ and } \Psi = \Psi_{\{ab\}} \\ \Psi_{\{\bar{a}b, a\bar{b}\}} & \text{if } \{\bar{a}b, a\bar{b}\} \subseteq \llbracket\alpha\rrbracket \text{ and } \Psi = \Psi_{\{\bar{a}b\}} \\ \Psi_{\min(\llbracket\alpha\rrbracket, \ll)} & \text{otherwise} \end{cases}$$

By Theorem 7.12, we obtain that ⊛ *is a generalized credibility-limited revision operator. A graphical representation of this operator is given in Figure 7.3.*

Note that ⊛ in Example 7.13 has properties that AGM revision operators do not have:

- The beliefs accepted for revision are not the full language $\mathcal{L}$.
- The selection of beliefs accepted for revision is done individually for each epistemic state.
- Inconsistent beliefs are only accepted for revision in selected epistemic states.

Moreover, ⊛ in Example 7.13 demonstrates that in contrast to the credibility-limited revision operators considered by Booth et al. [27], generalized credibility-limited revision operators, as defined in Definition 7.8, are able to deal with inconsistent input and with inconsistent epistemic states, and therefore are fully compatible with the Darwiche-Pearl framework, as introduced in Section 6.1. Furthermore, note that dealing with inconsistent belief states is a feature all theorems (which are close to Theorem 7.12) of the investigations by Hansson et al. [77] do not have[7].

7.5. Properties of Credibility-Limited Revision

The following proposition points out that our generalization approach is successful in the sense that every AGM revision operator for epistemic states is indeed a generalized credibility-limited revision operator in the sense of Definition 7.8.

Proposition 7.14. *Let $\mathcal{E}$ be a set of epistemic states and let $*$ be a belief change operator for $\mathcal{E}$. The operator $*$ is an AGM revision operator for $\mathcal{E}$ if and only if $*$ is a generalized credibility-limited revision operator for $\mathcal{E}$ which is revision-compatible with some faithful credibility-limited assignment $\Psi \mapsto (\preceq_\Psi, C_\Psi, b_\Psi)$ where $C_\Psi = \Omega$ and $b_\Psi = \bot$ for each $\Psi \in \mathcal{E}$.*

Proof. The straightforward way of mapping a faithful assignment $\Psi \mapsto \leq_\Psi$ to a faithful credibility-limited assignment $\Psi \mapsto (\preceq_\Psi, C_\Psi, b_\Psi)$ is by setting $C_\Psi = \Omega$, setting $\preceq_\Psi = \leq_\Psi$, and setting $b_\Psi = \bot$. This is a bijective function. Clearly, this function maps a faithful assignment, that is revision-compatible with $*$, to a faithful credibility-limited assignment, that is revision-compatible with $*$.

For the other direction, we have, inverse to the translation above, that a faithful revision-compatible assignment with the properties specified above is mapped to a faithful revision-compatible assignment $\Psi \mapsto \leq_\Psi$ by setting $\leq_\Psi = \preceq_\Psi$. We obtain again that compatibility is preserved, i.e., this translation maps a faithful credibility-limited assignment, that is revision-compatible with $*$, to a faithful assignment,

---

[7]   Hansson et al. consider only consistent belief sets for all theorems concerning sphere-based belief change [77]; see also Chapter 3 for a note on the relation between systems of spheres and total preorders.

that is revision-compatible with $*$. Consequently, the claim follows by Proposition 6.7 and Theorem 7.12. $\qquad\square$

Next, we show that generalized credibility-limited revision really extends credibility-limited revision for epistemic states as proposed in [27]. Therefore, we use Theorem 7.12 to characterize operators that satisfy (CL1)–(CL6), including (CL3), when there is no epistemic state with an inconsistent belief set (see global consistency, defined on p. 120).

Proposition 7.15. *Let $\mathcal{E}$ be a global consistent set of epistemic states and let $\circledast$ be a belief change operator for $\mathcal{E}$. The operator $\circledast$ satisfies (CL1)–(CL6) if and only if there is a credibility-limited assignment $\Psi \mapsto (\preceq_\Psi, C_\Psi, b_\Psi)$ that is revision-compatible with $\circledast$ such that $b_\Psi = \top$ for each $\Psi \in \mathcal{E}$.*

Proof. We consider both directions of the claim independently.

   The "$\Rightarrow$"-direction. If $\circledast$ satisfies (CL1)–(CL6), then (GCL1)–(GCL7) are satisfied (as (GCL3) and (GCL4) are implied by (CL3)). By Theorem 7.12, there exists some faithful credibility-limited assignment $\Psi \mapsto (\preceq_\Psi, C_\Psi, b_\Psi)$ that is revision-compatible with $\circledast$. Let $\Psi \in \mathcal{E}$ be an epistemic state. From (CL3) we obtain that $[\![\Psi \circledast \alpha]\!] \neq \emptyset$ for each $\alpha \in \mathcal{L}$. Consequently, we have $b_\Psi = \top$, as otherwise we would obtain $[\![\Psi \circledast \bot]\!] = \emptyset$ by revision-compatible.

   The "$\Leftarrow$"-direction. Suppose there is a credibility-limited assignment $\Psi \mapsto (\preceq_\Psi, C_\Psi, b_\Psi)$ that is revision-compatible with $\circledast$ such that $b_\Psi = \top$ for each $\Psi \in \mathcal{E}$. By Theorem 7.12, we obtain that $\circledast$ satisfies (CL1), (CL2), and (CL4)–(CL6). For satisfaction of (CL3) observe that by revision-compatibility we obtain $[\![\Psi \circledast \bot]\!] \neq \emptyset$ due to $b_\Psi = \top$ for each $\Psi \in \mathcal{E}$. For all consistent formula α we have $[\![\Psi \circledast \alpha]\!] \neq \emptyset$ due to the global consistency of $\mathcal{E}$. $\qquad\square$

We want to remark that there is *no* generalized credibility-limited revision operator $\circledast$ for $\mathcal{E}$ that satisfies (CL3) whenever $\mathcal{E}$ violates global consistency. The rationale is that for each Ψ with Bel(Ψ) is inconsistent, we will always have $\bot \in$ Bel($\Psi \circledast \bot$) due to (GCL1). Thus, the extension to generalized credibility-limited revision operators made the whole approach of credibility-limited revision available in strictly more sets of epistemic states. Moreover, in comparison to the case of AGM revision operators (see Theorem 6.8), a set of epistemic states $\mathcal{E}$ has to obey fewer restrictions to guarantee existence of a generalized credibility-limited revision operator for $\mathcal{E}$.

Proposition 7.16. *Let $\mathcal{E}$ be a set of epistemic states. There exists a generalized credibility-limited revision operator for $\mathcal{E}$ if and only if $\mathcal{E}$ satisfies, for each $\Psi \in \mathcal{E}$, the following:*

(CL-ES) *If $M \subseteq [\![\Psi]\!]$ with $M \neq \emptyset$, then there exists $\Psi_M \in \mathcal{E}$ such that $[\![\Psi_M]\!] = M$.*

Proof. We start by showing that the existence of a generalized credibility-limited revision operator $\circledast$ implies satisfaction of (CL-ES). For each $M \subseteq \Omega$ let φ_M be a formula such that $[\![\varphi_M]\!] = M$ holds. In the following let $\Psi \in \mathcal{E}$ be an epistemic state. If $[\![\Psi]\!] = \emptyset$ holds, then the statement of (CL-ES) is trivially true. We assume in the following that $[\![\Psi]\!] \neq \emptyset$ holds. Let $M \subsetneq [\![\Psi]\!]$ be such that $M \neq \emptyset$ holds. Clearly, because $\circledast$ satisfies (GCL2), revision of Ψ by φ_M yields an epistemic state $\Psi \circledast \varphi_M$ such that $[\![\Psi \circledast \varphi_M]\!] = M$ is satisfied. In summary, (CL-ES) is satisfied.

For the remaining direction, let $\mathcal{E}$ be a (non-empty) set of epistemic states that satisfies (CL-ES). For each $M \subseteq \Omega$ let Ψ_M denote a uniquely chosen epistemic state from $\mathcal{E}$ such that $[\![\Psi_M]\!] = M$ (as far as such an epistemic state Ψ_M exists in $\mathcal{E}$). We construct a belief change operator $\circledast$ for $\mathcal{E}$ as follows:

$$\Psi \circledast \alpha = \begin{cases} \Psi_{[\![\Psi]\!] \cap [\![\alpha]\!]} & \text{if } [\![\Psi]\!] \cap [\![\alpha]\!] \neq \emptyset \\ \Psi & \text{otherwise} \end{cases}$$

Considering (CL-ES) and the definition of $\circ$ shows that for all $\Psi \in \mathcal{E}$ and $\alpha \in \mathcal{L}$ the state $\Psi \circledast \alpha$ exists. Now let $\Psi \mapsto (\preceq_\Psi, C_\Psi, b_\Psi)$ be the function that yields, for each $\Psi \in \mathcal{E}$, the following:

$$C_\Psi = [\![\Psi]\!] \qquad \preceq_\Psi = [\![\Psi]\!] \times [\![\Psi]\!] \qquad b_\Psi = \top$$

Indeed, $\Psi \mapsto (\preceq_\Psi, C_\Psi, b_\Psi)$ is a faithful credibility-limited assignment. Moreover, $\Psi \mapsto (\preceq_\Psi, C_\Psi, b_\Psi)$ is revision-compatible with $\circledast$. By Theorem 7.12, we obtain that $\circledast$ is a generalized credibility-limited revision operator for $\mathcal{E}$. $\square$

7.6. Realizability and Credibility-Limited Revision

Not every acceptance description will give rise to a credibility-limited revision operator. In particular, we have already seen that a credibility-limited revision operator does *not* exist for every set of epistemic states (see Proposition 7.16), yet for every set of epistemic states an acceptance description exists.

Proposition 7.17. *Let $\mathcal{E}$ be a set of epistemic states and let $\circledast$ be a belief change operator for $\mathcal{E}$. If $\circledast$ is a generalized credibility-limited revision operator for $\mathcal{E}$, then $\mathrm{Bel}(\Psi) \subseteq Scp^{\circledast}(\Psi)$ and $Scp^{\circledast}(\Psi)$ satisfies single-sentence closure and disjunction completeness.*

Proof. Due to Theorem 7.12, there exists a faithful credibility-limited assignment $\Psi \mapsto (\preceq_{\Psi}, C_{\Psi}, b_{\Psi})$ that is revision-compatible with $\circledast$. Recall that $\preceq_{\Psi}$ is a relation over $C_{\Psi} \subseteq \Omega$. Because $\Psi \mapsto (\preceq_{\Psi}, C_{\Psi}, b_{\Psi})$ is revision-compatible with $\circledast$ and $[\![\Psi]\!] \subseteq C_{\Psi}$ holds, we obtain $Scp^{\circledast}(\Psi) = \{\alpha \mid [\![\alpha]\!] \cap C_{\Psi} \neq \emptyset\}$ whenever $b_{\Psi} = \top$. If $b_{\Psi} = \bot$, then $Scp^{\circledast}(\Psi) = \{\beta \mid \beta \equiv \bot\} \cup \{\alpha \mid [\![\alpha]\!] \cap C_{\Psi} \neq \emptyset\}$. In both cases, the case of $b_{\Psi} = \top$ and $b_{\Psi} = \bot$, we obtain that $Scp^{\circledast}(\Psi)$ satisfies single-sentence closure. Furthermore, disjunction completeness holds due to Proposition 7.3. $\square$

In the remaining part of this section, we will formally describe circumstances required for $\mathcal{A}$ to give rise to a credibility-limited revision operator. Therefore, consider the following notion.

Definition 7.18. *Let $\mathcal{E}$ be a set of epistemic states that satisfies (CL-ES) and let $\mathcal{A} : \mathcal{E} \to \mathcal{P}(\mathcal{L})$ be an acceptance description for $\mathcal{E}$. We say that $\mathcal{A}$ is credibility-limited revision compatible with $\mathcal{E}$ if the following is satisfied:*

(AD-CL1) $\mathrm{Bel}(\Psi) \subseteq \mathcal{A}(\Psi)$ *for each $\Psi \in \mathcal{E}$.*
(AD-CL2) *If $\mathrm{Bel}(\Psi) \neq \mathcal{L}$, then there exists $\Psi_{\omega} \in \mathcal{E}$ such that $\mathrm{Bel}(\Psi_{\omega}) = \mathrm{Cn}(\varphi_{\omega})$ for each $\omega \in \Omega$ with $\varphi_{\omega} \in \mathcal{A}(\Psi)$.*

The following proposition shows that credibility-limited revision compatibility is a sufficient condition for compliance of an acceptance description with some generalized credibility-limited revision operator.

Proposition 7.19. *Let $\mathcal{E}$ be a set of epistemic states that satisfies* (CL-ES). *For every credibility-limited revision compatible acceptance description* $\mathcal{A} : \mathcal{E} \to \mathcal{P}(\mathcal{L})$ *for $\mathcal{E}$ there exists a generalized credibility-limited revision operator $\circledast$ for $\mathcal{E}$ with*

$$Scp^{\circledast}(\Psi) = \mathcal{A}(\Psi)$$

for all $\Psi \in \mathcal{E}$.

Proof. Let $\mathcal{A} : \mathcal{E} \to \mathcal{P}(\mathcal{L})$ be a credibility-limited revision compatible acceptance description for $\mathcal{E}$. Recall that, according to Proposition 7.3, for each $L \subseteq \mathcal{L}$, that satisfies single-sentence closure and disjunction completeness, there exists a set of interpretations $M_L \subseteq \Omega$ such that $L \setminus \{\beta \mid \bot \equiv \beta\} = \{\psi \mid [\![\psi]\!] \cap M_L \neq \emptyset\}$. With $M_{\Psi} \subseteq \Omega$ we denote the following set of interpretations:

$$M_{\Psi} = \begin{cases} \emptyset & \text{if } \mathrm{Bel}(\Psi) = \mathcal{L} \\ M_{\mathcal{A}(\Psi)} & \text{otherwise} \end{cases}$$

Note that $\mathrm{Bel}(\Psi) = \mathcal{L}$ implies $\mathcal{A}(\Psi) = \mathcal{L}$ due to (AD-CL1). Moreover, for each $M \subseteq \Omega$ let Ψ_M denote a uniquely chosen epistemic state from $\mathcal{E}$, such that $[\![\Psi_M]\!] = M$ (as far as such an epistemic state exists).

In the following, let $\ll$ be an arbitrary (but fixed chosen) linear order on Ω. For each $\Psi \in \mathcal{E}$, we denote with $\ll_{\Psi}$ the linear order on M_{Ψ} such that

$$\ll_{\Psi} = \ll \cap (M_{\Psi} \times M_{\Psi})$$

holds, i.e., $\ll_{\Psi}$ is the restriction of $\ll$ to M_{Ψ}.

Let $\circledast : \mathcal{E} \times \mathcal{L} \to \mathcal{E}$ be the belief change operator given by:

$$\Psi \circledast \alpha = \begin{cases} \Psi_{[\![\alpha]\!] \cap [\![\Psi]\!]} & \text{if } [\![\alpha]\!] \cap [\![\Psi]\!] \neq \emptyset \\ \Psi_{\min([\![\alpha]\!], \ll_{\Psi})} & \text{if } [\![\alpha]\!] \cap [\![\Psi]\!] = \emptyset \text{ and } [\![\alpha]\!] \cap M_{\Psi} \neq \emptyset \\ \Psi_{\emptyset} & \text{if } [\![\alpha]\!] = \emptyset \text{ and } \bot \in \mathcal{A}(\Psi) \\ \Psi & \text{otherwise} \end{cases} \quad (\bigstar)$$

In order to proof that $\circledast$ exists it is sufficient to show that $\Psi \circledast \alpha$ exists for each $\Psi \in \mathcal{E}$ and for each $\alpha \in \mathcal{E}$. If $\mathrm{Bel}(\Psi) = \mathcal{L}$, then, because of (AD-CL2), we have $\mathcal{A}(\Psi) = \mathcal{L}$ and consequently $M_{\Psi} = \emptyset$. By setting $\Psi_{\emptyset} = \Psi$, we obtain that $\Psi \circledast \alpha$ exists for all relevant cases of $(\bigstar)$. For the case of $\mathrm{Bel}(\Psi) \neq \mathcal{L}$, we consider the three relevant cases of $(\bigstar)$:

The case of $[\![\alpha]\!] \cap [\![\Psi]\!] \neq \emptyset$. We obtain existence of $\Psi_{[\![\alpha]\!]\cap[\![\Psi]\!]}$ from (CL-ES).

The case of $[\![\alpha]\!] \cap [\![\Psi]\!] = \emptyset$ and $[\![\alpha]\!] \cap M_\Psi \neq \emptyset$. Note that $\ll_\Psi$ is a linear order, and thus, we have to show that for each $\omega \in M_\Psi$ the epistemic state $\Psi_{\{\omega\}}$ exists. Because we have (AD-CL2) from Definition 7.18, there exists Ψ_ω with $[\![\Psi_\omega]\!] = \{\omega\}$ for each $\omega \in M_\Psi$, which guarantees the existence of $\Psi_{\{\omega\}}$.

The case of $[\![\alpha]\!] = \emptyset$ and $\bot \in \mathcal{A}(\Psi)$. We obtain an epistemic state $\Psi_\bot$ from (AD-ES2) which satisfies $[\![\Psi_\bot]\!] = \emptyset$. This guarantees that the epistemic state $\Psi_\emptyset$ exists, as we could choose $\Psi_\emptyset = \Psi_\bot$.

In the following we show that $\circledast$ is a generalized credibility-limited revision operator. We will use Theorem 7.12 and show that $\circledast$ is revision-compatible with a faithful credibility-limited assignment. Let $\Psi \mapsto (\preceq_\Psi, C_\Psi, b_\Psi)$ be the function given by

$$C_\Psi = M_\Psi$$
$$\preceq_\Psi = (\ll_\Psi \setminus (\Omega \times [\![\Psi]\!])) \cup ([\![\Psi]\!] \times \Omega)$$
$$b_\Psi = \begin{cases} \bot & \text{if } \bot \in \mathcal{A}(\Psi) \text{ and } [\![\Psi]\!] \neq \emptyset \\ \top & \text{otherwise} \end{cases}$$

for each $\Psi \in \mathcal{E}$. We show that $\Psi \mapsto (\preceq_\Psi, C_\Psi, b_\Psi)$ is a faithful credibility-limited assignment that is revision-compatible with $\circledast$:

Faithful credibility-limited assignment. Note that $b_\Psi = \bot$ implies $\bot \in \mathcal{A}(\Psi)$ and $[\![\Psi]\!] \neq \emptyset$. Because $\mathcal{A}(\Psi)$ satisfies single-sentence closure, we obtain $\mathcal{A}(\Psi) = \mathcal{L}$ from $\bot \in \mathcal{A}(\Psi)$ in the case of $b_\Psi = \bot$. As given above, $\mathcal{A}(\Psi) = \mathcal{L}$ implies $M_\Psi = M_{\mathcal{A}(\Psi)} = \Omega$ (given $[\![\Psi]\!] \neq \emptyset$), and thus $b_\Psi = \bot$ implies $C_\Psi = \Omega$. This shows that $\Psi \mapsto (\preceq_\Psi, C_\Psi, b_\Psi)$ satisfies (CLA$_\bot$).

Moreover, because $\mathcal{A}$ is credibility-limited revision compatible with $\mathcal{E}$, we have (AD-CL2), which guarantees $[\![\Psi]\!] \subseteq M_\Psi$. Thus, the construction in ($\bigstar$) yields $[\![\Psi]\!] = \min(C_\Psi, \preceq_\Psi)$ if $[\![\Psi]\!] \neq \emptyset$. This shows that $\Psi \mapsto (\preceq_\Psi, C_\Psi, b_\Psi)$ is a faithful credibility-limited assignment (see Definition 7.10).

Revision-compatible. In order to show that $\Psi \mapsto (\preceq_\Psi, C_\Psi, b_\Psi)$ is revision-compatible with $\circledast$, we show that

$$[\![\Psi \circledast \alpha]\!] = \begin{cases} \min([\![\alpha]\!], \preceq_\Psi) & \text{if } [\![\alpha]\!] \cap C_\Psi \neq \emptyset \\ \emptyset & \text{if } [\![\alpha]\!] = \emptyset \text{ and } b_\Psi = \bot \qquad (\#) \\ [\![\Psi]\!] & \text{otherwise} \end{cases}$$

from Definition 7.11 complies with Equation ($\bigstar$). We consider each case of Equation ($\#$) individually:

$[\![\alpha]\!] \cap C_\Psi \neq \emptyset$. Due to the faithfulness of $\Psi \mapsto (\preceq_\Psi, C_\Psi, b_\Psi)$ we have $[\![\Psi]\!] \subseteq C_\Psi$. Inspecting Equation ($\bigstar$) yields $\Psi \circledast \alpha = \Psi_{[\![\alpha]\!] \cap [\![\Psi]\!]}$ whenever $[\![\alpha]\!] \cap [\![\Psi]\!] \neq \emptyset$. These observations yield $[\![\Psi_{[\![\alpha]\!] \cap [\![\Psi]\!]}]\!] = [\![\alpha]\!] \cap [\![\Psi]\!] = \min([\![\alpha]\!], \preceq_\Psi)$ for the case of $[\![\alpha]\!] \cap C_\Psi \cap [\![\Psi]\!] \neq \emptyset$. In the case of $[\![\alpha]\!] \cap C_\Psi \cap [\![\Psi]\!] = \emptyset$, we obtain $\Psi \circledast \alpha = \Psi_{\min([\![\alpha]\!], \ll_\Psi)}$ from Equation ($\bigstar$). For the following recall that $C_\Psi = M_{\mathcal{A}(\Psi)}$ holds. We obtain $\min([\![\alpha]\!], \preceq_\Psi) = \min([\![\alpha]\!], \ll_\Psi) = [\![\Psi_{\min([\![\alpha]\!], \ll_\Psi)}]\!]$ from the definition of $\preceq_\Psi$. Consequently, we have that $[\![\Psi \circledast \alpha]\!] = [\![\Psi_{\min([\![\alpha]\!], \ll_\Psi)}]\!] = \min([\![\alpha]\!], \preceq_\Psi)$ holds.

$[\![\alpha]\!] = \emptyset$ and $b_\Psi = \bot$. Note that $b_\Psi = \bot$ implies $\bot \in \mathcal{A}(\Psi)$ by definition of $\Psi \mapsto (\preceq_\Psi, C_\Psi, b_\Psi)$. Considering Equation ($\bigstar$) yields $[\![\Psi \circledast \alpha]\!] = \emptyset = [\![\Psi_\emptyset]\!]$.

None of the cases above applies. Whenever none of the cases above applies, only two cases remain. In the following we show that we obtain $[\![\Psi \circledast \alpha]\!] = [\![\Psi]\!]$ for both cases.

The case of α is consistent, yet $[\![\alpha]\!] \cap C_\Psi = \emptyset$ holds. Recall that $[\![\Psi]\!] \subseteq C_\Psi$ holds and $C_\Psi = M_{\mathcal{A}(\Psi)}$ holds. Consequently, we obtain $\Psi \circledast \alpha = \Psi$ from $[\![\alpha]\!] \cap C_\Psi = \emptyset$ and Equation ($\bigstar$).

The case of α is inconsistent and $b_\Psi = \top$ holds. Then, by definition of b_Ψ, we have $\bot \notin \mathcal{A}(\Psi)$ and thus, we obtain $\Psi \circledast \alpha = \Psi$ from Equation ($\bigstar$).

As the last step, we show that $Scp^\circledast(\Psi) = \mathcal{A}(\Psi)$ holds. First, observe that, due to Proposition 7.17, we have that $\mathrm{Bel}(\Psi) \subseteq Scp^\circledast(\Psi)$ and $Scp^\circledast(\Psi)$ satisfies single-sentence closure and disjunction completeness for all $\Psi \in \mathcal{E}$. Towards a contradiction, assume that $Scp^\circledast(\Psi) \neq \mathcal{A}(\Psi)$ holds. By using Proposition 7.3 and the proof of Proposition 7.17, we obtain that $Scp^\circledast(\Psi) \neq \mathcal{A}(\Psi)$ implies that (1) $C_\Psi \neq M_{\mathcal{A}(\Psi)}$ or (2) $b_\Psi = \bot$ and $\bot \notin \mathcal{A}(\Psi)$ or (3) $b_\Psi = \top$ and $\bot \in \mathcal{A}(\Psi)$. However, consulting the definition of $\Psi \mapsto (\preceq_\Psi, C_\Psi, b_\Psi)$ and by using the revision-compatibility of $\Psi \mapsto (\preceq_\Psi, C_\Psi, b_\Psi)$ with $\circledast$ yields that neither of (1)–(3) holds. Case (1) is impossible, because we have $C_\Psi = M_{\mathcal{A}(\Psi)}$ by definition. Moreover, by construction we have $b_\Psi = \bot$ if and only if $\bot \in \mathcal{A}(\Psi)$, ruling out the case (2) and the case (3). $\qquad\qquad$ □

Combining Proposition 7.17 and Proposition 7.19, we obtain the following statements about acceptance descriptions and generalized credibility-limited revision operators for epistemic states.

Theorem 7.20 (Strong Realizability). *Let $\mathcal{E}$ be a set of epistemic states that satisfies* (CL-ES). *Then the following statements hold:*

(a) Every credibility-limited revision compatible acceptance description for $\mathcal{E}$ complies with some generalized credibility-limited revision operator for $\mathcal{E}$.

(b) Every generalized credibility-limited revision operator for $\mathcal{E}$ complies with some credibility-limited revision compatible acceptance description for $\mathcal{E}$.

Proof. Statement (a) is given by Proposition 7.19. By employing Proposition 7.17, we obtain statement (b) from the following considerations. Due to Proposition 7.17, we obtain that (AD-CL1) holds for every acceptance description that complies with a generalized credibility-limited revision operator. Moreover, satisfaction of (AD-CL2) is guaranteed by (GCL1) and (GCL3). $\qquad\qquad$ □

Theorem 7.20 is very useful for the realization of generalized credibility-limited revision operators in arbitrary sets of epistemic states. Suppose we want to obtain an operator on an arbitrary $\mathcal{E}$ with certain restrictions regarding the acceptance of beliefs. According to Theorem 7.20, we could check if this is possible by checking whether $\mathcal{E}$ satisfies (CL-ES) and checking whether the properties mentioned in Definition 7.18 are satisfied.

7.7. Interim Conclusion

In this chapter, we started by introducing acceptance descriptions and established the goal of having a class of belief change operators that realizes every acceptance description. We considered the non-prioritized revision operation of credibility-limited revision, which we generalized to generalized credibility-limited revision operators for epistemic states such that AGM revision operators for epistemic states are also included. We provided a proof showing that generalized credibility-limited revision operators for epistemic states are characterized by faithful credibility-limited assignments.

Finally, we have seen in this chapter that neither AGM revision operators for epistemic states nor generalized credibility-limited revision operators, as shown by Proposition 7.5 and Theorem 7.20, allow operators that are compliant with every acceptance description. In the following chapter, we consider a family of belief change operators that realizes a broader variety of acceptance descriptions than generalized credibility-limited revision operators.

Chapter 8

Dynamic-Limited Revision

We have demonstrated in Chapter 7 that generalized credibility-limited revision operators for epistemic states are not able to comply with arbitrary acceptance descriptions. In this chapter, we will see that the way how (generalized) credibility-limited revision operators for epistemic states treat prior beliefs is a source of this incompatibility. We introduce dynamic-limited revision operators for epistemic states that generalize (generalized) credibility-limited revision operators such that a different treatment of prior beliefs is possible. Next, we characterize dynamic-limited revision operators for epistemic states semantically. Finally, we discuss limits of the standard relational approach which employs total preorders, that includes dynamic-limited revision operators, for realizing arbitrary sets of acceptance descriptions.

8.1. Acceptance and Treatment of Prior Beliefs

We start with investigating the incompatibility of generalized credibility-limited revision operators for epistemic states with arbitrary acceptance descriptions. As given by Theorem 7.20, the conditions (CL-ES), (AD-CL1) and (AD-CL2) characterize those situations where acceptance descriptions are realized by generalized credibility-limited revision operators. Note that both (CL-ES) and (AD-CL1) deal with the initial beliefs of a change and thus, it is likely that how the initial beliefs are treated by generalized credibility-limited operators gives rise to the incompatibility between arbitrary acceptance descriptions and these belief change operators.

Prioritization of Initial Beliefs by (GCL2). Generalized credibility-limited revision satisfies the postulate:

(GCL2) If $\mathrm{Bel}(\Psi) + \alpha$ is consistent, then $\mathrm{Bel}(\Psi \circ \alpha) = \mathrm{Bel}(\Psi) + \alpha$.

which can be semantically reformulated as follows:

(GCL2$_{\mathrm{sem}}$) If $[\![\Psi]\!] \cap [\![\alpha]\!] \neq \emptyset$, then $[\![\Psi \circ \alpha]\!] = [\![\Psi]\!] \cap [\![\alpha]\!]$.

In the following, we will consider an example that shows that (GCL2) is one reason why generalized credibility-limited revision operators for epistemic states are not complying with every acceptance description.

Example 8.1. *Let* $\Sigma = \{a, b\}$ *and thus we have* $\Omega = \{ab, a\bar{b}, \bar{a}b, \bar{a}\bar{b}\}$. *Furthermore, let* $\mathcal{E}$ *be the set of epistemic states with* $\mathcal{E} = \{\Psi_a, \Psi_{\bar{a}}\} \cup \{\Psi_\omega \mid \omega \in \Omega\}$ *such that the following holds for each* $\omega \in \Omega$:

$$[\![\Psi_a]\!] = \{ab, \ a\bar{b}\} \qquad [\![\Psi_{\bar{a}}]\!] = \{\bar{a}b, \ \bar{a}\bar{b}\} \qquad [\![\Psi_\omega]\!] = \{\omega\}$$

We consider the acceptance description $\mathcal{A}$ *for* $\mathcal{E}$ *given for each* $\omega \in \Omega$ *by:*

$$\mathcal{A}(\Psi_a) = \{\alpha \in \mathcal{L} \mid \bar{a}\bar{b} \models \alpha\}$$
$$\mathcal{A}(\Psi_{\bar{a}}) = \{\alpha \in \mathcal{L} \mid ab \models \alpha\}$$
$$\mathcal{A}(\Psi_\omega) = \{\alpha \in \mathcal{L} \mid \omega \models \alpha\}$$

Note that Proposition 7.3 guarantees that $\mathcal{A}(\Psi)$ *satisfies single-sentence closure and disjunction completeness for each* $\Psi \in \mathcal{E}$.

Let $\circ$ *be a belief change operator for* $\mathcal{E}$ *that complies with* $\mathcal{A}$ *(see Definition 7.6). As* $\circ$ *complies with* $\mathcal{A}$ *we obtain that the scope of* $\circ$ *with respect to* Ψ_a *consists of* $\mathrm{Bel}(\Psi_a)$ *and all beliefs* α *that have* $\bar{a}\bar{b}$ *as a model, i.e., we have that*

$$Scp^\circ(\Psi_a) = \mathrm{Bel}(\Psi_a) \cup \{\alpha \in \mathcal{L} \mid [\![\alpha]\!] \cap \{\bar{a}\bar{b}\} \neq \emptyset\} \qquad (\bigstar)$$
$$= \{\alpha \in \mathcal{L} \mid ab \models \alpha \text{ and } a\bar{b} \models \alpha\} \cup \{\alpha \in \mathcal{L} \mid \bar{a}\bar{b} \models \alpha\}$$

holds. Now, suppose that $\circ$ *satisfies* (GCL2). *Consequently, because* $\mathrm{Bel}(\Psi_a) + (a \wedge b)$ *is consistent, we obtain* $\mathrm{Bel}(\Psi_a \circ (a \wedge b)) = \mathrm{Bel}(\Psi_a) + (a \wedge b)$, *which implies* $a \wedge b \in \mathrm{Bel}(\Psi_a \circ (a \wedge b))$. *By considering the definition of* $Scp^\circ(\Psi_a)$, *Definition 7.4, this implies that we have* $a \wedge b \in$

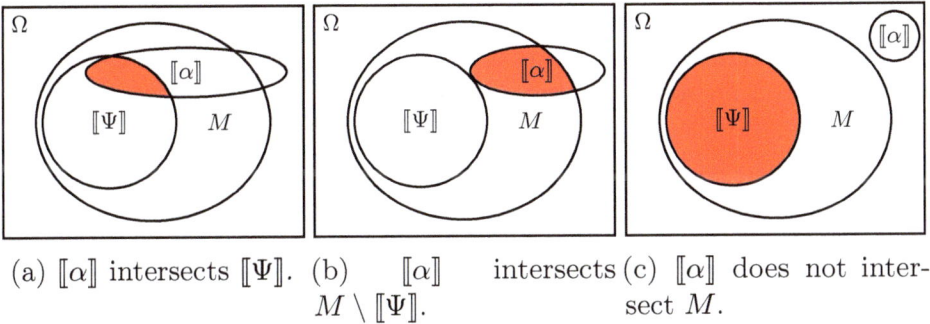

(a) $[\![\alpha]\!]$ intersects $[\![\Psi]\!]$. (b) $[\![\alpha]\!]$ intersects (c) $[\![\alpha]\!]$ does not inter-
$M \setminus [\![\Psi]\!]$. sect M.

Figure 8.1: Elements in $[\![\Psi \circ \alpha]\!]$ (red area) depending on how $[\![\alpha]\!]$, $[\![\Psi]\!]$ and M are related. This figure illustrates the case of $[\![\Psi]\!] \subseteq M$ as it appears for generalized credibility-limited revision operators for epistemic states.

$Scp^\circ(\Psi_a)$. *This is a contradiction to* (★), *because neither* $a \wedge b \in$ $Bel(\Psi_a)$ *nor* $a \wedge b \in \{\alpha \in \mathcal{L} \mid \overline{a}\overline{b} \models \alpha\}$ *holds, and thus, we obtain* $a \wedge b \notin Scp^\circ(\Psi_a)$ *according to* (★).

Example 8.1 demonstrates that the dynamics of generalized credibility-limited revision operators is incompatible with some acceptance descriptions $\mathcal{A}$. In particular, there are situations where a new belief α is consistent with $Bel(\Psi)$ but neither $\alpha \in Bel(\Psi)$ nor $\alpha \in \mathcal{A}(\Psi)$ holds. Dynamic-limited revision operators will be similar to credibility-limited revision operators for epistemic states but will be able to deal with such situations. Before we introduce dynamic-limited revision operators in the next section, we consider how prior beliefs are treated according to (GCL2).

A closer look on (GCL2). Recall that for a generalized credibility-limited revision operator ⊛ for epistemic states we have that $[\![\Psi \circledast \alpha]\!]$ is equivalent to $[\![\Psi]\!]$ or we have that $[\![\Psi \circledast \alpha]\!]$ is a subset of some set C_Ψ of interpretations (see Definition 7.11 in Section 7.4). The postulate (GCL2) particularity enforces that $[\![\Psi]\!]$ lower-bounds the set C_Ψ, i.e., we have $[\![\Psi]\!] \subseteq C_\Psi$ (see also Definition 7.9), and that $[\![\Psi \circledast \alpha]\!]$ contains elements from $[\![\Psi]\!]$, whenever this is possible due to success of revision. This establishes the dynamics illustrated in Figure 8.1 (where C_Ψ corresponds to M in this figure).

The postulate (GCL2) goes back to the original approach by AGM[1]

---

[1] The postulate (GCL2) corresponds to (R2), respectively (KM2), which is

and regulates how a belief revision operator threats prior beliefs [63, 79]. In particular, according to (GCL2) the initial beliefs are changed as minimally as possible, whenever the initial beliefs are consistent with the new information. The semantic formulation (GCL2$_\text{sem}$) exhibits three characteristics of minimal change of prior beliefs according to (GCL2), by showing how models of Bel(Ψ), i.e., the elements of $[\![\Psi]\!]$, are treated in the course of change:

> *Exclusiveness of* $[\![\Psi]\!]$. This means that if $[\![\Psi \circ \alpha]\!]$ contains elements from $[\![\Psi]\!]$, then $[\![\Psi \circ \alpha]\!]$ contains only elements from $[\![\Psi]\!]$.
>
> *Equal Treatment of Elements in* $[\![\Psi]\!]$. There is no internal preference over the elements in $[\![\Psi]\!]$. For revision operators this means that if $[\![\Psi \circ \alpha]\!] \cap [\![\Psi]\!] \cap [\![\alpha]\!] \neq \emptyset$, then $[\![\Psi]\!] \cap [\![\alpha]\!] \subseteq [\![\Psi \circ \alpha]\!]$.
>
> *Prioritization of* $[\![\Psi]\!]$. The set $[\![\Psi \circ \alpha]\!]$ contains elements of $[\![\Psi]\!]$, whenever that is possible. For revision this means that $[\![\Psi]\!] \cap [\![\alpha]\!] \neq \emptyset$ implies that $[\![\Psi \circ \alpha]\!] \cap [\![\Psi]\!] \cap [\![\alpha]\!] \neq \emptyset$ holds.

This specific treatment of elements in $[\![\Psi]\!]$ is especially reflected by the respective *faithfulness* conditions used in the semantic characterization of generalized credibility-limited revision operators for epistemic states (see Definition 7.10 on p. 144). Regarding Example 8.1, we see that exclusiveness of $[\![\Psi]\!]$ is not in conflict with ∘ in Example 8.1. However, we have that the prioritization of elements of $[\![\Psi]\!]$ and equal treatment of elements in $[\![\Psi]\!]$, respectively, are conflicting with ∘ in Example 8.1.

8.2. Dynamic-Limited Revision Operators

The following introduces dynamic-limited revision operators for epistemic states by syntactic postulates. We characterize dynamic-limited revision operators for epistemic states similarly as we characterized generalized credibility-limited revision operators for epistemic states. In the subsequent section we will motivate and explain the design choices made for dynamic-limited revision operators.

---

the fusion of the postulates (AGM∗2) (Inclusion) and (AGM∗3) (Vacuity) of AGM revision (see p. 27).

Definition 8.2. *Let $\mathcal{E}$ be a set of epistemic states. A belief change operator $\star$ for $\mathcal{E}$ is called a dynamic-limited revision operator for $\mathcal{E}$ if $\star$ satisfies the following postulates[2].:*

(DL0) $\mathrm{Bel}(\Psi \star \alpha) = \mathrm{Bel}(\Psi)$ *or* $\alpha \in \mathrm{Bel}(\Psi \star \alpha)$.

(DL1) *If* $\mathrm{Bel}(\Psi) \cup \mathrm{Bel}(\Psi \star \alpha)$ *is consistent, then* $\mathrm{Bel}(\Psi) \subseteq \mathrm{Bel}(\Psi \star \alpha)$.

(DL2) *If* $\mathrm{Bel}(\Psi) \cup \mathrm{Bel}(\Psi \star (\alpha \wedge \beta))$ *is consistent and* $\mathrm{Bel}(\Psi) \neq \mathrm{Bel}(\Psi \star (\alpha \wedge \beta))$,
   then $\mathrm{Bel}(\Psi \star \alpha) \cup \mathrm{Bel}(\Psi \star \beta)$ *is consistent.*

(DL3) *If* $\mathrm{Bel}(\Psi) \cup \mathrm{Bel}(\Psi \star \alpha)$ *and* $\mathrm{Bel}(\Psi) + \alpha$ *are consistent, and* $\alpha \models \gamma$ *and* $\mathrm{Bel}(\Psi \star \gamma) \not\subseteq \mathrm{Cn}(\alpha)$ *holds, then consistency of* β *and inconsistency of* $\mathrm{Bel}(\Psi) \cup \mathrm{Bel}(\Psi \star \beta)$ *together imply that* $\mathrm{Bel}(\Psi) \cup \mathrm{Bel}(\Psi \star (\alpha \vee \beta))$ *is inconsistent.*

(DL4) *If* $\mathrm{Bel}(\Psi)$ *and* α *are consistent, then* $\mathrm{Bel}(\Psi \star \alpha)$ *is consistent.*

(DL5) *If* $\mathrm{Bel}(\Psi \star \alpha)$ *is consistent and* $\alpha \models \beta$, *then* $\mathrm{Bel}(\Psi \star \beta)$ *is consistent.*

(DL6) *If* $\alpha \equiv \beta$, *then* $\mathrm{Bel}(\Psi \star \alpha) = \mathrm{Bel}(\Psi \star \beta)$.

(DL7) *If* α *is consistent and* $\alpha \in \mathrm{Bel}(\Psi \star \alpha)$, *then* $\alpha \models \beta$ *implies* $\beta \in \mathrm{Bel}(\Psi \star \beta)$.

(DL8) *If* α, β *are consistent and* $\mathrm{Bel}(\Psi \star \alpha) \neq \mathrm{Bel}(\Psi)$ *and* $\mathrm{Bel}(\Psi \star \beta) = \mathrm{Bel}(\Psi)$, *then* $\beta \notin \mathrm{Bel}(\Psi)$ *implies* $\mathrm{Bel}(\Psi \star (\alpha \vee \beta)) + \beta$ *is inconsistent.*

(DL9) $\mathrm{Bel}(\Psi \star (\alpha \vee \beta)) = \begin{cases} \mathrm{Bel}(\Psi \star \alpha) & or \\ \mathrm{Bel}(\Psi \star \beta) & or \\ \mathrm{Bel}(\Psi \star \alpha) \cap \mathrm{Bel}(\Psi \star \beta) \end{cases}$.

Next, we now adapt the formal notions for the semantic characterizations of revision by Darwiche and Pearl [41], which was also used for the characterization of generalized credibility-limited revision, to operators that maintain a total preorder only over a limited set of worlds. In particular, we start by restricting the total preorders in assignments to $\mathcal{S}_\Psi$, a subset of Ω. The set $\mathcal{S}_\Psi$ is supposed to hold the models of beliefs from the scope which are not in $\mathrm{Bel}(\Psi)$. It will turn out that these are the elements for a semantic characterization of dynamic-limited revision operators.

---

[2]   The abbreviation *DL* stands for *dynamic-limited* revision

Definition 8.3 (Limited Assignment). *Let $\mathcal{E}$ be a set of epistemic states. A function $\Psi \mapsto (\preceq_\Psi, \mathcal{S}_\Psi, b_\Psi)$ is called a* limited assignment *for $\mathcal{E}$ if $\mathcal{S}_\Psi \subseteq \Omega$ is a set of interpretations, and $\preceq_\Psi$ is a total preorder over $\mathcal{S}_\Psi$, and $b_\Psi \in \{\top, \bot\}$.*

Like credibility-limited assignments (see Definition 7.9), limited assignments carry two kinds of information. The set $\mathcal{S}_\Psi$ is meant to describe semantically all consistent beliefs that the agent will accept for revision and b_Ψ represents whether an inconsistent formula is accepted for revision or not. Note that $\mathcal{S}_\Psi$ depends on the state, thus, for each state Ψ the set $\mathcal{S}_\Psi$ might be a completely different subset of Ω. Moreover, in contrast to C_Ψ of credibility-limited assignments, $\mathcal{S}_\Psi$ is a relation over an arbitrary subset of Ω. Second, the total preorder $\preceq_\Psi$ serves to same purpose as for revision: representing the preferences of the agent. As stated before, for a relation $\preceq_\Psi$ over a subset of Ω, we denote with $\prec_\Psi$ the strict part of $\preceq_\Psi$ and with $\simeq_\Psi$ the equivalent part of $\preceq_\Psi$ (see Chapter 2). We link limited assignments and belief change operators similar to the approaches of credibility-limited revision in Theorem 7.12.

Definition 8.4 (Revision-Compatible). *Let $\mathcal{E}$ be a set of epistemic states and let $\star$ be a belief change operator for $\mathcal{E}$. A limited assignment $\Psi \mapsto (\preceq_\Psi, \mathcal{S}_\Psi, b_\Psi)$ for $\mathcal{E}$ is called* (dynamic-limited) revision-compatible *with $\star$ if the following holds:*

$$[\![\Psi \star \alpha]\!] = \begin{cases} \min([\![\alpha]\!], \preceq_\Psi) & \text{if } [\![\alpha]\!] \cap \mathcal{S}_\Psi \neq \emptyset \\ \emptyset & \text{if } [\![\alpha]\!] = \emptyset \text{ and } b_\Psi = \bot \\ [\![\Psi]\!] & \text{otherwise} \end{cases}$$

(revision-compatible)

To reflect that in general $[\![\Psi]\!]$ and $\mathcal{S}_\Psi$ do not share the same interpretations, we adapt the concept of faithfulness.

Definition 8.5 (Faithful Limited Assignment). *Let $\mathcal{E}$ be a set of epistemic states. A limited assignment $\Psi \mapsto (\preceq_\Psi, \mathcal{S}_\Psi, b_\Psi)$ for $\mathcal{E}$ is called* faithful *if for each Ψ the following conditions hold:*

(FLA1) *If $[\![\Psi]\!] \cap \mathcal{S}_\Psi \neq \emptyset$, then $\min(\mathcal{S}_\Psi, \preceq_\Psi) = [\![\Psi]\!] \cap \mathcal{S}_\Psi$.*
(FLA2) *If $|[\![\Psi]\!]| = 1$, then $\mathcal{S}_\Psi \neq [\![\Psi]\!]$.*
(FLA3) *If $[\![\Psi]\!] = \emptyset$, then $b_\Psi = \top$.*

The faithfulness condition (FLA1) states that minimal elements of $\preceq_\Psi$ are models of Ψ (if $\llbracket\Psi\rrbracket$ shares elements with $\mathcal{S}_\Psi$), but $\min(\mathcal{S}_\Psi, \preceq_\Psi)$ does *not* necessarily contain all models of Ψ. The conditions (FLA2) and (FLA3) rule out semantically ambiguous cases. Clearly, limited assignments are a generalization of Darwiche and Pearl's assignments (see Definition 6.5), because if $\mathcal{S}_\Psi = \Omega$ for every $\Psi \in \mathcal{E}$, then a (faithful) limited assignment is a (faithful) assignment. Moreover, they subsume credibility-limited assignments (see Definition 7.9).

The following theorem shows that dynamic-limited revision operators are exactly captured by the semantic concepts we just introduced.

Theorem 8.6. *Let $\mathcal{E}$ be a set of epistemic states and let $\star$ be a belief change operator for $\mathcal{E}$. Then $\star$ is a dynamic-limited revision operator if and only if $\star$ is revision-compatible with some faithful limited-assignment for $\mathcal{E}$.*

The outline of proof of Theorem 8.6 follows the proof of Theorem 7.12. However, the different postulates require different treatment of the cases, especially in those cases, where the models of $\mathrm{Bel}(\Psi)$ or the faithfulness of the assignment are involved.

Proof. We consider both directions of the claim independently. For the "$\Rightarrow$"-direction, we will construct a faithful limited-assignment that is revision-compatible with a given dynamic-limited revision operator $\star$. We proceed in several steps:

[Step 1 – Construction]
This step describes how $\Psi \mapsto (\preceq_\Psi, \mathcal{S}_\Psi, b_\Psi)$ is constructed.
[Step 2 – Limited Assignment]
We show that $\Psi \mapsto (\preceq_\Psi, \mathcal{S}_\Psi, b_\Psi)$ is a limited assignment (Definition 8.3).
[Step 3 – Faithfulness]
We show that $\Psi \mapsto (\preceq_\Psi, \mathcal{S}_\Psi, b_\Psi)$ is faithful (Definition 8.5).
[Step 4 – Revision-Compatibility]
We show that $\Psi \mapsto (\preceq_\Psi, \mathcal{S}_\Psi, b_\Psi)$ is revision-compatible with $\star$ (Definition 8.4).

For the "$\Leftarrow$"-direction, we start from a belief change operator $\star$ that is revision-compatible with a faithful limited-assignment and show step by step that each of the postulates (DL0)–(DL9) is satisfied. Next, we start with the actual proof.

The "⇒"-direction. Let $\star$ be a dynamic-limited revision operator for $\mathcal{E}$.

[**Step 1 – Construction**] At first, we construct a function $\Psi \mapsto (\preceq_\Psi, \mathcal{S}_\Psi, b_\Psi)$, for which we will show that this function is a faithful limited-assignment that is revision-compatible with $\star$. We set $\mathcal{S}_\Psi$ as follows

$$\mathcal{S}'_\Psi = \{\omega \mid [\![\varphi_\omega]\!] = [\![\Psi \star \varphi_\omega]\!]\},$$

$$\mathcal{S}_\Psi = \begin{cases} \emptyset & \text{if } |[\![\Psi]\!]| = 1 \text{ and } [\![\Psi]\!] = \mathcal{S}'_\Psi \\ \mathcal{S}'_\Psi \setminus [\![\Psi]\!] & \text{if } [\![\Psi]\!] = \{\omega\} \text{ and } [\![\Psi]\!] \subsetneq \mathcal{S}'_\Psi \text{ and} \\ & \quad \text{there exists } \omega \models \alpha \text{ such that } \omega \notin [\![\Psi \star \alpha]\!] \\ \mathcal{S}'_\Psi & \text{otherwise} \end{cases}$$

$$(\star)$$

for each $\Psi \in \mathcal{E}$, where φ_ω denotes a formula with $[\![\varphi_\omega]\!] = \{\omega\}$. If $[\![\Psi]\!] \neq \emptyset$ and $\perp \in \text{Bel}(\Psi \star \perp)$, then we set $b_\Psi = \perp$; otherwise we set $b_\Psi = \top$. For each $\Psi \in \mathcal{E}$ let $\preceq_\Psi \subseteq \mathcal{S}_\Psi \times \mathcal{S}_\Psi$ be the relation such that

$$\omega_1 \preceq_\Psi \omega_2 \text{ if and only if } \omega_1 \in [\![\Psi \star \varphi_{\omega_1,\omega_2}]\!]$$

holds, where $\varphi_{\omega_1,\omega_2}$ denotes a formula with $[\![\varphi_{\omega_1,\omega_2}]\!] = \{\omega_1, \omega_2\}$.

[**Step 2 – Limited Assignment**] To show that $\Psi \mapsto (\preceq_\Psi, \mathcal{S}_\Psi, b_\Psi)$ is a limited assignment (see Definition 8.3) it is sufficient to show that $\preceq_\Psi$ is a total preorder on $\mathcal{S}_\Psi$:

Reflexivity and Totality. Reflexivity is a direct consequence of totality, thus in the following we show only totality. Let $\omega_1, \omega_2 \in \mathcal{S}_\Psi$. We show totality by contradiction. Therefore, assume $\omega_1 \not\preceq_\Psi \omega_2$ and $\omega_2 \not\preceq_\Psi \omega_1$ in the following. From the definition of $\preceq_\Psi$ we obtain $\omega_1, \omega_2 \notin [\![\Psi \star \varphi_{\omega_1,\omega_2}]\!]$, where $\varphi_{\omega_1,\omega_2}$ is a formula such that $[\![\Psi \star \varphi_{\omega_1,\omega_2}]\!] = \{\omega_1, \omega_2\}$. From (DL6), we obtain that $[\![\Psi \star \varphi_{\omega_1,\omega_2}]\!] = [\![\Psi \star (\varphi_{\omega_1} \vee \varphi_{\omega_2})]\!]$ holds. By (DL9) we have that $[\![\Psi \star (\varphi_{\omega_1} \vee \varphi_{\omega_2})]\!]$ is equivalent to either $[\![\Psi \star \varphi_{\omega_1}]\!]$ or $[\![\Psi \star \varphi_{\omega_2}]\!]$ or $[\![\Psi \star \varphi_{\omega_1}]\!] \cup [\![\Psi \star \varphi_{\omega_2}]\!]$. From the definition of $\mathcal{S}_\Psi$ we obtain $[\![\Psi \star \varphi_{\omega_1}]\!] = \{\omega_1\}$ and $[\![\Psi \star \varphi_{\omega_2}]\!] = \{\omega_2\}$. Consequently, we obtain that $\omega_1 \in [\![\Psi \star \varphi_{\omega_1,\omega_2}]\!]$ or

$\omega_2 \in [\![\Psi \star \varphi_{\omega_1,\omega_2}]\!]$ holds, which is a contradiction to our prior observation of $\omega_1, \omega_2 \notin [\![\Psi \star \varphi_{\omega_1,\omega_2}]\!]$.

Transitivity. Let $\omega_1, \omega_2, \omega_3 \in \mathcal{S}_\Psi$. We show totality by contradiction. Therefore, we assume $\omega_1 \preceq_\Psi \omega_2$ and $\omega_2 \preceq_\Psi \omega_3$ and $\omega_1 \npreceq_\Psi \omega_3$ in the following. The latter assumption and the definition of $\preceq_\Psi$ yields $\omega_1 \notin [\![\Psi \star \varphi_{\omega_1,\omega_3}]\!]$. By the definition of $\mathcal{S}_\Psi$, and using (DL6) and (DL9), we obtain $[\![\Psi \star \varphi_{\omega_1,\omega_3}]\!] = \{\omega_3\}$. In the following let $\varphi_{\omega_1,\omega_2,\omega_3}$ be a formula such that $[\![\varphi_{\omega_1,\omega_2,\omega_3}]\!] = \{\omega_1, \omega_2, \omega_3\}$. Recall that by the definition of $\mathcal{S}_\Psi$ we have $[\![\Psi \star \varphi_\omega]\!] = \{\omega\}$ for each $\omega \in \{\omega_1, \omega_2, \omega_3\}$. We consider two subcases:

The case of $[\![\Psi \star \varphi_{\omega_1,\omega_2,\omega_3}]\!] = \{\omega_3\}$. Using (DL6) we obtain $[\![\Psi \star \varphi_{\omega_1,\omega_2,\omega_3}]\!] = [\![\Psi \star (\varphi_{\omega_1} \vee \varphi_{\omega_2,\omega_3})]\!]$. Because we have $\omega_3 \notin [\![\Psi \star \varphi_{\omega_1}]\!]$, we obtain $[\![\Psi \star \varphi_{\omega_1,\omega_2,\omega_3}]\!] = [\![\Psi \star \varphi_{\omega_2,\omega_3}]\!]$ from (DL9). Using the definition of $\preceq_\Psi$ and $[\![\Psi \star \varphi_{\omega_1,\omega_2,\omega_3}]\!] = \{\omega_3\}$ we obtain the contradiction $\omega_2 \npreceq_\Psi \omega_3$.

The case of $[\![\Psi \star \varphi_{\omega_1,\omega_2,\omega_3}]\!] \neq \{\omega_3\}$. By using (DL6) we obtain $[\![\Psi \star \varphi_{\omega_1,\omega_2,\omega_3}]\!] = [\![\Psi \star (\varphi_{\omega_1,\omega_2} \vee \varphi_{\omega_1,\omega_3})]\!]$. Because we have $[\![\Psi \star \varphi_{\omega_1,\omega_3}]\!] = \{\omega_3\}$ and $[\![\Psi \star \varphi_{\omega_1,\omega_2,\omega_3}]\!] \neq \{\omega_3\}$, we obtain $[\![\Psi \star \varphi_{\omega_1,\omega_2}]\!] \subseteq [\![\Psi \star \varphi_{\omega_1,\omega_2,\omega_3}]\!]$ from (DL9). By using the definition of $\preceq_\Psi$ and $\omega_1 \preceq_\Psi \omega_2$ we obtain $\omega_1 \in [\![\Psi \star \varphi_{\omega_1,\omega_2}]\!]$. Consequently, we have $\omega_1 \in [\![\Psi \star \varphi_{\omega_1,\omega_2,\omega_3}]\!]$.

By using (DL6) again, we obtain $[\![\Psi \star \varphi_{\omega_1,\omega_2,\omega_3}]\!] = [\![\Psi \star (\varphi_{\omega_2} \vee \varphi_{\omega_1,\omega_3})]\!]$. Because we have $\omega_1 \in [\![\Psi \star \varphi_{\omega_1,\omega_2,\omega_3}]\!]$ and $[\![\Psi \star \varphi_{\omega_2}]\!] = \{\omega_2\}$, we obtain $[\![\Psi \star \varphi_{\omega_1,\omega_2,\omega_3}]\!] \cap \{\omega_1, \omega_3\} = [\![\Psi \star \varphi_{\omega_1,\omega_3}]\!]$ from (DL9). Consequently, we obtain $\omega_1 \in [\![\Psi \star \varphi_{\omega_1,\omega_3}]\!]$, which yields the contradiction $\omega_1 \preceq_\Psi \omega_3$.

In summary, $\Psi \mapsto (\preceq_\Psi, \mathcal{S}_\Psi, b_\Psi)$ is a limited assignment.

[Step 3 – Faithfulness] Next, we show that $\Psi \mapsto (\preceq_\Psi, \mathcal{S}_\Psi, b_\Psi)$ is a faithful limited assignment by showing that the conditions (FLA1)–(FLA3) from Definition 8.5 are satisfied:

(FLA1) Suppose that $[\![\Psi]\!] \cap \mathcal{S}_\Psi \neq \emptyset$. Let $\omega_1 \in [\![\Psi]\!]$ and $\omega_1, \omega_2 \in \mathcal{S}_\Psi$. We consider two cases.

The case of $\omega_2 \in [\![\Psi]\!]$. We immediately obtain $[\![\Psi \star \varphi_{\omega_1}]\!] = \{\omega_1\} \subsetneq [\![\Psi]\!]$ from $\omega_1, \omega_2 \in [\![\Psi]\!]$. From the satisfaction of (DL2) and (DL6) by $\star$ and $[\![\Psi \star \varphi_{\omega_1}]\!] = \{\omega_1\} \subsetneq [\![\Psi]\!]$, we obtain $\omega_1 \in [\![\Psi \star \varphi_{\omega_1,\omega_2}]\!]$ by setting $\alpha = \varphi_{\omega_1}$ and $\beta = \varphi_{\omega_1,\omega_2}$ in (DL2). By an analogue argumentation, we obtain $\omega_2 \in [\![\Psi \star \varphi_{\omega_1,\omega_2}]\!]$.

Then, applying the definition of $\preceq_\Psi$ yields $\omega_1 \simeq_\Psi \omega_2$, i.e., $\omega_1 \preceq_\Psi \omega_2$ and $\omega_2 \preceq_\Psi \omega_1$.

The case of $\omega_2 \notin [\![\Psi]\!]$. Observe that $\star$ satisfies (DL0), and thus we have $[\![\Psi \star \varphi_{\omega_1,\omega_2}]\!] = [\![\Psi]\!]$ or $[\![\Psi \star \varphi_{\omega_1,\omega_2}]\!] \subseteq \{\omega_1, \omega_2\}$. In the former case, the case of $[\![\Psi \star \varphi_{\omega_1,\omega_2}]\!] = [\![\Psi]\!]$, we obtain $\omega_2 \notin [\![\Psi \star \varphi_{\omega_1,\omega_2}]\!]$. For the case of $[\![\Psi \star \varphi_{\omega_1,\omega_2}]\!] \subseteq \{\omega_1, \omega_2\}$, note that (DL5) yields that $[\![\Psi \star \varphi_{\omega_1,\omega_2}]\!]$ is non-empty. We show that $\omega_1 \in [\![\Psi \star \varphi_{\omega_1,\omega_2}]\!]$. Towards a contradiction, suppose that $\omega_1 \notin [\![\Psi \star \varphi_{\omega_1,\omega_2}]\!]$ and thus, $\omega_2 \in [\![\Psi \star \varphi_{\omega_1,\omega_2}]\!]$ holds. We consider $(\bigstar)$, and obtain the two cases of $[\![\Psi]\!] = [\![\omega_1]\!]$ and $|[\![\Psi]\!]| > 1$. If $[\![\Psi]\!] = [\![\omega_1]\!]$, then we obtain a contradiction to $\omega_1 \in \mathcal{S}_\Psi$ immediately from $\omega_1 \notin [\![\Psi \star \varphi_{\omega_1,\omega_2}]\!]$ and $(\bigstar)$. In the case of $|[\![\Psi]\!]| > 1$, we employ (DL2) and (DL6), and obtain that $[\![\Psi \star \varphi_{\omega_1,\omega_2}]\!] \cap [\![\Psi \star \varphi_{\omega_1}]\!] \neq \emptyset$ holds from $[\![\Psi \star \varphi_{\omega_1}]\!] = \{\omega_1\}$. Consequently, we obtain that $\omega_1 \in [\![\Psi \star \varphi_{\omega_1,\omega_2}]\!]$ holds. This last observation shows that $[\![\Psi \star \varphi_{\omega_1,\omega_2}]\!] \cap [\![\Psi]\!] \neq \emptyset$, and thus, we obtain $\omega_2 \notin [\![\Psi \star \varphi_{\omega_1,\omega_2}]\!]$ from (DL1) and $\omega_2 \notin [\![\Psi]\!]$.

Thus, we have shown that $\omega_2 \notin [\![\Psi \star \varphi_{\omega_1,\omega_2}]\!]$ holds, regardless of whether $[\![\Psi \star \varphi_{\omega_1,\omega_2}]\!] = [\![\Psi]\!]$ or $[\![\Psi \star \varphi_{\omega_1,\omega_2}]\!] \subseteq \{\omega_1, \omega_2\}$ holds. From the definition of $\preceq_\Psi$ and totality of $\preceq_\Psi$, we obtain $\omega_1 \prec_\Psi \omega_2$ from $\omega_2 \notin [\![\Psi]\!]$.

In summary, we have that $\omega_2 \in [\![\Psi]\!]$ holds if and only if $\omega_1 \preceq_\Psi \omega_2$ and $\omega_2 \preceq_\Psi \omega_1$ hold. Combining these observations yields the desired result $[\![\Psi]\!] \cap \mathcal{S}_\Psi = \min(\mathcal{S}_\Psi, \preceq_\Psi)$.

(FLA2) Satisfaction of this condition is given by the case-distinction in $(\bigstar)$.

(FLA3) As given above, the construction of $\Psi \mapsto (\preceq_\Psi, \mathcal{S}_\Psi, b_\Psi)$ guarantees that whenever $b_\Psi = \bot$ holds, we have $[\![\Psi]\!] \neq \emptyset$. Consequently, condition (FLA3) is satisfied by $\Psi \mapsto (\preceq_\Psi, \mathcal{S}_\Psi, b_\Psi)$.

[Step 4 – Revision-Compatibility] We show that $\Psi \mapsto (\preceq_\Psi, \mathcal{S}_\Psi, b_\Psi)$ is revision-compatible with $\star$. For that, we consider four cases in the following: **[Step 4.1]** the case of $[\![\alpha]\!] \cap \mathcal{S}_\Psi \neq \emptyset$, **[Step 4.2]** the case of $[\![\alpha]\!] = \emptyset$ and $b_\Psi = \bot$, **[Step 4.3]** the case of $[\![\alpha]\!] = \emptyset$ and $b_\Psi = \top$, and **[Step 4.4]** the case of $[\![\alpha]\!] \neq \emptyset$ and $[\![\alpha]\!] \cap \mathcal{S}_\Psi = \emptyset$. We continue by considering these cases.

[Step 4.1] *The case of $[\![\alpha]\!] \cap \mathcal{S}_\Psi \neq \emptyset$.* In this case, we directly obtain that α is consistent. Moreover, from $[\![\alpha]\!] \cap \mathcal{S}_\Psi \neq \emptyset$ we obtain an interpretation $\omega \in [\![\alpha]\!] \cap S_\Psi$. The definition of S_Ψ yields $[\![\Psi \star \varphi_\omega]\!] = \{\omega\}$. We obtain $[\![\Psi \star \alpha]\!] \neq \emptyset$ from (DL5) and $\varphi_\omega \models \alpha$, and from (DL7) that $[\![\Psi \star \alpha]\!] \subseteq [\![\alpha]\!]$ holds. We show that $\min([\![\alpha]\!], \preceq_\Psi) = [\![\Psi \star \alpha]\!]$ holds by showing independently that **[Step 4.1.1]** $\min([\![\alpha]\!], \preceq_\Psi) \subseteq [\![\Psi \star \alpha]\!]$ and **[Step 4.1.2]** $[\![\Psi \star \alpha]\!] \subseteq \min([\![\alpha]\!], \preceq_\Psi)$.

[Step 4.1.1] As next step, we show $\min([\![\alpha]\!], \preceq_\Psi) \subseteq [\![\Psi \star \alpha]\!]$ by contradiction. Suppose that there exists some $\omega \in \min([\![\alpha]\!], \preceq_\Psi)$ such that $\omega \notin [\![\Psi \star \alpha]\!]$ holds. We consider two subcases.

$\omega \in [\![\Psi]\!]$. Recall that $\omega \in S_\Psi$ implies that $[\![\Psi \star \varphi_\omega]\!] = \{\omega\}$ holds. From this and $\omega \in [\![\Psi]\!]$ we obtain that $\mathrm{Bel}(\Psi) \cup \mathrm{Bel}(\Psi \star \varphi_\omega)$ is consistent. Because $\mathrm{Bel}(\Psi) \cup \mathrm{Bel}(\Psi \star \varphi_\omega)$ is consistent and because we have $\omega \models \alpha$, we also have that $\mathrm{Bel}(\Psi) \cup \mathrm{Bel}(\Psi \star (\varphi_\omega \wedge \alpha))$ is consistent, as $\star$ satisfies (DL6). Using (DL2) and the consistency of $\mathrm{Bel}(\Psi) \cup \mathrm{Bel}(\Psi \star (\varphi_\omega \wedge \alpha))$ yields that $\mathrm{Bel}(\Psi \star \alpha) \cup \mathrm{Bel}(\Psi \star \varphi_\omega)$ is consistent. From this observation and $[\![\Psi \star \varphi_{\omega_1}]\!] = \{\omega_1\} = [\![\Psi \star (\varphi_\omega \wedge \alpha)]\!]$, we obtain $\omega \in [\![\Psi \star \alpha]\!]$.

$\omega \notin [\![\Psi]\!]$. Because of $[\![\Psi \star \alpha]\!] \neq \emptyset$ there exists some $\omega' \in [\![\Psi \star \alpha]\!]$. In the following, we consider several cases.

The case of $\omega' \notin S_\Psi$ and $\omega' \in [\![\Psi]\!]$. Because φ_ω is consistent, we have that $[\![\varphi_\omega]\!] = \{\omega\}$ and $\varphi_\omega \models \varphi_{\omega,\omega'}$ hold. By employing these observations, we obtain $[\![\Psi \star \varphi_{\omega,\omega'}]\!] \subseteq \{\omega, \omega'\}$ from (DL7). Moreover, because (DL5) holds, $[\![\varphi_\omega]\!] = \{\omega\}$ and $\varphi_\omega \models \varphi_{\omega,\omega'}$ together imply $[\![\Psi \star \varphi_{\omega,\omega'}]\!] \neq \emptyset$.

We will now show that $\omega' \in [\![\Psi \star \varphi_{\omega,\omega'}]\!]$ holds. Therefore, observe that due to (DL0) either $[\![\Psi \star \varphi_{\omega'}]\!] = [\![\Psi]\!]$ or $[\![\Psi \star \varphi_{\omega'}]\!] \subseteq \{\omega'\}$ holds. The former case yields $\omega' \in [\![\Psi \star \varphi_{\omega'}]\!]$, as we have $\omega' \in [\![\Psi]\!]$. In the latter case, we obtain $[\![\Psi \star \varphi_{\omega'}]\!] = \{\omega'\}$, because $\star$ satisfies (DL4) and thus, consistency of $\mathrm{Bel}(\Psi)$ and consistency of $\varphi_{\omega'}$ yields $[\![\Psi \star \varphi_{\omega'}]\!] \neq \emptyset$. Now observe that $[\![\Psi \star \varphi_{\omega'}]\!] = [\![\Psi \star (\varphi_{\omega'} \wedge \varphi_{\omega,\omega'})]\!]$, because $\star$ satisfies (DL4). By using (DL4) we obtain $[\![\Psi \star \varphi_{\omega'}]\!] \cap [\![\Psi \star \varphi_{\omega,\omega'}]\!] \neq \emptyset$, which yields $\omega' \in [\![\Psi \star \varphi_{\omega,\omega'}]\!]$.

Because we have $\omega' \in [\![\Psi \star \varphi_{\omega,\omega'}]\!]$, we obtain $[\![\Psi]\!] \cap [\![\Psi \star \varphi_{\omega,\omega'}]\!] \neq \emptyset$ from $\omega' \in [\![\Psi]\!]$. Consequently, satisfaction of (DL1) by $\star$ yields that $[\![\Psi \star \varphi_{\omega,\omega'}]\!] \subseteq [\![\Psi]\!]$ holds. As

$\omega \notin [\![\Psi]\!]$ and $[\![\Psi \star \varphi_{\omega,\omega'}]\!] \subseteq \{\omega, \omega'\}$ holds, we obtain $[\![\Psi \star \varphi_{\omega,\omega'}]\!] = \{\omega'\}$ from $\omega' \in [\![\Psi \star \varphi_{\omega,\omega'}]\!]$.

By employing (DL6) we obtain that $[\![\Psi \star \varphi_{\omega,\omega'}]\!] = [\![\Psi \star (\varphi_\omega \vee \varphi_{\omega'})]\!]$ holds. Thus, (DL9) yields that $[\![\Psi \star \varphi_{\omega,\omega'}]\!]$ is either equivalent to $[\![\Psi \star \varphi_\omega]\!]$ or $[\![\Psi \star \varphi_{\omega'}]\!]$ or $[\![\Psi \star \varphi_\omega]\!] \cup [\![\Psi \star \varphi_{\omega'}]\!]$. Now recall that we have $[\![\Psi \star \varphi_\omega]\!] = \{\omega\}$. Because of this and because we have $\omega \notin [\![\Psi \star \varphi_{\omega,\omega'}]\!]$, the only possibility is $[\![\Psi \star \varphi_{\omega,\omega'}]\!] = [\![\Psi \star \varphi_{\omega'}]\!] = \{\omega'\}$.

If $[\![\Psi]\!] \neq \{\omega'\}$, then the observation $[\![\Psi \star \varphi_{\omega'}]\!] = \{\omega'\}$ yields the contradiction $\omega' \in \mathcal{S}_\Psi$.

If $[\![\Psi]\!] = \{\omega'\}$, then we obtain that $\omega' \in \mathcal{S}_\Psi$ holds from $[\![\Psi \star \varphi_{\omega'}]\!] = [\![\Psi \star \varphi_{\omega,\omega'}]\!] = \{\omega'\}$ by using (DL3) and the definition of $\mathcal{S}_\Psi$. Note that $\omega' \notin \mathcal{S}_\Psi$ and $[\![\Psi]\!] = \{\omega'\}$ would imply existence of some γ with $\varphi_{\omega'} \models \gamma$ and $\omega' \notin [\![\Psi \star \gamma]\!]$. Then, by using (DL3), consistency of φ_ω and inconsistency of $\mathrm{Bel}(\Psi \star \varphi_\omega) \cup \mathrm{Bel}(\Psi)$ yields inconsistency of $\mathrm{Bel}(\Psi \star (\varphi_\omega \vee \varphi_{\omega'})) \cup \{\varphi_{\omega'}\}$. Due to (DL6), this would lead to the contradiction $\omega' \notin [\![\Psi \star \varphi_{\omega,\omega'}]\!]$.

The case of $\omega' \notin \mathcal{S}_\Psi$ and $\omega' \notin [\![\Psi]\!]$. Let γ be a formula with $\alpha \equiv \gamma \vee \varphi_{\omega'}$ and $\omega' \not\models \gamma$. Using (DL6) we obtain that $[\![\Psi \star \alpha]\!] = [\![\Psi \star (\gamma \vee \varphi_{\omega'})]\!]$ holds. Note that by (DL0) we have $[\![\Psi \star \gamma]\!] = [\![\Psi]\!]$ or $[\![\Psi \star \gamma]\!] \subseteq [\![\gamma]\!]$. This implies that we have $\omega' \notin [\![\Psi \star \gamma]\!]$. Consequently, we obtain $\omega' \in [\![\Psi \star \varphi_{\omega'}]\!]$ from (DL9). Using $\omega' \notin [\![\Psi]\!]$, $\omega' \in [\![\Psi \star \varphi_{\omega'}]\!]$ and (DL0), we obtain $[\![\Psi \star \varphi_{\omega'}]\!] = \{\omega'\}$, which yields the contradiction $\omega' \in \mathcal{S}_\Psi$ according to ($\bigstar$).

The case of $\omega' \in \mathcal{S}_\Psi$. Because of $\omega \in \min([\![\alpha]\!], \preceq_\Psi)$ we have $\omega \preceq_\Psi \omega'$. Moreover, from faithfulness and $\omega \notin [\![\Psi]\!]$, we obtain $\omega' \notin [\![\Psi]\!]$ from $\omega \in \min([\![\alpha]\!], \preceq_\Psi)$. From the definition of $\preceq_\Psi$ we obtain $\omega \in [\![\Psi \star \varphi_{\omega,\omega'}]\!]$. Now let γ be a formula such that $\omega, \omega' \notin [\![\gamma]\!]$ and $\alpha \equiv \gamma \vee \varphi_{\omega,\omega'}$. Note that by (DL0) we have $[\![\Psi \star \gamma]\!] = [\![\Psi]\!]$ or $[\![\Psi \star \gamma]\!] \subseteq [\![\gamma]\!]$. This together with $\omega, \omega' \notin [\![\Psi]\!]$ implies $\omega' \notin [\![\Psi \star \gamma]\!]$. Using (DL6) we obtain that $[\![\Psi \star \alpha]\!] = [\![\Psi \star (\gamma \vee \varphi_{\omega,\omega'})]\!]$ holds. Because $\star$ satisfies (DL9) and $\omega' \notin [\![\Psi \star \gamma]\!]$ holds, we have $[\![\Psi \star \alpha]\!] = [\![\Psi \star \varphi_{\omega,\omega'}]\!]$ or $[\![\Psi \star \alpha]\!] = [\![\Psi \star \gamma]\!] \cup [\![\Psi \star \varphi_{\omega,\omega'}]\!]$. In both cases we obtain $\omega \in [\![\Psi \star \alpha]\!]$ from $\omega \in [\![\Psi \star \varphi_{\omega,\omega'}]\!]$.

In summary, $\min([\![\alpha]\!], \preceq_\Psi) \subseteq [\![\Psi \star \alpha]\!]$ holds.

[Step 4.1.2] In the following, we show by contradiction

that $[\![\Psi \star \alpha]\!] \subseteq \min([\![\alpha]\!], \preceq_\Psi)$ holds. Suppose that there exists some $\omega_1 \in [\![\Psi \star \alpha]\!]$ such that $\omega_1 \notin \min([\![\alpha]\!], \preceq_\Psi)$. From $[\![\alpha]\!] \cap \mathcal{S}_\Psi \neq \emptyset$ we obtain that there exists some $\omega_2 \in \Omega$ with $\omega_2 \in \min([\![\alpha]\!], \preceq_\Psi)$. As shown before, we have $\omega_2 \in [\![\Psi \star \alpha]\!]$. The following distinguishes between the case of $\omega_1 \in [\![\Psi]\!]$ and $\omega_1 \notin [\![\Psi]\!]$.

$\omega_1 \in [\![\Psi]\!]$. If $\omega_1 \in \mathcal{S}_\Psi$ holds, then the faithfulness of $\Psi \mapsto (\preceq_\Psi, \mathcal{S}_\Psi, b_\Psi)$ immediately implies $\omega_1 \in \min([\![\alpha]\!], \preceq_\Psi)$. In the following, we consider the case of $\omega_1 \notin \mathcal{S}_\Psi$.

Because $\star$ satisfies (DL1), we obtain $[\![\Psi \star \alpha]\!] \subseteq [\![\Psi]\!]$ from $\omega_1 \in [\![\Psi]\!]$ and $\omega_1 \in [\![\Psi \star \alpha]\!]$. Consequently, our prior observation $\omega_2 \in [\![\Psi \star \alpha]\!]$ yields $\omega_2 \in [\![\Psi]\!]$. Furthermore, because $\text{Bel}(\Psi)$ and φ_{ω_1} are consistent, we obtain $[\![\Psi \star \varphi_{\omega_1}]\!] \neq \emptyset$ from (DL4). By using (DL0), we obtain that either $[\![\Psi \star \varphi_{\omega_1}]\!] = [\![\Psi]\!]$ or $[\![\Psi \star \varphi_{\omega_1}]\!] = \{\omega_1\}$. Note that we have $|[\![\Psi]\!]| > 1$ and thus, due to ($\bigstar$), the latter case would yield a contradiction to our assumption of $\omega_1 \in \mathcal{S}_\Psi$. Consequently, the only possibility is that we have $[\![\Psi \star \varphi_{\omega_1}]\!] = [\![\Psi]\!]$.

In the following, we consider two disjoint cases:

The case of $[\![\Psi \star \alpha]\!] \neq [\![\Psi]\!]$. We show that applying (DL8) in this case yields the contradiction $\omega_1 \notin [\![\Psi \star \alpha]\!]$. Recall that φ_{ω_1} and α are consistent. Moreover, observe that we have $\varphi_{\omega_1} \notin \text{Bel}(\Psi)$, as $\omega_2 \in [\![\Psi]\!]$, but $\omega_2 \not\models \varphi_{\omega_1}$. Consequently, by using these observations and (DL8), we obtain $[\![\Psi \star (\alpha \vee \varphi_{\omega_1})]\!] \cap [\![\varphi_{\omega_1}]\!] = \emptyset$ from $[\![\Psi \star \alpha]\!] \neq [\![\Psi]\!]$ and $[\![\Psi \star \varphi_{\omega_1}]\!] = [\![\Psi]\!]$, by setting $\beta = \varphi_{\omega_1}$ in (DL8). From (DL6) and $\varphi_{\omega_1} \models \alpha$ we obtain $[\![\Psi \star (\alpha \vee \varphi_{\omega_1})]\!] = [\![\Psi \star \alpha]\!]$. Because we have $\omega_1 \in [\![\varphi_{\omega_1}]\!] = [\![\Psi]\!]$, the combination of these observations yields $\omega_1 \notin [\![\Psi \star \alpha]\!]$.

The case of $[\![\Psi \star \alpha]\!] = [\![\Psi]\!]$. Let γ be a formula such that $\omega_2 \not\models \gamma$ and $\alpha \equiv \gamma \vee \varphi_{\omega_2}$. Because $\star$ satisfies (DL6), we have $[\![\Psi \star \alpha]\!] = [\![\Psi \star (\gamma \vee \varphi_{\omega_2})]\!]$ is equivalent to either $[\![\Psi \star \gamma]\!]$ or $[\![\Psi \star \varphi_{\omega_2}]\!]$ or $[\![\Psi \star \gamma]\!] \cup [\![\Psi \star \varphi_{\omega_2}]\!]$. As $\omega_1 \notin [\![\Psi \star \varphi_{\omega_2}]\!]$ holds, yet $\omega_1 \in [\![\Psi \star (\gamma \vee \varphi_{\omega_2})]\!]$ does hold, it must be the case that $\omega_1 \in [\![\Psi \star \gamma]\!]$ and $[\![\Psi \star \gamma]\!] \subseteq [\![\Psi \star (\gamma \vee \varphi_{\omega_2})]\!]$ hold. Note that this implies also that γ is consistent, as otherwise, due to (DL6), we would obtain $[\![\Psi \star (\gamma \vee \varphi_{\omega_2})]\!] = \{\omega_2\}$. There are two subcases two consider.

The case of $[\![\Psi \star \gamma]\!] \neq [\![\Psi]\!]$. First, recall that $\omega_1, \omega_2 \in$

$[\![\Psi]\!]$ holds, and thus, we obtain that $\varphi_{\omega_1} \notin \mathrm{Bel}(\Psi)$ holds. We employ (DL8) to obtain $\omega_1 \notin [\![\Psi \star (\gamma \vee \varphi_{\omega_1})]\!]$ from $[\![\Psi \star \gamma]\!] \neq [\![\Psi]\!]$ and $[\![\Psi \star \varphi_{\omega_1}]\!] = [\![\Psi]\!]$ by setting $\alpha = \gamma$ and $\beta = \varphi_{\omega_1}$ in (DL8). Because $\star$ satisfies (DL6) and $\varphi_{\omega_1} \models \gamma$, we obtain the contradiction $\omega_1 \notin [\![\Psi \star (\gamma \vee \varphi_{\omega_1})]\!] = [\![\Psi \star \gamma]\!]$.

The case of $[\![\Psi \star \gamma]\!] = [\![\Psi]\!]$. Note that $\omega_2 \in [\![\Psi]\!]$ and $\omega_2 \not\models \gamma$ together imply $\gamma \notin \mathrm{Bel}(\Psi)$. Applying (DL8) to φ_{ω_2} and γ yields $[\![\Psi \star (\gamma \vee \varphi_{\omega_2})]\!] \cap [\![\gamma]\!] = \emptyset$. Consequently, we obtain that $\omega_1 \notin [\![\Psi \star (\gamma \vee \varphi_{\omega_2})]\!]$. Because $\star$ satisfies (DL6) and we have $\alpha \equiv \gamma \vee \varphi_{\omega_2}$, our last observation yields the contradiction $\omega_1 \notin [\![\Psi \star \alpha]\!] = [\![\Psi]\!]$.

This completes the case of $[\![\Psi \star \alpha]\!] \neq [\![\Psi]\!]$. In summary, if $\omega_1 \in [\![\Psi]\!]$, we obtain a contradiction to $\omega_1 \notin \min([\![\alpha]\!], \preceq_\Psi)$ in all possible cases.

$\omega_1 \notin [\![\Psi]\!]$. We start by showing that $\omega_2 \notin [\![\Psi]\!]$ holds. Suppose that we have $\omega_2 \in [\![\Psi]\!]$. Because we have $\omega_2 \in [\![\Psi \star \alpha]\!]$, we obtain that $\mathrm{Bel}(\Psi) \cup \mathrm{Bel}(\Psi \star \alpha)$ is consistent from $\omega_2 \in [\![\Psi]\!]$. Consequently, satisfaction of (DL1) by $\star$ implies $[\![\Psi \star \alpha]\!] \subseteq [\![\Psi]\!]$. This yields a contradiction, as $\omega_1 \notin [\![\Psi]\!]$ does hold, yet we have $\omega_1 \in [\![\Psi \star \alpha]\!]$. Consequently, the only possibility is that $\omega_2 \notin [\![\Psi]\!]$ holds.

Now let γ be a formula such that $\alpha \equiv \gamma \vee \varphi_{\omega_1,\omega_2}$ and $\omega_1, \omega_2 \notin [\![\gamma]\!]$. Satisfaction of (DL0) by $\star$ yields that either $[\![\Psi \star \gamma]\!] = [\![\Psi]\!]$ or $[\![\Psi \star \gamma]\!] \subseteq [\![\gamma]\!]$ holds. This together with $\omega_1, \omega_2 \notin [\![\Psi]\!]$ implies $\omega_1, \omega_2 \notin [\![\Psi \star \gamma]\!]$. Using (DL6) we obtain that $[\![\Psi \star \alpha]\!] = [\![\Psi \star (\gamma \vee \varphi_{\omega,\omega'})]\!]$ holds. Because $\star$ satisfies (DL9) and $\omega_1, \omega_2 \notin [\![\Psi \star \gamma]\!]$ holds, we have $[\![\Psi \star \alpha]\!] = [\![\Psi \star \varphi_{\omega_1,\omega_2}]\!]$ or $[\![\Psi \star \alpha]\!] = [\![\Psi \star \gamma]\!] \cup [\![\Psi \star \varphi_{\omega_1,\omega_2}]\!]$. We obtain $[\![\Psi \star \alpha]\!] \cap \{\omega_1, \omega_2\} = [\![\Psi \star \varphi_{\omega_1,\omega_2}]\!] = \{\omega_1, \omega_2\}$. Applying (DL6) and (DL9) again yields $[\![\Psi \star \varphi_{\omega_1,\omega_2}]\!] = [\![\Psi \star \varphi_{\omega_1}]\!] \cup [\![\Psi \star \varphi_{\omega_2}]\!]$. This together with $\omega_1 \notin [\![\Psi]\!]$ and (DL0) yields $[\![\Psi \star \varphi_{\omega_1}]\!] = \{\omega_1\}$. By the definition of $\mathcal{S}_\Psi$ in $(\bigstar)$, we obtain $\omega_1 \in \mathcal{S}_\Psi$ from $\omega_1 \notin [\![\Psi]\!]$ and $[\![\Psi \star \varphi_{\omega_1}]\!] = \{\omega_1\}$. Moreover, from $[\![\Psi \star \varphi_{\omega_1,\omega_2}]\!] = \{\omega_1, \omega_2\}$ we obtain $\omega_1 \preceq_\Psi \omega_2$ from the definition of $\preceq_\Psi$. This last observation together with $\omega_2 \in \min([\![\alpha]\!], \preceq_\Psi)$ implies the contradiction $\omega_1 \in \min([\![\alpha]\!], \preceq_\Psi)$.

This completes the case of $[\![\alpha]\!] \cap \mathcal{S}_\Psi \neq \emptyset$, for which we have seen that $[\![\Psi \star \alpha]\!] = \min([\![\alpha]\!], \preceq_\Psi)$ holds.

[Step 4.2] *The case of* $[\![\alpha]\!] = \emptyset$ *and* $b_\Psi = \bot$. We show $\alpha \in$

$\mathrm{Bel}(\Psi \star \alpha)$, i..e, $[\![\Psi \star \alpha]\!] = \emptyset$. From the definition of b_Ψ we obtain $\bot \in \mathrm{Bel}(\Psi \star \bot)$ from $b_\Psi = \bot$. Because $\star$ satisfies (DL6), we obtain $\alpha \in \mathrm{Bel}(\Psi \star \alpha)$.

[Step 4.3] *The case of* $[\![\alpha]\!] = \emptyset$ *and* $b_\Psi = \top$. We show $\mathrm{Bel}(\Psi \star \alpha) = \mathrm{Bel}(\Psi)$, i.e., $[\![\Psi \star \alpha]\!] = [\![\Psi]\!]$. Consulting (DL0) yields that $\alpha \in \mathrm{Bel}(\Psi \star \alpha)$ is the only non-trivial case to consider. Because $\star$ satisfies (DL6) we obtain $\bot \in \mathrm{Bel}(\Psi \star \bot)$. From the definition of b_Ψ, and from $b_\Psi = \top$ and $\bot \in \mathrm{Bel}(\Psi \star \bot)$, we obtain $[\![\Psi]\!] = \emptyset$. Consequently, we have $\mathrm{Bel}(\Psi \star \alpha) = \mathrm{Bel}(\Psi)$.

[Step 4.4] *The case of* $[\![\alpha]\!] \neq \emptyset$ *and* $[\![\alpha]\!] \cap \mathcal{S}_\Psi = \emptyset$. We show that $\mathrm{Bel}(\Psi \star \alpha) = \mathrm{Bel}(\Psi)$ holds. Towards a contradiction, we assume that the contrary holds, i.e., that we have $[\![\Psi]\!] \neq [\![\Psi \star \alpha]\!]$. Because $\star$ satisfies (DL0), this assumption yields $[\![\Psi \star \alpha]\!] \subseteq [\![\alpha]\!]$. We consider the case of **[Step 4.4.1]** $[\![\Psi \star \alpha]\!] \cap [\![\Psi]\!] \neq \emptyset$ and the case of **[Step 4.4.2]** $[\![\Psi \star \alpha]\!] \cap [\![\Psi]\!] = \emptyset$ independently.

[Step 4.4.1] $[\![\Psi \star \alpha]\!] \cap [\![\Psi]\!] \neq \emptyset$. At first, we consider the case of $[\![\Psi \star \alpha]\!] \cap [\![\Psi]\!] \neq \emptyset$, i.e., there is some interpretation $\omega \in \Omega$ with $\omega \in [\![\Psi \star \alpha]\!] \cap [\![\Psi]\!] \neq \emptyset$. Note that we have $\omega \in [\![\alpha]\!]$ and $\omega \in [\![\Psi \star \alpha]\!]$ and $\omega \in [\![\Psi]\!]$. In the following, we consider two subcases for φ_ω, which are the only two possible cases according to (DL0).

The subcase of $[\![\Psi \star \varphi_\omega]\!] = [\![\Psi]\!]$. For this case, we consider two subcases.

If $[\![\Psi]\!] = [\![\varphi_\omega]\!]$, then we have $[\![\Psi]\!] = \{\omega\}$. Because of $\omega \in [\![\Psi \star \alpha]\!]$, we obtain $[\![\Psi \star \alpha]\!] \subseteq [\![\Psi]\!]$ from (DL1). This last observation yields a contradiction, as this observation implies $[\![\Psi \star \alpha]\!] = [\![\Psi]\!]$, but we assumed $[\![\Psi]\!] \neq [\![\Psi \star \alpha]\!]$.

The case of $[\![\Psi]\!] \neq [\![\varphi_\omega]\!]$. Note that φ_ω and α are both consistent. Thus, by using (DL8), we obtain that $[\![\Psi \star (\alpha \vee \varphi_\omega)]\!] \cap \{\omega\} = \emptyset$ holds from $[\![\Psi \star \alpha]\!] \cap [\![\Psi]\!] \neq \emptyset$ and $[\![\varphi_\omega]\!] = [\![\Psi]\!]$. As $[\![\varphi_\omega]\!] = \{\omega\}$, we obtain that $\omega \notin [\![\Psi \star (\alpha \vee \varphi_\omega)]\!]$ holds. Moreover, because $\star$ satisfies (DL6), we obtain $[\![\Psi \star (\alpha \vee \varphi_\omega)]\!] = [\![\Psi \star \alpha]\!]$ from $\omega \in [\![\alpha]\!]$. Consequently, we have shown the contradiction $\omega \notin [\![\Psi \star \alpha]\!]$.

The subcase of $[\![\Psi \star \varphi_\omega]\!] \subseteq \{\omega\}$ *and* $[\![\Psi]\!] \neq [\![\varphi_\omega]\!]$. Because $[\![\Psi]\!] \neq \emptyset$ and φ_ω is consistent, we obtain $[\![\Psi \star \varphi_\omega]\!] \neq \emptyset$ from (DL4). Combining this observation with $[\![\Psi \star \varphi_\omega]\!] \subseteq \{\omega\}$

implies $[\![\Psi \star \varphi_\omega]\!] = \{\omega\}$, which shows that we have $\omega \in \mathcal{S}_\Psi$. This yields a contradiction, as we have $\omega \models \alpha$ and thus, we obtain $[\![\alpha]\!] \cap \mathcal{S}_\Psi \neq \emptyset$.

[Step 4.4.2] *The case of* $[\![\Psi \star \alpha]\!] \cap [\![\Psi]\!] = \emptyset$. In the following, we consider the case of $[\![\Psi \star \alpha]\!] \cap [\![\Psi]\!] = \emptyset$.

If $[\![\alpha]\!] = \{\omega\}$ is a singleton set, then $[\![\Psi \star \alpha]\!] \subseteq [\![\alpha]\!]$ implies that we have either $[\![\Psi \star \alpha]\!] = \{\omega\}$ or $[\![\Psi \star \alpha]\!] = \emptyset$. The former case implies that $\omega \in \mathcal{S}_\Psi$ holds and thus we obtain the contradiction $[\![\alpha]\!] \cap \mathcal{S}_\Psi \neq \emptyset$ for this case. We consider the case of $[\![\Psi \star \alpha]\!] = \emptyset$. From consistency of α and (DL4) we obtain that $\mathrm{Bel}(\Psi)$ is inconsistent, showing that $[\![\Psi]\!] = [\![\Psi \star \alpha]\!]$ holds.

We consider the remaining case of $|[\![\alpha]\!]| > 1$, for which we consider two subcases:

The subcase of $[\![\Psi \star \alpha]\!] = \emptyset$. As before, the consistency of α and satisfaction of (DL4) by $\star$ yields that $\mathrm{Bel}(\Psi)$ is inconsistent, which shows that $[\![\Psi]\!] = [\![\Psi \star \alpha]\!]$ holds.

The subcase of $[\![\Psi \star \alpha]\!] \neq \emptyset$. Let $\omega \in [\![\Psi \star \alpha]\!]$ and let γ_ω be a formula such that $\alpha \equiv \gamma_\omega \vee \varphi_\omega$ and $\omega \notin [\![\gamma_\omega]\!]$ holds. Note that by (DL0) we have $[\![\Psi \star \gamma_\omega]\!] = [\![\Psi]\!]$ or $[\![\Psi \star \gamma_\omega]\!] \subseteq [\![\gamma_\omega]\!]$. This together with $\omega \notin [\![\Psi]\!]$ implies $\omega \notin [\![\Psi \star \gamma_\omega]\!]$. By (CL4) we obtain $[\![\Psi \star \alpha]\!] = [\![\Psi \star (\gamma_\omega \vee \varphi_\omega)]\!]$. Because $\star$ satisfies (CL6) and $\omega \notin [\![\Psi \star \gamma_\omega]\!]$ holds, we have $[\![\Psi \star \alpha]\!] = [\![\Psi \star \varphi_\omega]\!]$ or $[\![\Psi \star \alpha]\!] = [\![\Psi \star \gamma_\omega]\!] \cup [\![\Psi \star \varphi_\omega]\!]$. From this observation, we obtain $[\![\Psi \star \alpha]\!] \cap \{\omega\} = [\![\Psi \star \varphi_\omega]\!] = \{\omega\}$, which yields $\omega \in [\![\Psi \star \varphi_\omega]\!]$. Because $\star$ satisfies (DL0) and we have $\omega \notin [\![\Psi]\!]$, we obtain $[\![\Psi \star \varphi_\omega]\!] = \{\omega\}$ from $\omega \in [\![\Psi \star \varphi_\omega]\!]$, a contradiction to $[\![\Psi \star \varphi_\omega]\!] \neq \{\omega\}$.

This completes the "$\Rightarrow$"-direction of the proof, i.e., we have shown that every dynamic-limited revision operator for $\mathcal{E}$ is revision-compatible with some faithful limited-assignment for $\mathcal{E}$, namely the assignment $\Psi \mapsto (\preceq_\Psi, \mathcal{S}_\Psi, b_\Psi)$ that we constructed at the beginning.

The "$\Leftarrow$"-direction. Let $\star$ be a belief change operator for $\mathcal{E}$ and let $\Psi \mapsto (\preceq_\Psi, \mathcal{S}_\Psi, b_\Psi)$ be a faithful limited assignment that is revision-compatible with $\star$. We show satisfaction of (DL0)–(DL8). We start with (DL6) and continue with the remaining postulates in ascending order.

(DL6) Let $\alpha \equiv \beta$, i.e., $[\![\alpha]\!] = [\![\beta]\!]$. From revision-compatibility of

$\Psi \mapsto (\preceq_\Psi, \mathcal{S}_\Psi, b_\Psi)$ with $\star$ we immediately obtain $[\![\Psi \star \alpha]\!] = [\![\Psi \star \beta]\!]$.

(DL0) We have to show that either $\mathrm{Bel}(\Psi \star \alpha) = \mathrm{Bel}(\Psi)$ or $\alpha \in \mathrm{Bel}(\Psi \star \alpha)$ holds. Due to the revision-compatibility of $\Psi \mapsto (\preceq_\Psi, \mathcal{S}_\Psi, b_\Psi)$ with $\star$ there are three cases to consider. If $[\![\alpha]\!] \cap \mathcal{S}_\Psi \neq \emptyset$, we obtain $[\![\Psi \star \alpha]\!] \subseteq [\![\alpha]\!]$. Consequently, we have that $\alpha \in \mathrm{Bel}(\Psi \star \alpha)$. If $[\![\alpha]\!] = \emptyset$ and $b_\Psi = \perp$ holds, we obtain $[\![\Psi \star \alpha]\!] = \emptyset$. Consequently, we have $\mathrm{Bel}(\Psi \star \alpha) = \mathrm{Cn}(\perp)$, and thus $\alpha \in \mathrm{Bel}(\Psi \star \alpha)$ holds. If none of the cases above applies, we obtain $[\![\Psi \star \alpha]\!] = [\![\Psi]\!]$, which is equivalent to $\mathrm{Bel}(\Psi \star \alpha) = \mathrm{Bel}(\Psi)$.

(DL1) Suppose that $\mathrm{Bel}(\Psi) \cup \mathrm{Bel}(\Psi \star \alpha)$ is consistent, i.e., $[\![\Psi]\!] \cap [\![\Psi \star \alpha]\!]$ is non-empty. We have to show that $\mathrm{Bel}(\Psi) \subseteq \mathrm{Bel}(\Psi \star \alpha)$ holds. Due to the revision-compatibility of $\Psi \mapsto (\preceq_\Psi, \mathcal{S}_\Psi, b_\Psi)$ with $\star$ there are three cases to consider. If $[\![\alpha]\!] \cap \mathcal{S}_\Psi \neq \emptyset$, then $\mathrm{Bel}(\Psi) \cup \mathrm{Bel}(\Psi \star \alpha)$ implies that $\mathcal{S}_\Psi \cap [\![\Psi]\!] \neq \emptyset$ and $[\![\Psi \star \alpha]\!] = \min([\![\alpha]\!], \preceq_\Psi)$. From faithfulness of $\Psi \mapsto (\preceq_\Psi, \mathcal{S}_\Psi, b_\Psi)$ we obtain $\min([\![\alpha]\!], \preceq_\Psi) \subseteq [\![\Psi]\!]$, which shows satisfaction of (DL1) for this case. If $[\![\alpha]\!] = \emptyset$ and $b_\Psi = \perp$ holds, we obtain $[\![\Psi \star \alpha]\!] = \emptyset \subseteq [\![\Psi]\!]$. If none of the cases above applies, we obtain $[\![\Psi \star \alpha]\!] = [\![\Psi]\!]$, which is equivalent to $\mathrm{Bel}(\Psi \star \alpha) = \mathrm{Bel}(\Psi)$.

(DL2) Suppose that $\mathrm{Bel}(\Psi) \cup \mathrm{Bel}(\Psi \star (\alpha \wedge \beta))$ is consistent and $\mathrm{Bel}(\Psi \star (\alpha \wedge \beta)) \neq \mathrm{Bel}(\Psi)$. We have to show that $\mathrm{Bel}(\Psi \star \alpha) \cup \mathrm{Bel}(\Psi \star \beta)$ is consistent. Due to the revision-compatibility of $\Psi \mapsto (\preceq_\Psi, \mathcal{S}_\Psi, b_\Psi)$ with $\star$, we have that $\mathrm{Bel}(\Psi \star (\alpha \wedge \beta)) \neq \mathrm{Bel}(\Psi)$ implies that either $[\![\alpha \wedge \beta]\!] \cap \mathcal{S}_\Psi \neq \emptyset$ or $[\![\alpha \wedge \beta]\!] = \emptyset$ holds. The latter case is impossible, as this case, together with the consistency of $\mathrm{Bel}(\Psi) \cup \mathrm{Bel}(\Psi \star (\alpha \wedge \beta))$, would yield $\mathrm{Bel}(\Psi \star (\alpha \wedge \beta)) = \mathrm{Bel}(\Psi)$. For the case of $[\![\alpha \wedge \beta]\!] \cap \mathcal{S}_\Psi = \emptyset$ we obtain $[\![\alpha]\!] \cap \mathcal{S}_\Psi = \emptyset$ and $[\![\beta]\!] \cap \mathcal{S}_\Psi = \emptyset$. Because $\mathrm{Bel}(\Psi) \cup \mathrm{Bel}(\Psi \star (\alpha \wedge \beta))$ is consistent, we also have $\min([\![\alpha \wedge \beta]\!], \preceq_\Psi) \subseteq [\![\Psi]\!]$. Thus, because $\Psi \mapsto (\preceq_\Psi, \mathcal{S}_\Psi, b_\Psi)$ is faithful, we obtain that $\min([\![\alpha]\!], \preceq_\Psi) \subseteq [\![\Psi]\!]$ and $\min([\![\beta]\!], \preceq_\Psi) \subseteq [\![\Psi]\!]$ hold. We obtain $\min([\![\alpha \wedge \beta]\!], \preceq_\Psi) = \min([\![\alpha]\!], \preceq_\Psi) \cap \min([\![\beta]\!], \preceq_\Psi)$, which implies that $\mathrm{Bel}(\Psi \star \alpha) \cup \mathrm{Bel}(\Psi \star \beta)$ is consistent.

(DL3) Suppose that $[\![\Psi]\!] \cap [\![\alpha]\!] \neq \emptyset$ and $[\![\Psi]\!] \cup [\![\Psi \star \alpha]\!] \neq \emptyset$ and $\alpha \models \gamma$ and $[\![\alpha]\!] \not\subseteq [\![\Psi \star \gamma]\!]$ holds. Furthermore, suppose that β is consistent and that $[\![\Psi]\!] \cap [\![\Psi \star \beta]\!] = \emptyset$ holds. We show that $[\![\Psi \star (\alpha \vee \beta)]\!] \cap [\![\Psi]\!] = \emptyset$ holds.

As an intermediate step, we show that $[\![\alpha]\!] \cap \mathcal{S}_\Psi = \emptyset$ holds. We obtain consistency of α from $[\![\Psi]\!] \cap [\![\alpha]\!] \neq \emptyset$. Considering Definition 8.4 and the revision-compatibility of $\Psi \mapsto (\preceq_\Psi, \mathcal{S}_\Psi, b_\Psi)$ with $\star$, we obtain exactly two cases from the consistency of α and $[\![\Psi]\!] \cup [\![\Psi \star \alpha]\!] \neq \emptyset$:

The case of $[\![\alpha]\!] \cap \mathcal{S}_\Psi = \emptyset$. Then we obtain the desired result $[\![\alpha]\!] \cap \mathcal{S}_\Psi = \emptyset$.

The case of $[\![\alpha]\!] \cap \mathcal{S}_\Psi \neq \emptyset$. We have $[\![\Psi]\!] = [\![\Psi \star \alpha]\!]$ for this case. Using faithfulness of $\Psi \mapsto (\preceq_\Psi, \mathcal{S}_\Psi, b_\Psi)$ and the revision-compatibility of $\Psi \mapsto (\preceq_\Psi, \mathcal{S}_\Psi, b_\Psi)$ with $\star$, we obtain $[\![\Psi]\!] \subseteq [\![\alpha]\!] \cap \mathcal{S}_\Psi$ from $[\![\Psi]\!] = [\![\Psi \star \alpha]\!]$. Moreover, $[\![\Psi]\!] = [\![\Psi \star \alpha]\!]$ implies that we have $[\![\Psi]\!] = [\![\Psi \star \alpha]\!] = \min([\![\alpha]\!], \preceq_\Psi)$. Because $\Psi \mapsto (\preceq_\Psi, \mathcal{S}_\Psi, b_\Psi)$ is faithful, this implies also that $\{\min([\![\alpha]\!], \preceq_\Psi)\} \subseteq \min(\mathcal{S}_\Psi, \preceq_\Psi)$ holds. Consequently, $\alpha \models \gamma$ implies that $\min([\![\alpha]\!], \preceq_\Psi) \subseteq \min([\![\gamma]\!], \preceq_\Psi)$ holds. By employing the revision-compatibility of $\Psi \mapsto (\preceq_\Psi, \mathcal{S}_\Psi, b_\Psi)$ with $\star$ again, we obtain the contradiction $\min([\![\alpha]\!], \preceq_\Psi) \subseteq [\![\Psi \star \gamma]\!]$.

In summary, the only possibility is that $[\![\alpha]\!] \cap \mathcal{S}_\Psi = \emptyset$ holds.

Now, we show that $[\![\Psi \star (\alpha \vee \beta)]\!] \not\subseteq [\![\Psi]\!]$ holds. By employing the revision-compatibility of $\Psi \mapsto (\preceq_\Psi, \mathcal{S}_\Psi, b_\Psi)$ with $\star$ we obtain $[\![\beta]\!] \cap \mathcal{S}_\Psi \neq \emptyset$ from $[\![\Psi]\!] \cap [\![\Psi \star \beta]\!] = \emptyset$. Furthermore, this last result implies $[\![\Psi \star (\beta)]\!] = \min([\![\beta]\!], \preceq_\Psi)$. Consequently, from this and $[\![\alpha]\!] \cap \mathcal{S}_\Psi = \emptyset$, we obtain $[\![\beta]\!] \cap \mathcal{S}_\Psi = [\![\alpha \vee \beta]\!] \cap \mathcal{S}_\Psi \neq \emptyset$. We obtain that $[\![\Psi \star (\alpha \vee \beta)]\!] = \min([\![\alpha \vee \beta]\!], \preceq_\Psi) = \min([\![\beta]\!], \preceq_\Psi)$ holds. Finally, by employing $[\![\Psi \star \beta]\!] = \min([\![\beta]\!], \preceq_\Psi)$, we obtain $[\![\Psi \star (\alpha \vee \beta)]\!] \cap [\![\Psi]\!] = \emptyset$ from $[\![\Psi]\!] \cap [\![\Psi \star \beta]\!] = \emptyset$.

(DL4) Suppose that $\mathrm{Bel}(\Psi \star \alpha)$ is inconsistent. We show that $\mathrm{Bel}(\Psi)$ is inconsistent or α is inconsistent, by obtaining a contradiction when assuming the contrary, i.e., $\mathrm{Bel}(\Psi)$ is consistent and α is consistent. From revision-compatibility of $\Psi \mapsto (\preceq_\Psi, \mathcal{S}_\Psi, b_\Psi)$ with $\star$ and consistency of α, we obtain $[\![\Psi \star \alpha]\!] = [\![\Psi]\!]$, a contradiction between the inconsistency of $\mathrm{Bel}(\Psi \star \alpha)$ and the consistency of $\mathrm{Bel}(\Psi)$.

(DL5) Suppose that $\mathrm{Bel}(\Psi \star \alpha)$ is consistent and $\alpha \models \beta$ holds, i.e., we have $[\![\Psi \star \alpha]\!] \neq \emptyset$ and $[\![\alpha]\!] \subseteq [\![\beta]\!]$. We show that $\mathrm{Bel}(\Psi \star \beta)$ is consistent. If $\alpha \equiv \beta$, we obtain the claim directly from (DL6). In the following we assume $[\![\alpha]\!] \subsetneq [\![\beta]\!]$. Consequently, we have that β is consistent. From the revision-compatibility of $\Psi \mapsto (\preceq_\Psi, \mathcal{S}_\Psi, b_\Psi)$ with $\star$ and consistency of $[\![\Psi \star \alpha]\!]$ we obtain that either $[\![\Psi \star \alpha]\!] = \min([\![\alpha]\!], \preceq_\Psi)$ or $[\![\Psi \star \alpha]\!] = [\![\Psi]\!]$ holds. We consider three cases.

α *is inconsistent.* In this case, we have $[\![\Psi \star \alpha]\!] = [\![\Psi]\!]$. As a direct consequence, we obtain from the revision-compatibility of $\star$ with $\Psi \mapsto (\preceq_\Psi, \mathcal{S}_\Psi, b_\Psi)$ that $[\![\Psi]\!] \neq \emptyset$ holds. Recalling that β is consistent, consultation of revision-compatibility reveals that $\mathrm{Bel}(\Psi \star \beta)$ is consistent in all cases.

α *is consistent and* $[\![\Psi \star \alpha]\!] = \min([\![\alpha]\!], \preceq_\Psi)$. From revision-compatibility of $\Psi \mapsto (\preceq_\Psi, \mathcal{S}_\Psi, b_\Psi)$ with $\star$ we obtain $[\![\alpha]\!] \cap \mathcal{S}_\Psi \neq \emptyset$. Consequently, we also have $[\![\beta]\!] \cap \mathcal{S}_\Psi \neq \emptyset$. Consulting revision-compatibility yields that $\mathrm{Bel}(\Psi \star \beta)$ is consistent.

α *is consistent and* $[\![\Psi \star \alpha]\!] = [\![\Psi]\!]$. From consistency of α we obtain consistency of β. Thus, by revision-compatibility, we obtain that $\mathrm{Bel}(\Psi \star \beta)$ is consistent.

(DL7) Suppose α is consistent and $\alpha \in \mathrm{Bel}(\Psi \star \alpha)$ and $\alpha \models \beta$, i.e., $[\![\Psi \star \alpha]\!] \subseteq [\![\alpha]\!]$ and $\emptyset \neq [\![\alpha]\!] \subseteq [\![\beta]\!]$. The latter implies that β is consistent as well. We show that $\beta \in \mathrm{Bel}(\Psi \star \beta)$ holds. If $[\![\beta]\!] \cap \mathcal{S}_\Psi$ is non-empty, then we obtain $\beta \in \mathrm{Bel}(\Psi \star \beta)$. In the remaining case of $[\![\beta]\!] \cap \mathcal{S}_\Psi = \emptyset$ and β is consistent, we obtain $[\![\alpha]\!] \cap \mathcal{S}_\Psi = \emptyset$ from $[\![\alpha]\!] \subseteq [\![\beta]\!]$. From $[\![\Psi \star \alpha]\!] \subseteq [\![\alpha]\!]$ and the revision-compatibility of $\Psi \mapsto (\preceq_\Psi, \mathcal{S}_\Psi, b_\Psi)$ with $\star$ we obtain two cases:

$[\![\Psi \star \alpha]\!] = [\![\Psi]\!]$. Using the consistency of β and the revision-compatibility of $\Psi \mapsto (\preceq_\Psi, \mathcal{S}_\Psi, b_\Psi)$ with $\star$ again, we obtain $[\![\Psi \star \beta]\!] = [\![\Psi]\!]$. From $[\![\Psi]\!] = [\![\Psi \star \alpha]\!] \subseteq [\![\alpha]\!]$ and $[\![\alpha]\!] \subseteq [\![\beta]\!]$ we obtain $[\![\Psi \star \alpha]\!] = [\![\Psi]\!] = [\![\Psi \star \beta]\!] \subseteq [\![\beta]\!]$.

$[\![\alpha]\!] = \emptyset$ *and* $b_\Psi = \bot$. Because β is consistent and $(\mathrm{CLA}_\bot)$ holds, we obtain $\mathcal{S}_\Psi = \Omega$, which is a contradiction to $[\![\beta]\!] \cap \mathcal{S}_\Psi = \emptyset$.

(DL8) Suppose that α, β are consistent and $\beta \notin \mathrm{Bel}(\Psi)$. Moreover, suppose that $[\![\Psi \star \alpha]\!] \neq [\![\Psi]\!]$ and $[\![\Psi \star \beta]\!] = [\![\Psi]\!]$. We show that $[\![\Psi \star (\alpha \vee \beta)]\!] \cap [\![\beta]\!] = \emptyset$ holds. The revision-compatibility of $\Psi \mapsto (\preceq_\Psi, \mathcal{S}_\Psi, b_\Psi)$ with $\star$ yields the following two conclusions. First, because α is consistent and we have $[\![\Psi \star \alpha]\!] \neq [\![\Psi]\!]$, we obtain $[\![\alpha]\!] \cap \mathcal{S}_\Psi \neq \emptyset$. Second, because β is consistent and we have $[\![\Psi \star \beta]\!] = [\![\Psi]\!]$, yet $\beta \notin \mathrm{Bel}(\Psi)$ holds, we obtain $[\![\beta]\!] \cap \mathcal{S}_\Psi = \emptyset$. Consequently, we obtain $[\![\alpha]\!] \cap \mathcal{S}_\Psi = [\![\alpha \vee \beta]\!] \cap \mathcal{S}_\Psi$ and thus that $\min([\![\alpha \vee \beta]\!], \preceq_\Psi) = \min([\![\alpha]\!], \preceq_\Psi)$ holds. From

$[\![\alpha \vee \beta]\!] \cap \mathcal{S}_\Psi \neq \emptyset$ and the revision-compatibility of $\Psi \mapsto (\preceq_\Psi, \mathcal{S}_\Psi, b_\Psi)$ with $\star$, we obtain $[\![\Psi \star (\alpha \vee \beta)]\!] = \min([\![\alpha \vee \beta]\!], \preceq_\Psi)$. This last observation together with $[\![\beta]\!] \cap \mathcal{S}_\Psi = \emptyset$ yields $[\![\Psi \star (\alpha \vee \beta)]\!] \cap [\![\beta]\!] = \emptyset$.

(DL9) In the following, suppose that α, β are formulas. We show that $[\![\Psi \star (\alpha \vee \beta)]\!] = [\![\Psi \star \alpha]\!]$ or $[\![\Psi \star (\alpha \vee \beta)]\!] = [\![\Psi \star \beta]\!]$ or $[\![\Psi \star (\alpha \vee \beta)]\!] = [\![\Psi \star \alpha]\!] \cup [\![\Psi \star \beta]\!]$ holds. Note that by revision-compatibility of $\Psi \mapsto (\preceq_\Psi, \mathcal{S}_\Psi, b_\Psi)$ with $\star$ there are several cases for each of α and β. In the following, we consider (potentially overlapping) cases, all other not explicitly mentioned cases will follow by (DL6) or symmetry:

The case of $[\![\alpha]\!] \cap \mathcal{S}_\Psi \neq \emptyset$ *and* $[\![\beta]\!] \cap \mathcal{S}_\Psi \neq \emptyset$. For this case observe that $[\![\alpha \vee \beta]\!] \cap \mathcal{S}_\Psi = ([\![\alpha]\!] \cap \mathcal{S}_\Psi) \cup ([\![\beta]\!] \cap \mathcal{S}_\Psi)$ holds. We obtain satisfaction of (DL9) by Lemma 2.1.

The case of $[\![\alpha]\!] \cap \mathcal{S}_\Psi \neq \emptyset$ *and* $[\![\beta]\!] \cap \mathcal{S}_\Psi = \emptyset$. In this case, we obtain $[\![\alpha \vee \beta]\!] \cap \mathcal{S}_\Psi = [\![\alpha]\!] \cap \mathcal{S}_\Psi$ from $[\![\alpha]\!] \cap \mathcal{S}_\Psi \neq \emptyset$. Considering revision-compatibility yields that $[\![\Psi \star (\alpha \vee \beta)]\!] = [\![\Psi \star \alpha]\!]$ holds.

The case of $[\![\alpha]\!] \cap \mathcal{S}_\Psi = \emptyset$, *and* $[\![\beta]\!] \cap \mathcal{S}_\Psi = \emptyset$ *and* $[\![\alpha]\!] \neq [\![\beta]\!]$. We obtain $[\![\alpha \vee \beta]\!] = [\![\alpha]\!] \cup [\![\beta]\!] \neq \emptyset$ from $[\![\alpha]\!] \neq [\![\beta]\!]$. Because $[\![\alpha]\!] \cap \mathcal{S}_\Psi = \emptyset$ and $[\![\beta]\!] \cap \mathcal{S}_\Psi = \emptyset$ holds, we have $[\![\alpha \vee \beta]\!] \cap \mathcal{S}_\Psi = \emptyset$. We obtain $[\![\Psi \star (\alpha \vee \beta)]\!] = [\![\Psi]\!]$. Moreover, we have that $[\![\alpha]\!] \neq \emptyset$ or $[\![\beta]\!] \neq \emptyset$ holds. This implies that $[\![\Psi \star \alpha]\!] = [\![\Psi]\!]$ or $[\![\Psi \star \beta]\!] = [\![\Psi]\!]$ holds. We obtain that at last one of $[\![\Psi \star (\alpha \vee \beta)]\!] = [\![\Psi \star \alpha]\!]$ or $[\![\Psi \star (\alpha \vee \beta)]\!] = [\![\Psi \star \beta]\!]$ holds.

This completes the proof of Theorem 8.6.   □

In the following section, we consider the postulates of dynamic-limited revision operators.

8.3. The Postulates of Dynamic-Limited Revision

Dynamic-limited revision operators have many postulates in common with generalized credibility-limited revision operators (operators that satisfy (GCL1)–(GCL7) from p. 143). This is intended, as dynamic-limited revision operator are a generalization of generalized credibility-limited revision operators that comply with arbitrary acceptance descriptions.

Before considering the postulates (DL0)–(DL9) in detail and the differences to (GCL1)–(GCL7), recall that compliance of $\star$ with some acceptance descriptions means that we obtain

$$Scp^{\star}(\Psi) = \mathrm{Bel}(\Psi) \cup \{\alpha \mid \alpha \in \mathrm{Bel}(\Psi \star \alpha)\}$$

where $\{\alpha \mid \alpha \in \mathrm{Bel}(\Psi \star \alpha)\}$ satisfies single-sentence closure and disjunction completeness. Proposition 7.3 showed that $\{\alpha \mid \alpha \in \mathrm{Bel}(\Psi \star \alpha)\}$ satisfies single-sentence closure and disjunction completeness if there is (in most cases) some set of interpretations M such that $\{\alpha \mid \alpha \in \mathrm{Bel}(\Psi \star \alpha)\} = \{\alpha \mid [\![\alpha]\!] \cap M \neq \emptyset\}$. Dynamic-limited revision operators fit very well to this property, as we have shown in Theorem 8.6 that semantically, each dynamic-limited revision operator $\star$ maintains some set of interpretations $\mathcal{S}_{\Psi}$ for each epistemic state Ψ and either yields $[\![\Psi \star \alpha]\!] \subseteq \mathcal{S}_{\Psi}$ whenever $[\![\alpha]\!] \cap \mathcal{S}_{\Psi} \neq \emptyset$ and otherwise falls back to the prior situation, i.e., $[\![\Psi \star \alpha]\!] = [\![\Psi]\!]$. In the following we consider the postulates (DL0)–(DL9) in detail.

Treatment of New Beliefs. The first postulate, the postulate

(DL0) $\mathrm{Bel}(\Psi \star \alpha) = \mathrm{Bel}(\Psi)$ or $\alpha \in \mathrm{Bel}(\Psi \star \alpha)$.

describes that the new information α is accepted for revision (the case of $\alpha \in \mathrm{Bel}(\Psi \star \alpha)$) or the agent falls back to her prior beliefs (the case of $\mathrm{Bel}(\Psi \star \alpha) = \mathrm{Bel}(\Psi)$). Clearly, (DL0) is the same as (GCL1) of generalized credibility-limited revision operators. Regarding compliance with acceptance descriptions, this postulate ensures that the scope of every dynamic-limited revision operator $\star$ falls into the scheme of Definition 7.6, i.e., we obtain:

$$Scp^{\star}(\Psi) = \mathrm{Bel}(\Psi) \cup \{\alpha \mid \alpha \in \mathrm{Bel}(\Psi \star \alpha)\}$$

Note that having only (DL0) does not ensure that $\star$ complies with some acceptance description, because (DL0) does not imply that $\{\alpha \mid \alpha \in \text{Bel}(\Psi \star \alpha)\}$ satisfies single-sentence closure and disjunction completeness. Furthermore, note that according to (DL0) for dynamic-limited revision operators the only beliefs that change the beliefs of an agent are those beliefs that get accepted for revision.

Treatment of Prior Beliefs. For (generalized) credibility-limited revision operators for epistemic states, the postulate (GCL2) determines how prior beliefs are treated. The postulates (DL1)–(DL3) are meant to implement a more flexible treatment of prior beliefs than (GCL2). As discussed in the previous section, in particular in and after Example 8.1, (GCL2) leads to incompatibilities with some acceptance descriptions. The rationale is that (GCL2) enforces acceptance of beliefs that are impossible to accept according to every acceptance description. Semantically, we have seen that the reason for this is that $\llbracket \Psi \rrbracket$ is always part of $\mathcal{S}_\Psi$ (as illustrated in Figure 8.1, where $\mathcal{S}_\Psi$ corresponds to M). As shown by Theorem 8.6, for dynamic-limited revision it is not mandatory that $\llbracket \Psi \rrbracket \subseteq \mathcal{S}_\Psi$ holds (but it is also possible to have this behaviour).

Instead, dynamic-limited revision operators yield a subset of $\mathcal{S}_\Psi$ when a new belief shares models with $\mathcal{S}_\Psi$. We obtain the dynamics that is illustrated in Figure 8.2 and Figure 8.3 (where $\mathcal{S}_\Psi$ corresponds to M). The syntactic postulates (DL1)–(DL3) give rise to this dynamics. In the following, we discuss how each of these postulates corresponds to one of the core aspects of (GCL2), identified at the end of Section 8.1, and how (DL1)–(DL3) implement the dynamics illustrated in Figure 8.2 and Figure 8.3. We start with the first condition.

> *Exclusiveness of* $\llbracket \Psi \rrbracket$. The models of $\text{Bel}(\Psi)$ have an exclusive status when it comes to revision. If $\text{Bel}(\Psi \star \alpha)$ is consistent with the prior beliefs, then the revision should preserve all prior beliefs. This is directly expressed by the first postulate:
>
> (DL1) If $\text{Bel}(\Psi) \cup \text{Bel}(\Psi \star \alpha)$ is consistent, then $\text{Bel}(\Psi) \subseteq \text{Bel}(\Psi \star \alpha)$.

A characteristic of beliefs that gets accepted for revision is that these are the only beliefs that are capable of changing the beliefs of an agent,

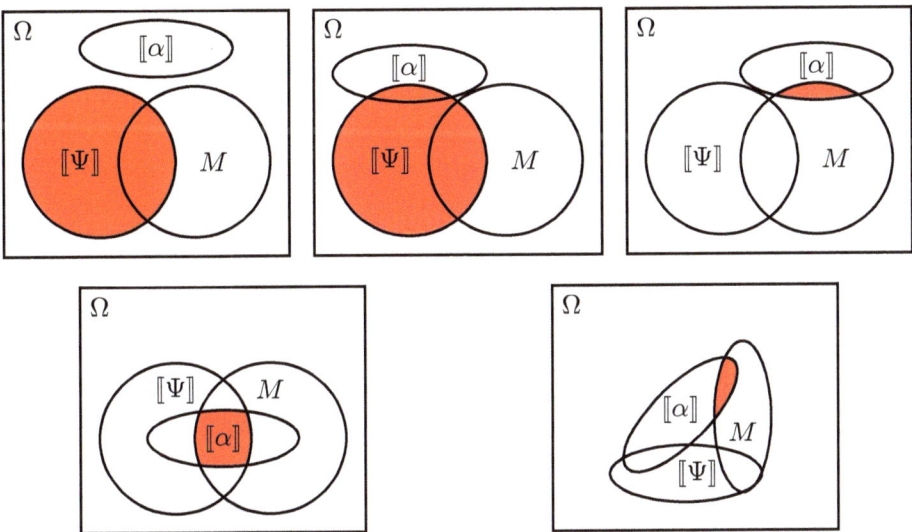

Figure 8.2: Elements in $\llbracket \Psi \circ \alpha \rrbracket$ (red area) depending on how $\llbracket \alpha \rrbracket$, $\llbracket \Psi \rrbracket$ and M are related. This figure illustrates the case of $\llbracket \Psi \rrbracket \cap M \neq \emptyset$ and $\llbracket \Psi \rrbracket \setminus M \neq \emptyset$.

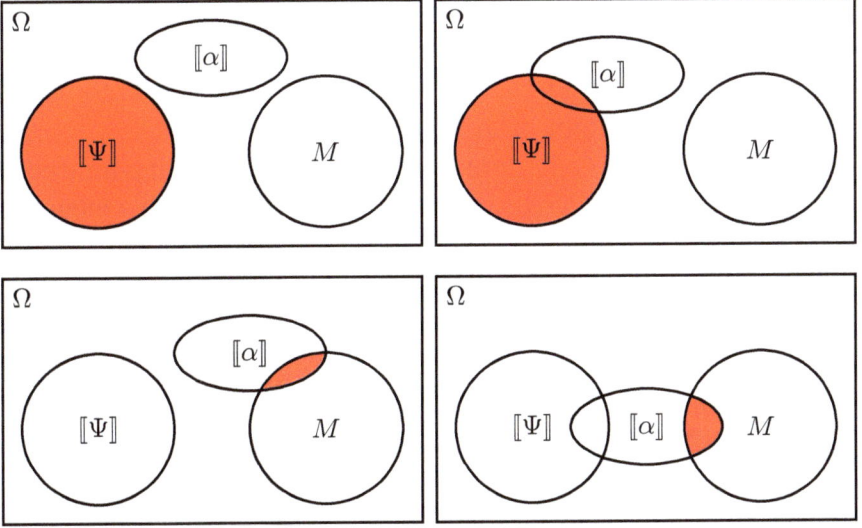

Figure 8.3: Elements in $\llbracket \Psi \circ \alpha \rrbracket$ (red area) depending on how $\llbracket \alpha \rrbracket$, $\llbracket \Psi \rrbracket$ and M are related. This figure illustrates the case of $\llbracket \Psi \rrbracket \cap M = \emptyset$.

i.e., $\mathrm{Bel}(\Psi \star \alpha) \neq \mathrm{Bel}(\alpha)$ implies that α get accepted for revision[3]. The remaining postulates (DL2) and (DL3) make use of this property.

Equal Treatment of Elements in $[\![\Psi]\!] \cap \mathcal{S}_\Psi$. The original principle (implied by (GCL2)) expresses that is no internal preference between the elements of $[\![\Psi]\!]$, in the sense that if $[\![\Psi \circ \alpha]\!] \cap [\![\Psi]\!] \cap [\![\alpha]\!] \neq \emptyset$ holds, we would obtain $[\![\Psi]\!] \cap [\![\alpha]\!] \subseteq [\![\Psi \circ \alpha]\!]$. However, dynamic-limited revision operators give priority to elements of $\mathcal{S}_\Psi$, which might include a (strict) subset of $[\![\Psi]\!]$. We adapt the equal treatment of elements to dynamic-limited revision operators to be restricted to elements of $\mathcal{S}_\Psi$. This means if $[\![\Psi \circ \alpha]\!] \cap [\![\Psi]\!] \cap [\![\alpha]\!] \cap \mathcal{S}_\Psi \neq \emptyset$ holds, then $[\![\Psi]\!] \cap [\![\alpha]\!] \cap \mathcal{S}_\Psi \subseteq [\![\Psi \circ \alpha]\!]$. The postulate

(DL2) If $\mathrm{Bel}(\Psi) \cup \mathrm{Bel}(\Psi \star (\alpha \wedge \beta))$ is consistent and $\mathrm{Bel}(\Psi) \neq \mathrm{Bel}(\Psi \star (\alpha \wedge \beta))$, then $\mathrm{Bel}(\Psi \star \alpha) \cup \mathrm{Bel}(\Psi \star \beta)$ is consistent.

expresses this rather implicitly. Informally, the postulate (DL2) could be read as follows:

> If $[\![\Psi \circ (\alpha \wedge \beta)]\!]$ shares models with $[\![\Psi]\!] \cap \mathcal{S}_\Psi$, i.e., $[\![\Psi \circ (\alpha \wedge \beta)]\!] \cap [\![\Psi]\!] \cap [\![\alpha]\!] \cap [\![\beta]\!] \neq \emptyset$ holds, then $[\![\Psi \circ \alpha]\!]$ and $[\![\Psi \circ \beta]\!]$ share elements.

As both, $[\![\Psi \circ \alpha]\!]$ and $[\![\Psi \circ \beta]\!]$, contain elements of $[\![\Psi]\!] \cap \mathcal{S}_\Psi$ (under the given precondition), we will finally obtain that the models in $[\![\Psi \circ (\alpha \wedge \beta)]\!]$ are also included in $[\![\Psi \circ \alpha]\!]$ and $[\![\Psi \circ \beta]\!]$. This guarantees that there are no elements in $[\![\Psi]\!] \cap \mathcal{S}_\Psi$ that are more preferred than other elements in $[\![\Psi]\!] \cap \mathcal{S}_\Psi$.

Prioritization of $[\![\Psi]\!] \cap \mathcal{S}_\Psi$. For (generalized) credibility-limited revision operators we have that the set $[\![\Psi \circ \alpha]\!]$ contains elements of $[\![\Psi]\!]$, whenever that is possible, i.e., we have that $[\![\Psi]\!] \cap [\![\alpha]\!] \neq \emptyset$ implies that $[\![\Psi \circ \alpha]\!] \cap [\![\Psi]\!] \cap [\![\alpha]\!] \neq \emptyset$ holds. As dynamic-limited revision operators prioritize elements of $\mathcal{S}_\Psi$ over $[\![\Psi]\!]$ we restrict this property to $[\![\Psi]\!] \cap \mathcal{S}_\Psi$. Consequently, whenever $[\![\Psi]\!] \cap [\![\alpha]\!] \cap \mathcal{S}_\Psi \neq \emptyset$ holds, we have that also $[\![\Psi \circ \alpha]\!] \cap [\![\Psi]\!] \cap \mathcal{S}_\Psi \cap [\![\alpha]\!] \neq \emptyset$ holds. The postulate

(DL3) If $\mathrm{Bel}(\Psi) \cup \mathrm{Bel}(\Psi \star \alpha)$ and $\mathrm{Bel}(\Psi) + \alpha$ are consistent, and $\alpha \models \gamma$ and $\mathrm{Bel}(\Psi \star \gamma) \not\subseteq \mathrm{Cn}(\alpha)$ holds, then consistency of β and inconsistency of $\mathrm{Bel}(\Psi) \cup \mathrm{Bel}(\Psi \star \beta)$ together imply

---

[3]   In Section 8.4 we will exactly characterize what it means to get "accepted for revision" by a dynamic-limited revision operator.

that $\text{Bel}(\Psi) \cup \text{Bel}(\Psi \star (\alpha \vee \beta))$ is inconsistent.

implies prioritization of $\llbracket \Psi \rrbracket \cap \mathcal{S}_\Psi$, but describes this in a contra-positive way. We provide some intuition for (DL3) by describing the postulate informally. First, the premise of (DL3),

$\text{Bel}(\Psi) \cup \text{Bel}(\Psi \star \alpha)$ and $\text{Bel}(\Psi) + \alpha$ are consistent, and $\alpha \models \gamma$ and $\text{Bel}(\Psi \star \gamma) \not\subseteq \text{Cn}(\alpha)$,

implies that α is consistent with $\text{Bel}(\Psi)$ and describes that models of α are not absolutely preferred (this is attested by $\alpha \models \gamma$ and $\text{Bel}(\Psi \star \gamma) \not\subseteq \text{Cn}(\alpha)$). The next part of (DL3),

consistency of β and inconsistency of $\text{Bel}(\Psi) \cup \text{Bel}(\Psi \star \beta)$,

describes that β is not consistent with $\text{Bel}(\Psi)$. This implies $\text{Bel}(\Psi) \neq \text{Bel}(\Psi \star \beta)$, and consequently, that β is accepted for revision (as discussed for (DL0)). The consequence of (DL3),

$\text{Bel}(\Psi) \cup \text{Bel}(\Psi \star (\alpha \vee \beta))$ is inconsistent,

states that $\llbracket \Psi \star (\alpha \vee \beta) \rrbracket$ contains no models from $\llbracket \Psi \rrbracket$. Thus, informally, (DL3) could be read as a postulate describing that if there is a witness (the formula γ) that shows that the models of $\llbracket \Psi \rrbracket$ are not preferred, then they will never be preferred (which is expressed by β).

Specifics of Accepted Beliefs. According to the single-sentence closure property of acceptance descriptions, acceptance of a sentence α carries over to all sentences implied by α. The following postulate of dynamic-limited revision operators ensures this behaviour for all consistent beliefs:

(DL7) If α is consistent and $\alpha \in \text{Bel}(\Psi \star \alpha)$, then $\alpha \models \beta$ implies that $\beta \in \text{Bel}(\Psi \star \beta)$.

As shown by Theorem 8.6 for a dynamic-limited revision operator $\star$ we have that $\mathcal{S}_\Psi$ contains exactly the models that yield (see also Proposition 7.3) the set of consistent beliefs that are accepted for revision, i.e., the set of beliefs $\{\alpha \mid \alpha \in \text{Bel}(\Psi \star \alpha)\} = \{\alpha \mid \llbracket \alpha \rrbracket \cap \mathcal{S}_\Psi \neq \emptyset\}$. Moreover, by design, $\llbracket \Psi \star \alpha \rrbracket \neq \llbracket \Psi \rrbracket$ should imply that $\llbracket \Psi \star \alpha \rrbracket$ has only elements of $\mathcal{S}_\Psi$. The following postulate guarantees this last property:

(DL8) If α, β are consistent and $\mathrm{Bel}(\Psi \star \alpha) \neq \mathrm{Bel}(\Psi)$ and $\mathrm{Bel}(\Psi \star \beta) = \mathrm{Bel}(\Psi)$, then $\beta \notin \mathrm{Bel}(\Psi)$ implies that $\mathrm{Bel}(\Psi \star (\alpha \vee \beta)) + \beta$ is inconsistent.

For an informal explanation of (DL8) recall that $\mathrm{Bel}(\Psi \star \alpha) \neq \mathrm{Bel}(\Psi)$ implies that α is accepted for revision, i.e., we have $[\![\alpha]\!] \cap \mathcal{S}_\Psi \neq \emptyset$. Conversely, $\mathrm{Bel}(\Psi \star \beta) = \mathrm{Bel}(\Psi)$ and $\beta \notin \mathrm{Bel}(\Psi)$ together imply that β is not accepted for revision. Consequently, the consequence of (DL8), i.e., $\mathrm{Bel}(\Psi \star (\alpha \vee \beta)) + \beta$, expresses informally that $\mathrm{Bel}(\Psi \star (\alpha \vee \beta))$ (and finally also $\mathrm{Bel}(\Psi \star \alpha)$) contains no models of sentences that are not accepted for revision (the models of β).

Semantic Organization and Consistency Management. The remaining postulates (DL4), (DL5), (DL6) and (DL9) are also postulates of generalized credibility-limited revision operators. The postulates

(DL6) If $\alpha \equiv \beta$, then $\mathrm{Bel}(\Psi \star \alpha) = \mathrm{Bel}(\Psi \star \beta)$.

$$(\mathrm{DL9})\ \ \mathrm{Bel}(\Psi \star (\alpha \vee \beta)) = \begin{cases} \mathrm{Bel}(\Psi \star \alpha) \text{ or} \\ \mathrm{Bel}(\Psi \star \beta) \text{ or} \\ \mathrm{Bel}(\Psi \star \alpha) \cap \mathrm{Bel}(\Psi \star \beta) \end{cases}.$$

correspond to (GCL4) and (GCL7), respectively, and ensure that only semantic content matters and that $\preceq_\Psi$ is indeed a total preorder. As the postulates (CL3wcp) and (CL3u) for generalized credibility-limited revision operators, the postulates

(DL4) If $\mathrm{Bel}(\Psi)$ and α are consistent, then $\mathrm{Bel}(\Psi \star \alpha)$ is consistent.

(DL5) If $\mathrm{Bel}(\Psi \star \alpha)$ is consistent and $\alpha \models \beta$, then $\mathrm{Bel}(\Psi \star \beta)$ is consistent.

rule out certain cases where the operator yields unexpected consistent or inconsistent states. For a discussion of these postulates we refer to Example 7.7 (on p. 140) and the subsequent discussion after Example 7.7.

8.4. Properties of Dynamic-Limited Revision

In this section we consider properties of dynamic-limited revision operators. Especially, we consider the internal structure of subclasses of dynamic-limited revision operators.

Remark on Faithfulness. First, we consider how the faithfulness property (Definition 8.5) is related to dynamic-limited revision operators. The faithfulness condition (FLA1) encodes semantically how elements of $[\![\Psi]\!] \cap \mathcal{S}_\Psi$ are treated by dynamic-limited revision operators. Besides of that, condition (FLA2) and condition (FLA3) in Definition 8.5 are chosen to rule out situations where the information in $\mathcal{S}_\Psi$ has no effect on the operation of $\circ$. Consequently, semantic information will have a meaning for the revision process. In particular, without (FLA2) and (FLA3), the following proposition would not hold.

Proposition 8.7. *Let $\mathcal{E}$ be a set of epistemic states and let $\Psi \mapsto (\preceq_\Psi , \mathcal{S}_\Psi, b_\Psi)$ be a faithful limited assignment for $\mathcal{E}$. For each belief change operator $\circ$ for $\mathcal{E}$ that is revision-compatible with $\Psi \mapsto (\preceq_\Psi, \mathcal{S}_\Psi, b_\Psi)$ the following two statements hold:*

(a) $\mathcal{S}_\Psi \neq \emptyset$ if and only if there exists a consistent $\alpha \in \mathcal{L}$ with $\mathrm{Bel}(\Psi \circ \alpha) \neq \mathrm{Bel}(\Psi)$

(b) $b_\Psi = \bot$ if and only if $\mathrm{Bel}(\Psi \circ \bot) \neq \mathrm{Bel}(\Psi)$

Proof. For each of (a) and (b) we consider both directions independently and start with statement (a).

> *From $\mathcal{S}_\Psi \neq \emptyset$ to α.* Assume that $\mathcal{S}_\Psi \neq \emptyset$ holds. We consider three cases:
> *The case of $[\![\Psi]\!] = \mathcal{S}_\Psi$.* From (FLA2) and $\mathcal{S}_\Psi \neq \emptyset$ we obtain that there are at least two interpretations $\omega, \omega' \in [\![\Psi]\!]$. From revision-compatibility and $\omega \in \mathcal{S}_\Psi$, we obtain $[\![\Psi \circ \varphi_\omega]\!] = \{\omega\} \neq [\![\Psi]\!]$.
> *The case of $\mathcal{S}_\Psi \setminus [\![\Psi]\!] \neq \emptyset$.* Let $\omega \in \mathcal{S}_\Psi \setminus [\![\Psi]\!]$. Because $\circ$ is revision-compatible with $\Psi \mapsto (\preceq_\Psi, \mathcal{S}_\Psi, b_\Psi)$, we obtain $[\![\Psi \circ \varphi_\omega]\!] = \{\omega\} \neq [\![\Psi]\!]$.
> *The case of $[\![\Psi]\!] \setminus \mathcal{S}_\Psi \neq \emptyset$.* Let $\omega \in [\![\Psi]\!] \setminus \mathcal{S}_\Psi$ and α be a formula such that $[\![\alpha]\!] = \mathcal{S}_\Psi$ holds. Because $\circ$ is revision-compatible with $\Psi \mapsto (\preceq_\Psi, \mathcal{S}_\Psi, b_\Psi)$, we obtain $\omega \notin [\![\Psi \circ \alpha]\!]$ from $\omega \notin \mathcal{S}_\Psi$. This last observation immediately yields $[\![\Psi \circ \varphi_\omega]\!] \neq \{\omega\} \neq [\![\Psi]\!]$).
> In summary, we have shown that $\mathcal{S}_\Psi \neq \emptyset$ implies the existence of some formula α such that $\mathrm{Bel}(\Psi \circ \alpha) \neq \mathrm{Bel}(\Psi)$.
> *From α to $\mathcal{S}_\Psi \neq \emptyset$.* Assume that there exists a consistent formula $\alpha \in \mathcal{L}$ such that $\mathrm{Bel}(\Psi \circ \alpha) \neq \mathrm{Bel}(\Psi)$ holds. Because $\circ$ is revision-compatible with $\Psi \mapsto (\preceq_\Psi, \mathcal{S}_\Psi, b_\Psi)$, we obtain $[\![\alpha]\!] \cap \mathcal{S}_\Psi \neq \emptyset$ from

the consistency of α and $\mathrm{Bel}(\Psi \circ \alpha) \neq \mathrm{Bel}(\Psi)$. Consequently, we obtain $\mathcal{S}_\Psi \neq \emptyset$ from $[\![\alpha]\!] \cap \mathcal{S}_\Psi \neq \emptyset$.

This completes the proof of (a). Next, we show that statement (b) holds. Again we consider both directions of the claim independently.

> *From $b_\Psi = \bot$ to $\mathrm{Bel}(\Psi \circ \bot) \neq \mathrm{Bel}(\Psi)$.* Assume that $b_\Psi = \bot$ holds. Because $\Psi \mapsto (\preceq_\Psi, \mathcal{S}_\Psi, b_\Psi)$ is faithful, (FLA3) is satisfied, and thus, $b_\Psi = \bot$ implies $[\![\Psi]\!] \neq \emptyset$. Because $\circ$ is revision-compatible with $\Psi \mapsto (\preceq_\Psi, \mathcal{S}_\Psi, b_\Psi)$, we obtain $[\![\Psi \circ \bot]\!] = \emptyset$ from $b_\Psi = \bot$. Consequently, we have $\mathrm{Bel}(\Psi \circ \bot) \neq \mathrm{Bel}(\Psi)$.
>
> *From $\mathrm{Bel}(\Psi \circ \bot) \neq \mathrm{Bel}(\Psi)$ to $b_\Psi = \bot$.* Suppose that we have $\mathrm{Bel}(\Psi \circ \bot) \neq \mathrm{Bel}(\Psi)$. Because $\circ$ is revision-compatible with $\Psi \mapsto (\preceq_\Psi, \mathcal{S}_\Psi, b_\Psi)$, we obtain $b_\Psi = \bot$ immediately from $[\![\bot]\!] = \emptyset$ and $[\![\Psi \circ \bot]\!] \neq [\![\Psi]\!]$.   □

Special Treatment of Inconsistent Beliefs. We will make use of the following subclass of dynamic-limited revision operators.

Definition 8.8 ($\bot$-closed)**.** *Let $\mathcal{E}$ be a set of epistemic states. A limited assignment $\Psi \mapsto (\preceq_\Psi, \mathcal{S}_\Psi, b_\Psi)$ for $\mathcal{E}$ is called $\bot$-closed if the following properties are satisfied:*

(FLA1$_\bot$) *If $b_\Psi = \bot$ and $|[\![\Psi]\!]| \neq 1$, then $\mathcal{S}_\Psi = \Omega$.*
(FLA2$_\bot$) *If $b_\Psi = \bot$ and $|[\![\Psi]\!]| = 1$, then $\mathcal{S}_\Psi \cup [\![\Psi]\!] = \Omega$.*

A dynamic-limited revision operator $\star$ for $\mathcal{E}$ is called $\bot$-closed if $\star$ is revision-compatible with a $\bot$-closed faithful limited assignment.

Note that for generalized credibility-limited revision operators the semantic properties (CLA$_\bot$) corresponds to (GCL6) (see p. 143). For dynamic-limited revision operators, (CLA$_\bot$) is not sufficient to obtain (GCL6). The following proposition shows that the properties of $\bot$-closed dynamic-limited revision operators in Definition 8.8 correspond to (GCL6) (in addition to (DL0)–(DL8)).

Proposition 8.9. *Let $\mathcal{E}$ be a set of epistemic states and $\star$ be a belief change operator for $\mathcal{E}$. The operator $\star$ is a $\bot$-closed dynamic-limited revision operator if and only if $\star$ satisfies (DL0)–(DL6), (DL8), (DL9) and (GCL6).*

Proof. Observe that (GCL6) implies satisfaction of (DL7). Consequently, we obtain that $\star$ is a dynamic-limited revision operator as $\star$ satisfies (DL0)–(DL9). Because $\star$ is a dynamic-limited revision operator there exists some limited assignment $\Psi \mapsto (\preceq_\Psi, \mathcal{S}_\Psi, b_\Psi)$ that is revision-compatible with $\star$ (see Theorem 8.6). We show that satisfaction of (GCL6) corresponds to $\perp$-closure of $\star$, i.e., that (FLA1$_\perp$) and (FLA2$_\perp$) are satisfied.

From (GCL6) *to* $\perp$-*closed.* First, assume that there is some $\Psi \in \mathcal{E}$ such that (FLA1$_\perp$) is violated, i.e., $b_\Psi = \perp$ and $|[\![\Psi]\!]| \neq 1$ and $\mathcal{S}_\Psi \neq \Omega$. Let $\omega \in \Omega$ with $\omega \notin \mathcal{S}_\Psi$. We consider two cases:

The case of $\varphi_\omega \notin [\![\Psi \star \varphi_\omega]\!]$. Because of $b_\Psi = \perp$ we obtain that $\perp \in \mathrm{Bel}(\Psi \star \perp)$ holds. By using (GCL6), we obtain the contradiction $\varphi_\omega \in [\![\Psi \star \varphi_\omega]\!]$ from $\perp \in \mathrm{Bel}(\Psi \star \perp)$.

The case of $\varphi_\omega \in [\![\Psi \star \varphi_\omega]\!]$. This implies that $[\![\Psi]\!] = \{\omega\}$ or $[\![\Psi]\!] = \emptyset$ holds. Note that due to the faithfulness of $\Psi \mapsto (\preceq_\Psi, \mathcal{S}_\Psi, b_\Psi)$ the latter case is impossible due to $b_\Psi = \perp$. The former case of $[\![\Psi]\!] = \{\omega\}$ is also impossible due to $|[\![\Psi]\!]| \neq 1$.

Next, assume that there is some $\Psi \in \mathcal{E}$ such that (FLA2$_\perp$) is violated, i.e., $b_\Psi = \perp$ and $|[\![\Psi]\!]| = 1$ and $\mathcal{S}_\Psi \cup [\![\Psi]\!] \neq \Omega$. Let $\omega \in \Omega$ with $\omega \notin \mathcal{S}_\Psi \cup [\![\Psi]\!]$. Clearly, we obtain that $\varphi_\omega \notin [\![\Psi \star \varphi_\omega]\!]$ holds. Moreover, because of $b_\Psi = \perp$ we obtain that $\perp \in \mathrm{Bel}(\Psi \star \perp)$ holds. By using (GCL6), we obtain the contradiction $\varphi_\omega \in [\![\Psi \star \varphi_\omega]\!]$ from $\perp \in \mathrm{Bel}(\Psi \star \perp)$.

From $\perp$-*closed to* (GCL6). Note that $\star$ satisfies (DL7), and thus, for all consistent α, β the postulate (GCL6) is satisfied. We consider the only non-trivial case of $\alpha \equiv \perp$ and β is consistent. Therefore, assume that the preconditions of (GCL6) holds, i.e., we have that $\alpha \in \mathrm{Bel}(\Psi \star \alpha)$ and $\alpha \models \beta$ hold. We show that $\beta \in \mathrm{Bel}(\Psi \star \beta)$ holds by considering two cases:

The case of $\beta \in \mathrm{Bel}(\Psi)$. For this case we obtain that $\beta \in \mathrm{Bel}(\Psi \star \beta)$ is satisfied immediately from the fact that $\star$ satisfies (DL0).

The case of $\beta \notin \mathrm{Bel}(\Psi)$. We obtain that $[\![\Psi]\!] \neq \emptyset$ holds. By employing Theorem 8.6, we obtain that $b_\Psi = \perp$ holds from $\perp \in \mathrm{Bel}(\Psi \star \perp)$ and consistency of $\mathrm{Bel}(\Psi)$. As $\star$ is $\perp$-closed the postulates (FLA1$_\perp$) and (FLA2$_\perp$) are satisfied. Consequently, we have that $\mathcal{S}_\Psi \cup [\![\Psi]\!] = \Omega$ holds. This and $\beta \notin \mathrm{Bel}(\Psi)$ together imply that $[\![\beta]\!] \cap \mathcal{S}_\Psi \neq \emptyset$ holds. Employing Theorem 8.6 again yields $\beta \in \mathrm{Bel}(\Psi \star \beta)$. $\qquad\square$

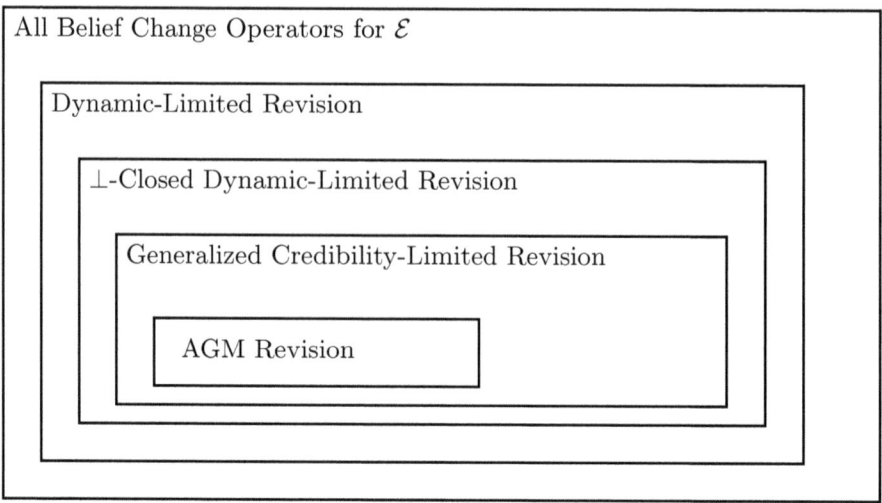

Figure 8.4: Interrelations among the families of belief change operators considered in Part II.

Existence of Dynamic-Limited Revision Operators. The semantic characterization of dynamic-limited revision operators given by Theorem 8.6 yields (by choosing $\mathcal{S}_\Psi = \emptyset$) that some dynamic-limited revision operators do not accept any belief for revision, i.e, operators that do not alter the beliefs at all. As given in Section 6.1 such operators are called neutral.

Proposition 8.10. *Let $\mathcal{E}$ be a set of epistemic states. Every neutral belief change operator for $\mathcal{E}$ is a dynamic-limited revision operator.*

Proof. Construct a faithful limited assignment $\Psi \mapsto (\preceq_\Psi, \mathcal{S}_\Psi, b_\Psi)$ such that $\mathcal{S}_\Psi = \emptyset$ and $b_\Psi = \top$ for each $\Psi \in \mathcal{E}$. This assignment is revision-compatible with any neutral revision operator for $\mathcal{E}$, and thus, due to Theorem 8.19, a dynamic-limited revision operator. $\qquad\square$

An immediate consequence is that in each set of epistemic states a dynamic-limited revision operator exists.

Corollary 8.11. *For each set of epistemic states $\mathcal{E}$ there exists at least one dynamic-limited revision operator for $\mathcal{E}$.*

Relation to other Families of Belief Operators. From Theorem 8.6, we directly obtain the following proposition which describes the interrelations among AGM revision, generalized credibility-limited and dynamic-limited revision in the Darwiche-Pearl framework (see Figure 8.4 for an illustration).

Proposition 8.12. *Let $\mathcal{E}$ be a set of epistemic states and $\circ$ be a belief change operator for $\mathcal{E}$. If*

- *the operator $\circ$ is a generalized credibility-limited revision operator for $\mathcal{E}$, or*
- *the operator $\circ$ is an AGM revision for for $\mathcal{E}$,*

then is $\circ$ a $\perp$-closed dynamic-limited revision operator for $\mathcal{E}$. Furthermore, there is a set of epistemic states $\mathcal{E}$ and a $\perp$-closed dynamic-limited revision operator for $\mathcal{E}$ that is not a generalized credibility-limited revision operator for $\mathcal{E}$.

Finally, note that even in the sense of the original definition by Hansson et al. [77, Def. 1], dynamic-limited revisions operators exceed what is denoted as credibility-limited revision. The reason for this is that credibility-limited revision in the sense of Hansson et al. [77, Def. 1] always satisfies the inclusion postulate (AGM*2), but this is not the case for dynamic-limited revisions operators, i.e., the following postulate is *not* satisfied by a dynamic-limited revision operator $\star$ in general:

(ES-Inclusion) $\mathrm{Bel}(\Psi \star \alpha) \subseteq \mathrm{Bel}(\Psi) + \alpha.$

The following example presents a dynamic-limited revision operator that violates (ES-Inclusion).

Example 8.13. *Assume that $\Sigma = \{a, b\}$ and $\Omega = \{ab, \ a\overline{b}, \ \overline{a}b, \ \overline{a}\overline{b}\}$ hold. As in Example 8.1, let $\mathcal{E}$ be the set of epistemic states with $\mathcal{E} = \{\Psi_a, \Psi_{\overline{a}}\} \cup \{\Psi_\omega \mid \omega \in \Omega\}$ such that the following holds for each $\omega \in \Omega$:*

$$\llbracket \Psi_a \rrbracket = \{ab, \ a\overline{b}\} \qquad \llbracket \Psi_{\overline{a}} \rrbracket = \{\overline{a}b, \ \overline{a}\overline{b}\} \qquad \llbracket \Psi_\omega \rrbracket = \{\omega\}$$

Consider the acceptance description $\mathcal{A}$ for $\mathcal{E}$ from Example 8.1 given

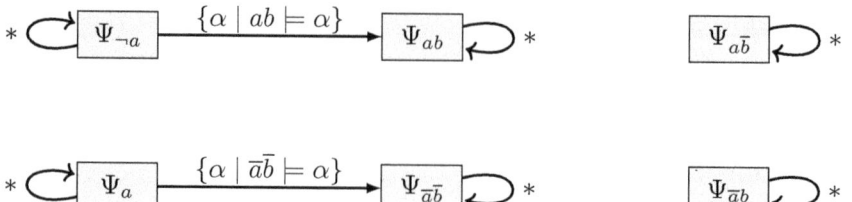

Figure 8.5: Graphical representation of the revision operator $\star$ for $\mathcal{E}$ given in Example 8.13 that complies with the acceptance description $\mathcal{A}$ for $\mathcal{E}$ from Example 8.1.

for each $\omega \in \Omega$ by:

$$\mathcal{A}(\Psi_a) = \{\alpha \in \mathcal{L} \mid \overline{a}\overline{b} \models \alpha\}$$
$$\mathcal{A}(\Psi_{\overline{a}}) = \{\alpha \in \mathcal{L} \mid ab \models \alpha\}$$
$$\mathcal{A}(\Psi_\omega) = \{\alpha \in \mathcal{L} \mid \omega \models \alpha\}$$

We employ Theorem 8.6 and specify a dynamic-limited revision operator $\star$ for $\mathcal{E}$ semantically by a faithful limited assignment $\Psi \mapsto (\preceq_\Psi, \mathcal{S}_\Psi, b_\Psi)$. We set $b_\Psi = \top$ for each $\Psi \in \mathcal{E}$ and set $\mathcal{S}_\Psi$ and $\preceq_\Psi$ for each $\omega \in \Omega$ as follows:

$$\mathcal{S}_{\Psi_a} = \{\overline{a}\overline{b}\} \qquad \mathcal{S}_{\Psi_{\overline{a}}} = \{ab\} \qquad \mathcal{S}_{\Psi_\omega} = \emptyset$$
$$\preceq_{\Psi_a} = \{(\overline{a}\overline{b}, \overline{a}\overline{b})\} \qquad \preceq_{\Psi_{\overline{a}}} = \{(ab, ab)\} \qquad \preceq_{\Psi_\omega} = \emptyset$$

Note that $\mathcal{S}_\Psi$ contains at most one element for each $\Psi \in \mathcal{E}$. Consulting Definition 8.5 reveals that $\Psi \mapsto (\preceq_\Psi, \mathcal{S}_\Psi, b_\Psi)$ is indeed a faithful limited assignment. Let $\star$ be the unique belief change operator that is revision-compatible with $\Psi \mapsto (\preceq_\Psi, \mathcal{S}_\Psi, b_\Psi)$. Figure 8.5 provides a graphical illustration of $\star$.

The dynamics given in Definition 8.4 reveals that $\star$ complies with $\mathcal{A}$. In particular, we have that $[\![\Psi_{\overline{a}} \star b]\!] = \{ab\}$ holds, while having at the same time that $[\![\Psi_{\overline{a}}]\!] \cap [\![b]\!] = \{\overline{a}b\}$ holds. This means we have $\mathrm{Bel}(\Psi_{\overline{a}} \star b) \not\subseteq \mathrm{Bel}(\Psi_{\overline{a}}) + b$ and consequently $\star$ violates (ES-Inclusion).

8.5. Acceptance and Dynamic-Limited Revision

In this section we capture the nature of beliefs accepted for revision by dynamic-limited revision operators. We start by considering a syntactic interpretation for the semantic concept of $\mathcal{S}_\Psi$ for dynamic-limited revision operators.

Definition 8.14. *Let $\mathcal{E}$ be a set of epistemic states and let $\circ$ be a belief change operator for $\mathcal{E}$. Moreover, let $\Psi \in \mathcal{E}$ be an epistemic state. For a belief $\alpha \in \mathcal{L}$ we define the following conditions:*

(S1) *If $\mathrm{Bel}(\Psi) + \alpha$ is consistent, then $\mathrm{Bel}(\Psi \circ \beta) \subseteq \mathrm{Bel}(\Psi \circ \alpha)$ for all β with $\alpha \models \beta$.*

(S2) *If $\mathrm{Bel}(\Psi) + \alpha$ is consistent, then there exists some $\beta \not\models \neg\alpha$ with $\mathrm{Bel}(\Psi \circ \beta) \neq \mathrm{Bel}(\Psi)$.*

(S3) *For all β, $\mathrm{Bel}(\Psi \circ \beta) \subseteq \mathrm{Bel}(\Psi \circ \alpha)$ implies consistency of $\mathrm{Bel}(\Psi \circ \beta) + \alpha$.*

Condition (S1) states that if α is consistent with the prior beliefs, then a change by a more general belief results in the beliefs of $\mathrm{Bel}(\Psi \circ \alpha)$ or fewer beliefs. Condition (S2) states that if α is consistent with the prior beliefs, then there is some β that is consistent with α that changes the current beliefs. Condition (S3) expresses (in the contrapositive version) that when changing by a belief α, which is inconsistent with the result of a change with a belief β, then the result will never contain all beliefs obtained by the change with β.

We will now show that conditions (S1)–(S3) allow capturing the interpretations in $\mathcal{S}_\Psi$. The conditions (S1) and (S2) describe elements of $\mathcal{S}_\Psi \cap [\![\Psi]\!]$ and condition (S3) describes elements of $\mathcal{S}_\Psi \setminus [\![\Psi]\!]$.

Lemma 8.15. *Let $\mathcal{E}$ be a set of epistemic states, let $\star$ be a dynamic-limited revision operator for $\mathcal{E}$ and let $\Psi \mapsto (\preceq_\Psi, \mathcal{S}_\Psi, b_\Psi)$ be a faithful limited assignment that is revision-compatible with $\star$. The following holds:*

(a) *If $\omega \in [\![\Psi]\!]$, then $\omega \in \mathcal{S}_\Psi$ iff φ_ω satisfies (S1) and (S2) in Ψ.*

(b) *If $\omega \notin [\![\Psi]\!]$, then $\omega \in \mathcal{S}_\Psi$ iff φ_ω satisfies (S3) in Ψ.*

Proof. We show (a) and (b) independently.

Statement (a). Let ω be an interpretation with $\omega \in [\![\Psi]\!]$. We consider both directions of the claim independently:

From $\omega \in \mathcal{S}_{\Psi}$ to (S1) *and* (S2). By the faithfulness of $\Psi \mapsto (\preceq_{\Psi}, \mathcal{S}_{\Psi}, b_{\Psi})$ we obtain that (FLA1)–(FLA3) are satisfied. We obtain $\omega \in \min(\mathcal{S}_{\Psi}, \preceq_{\Psi})$ from (FLA1). This implies $\omega \in \min([\![\beta]\!], \preceq_{\Psi}) = [\![\Psi \circ \beta]\!]$ for each β with $\omega \models \beta$, thus, (S1) is satisfied by φ_{ω}. If $|[\![\Psi]\!]| = 1$, then we obtain $[\![\Psi]\!] \neq \{\omega\}$ from (FLA2). Furthermore, for $|[\![\Psi]\!]| > 1$ there exist some $\omega' \neq \omega$ with $\omega' \in [\![\Psi]\!]$, and we obtain again $[\![\Psi]\!] \neq \{\omega\}$. Because $\star$ is revision-compatible with $\Psi \mapsto (\preceq_{\Psi}, \mathcal{S}_{\Psi}, b_{\Psi})$, we obtain $[\![\Psi]\!] \neq [\![\Psi \star \varphi_{\omega}]\!]$ from $\omega \in \mathcal{S}_{\Psi}$ and $[\![\Psi]\!] \neq \{\omega\}$. As $\varphi_{\omega} \not\models \neg\varphi_{\omega}$, we obtain that (S2) is satisfied by φ_{ω}.

From (S1) *and* (S2) *to $\omega \in \mathcal{S}_{\Psi}$.* We show this direction by contraposition, i.e., we show that $\omega \notin \mathcal{S}_{\Psi}$ implies that (S1) or (S2) is violated. Recall that $\mathrm{Bel}(\Psi) + \varphi_{\omega}$ is consistent, because we have $\omega \in [\![\Psi]\!]$. We consider two cases:

The case of $\mathcal{S}_{\Psi} = \emptyset$. Because $\star$ is revision-compatible with $\Psi \mapsto (\preceq_{\Psi}, \mathcal{S}_{\Psi}, b_{\Psi})$, we obtain that $\mathcal{S}_{\Psi} = \emptyset$ implies that $[\![\Psi]\!] = [\![\Psi \star \alpha]\!]$ holds for all consistent $\alpha \in \mathcal{L}$. Consequently, there is no formula β such that $\beta \not\models \neg\varphi_{\omega}$ and $[\![\Psi \star \beta]\!] \neq [\![\Psi]\!]$. This yields a violation of (S2) by φ_{ω} because $\mathrm{Bel}(\Psi) + \varphi_{\omega}$ is consistent.

The case of $\mathcal{S}_{\Psi} \neq \emptyset$. There exists some interpretation ω' with $\omega' \in \mathcal{S}_{\Psi}$. Now let β be a formula such that $[\![\beta]\!] = \{\omega, \omega'\}$. We obtain $[\![\Psi \star \beta]\!] = \{\omega'\}$ from $\omega' \in \mathcal{S}_{\Psi}$ and the revision-compatibility of $\star$ with $\Psi \mapsto (\preceq_{\Psi}, \mathcal{S}_{\Psi}, b_{\Psi})$. As $\mathrm{Bel}(\Psi) + \varphi_{\omega}$ is consistent, this yields that φ_{ω} violates (S1).

Statement (b). Let ω be an interpretation with $\omega \notin [\![\Psi]\!]$. We consider both directions of the claim independently:

From $\omega \in \mathcal{S}_{\Psi}$ to (S3). Because $\star$ is revision-compatible with $\Psi \mapsto (\preceq_{\Psi}, \mathcal{S}_{\Psi}, b_{\Psi})$, we obtain $[\![\Psi \star \varphi_{\omega}]\!] = \{\omega\}$ from $\omega \in \mathcal{S}_{\Psi}$. Now let β be a formula such that $[\![\Psi \star \varphi_{\omega}]\!] \subseteq [\![\Psi \star \beta]\!]$. We obtain $\omega \in [\![\Psi \star \beta]\!]$ from $[\![\Psi \star \varphi_{\omega}]\!] = \{\omega\}$. Consequently, we have that $[\![\Psi \star \beta]\!] + \varphi_{\omega}$ is consistent. This shows that (S3) is satisfied.

From (S3) *to $\omega \in \mathcal{S}_{\Psi}$.* We show this direction by contraposition, i.e., we show that $\omega \notin \mathcal{S}_{\Psi}$ implies that (S3) is violated.

The case of $[\![\Psi]\!] = \emptyset$. Because $\star$ is revision-compatible with $\Psi \mapsto (\preceq_{\Psi}, \mathcal{S}_{\Psi}, b_{\Psi})$, we obtain from $\omega \notin \mathcal{S}_{\Psi}$ that $[\![\Psi]\!] = [\![\Psi \circ \varphi_{\omega}]\!]$ is inconsistent. Now choose $\beta = \varphi_{\omega}$, and thus we have $[\![\Psi \circ \beta]\!] + \varphi_{\omega}$ is inconsistent. Towards a contradiction, suppose that (S3) is satisfied by φ_ω. Then, by reading (S3) contrapositively, we obtain $[\![\Psi \circ \varphi_\omega]\!] \not\subseteq [\![\Psi \circ \beta]\!]$ from (S3) and the inconsistency of $[\![\Psi \circ \beta]\!] + \varphi_\omega$. This is a contradiction to $[\![\Psi \circ \varphi_\omega]\!] = [\![\Psi \circ \beta]\!]$, which yields that (S3) is violated.

The case of $[\![\Psi]\!] \neq \emptyset$. Let ω' be a model of $\mathrm{Bel}(\Psi)$, i.e., we have $\omega' \in [\![\Psi]\!]$. Because $\omega \notin [\![\Psi]\!]$ holds, we obtain that $\mathrm{Bel}(\Psi \circ \varphi_{\omega'}) + \varphi_\omega$ is inconsistent. From $\omega \notin \mathcal{S}_\Psi$ and the revision-compatibility of $\star$ with $\Psi \mapsto (\preceq_\Psi, \mathcal{S}_\Psi, b_\Psi)$, we obtain that $[\![\Psi \circ \varphi_\omega]\!] = [\![\Psi]\!]$ holds. As in the case of $[\![\Psi]\!] = \emptyset$, by reading (S3) contrapositively, we obtain that the formula φ_ω violates (S3). $\qquad\square$

By employing Lemma 8.15 we obtain the following proposition.

Proposition 8.16. *Let $\mathcal{E}$ be a set of epistemic states and let $\star$ be a dynamic-limited revision operator for $\mathcal{E}$ that is revision-compatible with a faithful limited assignment $\Psi \mapsto (\preceq_\Psi, \mathcal{S}_\Psi, b_\Psi)$. Then $\omega \in \mathcal{S}_\Psi$ if and only if φ_ω satisfies (S1)–(S3) in Ψ.*

Proof. If $\omega \in [\![\Psi]\!]$, then we obtain either $[\![\Psi \star \varphi_\omega]\!] = [\![\Psi]\!]$ or $[\![\Psi \star \varphi_\omega]\!] = \{\omega\}$. In both cases we have $\omega \in [\![\Psi \star \varphi_\omega]\!]$, and thus, $[\![\Psi \star \varphi_\omega]\!] \subseteq [\![\Psi \star \beta]\!]$ implies consistency of $\mathrm{Bel}(\Psi \star \beta) + \varphi_\omega$. If $\omega \notin [\![\Psi]\!]$, then we immediately obtain that φ_ω satisfies (S1) and (S2). Consequently, by using Lemma 8.15, we obtain that $\omega \in \mathcal{S}_\Psi$ if and only if φ_ω satisfies (S1)–(S3) in Ψ. $\qquad\square$

As shown by Proposition 8.16, the properties (S1)–(S3) syntactically characterize the elements of $\mathcal{S}_\Psi$. This gives rise to the following notions.

Definition 8.17. *Let $\circ$ be a belief change operator and Ψ be an epistemic state. A belief $\alpha \in \mathcal{L}$ is said to*

- *satisfy (AR1) in Ψ if α satisfies (S1)–(S3) and every consistent β with $\beta \models \alpha$ satisfies (S1)–(S3) in Ψ.*
- *satisfy (AR2) in Ψ if $\alpha \equiv \alpha_1 \vee \ldots \vee \alpha_n$ where each α_i satisfies (AR1) in Ψ.*
- *be accepted for revision in Ψ by $\circ$ if $\beta \models \alpha$ for some β that satisfies (AR2) in Ψ.*

The notions of (AR1) and (AR2) are helpful, as they capture those beliefs whose models are elements in $\mathcal{S}_\Psi$.

Proposition 8.18. *Let $\mathcal{E}$ be a set of epistemic states and let $\star$ be a dynamic-limited revision operator for $\mathcal{E}$ that is revision-compatible with a faithful limited assignment $\Psi \mapsto (\preceq_\Psi, \mathcal{S}_\Psi, b_\Psi)$. A belief α satisfies (AR2) in Ψ if and only if $[\![\alpha]\!] \subseteq \mathcal{S}_\Psi$ and α is consistent.*

Proof. We consider both directions of the claim independently:

> *From α satisfies (AR2) in Ψ to $[\![\alpha]\!] \subseteq \mathcal{S}_\Psi$ and α is consistent.*
> First, we show that α is consistent. Towards a contradiction, suppose the contrary, i.e, that α is inconsistent. Then α satisfies (AR1) in Ψ, and thus satisfies (S1)–(S3) in Ψ. Using that α satisfies (S3) in Ψ yields that $\text{Bel}(\Psi \star \alpha) + \alpha$ is consistent, by choosing $\beta = \alpha$ in (S3). As α is inconsistent, the latter is impossible and thus, α is consistent.
>   Next, we show that $[\![\alpha]\!] \subseteq \mathcal{S}_\Psi$ holds. Because α satisfies (AR2) in Ψ and α is consistent, we obtain φ_ω that satisfies (AR1) in Ψ for each $\omega \in [\![\alpha]\!]$. From Proposition 8.16, we obtain that $\omega \in \mathcal{S}_\Psi$ for each $\omega \in [\![\alpha]\!]$.
> *From $[\![\alpha]\!] \subseteq \mathcal{S}_\Psi$ and α is consistent to α satisfies (AR2) in Ψ.*
> Let α be a consistent formula such that $[\![\alpha]\!] \subseteq \mathcal{S}_\Psi$. By using Proposition 8.16, we obtain that φ_ω satisfies (AR1) in Ψ for each $\omega \in \mathcal{S}_\Psi$. Consequently, for each $\omega \in [\![\alpha]\!]$, we obtain that φ_ω satisfies (AR1) in Ψ from $[\![\alpha]\!] \subseteq \mathcal{S}_\Psi$. By using finiteness of Ω, we obtain $\alpha \equiv \varphi_{\omega_1} \vee \ldots \vee \varphi_{\omega_n}$ with $[\![\alpha]\!] = \{\omega_1, \ldots, \omega_n\}$. This shows that α satisfies (AR2) in Ψ. $\square$

From Proposition 8.18, we obtain the following theorem.

Theorem 8.19. *Let $\mathcal{E}$ be a set of epistemic states and let $\star$ be a dynamic-limited revision operator for $\mathcal{E}$ that is revision-compatible with a faithful limited assignment $\Psi \mapsto (\preceq_\Psi, \mathcal{S}_\Psi, b_\Psi)$. For each consistent belief $\alpha \in \mathcal{L}$ we have:*

α is accepted for revision in Ψ by $\star$ if and only if $[\![\alpha]\!] \cap \mathcal{S}_\Psi \neq \emptyset$ holds

As the last step of this section, we characterize the scope of dynamic-limited revision operators for epistemic states.

Proposition 8.20. *Let $\mathcal{E}$ be a set of epistemic states and let $\star$ be a belief change operator for $\mathcal{E}$. If $\star$ is a dynamic-limited revision operator for $\mathcal{E}$, then there exists a set $X \subseteq \mathcal{L}$ that satisfies single-sentence closure and disjunction completeness such that:*

$$\mathrm{Bel}(\Psi) \cup X \subseteq Scp^\star(\Psi) \subseteq \mathrm{Bel}(\Psi) \cup X \cup \{\beta \in \mathcal{L} \mid \beta \equiv \bot\}$$

Proof. Let $\Psi \mapsto (\preceq_\Psi, C_\Psi, b_\Psi)$ be a faithful limited assignment that is revision-compatible with $\star$. Recall that $\preceq_\Psi$ is a relation over $\mathcal{S}_\Psi \subseteq \Omega$. If $Scp^\star(\Psi) = \mathcal{L}$, then the claim is trivially satisfied, because $\mathcal{L}$ satisfies single-sentence closure and disjunction completeness.

In the following, we assume $Scp^\star(\Psi) \neq \mathcal{L}$. Let X be the set given by $X = \{\alpha \in \mathcal{L} \mid [\![\alpha]\!] \cap \mathcal{S}_\Psi \neq \emptyset\}$. Using Proposition 7.2, we obtain that X satisfies single-sentence closure and disjunction completeness. We show that $\mathrm{Bel}(\Psi) \cup X \subseteq Scp^\star(\Psi)$ holds, i.e. we show that for each $\alpha \in \mathrm{Bel}(\Psi) \cup X$ we have $\alpha \in \mathrm{Bel}(\Psi \star \alpha)$.

From $\alpha \in X$ to $\alpha \in Scp^\star(\Psi)$. Considering the definition of X yields that $\alpha \in X$ implies $[\![\alpha]\!] \cap \mathcal{S}_\Psi \neq \emptyset$. Because of this and because $\star$ is revision-compatible with $\Psi \mapsto (\preceq_\Psi, C_\Psi, b_\Psi)$, we obtain $\alpha \in \mathrm{Bel}(\Psi \star \alpha)$ from $\alpha \in X$. Consequently, we have that $\alpha \in Scp^\star(\Psi)$ holds.

From $\alpha \in \mathrm{Bel}(\Psi)$ to $\alpha \in Scp^\star(\Psi)$. We consider three subcases based on the revision-compatibility of $\Psi \mapsto (\preceq_\Psi, C_\Psi, b_\Psi)$ with $\star$. If $[\![\alpha]\!] \cap \mathcal{S}_\Psi \neq \emptyset$, then we obtain $\alpha \in X$, for which we have already shown that $\alpha \in Scp^\star(\Psi)$ holds. If $[\![\alpha]\!] = \emptyset$ and $b_\Psi = \bot$, then we obtain $[\![\Psi \star \alpha]\!] = \emptyset$, which implies $\alpha \in \mathrm{Bel}(\Psi \star \alpha)$. For all other cases we obtain $\Psi \star \alpha = \Psi$, and thus, $\alpha \in \mathrm{Bel}(\Psi)$ implies $\alpha \in \mathrm{Bel}(\Psi \star \alpha)$.

Considering the revision-compatibility of $\Psi \mapsto (\preceq_\Psi, C_\Psi, b_\Psi)$ with $\star$ reveals that every α with $\alpha \in \mathrm{Bel}(\Psi \star \alpha)$ satisfies one of the following conditions: (1) $[\![\alpha]\!] \cap \mathcal{S}_\Psi \neq \emptyset$ or (2) $[\![\alpha]\!] = \emptyset$ and $b_\Psi = \bot$ or (3) $\alpha \in \mathrm{Bel}(\Psi)$. Note that if α satisfies (1), we obtain $\alpha \in X$. We obtain that $Scp^\star(\Psi) \subseteq \mathrm{Bel}(\Psi) \cup X \cup \{\beta \in \mathcal{L} \mid \beta \equiv \bot\}$ holds. $\square$

8.6. Realizability and Dynamic-Limited Revision

We will now consider the acceptance descriptions dynamic-limited revision operators comply with. As shown in Proposition 8.20, the scope of general dynamic-limited revision operators does not match with the condition for compliance given in Definition 7.6. In this section, we will consider only $\perp$-closed dynamic-limited revision operators. The rationale for this is that the $\perp$-closed operators are the subfamily of dynamic-limited revision operators that match with the condition for compliance given in Definition 7.6.

Proposition 8.21. *Let $\mathcal{E}$ be a set of epistemic states and let $\star$ be a belief change operator for $\mathcal{E}$. If $\star$ is a $\perp$-closed dynamic-limited revision operator for $\mathcal{E}$, then there exists a set $X \subseteq \mathcal{L}$ that satisfies single-sentence closure and disjunction completeness such that:*

$$Scp^\star(\Psi) = \mathrm{Bel}(\Psi) \cup X$$

Proof. From Proposition 8.20, we obtain a set $X_\Psi \subseteq \mathcal{L}$ that satisfies single-sentence closure and disjunction completeness such that

$$\mathrm{Bel}(\Psi) \cup X_\Psi \subseteq Scp^\star(\Psi) \subseteq \mathrm{Bel}(\Psi) \cup X_\Psi \cup \{\beta \in \mathcal{L} \mid \beta \equiv \perp\} \quad (\bigstar)$$

holds for every $\Psi \in \mathcal{E}$. If $\{\beta \in \mathcal{L} \mid \beta \equiv \perp\} \not\subseteq Scp^\star(\Psi)$, then we obtain $Scp^\star(\Psi) = \mathrm{Bel}(\Psi) \cup X_\Psi$ from Equation $(\bigstar)$.

We consider the case of $\{\beta \in \mathcal{L} \mid \beta \equiv \perp\} \subseteq Scp^\star(\Psi)$. Because $\star$ is a $\perp$-closed dynamic-limited revision operator, we obtain that (GCL6) is satisfied from Proposition 8.9. The postulates (GCL6) yield that whenever $\{\beta \in \mathcal{L} \mid \beta \equiv \perp\} \subseteq Scp^\star(\Psi)$ holds, then we also have $Scp^\star(\Psi) = \mathcal{L}$. Thus, by considering Equation $(\bigstar)$, we obtain that $\{\beta \in \mathcal{L} \mid \beta \equiv \perp\} \subseteq Scp^\star(\Psi)$ implies $X_\Psi = Scp^\star(\Psi) = \mathcal{L}$. $\square$

Next, we introduce those acceptance descriptions the $\perp$-closed dynamic-limited revision operators exactly comply with. In the following definition, let $\mu_{\mathcal{A}(\Psi)}$ be a formula with $[\![\mu_{\mathcal{A}(\Psi)}]\!] = M_{\mathcal{A}(\Psi)}$, where $\mathcal{A}$ is an acceptance description and $M_{\mathcal{A}(\Psi)}$ is the set of interpretations guaranteed by Proposition 7.3 for $\mathcal{A}(\Psi)$, i.e., we have $\mathcal{A}(\Psi) \setminus \{\beta \mid \beta \equiv \perp\} = \{\alpha \mid \alpha \wedge \mu_{\mathcal{A}(\Psi)}$ is consistent$\}$.

Definition 8.22. *Let $\mathcal{E}$ be a set of epistemic states and let $\mathcal{A} : \mathcal{E} \to \mathcal{P}(\mathcal{L})$ be an acceptance description for $\mathcal{E}$. We say that $\mathcal{A}$ is dynamic-limited revision compatible with $\mathcal{E}$ if the following is satisfied:*

(AD-DL1) *If $\mathrm{Bel}(\Psi)$ is consistent, then for each consistent $\alpha \in \mathcal{A}(\Psi)$ there exists $\Psi_\alpha \in \mathcal{E}$ with $\alpha \in \mathrm{Bel}(\Psi_\alpha)$ and $\mathrm{Bel}(\Psi_\alpha)$ is consistent.*
(AD-DL2) *If $\mathrm{Bel}(\Psi) + (\alpha \wedge \mu_{\mathcal{A}(\Psi)})$ is consistent, then there exists $\Psi_\alpha \in \mathcal{E}$ with $\mathrm{Bel}(\Psi_\alpha) = \mathrm{Bel}(\Psi) + (\alpha \wedge \mu_{\mathcal{A}(\Psi)})$.*

Note that there is a qualitative difference between the restrictions (AD-DL1) and (AD-DL2) for dynamic-limited revision, and the restriction (AD-CL1) in Definition 7.18 for credibility-limited revision operators. The conditions (AD-DL1) and (AD-DL2) guarantee the existence of certain epistemic states, while (AD-CL1) restricts the elements of $\mathcal{A}(\Psi)$ itself. The following proposition shows that every ($\bot$-closed) dynamic-limited revision operator complies with some dynamic-limited revision compatible acceptance description.

Proposition 8.23. *Let $\mathcal{E}$ be a set of epistemic states and let $\star$ be a belief change operator for $\mathcal{E}$. If $\star$ is a $\bot$-closed dynamic-limited revision operator for $\mathcal{E}$, then there exists a dynamic-limited revision compatible acceptance description for $\mathcal{E}$ that complies with $\star$.*

Proof. Proposition 8.21 yields that there is an acceptance description $\mathcal{A}$ for $\mathcal{E}$ that complies with $\star$ by setting $\mathcal{A}(\Psi) = X_\Psi$ for each $\Psi \in \mathcal{E}$. We show that $\mathcal{A}$ is dynamic-limited revision compatible.

(AD-DL1) Because $\star$ satisfies (DL4), we obtain for each consistent $\alpha \in X_\Psi$ that $\mathrm{Bel}(\Psi \star \alpha)$ is consistent. This attests the existence of $\Psi_\alpha = \Psi \star \alpha$ as demanded by (AD-DL1).
(AD-DL2) We consider dynamic-limited revision operators semantically. The proof of Proposition 8.20 shows that $\mathcal{S}_\Psi$ corresponds to $\mu_{\mathcal{A}(\Psi)}$ used in Definition 8.22, i.e., $[\![\mu_{\mathcal{A}(\Psi)}]\!] = \mathcal{S}_\Psi$. Furthermore, the faithfulness condition (FLA1) demands that $[\![\Psi]\!] \cap \mathcal{S}_\Psi = \min(\mathcal{S}_\Psi, \preceq_\Psi)$ holds whenever we have $[\![\Psi]\!] \cap \mathcal{S}_\Psi \neq \emptyset$. Thus, from Theorem 8.6 we obtain that consistency of $\mathrm{Bel}(\Psi) + (\alpha \wedge \mu_{\mathcal{A}(\Psi)})$ implies that $\mathrm{Bel}(\Psi \star \alpha) = \mathrm{Bel}(\Psi) + (\alpha \wedge \mu_{\mathcal{A}(\Psi)})$. Consequently, $\Psi_\alpha = \Psi \star \alpha$ exists, as demanded by (AD-DL2). $\square$

Note that the proof of Proposition 8.23 reveals that (AD-DL1) is linked with (DL4) of dynamic-limited revision operators. Recall that the postulate (DL4) demands that for a consistent belief set $\mathrm{Bel}(\Psi)$ and a consistent belief α that get accepted for revision, $\mathrm{Bel}(\Psi \star \alpha)$ is also consistent. In line with (DL4), the condition (AD-DL1) expresses the demand of an epistemic state $\Psi \star \alpha$ such that $\mathrm{Bel}(\Psi \star \alpha)$ is consistent. Similarly, the faithfulness condition (FLA1) demands (and implies) that (AD-DL2) is satisfied.

Proposition 8.24. *Let $\mathcal{E}$ be a set of epistemic states. For every dynamic-limited revision compatible acceptance description $\mathcal{A} : \mathcal{E} \to \mathcal{P}(\mathcal{L})$ for $\mathcal{E}$ there exists a $\perp$-closed dynamic-limited revision operator $\star$ for $\mathcal{E}$ with*

$$Scp^\star(\Psi) = \mathrm{Bel}(\Psi) \cup \mathcal{A}(\Psi)$$

for all $\Psi \in \mathcal{E}$.

Proof. The proof has a similar outline as the proof for Proposition 7.19. For the sake of completeness, we present the full proof.

Let $\mathcal{A} : \mathcal{E} \to \mathcal{P}(\mathcal{L})$ be a dynamic-limited revision compatible acceptance description for $\mathcal{E}$. Recall that $\mathcal{A}(\Psi)$ satisfies single-sentence closure and disjunction completeness for each $\Psi \in \mathcal{E}$. Thus, as stated by Proposition 7.3, for each $\mathcal{A}(\Psi)$ there exists some set $M_{\mathcal{A}(\Psi)}$ such that $\mathcal{A}(\Psi) \setminus \{\beta \mid \perp \equiv \beta\} = \{\psi \mid [\![\psi]\!] \cap M_{\mathcal{A}(\Psi)} \neq \emptyset\}$ holds. In the following, we denote with $M_\Psi \subseteq \Omega$ the following set of interpretations:

$$M_\Psi = \begin{cases} \emptyset & \text{if } \mathrm{Bel}(\Psi) = \mathcal{L} \\ M_{\mathcal{A}(\Psi)} & \text{otherwise} \end{cases}$$

Moreover, for each $M \subseteq \Omega$ let Ψ_M denote a uniquely chosen epistemic state from $\mathcal{E}$, such that $[\![\Psi_M]\!] = M$ (as far as such an epistemic state exists).

In the following, let $\ll$ be an arbitrary (but fixed chosen) linear order on Ω. With $\ll_\Psi$ we denote the linear order on M_Ψ for each $\Psi \in \mathcal{E}$ such that

$$\ll_\Psi = \ll \cap (M_\Psi \times M_\Psi)$$

holds, i.e., $\ll_\Psi$ is the restriction of $\ll$ to M_Ψ.

Let $\star : \mathcal{E} \times \mathcal{L} \to \mathcal{E}$ be the belief change operator given by:

$$
\Psi \star \alpha = \begin{cases}
\Psi_{[\![\alpha]\!] \cap M_\Psi} & \text{if } [\![\alpha]\!] \cap [\![\Psi]\!] \cap M_\Psi \neq \emptyset \\
\Psi_{\min([\![\alpha]\!], \ll_\Psi)} & \text{if } [\![\alpha]\!] \cap [\![\Psi]\!] = \emptyset \text{ and } [\![\alpha]\!] \cap M_\Psi \neq \emptyset \\
\Psi_\emptyset & \text{if } [\![\alpha]\!] = \emptyset \text{ and } \bot \in \mathcal{A}(\Psi) \\
\Psi & \text{otherwise}
\end{cases} \quad (\bigstar)
$$

In order to proof that $\star$ exists it is sufficient to show that $\Psi \star \alpha$ exists for each $\Psi \in \mathcal{E}$ and for each $\alpha \in \mathcal{E}$. We consider the three relevant cases of $(\bigstar)$:

The case of $[\![\alpha]\!] \cap [\![\Psi]\!] \cap M_\Psi \neq \emptyset$. We obtain existence of $\Psi_{[\![\alpha]\!] \cap M_\Psi}$ from (AD-DL2).

The case of $[\![\alpha]\!] \cap [\![\Psi]\!] = \emptyset$ *and* $[\![\alpha]\!] \cap M_\Psi \neq \emptyset$. Note that $\ll_\Psi$ is a linear order, and thus, we have to show that for each $\omega \in M_{\mathcal{A}(\Psi)}$ the epistemic state $\Psi_{\{\omega\}}$ exists. Because we have (AD-DL1) from Definition 7.18, there exists Ψ_ω with $[\![\Psi_\omega]\!] = \{\omega\}$ for each $\omega \in M_{\mathcal{A}(\Psi)}$, which guarantees the existence of $\Psi_{\{\omega\}}$.

The case of $[\![\alpha]\!] = \emptyset$ *and* $\bot \in \mathcal{A}(\Psi)$. We obtain an epistemic state $\Psi_\bot$ from (AD-ES2) which satisfies $[\![\Psi_\bot]\!] = \emptyset$. This guarantees that the epistemic state $\Psi_\emptyset$ exists, as we could choose $\Psi_\emptyset = \Psi_\bot$.

In the following we show that $\star$ is a dynamic-limited revision operator. Therefore, we will make use of the following limited assignment $\Psi \mapsto (\preceq_\Psi, \mathcal{S}_\Psi, b_\Psi)$ given by

$$
\mathcal{S}_\Psi = M_\Psi
$$
$$
\preceq_\Psi = (\ll_\Psi \setminus (\Omega \times [\![\Psi]\!])) \cup ([\![\Psi]\!] \times \Omega)
$$
$$
b_\Psi = \begin{cases}
\bot & \text{if } \bot \in \mathcal{A}(\Psi) \text{ and } [\![\Psi]\!] \neq \emptyset \\
\top & \text{otherwise}
\end{cases}
$$

for each $\Psi \in \mathcal{E}$ such that $|[\![\Psi]\!]| \neq 1$ or $M_\Psi \neq [\![\Psi]\!]$. If $|[\![\Psi]\!]| = 1$ and $M_\Psi = [\![\Psi]\!]$, then we choose $(\preceq_\Psi, \mathcal{S}_\Psi, b_\Psi)$ as follows:

$$
\mathcal{S}_\Psi = \emptyset \qquad\qquad \preceq_\Psi = \emptyset \qquad\qquad b_\Psi = \top
$$

Clearly, $\Psi \mapsto (\preceq_\Psi, \mathcal{S}_\Psi, b_\Psi)$ is a limited assignment (cf. Definition 8.3). Note that satisfaction of the three conditions (FLA1)–(FLA3) is guaranteed by construction of $\Psi \mapsto (\preceq_\Psi, \mathcal{S}_\Psi, b_\Psi)$, which yields that $\Psi \mapsto (\preceq_\Psi, \mathcal{S}_\Psi, b_\Psi)$ is a faithful limited assignment.

Revision-compatibility. We show that $\Psi \mapsto (\preceq_\Psi, \mathcal{S}_\Psi, b_\Psi)$ is a faithful limited assignment that is revision-compatible with $\star$, i.e., we show that

$$[\![\Psi \star \alpha]\!] = \begin{cases} \min([\![\alpha]\!], \preceq_\Psi) & \text{if } [\![\alpha]\!] \cap \mathcal{S}_\Psi \neq \emptyset \\ \emptyset & \text{if } [\![\alpha]\!] = \emptyset \text{ and } b_\Psi = \bot \qquad (\#) \\ [\![\Psi]\!] & \text{otherwise} \end{cases}$$

from Definition 8.4 complies with Equation ($\bigstar$). If $|[\![\Psi]\!]| = 1$ and $M_\Psi = [\![\Psi]\!]$, then we obtain $[\![\Psi \star \alpha]\!] = [\![\Psi]\!]$ for every $\alpha \in \mathcal{L}$, which shows the claim. For the case of $|[\![\Psi]\!]| \neq 1$ or $M_\Psi \neq [\![\Psi]\!]$, we consider each case of Equation ($\#$) individually:

$[\![\alpha]\!] \cap \mathcal{S}_\Psi \neq \emptyset$. If $[\![\Psi]\!] \cap M_\Psi \neq \emptyset$, then, due to the faithfulness of $\Psi \mapsto (\preceq_\Psi, \mathcal{S}_\Psi, b_\Psi)$, we have $\min(M_\Psi, \preceq_\Psi) = [\![\Psi]\!] \cap M_\Psi$. This and the construction of $\preceq_\Psi$ yields that $[\![\Psi \star \alpha]\!] = \min([\![\alpha]\!], \preceq_\Psi) = [\![\Psi]\!] \cap M_\Psi \cap [\![\alpha]\!]$ holds for each $\alpha \in \mathcal{L}$ with $[\![\alpha]\!] \cap [\![\Psi]\!] \cap M_\Psi \neq \emptyset$.

For each α with $[\![\alpha]\!] \cap [\![\Psi]\!] \cap M_\Psi = \emptyset$, we obtain $[\![\Psi \star \alpha]\!] = \min([\![\alpha]\!], \ll_\Psi)$ from ($\bigstar$). Considering the construction of $\preceq_\Psi$ and ($\#$) yields $[\![\Psi \star \alpha]\!] = \min([\![\alpha]\!], \ll_\Psi) = \min([\![\alpha]\!], \preceq_\Psi)$.

$[\![\alpha]\!] = \emptyset$ *and* $b_\Psi = \bot$. Note that $b_\Psi = \bot$ implies $\bot \in \mathcal{A}(\Psi)$ by definition of $\Psi \mapsto (\preceq_\Psi, \mathcal{S}_\Psi, b_\Psi)$. Considering Equation ($\bigstar$) yields $[\![\Psi \star \alpha]\!] = \emptyset = [\![\Psi_\emptyset]\!]$.

None of the cases above applies. Whenever none of the cases above applies, only two cases remain. In the following we show that we obtain $[\![\Psi \star \alpha]\!] = [\![\Psi]\!]$ for both cases.

The case of α is consistent, yet $[\![\alpha]\!] \cap \mathcal{S}_\Psi = \emptyset$ holds. In this case, we obtain $\Psi \star \alpha = \Psi$ from $\mathcal{S}_\Psi = M_\Psi$, Equation ($\bigstar$) and $[\![\alpha]\!] \cap \mathcal{S}_\Psi = \emptyset$.

The case of α is inconsistent and $b_\Psi = \top$ holds. Then, by definition of b_Ψ, we have $\bot \notin \mathcal{A}(\Psi)$ or $[\![\Psi]\!] = \emptyset$ and thus, we obtain $\Psi \star \alpha = \Psi$ from Equation ($\bigstar$).

Next, we show that $\star$ is $\bot$-closed, i.e., we show that $b_\Psi = \bot$ implies $\mathcal{S}_\Psi = \Omega$. In the following we assume that $b_\Psi = \bot$ holds. Observe that $b_\Psi = \bot$ implies $\mathcal{A}(\Psi) = \mathcal{L}$ and $[\![\Psi]\!] \neq \emptyset$. Because of $[\![\Psi]\!] \neq \emptyset$, we obtain $M_\Psi = M_{\mathcal{A}(\Psi)}$. Thus, by using Proposition 7.3 and $\mathcal{A}(\Psi) = \mathcal{L}$, we obtain $M_{\mathcal{A}(\Psi)} = \Omega$. As we have $\mathcal{S}_\Psi = M_\Psi$, we obtain $[\![\Psi]\!] = \Omega$.

We show that $Scp^\star(\Psi) = \text{Bel}(\Psi) \cup \mathcal{A}(\Psi)$ holds. First, observe that due to Equation ($\#$) we have $\alpha \in \text{Bel}(\Psi \star \alpha)$ or $\text{Bel}(\Psi \star \alpha) = \text{Bel}(\Psi)$ for each

$\alpha \in \mathcal{L}$. This implies that we have $\alpha \in \text{Bel}(\Psi \star \alpha)$ for each $\alpha \in \text{Bel}(\alpha)$. Consequently, we obtain $\text{Bel}(\Psi) \subseteq Scp^\star(\Psi)$. Now let $X_\Psi = \{\alpha \mid [\![\alpha]\!] \cap \mathcal{S}_\Psi \neq \emptyset\}$ for each $\Psi \in \mathcal{E}$. By using Proposition 7.3, we obtain that X_Ψ satisfies single-sentence closure and disjunction completeness for all $\Psi \in \mathcal{E}$. From Equation (#), we have that $Scp^\star(\Psi) = \text{Bel}(\Psi) \cup X_\Psi$. Consulting the definition of $\Psi \mapsto (\preceq_\Psi, \mathcal{S}_\Psi, b_\Psi)$ and by using revision-compatibility of $\Psi \mapsto (\preceq_\Psi, \mathcal{S}_\Psi, b_\Psi)$ with $\star$ yields that $X_\Psi = \mathcal{A}(\Psi)$ holds. $\qquad\square$

Combining Proposition 8.23 and Proposition 8.24 yields the following theorem.

Theorem 8.25 (Strong Realizability). *Let $\mathcal{E}$ be a set of epistemic states. Then the following statements hold:*

(a) Every dynamic-limited revision compatible acceptance description for $\mathcal{E}$ complies with some dynamic-limited revision operator for $\mathcal{E}$.

(b) Every $\perp$-closed dynamic-limited revision operator for $\mathcal{E}$ complies with some dynamic-limited revision compatible acceptance description for $\mathcal{E}$.

8.7. Challenges for the Relational Approach

In the course of this Part, we have considered AGM revision operators, credibility-limited revision operators and dynamic-limited revision operators. For all these families of belief change operators, we have considered semantic characterizations that follow the same pattern. The result of a revision is semantically given by the minimal elements of a total preorder over interpretations assigned to the initial epistemic state. Moreover, the characterizing assignment of total preorders to epistemic states has to be faithful and compatible with the operator.

As shown by Theorem 8.25 even the very general class of dynamic-limited revision operators do have certain limitations (those mentioned in Definition 8.22) regarding realization of arbitrary acceptance descriptions. A natural step to overcome incompatibilities with arbitrary acceptance descriptions could be to generalize dynamic-limited revision operators further. While further generalization are conceivable, realization of arbitrary acceptance descriptions will probably be challenging for the relational assignment-based approach.

The rationale is that there are sets of epistemic states $\mathcal{E}$ such that *not* for every set of interpretations M an epistemic state in $\mathcal{E}$ exits which has M as models set, i.e., such that $[\![\Psi]\!] = M$ holds. Consider the following example.

Example 8.26. *Let Σ be a signature with two elements, and thus we have $\Omega = \{\omega_1, \omega_2, \omega_3, \omega_4\}$. Furthermore, let $\mathcal{E} = \{\Psi_{\{\omega_1,\omega_2\}}, \Psi_{\{\omega_2,\omega_3\}}, \Psi_{\{\omega_4\}}, \Psi_\emptyset\}$ be a set of epistemic states such that the following holds*

$$[\![\Psi_{\{\omega_1,\omega_2\}}]\!] = \{\omega_1, \omega_2\} \qquad\qquad [\![\Psi_{\{\omega_4\}}]\!] = \{\omega_4\}$$
$$[\![\Psi_{\{\omega_2,\omega_3\}}]\!] = \{\omega_2, \omega_3\} \qquad\qquad [\![\Psi_\emptyset]\!] = \emptyset$$

Now we consider the epistemic state $\Psi_{\{\omega_4\}}$ in more detail. Let $\mathcal{A}$ be an acceptance description for $\mathcal{E}$ such that:

$$\mathcal{A}(\Psi_{\{\omega_4\}}) = \{\alpha \mid [\![\alpha]\!] \cap \{\omega_1, \omega_2, \omega_3\} \neq \emptyset\}$$

For all other epistemic states $\Psi \in \mathcal{E} \setminus \{\Psi_{\{\omega_4\}}\}$ just set $\mathcal{A}(\Psi) = \emptyset$. Note that $\mathcal{A}$ is indeed an acceptance description for $\mathcal{E}$ as given in Definition 7.1:

- *We obtain that (AD-ES1) is satisfied, because $\mathcal{A}(\Psi_{\{\omega_4\}})$ satisfies single-sentence closure and disjunction completeness, and*
- *we obtain that (AD-ES2) is satisfied, because for every $\alpha \in \mathcal{A}(\Psi_{\{\omega_4\}})$ we have that there exists some $\Psi \in \mathcal{E}$ with $\alpha \in \mathrm{Bel}(\Psi)$ (the trivial witness is $\Psi_\emptyset$).*

The situation given in Example 8.26 reveals two problems that appear in general sets of epistemic states:

- For several beliefs α, e.g., for $\alpha = \varphi_{\omega_2}$ in Example 8.26, the only epistemic state Ψ with $\alpha \in \mathrm{Bel}(\Psi)$ has an inconsistent belief set (the state $\Psi_\emptyset$). However, there is no total preorder $\leq$ over $\{\omega_1, \omega_2, \omega_3\}$ such that $\min([\![\alpha]\!], \leq) = \emptyset$ holds[4].
- Total preorders are hardly usable as representation when only few epistemic states exists. One would expect that revising $\Psi_{\{\omega_4\}}$ by $\varphi_{\omega_1,\omega_2}$ yields $\Psi_{\{\omega_1,\omega_2\}}$, and revising $\Psi_{\{\omega_4\}}$ by $\varphi_{\omega_2,\omega_3}$

---

4   A way to overcome this issue might be given in the approach by Fermé and Wassermann [59], where the authors deal with the semantic representation of inconsistent beliefs.

yields $\Psi_{\{\omega_2,\omega_3\}}$ in Example 8.26. But for any relation $\leq$ that would yield $\min(\{\omega_1,\omega_2\}, \leq) = \{\omega_1,\omega_2\}$ and $\min(\{\omega_2,\omega_3\}, \leq) = \{\omega_2,\omega_3\}$ would also yield $\min(\{\omega_1,\omega_2,\omega_3\}, \leq) = \{\omega_1,\omega_2,\omega_3\}$ or $\min(\{\omega_1\}, \leq) = \{\omega_1\}$ (for which both no corresponding epistemic state in Example 8.26 exists).

A solution for these problems might be obtained by adapting the Darwiche-Pearl framework according to ideas[5] on the connection between belief change and orderings of propositions [36, 107]. We leave it as future work to find the right semantic construction to deal with these problems.

8.8. Summary

In this part, we considered revision and non-prioritized revision operators in the Darwiche-Pearl framework for belief change operators for epistemic states. We evaluated how operators could realize arbitrary acceptance descriptions.

In Chapter 6 we introduced the Darwiche-Pearl framework and considered AGM revision operators for epistemic states. The specifics of this framework are that arbitrary (abstract) sets of epistemic states are considered. Theorem 6.8 clarifies in which sets of epistemic states AGM revision operators exist.

In Chapter 7 we introduced acceptance descriptions as a thought experiment. We considered how credibility-limited revision could be generalized to generalized credibility-limited revision operators for epistemic states such that these operators also encompass AGM revision operators for epistemic states. In particular, generalized credibility-limited revision operators are given by postulates that express in which situations an operator yields a consistent or inconsistent set of beliefs. We proved a characterization theorem for generalized credibility-limited revision operators. Furthermore, we found exactly those acceptance descriptions that are realized by generalized credibility-limited revision operators.

---

[5]   Thanks to Eduardo Fermé for pointing to the work by Cantwell [36] at the 5th Madeira Workshop on Belief Revision, Argumentation, Ontologies, and Norms (BRAON'22).

In Chapter 8 we identified that generalized credibility-limited revision operators treat prior beliefs in a way such that generalized credibility-limited revision operators are unable to realize all acceptance descriptions. We relaxed generalized credibility-limited revision operators to dynamic-limited revision operators for epistemic states. In particular, in Section 8.3 we discussed the postulates of dynamic-limited revision operators for epistemic states in detail. We showed how dynamic-limited revision operators for epistemic states and generalized credibility-limited revision operators are related and considered properties of dynamic-limited revision operators. Finally, we characterized exactly those acceptance descriptions that are realized by dynamic-limited credibility-limited revision operators. We closed this Part with the challenges of realizing arbitrary acceptance descriptions with a relation approach as dynamic-limited revision operators for epistemic states.

Part III

Iteration Principles for Contraction

Introduction to Part III

In this part, we investigate iteration principles for contraction by considering several contraction-analogues of iteration principles for revision. We present a three-fold view on iteration principles for contraction that encompasses the change of *beliefs*, the change of *conditional beliefs*, and the change of *relations over possible worlds*. For this, we use specific conditionals for contraction, called *contractionals*, which were first studied by Bochman [24].

Due to the seminal work by Darwiche and Pearl [41], it is standard that principles for iterated revision and change of conditional beliefs are considered as two sides of the same coin. However, for iterated contraction, the situation is different, as there are only a small amount of iteration principles present in the literature, and for none of these iterated principles for contraction, there is a known equivalent formulation in terms of change of conditional beliefs. This part closes this gap.

In course of this part we will consider three main groups of iteration principles for contraction:

Syntactic Darwiche-Pearl Inspired Principles. We consider postulates for iterated contraction that are similar to the syntactic versions of the Darwiche-Pearl postulates for iterated revision. We obtain that a straightforward way of reformulation leads either to (partially) implausible postulates or to postulates not covering all cases one might expect. Whenever possible, we provide characterization theorems for these new postulates.

Semantic Darwiche-Pearl Inspired Principles. We consider postulates that are analogue to the semantic version of the Darwiche-Pearl

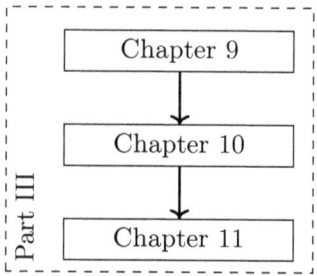

Overview of the organization of Part III.

postulates. We show that this new set of postulates and the set
of postulates given by Konieczny and Pino Pérez [98] define the
same subclass of AGM contraction operators for epistemic states.
However, we argue that our new postulates highlight new aspects
of iterated contraction operators. Especially, the new postulates
highlight the specific role of conditionals in the same manner as
the postulates for iterative revision by Darwich and Pearl do. For
some of the new postulates, we make use of a novel equivalence
relation for epistemic states with respect to a proposition α,
called α-equivalence, yielding an alternative formulation of these
postulates. Furthermore, we argue that our new postulates are
more succinct than the postulates by Konieczny and Pino Pérez
[98] because they deal less with changes of disjunctive beliefs.

Special Contraction Strategies. We explore a notion of independence
for contraction in the sense of independence for revision by Jin
and Thielischer [82] and show that this notion of independence
rules out trivial contraction operators. Moreover, we employ
contractionals to give alternative characterizations for natural
contraction and moderate contraction [112, 111, 123].

This part is organized in three chapters:

Chapter 9. In this chapter, we provide the technical background
and how conditionals are related to revision and contraction.
We briefly repeat the Darwiche-Pearl framework (but advice to
read Chapter 6 for a full introduction) and present the common
approach to iterated belief contraction in the Darwiche-Pearl
framework. We recall Ramsey-test conditionals for revision and
introduce contractionals as contraction counterparts thereof.

Chapter 10. In this chapter, we start by presenting the iteration principles for revision by Darwiche-Pearl. Furthermore, we consider contraction analogues to the syntactic Darwiche-Pearl postulates. Afterwards, we consider postulates for iterated contraction derived from the semantic Darwiche-Pearl postulates. We characterize all principles from the viewpoint of changing of beliefs, changing of conditional beliefs, and changing of relations over possible worlds.

Chapter 11. We consider natural and lexicographic revision, and independence for revision. For these specific kinds of revisions we consider counter-parts for contraction. We characterize those counter-parts from the viewpoint of change of beliefs, change of conditional beliefs, and change of relations over possible worlds.

Bibliographic Remark. Some results presented in this part have already been published in joint work with Gabriele Kern-Isberner and Christoph Beierle (see Section 1.4).

Remark on Epistemic States and the Underlying Logic. As stated in Chapter 6, we assume that $\mathcal{E}$ is a non-empty set of epistemic states (over some logical language $\mathcal{L}$). Moreover, as in Part II, $\mathcal{L}$ always denotes a propositional logic over an arbitrary but fixed chosen signature Σ, where Ω denotes the set of interpretations (see also the remarks on logic in Chapter 6).

Note on the Naming-Pattern for Postulates. In the course of this part, we consider several principles for iterated revision and counterparts for these principles for contraction. Because of the number of postulates and in order to underline the direct correspondence between revision and contraction postulates, we will use the following naming scheme. Postulates for *iterated revision* are denoted by IR; postulates for *iterated contraction* will be abbreviated by IC. Moreover, we will consider postulates for the change of beliefs (formulas), change of conditional beliefs, and the change of relations. To highlight the difference, we denote iteration postulates for revision with a *conditional* viewpoint by IR^{cond}, and IR^{rel} stands for considering a *relational* point of view. When considering change of beliefs, we denote the postulates by IR without superscript. Iteration postulates for contractions with a *contractional* viewpoint are denoted by IC^{cond}, and IC^{rel} stands for considering a *relational* point of view. When considering change of beliefs, we denote the postulates by IC without superscript.

Chapter 9

Contraction over Epistemic States and Conditionals

The purpose of this chapter is to provide the background for investigating iteration principles for contraction from a semantic and conditional point of view in the following chapters. Revision has a conditional semantics via the Ramsey-test for revision [148] and this was used by Darwiche and Pearl for introducing postulates for iterated revision [41]. We will adapt this approach to iterated contraction, and in the following we start by presenting the Darwiche-Pearl framework. Then we will introduce the Ramsey-test for revision and introduce contractionals, a special form of conditionals which we will use for our investigations on iterated contraction. Change of conditional beliefs is also connected with α-equivalence, a notion we will use for the succinct formulation of postulates.

9.1. Darwiche-Pearl Framework – Brief Overview

Remark. *We introduced the Darwiche-Pearl framework in detail in Chapter 6, including revision in this framework (see Section 6.3). This section only briefly recalls the basic ideas and concepts of this framework and AGM revision operators for epistemic states.*

The Darwiche-Pearl framework [41] abstracts from concrete representations for belief states and considers *epistemic states*. Furthermore, the Darwiche-Pearl framework focusses on propositional logics and thus, in this part we only consider propositional logic over finitely many atoms (as introduced in Chapter 2). We denote the set of all epistemic states with $\mathcal{E}$, for which we assume non-emptiness. Belief change operators in this framework obey the following definition.

Definition 6.2. Let $\mathcal{E}$ be a set of epistemic states. A *belief change operator (for epistemic states) over $\mathcal{E}$ (and $\mathcal{L}$)* is a function $\circ : \mathcal{E} \times \mathcal{L} \to \mathcal{E}$.

The framework has the assumption that every epistemic state $\Psi \in \mathcal{E}$ induces a set of beliefs $\mathrm{Bel}(\Psi) \subseteq \mathcal{L}$, which is a deductively closed set with respect to $\mathcal{L}$. We write $\Psi \models \alpha$ if $\alpha \in \mathrm{Bel}(\Psi)$ and we use $[\![\Psi]\!]$ as shorthand for $[\![\mathrm{Bel}(\Psi)]\!]$. Moreover, in this part, sometimes we additionally assume that $\mathcal{E}$ satisfies unbiasedness (see p. 119), which guarantees that for every belief set L there exists at least one epistemic state Ψ such that $\mathrm{Bel}(\Psi) = L$.

A primary means to characterize operator classes in the Darwiche-Pearl framework is by faithful assignments.

Definition 6.5. Let $\mathcal{E}$ be a set of epistemic states. A function $\Psi \mapsto \leq_\Psi$ that maps each epistemic state from $\mathcal{E}$ to a total preorder on interpretations is said to be a *faithful assignment (for $\mathcal{E}$)* if the following holds:

(FA1) If $\omega_1 \in [\![\Psi]\!]$ and $\omega_2 \in [\![\Psi]\!]$, then $\omega_1 \simeq_\Psi \omega_2$.
(FA2) If $\omega_1 \in [\![\Psi]\!]$ and $\omega_2 \notin [\![\Psi]\!]$, then $\omega_1 <_\Psi \omega_2$.

AGM revision (see Chapter 3) has a counter-part in the Darwiche-Pearl framework, characterized by selecting minimal models with respect to a faithful assignment.

Proposition 6.7. Let $\mathcal{E}$ be a set of epistemic states and let $*$ be a belief change operator $*$ for $\mathcal{E}$. The operator $*$ is an *AGM revision operator for $\mathcal{E}$* if and only if there is a faithful assignment $\Psi \mapsto \leq_\Psi$ for $\mathcal{E}$ which is revision-compatible with $*$, i.e., the following is satisfied:

$$[\![\Psi * \alpha]\!] = \min([\![\alpha]\!], \leq_\Psi)$$

9.2. Contraction in Epistemic States

Contraction is the process of withdrawing beliefs. In the following, we introduce the counter-part of AGM contraction for epistemic states, present a semantic characterization and consider some properties thereof.

AGM Contraction for Epistemic State. Postulates for AGM contraction [2] where first adapted by Caridroit, Konieczny and Marquis [37] to the setting of propositional logic (see Chapter 3). Based on the reformulation of AGM contraction postulates for propositional logic, Konieczny and Pino Pérez provided an adapted version of these postulates for the framework of epistemic states [98]:

Definition 9.1 (AGM Contraction Operator for Epistemic States). *Let $\mathcal{E}$ be a set of epistemic states. A belief change operator $\div$ (for $\mathcal{E}$) is called an AGM contraction operator for $\mathcal{E}$ if the following postulates are satisfied[1]:*

(C1) $\mathrm{Bel}(\Psi \div \alpha) \subseteq \mathrm{Bel}(\Psi)$.
(C2) If $\alpha \notin \mathrm{Bel}(\Psi)$, then $\mathrm{Bel}(\Psi) \subseteq \mathrm{Bel}(\Psi \div \alpha)$.
(C3) If $\alpha \not\equiv \top$, then $\alpha \notin \mathrm{Bel}(\Psi \div \alpha)$.
(C4) $\mathrm{Bel}(\Psi) \subseteq \mathrm{Bel}(\Psi \div \alpha) + \alpha$.
(C5) If $\alpha \equiv \beta$, then $\mathrm{Bel}(\Psi \div \alpha) = \mathrm{Bel}(\Psi \div \beta)$.
(C6) $\mathrm{Bel}(\Psi \div \alpha) \cap \mathrm{Bel}(\Psi \div \beta) \subseteq \mathrm{Bel}(\Psi \div (\alpha \wedge \beta))$.
(C7) If $\beta \notin \mathrm{Bel}(\Psi \div (\alpha \wedge \beta))$, then $\mathrm{Bel}(\Psi \div (\alpha \wedge \beta)) \subseteq \mathrm{Bel}(\Psi \div \beta)$.

If no specific set of epistemic states $\mathcal{E}$ is considered, or $\mathcal{E}$ is clear from the context, we also use *AGM contraction operator for epistemic states* instead of AGM contraction operator for $\mathcal{E}$. The postulates (C1)–(C7) directly correspond to (CKM1)–(CKM7) (see Chapter 3). Note the specific difference between postulate (C5) and (CKM4), which reflects the intention that additional meta-information in the epistemic state might have influence on the change. Moreover, note that the postulates (C1)–(C7) do not state how one should maintain the contraction strategy in the case of iteration.

As an aside, we want to remark that Chopra, Ghose, Meyer and Wong [40] gave also a reformulation of AGM contraction for the framework

---

[1] The abbreviation C stands for *contraction*.

of epistemic states, similar to the one used by Konieczny and Pino Pérez. However, there are subtle differences between these two similar, but slightly different groups of postulates[2]. We use the postulates by Konieczny and Pino Pérez here, because they are more general.

Semantic Characterization. For a semantic characterization by faithful assignments, we link contraction operators and faithful assignments by a notion of compatibility, like we did for revision (c.f. Definition 6.6).

Definition 9.2 (Contraction-Compatibility). *Let $\mathcal{E}$ be a set of epistemic states. A faithful assignment $\Psi \mapsto \leq_\Psi$ (for $\mathcal{E}$) is called* contraction-compatible *with a belief change operator $\div$ for $\mathcal{E}$ if the following holds:*

$$\llbracket \Psi \div \alpha \rrbracket = \llbracket \Psi \rrbracket \cup \min(\llbracket \neg\alpha \rrbracket, \leq_\Psi) \qquad \text{(contraction-compatible)}$$

A characterization in terms of total preorders on epistemic states is given by the following proposition.

Proposition 9.3 (Characterization of AGM Contraction Operators [98]). *Let $\mathcal{E}$ be a set of epistemic states and let $\div$ be a belief change operator for $\mathcal{E}$. The operator $\div$ is an AGM contraction operator for $\mathcal{E}$ if and only if there is a faithful assignment $\Psi \mapsto \leq_\Psi$ for $\mathcal{E}$ which is contraction-compatible with $\div$.*

Examples. The following examples demonstrate that AGM contraction operators for epistemic states can be simple.

Example 9.4. *Let $\Sigma = \{a\}$ and thus $\Omega = \{a, \bar{a}\}$. Consider the following set of epistemic states $\mathcal{E} = \{\Psi_a, \Psi_{\bar{a}}, \Psi_\top\}$ with:*

$$\llbracket \Psi_a \rrbracket = \{a\} \qquad \llbracket \Psi_{\bar{a}} \rrbracket = \{\bar{a}\} \qquad \llbracket \Psi_\top \rrbracket = \Omega$$

---

[2]   The subtle, but yet powerful difference is that Chopra, Ghose, Meyer and Wong (CGMW) use a stronger syntax independence postulate in comparison to the postulate (C5) by Konieczny and Pino Pérez (KPP). For an epistemic state Ψ, the CGMW-postulate states that for equivalent formulas, contraction on Ψ yields the same epistemic state, while the KPP-postulate (C5) states that for equivalent formulas, contraction on Ψ yields the same belief set (but not necessarily the same epistemic state). All other postulates are the same. Consequently, every belief change operator that satisfies the CGMW-postulates satisfies the KPP-postulates.

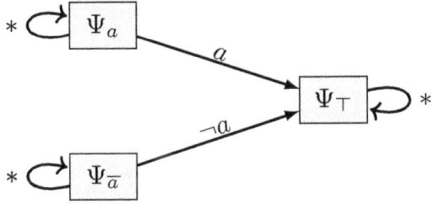

Figure 9.1: Graphical representation of the AGM contraction operator $\div$ for $\mathcal{E}$ given in Example 9.4.

The set $\mathcal{E}$ contains only epistemic states for which the beliefs are consistent, i.e., $[\![\Psi]\!] \neq \emptyset$ for all $\Psi \in \mathcal{E}$. Let $\div$ be a belief change operator for $\mathcal{E}$ given as follows for all $\Psi \in \mathcal{E}$ and $\alpha \in \mathcal{L}$:

$$\Psi \div \alpha = \begin{cases} \Psi_\top & \text{, if } \alpha \in \mathrm{Bel}(\Psi) \\ \Psi & \text{, otherwise} \end{cases}$$

For a graphical representation of $\div$ consider Figure 9.1. To demonstrate that $\div$ is an AGM contraction operator for $\mathcal{E}$, we use Proposition 9.3 and provide a faithful assignment which is contraction-compatible with $\div$. Let $\Psi \mapsto \leq_\Psi$ be the mapping where for each $\Psi \in \mathcal{E}$ the relation $\leq_\Psi$ is a total preorder determined by:

$$a <_{\Psi_a} \overline{a} \qquad\qquad \overline{a} <_{\Psi_{\overline{a}}} a \qquad\qquad a \simeq_{\Psi_\top} \overline{a}$$

The function $\Psi \mapsto \leq_\Psi$ is a faithful assignment for $\mathcal{E}$, as $[\![\Psi]\!] = \min(\Omega, \leq_\Psi)$ holds for each $\Psi \in \mathcal{E}$. Moreover, one can check quickly that $\Psi \mapsto \leq_\Psi$ is contraction-compatible with $\div$. Observer that the operator $\div$ is the only possible AGM contraction for $\mathcal{E}$.

In the course of this part, we will encounter two specific types of AGM contraction operators for epistemic states which we introduce in the following. We start with the very radical class of full meet AGM contraction operators for epistemic states.

Definition 9.5. *Let $\mathcal{E}$ be a set of epistemic states. An AGM contraction operator $\div$ for $\mathcal{E}$ said to be a* full meet[3] *contraction operator if the following is satisfied:*

$$\mathrm{Bel}(\Psi \div \alpha) = \begin{cases} \mathrm{Bel}(\Psi) & \textit{if } \alpha \notin \mathrm{Bel}(\Psi) \\ \mathrm{Bel}(\Psi) \cap \mathrm{Cn}(\neg\alpha) & \textit{otherwise} \end{cases} \qquad \text{(full meet)}$$

Thus, if α is believed previously in Ψ, then after contraction by α a full meet contraction operator yields always a new state that only retains beliefs that are consequences of $\neg\alpha$. Semantically, a full meet contraction operator adds all possible counter-models of α to $[\![\Psi]\!]$ in the process of contraction by α, i.e.:

$$[\![\Psi \div \alpha]\!] = \begin{cases} [\![\Psi]\!] & \text{if } [\![\Psi]\!] \cap [\![\neg\alpha]\!] \neq \emptyset \\ [\![\Psi]\!] \cup [\![\neg\alpha]\!] & \text{otherwise} \end{cases}$$

Every full meet AGM contraction operator $\div$ for $\mathcal{E}$ is contraction-compatible with the following faithful assignment $\Psi \mapsto \leq_\Psi^{\mathrm{flat}}$, which we denote as the *flat faithful assignment for $\mathcal{E}$*, given by

$$\omega_1 \leq_\Psi^{\mathrm{flat}} \omega_2 \quad \text{if} \quad \omega_1 \in [\![\Psi]\!] \text{ or } \omega_2 \notin [\![\Psi]\!]$$

for each $\Psi \in \mathcal{E}$. Typically, $\leq_\Psi^{\mathrm{flat}}$ will have two layers, the lowermost layer consists of $[\![\Psi]\!]$ (if $[\![\Psi]\!] \neq \emptyset$), and the other layer contains all elements of $\Omega \setminus [\![\Psi]\!]$. The name "flat" refers to the fact that $\leq_\Psi^{\mathrm{flat}}$ has the least number of layers for each $\Psi \in \mathcal{E}$ compared to all other faithful assignments for $\mathcal{E}$.

Proposition 9.6. *Let $\mathcal{E}$ be a set of epistemic states and let $\div$ be an AGM contraction operator for $\mathcal{E}$. The operator $\div$ is a full meet AGM contraction operator for $\mathcal{E}$ if and only if $\div$ is contraction-compatible with the flat faithful assignment for $\mathcal{E}$.*

Proof. This is immediately given by Proposition 6.7 . □

---

3 While "full meet" denotes here a property of $\div$, the name full meet refers to the fact that every change from the belief set $\mathrm{Bel}(\Psi)$ to the belief set $\mathrm{Bel}(\Psi \div \alpha)$ is indeed a full meet contraction in the sense of belief changes for belief sets which are constructed from reminder sets and selection functions [73].

Second, we consider AGM contraction operators for epistemic states where the behaviour is partially given by a linear order on the possible worlds.

Definition 9.7 (linear, maxichoice). *Let $\mathcal{E}$ be a set of epistemic states and let $\div$ be an AGM contraction operator for $\mathcal{E}$. The operator $\div$ is called* linear *if there exists a linear order $\ll^{\div}$ on Ω such that the following is satisfied for each $\Psi \in \mathcal{E}$ and $\alpha \in \mathcal{L}$:*

$$[\![\Psi \div \alpha]\!] = \begin{cases} [\![\Psi]\!] & \text{if } \alpha \notin \mathrm{Bel}(\Psi) \\ [\![\Psi]\!] \cup \min([\![\neg\alpha]\!], \ll^{\div}) & \text{otherwise} \end{cases} \quad \text{(linear)}$$

The operator $\div$ is called maxichoice[4] *if for each $\Psi \in \mathcal{E}$ there exists a linear order $\ll^{\div}_{\Psi}$ on Ω such that the following is satisfied for each $\alpha \in \mathcal{L}$:*

$$[\![\Psi \div \alpha]\!] = \begin{cases} [\![\Psi]\!] & \text{if } \alpha \notin \mathrm{Bel}(\Psi) \\ [\![\Psi]\!] \cup \min([\![\neg\alpha]\!], \ll^{\div}_{\Psi}) & \text{otherwise} \end{cases} \quad \text{(maxichoice)}$$

Note that the relation $\ll^{\div}$ of a linear AGM contraction operator $\div$ is *independent of a particular epistemic state* and thus, a linear AGM contraction operator $\div$ has globally the same behaviour for every epistemic state Ψ (possibly except for elements of $\mathrm{Bel}(\Psi)$). On the other hand, for maxichoice AGM contraction operators we have that $\ll^{\div}_{\Psi}$ is state-dependent, and thus, a maxichoice AGM contraction operator may behave differently for each epistemic state. Consequently, every linear AGM contraction operator for epistemic states is also a maxichoice AGM contraction operator for epistemic states. At the end of this section, we will see that linear AGM contraction operators for epistemic states could be considered as basal AGM contraction operators for epistemic states.

We characterize maxichoice AGM contraction operator for epistemic states. For a linear order $\ll$ on Ω, let $\leq^{\lll}_{\Psi}$ denote the relation

$$\leq^{\lll}_{\Psi} = (\ll \setminus (\Omega \times [\![\Psi]\!])) \cup ([\![\Psi]\!] \times \Omega)$$

in the following proposition, i.e., the total preorder Ω such that $[\![\Psi]\!]$ is the set of the lowermost interpretations in $\leq_{\Psi}$ (if $[\![\Psi]\!] \neq \emptyset$), and the remaining interpretations are ordered according to $\ll$.

---

[4]   This refers to the fact that for these operators all the changes from one belief set $\mathrm{Bel}(\Psi)$ to another belief set $\mathrm{Bel}(\Psi \div \alpha)$ are *maxichoice* contractions [73] (see also Footnote 3).

Proposition 9.8. *Let $\mathcal{E}$ be a set of epistemic states and let $\div$ be an AGM contraction operator for $\mathcal{E}$. The operator $\div$ is a maxichoice AGM contraction operator for $\mathcal{E}$ if and only if $\div$ is contraction-compatible with the faithful assignment $\Psi \mapsto \leq_\Psi^{\ll_\Psi^{\div}}$ for $\mathcal{E}$, where each $\ll_\Psi^{\div}$ is a linear order on Ω.*

Proof. This is immediately given by Proposition 6.7 . □

In general, not every maxichoice AGM contraction operator for epistemic states is a linear AGM contraction operator for epistemic states. This highlights again the difference between the iterative reading of belief change and the one-shot reading of belief change (see Chapter 3), as, in the one-shot reading, a differentiation between linear and maxichoice AGM contraction operators is *not* possible.

The AGM contraction operator for epistemic states given in Example 9.4 is linear. In the following examples we consider a maxichoice AGM contraction operator for epistemic states that is not linear.

Example 9.9. *Let $\Sigma = \{a, b\}$ and thus $\Omega = \{ab, \bar{a}b, a\bar{b}, \bar{a}\bar{b}\}$. Consider the following set of epistemic states $\mathcal{E} = \{\Psi_M \mid \emptyset \neq M \subseteq \Omega\}$ with $[\![\Psi_M]\!] = M$ for each $\emptyset \neq M \subseteq \Omega$. For every non-empty subset of Ω, the set $\mathcal{E}$ contains exactly one epistemic state having this set as model set. Furthermore, let $\ll$ and $\prec\!\!\!\prec$ be linear orders on Ω with*

$$ab \ll \bar{a}b \ll a\bar{b} \ll \bar{a}\bar{b} \qquad and \qquad ab \prec\!\!\!\prec a\bar{b} \prec\!\!\!\prec \bar{a}b \prec\!\!\!\prec \bar{a}\bar{b} .$$

Let $\div$ be a belief change operator for $\mathcal{E}$ given as follows for all $\Psi \in \mathcal{E}$ and $\alpha \in \mathcal{L}$:

$$\Psi \div \alpha = \begin{cases} \Psi & , if \ \alpha \in \mathrm{Bel}(\Psi) \\ \Psi_{[\![\Psi]\!] \cup \min([\![\neg\alpha]\!], \prec\!\!\!\prec)} & , if \ \alpha \notin \mathrm{Bel}(\Psi) \ and \ \Psi = \Psi_{\{ab\}} \quad (9.1) \\ \Psi_{[\![\Psi]\!] \cup \min([\![\neg\alpha]\!], \ll)} & , otherwise \end{cases}$$

For a graphical illustration of $\div$ consider Figure 9.2. From Proposition 9.8, we obtain that $\div$ is a maxichoice AGM contraction operator for $\mathcal{E}$.

We will now show that $\div$ is not a linear AGM contraction operator for $\mathcal{E}$. Suppose that there exists a linear order $\ll^{\div}$ on Ω (as demanded in

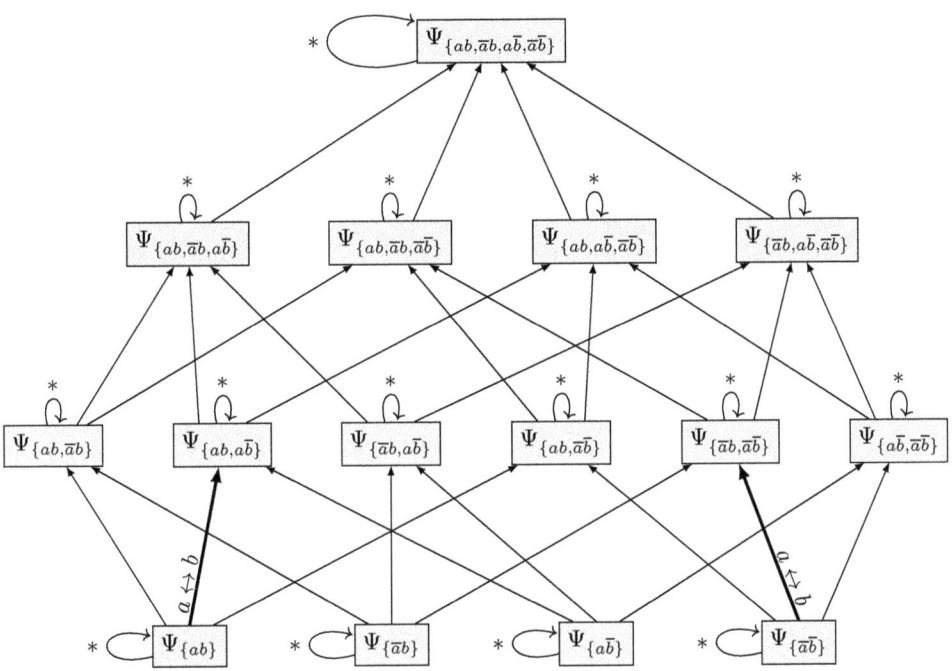

Figure 9.2: Graphical illustration of the AGM contraction operator ÷ for $\mathcal{E}$ given in Example 9.9. For the sake of clarity, most edges are only sketched. Only the edges with $\alpha \equiv a \leftrightarrow b$ for $\Psi_{\{ab\}}$ and $\Psi_{\{\overline{a}\overline{b}\}}$ from Example 9.9 are explicitly given. As it is typical for maxichoice contractions, each contraction adds at most one additional model.

Definition 9.7) such that for all $\Psi \in \mathcal{E}$ the following holds:

$$[\![\Psi \div \alpha]\!] = \begin{cases} [\![\Psi]\!] & \text{if } \alpha \notin \mathrm{Bel}(\Psi) \\ [\![\Psi]\!] \cup \min([\![\neg\alpha]\!], \ll^{\div}) & \text{otherwise} \end{cases} \quad (9.2)$$

In the following, let α be a formula such that $[\![\neg\alpha]\!] = \{a\overline{b}, \overline{a}b\}$ holds, i.e., $\alpha \equiv a \leftrightarrow b$. Consequently, we have $\alpha \in \mathrm{Bel}(\Psi_{\{ab\}})$ and $\alpha \in \mathrm{Bel}(\Psi_{\{\overline{a}\overline{b}\}})$. By using Equation (9.1), we obtain $[\![\Psi_{\{ab\}} \div \alpha]\!] = \{ab, a\overline{b}\}$ and $[\![\Psi_{\{\overline{a}\overline{b}\}} \div \alpha]\!] = \{\overline{a}b, \overline{a}\overline{b}\}$. This yields a conflict with Equation (9.2), as all prior observations together imply that $a\overline{b} \ll^{\div} \overline{a}b$ and $\overline{a}b \ll^{\div} a\overline{b}$ hold at the same time, which is impossible whenever $\ll^{\div}$ is a linear order. In summary, $\div$ is a maxichoice, but not linear, AGM contraction operator for $\mathcal{E}$.

Further Remarks. Comparing Proposition 6.7 and Proposition 9.3 reveals that contraction is a unique form of changing. As in the general Darwiche-Pearl framework, unlike in the classical setting (see Chapter 3), there are specific situations where revision and contraction are not interdefinable, as shown by Konieczny and Pino Pérez.

Proposition 9.10 ([98])**.** *There exists a set of epistemic states $\mathcal{E}$ such that there exist more[5] AGM revision operators for $\mathcal{E}$ than AGM contraction operators for $\mathcal{E}$.*

The matter becomes even more complex, as the converse to Proposition 9.10 is also true in certain situations.

Proposition 9.11. *There exists a set of epistemic states $\mathcal{E}$ such that there exist more[6] AGM contraction operators for $\mathcal{E}$ than AGM revision operators for $\mathcal{E}$.*

Proof. Consider $\mathcal{E}$ and $\div$ from Example 9.4. Recall that $\div$ is an AGM contraction operator for $\mathcal{E}$. By Theorem 6.8 there exists no AGM revision operator for $\mathcal{E}$. □

Besides of Proposition 9.10 and Proposition 9.11, we leave it open to systematically studying the relation between AGM revision and AGM contraction in different setups of epistemic states.

The following proposition fully captures those sets of epistemic states $\mathcal{E}$ for which an AGM contraction operator for $\mathcal{E}$ exists.

Proposition 9.12. *Let $\mathcal{E}$ be a set of epistemic states. There exists an AGM contraction operator $\div$ for $\mathcal{E}$ if and only if $\mathcal{E}$ satisfies the following postulate:*

(AGM-ES3) *For each $\Psi \in \mathcal{E}$ and for each $M \subseteq \Omega$ with $\llbracket \Psi \rrbracket \subseteq M$ there exists $\Psi_M \in \mathcal{E}$ such that $\llbracket \Psi_M \rrbracket = M$.*

Proof. We start by showing that the existence of $\div$ implies satisfaction of (AGM-ES3). For each $\omega \in \Omega$ let $\varphi_{\overline{\omega}}$ be a formula such that $\llbracket \varphi_{\overline{\omega}} \rrbracket = \Omega \backslash \{\omega\}$ holds. Let $\Psi \in \mathcal{E}$ be an arbitrary epistemic state and $M \subseteq \Omega$ be such that $\llbracket \Psi \rrbracket \subsetneq M$ holds. In the following let $M \backslash \llbracket \Psi \rrbracket = \{\omega_1, \ldots, \omega_n\}$.

---

[5]   In terms of cardinality, i.e., the set of all AGM revision operators for $\mathcal{E}$ has strictly more elements than the set of all AGM contraction operators for $\mathcal{E}$.

[6]   In terms of cardinality, see also Footnote 5.

Using Proposition 9.3 we obtain that $\Psi_M = (((\Psi \div \varphi_{\overline{\omega_1}}) \div \varphi_{\overline{\omega_2}}) \ldots) \div \varphi_{\overline{\omega_n}}$ is an epistemic state with $[\![\Psi_M]\!] = M$.

For the remaining direction, let $\mathcal{E}$ be a (non-empty) set of epistemic states that satisfies (AGM-ES3). We construct a linear AGM contraction operator for $\mathcal{E}$. Let $\ll$ be an arbitrary linear order on Ω, and for each $\omega \in \Omega$ let $\Psi_{\{\omega\}}$ denote a uniquely chosen epistemic state from $\mathcal{E}$ such that $[\![\Psi_{\{\omega\}}]\!] = [\![\Psi]\!] \cup \{\omega\}$. Let $\div$ be the belief change operator for $\mathcal{E}$ given as follows:

$$\Psi \div \alpha = \begin{cases} \Psi & \text{if } \alpha \notin \mathrm{Bel}(\Psi) \\ \Psi_{\min([\![\neg\alpha]\!], \ll)} & \text{otherwise} \end{cases}$$

Because $\mathcal{E}$ satisfies (AGM-ES3), we have that for each $\Psi \in \mathcal{E}$ and $\alpha \in \mathcal{L}$ the epistemic state $\Psi \div \alpha$ exists, i.e., $\Psi \div \alpha \in \mathcal{E}$. Now let $\Psi \mapsto \leq_\Psi$ be defined for each $\Psi \in \mathcal{E}$ as follows (see also Proposition 9.8):

$$\leq_\Psi = (\ll \setminus (\Omega \times [\![\Psi]\!])) \cup ([\![\Psi]\!] \times \Omega).$$

Indeed, $\Psi \mapsto \leq_\Psi$ is a faithful assignment. Moreover, $\Psi \mapsto \leq_\Psi$ is contraction-compatible with $\div$. By Proposition 9.3, we obtain that $\div$ is an AGM contraction operator for $\mathcal{E}$.   □

From the proof of Proposition 9.11, we obtain that linear AGM contraction operators for epistemic states are in some way basic AGM contraction operators for epistemic states. They exist for a set of epistemic states $\mathcal{E}$, whenever any AGM contraction operator for E exists at all. The following corollary formally describes this observation.

Corollary 9.13. *Let $\mathcal{E}$ be a set of epistemic states. If there exists an AGM contraction operator for $\mathcal{E}$, then there exists also a linear AGM contraction operator for $\mathcal{E}$.*

Note that Corollary 9.13 might have application in algorithms that compute, for a set of epistemic states $\mathcal{E}$, whether an AGM contraction operator for $\mathcal{E}$ exists.

9.3. Ramsey Test Conditionals and Revision

For the matter of this part, a conditional is a syntactic object $(\beta \,|\, \alpha)$, where $\alpha, \beta \in \mathcal{L}$. A typical informal interpretation of a conditional

$(\beta\,|\,\alpha)$ is that $(\beta\,|\,\alpha)$ stands for "if α, then usually β", establishing conditionals as fundamental objects in non-monotonic reasoning [99]. The *Ramsey test* [148] provides an alternative semantics for conditionals by stating that one should believe $(\beta\,|\,\alpha)$ if and only if one believes β after revision by α. We use the Ramsey test here in the following formulation:

(RT) $\Psi \models (\beta\,|\,\alpha)$ if and only if $\Psi * \alpha \models \beta$

One application of (RT) in the setting of iterated belief change is that (RT) makes it possible to use conditionals as a syntactic means to describe (partially) how a belief revision operator $*$ behaves with respect to a particular epistemic state. More precisely, given the set $C(\Psi)$ of all conditionals $(\beta\,|\,\alpha)$ with $\Psi \models (\beta\,|\,\alpha)$, in the presence of (RT), we can determine $\mathrm{Bel}(\Psi * \alpha)$ just from $C(\Psi)$ and α. Note that in general, we can not determine $\Psi * \alpha$ just from the set of conditionals $C(\Psi)$ and α.

When considering an AGM revision operator $*$ for $\mathcal{E}$, we obtain from Proposition 6.7 that $\leq_\Psi$ has similar properties as $C(\Psi)$, i.e., for each epistemic state Ψ, the total preorder $\leq_\Psi$ and α determine $\mathrm{Bel}(\Psi * \alpha)$ entirely. This gives rationale to consider $\leq_\Psi$ as a semantic counter-part of $C(\Psi)$, which is indeed given by the following. First, we formally introduce notions of acceptance of a conditional by an epistemic state and by a total preorder.

Definition 9.14. *Let $\Psi \in \mathcal{E}$ be an epistemic state and let $\leq$ be a total preorder over Ω. We say a conditional $(\beta\,|\,\alpha)$ is accepted by Ψ (and $*$), written $\Psi \models (\beta\,|\,\alpha)$, if $\Psi * \alpha \models \beta$. Moreover, we say a conditional $(\beta\,|\,\alpha)$ is accepted by $\leq$ if for each $\omega \in [\![\alpha \wedge \neg\beta]\!]$ there exists $\omega' \in [\![\alpha \wedge \beta]\!]$ such that $\omega' < \omega$.*

The definition of $\Psi \models (\beta\,|\,\alpha)$ is just the right-hand side of (RT). Clearly, acceptance of the conditional $(\beta\,|\,\alpha)$ by Ψ depends on $*$, but we write $\Psi \models (\beta\,|\,\alpha)$ instead of $\Psi \models^* (\beta\,|\,\alpha)$, omitting the superscript on $\models^*$, since $*$ will be always clear by the context. Acceptance by a total preorder is chosen such that it is compatible with revision-compatibility (cf. Definition 6.6). The following proposition presents formally the correspondence between the acceptance by Ψ and the acceptance by $\leq_\Psi$.

Proposition 9.15. *Let $\mathcal{E}$ be a set of epistemic states and let $*$ be an AGM revision operator for $\mathcal{E}$ that is revision-compatible with a faithful assignment $\Psi \mapsto \leq_\Psi$. For each $\Psi \in \mathcal{E}$ and $\alpha, \beta \in \mathcal{L}$ the following statements are equivalent:*

(a) $\Psi * \alpha \models \beta$

(b) $(\beta \mid \alpha)$ is accepted by $\leq_\Psi$

(c) $(\beta \mid \alpha)$ is accepted by Ψ and $*$

Proof. The equivalence of (a) and (c) is given by definition. From Proposition 6.7, we obtain $\beta \in \mathrm{Bel}(\Psi * \alpha)$ if and only if $\min(\llbracket \alpha \rrbracket, \leq_\Psi) \subseteq \llbracket \beta \rrbracket$. The latter is exactly the case if and only if $(\beta \mid \alpha)$ is accepted by $\leq_\Psi$. We obtain that (a) and (b) are equivalent. $\qquad \square$

9.4. Iterated Contraction and Conditionals

In this section we prepare the ground for our investigations on iteration principles for contraction from a conditional perspective. Therefore, we will use AGM contraction operators for epistemic states to provide a semantics for conditionals in the same fashion as revision operators provide a semantics of conditionals via the Ramsey-test (cf. Section 9.3). The approach we follow is that we replace the revision operator in (RT) by a contraction operator. To distinguish conditionals which have a semantics by revision operators, sometimes called *RT-conditionals* in the sequel, from conditionals which use contraction operators as semantics, we will call the latter *contractionals* (as proposed by Bochman [24]) and denote them by $[\beta \mid \alpha]$. We obtain the following reformulation of (RT) for contractionals:

(Contractional) $\Psi \models [\beta \mid \alpha]$ if and only if $\Psi \div \alpha \models \beta$

For the rest of Part III, we assume that $\div$ is always an AGM contraction operator for epistemic states, and given this class of operators, we will investigate the properties of contractionals. We start with some intuition for contractionals by suggesting to read a contractional $[\beta \mid \alpha]$ as:

believe β even in the absence of α.

More specifically, a contractional $[\beta \,|\, \alpha]$ encodes two aspects: (1) β is believed, and (2) believing of β is independent of believing in α. The rationale for this interpretation is given by the AGM contraction postulates (C1)–(C7):

- The rationale for (1) is that $\div$ satisfies inclusion (C1), by which a contraction never introduces new beliefs. Thus, it is unavoidable that $\Psi \models [\beta \,|\, \alpha]$ holds only if $\beta \in \mathrm{Bel}(\Psi)$.
- Aspect (2) is given by the success condition (C3), encoding the overall goal of contraction by α to remove all beliefs that imply α. Consequently, if $\Psi \models [\beta \,|\, \alpha]$, then β is a belief that is unrelated to α in the sense that believing in β gives no rationale to believe in α. In other words, β is independent of α in the sense that when α is given up the belief β is not given up.

Consider the following example for a comparison of the meaning of contractionals to Ramsey test conditionals.

Example 9.16. *Let f have the intended meaning that something is "able to fly" and p the intended meaning that something is a "penguin". Then the acceptance of a (Ramsey test) conditional $(\neg f \,|\, p)$ states that if the agent learns that something is a penguin, she will believe that it is not able to fly. In contrast, the acceptance of a contractional $[\neg f \,|\, p]$ states that the agent keeps the belief that something is not able to fly, even if the agent gives up her belief that it is a penguin.*

We continue by investigating contractionals more formally. Like in the previous section, we define a notion of acceptance of a contractional by an epistemic state Ψ and a notion of acceptance by a total preorder over worlds.

Definition 9.17. *Let $\mathcal{E}$ be a set of epistemic states and let $\div$ be an AGM contraction operator for $\mathcal{E}$. Furthermore, let $\Psi \in \mathcal{E}$ be an epistemic state and let $\leq$ be a total preorder over Ω. We say a contractional $[\beta \,|\, \alpha]$ is accepted by Ψ (and $\div$), written $\Psi \models [\beta \,|\, \alpha]$, if $\Psi \div \alpha \models \beta$. Moreover, we say a contractional $[\beta \,|\, \alpha]$ is accepted by $\leq$ if $\min(\Omega, \leq) \subseteq [\![\beta]\!]$ and for every $\omega_1 \in [\![\neg\alpha \wedge \neg\beta]\!]$ there exists $\omega_2 \in [\![\neg\alpha \wedge \beta]\!]$ such that $\omega_2 < \omega_1$.*

Note that the notion of acceptance of a contractional $[\beta \,|\, \alpha]$ by a total preorder is chosen to be compliant with the notion of contraction-compatibility used in Proposition 9.3. Analogously to Proposition 9.15, we obtain that acceptance by an epistemic state and acceptance by a total preorder of a contractional are equivalent.

Proposition 9.18. *Let $\mathcal{E}$ be a set of epistemic states and let $\div$ be an AGM contraction operator for $\mathcal{E}$ that is contraction-compatible with a faithful assignment $\Psi \mapsto \leq_\Psi$. For each $\Psi \in \mathcal{E}$ and $\alpha, \beta \in \mathcal{L}$ the following statements are equivalent:*

(a) $\Psi \div \alpha \models \beta$

(b) $[\beta \,|\, \alpha]$ *is accepted by* $\leq_\Psi$

(c) $[\beta \,|\, \alpha]$ *is accepted by* Ψ *and* $\div$

Proof. The equivalence of (a) and (c) is given by definition. From Proposition 9.3, we obtain $\beta \in \mathrm{Bel}(\Psi * \alpha)$ if and only if $[\![\Psi]\!] \cup \min([\![\alpha]\!], \leq_\Psi) \subseteq [\![\beta]\!]$. The latter is exactly the case if and only if $(\beta \,|\, \alpha)$ is accepted by $\leq_\Psi$. We obtain that (a) and (b) are equivalent. $\square$

As an application of Proposition 9.18, we consider the inclusion postulate (C1) from the set of basic postulates for AGM contraction, stating that a contraction does not yield new beliefs. The following property is a consequence of the inclusion property and the recovery condition (C4).

Proposition 9.19. *Let $\mathcal{E}$ be a set of epistemic states and let $-$ be a belief change operator for $\mathcal{E}$ that satisfies (C1) and (C4). If $\alpha, \beta, \gamma \in \mathcal{L}$, then $\gamma \in \mathrm{Bel}(\Psi - \alpha - \beta)$ implies $\gamma \in \mathrm{Bel}(\Psi - \top)$.*

Proof. Because $-$ satisfies (C1), we obtain $\gamma \in \mathrm{Bel}(\Psi)$ from $\gamma \in \mathrm{Bel}(\Psi - \alpha - \beta)$. Now note that $\top \in \mathrm{Bel}(\Psi - \top)$, because $\top$ is element of every deductively closed set. Consequently, we have $\mathrm{Bel}(\Psi - \top) + \top = \mathrm{Bel}(\Psi - \top)$. From this last observation and (C4) we obtain $\mathrm{Bel}(\Psi) \subseteq \mathrm{Bel}(\Psi - \top)$. $\square$

By employing Proposition 9.18, from Proposition 9.19 we obtain that every AGM contraction operator for $\mathcal{E}$ satisfies the following:

If $\alpha, \beta, \gamma \in \mathcal{L}$, then $\Psi \div \alpha \models [\gamma \,|\, \beta] \Rightarrow \Psi \models [\gamma \,|\, \top]$.

9.5. α-Equivalence

For the case of iterated contraction, we need to constrain the notion of equivalence of formulas to specific cases. For expressing such constraints, we propose a notion of equivalence which is relative to a proposition α, which we call α-equivalence.

Definition 9.20 (α-equivalence). *For two sets of interpretations* $\Omega_1, \Omega_2 \subseteq \Omega$ *and a formula* α *we say* Ω_1 *is* α-equivalent *to* Ω_2, *written* $\Omega_1 =_\alpha \Omega_2$, *if* Ω_1 *and* Ω_2 *contain the same set of models of* α, *i.e.* $\Omega_1 \cap [\![\alpha]\!] = \Omega_2 \cap [\![\alpha]\!]$.

This is lifted to sets of formulas X, Y, by saying X is α-*equivalent* to Y, written $X =_\alpha Y$, if $[\![X]\!] =_\alpha [\![Y]\!]$. For sets of formulas an alternative formulation is possible:

Proposition 9.21. *Two sets of formulas* X *and* Y *are* α-*equivalent if and only if* $Cn(X \cup \{\alpha\}) = Cn(Y \cup \{\alpha\})$.

Intuitively, X and Y are α-equivalent if they agree on everything about α. In the following, we give an example which demonstrates α-equivalence.

Example 9.22. *Suppose a scenario about birds (b), penguins (p) and flying (f). Let* $X = Cn(b \wedge f, p \rightarrow f)$ *and* $Y = Cn(b \wedge f, p \rightarrow \neg f)$ *be belief sets which differ mainly in their beliefs about whether a penguin can fly or not. The models of these two belief sets are* $[\![X]\!] = \{bfp, bf\overline{p}\}$ *and* $[\![Y]\!] = \{bf\overline{p}\}$. *Then* X *and* Y *agree in their view on birds that are no penguins,* $X =_{b \wedge \neg p} Y$, *but they do not agree in everything about birds,* $X \neq_b Y$.

We will use the notion of α-equivalence as a tool to describe invariants for belief changes. As an example, consider the following proposition, holding for every AGM contraction.

Proposition 9.23. *Let* $\mathcal{E}$ *be a set of epistemic states. For every AGM contraction operator* $\div$ *for* $\mathcal{E}$ *and all propositions* α, β *the following postulate holds:*

(Invariance) *If* $\neg \alpha \wedge \beta \equiv \bot$, *then* $\mathrm{Bel}(\Psi) =_\beta \mathrm{Bel}(\Psi \div \alpha)$.

Proof. Assume α, β such that $\neg \alpha \wedge \beta \equiv \bot$. By Proposition 9.3 there is a faithful assignment $\Psi \mapsto \leq_\Psi$ such that (contraction-compatible) is fulfilled. Since $\neg\alpha \wedge \beta \equiv \bot$ holds, $\neg\alpha$ and β have no models in common. Therefore, we can infer that the set $\min(\llbracket\neg\alpha\rrbracket, \leq_{\Psi})$ contains no models of β. Thus from $\llbracket\Psi \div \alpha\rrbracket = \llbracket\Psi\rrbracket \cup \min(\llbracket\neg\alpha\rrbracket, \leq_{\Psi})$ we can derive $\llbracket\Psi \div \alpha\rrbracket =_{\beta} \llbracket\Psi\rrbracket$, which is equivalent to $\mathrm{Bel}(\Psi) =_{\beta} \mathrm{Bel}(\Psi \div \alpha)$. $\qquad \square$

The following proposition relates α-equivalence of beliefs to the acceptance of contractionals.

Proposition 9.24. *Let $\mathcal{E}$ be a set of epistemic states, let $\div$ be an AGM contraction operator for $\mathcal{E}$, let $\Psi, \Phi \in \mathcal{E}$ be epistemic states and let $\alpha, \beta \in \mathcal{L}$ be propositions. Then $\mathrm{Bel}(\Psi \div \beta) =_{\alpha} \mathrm{Bel}(\Phi \div \beta)$ holds if and only if for all propositions γ we have:*

$$\Psi \models [\alpha \rightarrow \gamma \mid \beta] \ \text{if and only if} \ \Phi \models [\alpha \rightarrow \gamma \mid \beta]$$

Proof. We consider both directions of the claim independently.

The "$\Rightarrow$"-direction. For this direction let $\mathrm{Bel}(\Psi \div \beta) =_{\alpha} \mathrm{Bel}(\Phi \div \beta)$. This is equivalent to:

$$\llbracket\Psi \div \beta\rrbracket \cap \llbracket\alpha\rrbracket = \llbracket\Phi \div \beta\rrbracket \cap \llbracket\alpha\rrbracket \qquad (9.3)$$

Assume now (without loss of generality) that $\Psi \models [\gamma \vee \neg\alpha \mid \beta]$ and $\Phi \not\models [\gamma \vee \neg\alpha \mid \beta]$. Then we get a contradiction, since there must be a world $w \in \llbracket\neg\gamma \wedge \alpha\rrbracket$ such that $w \in \llbracket\Phi \div \beta\rrbracket$, which contradicts the assumption in combination with Equation (9.3).

The "$\Leftarrow$"-direction. For all propositions γ it holds hat $\Psi \models [\gamma \vee \neg\alpha \mid \beta] \Leftrightarrow \Phi \models [\gamma \vee \neg\alpha \mid \beta]$. Towards a contradiction assume now that $\llbracket\Psi \div \beta\rrbracket \cap \llbracket\alpha\rrbracket \neq \llbracket\Phi \div \beta\rrbracket \cap \llbracket\alpha\rrbracket$. This implies (without loss of generality) that there is a world w such that $w \notin \llbracket\Psi \div \beta\rrbracket \cap \llbracket\alpha\rrbracket$ but $w \in \llbracket\Phi \div \beta\rrbracket \cap \llbracket\alpha\rrbracket$. Now let γ be a formula such that $\llbracket\gamma\rrbracket = \llbracket\Psi \div \beta\rrbracket \cap \llbracket\alpha\rrbracket$. Clearly, it holds that $\Psi \div \beta \models \gamma \vee \neg\alpha$ and $\Phi \div \beta \not\models \gamma \vee \neg\alpha$. By the correspondence between contractionals and contractions this is a contradiction the our assumption. $\qquad \square$

In the following chapters we investigate and evaluate iteration principles for AGM contraction operators. We consider mainly two groups of iteration principles which are analogues to the Darwiche-Pearl iteration principles for AGM revision operators for epistemic states. The first group are counter-parts for AGM contraction operators to the syntactic versions (IR1)–(IR4), respectively (IR1^{cond})–(IR4^{cond}), of the Darwiche-Pearl iteration principles. Secondly, we consider counter-parts for AGM contraction operators to the semantic versions (IR1^{rel})–(IR4^{rel}) of the Darwiche-Pearl iteration principles. We will employ α-equivalence as a means for the succinct formulation of postulates. For both groups of principles we consider the impact of conditional beliefs, i.e., how acceptance of contractions evolves in the process of contraction. Finally, we consider conditional beliefs in the context of concrete strategies for AGM contraction operators. In particular, we consider minimization in the change of conditional beliefs.

Chapter 10

Cautious Iterated Contraction

In this chapter, we will investigate iteration principles for contraction. Therefore, we take inspiration from the iteration principles by Darwiche and Pearl for iterated revision. The specific feature of these revision principles is that they are widely considered as postulates which respect conditional beliefs in a natural and *cautious* way [41].

In the following section, we start by introducing the iteration principles by Darwiche and Pearl. These principles will be given as postulates for change of beliefs (which provides a syntactic point of view), and equivalently, as postulates for changing relations on possible worlds (which provides a semantic point of view). In addition, we consider postulates for the change of conditional beliefs, which also describe the iteration principles by Darwiche and Pearl. Based on these postulates for revision, we will consider two kinds of iteration principles for contraction in the course of this chapter:

- Iteration principles for contraction given by postulates that are analogue to the postulates for iterated revision by Darwiche and Pearl and that consider the change of (conditional) beliefs.
- Iteration principles for contraction given by postulates that are analogue to the postulates for iterated revision by Darwiche and Pearl and that consider the change of relations on possible worlds.

		Revision – first Darwiche-Pearl principle
Conditional	(IR1^{cond})	If $\beta \models \alpha$, then $\Psi \models (\gamma \mid \beta) \Leftrightarrow \Psi * \alpha \models (\gamma \mid \beta)$
Belief	(IR1)	If $\beta \models \alpha$, then $\text{Bel}(\Psi * \alpha * \beta) = \text{Bel}(\Psi * \beta)$
Relational	(IR1^{rel})	If $\omega_1, \omega_2 \in [\![\alpha]\!]$, then $\omega_1 \leq_\Psi \omega_2 \Leftrightarrow \omega_1 \leq_{\Psi * \alpha} \omega_2$
		Contraction analogues to the first Darwiche-Pearl principle
Contractional	(IC1$^{\text{cond}}_{\text{ca}}$)	If $\neg\alpha \models \beta$, then $\Psi \div \alpha \models [\gamma \mid \beta] \Leftrightarrow \Psi \models [\gamma \mid \beta]$
Belief	(IC1$_{\text{ca}}$)	If $\neg\alpha \models \beta$, then $\text{Bel}(\Psi \div \alpha \div \beta) = \text{Bel}(\Psi \div \beta)$
Relational		no AGM contraction operator (Proposition 10.5)
Contractional	(IC1$^{\text{cond}}_{\Leftarrow}$)	If $\neg\alpha \models \beta$, then $\Psi \models [\gamma \mid \beta] \Rightarrow \Psi \div \alpha \models [\gamma \mid \beta]$
Belief		If $\neg\alpha \models \beta$, then $\Psi \div \beta \models \gamma \Rightarrow \Psi \div \alpha \div \beta \models \gamma$
Relational		no AGM contraction operator (Proposition 10.5)
Contractional	(IC1$^{\text{cond}}_{\Rightarrow}$)	If $\neg\alpha \models \beta$, then $\Psi \div \alpha \models [\gamma \mid \beta] \Rightarrow \Psi \models [\gamma \mid \beta]$
Belief		If $\neg\alpha \models \beta$, then $\Psi \div \alpha \div \beta \models \gamma \Rightarrow \Psi \div \beta \models \gamma$
Relational	(IC1$^{\text{rel}}_{\Rightarrow}$)	If $\omega_1, \omega_2 \in [\![\alpha]\!]$, then $\omega_1 \leq_\Psi \omega_2 \Rightarrow \omega_1 \leq_{\Psi \div \alpha} \omega_2$
Contractional	(IC1^{cond})	If $\neg\alpha \models \beta$, then $\Psi \div \alpha \models [\alpha \rightarrow \gamma \mid \beta] \Leftrightarrow \Psi \models [\alpha \rightarrow \gamma \mid \beta]$
Belief	(IC1)	If $\neg\alpha \models \beta$, then $\text{Bel}(\Psi \div \alpha \div \beta) =_\alpha \text{Bel}(\Psi \div \beta)$
Relational	(IC1^{rel})	If $\omega_1, \omega_2 \in [\![\alpha]\!]$, then $\omega_1 \leq_\Psi \omega_2 \Leftrightarrow \omega_1 \leq_{\Psi \div \alpha} \omega_2$
		Revision – third Darwiche-Pearl principle
Conditional	(IR3^{cond})	If $\Psi \models (\alpha \mid \beta)$, then $\Psi * \alpha \models (\alpha \mid \beta)$
Belief	(IR3)	If $\Psi * \beta \models \alpha$, then $\Psi * \alpha * \beta \models \alpha$
Relational	(IR3^{rel})	If $\omega_1 \in [\![\alpha]\!]$ and $\omega_2 \in [\![\neg\alpha]\!]$, then $\omega_1 <_\Psi \omega_2 \Rightarrow \omega_1 <_{\Psi * \alpha} \omega_2$
		Contraction analogues to the third Darwiche-Pearl principle
Contractional	(IC3$^{\text{cond}}_{\text{ca}}$)	If $\Psi \models [\neg\alpha \mid \beta]$, then $\Psi \div \alpha \models [\neg\alpha \mid \beta]$
Belief	(IC3$_{\text{ca}}$)	If $\Psi \div \beta \models \neg\alpha$, then $\Psi \div \alpha \div \beta \models \neg\alpha$
Relational	(IC3$^{\text{rel}}_{\text{ca}}$)	If $\omega_1 \in [\![\neg\alpha]\!], \omega_2 \in [\![\alpha]\!]$ and $[\![\Psi]\!] \subseteq [\![\neg\alpha]\!]$, then $\omega_1 <_\Psi \omega_2 \Rightarrow \omega_1 <_{\Psi \div \alpha} \omega_2$
Contractional	(IC3^{cond})	If $\gamma \models \beta$, then $\Psi \models [\alpha \rightarrow \gamma \mid \beta] \Rightarrow \Psi \div \alpha \models [\alpha \rightarrow \gamma \mid \beta]$
Belief	(IC3)	If $\gamma \models \beta$, then $\Psi \div \beta \models \alpha \rightarrow \gamma \Rightarrow \Psi \div \alpha \div \beta \models \alpha \rightarrow \gamma$
Relational	(IC3^{rel})	If $\omega_1 \in [\![\neg\alpha]\!]$ and $\omega_2 \in [\![\alpha]\!]$, then $\omega_1 <_\Psi \omega_2 \Rightarrow \omega_1 <_{\Psi \div \alpha} \omega_2$

Table 10.1: Overview of different iteration principles considered for AGM contraction operators for epistemic states which are counterparts to the postulates of the first and the third principle by Darwiche and Pearl. The three postulates in each of the groups are equivalent postulates given that $\div$ is an AGM contraction operator and that $*$ is an AGM revision operator, respectively.

		Revision – second Darwiche-Pearl principle
Conditional	(IR2^{cond})	If $\beta \models \neg\alpha$, then $\Psi \models (\gamma \mid \beta) \Leftrightarrow \Psi * \alpha \models (\gamma \mid \beta)$
Belief	(IR2)	If $\beta \models \neg\alpha$, then $\text{Bel}(\Psi * \alpha * \beta) = \text{Bel}(\Psi * \beta)$
Relational	(IR2^{rel})	If $\omega_1, \omega_2 \in [\![\neg\alpha]\!]$, then $\omega_1 \leq_\Psi \omega_2 \Leftrightarrow \omega_1 \leq_{\Psi*\alpha} \omega_2$

		Contraction analogues to the second Darwiche-Pearl principle
Contractional	(IC2$^{\text{cond}}_{\text{ca}}$)	If $\alpha \models \beta$, then $\Psi \div \alpha \models [\gamma \mid \beta] \Leftrightarrow \Psi \models [\gamma \mid \beta]$
Belief	(IC2$_{\text{ca}}$)	If $\alpha \models \beta$, then $\text{Bel}(\Psi \div \alpha \div \beta) = \text{Bel}(\Psi \div \beta)$
Relational		no AGM contraction operator (Proposition 10.8)

Contractional	(IC2$^{\text{cond}}_{\Leftarrow}$)	If $\alpha \models \beta$, then $\Psi \models [\gamma \mid \beta] \Rightarrow \Psi \div \alpha \models [\gamma \mid \beta]$
Belief		If $\alpha \models \beta$, then $\Psi \div \beta \models \gamma \Rightarrow \Psi \div \alpha \div \beta \models \gamma$
Relational		no AGM contraction operator (Proposition 10.8)

Contractional	(IC2$^{\text{cond}}_{\Rightarrow}$)	If $\alpha \models \beta$, then $\Psi \div \alpha \models [\gamma \mid \beta] \Rightarrow \Psi \models [\gamma \mid \beta]$
Belief		If $\alpha \models \beta$, then $\Psi \div \alpha \div \beta \models \gamma \Rightarrow \Psi \div \beta \models \gamma$
Relational	(IC2$^{\text{rel}}_{\Rightarrow}$)	If $\omega_1, \omega_2 \in [\![\neg\alpha]\!]$, then $\omega_1 \leq_\Psi \omega_2 \Rightarrow \omega_1 \leq_{\Psi\div\alpha} \omega_2$

Contractional	(IC2^{cond})	If $\alpha \models \beta$, then $\Psi \div \alpha \models [\neg\beta \to \gamma \mid \beta] \Leftrightarrow \Psi \models [\neg\beta \to \gamma \mid \beta]$
Belief	(IC2)	If $\alpha \models \beta$, then $\text{Bel}(\Psi \div \alpha \div \beta) =_{\neg\beta} \text{Bel}(\Psi \div \beta)$
Relational	(IC2^{rel})	If $\omega_1, \omega_2 \in [\![\neg\alpha]\!]$, then $\omega_1 \leq_\Psi \omega_2 \Leftrightarrow \omega_1 \leq_{\Psi\div\alpha} \omega_2$

		Revision – fourth Darwiche-Pearl principle
Conditional	(IR4^{cond})	If $\Psi \not\models (\neg\alpha \mid \beta)$, then $\Psi * \alpha \not\models (\neg\alpha \mid \beta)$
Belief	(IR4)	If $\Psi * \beta \not\models \neg\alpha$, then $\Psi * \alpha * \beta \not\models \neg\alpha$
Relational	(IR4^{rel})	If $\omega_1 \in [\![\alpha]\!]$ and $\omega_2 \in [\![\neg\alpha]\!]$, then $\omega_1 \leq_\Psi \omega_2 \Rightarrow \omega_1 \leq_{\Psi*\alpha} \omega_2$

		Contraction analogues to the fourth Darwiche-Pearl principle
Contractional	(IC4$^{\text{cond}}_{\text{weak}}$)	If $\Psi \models \neg\alpha$, then $\Psi \not\models [\neg\alpha \to \beta \mid \beta] \Rightarrow \Psi \div \alpha \not\models [\neg\alpha \to \beta \mid \beta]$
Belief	(IC4$_{\text{weak}}$)	If $\Psi \models \neg\alpha$, then $\Psi \div \beta \not\models \neg\alpha \to \beta \Rightarrow \Psi \div \alpha \div \beta \not\models \neg\alpha \to \beta$
Relational	(IC4$^{\text{rel}}_{\text{weak}}$)	If $\omega_1 \in [\![\neg\alpha]\!]$, $\omega_2 \in [\![\alpha]\!]$ and $[\![\Psi]\!] \subseteq [\![\neg\alpha]\!]$, then $\omega_1 \leq_\Psi \omega_2 \Rightarrow \omega_1 \leq_{\Psi\div\alpha} \omega_2$

Contractional	(IC4^{cond})	If $\gamma \models \beta$, then $\Psi \div \alpha \models [\neg\alpha \to \gamma \mid \beta] \Rightarrow \Psi \models [\neg\alpha \to \gamma \mid \beta]$
Belief	(IC4)	If $\gamma \models \beta$, then $\Psi \div \alpha \div \beta \models \neg\alpha \to \gamma \Rightarrow \Psi \div \beta \models \neg\alpha \to \gamma$
Relational	(IC4^{rel})	If $\omega_1 \in [\![\neg\alpha]\!]$ and $\omega_2 \in [\![\alpha]\!]$, then $\omega_1 \leq_\Psi \omega_2 \Rightarrow \omega_1 \leq_{\Psi\div\alpha} \omega_2$

Table 10.1 (continued).: Overview of different iteration principles considered for AGM contraction operators for epistemic states which are counter-parts to the postulates of the second and the fourth principle by Darwiche and Pearl. The three postulates in each of the groups are equivalent postulates given that $\div$ is an AGM contraction operator and that $*$ is an AGM revision operator, respectively.

For each iteration postulate for contraction that we obtain from an iteration postulate for revision, we provide an equivalent corresponding postulate from the viewpoint of change of beliefs, an equivalent corresponding postulate from the viewpoint of change of conditional beliefs, and an equivalent corresponding postulate from the viewpoint of change of relations over interpretations (if such meaningful postulates exist). Thus, we obtain (most of the time) groups of three postulates, one for each point of view. Table 10.1 on the following pages provides a summary of most of the groups of postulates we consider in this chapter. In the course of this chapter we will rigorously proof that the postulates in each of these groups of postulates given in Table 10.1 are equivalent.

10.1. Postulates for Iterated Revision

In the following, we introduce the iteration principles for revision by Darwiche and Pearl [41]. We consider three different groups of postulates, whereby each group describes those principles from a different point of view on changing: the perspective of change of beliefs, the perspective of change of conditional beliefs, and the perspective of change of relations of worlds. We consider the theorem by Darwiche and Pearl [41] which shows equivalence between these three groups of postulates for AGM revision operators.

Change of Beliefs. Darwiche and Pearl propose the following (denoted as "cautious" [41]) iteration postulates for revision [41]:

(IR1) If $\beta \models \alpha$, then $\mathrm{Bel}(\Psi * \alpha * \beta) = \mathrm{Bel}(\Psi * \beta)$.

(IR2) If $\beta \models \neg\alpha$, then $\mathrm{Bel}(\Psi * \alpha * \beta) = \mathrm{Bel}(\Psi * \beta)$.

(IR3) If $\Psi * \beta \models \alpha$, then $\Psi * \alpha * \beta \models \alpha$.

(IR4) If $\Psi * \beta \not\models \neg\alpha$, then $\Psi * \alpha * \beta \not\models \neg\alpha$.

Intuitively, (IR1) and (IR2) establish that revision by a more general belief α, respectively $\neg\alpha$, beforehand does not influence revision by a more specific belief β. The postulates (IR3) and (IR4) together state that revision by α does not influence the credibility of α with respect to subsequent changes.

Change of Conditional Beliefs. Darwiche and Pearl propose that arbitrary changes of conditional beliefs are undesirable, and propose to restrict the change of conditional beliefs in the course of iterative change by the following postulates:

(IR1^{cond}) If $\beta \models \alpha$, then $\Psi \models (\gamma\,|\,\beta) \Leftrightarrow \Psi * \alpha \models (\gamma\,|\,\beta)$.

(IR2^{cond}) If $\beta \models \neg\alpha$, then $\Psi \models (\gamma\,|\,\beta) \Leftrightarrow \Psi * \alpha \models (\gamma\,|\,\beta)$.

(IR3^{cond}) If $\Psi \models (\alpha\,|\,\beta)$, then $\Psi * \alpha \models (\alpha\,|\,\beta)$.

(IR4^{cond}) If $\Psi \not\models (\neg\alpha\,|\,\beta)$, then $\Psi * \alpha \not\models (\neg\alpha\,|\,\beta)$.

The postulate (IR1^{cond}), respectively (IR2^{cond}), states that revision by α does not influence conditional beliefs whose premise is more specific than α, respectively more specific than $\neg\alpha$. From (IR3^{cond}) and (IR4^{cond}) we obtain that revision by α does not introduce nor revoke conditional beliefs which have $\neg\alpha$ in its consequence.

Relational Viewpoint. The following postulates were given by Darwiche and Pearl for a semantic-based and plausibility-based perspective on change:

(IR1^{rel}) If $\omega_1, \omega_2 \in [\![\alpha]\!]$, then $\omega_1 \leq_\Psi \omega_2 \Leftrightarrow \omega_1 \leq_{\Psi*\alpha} \omega_2$.

(IR2^{rel}) If $\omega_1, \omega_2 \in [\![\neg\alpha]\!]$, then $\omega_1 \leq_\Psi \omega_2 \Leftrightarrow \omega_1 \leq_{\Psi*\alpha} \omega_2$.

(IR3^{rel}) If $\omega_1 \in [\![\alpha]\!]$ and $\omega_2 \in [\![\neg\alpha]\!]$, then $\omega_1 <_\Psi \omega_2 \Rightarrow \omega_1 <_{\Psi*\alpha} \omega_2$.

(IR4^{rel}) If $\omega_1 \in [\![\alpha]\!]$ and $\omega_2 \in [\![\neg\alpha]\!]$, then $\omega_1 \leq_\Psi \omega_2 \Rightarrow \omega_1 \leq_{\Psi*\alpha} \omega_2$.

The postulates (IR1^{rel}) and (IR1^{rel}) state together that the plausibility-relation of two possible worlds, which can not be distinguished by α, does not change when revising by α. By the postulates IR3^{rel} and (IR3^{rel}), it is ensured that the plausibility of counter-worlds of α is not improved when revising by α.

Due to Darwiche and Pearl, it is well-known that the three groups of postulates given above all describe the same principles.

Theorem 10.1 (Extended Characterization Theorem, [41]). *Let $\mathcal{E}$ be a set of epistemic states, let $\div$ be an AGM revision operator for $\mathcal{E}$, and let $\Psi \mapsto \leq_\Psi$ be a faithful assignment that is revision-compatible with $\div$. The following statements are equivalent:*

- *The operator $\div$ satisfies (IR1)–(IR4).*
- *The operator $\div$ satisfies (IR1^{rel})–(IR4^{rel}).*
- *The operator $\div$ satisfies (IR1^{cond})–(IR4^{cond}).*

In addition to Proposition 10.1 we like to remark that there is a direct correspondence between the postulates considered in this section. For each $i \in \{1, 2, 3, 4\}$ and for each AGM revision operator $*$ for epistemic states (and corresponding assignment $\Psi \mapsto \leq_\Psi$) we have:

$$* \text{ satisfies (IR}i) \quad \text{iff} \quad * \text{ satisfies (IR}i^{\text{cond}}) \quad \text{iff} \quad * \text{ satisfies (IR}i^{\text{rel}})$$

An advantage of these postulates is that they are very intuitive, regardless which of the three perspectives given here is considered. Most of the Darwiche-Pearl postulates for revision are widely accepted and have wide applications. However, the postulate (IR2) has sometimes been criticized [126], as, e.g, (IR2) is not satisfied in some situations [22].

In the next section, we examine (IR1)–(IR4) according to their suitability as postulates for iterated contraction.

10.2. (IR1)–(IR4) as Contraction Postulates

A compelling approach is to consider the syntactic Darwiche-Pearl postulates (IR1)–(IR4) as contraction postulates without undertaking any modifications, i.e, consideration of the following postulates[1,2]:

(IC1$_{\text{dca}}$) If $\beta \models \alpha$, then $\Psi \div \alpha \div \beta \models \gamma \Leftrightarrow \Psi \div \beta \models \gamma$.
(IC2$_{\text{dca}}$) If $\beta \models \neg\alpha$, then $\Psi \div \alpha \div \beta \models \gamma \Leftrightarrow \Psi \div \beta \models \gamma$.
(IC3$_{\text{dca}}$) If $\Psi \div \beta \models \alpha$, then $\Psi \div \alpha \div \beta \models \alpha$.
(IC4$_{\text{dca}}$) If $\Psi \div \alpha \div \beta \models \neg\alpha$, then $\Psi \div \beta \models \neg\alpha$.

---

[1]   The subscript *dca* stands for *direct contraction analogue*

Analogously, we obtain the following postulates from $(\text{IR1}^{\text{cond}})$–$(\text{IR4}^{\text{cond}})$ by considering contractionals instead of RT-conditionals[2]:

$(\text{IC1}^{\text{cond}}_{\text{dca}})$ If $\beta \models \alpha$, then $\Psi \div \alpha \models [\gamma \,|\, \beta] \Leftrightarrow \Psi \models [\gamma \,|\, \beta]$.
$(\text{IC2}^{\text{cond}}_{\text{dca}})$ If $\beta \models \neg\alpha$, then $\Psi \div \alpha \models [\gamma \,|\, \beta] \Leftrightarrow \Psi \models [\gamma \,|\, \beta]$.
$(\text{IC3}^{\text{cond}}_{\text{dca}})$ If $\Psi \models [\alpha \,|\, \beta]$, then $\Psi \div \alpha \models [\alpha \,|\, \beta]$.
$(\text{IC4}^{\text{cond}}_{\text{dca}})$ If $\Psi \div \alpha \models [\neg\alpha \,|\, \beta]$, then $\Psi \models [\neg\alpha \,|\, \beta]$.

Clearly, due to Proposition 9.18, $(\text{IC1}^{\text{cond}}_{\text{dca}})$–$(\text{IC4}^{\text{cond}}_{\text{dca}})$ are equivalent to $(\text{IC1}_{\text{dca}})$–$(\text{IC4}_{\text{dca}})$ in the context of AGM contraction operators for epistemic sates. In the following, we will demonstrate that most of these postulates unfortunately do not comply with AGM contraction.

As a first result, we show that the postulates $(\text{IC1}_{\text{dca}})$–$(\text{IC3}_{\text{dca}})$ are incompatible with AGM contraction operators for epistemic states in a very general sense.

Proposition 10.2 (Impossibility Result)**.** *Let $\mathcal{E}$ be a set of epistemic states that contains at least one epistemic state $\Psi_{\mathcal{Q}} \in \mathcal{E}$ with $[\![\Psi_{\mathcal{Q}}]\!] \neq \Omega$. There is no AGM contraction operator for $\mathcal{E}$ that satisfies at least one of $(\text{IC1}_{\text{dca}})$–$(\text{IC3}_{\text{dca}})$.*

Proof. The proof is by contradiction. Let $\div$ be an AGM contraction operator for $\mathcal{E}$. From the existence of $\div$, from $[\![\Psi_{\mathcal{Q}}]\!] \neq \Omega$ and from Proposition 9.12 we obtain that there exists an epistemic state $\Psi^{\not\ell}_{\mathcal{Q}} \in \mathcal{E}$ with $\emptyset \neq [\![\Psi^{\not\ell}_{\mathcal{Q}}]\!] \neq \Omega$. Because $\div$ is an AGM contraction operator for epistemic states, we have that $\div$ satisfies (C1)–(C3). In the following, we consider each of $(\text{IC1}_{\text{dca}})$–$(\text{IC3}_{\text{dca}})$ independently.

$(\text{IC1}_{\text{dca}})$ In the following let $\omega \in \Omega \setminus [\![\Psi^{\not\ell}_{\mathcal{Q}}]\!]$. Furthermore, let α be a formula with $[\![\neg\alpha]\!] = \{\omega\}$, and let β be formula such that $[\![\neg\beta]\!] = \{\omega\} \cup [\![\Psi^{\not\ell}_{\mathcal{Q}}]\!]$ holds, and let γ be a formula such that $[\![\gamma]\!] = [\![\Psi]\!]$ holds. Note that we have $\beta \models \alpha$, $\Psi \models \gamma$ and $\beta \notin \text{Bel}(\Psi)$. From (C1) and (C2) we obtain $[\![\Psi]\!] = [\![\gamma]\!] = [\![\Psi \div \beta]\!]$. This last observation implies $\Psi \div \beta \models \gamma$. We obtain $\Psi \div \alpha \div \beta \models \gamma$ from $(\text{IC1}_{\text{dca}})$, and thus $[\![\Psi \div \alpha \div \beta]\!] = [\![\Psi]\!] = [\![\Psi \div \beta]\!]$. From $\omega \in \Omega \setminus [\![\Psi^{\not\ell}_{\mathcal{Q}}]\!]$ and $[\![\neg\alpha]\!] = \{\omega\}$, we obtain $\Psi \models \alpha$. Putting all observations together, we obtain $\Psi \div \alpha \div \beta \models \alpha$. Using (C1) we obtain $\text{Bel}(\Psi \div \alpha \div \beta) \subseteq \text{Bel}(\Psi \div \alpha) \subseteq \text{Bel}(\Psi)$, which implies $\alpha \in \text{Bel}(\Psi \div \alpha)$. This last observation contradicts (C3).

(IC2$_{\text{dca}}$) In the following let β be a formula such that $[\![\beta]\!] = \Omega \setminus [\![\Psi_{\widehat{\Omega}}^{\not\vdash}]\!]$ holds, i.e., $[\![\neg\beta]\!] = [\![\Psi]\!]$, and let γ be a formula such that $[\![\gamma]\!] = [\![\Psi]\!]$ holds. By our assumptions of $\Psi_{\widehat{\Omega}}^{\not\vdash}$, we obtain that $\emptyset \neq [\![\beta]\!] \neq \Omega$ and $\beta \notin \text{Bel}(\Psi)$ holds. Consequently, (C1) and (C2), together with $\beta \notin \text{Bel}(\Psi)$, imply $[\![\Psi]\!] = [\![\neg\beta]\!] = [\![\Psi \div \beta]\!]$. Observe that we have $\beta \models \neg\gamma$ and $\Psi \div \beta \models \gamma$. Because $\div$ satisfies (IC2$_{\text{dca}}$), we obtain $\Psi \div \gamma \div \beta \models \gamma$ from (IC2$_{\text{dca}}^{\text{cond}}$) by substituting α by γ in (IC2$_{\text{dca}}^{\text{cond}}$). Using (C1) we obtain $\text{Bel}(\Psi \div \gamma \div \beta) \subseteq \text{Bel}(\Psi \div \gamma) \subseteq \text{Bel}(\Psi)$, which implies $\gamma \in \text{Bel}(\Psi \div \gamma)$. This last observation contradicts (C3).

(IC3$_{\text{dca}}$) In the following let $\omega \in \Omega \setminus [\![\Psi_{\widehat{\Omega}}^{\not\vdash}]\!]$. Furthermore, let α be a formula with $[\![\neg\alpha]\!] = \{\omega\}$, and let β be formula such that $[\![\neg\beta]\!] = \{\omega\} \cup [\![\Psi_{\widehat{\Omega}}^{\not\vdash}]\!]$ holds. By using (C1)–(C3), we obtain $\Psi \div \beta \models \alpha$ and $\Psi \div \alpha \div \beta \not\models \alpha$. This is a contradiction to (IC3$_{\text{dca}}$). □

While there is no AGM contraction operator for epistemic states that is compatible with one of the postulates (IC1$_{\text{dca}}$)–(IC3$_{\text{dca}}$), the situation if different for (IC4$_{\text{dca}}$). The following proposition characterizes (IC4$_{\text{dca}}$) semantically for AGM contraction operators for epistemic states.

Proposition 10.3. *Let $\mathcal{E}$ be a set of epistemic states, let $\div$ be an AGM contraction operator for $\mathcal{E}$, and let $\Psi \mapsto \leq_\Psi$ be a faithful-assignment that is contraction-compatible with $\div$. The belief change operator $\div$ satisfies* (IC4$_{\text{dca}}$) *if and only if the following is satisfied:*

(IC4$_{\text{dca}}^{\text{rel}}$) *If $\omega_1 \in [\![\neg\alpha]\!]$, $\omega_2 \in [\![\alpha]\!]$ and $[\![\Psi]\!] \subseteq [\![\neg\alpha]\!]$, then $\omega_2 \leq_\Psi \omega_1 \Rightarrow \omega_2 \leq_{\Psi \div \alpha} \omega_1$.*

Proof. We consider both directions of Proposition 10.3 independently.

From (IC4$_{\text{dca}}^{\text{rel}}$) *to* (IC4$_{\text{dca}}$). Towards a contradiction we suppose that (IC4$_{\text{dca}}$) is not satisfied, i.e., $\Psi \div \beta \not\models \neg\alpha$ and $\Psi \div \alpha \div \beta \models \neg\alpha$ holds. If $[\![\Psi]\!] \cap [\![\alpha]\!] \neq \emptyset$, then we obtain (IC4$_{\text{dca}}$) directly from (C1). Thus, we have $[\![\Psi]\!] \subseteq [\![\neg\alpha]\!]$. Using $\Psi \div \beta \not\models \neg\alpha$ and Proposition 9.3, we obtain that there is some interpretation $\omega_2 \in \min([\![\neg\beta]\!], \leq_\Psi)$ such that $\omega_2 \in [\![\alpha]\!]$ holds.

Likewise, $\Psi \div \alpha \div \beta \models \neg\alpha$ and Proposition 9.3 together imply that there is some interpretation $\omega_1 \in \min([\![\neg\beta]\!], \leq_\Psi)$ such that $\omega_2 \in [\![\neg\alpha]\!]$ holds. From the latter, we obtain that $\omega_1 <_{\Psi \div \alpha} \omega_2$ holds. Application of the contraposition of $(\mathrm{IC4}^{\mathrm{rel}}_{\mathrm{dca}})$ yields $\omega_1 <_\Psi \omega_2$, and thus we have $\omega_2 \notin \min([\![\neg\beta]\!], \leq_\Psi)$. The latter is a contradiction to the minimality of ω_2 in $[\![\neg\beta]\!]$ with respect to $\leq_\Psi$.

From $(\mathrm{IC4}_{\mathrm{dca}})$ *to* $(\mathrm{IC4}^{\mathrm{rel}}_{\mathrm{dca}})$. Let $\omega_2 \in [\![\alpha]\!]$ and $\omega_1 \in [\![\neg\alpha]\!]$ and $[\![\Psi]\!] \subseteq [\![\neg\alpha]\!]$. Towards a contradiction we suppose that we have $\omega_2 \leq_\Psi \omega_1$ and $\omega_1 <_{\Psi \div \alpha} \omega_2$. Because (C1) is satisfied, we obtain $\omega_2, \omega_1 \in [\![\Psi]\!]$ from $\omega_1 <_{\Psi \div \alpha} \omega_2$ and faithfulness of $\Psi \mapsto \leq_\Psi$. Now let β be such that $[\![\neg\beta]\!] = \{\omega_2, \omega_1\}$ holds. Since $\Psi \mapsto \leq_\Psi$ is contraction-compatible with $\div$, our assumptions $\omega_2 \leq_\Psi \omega_1$ and $\omega_1 <_{\Psi \div \alpha} \omega_2$ together yield that $\omega_2 \in [\![\Psi \div \beta]\!]$ and $\omega_2 \notin [\![\Psi \div \beta]\!]$ holds. We obtain the contradiction $\Psi \div \beta \not\models \neg\alpha$, but $\Psi \div \alpha \div \beta \models \neg\alpha$. $\square$

Proposition 10.3 yields that $(\mathrm{IC4}_{\mathrm{dca}})$, i.e., the postulate (IR4), is an iteration principle which is compatible with AGM contraction operators for epistemic states. Furthermore, Proposition 10.3 points out that $(\mathrm{IC4}_{\mathrm{dca}})$ prevents strict improvement of counter-worlds for α when contracting by α, which could be considered as counter-intuitive for the process of contraction.

In this section, we investigated the naive approach of treating the Darwiche-Pearl postulates (IR1)–(IR4) for revision as contraction postulates $(\mathrm{IC1}_{\mathrm{dca}})$–$(\mathrm{IC4}_{\mathrm{dca}})$. We showed that each of these revision postulates (IR1)–(IR3), when viewed as a contraction postulate $(\mathrm{IC1}_{\mathrm{dca}})$–$(\mathrm{IC3}_{\mathrm{dca}})$, is incompatible with AGM contraction operators for epistemic states. Moreover, the semantic characterization of the revision postulate (IR4) reveals that this postulate, when viewed as a postulate for contraction $(\mathrm{IC4}_{\mathrm{dca}})$, is counter-intuitive for AGM contraction. In the next section, we consider postulates that are similar to (IR1)–(IR4), but are adapted to better fit the overall intention of contraction.

10.3. Contraction Analogues to (IR1)–(IR4)

In the previous section, we established that the postulates (IR1)–(IR3) are non-valid iteration principles for AGM contraction operators for epistemic states. In this section, we consider contraction analogues to

the syntactic iteration postulates (IR1)–(IR4) given by Darwiche and
Pearl. We consider slightly modified versions of (IR1)–(IR4) which will
match better the intensional behaviour of AGM contraction. Again,
we will see that these postulates are only partially compatible with
AGM contraction operators for epistemic states.

10.3.1. Adapting $(\text{IR1}^{\text{cond}})$–$(\text{IR4}^{\text{cond}})$ to a Contraction Attitude

To adapt the Darwiche-Pearl principles for iterated revision, we will
use the conditional formulations $(\text{IR1}^{\text{cond}})$–$(\text{IR4}^{\text{cond}})$ as starting point.
The rationale is that the correspondence between $(\text{IR1}^{\text{cond}})$–$(\text{IR4}^{\text{cond}})$
and our new contraction postulates will be evident.

We start with the first two postulates, which we obtain from $(\text{IR1}^{\text{cond}})$
and $(\text{IR2}^{\text{cond}})$ by replacing the preconditions of these postulates as
follows[3]:

$(\text{IC1}_{\text{ca}}^{\text{cond}})$ If $\neg\alpha \models \beta$, then $\Psi \div \alpha \models [\gamma \mid \beta] \Leftrightarrow \Psi \models [\gamma \mid \beta]$.
   Explanation: If β is believed whenever the negation of α is believed,
   then contraction by α does not influence whether an agent believes
   γ, even in the absence of β.
$(\text{IC2}_{\text{ca}}^{\text{cond}})$ If $\alpha \models \beta$, then $\Psi \div \alpha \models [\gamma \mid \beta] \Leftrightarrow \Psi \models [\gamma \mid \beta]$.
   Explanation: If β is believed whenever α is believed, then contrac-
   tion by α does not influence whether an agent believes γ, even in
   the absence of β.

As explained in Section 10.1, in the view of AGM revision, the postu-
lates $(\text{IR1}^{\text{cond}})$ and $(\text{IR2}^{\text{cond}})$ state that revision of a belief does not
affect revisions by more specific beliefs. The postulates $(\text{IC1}_{\text{ca}}^{\text{cond}})$ and
$(\text{IC2}_{\text{ca}}^{\text{cond}})$ provide the similar, but dual, restriction, that a contraction
of specific beliefs does not affect a contraction by a more general belief.

We continue with analogues[4] to $(\text{IR3}^{\text{cond}})$ and $(\text{IR4}^{\text{cond}})$, which we
obtain from $(\text{IR3}^{\text{cond}})$ and $(\text{IR4}^{\text{cond}})$ by replacing the consequence of
conditionals in these postulates by its negation as in the following:

---

3   The subscript *ca* stands for *contractional analogue.*
4   We are reading $(\text{IR4}^{\text{cond}})$ contrapositively.

(IC3$_{ca}^{cond}$) If $\Psi \models [\neg\alpha \,|\, \beta]$, then $\Psi \div \alpha \models [\neg\alpha \,|\, \beta]$.

    Explanation: If $\neg\alpha$ is believed even in the absence of β, then contraction by α does not revoke this relation between $\neg\alpha$ and β.

(IC4$_{ca}^{cond}$) If $\Psi \div \alpha \models [\alpha \,|\, \beta]$, then $\Psi \models [\alpha \,|\, \beta]$.

    Explanation: If posterior to a contraction with α an agent is convinced that α should be believed even in the absence of β, then the agent was convinced previously about this relation between α and β.

The Postulates (IC3$_{ca}^{cond}$) and (IC4$_{ca}^{cond}$) have a similar intention as (IR3^{cond}) and (IR4^{cond}). Recall that (IR3^{cond}) and (IR4^{cond}) limit revision operators in a way such that a revision by α does not affect the credibility of α in subsequent revisions. Similarly, (IC3$_{ca}^{cond}$) and (IC4$_{ca}^{cond}$) state that a contraction by α does not influence the credibility of the negation of α, and, moreover, contracting by α does not influence whether believing in α depends on some other belief β.

In the remaining part of this section, we discuss the postulates (IC1$_{ca}^{cond}$) to (IC4$_{ca}^{cond}$). We will not only consider a technical viewpoint on contractionals, but also discuss the meaning of these postulates.

10.3.2. Evaluation of (IC1$_{ca}^{cond}$) and (IC2$_{ca}^{cond}$)

We will now argue that (IC1$_{ca}^{cond}$) is a too strong postulate to be applicable in every case. Consider the following example, which provides a case where (IC1$_{ca}^{cond}$) is too strong.

Example 10.4. *Consider the following three propositions*

$$\alpha : Alice\ attends\ the\ party$$
$$\beta : Bernd\ attends\ the\ party$$
$$\gamma : Gavin\ attends\ the\ party$$

about believing whether Alice, Bernd and Gavin attending to a party. Bernd loves parties but seems not to like Alice, thus he is surely joining the party if Alice is not attending the party ($\neg\alpha \models \beta$). Moreover, Gavin seems not to like parties, but Gavin likes Alice, and he is only attending the party when Alice attends the party ($\gamma \models \alpha$).

Suppose in the following that our agent believes initially that Gavin is attending the party, i.e., we have $\gamma \in Bel(\Psi)$. Moreover, assume in *the following, that the agent believes that Gavin does not know Bernd, and thus is convinced that Gavin will join the party, even if Bernd does not attend the party, i.e., we have $\Psi \models [\gamma \,|\, \beta]$. Recall that $[\gamma \,|\, \beta]$ expresses that the contraction of β does not influence the belief in γ.*

Our agent arrives at the party, and one of the other guests lets her know that Alice will not join the party. The agent will update her beliefs according to this new information, i.e., we have $\Psi \div \alpha$. Given the background knowledge, the agent will conclude that Gavin will not attend the party, i.e., we have $\gamma \notin \mathrm{Bel}(\Psi \div \alpha)$. In this new situation the connection between Gavin and Bernd becomes irrelevant, i.e, we have that $\gamma \notin \mathrm{Bel}(\Psi \div \alpha)$ implies $\Psi \div \alpha \not\models [\gamma \,|\, \beta]$. Note that this conflicts with $(\mathrm{IC1}_{\mathrm{ca}}^{\mathrm{cond}})$, as $(\mathrm{IC1}_{\mathrm{ca}}^{\mathrm{cond}})$ demands $\Psi \div \alpha \models [\gamma \,|\, \beta]$.

Example 10.4 indicates that at least the "$\Leftarrow$"-part of the postulate $(\mathrm{IC1}_{\mathrm{ca}}^{\mathrm{cond}})$ is implausible. The following proposition shows that this is even reflected by the formal framework.

Proposition 10.5. *Let $\mathcal{E}$ be a set of epistemic states that contains at least one epistemic state $\Psi_{\mathfrak{A}} \in \mathcal{E}$ with $[\![\Psi_{\mathfrak{A}}]\!] \neq \Omega$. There is no AGM contraction operator $\div$ for $\mathcal{E}$ that satisfies:*

$(\mathrm{IC1}_{\Leftarrow}^{\mathrm{cond}})$ *If $\neg\alpha \models \beta$, then $\Psi \div \alpha \models [\gamma \,|\, \beta] \Leftarrow \Psi \models [\gamma \,|\, \beta]$.*

Proof. The proof is by contradiction. Let $\div$ be an AGM contraction operator for $\mathcal{E}$ that satisfies $(\mathrm{IC1}_{\Leftarrow}^{\mathrm{cond}})$. Because $\div$ is an AGM contraction operator for epistemic states, we have that $\div$ satisfies (C1)–(C3).

From $[\![\Psi_{\mathfrak{A}}]\!] \neq \Omega$ we obtain that there exists $\omega \in \Omega$ with $\omega \notin [\![\Psi_{\mathfrak{A}}]\!]$. In the following let $\alpha, \beta, \gamma \in \mathcal{L}$ be formulas such that the following holds:

$$[\![\alpha]\!] = \Omega \setminus \{\omega\} \qquad [\![\beta]\!] = \Omega \setminus [\![\Psi_{\mathfrak{A}}]\!] \qquad [\![\gamma]\!] = [\![\Psi_{\mathfrak{A}}]\!]$$

We obtain $\neg\alpha \models \beta$, and $\beta \notin [\![\Psi_{\mathfrak{A}}]\!]$ and $\alpha, \gamma \in \mathrm{Bel}(\Psi_{\mathfrak{A}})$. Consequently, by (C1) and (C2), we have $[\![\Psi_{\mathfrak{A}} \div \beta]\!] = [\![\Psi_{\mathfrak{A}}]\!]$ and $\gamma \in \mathrm{Bel}(\Psi_{\mathfrak{A}} \div \beta)$. The latter is, due to Proposition 9.18, equivalent to $\Psi_{\mathfrak{A}} \models [\gamma \,|\, \beta]$. Moreover, because $\div$ satisfies $(\mathrm{IC1}_{\Leftarrow}^{\mathrm{cond}})$, we obtain $\gamma \in \mathrm{Bel}(\Psi_{\mathfrak{A}} \div \alpha \div \beta)$ from Proposition 9.18. Due to $[\![\gamma]\!] = [\![\Psi_{\mathfrak{A}}]\!]$, a repeated application of (C1) yields $[\![\Psi_{\mathfrak{A}}]\!] = [\![\Psi_{\mathfrak{A}} \div \alpha]\!] = [\![\Psi_{\mathfrak{A}} \div \alpha \div \beta]\!]$. We obtain $\alpha \in \mathrm{Bel}(\Psi_{\mathfrak{A}} \div \alpha)$ from $\alpha \in \mathrm{Bel}(\Psi_{\mathfrak{A}})$. However, because of $\alpha \not\equiv \top$, we obtain the contradiction $\alpha \notin \mathrm{Bel}(\Psi_{\mathfrak{A}})$ from (C1). $\qquad\square$

While one direction of $(\text{IC1}^{\text{cond}}_{\text{ca}})$ is incompatible with AGM contraction operators for epistemic states, the other direction of $(\text{IC1}^{\text{cond}}_{\text{ca}})$ seems to be reasonable and has an intuitive semantic counterpart, as the following proposition shows.

Proposition 10.6. *Let $\mathcal{E}$ be a set of epistemic states, let $\div$ be an AGM contraction operator for $\mathcal{E}$, and let $\Psi \mapsto \leq_\Psi$ be a faithful-assignment that is contraction-compatible with $\div$. The postulate*

$(\text{IC1}^{\text{cond}}_{\Rightarrow})$ *If $\neg\alpha \models \beta$, then $\Psi \div \alpha \models [\gamma \,|\, \beta] \Rightarrow \Psi \models [\gamma \,|\, \beta]$.*
   Explanation: *If the negation of α is more specific than β, then a contraction with α does not influence whether γ is believed in the absence of β or not.*

is satisfied by $\div$ if and only if the following holds:

$(\text{IC1}^{\text{rel}}_{\Rightarrow})$ *If $\omega_1, \omega_2 \in [\![\alpha]\!]$, then $\omega_1 \leq_\Psi \omega_2 \Rightarrow \omega_1 \leq_{\Psi \div \alpha} \omega_2$.*

Proof. We consider both directions of the claim independently.

   From $(\text{IC1}^{\text{cond}}_{\Rightarrow})$ *to* $(\text{IC1}^{\text{rel}}_{\Rightarrow})$. Let $\omega_1, \omega_2 \in [\![\alpha]\!]$ and let $\omega_1 \leq_\Psi \omega_2$. Towards a contradiction, we suppose that $\omega_2 <_{\Psi \div \alpha} \omega_1$ holds. Now choose $\beta \in \mathcal{L}$ such that $[\![\beta]\!] = \Omega \setminus \{\omega_1, \omega_2\}$ holds, and choose γ such that $[\![\gamma]\!] = \Omega \setminus \{\omega_1\}$ holds. Because $\Psi \mapsto \leq_\Psi$ is contraction-compatible with $\div$, we obtain $\omega_1 \in [\![\Psi \div \beta]\!]$ from $\omega_2 <_{\Psi \div \alpha} \omega_1$, and from $\omega_2 <_{\Psi \div \alpha} \omega_1$ we obtain $\omega_1 \notin [\![\Psi \div \alpha \div \beta]\!]$. Consequently, we have $\gamma \notin \text{Bel}(\Psi \div \beta)$ and $\gamma \in \text{Bel}(\Psi \div \alpha \div \beta)$. This contradicts the satisfaction of $(\text{IC1}^{\text{cond}}_{\Rightarrow})$.
   From $(\text{IC1}^{\text{rel}}_{\Rightarrow})$ *to* $(\text{IC1}^{\text{cond}}_{\Rightarrow})$. Now assume that $(\text{IC1}^{\text{rel}}_{\Rightarrow})$ is satisfied. We show that $(\text{IC1}^{\text{cond}}_{\Rightarrow})$ holds. Let $\neg\alpha \models \beta$ and $\Psi \div \alpha \models [\gamma \,|\, \beta]$. By Proposition 9.3, we obtain $[\![\Psi]\!] \cup \min([\![\neg\beta]\!], \leq_{\Psi \div \alpha}) \subseteq [\![\gamma]\!]$. Towards a contradiction assume $\Psi \not\models [\gamma \,|\, \beta]$, i.e., $\gamma \notin \text{Bel}(\Psi \div \beta)$. Proposition 9.3 yields $\min([\![\neg\beta]\!], \leq_\Psi) \not\subseteq [\![\gamma]\!]$. Therefore, there exist some $\omega_1 \in \min([\![\neg\beta]\!], \leq_\Psi)$ such that $\omega_1 \notin [\![\gamma]\!]$ and $\omega_1 \notin \min([\![\neg\beta]\!], \leq_{\Psi \div \alpha})$. Because $\min([\![\neg\beta]\!], \leq_{\Psi \div \alpha})$ is non-empty, there is some $\omega_2 \in \min([\![\neg\beta]\!], \leq_{\Psi \div \alpha})$. From $\omega_1 \in \min([\![\neg\beta]\!], \leq_\Psi)$ and $\omega_2 \in [\![\neg\beta]\!]$ we immediately obtain $\omega_1 \leq_\Psi \omega_2$. Moreover, from $\omega_2 \in \min([\![\neg\beta]\!], \leq_{\Psi \div \alpha})$ and $\omega_1 \notin \min([\![\neg\beta]\!], \leq_{\Psi \div \alpha})$ we conclude that $\omega_2 <_{\Psi \div \alpha} \omega_1$ holds. Recall that $\omega_1, \omega_2 \in [\![\alpha]\!]$, and thus, because $\div$ satisfies $(\text{IC1}^{\text{rel}}_{\Rightarrow})$, we obtain $\omega_2 <_\Psi \omega_1$ from the

contraposition of (IC1$^{\text{rel}}_{\Rightarrow}$) and $\omega_2 <_{\Psi \div \alpha} \omega_1$. However, this last observation contradicts our previous observation that we have $\omega_1 \leq_\Psi \omega_2$. □

For the postulate (IC2$^{\text{cond}}_{\text{ca}}$) we obtain similar results. We begin with the compatible half of the postulate.

Proposition 10.7. *Let $\mathcal{E}$ be a set of epistemic states, let $\div$ be an AGM contraction operator for $\mathcal{E}$, and let $\Psi \mapsto \leq_\Psi$ be a faithful-assignment that is contraction-compatible with $\div$. The following holds*

(IC2$^{\text{cond}}_{\Rightarrow}$) *If $\alpha \models \beta$, then $\Psi \div \alpha \models [\gamma \mid \beta] \Rightarrow \Psi \models [\gamma \mid \beta]$.*
   Explanation: *If α is more specific than β, then a contraction with α does not influence whether γ is believed in the absence of β or not.*

if and only if the following holds:

(IC2$^{\text{rel}}_{\Rightarrow}$) *If $\omega_1, \omega_2 \in [\![\neg\alpha]\!]$, then $\omega_1 \leq_\Psi \omega_2 \Rightarrow \omega_1 \leq_{\Psi \div \alpha} \omega_2$.*

Proof. We consider both directions of the claim independently.

From (IC2$^{\text{cond}}_{\Rightarrow}$) *to* (IC2$^{\text{rel}}_{\Rightarrow}$). Assume satisfaction of (IC2$^{\text{cond}}_{\Rightarrow}$). We show satisfaction of (IC2$^{\text{rel}}_{\Rightarrow}$) by contradiction. Let $\omega_1, \omega_2 \in [\![\neg\alpha]\!]$ with $\omega_1 \leq_\Psi \omega_2$. Towards a contradiction, assume $\omega_2 <_{\Psi \div \alpha} \omega_1$. First, choose $\beta \in \mathcal{L}$ such that $[\![\beta]\!] = \Omega \setminus \{\omega_1, \omega_2\}$ and γ such that $[\![\gamma]\!] = \Omega \setminus \{\omega_1\}$. From our assumptions about $\leq_{\Psi \div \alpha}$ and the faithfulness of $\leq_{\Psi \div \alpha}$ we obtain $\omega_1 \notin [\![\Psi \div \alpha \div \beta]\!]$ and $\omega_1 \in [\![\Psi \div \beta]\!]$. By Proposition 9.3, we obtain $\gamma \in \text{Bel}(\Psi \div \alpha \div \beta)$ and $\gamma \notin \text{Bel}(\Psi \div \beta)$. Note that $\alpha \models \beta$, and therefore we obtain a contradiction to (IC2$^{\text{cond}}_{\Rightarrow}$).

From (IC2$^{\text{rel}}_{\Rightarrow}$) *to* (IC2$^{\text{cond}}_{\Rightarrow}$). For the other direction, assume satisfaction of (IC2$^{\text{rel}}_{\Rightarrow}$). We show satisfaction of (IC2$^{\text{cond}}_{\Rightarrow}$). Let $\alpha \models \beta$ and $\gamma \in \text{Bel}(\Psi \div \alpha \div \beta)$. Now suppose $\gamma \notin \text{Bel}(\Psi \div \beta)$. This implies the existence of interpretations ω_1, ω_2 such that $\omega_1 \in \min([\![\neg\beta]\!], \leq_{\Psi \div \alpha})$ and $\omega_2 \notin \min([\![\neg\beta]\!], \leq_{\Psi \div \alpha})$ and $\omega_2 \in \min([\![\neg\beta]\!], \leq_\Psi)$. We obtain $\omega_1 <_{\Psi \div \alpha} \omega_2$ and $\omega_2 \leq_\Psi \omega_1$. Now note that $[\![\neg\beta]\!] \subseteq [\![\neg\alpha]\!]$, which implies a contradiction to (IC2$^{\text{rel}}_{\Rightarrow}$). □

The following proposition shows that the other "half" of $(IC2_{ca}^{cond})$ is incompatible with AGM contraction operators for epistemic states.

Proposition 10.8. *Let $\mathcal{E}$ be a set of epistemic states that contains at least one epistemic state $\Psi_{\mathcal{Q}} \in \mathcal{E}$ with $[\![\Psi_{\mathcal{Q}}]\!] \neq \Omega$. There is no AGM contraction operator $\div$ for $\mathcal{E}$ that satisfies:*

$(IC2_{\Leftarrow}^{cond})$ *If $\alpha \models \beta$, then $\Psi \div \alpha \models [\gamma \,|\, \beta] \Leftarrow \Psi \models [\gamma \,|\, \beta]$.*

Proof. The proof is by contradiction. Let $\div$ be an AGM contraction operator for $\mathcal{E}$ that satisfies $(IC2_{\Leftarrow}^{cond})$. Because $\div$ is an AGM contraction operator for epistemic states, we have that $\div$ satisfies (C1)–(C3). From $[\![\Psi_{\mathcal{Q}}]\!] \neq \Omega$ we obtain that there exists $w \in \Omega$ with $w \notin [\![\Psi_{\mathcal{Q}}]\!]$. In the following let $\alpha, \gamma \in \mathcal{L}$ be formulas such that the following holds:

$$[\![\alpha]\!] = \Omega \setminus \{w\} \qquad\qquad [\![\gamma]\!] = [\![\Psi_{\mathcal{Q}}]\!]$$

We obtain $\alpha, \gamma \in \mathrm{Bel}(\Psi_{\mathcal{Q}})$. From Proposition 9.3, we obtain $[\![\Psi_{\mathcal{Q}} \div \top]\!] = [\![\Psi_{\mathcal{Q}}]\!]$ and $\gamma \in \mathrm{Bel}(\Psi_{\mathcal{Q}} \div \top)$. The latter is, due to Proposition 9.18, equivalent to $\Psi_{\mathcal{Q}} \models [\gamma \,|\, \beta]$. Moreover, because $\div$ satisfies $(IC2_{\Leftarrow}^{cond})$, we obtain $\gamma \in \mathrm{Bel}(\Psi_{\mathcal{Q}} \div \alpha \div \top)$ from Proposition 9.18, by substituting β with $\top$ in $(IC2_{\Leftarrow}^{cond})$. Due to $[\![\gamma]\!] = [\![\Psi_{\mathcal{Q}}]\!]$, a repeated application of (C1) yields $[\![\Psi_{\mathcal{Q}}]\!] = [\![\Psi_{\mathcal{Q}} \div \alpha]\!] = [\![\Psi_{\mathcal{Q}} \div \alpha \div \top]\!]$. We obtain $\alpha \in \mathrm{Bel}(\Psi_{\mathcal{Q}} \div \alpha)$ from $\alpha \in \mathrm{Bel}(\Psi_{\mathcal{Q}})$. However, because of $\alpha \not\equiv \top$, we obtain the contradiction $\alpha \notin \mathrm{Bel}(\Psi_{\mathcal{Q}})$ from (C1). $\qquad\square$

To illustrate the incompatibility given by Proposition 10.8 consider a variation of Example 10.4.

Example 10.9. *Reconsider Example 10.4 about Alice, Bernd and Gavin. The specific personal relationship between Alice and Bernd seems to be not very important for Example 10.4. Thus, the example scenario also holds when replacing $\neg\alpha \models \beta$ by $\alpha \models \beta$. In terms of the example scenario: assume that Bernd is indifferent about parties, but seems to like Alice; then he is surely joining the party if Alice is attending the party ($\alpha \models \beta$).*

10.3.3. Evaluation of $(IC3_{ca}^{cond})$ and $(IC4_{ca}^{cond})$, and $(IC4_{dca}^{cond})$

In the following, we consider $(IC3_{ca}^{cond})$ and $(IC4_{ca}^{cond})$ in more detail. We start by showing that $(IC4_{ca}^{cond})$ is satisfied by every AGM contraction operator for epistemic states.

Proposition 10.10. *Let $\mathcal{E}$ be a set of epistemic states. Every AGM contraction operator for $\mathcal{E}$ satisfies* (IC4$_{\text{ca}}^{\text{cond}}$).

Proof. Let $\div$ be an AGM contraction operator for $\mathcal{E}$ and $\alpha, \beta \in \mathcal{L}$. We consider two cases:

The case of $\alpha \equiv \top$. In this case, (IC4$_{\text{ca}}^{\text{cond}}$) is trivially satisfied, as we have $\top \in \text{Bel}(\Phi)$ for each $\Phi \in \mathcal{E}$. Consequently, we obtain $\top \in \text{Bel}(\Psi \div \beta)$ for each $\Psi \in \mathcal{E}$, yielding that (IC4$_{\text{ca}}^{\text{cond}}$) is satisfied.

The case of $\alpha \not\equiv \top$. For this case, recall that (C3) is satisfied by $\div$, and thus $\alpha \not\equiv \top$ implies $\alpha \notin \text{Bel}(\Psi \div \alpha)$. Because $\div$ satisfies (C1), we obtain $\alpha \notin \text{Bel}(\Psi \div \alpha \div \beta)$ from $\alpha \notin \text{Bel}(\Psi \div \alpha)$. By Proposition 9.18, the last observation is equivalent to $\Psi \div \alpha \not\models [\alpha \,|\, \beta]$. Consequently, (IC4$_{\text{ca}}^{\text{cond}}$) is satisfied. $\square$

For the sake of completeness, note that due to Proposition 9.18 the postulate (IC3$_{\text{ca}}^{\text{cond}}$) is equivalent to:

(IC3$_{\text{ca}}$) If $\Psi \div \beta \models \neg\alpha$, then $\Psi \div \alpha \div \beta \models \neg\alpha$.

The following proposition characterizes (IC3$_{\text{ca}}^{\text{cond}}$) semantically.

Proposition 10.11. *Let $\mathcal{E}$ be a set of epistemic states, let $\div$ be an AGM contraction operator for $\mathcal{E}$, and let $\Psi \mapsto \,\leq_\Psi$ be a faithful-assignment which is contraction-compatible with $\div$. Then, the operator $\div$ satisfies* (IC3$_{\text{ca}}^{\text{cond}}$) *if and only if the following holds:*

(IC3$_{\text{ca}}^{\text{rel}}$) If $\omega_1 \in [\![\neg\alpha]\!]$, $\omega_2 \in [\![\alpha]\!]$ and $[\![\Psi]\!] \subseteq [\![\neg\alpha]\!]$, then $\omega_1 <_\Psi \omega_2 \Rightarrow \omega_1 <_{\Psi \div \alpha} \omega_2$.

Proof. We consider both directions of the claim independently.

From (IC3$_{\text{ca}}^{\text{cond}}$) *to* (IC3$_{\text{ca}}^{\text{rel}}$). Assume satisfaction of (IC3$_{\text{ca}}^{\text{cond}}$). We show satisfaction of (IC3$_{\text{ca}}^{\text{rel}}$) by contradiction. Let $\omega_1 \in [\![\neg\alpha]\!]$ and $\omega_2 \in [\![\alpha]\!]$ and $[\![\Psi]\!] \subseteq [\![\neg\alpha]\!]$. Suppose that $\omega_1 <_\Psi \omega_2$ and $\omega_2 \leq_{\Psi \div \alpha} \omega_1$. Now choose β such that $[\![\beta]\!] = \Omega \setminus \{\omega_1, \omega_2\}$. Using Proposition 9.3, we obtain $\neg\alpha \in \text{Bel}(\Psi \div \beta)$ and $\neg\alpha \notin \text{Bel}(\Psi \div \alpha \div \beta)$, a direct contradiction to (IC3$_{\text{ca}}^{\text{cond}}$).

From (IC3$^{\text{rel}}_{\text{ca}}$) *to* (IC3$^{\text{cond}}_{\text{ca}}$). For the other direction, assume satisfaction of (IC3$^{\text{rel}}_{\text{ca}}$). We show satisfaction of (IC3$^{\text{cond}}_{\text{ca}}$). Let $\neg\alpha \in \text{Bel}(\Psi \div \beta)$ and $\neg\alpha \notin \text{Bel}(\Psi \div \alpha \div \beta)$. Because of Proposition 9.3 we obtain $[\![\Psi]\!] \subseteq [\![\neg\alpha]\!]$ and $\min(\neg\beta, \leq_\Psi) \subseteq [\![\neg\alpha]\!]$. Moreover, Proposition 9.3 implies the existence of an interpretation ω_2 such that $\omega_2 \notin [\![\neg\alpha]\!]$ and $\omega_2 \in \min([\![\neg\beta]\!], \leq_{\Psi \div \alpha})$. Because ω_2 exists, there exists another interpretation ω_1 such that $\omega_1 \in \min(\neg\beta, \leq_\Psi)$ and thus, $\omega_1 \in [\![\neg\alpha]\!]$. We obtain that $\omega_1 <_\Psi \omega_2$ and $\omega_2 \leq_{\Psi \div \alpha} \omega_1$, which contradicts (IC3$^{\text{rel}}_{\text{ca}}$). □

Because (IC4$^{\text{cond}}_{\text{ca}}$) is trivial for AGM contraction operators, as we have seen in Proposition 10.10, in the following we discuss the combination of (IC3$^{\text{cond}}_{\text{ca}}$) and (IC4$^{\text{cond}}_{\text{dca}}$) (see p. 239). Both postulates establish generally non-trivial principles for contraction, stating together that a contraction of a belief α does not change the independence of believing in $\neg\alpha$ from believing in β, i.e. (IC3$^{\text{cond}}_{\text{ca}}$) and (IC4$^{\text{cond}}_{\text{dca}}$) together are equivalent to:

$$\Psi \models [\,\neg\alpha \,|\, \beta\,] \text{ if and only if } \Psi \div \alpha \models [\,\neg\alpha \,|\, \beta\,]$$

To illustrate (IC3$^{\text{cond}}_{\text{ca}}$) and (IC4$^{\text{cond}}_{\text{dca}}$) we present the following example, which makes use of the contraposition of (IC4$^{\text{cond}}_{\text{dca}}$):

$$\text{If } \Psi \not\models [\,\neg\alpha \,|\, \beta\,] \text{ then } \Psi \div \alpha \not\models [\,\neg\alpha \,|\, \beta\,].$$

Example 10.12. *Let α, β be the following propositions:*

$$\alpha : \text{\textit{Arnold likes pop music}}$$
$$\beta : \text{\textit{Arnold likes classical music}}$$

about Arnold's taste of music. Suppose that an agent believes that Arnold does not like Pop music ($\neg\alpha \in \text{Bel}(\Psi)$) and likes classical music ($\beta \in \text{Bel}(\Psi)$). In the following, we consider two approaches to the dependences between believing in $\neg\alpha$ and β.

For (IC3$^{\text{cond}}_{\text{ca}}$): *Suppose that the agent is convinced that Arnold's tastes of music for different music genres are independent of each other; in particular, the agent's belief that Arnold does not like pop music does not depend on whether Arnold likes classical music or not ($\Psi \models [\,\neg\alpha \,|\, \beta\,]$).*

For (IC4$_{\text{dca}}^{\text{cond}}$): *Suppose that the agent is convinced that Arnold's tastes of music for different music genres depend on each other. In particular, believing that Arnold does not like pop music depends on believing that Arnold likes classical music ($\Psi \not\models [\neg\alpha \,|\, \beta]$).*

In both cases, when for some reason the agent gives up the belief that Arnold does like pop music ($\Psi \div \alpha$), it would be implausible that the agent changes generally her opinion on the interrelation between tastes of music. This is reflected by (IC3$_{\text{ca}}^{\text{cond}}$), *respectively* (IC4$_{\text{dca}}^{\text{cond}}$), *and we would obtain $\Psi \div \alpha \models [\neg\alpha \,|\, \beta]$, respectively $\Psi \div \alpha \not\models [\neg\alpha \,|\, \beta]$.*

By what we have seen so-far, (IC3$_{\text{ca}}^{\text{cond}}$) and (IC4$_{\text{dca}}^{\text{cond}}$) seem to be viable postulates. However, considering the semantic characterizations of (IC3$_{\text{ca}}^{\text{cond}}$) and (IC4$_{\text{dca}}^{\text{cond}}$) highlights the limitation of these postulates. Recall that (IC4$_{\text{dca}}^{\text{cond}}$) is, as shown in Proposition 10.3, semantically characterized by

(IC4$_{\text{dca-c}}^{\text{rel}}$) If $\omega_1 \in [\![\neg\alpha]\!]$, $\omega_2 \in [\![\alpha]\!]$ and $[\![\Psi]\!] \subseteq [\![\neg\alpha]\!]$, then $\omega_1 <_{\Psi\div\alpha} \omega_2 \Rightarrow \omega_1 <_\Psi \omega_2$.

, which we obtain by contraposition from (IC4$_{\text{dca}}^{\text{rel}}$). As shown in Proposition 10.11, the postulate (IC3$_{\text{ca}}^{\text{cond}}$) is characterized by:

(IC3$_{\text{ca}}^{\text{rel}}$) If $\omega_1 \in [\![\neg\alpha]\!]$, $\omega_2 \in [\![\alpha]\!]$ and $[\![\Psi]\!] \subseteq [\![\neg\alpha]\!]$, then $\omega_1 <_\Psi \omega_2 \Rightarrow \omega_1 <_{\Psi\div\alpha} \omega_2$.

The postulates (IC4$_{\text{dca-c}}^{\text{rel}}$) and (IC3$_{\text{ca}}^{\text{rel}}$) have different consequences, but share the same precondition. Considering the precondition of (IC4$_{\text{dca-c}}^{\text{rel}}$) and (IC3$_{\text{ca}}^{\text{rel}}$) reveals that these postulates only apply to contractions by α, where α is anyway not believed in the prior belief state, i.e., we have $\alpha \notin \text{Bel}(\Psi)$.

Just for the sake of completeness, we consider a characterization theorem for the semantic postulate

(IC4$_{\text{weak}}^{\text{rel}}$) If $\omega_1 \in [\![\neg\alpha]\!]$, $\omega_2 \in [\![\alpha]\!]$ and $[\![\Psi]\!] \subseteq [\![\neg\alpha]\!]$, then $\omega_1 \leq_\Psi \omega_2 \Rightarrow \omega_1 \leq_{\Psi\div\alpha} \omega_2$.

The precondition of (IC4$_{\text{weak}}^{\text{rel}}$) is the same as the precondition of (IC4$_{\text{dca-c}}^{\text{rel}}$) and the precondition of (IC3$_{\text{ca}}^{\text{rel}}$), but the postulates have different consequences. The rationale to consider $(IC4_{\text{weak}}^{\text{rel}})$ is that this postulate is related to $(IC3_{\text{ca}}^{\text{rel}})$ as $(IR4^{\text{rel}})$ is related to $(IR3^{\text{rel}})$ (see Section 10.1). Especially, note that $(IC4_{\text{weak}}^{\text{rel}})$ has the same consequence as $(IR4^{\text{rel}})$, and $(IC3_{\text{ca}}^{\text{rel}})$ has the same consequence as $(IR3^{\text{rel}})$.

Proposition 10.13. *Let $\mathcal{E}$ be a set of epistemic states, let $\div$ be an AGM contraction operator for $\mathcal{E}$, and let $\Psi \mapsto \leq_{\Psi}$ be a faithful-assignment which is contraction-compatible with $\div$. Then the operator $\div$ satisfies*

$(IC4_{\text{weak}})$ *If $\Psi \models \neg\alpha$ and $\Psi \div \beta \not\models \neg\alpha{\rightarrow}\beta$, then $\Psi \div \alpha \div \beta \not\models \neg\alpha{\rightarrow}\beta$.*

if and only if the following holds:

$(IC4_{\text{weak}}^{\text{rel}})$ *If $\omega_1 \in [\![\neg\alpha]\!]$, $\omega_2 \in [\![\alpha]\!]$ and $[\![\Psi]\!] \subseteq [\![\neg\alpha]\!]$, then $\omega_1 \leq_{\Psi} \omega_2 \Rightarrow$ $\omega_1 \leq_{\Psi \div \alpha} \omega_2$.*

Proof. We consider both directions of the claim independently.

From $(IC4_{\text{weak}})$ to $(IC4_{\text{weak}}^{\text{rel}})$. We show satisfaction of the contraposition of $(IC4_{\text{weak}})$, i.e., that the following holds:

$$\text{if } \omega_1 \in [\![\neg\alpha]\!], \ \omega_2 \in [\![\alpha]\!] \text{ and } [\![\Psi]\!] \subseteq [\![\neg\alpha]\!],$$
$$\text{then } \omega_2 <_{\Psi \div \alpha} \omega_1 \Rightarrow \omega_2 <_{\Psi} \omega_1$$

In the following, let $\omega_1 \in [\![\neg\alpha]\!]$ and $\omega_2 \in [\![\alpha]\!]$ and $[\![\Psi]\!] \subseteq [\![\neg\alpha]\!]$. Assume that $\omega_2 <_{\Psi \div \alpha} \omega_1$ holds. Towards a contradiction suppose that we have $\omega_1 \not<_{\Psi} \omega_2$, i.e., we have $\omega_1 \simeq_{\Psi} \omega_2$. Now choose β such that $[\![\neg\beta]\!] = \{\omega_1, \omega_2\}$ holds. We obtain $\omega_1, \omega_2 \in \min([\![\neg\beta]\!], \leq_{\Psi})$ from $\omega_1 \simeq_{\Psi} \omega_2$ and $[\![\neg\beta]\!] = \{\omega_1, \omega_2\}$. This together with $[\![\Psi]\!] \subseteq [\![\neg\alpha]\!]$ implies $\omega_1, \omega_2 \notin [\![\Psi]\!]$ and $\omega_1, \omega_2 \in [\![\Psi \div \beta]\!]$, since $\Psi \mapsto \leq_{\Psi}$ is contraction-compatible with $\div$. Note that the contraction-compatibility of $\Psi \mapsto \leq_{\Psi}$ with $\div$ yields $[\![\Psi \div \alpha]\!] = [\![\Psi]\!] \cup \min([\![\neg\alpha]\!], \leq_{\Psi})$. By using the latter, $\omega_1, \omega_2 \notin [\![\Psi]\!]$ and $\omega_2 <_{\Psi \div \alpha} \omega_1$, we obtain $\omega_1, \omega_2 \notin [\![\Psi \div \alpha]\!]$ and $[\![\Psi \div \alpha]\!] \subseteq [\![\neg\alpha]\!]$ from the faithfulness of $\Psi \mapsto \leq_{\Psi}$. Employing contraction-compatible of $\Psi \mapsto \leq_{\Psi}$ with $\div$ again, we obtain $[\![\Psi \div \alpha \div \beta]\!] = [\![\Psi \div \alpha]\!] \cup \{\omega_2\}$ from $\omega_2 <_{\Psi \div \alpha} \omega_1$. Our last observation implies $\Psi \div \alpha \div \beta \models \neg\alpha \rightarrow \beta$. Recall that we have shown $\omega_1, \omega_2 \in [\![\Psi \div \beta]\!]$, and thus $\Psi \div \beta \not\models \neg\alpha \rightarrow \beta$

holds. Consequently, because $\div$ satisfies (IC4$_{\text{weak}}$), we obtain the contradiction $\Psi \div \alpha \div \beta \not\models \neg\alpha \to \beta$ from $[\![\Psi]\!] \subseteq [\![\neg\alpha]\!]$.

From (IC4$_{\text{weak}}^{\text{rel}}$) *to* (IC4$_{\text{weak}}$). Suppose that $[\![\Psi]\!] \subseteq [\![\neg\alpha]\!]$ and $\Psi \div \beta \not\models \neg\alpha \to \beta$ holds. From the contraction-compatibility of $\Psi \mapsto \leq_\Psi$ with $\div$ we obtain that there exists $\omega \in [\![\Psi \div \beta]\!]$ with $\omega \models \neg\alpha \wedge \neg\beta$ such that $\omega \in [\![\Psi]\!]$ or $\omega \in \min([\![\neg\beta]\!], \leq_\Psi)$ holds. Towards a contradiction, we assume $\Psi \div \alpha \div \beta \models \neg\alpha \to \beta$. Note that $\div$ satisfies (C1), and thus, $\omega \in [\![\Psi]\!]$ or $\omega \in [\![\Psi \div \alpha]\!]$ or $\omega \in [\![\Psi \div \alpha \div \beta]\!]$ would imply $\Psi \div \alpha \div \beta \not\models \neg\alpha \to \beta$. Consequently, we have $\omega \notin [\![\Psi]\!]$ and $\omega \in \min([\![\neg\beta]\!], \leq_\Psi)$. Moreover, by the same argumentation, we obtain $\omega \notin \min([\![\neg\alpha]\!], \leq_\Psi)$ and $\omega \notin \min([\![\neg\beta]\!], \leq_{\Psi \div \alpha})$ from (C1). From the contraction-compatibility of $\Psi \mapsto \leq_\Psi$ with $\div$ we obtain $\min([\![\neg\beta]\!], \leq_{\Psi \div \alpha}) \subseteq [\![\Psi \div \alpha \div \beta]\!]$. Consequently, because of $\Psi \div \alpha \div \beta \models \neg\alpha \to \beta$ and $\neg\alpha \to \beta \equiv \neg\beta \to \alpha$, we have $\omega' \models \alpha$ for each $\omega' \in \min([\![\neg\beta]\!], \leq_{\Psi \div \alpha})$. As $\min([\![\neg\beta]\!], \leq_{\Psi \div \alpha})$ is non-empty, there exists some $\omega' \in \min([\![\neg\beta]\!], \leq_{\Psi \div \alpha})$. Because of $\omega \notin \min([\![\neg\beta]\!], \leq_{\Psi \div \alpha})$, we obtain $\omega' <_{\Psi \div \alpha} \omega$. As we have $[\![\Psi]\!] \subseteq [\![\neg\alpha]\!]$, we obtain $\omega' <_\Psi \omega$ from (IC4$_{\text{weak}}^{\text{rel}}$) and $\omega' <_{\Psi \div \alpha} \omega$. This observation yields a contradiction to $\omega \in \min([\![\neg\beta]\!], \leq_\Psi)$. $\square$

Employing Proposition 9.18 again yields that the postulate (IC4$_{\text{weak}}$) is equivalent to the following postulate for the change of conditional beliefs:

(IC4$_{\text{weak}}^{\text{cond}}$) If $\Psi \models \neg\alpha$ and $\Psi \not\models [\neg\alpha \to \beta \mid \beta]$, then $\Psi \div \alpha \not\models [\neg\alpha \to \beta \mid \beta]$.

In summary, this section presented and discussed postulates based on the translation of the syntactic Darwiche-Pearl postulates for revision to contraction. In the following section, we will consider semantic postulates and describe syntactic counterparts for them. This includes postulates which are similar to (IC3$_{\text{ca}}$) and (IC4$_{\text{weak}}^{\text{cond}}$), yet do not suffer from the restriction to contractions by those formulas α, where α is not believed previously.

10.4. Contraction Analogues to (IR1^{rel})–(IR4^{rel})

In this section, we consider contraction analogues to the semantic Darwiche-Pearl postulates (IR1^{rel})–(IR4^{rel}) (see Section 10.1) and propose a syntactic characterization for them. We will also present equivalent formulations of these new syntactic characterizations of the contraction postulates with and without employing contractionals. Table 10.2 summarizes most of the postulates we consider in this section.

The starting point for our investigations in this section is the following group of semantic contraction postulates, which were presented first by Chopra, Ghose, Meyer and Wong [40]:

(IC1^{rel}) If $\omega_1, \omega_2 \in [\![\alpha]\!]$, then $\omega_1 \leq_\Psi \omega_2 \Leftrightarrow \omega_1 \leq_{\Psi \div \alpha} \omega_2$.

(IC2^{rel}) If $\omega_1, \omega_2 \in [\![\neg\alpha]\!]$, then $\omega_1 \leq_\Psi \omega_2 \Leftrightarrow \omega_1 \leq_{\Psi \div \alpha} \omega_2$.

(IC3^{rel}) If $\omega_1 \in [\![\neg\alpha]\!]$ and $\omega_2 \in [\![\alpha]\!]$, then $\omega_1 <_\Psi \omega_2 \Rightarrow \omega_1 <_{\Psi \div \alpha} \omega_2$.

(IC4^{rel}) If $\omega_1 \in [\![\neg\alpha]\!]$ and $\omega_2 \in [\![\alpha]\!]$, then $\omega_1 \leq_\Psi \omega_2 \Rightarrow \omega_1 \leq_{\Psi \div \alpha} \omega_2$.

The postulates (IC1^{rel}) and (IC2^{rel}) ensure that the order of worlds does not change if they are equivalent with respect to the new information received [92]. The postulates (IC3^{rel}) and (IC4^{rel}) together enforce that the plausibility of models of α is not improved whenever contracting by α.

Moreover, these postulates are well-behaving as they are, e.g., compatible with full meet and linear AGM contraction operators for epistemic states. Recall that we identified linear AGM contraction operators as a basic type of AGM contraction operators for epistemic states in Section 9.2.

Proposition 10.14. *Let $\mathcal{E}$ be a set of epistemic states, let $\div$ be an AGM contraction operator for $\mathcal{E}$, and let $\Psi \mapsto \leq_\Psi$ be a faithful assignment that is contraction-compatible with $\div$. If $\div$ is linear or full meet, then (IC1^{rel})–(IC4^{rel}) are satisfied.*

Proof. Observe that by Definition 9.7 and Proposition 9.6 we have $\omega_1 \leq_\Psi \omega_2$ if and only if $\omega_1 \leq_{\Psi \div \alpha} \omega_2$ for all $\omega_1, \omega_2 \notin [\![\Psi \div \alpha]\!]$. This, together with the contraction-compatibility of $\div$ with $\Psi \mapsto \leq_\Psi$ yields the claim. $\square$

A consequence of this observation is that there exists an AGM contraction operator for $\mathcal{E}$ that satisfies (IC1^{rel})–(IC4^{rel}) whenever there exists an AGM contraction operator for $\mathcal{E}$ at all (cf. Corollary 9.13).

Semantic	(IC1^{rel})	If $\omega_1, \omega_2 \in [\![\alpha]\!]$, then $\omega_1 \leq_\Psi \omega_2 \Leftrightarrow \omega_1 \leq_{\Psi \div \alpha} \omega_2$
Contractional	(IC1^{cond})	If $\neg\alpha \models \beta$, then $\Psi \div \alpha \models [\alpha{\to}\gamma \,|\, \beta] \Leftrightarrow \Psi \models [\alpha{\to}\gamma \,|\, \beta]$
Syntactic	(IC1)	If $\neg\alpha \models \beta$, then $\text{Bel}(\Psi \div \alpha \div \beta) =_\alpha \text{Bel}(\Psi \div \beta)$
Semantic	(IC2^{rel})	If $\omega_1, \omega_2 \in [\![\neg\alpha]\!]$, then $\omega_1 \leq_\Psi \omega_2 \Leftrightarrow \omega_1 \leq_{\Psi \div \alpha} \omega_2$
Contractional	(IC2^{cond})	If $\alpha \models \beta$, then $\Psi \div \alpha \models [\neg\beta{\to}\gamma \,|\, \beta] \Leftrightarrow \Psi \models [\neg\beta{\to}\gamma \,|\, \beta]$
Syntactic	(IC2)	If $\alpha \models \beta$, then $\text{Bel}(\Psi \div \alpha \div \beta) =_{\neg\beta} \text{Bel}(\Psi \div \beta)$
Semantic	(IC3^{rel})	If $\omega_1 \in [\![\neg\alpha]\!]$ and $\omega_2 \in [\![\alpha]\!]$, then $\omega_1 <_\Psi \omega_2 \Rightarrow \omega_1 <_{\Psi \div \alpha} \omega_2$
Contractional	(IC3^{cond})	If $\gamma \models \beta$, then $\Psi \models [\alpha{\to}\gamma \,|\, \beta] \Rightarrow \Psi \div \alpha \models [\alpha{\to}\gamma \,|\, \beta]$
Syntactic	(IC3)	If $\gamma \models \beta$, then $\Psi \div \beta \models \alpha{\to}\gamma \Rightarrow \Psi \div \alpha \div \beta \models \alpha{\to}\gamma$
Semantic	(IC4^{rel})	If $\omega_1 \in [\![\neg\alpha]\!]$ and $\omega_2 \in [\![\alpha]\!]$, then $\omega_1 \leq_\Psi \omega_2 \Rightarrow \omega_1 \leq_{\Psi \div \alpha} \omega_2$
Contractional	(IC4^{cond})	If $\gamma \models \beta$, then $\Psi \div \alpha \models [\neg\alpha{\to}\gamma \,|\, \beta] \Rightarrow \Psi \models [\neg\alpha{\to}\gamma \,|\, \beta]$
Syntactic	(IC4)	If $\gamma \models \beta$, then $\Psi \div \alpha \div \beta \models \neg\alpha{\to}\gamma \Rightarrow \Psi \div \beta \models \neg\alpha{\to}\gamma$

Table 10.2: Overview of the different principles proposed in Section 10.4 and their different representations shown here.

Next, we consider characterizations of (IC1^{rel})–(IC4^{rel}) presented in the literature.

10.4.1. Characterization by Konieczny and Pino Pérez

The first syntactic characterization of the postulates (IC1^{rel}) and (IC4^{rel}) was given by involving a revision operator [40]. A characterization which does not depend on other operators was given by Konieczny and Pino Pérez [98]. They proposed the following postulates for iterated contraction[5]:

(IC1$_{\text{KPP}}$) If $\neg\alpha \models \gamma$, then $\text{Bel}(\Psi \div \alpha) \subseteq \text{Bel}(\Psi \div (\alpha \vee \beta)) \Leftrightarrow \text{Bel}(\Psi \div \gamma \div \alpha) \subseteq \text{Bel}(\Psi \div \gamma \div (\alpha \vee \beta))$.

(IC2$_{\text{KPP}}$) If $\gamma \models \alpha$, then $\text{Bel}(\Psi \div \alpha) \subseteq \text{Bel}(\Psi \div (\alpha \vee \beta)) \Leftrightarrow \text{Bel}(\Psi \div \gamma \div \alpha) \subseteq \text{Bel}(\Psi \div \gamma \div (\alpha \vee \beta))$.

(IC3$_{\text{KPP}}$) If $\neg\beta \models \gamma$, then $\text{Bel}(\Psi \div \gamma \div \alpha) \subseteq \text{Bel}(\Psi \div \gamma \div (\alpha \vee \beta)) \Rightarrow \text{Bel}(\Psi \div \alpha) \subseteq \text{Bel}(\Psi \div (\alpha \vee \beta))$.

(IC4$_{\text{KPP}}$) If $\gamma \models \beta$, then $\text{Bel}(\Psi \div \gamma \div \alpha) \subseteq \text{Bel}(\Psi \div \gamma \div (\alpha \vee \beta)) \Rightarrow \text{Bel}(\Psi \div \alpha) \subseteq \text{Bel}(\Psi \div (\alpha \vee \beta))$.

---

[5]   The subscript *KPP* stands for *Konieczny and Pino Pérez*. The original formulation of these postulates makes use of a formula $B(\Psi)$ instead of a belief set $\text{Bel}(\Psi)$ [98].

For an explanation of $(\text{IC1}_{\text{KPP}})$–$(\text{IC4}_{\text{KPP}})$ we refer to Konieczny and Pino Pérez [98]. The class of operators fulfilling these postulates is captured semantically by the following characterization theorem.

Proposition 10.15 ([98]). *Let $\mathcal{E}$ be a set of epistemic states, let $\div$ be an AGM contraction operator for $\mathcal{E}$, and let $\Psi \mapsto \leq_\Psi$ be a faithful assignment that is contraction-compatible with $\div$. Then $\div$ satisfies $(\text{IC1}_{\text{KPP}})$–$(\text{IC4}_{\text{KPP}})$ if and only $(\text{IC1}^{\text{rel}})$–$(\text{IC4}^{\text{rel}})$ are satisfied.*

The postulates $(\text{IC1}_{\text{KPP}})$–$(\text{IC4}_{\text{KPP}})$ focus on the role of disjunctive beliefs. However, they do not give a direct overview of the impact of $(\text{IC1}^{\text{rel}})$–$(\text{IC4}^{\text{rel}})$ on the dynamics of conditional beliefs in the process of iterated contraction. In the remaining sections of this chapter, we consider postulates which actually do provide insight in the dynamics of conditional beliefs, and we will show that these postulates characterize $(\text{IC1}^{\text{rel}})$–$(\text{IC4}^{\text{rel}})$. Next, we use α-equivalence as formal means to describe these postulates in a succinct manner.

10.4.2. Syntactic Characterization of $(\text{IC1}^{\text{rel}})$ and $(\text{IC2}^{\text{rel}})$

In the following, we present two principles (IC1) and (IC2) which will be postulates in the fashion of (IR1) and (IR2), specifying situations in which beliefs after a contraction are not influenced by specific prior contractions. Recall that the postulates $(\text{IC1}_{\text{ca}}^{\text{cond}})$ and $(\text{IC2}_{\text{ca}}^{\text{cond}})$ already describe such situations, but are shown to be incompatible with AGM contraction operators for epistemic states (cf. Section 10.3). Due to Proposition 9.18, the following postulates are equivalent to $(\text{IC1}_{\text{ca}}^{\text{cond}})$ and $(\text{IC2}_{\text{ca}}^{\text{cond}})$:

(IC1_{ca}) If $\neg\alpha \models \beta$, then $\text{Bel}(\Psi \div \alpha \div \beta) = \text{Bel}(\Psi \div \beta)$.

(IC2_{ca}) If $\alpha \models \beta$, then $\text{Bel}(\Psi \div \alpha \div \beta) = \text{Bel}(\Psi \div \beta)$.

The postulates (IC1) and (IC2) we propose below are similar to (IC1_{ca}) and (IC2_{ca}), but make use of α-equivalence to restrict (IC1_{ca}) and (IC2_{ca}) to specific cases such that (IC1) and (IC2) are compatible with AGM contraction operators for epistemic states. Moreover, we chose this restriction such that (IC1) and (IC2) are equivalent to $(\text{IC1}^{\text{rel}})$ and $(\text{IC2}^{\text{rel}})$.

Remember that $(\text{IC1}^{\text{rel}})$ and $(\text{IC2}^{\text{rel}})$ require that all interpretations of a certain kind should not change their plausibility relative to each other in the process of contraction. The postulate (IC1^{rel}) enforces this condition for the models of α, and (IC2^{rel}) enforces the same condition for models of $\neg\alpha$, thus it is natural to specify the following postulates:

(IC1) If $\neg\alpha \models \beta$, then $\mathrm{Bel}(\Psi \div \alpha \div \beta) =_\alpha \mathrm{Bel}(\Psi \div \beta)$.
  Explanation: The beliefs about α after a contraction with β are independent of whether α was contracted previously or not, if β is more general than the negation of α.

(IC2) If $\alpha \models \beta$, then $\mathrm{Bel}(\Psi \div \alpha \div \beta) =_{\neg\beta} \mathrm{Bel}(\Psi \div \beta)$.
  Explanation: The beliefs about $\neg\beta$ after a contraction with β are independent of whether α was contracted previously or not, if β is more general than α.

We will now show that (IC1) and (IC2) are equivalent to (IC1^{rel}) and (IC2^{rel}) for AGM contraction operators for epistemic states. Note that (IC2) makes use of $\neg\beta$-equivalence, and the following proposition shows also that this is the right condition to capture (IC2^{rel}).

Proposition 10.16. *Let $\mathcal{E}$ be a set of epistemic states, let $\div$ be an AGM contraction operator for $\mathcal{E}$, and let $\Psi \mapsto \leq_\Psi$ be a faithful assignment that is contraction-compatible with $\div$. The operator $\div$ satisfies the postulate (IC1), respectively (IC2), if and only if (IC1^{rel}), respectively (IC2^{rel}), is satisfied.*

Proof. Let $\div$ be an AGM contraction operator for $\mathcal{E}$ for epistemic states, thus fulfilling (C1)–(C7), and let $\Psi \mapsto \leq_\Psi$ be a faithful assignment that is contraction-compatible with $\div$. The proof considers both directions of the claim independently.

  The "$\Leftarrow$"-direction. Suppose that (IC1^{rel}), respectively (IC2^{rel}), is satisfied. From the contraction-compatibility of $\Psi \mapsto \leq_\Psi$ with $\div$ we obtain

$$\llbracket \Psi \div \alpha \div \beta \rrbracket = \llbracket \Psi \rrbracket \cup \min(\llbracket \neg\alpha \rrbracket, \leq_\Psi) \cup \min(\llbracket \neg\beta \rrbracket, \leq_{\Psi \div \alpha}),$$
$$(10.1)$$

  for each $\alpha, \beta \in \mathcal{L}$. We show that (IC1), respectively (IC2), is satisfied by $\div$:

(IC1) Suppose that $\neg\beta \models \alpha$ holds, which is equivalent to $[\![\neg\beta]\!] \subseteq [\![\alpha]\!]$. From (IC1^{rel}) and $[\![\neg\beta]\!] \subseteq [\![\alpha]\!]$ we obtain:

$$\min([\![\neg\beta]\!], \leq_\Psi) = \min([\![\neg\beta]\!], \leq_{\Psi \div \alpha}) \qquad (10.2)$$

Combining (10.1) with (10.2) yields:

$$[\![\Psi \div \alpha \div \beta]\!] = [\![\Psi]\!] \cup \min([\![\neg\alpha]\!], \leq_\Psi) \cup \min([\![\neg\beta]\!], \leq_\Psi) \ (10.3)$$

By using (10.3) and $[\![\Psi \div \beta]\!] = [\![\Psi]\!] \cup \min([\![\neg\beta]\!], \leq_\Psi)$, obtained from the contraction-compatibility of $\Psi \mapsto \leq_\Psi$ with $\div$ and using $\min([\![\neg\alpha]\!], \leq_\Psi) \cap [\![\alpha]\!] = \emptyset$, we conclude that $[\![\Psi \div \alpha \div \beta]\!] \cap [\![\alpha]\!] = [\![\Psi \div \beta]\!] \cap [\![\alpha]\!]$ holds, which is equivalent to the required result $\text{Bel}(\Psi \div \alpha \div \beta) =_\alpha \text{Bel}(\Psi \div \beta)$.

(IC2) Let $\neg\beta \models \neg\alpha$, which is equivalent to $\alpha \models \beta$. By (IC2^{rel}) and $\neg\beta \models \neg\alpha$ it holds that:

$$\min([\![\neg\beta]\!], \leq_\Psi) = \min([\![\neg\beta]\!], \leq_{\Psi \div \alpha}) \qquad (10.4)$$

Combining Equation (10.1) that holds for every α, β with (10.4) yields:

$$[\![\Psi \div \alpha \div \beta]\!] = [\![\Psi]\!] \cup \min([\![\neg\alpha]\!], \leq_\Psi) \cup \min([\![\neg\beta]\!], \leq_\Psi) \ (10.5)$$

By using $\neg\beta \models \neg\alpha$ we conclude that there are only two possible cases:

$$\min([\![\neg\alpha]\!], \leq_\Psi) \cap [\![\neg\beta]\!] = \emptyset, \text{ or} \qquad (10.6)$$
$$\min([\![\neg\alpha]\!], \leq_\Psi) \cap [\![\neg\beta]\!] = \min([\![\neg\beta]\!], \leq_\Psi) \cap [\![\neg\beta]\!]. \quad (10.7)$$

In both cases, (10.6) and (10.7), from (10.5) we directly infer:

$$[\![\Psi \div \alpha \div \beta]\!] \cap [\![\neg\beta]\!] = [\![\Psi]\!] \cup \min([\![\neg\beta]\!], \leq_\Psi) \cap [\![\neg\beta]\!] \ (10.8)$$

From (10.8) and $[\![\Psi \div \beta]\!] = [\![\Psi]\!] \cup \min([\![\neg\beta]\!], \leq_\Psi)$, obtained from the contraction-compatibility of $\Psi \mapsto \leq_\Psi$ with $\div$, we conclude that $[\![\Psi \div \alpha \div \beta]\!] \cap [\![\neg\beta]\!] = [\![\Psi \div \beta]\!] \cap [\![\neg\beta]\!]$ holds. This latter observation is equivalent to $\text{Bel}(\Psi \div \alpha \div \beta) =_{\neg\beta} \text{Bel}(\Psi \div \beta)$.

The "⇒"-direction. We assume that $\div$ satisfies (IC1), respectively (IC2). In the following we show that (IC1^{rel}), respectively (IC2^{rel}), is satisfied.

(IC1^{rel}) Suppose $\omega_1, \omega_2 \in [\![\alpha]\!]$. We choose $\beta = \neg(\omega_1 \vee \omega_2)$ and therefore, we have $\neg\alpha \models \beta$ and $\neg\beta \models \alpha$. By (IC1) we have $\text{Bel}(\Psi \div \alpha \div \beta) =_\alpha \text{Bel}(\Psi \div \beta)$, which implies:

$$[\![\Psi \div \beta]\!] =_\alpha [\![\Psi \div \alpha \div \beta]\!], \tag{10.9}$$

which is equivalent to $[\![\Psi \div \beta]\!] \cap [\![\alpha]\!] = [\![\Psi \div \alpha \div \beta]\!] \cap [\![\alpha]\!]$. From the contraction-compatibility of $\div$ with $\Psi \mapsto \leq_\Psi$, we obtain that

$$\begin{aligned} [\![\Psi \div \alpha \div \beta]\!] &= [\![\Psi \div \alpha]\!] \cup \min([\![\neg\beta]\!], \leq_{\Psi \div \alpha}) \\ &= [\![\Psi]\!] \cup \min([\![\neg\alpha]\!], \leq_\Psi) \cup \min([\![\neg\beta]\!], \leq_{\Psi \div \alpha}) \end{aligned} \tag{10.10}$$

and

$$[\![\Psi \div \beta]\!] = [\![\Psi]\!] \cup \min([\![\neg\beta]\!], \leq_\Psi). \tag{10.11}$$

Substituting (10.10) and (10.11) into Equation (10.9) leads to

$$[\![\Psi]\!] \cup \min([\![\neg\alpha]\!], \leq_\Psi) \cup \min([\![\neg\beta]\!], \leq_{\Psi \div \alpha}) =_\alpha [\![\Psi]\!] \cup \min([\![\neg\beta]\!], \leq_\Psi). \tag{10.12}$$

Equation (10.12) is equivalent to:

$$\begin{aligned} ([\![\Psi]\!] \cup \min([\![\neg\alpha]\!], \leq_\Psi) \cup \min([\![\neg\beta]\!], \leq_{\Psi \div \alpha})) \cap [\![\alpha]\!] \\ = ([\![\Psi]\!] \cup \min([\![\neg\beta]\!], \leq_\Psi)) \cap [\![\alpha]\!] \end{aligned} \tag{10.13}$$

Because $\min([\![\neg\alpha]\!], \leq_\Psi) \cap [\![\alpha]\!] = \emptyset$, Equation (10.13) is equivalent to:

$$([\![\Psi]\!] \cup \min([\![\neg\beta]\!], \leq_{\Psi \div \alpha})) \cap [\![\alpha]\!] = ([\![\Psi]\!] \cup \min([\![\neg\beta]\!], \leq_\Psi)) \cap [\![\alpha]\!] \tag{10.14}$$

Remember that $\neg\beta \models \alpha$ and therefore $[\![\neg\beta]\!] \subseteq [\![\alpha]\!]$. Equation (10.14) implies

$$([\![\Psi]\!] \cup \min([\![\neg\beta]\!], \leq_{\Psi \div \alpha})) \cap [\![\neg\beta]\!] = ([\![\Psi]\!] \cup \min([\![\neg\beta]\!], \leq_\Psi)) \cap [\![\neg\beta]\!], \tag{10.15}$$

which is equivalent to $[\![\Psi]\!] \cup \min([\![\neg\beta]\!], \leq_{\Psi \div \alpha}) =_{\neg\beta} [\![\Psi]\!] \cup \min([\![\neg\beta]\!], \leq_\Psi)$. Next, we will show that

$$\min([\![\neg\beta]\!], \leq_{\Psi \div \alpha}) = \min([\![\neg\beta]\!], \leq_\Psi) \tag{10.16}$$

holds, by considering two cases, the case of $[\![\Psi]\!] \cap [\![\neg\beta]\!]$ being non-empty and the case of $[\![\Psi]\!] \cap [\![\neg\beta]\!]$ being empty.

The case of $[\![\Psi]\!] \cap [\![\neg\beta]\!] \neq \emptyset$. Because $\Psi \mapsto \,\leq_\Psi$ is a faithful assignment we obtain

$$[\![\Psi]\!] \cap [\![\neg\beta]\!] = \min([\![\neg\beta]\!], \leq_\Psi) \qquad (10.17)$$

from $[\![\Psi]\!] \cap [\![\neg\beta]\!] \neq \emptyset$. Moreover, because $\div$ is contraction-compatible with $\Psi \mapsto \,\leq_\Psi$, we easily get

$$[\![\Psi \div \alpha]\!] \cap [\![\alpha]\!] = ([\![\Psi]\!] \cup \min([\![\neg\alpha]\!], \leq_\Psi)) \cap [\![\alpha]\!],$$

which is, because of $\min([\![\neg\alpha]\!], \leq_\Psi) \cap [\![\alpha]\!] = \emptyset$, equivalent to:

$$[\![\Psi \div \alpha]\!] \cap [\![\alpha]\!] = [\![\Psi]\!] \cap [\![\alpha]\!]$$

Since $\neg\beta \models \alpha$, the set $[\![\Psi \div \alpha]\!]$ contains the same models of $\neg\beta$ as $[\![\Psi]\!]$, i.e.:

$$[\![\Psi \div \alpha]\!] \cap [\![\neg\beta]\!] = [\![\Psi]\!] \cap [\![\neg\beta]\!] \qquad (10.18)$$

Due to our assumption $[\![\Psi]\!] \cap [\![\neg\beta]\!] \neq \emptyset$, we obtain $[\![\Psi \div \alpha]\!] \cap [\![\neg\beta]\!] \neq \emptyset$ from (10.18). Then, because $\Psi \mapsto \,\leq_\Psi$ is a faithful assignment, we have:

$$[\![\Psi \div \alpha]\!] \cap [\![\neg\beta]\!] = \min([\![\neg\beta]\!], \leq_{\Psi \div \alpha}) \qquad (10.19)$$

Combining Equations (10.17), (10.18) and (10.19) yields that Equation (10.16) is satisfied in this case.

The case of $[\![\Psi]\!] \cap [\![\neg\beta]\!] = \emptyset$. Since $\neg\beta \models \alpha$ and $\min([\![\neg\alpha]\!], \leq_\Psi)$ contains no models of α, it must be the case that

$$[\![\Psi]\!] \cup \min([\![\neg\beta]\!], \leq_{\Psi \div \alpha}) =_\alpha [\![\Psi]\!] \cup \min([\![\neg\beta]\!], \leq_\Psi). \ (10.20)$$

We directly conclude from Equation (10.20) that Equation (10.16) holds in this case.

In summary, we have shown that Equation (10.16) holds for all cases. Note that $[\![\neg\beta]\!]$ has only two elements, $[\![\neg\beta]\!] = \{\omega_1, \omega_2\} \subseteq [\![\alpha]\!]$, and thus information about the minima provides us the relative order of the two elements ω_1 and ω_2. Consequently, Equation (10.16) implies that $\omega_1 \leq_\Psi \omega_2$ holds if and only if $\omega_1 \leq_{\Psi \div \alpha} \omega_2$ holds. This observation shows that $(\text{IC1}^{\text{rel}})$ holds.

(IC2^{rel}) Suppose $\omega_1, \omega_2 \in [\![\neg\alpha]\!]$. We choose $\beta = \neg(\omega_1 \vee \omega_2)$ and therefore, we have $\alpha \models \beta$. By (IC2) we have $\text{Bel}(\Psi \div \alpha \div \beta) =_{\neg\beta} \text{Bel}(\Psi \div \beta)$, which implies:

$$[\![\Psi \div \beta]\!] \cap [\![\neg\beta]\!] = [\![\Psi \div \alpha \div \beta]\!] \cap [\![\neg\beta]\!] \qquad (10.21)$$

From the contraction-compatibility of $\div$ with $\Psi \mapsto \leq_\Psi$ we obtain that

$$[\![\Psi \div \alpha]\!] = [\![\Psi]\!] \cup \min([\![\neg\alpha]\!], \leq_\Psi), \qquad (10.22)$$
$$[\![\Psi \div \beta]\!] = [\![\Psi]\!] \cup \min([\![\neg\beta]\!], \leq_\Psi) \qquad (10.23)$$

holds. Likewise, applying the contraction-compatibility of $\div$ with $\Psi \mapsto \leq_\Psi$ twice yields:

$$[\![\Psi \div \alpha \div \beta]\!] = [\![\Psi]\!] \cup \min([\![\neg\alpha]\!], \leq_\Psi) \cup \min([\![\neg\beta]\!], \leq_{\Psi \div \alpha}). \qquad (10.24)$$

Substituting (10.24) and (10.23) into Equation (10.21) leads to

$$([\![\Psi]\!] \cup \min([\![\neg\beta]\!], \leq_\Psi)) \cap [\![\neg\beta]\!]$$
$$= ([\![\Psi]\!] \cup \min([\![\neg\alpha]\!], \leq_\Psi) \cup \min([\![\neg\beta]\!], \leq_{\Psi \div \alpha})) \cap [\![\neg\beta]\!]. \qquad (10.25)$$

Note that every model of $\neg\beta$ is a model of $\neg\alpha$, therefore, either one of the following holds:

$$\min([\![\neg\alpha]\!], \leq_\Psi) \cap [\![\neg\beta]\!] = \emptyset, \text{ or} \qquad (10.26)$$
$$\min([\![\neg\alpha]\!], \leq_\Psi) \cap [\![\neg\beta]\!] = \min([\![\neg\beta]\!], \leq_\Psi). \qquad (10.27)$$

Next, we show that

$$\min([\![\neg\beta]\!], \leq_{\Psi \div \alpha}) = \min([\![\neg\beta]\!], \leq_\Psi) \qquad (10.28)$$

holds, by considering the cases of (10.26) and (10.27) independently:

(10.26) For this case, Equation (10.25) reduces to

$$([\![\Psi]\!] \cup \min([\![\neg\beta]\!], \leq_\Psi)) \cap [\![\neg\beta]\!]$$
$$= ([\![\Psi]\!] \cup \min([\![\neg\beta]\!], \leq_{\Psi \div \alpha})) \cap [\![\neg\beta]\!].$$

Furthermore, from (10.26) and $\neg\beta \models \neg\alpha$ we conclude $[\![\Psi]\!] \cap [\![\neg\beta]\!] = \emptyset$. Combing these two observations, we obtain satisfaction of (10.28), i.e., $\min([\![\neg\beta]\!], \leq_{\Psi \div \alpha}) = \min([\![\neg\beta]\!], \leq_\Psi)$.

(10.27) For this case note that $\min(\llbracket \neg \alpha \rrbracket, \leq_\Psi) \subseteq \llbracket \Psi \div \alpha \rrbracket$ holds. Consequently, because Equation (10.27) holds, we also have:

$$\min(\llbracket \neg \beta \rrbracket, \leq_\Psi) \subseteq \llbracket \Psi \div \alpha \rrbracket$$

By using faithfulness of $\Psi \mapsto \leq_\Psi$ (in particular condition (FA1) in Definition 6.5) we have $\min(\llbracket \neg \beta \rrbracket, \leq_\Psi) = \min(\llbracket \neg \beta \rrbracket, \leq_{\Psi \div \alpha})$, because the minimal models of $\neg \beta$ with respect to $\leq_{\Psi \div \alpha}$ are contained in $\llbracket \Psi \div \alpha \rrbracket$ by (10.22) and (10.27).

In summary, in both cases, (10.26) and (10.27), we have shown that (10.28) holds. Note that $\llbracket \neg \beta \rrbracket$ has only two elements, $\llbracket \neg \beta \rrbracket = \{\omega_1, \omega_2\} \subseteq \llbracket \neg \alpha \rrbracket$, and thus information about the minima provides us the relative order of the two elements ω_1 and ω_2. Consequently, Equation (10.28) implies that $\omega_1 \leq_\Psi \omega_2$ holds if and only if $\omega_1 \leq_{\Psi \div \alpha} \omega_2$ holds. This observation shows that (IC2^{rel}) holds. $\qquad\square$

As (IC2^{rel}) explicitly restricts the dynamics of models of $\neg \alpha$, one might wonder why we do not use the following postulate as counter-part to (IC2^{rel}):

(IC2′) If $\alpha \models \beta$, then $\text{Bel}(\Psi \div \alpha \div \beta) =_{\neg \alpha} \text{Bel}(\Psi \div \beta)$.

The rationale is that (IC2^{rel}) is more permissive than (IC2′). Note that $\alpha \models \beta$ implies $\llbracket \neg \beta \rrbracket \subseteq \llbracket \neg \alpha \rrbracket$. Thus, a careful reading of (IC2′) shows that, semantically, (IC2′) imposes the additional condition that all minimal models of $\neg \alpha$ with respect to $\leq_\Psi$ have to be models of $\neg \beta$. The drastic consequence is that there is no AGM contraction operator which is compatible with (IC2′), for, e.g., unbiased sets of epistemic states. The following proposition and its proof provide this as a technical statement.

Proposition 10.17. *Let $\mathcal{E}$ be a set of epistemic states that contains at least one epistemic state $\Psi_\Omega \in \mathcal{E}$ with $\llbracket \Psi_\Omega \rrbracket \neq \Omega$. There is no AGM contraction operator for $\mathcal{E}$ that satisfies (IC2′).*

Proof. The proof is by contradiction. Let $\div$ be an AGM contraction operator for $\mathcal{E}$ that satisfies (IC2′). Because $\div$ is an AGM contraction operator for epistemic states, we have that $\div$ satisfies (C1)–(C3).

From $[\![\Psi_\mathfrak{R}]\!] \neq \Omega$ we obtain that there exists $\omega \in \Omega$ with $\omega \notin [\![\Psi_\mathfrak{R}]\!]$. In the following let $\alpha \in \mathcal{L}$ be a formula such that $[\![\alpha]\!] = \Omega \setminus \{\omega\}$ holds. In summary, we have:

$$[\![\Psi_\mathfrak{R}]\!] \subseteq [\![\alpha]\!] \qquad \omega \in [\![\neg\alpha]\!] \qquad \omega \notin [\![\Psi_\mathfrak{R}]\!]$$

From Proposition 9.3, we obtain $[\![\Psi_\mathfrak{R} \div \top]\!] = [\![\Psi_\mathfrak{R}]\!]$. The latter implies $\omega \notin [\![\Psi_\mathfrak{R} \div \top]\!]$ and $[\![\Psi_\mathfrak{R} \div \top]\!] \cap [\![\neg\alpha]\!] = [\![\Psi]\!] \cap [\![\neg\alpha]\!]$. Moreover, because $\div$ satisfies (IC2′), we obtain $\omega \notin [\![\Psi_\mathfrak{R} \div \alpha \div \top]\!]$ and $[\![\Psi_\mathfrak{R} \div \alpha \div \top]\!] \cap [\![\neg\alpha]\!] = [\![\Psi]\!] \cap [\![\neg\alpha]\!]$, by substituting β with $\top$ in (IC2′). A repeated application of (C1) yields

$$\omega \notin [\![\Psi_\mathfrak{R}]\!] \cap [\![\neg\alpha]\!] = [\![\Psi_\mathfrak{R} \div \alpha]\!] \cap [\![\neg\alpha]\!] = [\![\Psi_\mathfrak{R} \div \alpha \div \top]\!] \cap [\![\neg\alpha]\!].$$

Because of $\alpha \not\equiv \top$, we obtain $[\![\Psi_\mathfrak{R} \div \alpha]\!] \not\subseteq [\![\alpha]\!]$ from (C1). In summary, we obtain that both, $\omega \notin [\![\Psi_\mathfrak{R} \div \alpha]\!]$ and $\omega \in [\![\Psi_\mathfrak{R} \div \alpha]\!]$, hold at the same time, which is a contradiction. $\qquad\square$

The correspondence between contractionals and contractions from Section 9.5, in particular Proposition 9.24, allows us to give a conditional formulation of the postulates (IC1) and (IC2):

(IC1^{cond}) If $\neg\alpha \models \beta$, then $\Psi \div \alpha \models [\alpha \to \gamma \mid \beta] \Leftrightarrow \Psi \models [\alpha \to \gamma \mid \beta]$.

(IC2^{cond}) If $\alpha \models \beta$, then $\Psi \div \alpha \models [\neg\beta \to \gamma \mid \beta] \Leftrightarrow \Psi \models [\neg\beta \to \gamma \mid \beta]$.

We close this subsection with a formal statement about the interrelationship between the conditional and non-conditional variant for these postulates.

Proposition 10.18. *Let $\mathcal{E}$ be a set of epistemic states and let $\div$ be an AGM contraction operator for $\mathcal{E}$. The postulate (IC1), respectively (IC2), is satisfied by $\div$ if and only if (IC1^{cond}), respectively (IC2^{cond}), is satisfied.*

Next we consider postulates which will turn out to be syntactic counterparts to (IC3^{rel}) and (IC4^{rel}).

10.4.3. Syntactic Characterization of (IC3^{rel}) and (IC4^{rel})

The postulates (IC3^{rel}) and (IC4^{rel}) both ensure that by a contraction with α, models of α should not be improved with respect to models of $\neg\alpha$. We have seen that the postulates (IC3$^{\text{cond}}_{\text{ca}}$) and (IC4$^{\text{cond}}_{\text{ca}}$) already capture (IC3^{rel}) and (IC4^{rel}) for certain epistemic states (cf. Section 10.3.3 and Table 10.1). In this section, we will show that in the framework we are using here, (IC3^{rel}) and (IC4^{rel}) are fully characterized by the following postulates:

(IC3^{cond}) If $\gamma \models \beta$, then $\Psi \models [\alpha \rightarrow \gamma \,|\, \beta]$ implies $\Psi \div \alpha \models [\alpha \rightarrow \gamma \,|\, \beta]$.

> *Explanation:* A contraction with α preserves that the implication $\alpha \rightarrow \gamma$ is believed even in absence of β, if β is more general than γ.

(IC4^{cond}) If $\gamma \models \beta$, then $\Psi \div \alpha \models [\neg\alpha \rightarrow \gamma \,|\, \beta]$ implies $\Psi \models [\neg\alpha \rightarrow \gamma \,|\, \beta]$.

> *Explanation:* If β is more general than γ, then if the implication $\neg\alpha \rightarrow \gamma$ is believed even in absence of β after contraction with α, then this was also previously the case.

By using contraposition and the correspondence between contractionals and contractions given by Proposition 9.18, we obtain the following non-conditional formulation of the principles (IC4^{cond}) and (IC4^{cond}):

(IC3) If $\gamma \models \beta$, then $\Psi \div \beta \models \alpha \rightarrow \gamma$ implies $\Psi \div \alpha \div \beta \models \alpha \rightarrow \gamma$.

(IC4) If $\gamma \models \beta$, then $\Psi \div \alpha \div \beta \models \neg\alpha \rightarrow \gamma$ implies $\Psi \div \beta \models \neg\alpha \rightarrow \gamma$.

Note that AGM contraction operators for epistemic states fulfil the inclusion postulate (C1), and therefore no contraction can add additional beliefs. The postulates (IC3) and (IC4) constrain further which beliefs should be retained. The postulate (IC3) ensures that a contraction with α does not affect the retention of implications with antecedent α by (specific) subsequent contractions. Dually, the postulate (IC4) expresses that a contraction with α does not influence whether (specific) subsequent contractions withdraw implications with antecedent $\neg\alpha$. The latter becomes apparent when reading (IC4) contrapositively:

If $\gamma \models \beta$, then $\Psi \div \beta \not\models \neg\alpha \rightarrow \gamma$ implies $\Psi \div \alpha \div \beta \not\models \neg\alpha \rightarrow \gamma$.

The following proposition states equivalence between (IC3^{cond}) and (IC3), and equivalence between (IC4^{cond}) and (IC4).

Proposition 10.19. *Let $\mathcal{E}$ be a set of epistemic states and let $\div$ be an AGM contraction operator for $\mathcal{E}$. Then* (IC3^{cond}), *respectively* (IC4^{cond}), *is satisfied by $\div$ if and only if* (IC3^{cond}), *respectively* (IC4^{cond}), *is satisfied by $\div$.*

We show for the non-conditional postulates (IC3) and (IC3) that they characterize (IC3^{rel}) and (IC4^{rel}).

Proposition 10.20. *Let $\mathcal{E}$ be a set of epistemic states, let $\div$ be an AGM contraction operator for $\mathcal{E}$, and let $\Psi \mapsto \leq_\Psi$ be a faithful assignment that is contraction-compatible with $\div$. The operator $\div$ satisfies the postulate* (IC3), *respectively* (IC4), *if and only if* (IC3^{rel}), *respectively* (IC4^{rel}), *is satisfied.*

Proof. Let $\mathcal{E}$ be a set of epistemic states, let $\div$ be an AGM contraction operator for $\mathcal{E}$, i.e., $\div$ satisfies (C1)–(C7), and let $\Psi \mapsto \leq_\Psi$ be a faithful assignment that is contraction-compatible with $\div$. In the following, we will show the claim by considering the two directions of the claim independently.

The "$\Leftarrow$"-direction. Assume that (IC3^{rel}), respectively (IC4^{rel}), is satisfied. We will show that (IC3), respectively (IC4), is satisfied.

(IC3) Let $\gamma \models \beta$ and $\Psi \div \beta \models \alpha \to \gamma$. We show $\Psi \div \alpha \div \beta \models \alpha \to \gamma$ by contradiction, i.e., we conclude a contradiction from $\Psi \div \alpha \div \beta \not\models \alpha \to \gamma$. This implies that there exists some interpretation $\omega \in [\![\Psi \div \alpha \div \beta]\!]$ such that $\omega \not\models \alpha \to \gamma$ holds. Consequently, we have $\omega \models \neg\gamma \wedge \alpha$.

From the contraction-compatibility of $\div$ with $\Psi \mapsto \leq_\Psi$ we obtain the following two equations:

$$[\![\Psi \div \beta]\!] = [\![\Psi]\!] \cup \min([\![\neg\beta]\!], \leq_\Psi) \subseteq [\![\alpha \to \gamma]\!] \quad (10.29)$$

$$[\![\Psi \div \alpha \div \beta]\!] = [\![\Psi]\!] \cup \min([\![\neg\alpha]\!], \leq_\Psi) \cup \min([\![\neg\beta]\!], \leq_{\Psi \div \alpha}) \quad (10.30)$$

Following Equation (10.30), we have that either $\omega \in [\![\Psi]\!]$, $\omega \in \min([\![\neg\alpha]\!], \leq_\Psi)$ or $\omega \in \min([\![\neg\beta]\!], \leq_{\Psi \div \alpha})$ holds. For these three cases we have:

$\omega \in [\![\Psi]\!]$. If $\omega \in [\![\Psi]\!]$ we obtain the contradiction $\omega \models \alpha \to \gamma$ from Equation (10.29).

$\omega \in \min([\![\neg\alpha]\!], \leq_\Psi)$. Because we have $\omega \models \alpha$, this case is impossible.

$\omega \in \min([\![\neg\beta]\!], \leq_{\Psi\div\alpha})$. Because we already excluded $\omega \in [\![\Psi]\!]$, we assume $\omega \notin [\![\Psi]\!]$ in the following. Both together, $\omega \not\models \alpha \to \gamma$ and (10.29), imply that there exists some interpretation ω' with $\omega' \in \min([\![\neg\beta]\!], \leq_\Psi)$ and $\omega' <_\Psi \omega$. Using (10.29) we obtain that either $\omega' \models \neg\alpha$ or $\omega' \models \gamma$ holds. The latter case is impossible, as we have $\gamma \models \beta$ and $\omega' \models \neg\beta$. We consider the only remaining possibility of $\omega' \models \neg\alpha$. Because we have $\omega' \in [\![\neg\alpha]\!]$, $\omega \in [\![\alpha]\!]$ and $\omega' <_\Psi \omega$, we obtain $\omega' <_{\Psi\div\alpha} \omega$ from (IC3^{rel}). We obtain a contradiction to $\omega \in \min([\![\neg\alpha]\!], \leq_{\Psi\div\alpha})$.

In summary, in all possible cases we obtain a contradiction. This shows that (IC3^{rel}) implies (IC3).

(IC4) Let $\gamma \models \beta$ and $\Psi \div \alpha \div \beta \models \neg\alpha \to \gamma$, i.e, $[\![\Psi \div \alpha \div \beta]\!] \subseteq [\![\alpha]\!] \cup [\![\gamma]\!]$ holds. We show that $\Psi \div \beta \models \neg\alpha \to \gamma$ holds. Towards a contradiction, we assume that there exists $\omega \in [\![\Psi \div \beta]\!]$ with $\omega \not\models \neg\alpha \to \gamma$, i.e., $\omega \models \neg\alpha \land \neg\gamma$. Because $\div$ is contraction-compatible with $\Psi \mapsto \leq_\Psi$, we have either $\omega \in [\![\Psi]\!]$ or $\omega \in \min([\![\neg\beta]\!], \leq_\Psi)$. In the first case, we obtain $\omega \in [\![\Psi \div \alpha \div \beta]\!]$, which yields the contradiction $\Psi \div \alpha \div \beta \not\models \neg\alpha \to \gamma$.

We consider the remaining case of $\omega \in \min([\![\neg\beta]\!], \leq_\Psi)$ and $\omega \notin [\![\Psi]\!]$. Because $\div$ is contraction-compatible with $\Psi \mapsto \leq_\Psi$ we obtain $\Psi \models \beta$ and $\min([\![\neg\beta]\!], \leq_{\Psi\div\alpha}) \subseteq [\![\Psi \div \alpha \div \beta]\!]$. Moreover, from $\gamma \models \beta$ we obtain $[\![\neg\beta]\!] \subseteq [\![\neg\gamma]\!]$. Consequently, $[\![\Psi \div \alpha \div \beta]\!] \subseteq [\![\alpha]\!] \cup [\![\gamma]\!]$, together with $\min([\![\neg\beta]\!], \leq_{\Psi\div\alpha}) \subseteq [\![\Psi \div \alpha \div \beta]\!]$ and $[\![\neg\beta]\!] \subseteq [\![\neg\gamma]\!]$, yields that every interpretation of $\min([\![\neg\beta]\!], \leq_{\Psi\div\alpha})$ is contained in $[\![\alpha]\!]$. Thus, because $\min([\![\neg\beta]\!], \leq_{\Psi\div\alpha})$ is non-empty, there is an interpretation $\omega' \in [\![\Psi \div \alpha \div \beta]\!]$ with $\omega' \in \min([\![\neg\beta]\!], \leq_{\Psi\div\alpha})$ and $\omega' \in [\![\alpha]\!]$. From $\omega \models \neg\beta$, we obtain $\omega' <_{\Psi\div\alpha} \omega$. Because we have $\omega \in [\![\neg\alpha]\!]$, $\omega' \in [\![\alpha]\!]$ and $\omega' <_{\Psi\div\alpha} \omega$, we obtain $\omega' <_\Psi \omega$ from the contrapositive form of (IC4^{rel}). This last observation is a contradiction to the minimality of ω, i.e., a contradiction to $\omega \in \min([\![\neg\beta]\!], \leq_\Psi)$.

The "⇒"-direction. We suppose that $\div$ satisfies (IC3), respectively (IC4). In the following, we show that (IC3^{rel}), respectively (IC4^{rel}), is satisfied.

(IC3^{rel}) Suppose $\omega_1 \in [\![\neg\alpha]\!]$, $\omega_2 \in [\![\alpha]\!]$ and $\omega_1 <_\Psi \omega_2$. We show $\omega_1 <_{\Psi\div\alpha} \omega_2$ in the following. Because $\Psi \mapsto \leq_\Psi$ is a faithful assignment, we obtain $\omega_2 \notin [\![\Psi]\!]$ from (FA2) and $\omega_1 <_{\Psi\div\alpha} \omega_2$. Next, we consider the case of $\omega_1 \in [\![\Psi]\!]$ and $\omega_1 \notin [\![\Psi]\!]$ independently.

In the case of $\omega_1 \in [\![\Psi]\!]$ we obtain $\omega_1 \in [\![\Psi\div\alpha]\!]$ and $\omega_2 \notin [\![\Psi\div\alpha]\!]$ from the contraction-compatibility of $\div$ with $\Psi \mapsto \leq_\Psi$ and $\omega_2 \in [\![\alpha]\!]$. By using faithfulness of $\Psi \mapsto \leq_\Psi$, we obtain $\omega_1 <_{\Psi\div\alpha} \omega_2$.

For the remaining case of $\omega_1 \notin [\![\Psi]\!]$ let $\beta = \neg(\omega_1 \vee \omega_2)$ and γ such that $[\![\gamma]\!] = [\![\Psi]\!]$. Clearly, we have $\gamma \models \beta$ and $\Psi \div \beta \models \alpha \to \gamma$. By applying (IC3) we obtain $\Psi \div \alpha \div \beta \models \alpha \to \gamma$, which implies $\omega_2 \notin [\![\Psi \div \alpha \div \beta]\!]$. Note that we have $[\![\neg\beta]\!] = \{\omega_1, \omega_2\}$ and thus, the contraction-compatibility of $\div$ with $\Psi \mapsto \leq_\Psi$ yields that either $\omega_1 \in [\![\Psi \div \alpha \div \beta]\!]$ or $\omega_2 \in [\![\Psi \div \alpha \div \beta]\!]$ holds. Because we have $\omega_2 \notin [\![\Psi \div \alpha \div \beta]\!]$, the latter is impossible. This renders $\omega_1 \in [\![\Psi \div \alpha \div \beta]\!]$ as the only possible case. We obtain $\omega_1 <_{\Psi\div\alpha} \omega_2$.

(IC4^{rel}) We show that the contraposition of (IC4^{rel}) holds. Suppose $\omega_1 \in [\![\neg\alpha]\!]$, $\omega_2 \in [\![\alpha]\!]$ and $\omega_2 <_{\Psi\div\alpha} \omega_1$. We will show $\omega_2 <_\Psi \omega_1$.

Because $\Psi \mapsto \leq_\Psi$ is a faithful assignment, and thus fulfils especially (FA2), we have that $\omega_2 <_{\Psi\div\alpha} \omega_1$ implies $\omega_1 \notin [\![\Psi \div \alpha]\!]$. In the following, let $\beta = \neg(\omega_1 \vee \omega_2)$, i.e., $[\![\neg\beta]\!] = \{\omega_1, \omega_2\}$. By using the contraction-compatibility of $\div$ with $\Psi \mapsto \leq_\Psi$, we obtain $[\![\Psi\div\alpha\div\beta]\!] = [\![\Psi\div\alpha]\!] \cup \min([\![\neg\beta]\!], \leq_{\Psi\div\alpha})$. Consequently, because of $\omega_2 <_{\Psi\div\alpha} \omega_1$ and $[\![\neg\beta]\!] = \{\omega_1, \omega_2\}$, we have $[\![\Psi \div \alpha \div \beta]\!] = [\![\Psi \div \alpha]\!] \cup \{\omega_2\}$. By using the contraction-compatibility of $\div$ with $\Psi \mapsto \leq_\Psi$ again, we obtain $[\![\Psi \div \alpha]\!] = [\![\Psi]\!] \cup \min([\![\neg\alpha]\!], \leq_\Psi)$. We consider two different cases in the following.

The case of $\omega_2 \in [\![\Psi\div\alpha]\!]$. From $[\![\Psi\div\alpha]\!] = [\![\Psi]\!] \cup \min([\![\neg\alpha]\!], \leq_\Psi)$, we obtain $\omega_2 \in [\![\Psi]\!]$. By using $\omega_1 \notin [\![\Psi \div \alpha \div \beta]\!]$, we obtain $\omega_1 \notin [\![\Psi]\!]$. In summary, for $\omega_2 \in [\![\Psi\div\alpha]\!]$, we obtain $\omega_2 <_\Psi \omega_1$ from the faithfulness of $\Psi \mapsto \leq_\Psi$ and $\omega_2 \in [\![\Psi]\!]$ and $\omega_1 \notin [\![\Psi]\!]$.

The case of $\omega_2 \notin [\![\Psi \div \alpha]\!]$. Recall that $\omega_2 <_{\Psi\div\alpha} \omega_1$ yields

$\omega_2 \in \min(\llbracket \neg\beta \rrbracket, \leq_{\Psi \div \alpha})$. Moreover, we obtain $\omega_1 \notin \llbracket \Psi \div \alpha \rrbracket$ from $\omega_2 <_{\Psi \div \alpha} \omega_1$. Consequently, $\gamma \models \beta$ holds for γ with $\gamma \equiv \text{Bel}(\Psi \div \alpha)$. Because of $\llbracket \Psi \div \alpha \div \beta \rrbracket = \llbracket \Psi \div \alpha \rrbracket \cup \min(\llbracket \neg\beta \rrbracket, \leq_{\Psi \div \alpha})$, we have $\Psi \div \alpha \div \beta \models \neg\alpha \to \gamma$. Application of (IC4) yields $\Psi \div \beta \models \neg\alpha \to \gamma$. Remember that we have $\llbracket \neg\beta \rrbracket = \{\omega_1, \omega_2\}$, and consequently, the contraction-compatibility of $\div$ with $\Psi \mapsto \leq_\Psi$, implies that $\omega_1 \in \llbracket \Psi \div \beta \rrbracket$ or $\omega_2 \in \llbracket \Psi \div \beta \rrbracket$ holds. The case $\omega_1 \in \llbracket \Psi \div \beta \rrbracket$ is impossible due to $\omega_1 \not\models \neg\alpha \to \gamma$ and $\Psi \div \beta \models \neg\alpha \to \gamma$. The case of $\omega_2 \in \llbracket \Psi \div \beta \rrbracket$ remains the only possible case. Because of $\omega_1 \in \llbracket \Psi \div \beta \rrbracket$ and $\omega_2 \in \llbracket \Psi \div \beta \rrbracket$, we obtain $\omega_2 <_\Psi \omega_1$ from the faithfulness of $\Psi \mapsto \leq_\Psi$. $\square$

Next, we consider alternatives to (IC3^{cond}) and (IC4^{cond}) when (IC1) and (IC2) are given.

10.4.4. Alternatives for (IC3^{rel}) and (IC4^{rel}) in the Context of (IC1) and (IC2)

One might observe that (IC3^{cond}) and (IC4^{cond}) are more complex than (IC3$^{\text{cond}}_{\text{ca}}$) and (IC4$^{\text{cond}}_{\text{ca}}$), and also that (IC3^{cond}) and (IC4^{cond}) are more complex than their counter-parts for revision operators (IR3) and (IR4). In the following, we establish that if (IC1^{cond}) and (IC2^{cond}) are given, then the postulates (IC3^{cond}) and (IC4^{cond}) can be simplified. Consider the following postulates[6]:

(IC3$^{\text{cond}}_{\text{alt}}$) If $\neg\alpha \models \gamma$, then $\Psi \models [\gamma | \beta]$ implies $\Psi \div \alpha \models [\gamma | \beta]$.

 Explanation: A contraction with α preserves the acceptance of a contractional if its conclusion γ is more general than $\neg\alpha$.

(IC4$^{\text{cond}}_{\text{alt}}$) If $\alpha \models \gamma$, then $\Psi \div \alpha \models [\gamma | \beta]$ implies $\Psi \models [\gamma | \beta]$.

 Explanation: If a contractional whose conclusion γ is more general than α is accepted after a contraction with α, then the contractional should be accepted previously.

By using contraposition and the correspondence between contractionals and contractions, the following non-conditional formulation of the principles (IC3$^{\text{cond}}_{\text{alt}}$) and (IC4$^{\text{cond}}_{\text{alt}}$) can be obtained:

---

6 The subscript *alt* stands for *alternative*.

(IC3$_{\text{alt}}$) If $\neg\alpha \models \gamma$, then $\Psi \div \beta \models \gamma$ implies $\Psi \div \alpha \div \beta \models \gamma$.

(IC4$_{\text{alt}}$) If $\alpha \models \gamma$, then $\Psi \div \alpha \div \beta \models \gamma$ implies $\Psi \div \beta \models \gamma$.

The following proposition establishes equivalence of (IC3$_{\text{alt}}^{\text{cond}}$) and (IC3$_{\text{alt}}$), respectively equivalence between (IC4$_{\text{alt}}^{\text{cond}}$) and (IC4$_{\text{alt}}$).

Proposition 10.21. *Let $\mathcal{E}$ be a set of epistemic states and let $\div$ be an AGM contraction operator for $\mathcal{E}$. Then* (IC3$_{\text{alt}}$), *respectively* (IC4$_{\text{alt}}$), *is satisfied by $\div$ if and only if* (IC3$_{\text{alt}}^{\text{cond}}$), *respectively* (IC4$_{\text{alt}}^{\text{cond}}$), *is satisfied by $\div$.*

The following proposition shows that (IC3) and (IC4) are indeed equivalent to (IC3$_{\text{alt}}$) and (IC4$_{\text{alt}}$) in the context of (IC1) and (IC2).

Proposition 10.22. *Let $\mathcal{E}$ be a set of epistemic states and let $\div$ be an AGM contraction operator for $\mathcal{E}$. The following two statements hold:*

- *If $\div$ satisfies* (IC1), *then $\div$ satisfies* (IC3$_{\text{alt}}$) *if and only if $\div$ satisfies* (IC3).
- *If $\div$ satisfies* (IC2), *then $\div$ satisfies* (IC4$_{\text{alt}}$) *if and only if $\div$ satisfies* (IC4).

Proof. Let $\mathcal{E}$ be a set of epistemic states, let $\div$ be an AGM contraction operator for $\mathcal{E}$ and let $\Psi \mapsto \leq_\Psi$ be faithful assignment for $\mathcal{E}$ that is contraction-compatible with $\div$ (guaranteed by Proposition 9.3). Note that due to Proposition 10.16, satisfaction of (IC1) is equivalent to satisfaction of (IC1^{rel}), and satisfaction of (IC2) is equivalent to satisfaction of (IC2^{rel}), respectively. The general proof strategy is to show that (IC3$_{\text{alt}}$) is equivalent to (IC3^{rel}) in the light of (IC1^{rel}), and to show that (IC4$_{\text{alt}}$) is equivalent to (IC4^{rel}) in the light of (IC2^{rel}), respectively.

Next, we show that (IC3^{rel}) is satisfied when (IC3$_{\text{alt}}$) is satisfied, and we show satisfaction of (IC4^{rel}) when (IC4$_{\text{alt}}$) is satisfied, respectively.

(IC3^{rel}) Suppose $\omega_1 \in [\![\neg\alpha]\!]$, $\omega_2 \in [\![\alpha]\!]$ and $\omega_1 <_\Psi \omega_2$. We will show $\omega_1 <_{\Psi \div \alpha} \omega_2$. In the following let $\beta = \neg(\omega_1 \vee \omega_2)$. Since $\Psi \mapsto \leq_\Psi$ is a faithful assignment, we obtain $\omega_2 \notin [\![\Psi]\!]$ from (FA2). By using the contraction-compatibility of $\div$ with $\Psi \mapsto \leq_\Psi$, we obtain $\omega_2 \notin [\![\Psi \div \beta]\!]$ and $\omega_1 \in [\![\Psi \div \beta]\!]$. Now let $\gamma = \gamma' \vee \neg\alpha$, where γ' is a formula with $[\![\Psi \div \beta]\!] \cup \{\omega_1\} = [\![\gamma']\!]$. Consequently, we obtain $\neg\alpha \models \gamma$, and we have that $\omega_1 \models \gamma$ and $\omega_2 \not\models \gamma$ holds. From (IC3$_{\text{alt}}$) we conclude $\Psi \div \alpha \div \beta \models \gamma$. The latter observation implies $\omega_2 \notin [\![\Psi \div \alpha \div \beta]\!]$. Note that $[\![\neg\beta]\!] = \{\omega_1, \omega_2\}$ and thus, the contraction-compatibility of $\div$ with $\Psi \mapsto \leq_\Psi$ yields $\omega_1 \in [\![\Psi \div \alpha \div \beta]\!]$ or $\omega_2 \in [\![\Psi \div \alpha \div \beta]\!]$. Since the latter leads to a contradiction, $\omega_1 \in [\![\Psi \div \alpha \div \beta]\!]$ is the only possible case. We obtain $\omega_1 <_{\Psi \div \alpha} \omega_2$.

(IC4^{rel}) We show (IC4^{rel}) by contraposition. Suppose $\omega_1 \in [\![\neg\alpha]\!]$, $\omega_2 \in [\![\alpha]\!]$ and $\omega_2 <_{\Psi \div \alpha} \omega_1$. We will show $\omega_2 <_\Psi \omega_1$. Since $\Psi \mapsto \leq_\Psi$ is a faithful assignment, we obtain $\omega_1 \notin [\![\Psi \div \alpha]\!]$ from (FA2). Let $\beta = \neg(\omega_1 \vee \omega_2)$ in the following. Because $\div$ is contraction-compatible with $\Psi \mapsto \leq_\Psi$, we have $[\![\Psi \div \alpha \div \beta]\!] = [\![\Psi \div \alpha]\!] \cup \min([\![\neg\beta]\!], \leq_{\Psi \div \alpha})$. Consequently, $\omega_2 <_{\Psi \div \alpha} \omega_1$ implies $[\![\Psi \div \alpha \div \beta]\!] = [\![\Psi \div \alpha]\!] \cup \{\omega_2\}$. Now let $\gamma = \gamma' \vee \alpha$, where γ' is a formula with $[\![\gamma']\!] = [\![\Psi \div \alpha]\!] \cup \{\omega_2\}$. By definition of γ it is the case that $\Psi \div \alpha \div \beta \models \gamma$. Furthermore, by definition, we have $\alpha \models \gamma$ and $\omega_1 \not\models \gamma$ and $\omega_2 \models \gamma$. Because of these observations, we obtain $\Psi \div \beta \models \gamma$ from application of (IC4$_{\text{alt}}$). Recall that $\div$ is contraction-compatible with $\Psi \mapsto \leq_\Psi$, and therefore, at least one of $\omega_1 \in [\![\Psi \div \beta]\!]$ or $\omega_2 \in [\![\Psi \div \beta]\!]$ holds. Since we have $\Psi \div \beta \models \gamma$, the former case of $\omega_1 \in [\![\Psi \div \beta]\!]$ is not possible. From $\omega_2 \in [\![\Psi \div \beta]\!]$ and (FA2) we obtain $\omega_2 <_\Psi \omega_1$.

By employing Proposition 10.20, we obtain that (IC3$_{\text{alt}}$) implies (IC3), and that (IC3$_{\text{alt}}$) implies (IC4), respectively.

For the other direction, we will show that (IC3$_{\text{alt}}$) is satisfied when (IC1^{rel}) and (IC3^{rel}) are given, and we show that (IC4$_{\text{alt}}$) is satisfied when (IC2^{rel}) and (IC4^{rel}) are given, respectively.

(IC3$_{\text{alt}}$) Suppose that $\neg\alpha \models \gamma$ and $\Psi \div \beta \models \gamma$ holds. From the contraction-compatibility of $\div$ with $\Psi \mapsto \leq_\Psi$ we obtain the following two equations:

$$[\![\Psi \div \beta]\!] = [\![\Psi]\!] \cup \min([\![\neg\beta]\!], \leq_\Psi) \subseteq [\![\gamma]\!] \tag{10.31}$$
$$[\![\Psi \div \alpha \div \beta]\!] = [\![\Psi]\!] \cup \min([\![\neg\alpha]\!], \leq_\Psi) \cup \min([\![\neg\beta]\!], \leq_{\Psi \div \alpha}). \tag{10.32}$$

To show satisfaction of (IC3$_{\text{alt}}$), we show that every $\omega \in [\![\Psi \div \alpha \div \beta]\!]$ is a model of γ. By Equation (10.32), we have that either $\omega \in$

$\llbracket \Psi \rrbracket$, $\omega \in \min(\llbracket \neg \alpha \rrbracket, \leq_\Psi)$ or $\omega \in \min(\llbracket \neg \beta \rrbracket, \leq_{\Psi \div \alpha})$ holds. In the following we consider these three cases:

$\omega \in \llbracket \Psi \rrbracket$. For this case, we obtain $\omega \models \gamma$ from Equation (10.31).

$\omega \in \min(\llbracket \neg \alpha \rrbracket, \leq_\Psi)$. We obtain $\omega \in \llbracket \neg \alpha \rrbracket$ from $\omega \in \min(\llbracket \neg \alpha \rrbracket, \leq_\Psi)$. Consequently, the assumption $\neg \alpha \models \gamma$ implies $\omega \models \gamma$.

$\omega \in \min(\llbracket \neg \beta \rrbracket, \leq_{\Psi \div \alpha})$. As shown before, we have that $\omega \models \neg \alpha$ implies $\omega \models \gamma$. For the remaining case of $\omega \models \alpha$, we show $\omega \models \gamma$ by contradiction, i.e., we assume $\omega \models \neg \gamma$ in the following. Since $\min(\llbracket \neg \beta \rrbracket, \leq_\Psi)$ is non-empty and $\min(\llbracket \neg \beta \rrbracket, \leq_\Psi) \subseteq \llbracket \gamma \rrbracket$ holds, there must be an interpretation $\omega_1 \in \min(\llbracket \neg \beta \rrbracket, \leq_\Psi)$ with $\omega_1 <_\Psi \omega$. If $\omega_1, \omega \in \llbracket \alpha \rrbracket$, then $\omega_1 <_{\Psi \div \alpha} \omega$ by (IC1^{rel}). For $\omega_1 \in \llbracket \neg \alpha \rrbracket$ we conclude $\omega_1 <_{\Psi \div \alpha} \omega$ from $\omega \in \llbracket \alpha \rrbracket$ by using (IC3^{rel}). We have shown $\omega_1 <_{\Psi \div \alpha} \omega$ for all cases, which is a contradiction to the minimality of ω with respect to $\leq_{\Psi \div \alpha}$.

In summary, we obtain $\omega \models \gamma$, which implies $\Psi \div \alpha \div \beta \models \gamma$.

(IC4$_{\text{alt}}$) Suppose $\alpha \models \gamma$ and $\Psi \div \alpha \div \beta \models \gamma$. The contraction-compatibility of $\div$ with $\Psi \mapsto \leq_\Psi$ yields $\llbracket \Psi \rrbracket \subseteq \llbracket \gamma \rrbracket$ and $\min(\llbracket \neg \beta \rrbracket, \leq_{\Psi \div \alpha}) \subseteq \llbracket \gamma \rrbracket$. Let $\omega_1 \in \llbracket \neg \beta \rrbracket$ such that $\omega_1 \notin \min(\llbracket \neg \beta \rrbracket, \leq_{\Psi \div \alpha})$. We show that either $\omega_1 \notin \min(\llbracket \neg \beta \rrbracket, \leq_\Psi)$ or $\omega_1 \models \gamma$ holds, which is equivalent to showing that $\div$ satisfies (IC4$_{\text{alt}}$). Let $\omega_2 \in \min(\llbracket \neg \beta \rrbracket, \leq_{\Psi \div \alpha})$ and thus, $\omega_2 <_{\Psi \div \alpha} \omega_1$. We consider three cases:

The case of $\omega_1 \in \llbracket \alpha \rrbracket$. The assumption $\alpha \models \gamma$ yields $\omega \models \gamma$.

The case of $\omega_1 \in \llbracket \neg \alpha \rrbracket$ and $\omega_2 \in \llbracket \alpha \rrbracket$. By contraposition of (IC4^{rel}) we obtain $\omega_2 <_\Psi \omega_1$.

The case of $\omega_1, \omega_2 \in \llbracket \neg \alpha \rrbracket$. We conclude from (IC2^{rel}) that $\omega_2 <_\Psi \omega_1$ holds.

This shows that either $\omega_2 <_\Psi \omega_1$ or $\omega_1 \models \gamma$. The first case implies $\omega_1 \notin \min(\llbracket \neg \beta \rrbracket, \leq_\Psi)$, and thus yields $\min(\llbracket \neg \beta \rrbracket, \leq_\Psi) \subseteq \llbracket \gamma \rrbracket$. This shows that we have $\llbracket \Psi \div \beta \rrbracket = \llbracket \Psi \rrbracket \cup \min(\llbracket \neg \beta \rrbracket, \leq_\Psi) \subseteq \llbracket \gamma \rrbracket$.

In summary, we have shown the desired result.   □

10.5. Summary and Characterization Theorem

We started this chapter by considering the Darwiche-Pearl postulates for iterated revision. For iterated contraction, we undertook two syntactic approaches to obtain analogue postulates and we could demonstrate that these approaches do not lead to the desired results. We continued by considering the semantic postulates $(IC1^{rel})$–$(IC4^{rel})$ and showed step by step that (IC1)–(IC4) are appropriate counterparts that highlight also the role of contractional beliefs. To summarize the main results of these investigations, we present a characterization theorem for the sets of novel postulates presented.

Theorem 10.23 (Extended Characterization Theorem). *Let $\mathcal{E}$ be a set of epistemic states, let $\div$ be an AGM contraction operator for $\mathcal{E}$, and let $\Psi \mapsto \leq_\Psi$ be a faithful assignment for $\mathcal{E}$ that is contraction-compatible with $\div$.*
The following statements are equivalent:

- *The operator $\div$ satisfies (IC1)–(IC4).*
- *The operator $\div$ satisfies $(IC1^{cond})$–$(IC4^{cond})$.*
- *The operator $\div$ satisfies $(IC1^{rel})$–$(IC4^{rel})$.*
- *The operator $\div$ satisfies (IC1), (IC2), $(IC3_{alt})$ and $(IC4_{alt})$.*
- *The operator $\div$ satisfies $(IC1^{cond})$, $(IC2^{cond})$, $(IC3^{cond}_{alt})$ and $(IC4^{cond}_{alt})$.*
- *The operator $\div$ satisfies $(IC1_{KPP})$–$(IC4_{KPP})$.*

We have shown that all the groups of postulates considered in Theorem 10.23 are equivalent to $(IC1^{rel})$–$(IC4^{rel})$ in the context of AGM contraction operators for epistemic states. In particular, the class of AGM contraction operators for epistemic states which fulfil the iteration postulates $(IC1_{KPP})$ to $(IC4_{KPP})$ from Konieczny and Pino Pérez [98] for contraction can be expressed equivalently by any of the two groups of postulates (IC1) to (IC4) and $(IC1^{cond})$ to $(IC4^{cond})$ considered here in this chapter and summarized in Table 10.2. Moreover, results closely related to the equivalences between (IC1)–(IC4) and $(IC1^{rel})$–$(IC4^{rel})$ stated in Theorem 10.23 have been obtained independently by Eric Raidl and Hans Rott [122].

We want to highlight that each of (IC1)–(IC4) corresponds exactly to one of $(IC1^{rel})$–$(IC4^{rel})$. Thus, we have a situation similar as for AGM revision operators, where each (IR1)–(IR4) corresponds exactly to one of $(IR1^{rel})$–$(IR4^{rel})$. More precisely, for each $i \in \{1, 2, 3, 4\}$ and for each AGM contraction operator $\div$ for epistemic states (where $\Psi \mapsto \leq_\Psi$ is a corresponding assignment) we have:

$$\div \text{ satisfies (IC}i) \quad \text{iff} \quad \div \text{ satisfies (IC}i^{cond}) \quad \text{iff} \quad \div \text{ satisfies (IC}i^{rel})$$

The relation between (ICi) and (ICi^{rel}) is shown in Proposition 10.16 for (IC1) and (IC2), and for (IC3) and (IC4) in Proposition 10.20. The relation between (ICi) and (ICi^{cond}) is shown in Proposition 10.18 for (IC1) and (IC2), and for (IC3) and (IC4) in Proposition 10.19.

Finally, we want to remark that one could extend Theorem 10.23 by including also the syntactic postulates for iterated contractions by Chopra, Ghose, Meyer and Wong [40]. The rationale to not include their result is two-fold. First, their contraction postulates depend on a revision; this complicates specifying a class of operators, since for instance in the iterative case there are more revisions than contractions [98]. Moreover, the contraction postulates they are considering are slightly stronger, thus the exact relation is open to discover (cf. Section 9.2).

Chapter 11

Specific Contraction Strategies

The previous chapter, the Chapter 10, considers principles for the iteration of AGM contraction operators that cautiously restrict the change of conditional beliefs, as the Darwiche-Pearl postulates do for iterated revision. While the Darwiche-Pearl postulates are very popular, it has sometimes been argued [29, 82, 30] that using the Darwiche-Pearl postulates alone are not enough, as they are too liberal in the sense that they are not ruling out some potentially unwanted cases [82]. The research community considered several principles for iterated revision, by which the Darwiche-Pearl postulates can be accompanied, to restrict iterated revision furthermore. For iterated contraction only a few principles where discussed so-far [112, 111, 123].

In this chapter, we investigate principles for AGM contraction operators for epistemic states, that go beyond, yet are compatible with, the iteration postulates for contraction (the postulates (IC1)–(IC4)) we considered in the previous chapter. A motivation for these investigations is that one might argue that the principles we provided in the previous chapter for iterated contraction, especially those in Theorem 10.23, i.e., (IC1)–(IC4), inherit the drawback from the Darwiche-Pearl postulates of being too liberal. Our investigations take inspiration from three specific approaches for iterated revision: *natural revision* [32], *lexicographic revision* and the *independence principle* [82] for iterated revision. We consider corresponding counter-parts for contraction, i.e., for natural revision we consider *natural contraction* [112, 111, 123], and for lexicographic revision we consider *moderate contraction* [113].

A specific contribution of this chapter is a conditional perspective for natural and lexicographic counter-parts for iterated contraction. We discuss how to adapt the independence principle for revision to contraction. Moreover, we consider more gentle versions of natural contraction, moderate contraction and an independence principle for contraction. As in the previous chapter, we will characterize all considered contraction postulates by a syntactic perspective and by a semantic perspective, the change of belief, the change of conditional beliefs, and the change of relations over possible worlds. Finally, at the end of this chapter, connections between many postulates considered in this part are presented.

11.1. Specific Strategies for Revision

In the following, we briefly introduce natural revision, lexicographic revision and the independence principle for revision.

Minimal Change of Conditional Beliefs. As the first principle for revision, we consider the minimal change of conditional beliefs, which is given by the following postulates[1] [32]:

(IR_{min}^{cond}) If $\Psi * \alpha \models \neg\beta$, then $\Psi * \alpha \models (\gamma \mid \beta) \Leftrightarrow \Psi \models (\gamma \mid \beta)$.
(IR_{min}) If $\Psi * \alpha \models \neg\beta$, then $\mathrm{Bel}(\Psi * \alpha * \beta) = \mathrm{Bel}(\Psi * \beta)$.
(IR_{min}^{rel}) If $\omega_1, \omega_2 \notin [\![\Psi * \alpha]\!]$, then $\omega_1 \leq_\Psi \omega_2 \Leftrightarrow \omega_1 \leq_{\Psi * \alpha} \omega_2$.

Craig Boutilier proposed that minimality of change should be applied also to change of conditional beliefs [32], leading to the principle (IR_{min}^{cond}), which states that revision by α does not influence conditional beliefs for which the antecedence is inconsistent with the result of revision by α. AGM revision operators that satisfy (IR_{min}^{cond}) are sometimes also denoted as *natural revision* [29]. From Proposition 9.15 we obtain (IR_{min}), which is a counter-part to (IR_{min}^{cond}), which was already given in the literature [41]. The following proposition shows that when revising by α, satisfaction of (IR_{min}^{cond}) is equivalent to having that $\leq_{\Psi * \alpha}$ changes only minimally with respect to $\leq_\Psi$.

---

[1]   The subscript min stands for *minimization* of change in conditional beliefs.

Proposition 11.1 ([41]). *Let $\mathcal{E}$ be a set of epistemic states, let $*$ be an AGM revision operator for $\mathcal{E}$, and let $\Psi \mapsto \leq_\Psi$ be a faithful assignment that is revision-compatible with $*$. The following statements are equivalent:*

- *The operator $*$ satisfies $(\mathrm{IR}_{\min})$.*
- *The operator $*$ satisfies $(\mathrm{IR}_{\min}^{\mathrm{cond}})$.*
- *The postulate $(\mathrm{IR}_{\min}^{\mathrm{rel}})$ is satisfied.*

Darwiche and Pearl argue that absolute minimization of changes in conditional beliefs is not desirable for iterative belief revision [41], as it prevents evolution of the change strategy itself.

The Independence Principle. As the second principle, we consider *independence*, which is given by the following postulates[2] [82]:

$(\mathrm{IR}_{\mathrm{ind}})$ If $\Psi * \beta \not\models \neg\alpha$, then $\Psi * \alpha * \beta \models \alpha$.
$(\mathrm{IR}_{\mathrm{ind}}^{\mathrm{cond}})$ If $\Psi * \beta \not\models \neg\alpha$, then $\Psi * \alpha \models (\alpha \,|\, \beta)$.
$(\mathrm{IR}_{\mathrm{ind}}^{\mathrm{rel}})$ If $\omega_1 \in [\![\alpha]\!]$ and $\omega_2 \in [\![\neg\alpha]\!]$, then $\omega_1 \leq_\Psi \omega_2 \Rightarrow \omega_1 <_{\Psi*\alpha} \omega_2$.

The *independence* principle was introduced by Jin and Thielscher to avoid the introduction of unwanted dependencies between beliefs in the process of revision [82]. We skip an explanation of the notion of independence here and delegate this to the following section.

Due to Proposition 9.15 we obtain easily that $(\mathrm{IR}_{\mathrm{ind}}^{\mathrm{cond}})$ is an analogue to $(\mathrm{IR}_{\mathrm{ind}})$. It has been shown [29] that in the framework we consider here, $(\mathrm{IR}_{\mathrm{ind}})$ is equivalent to $(\mathrm{IR}_{\mathrm{ind}}^{\mathrm{rel}})$ whenever $*$ is an AGM revision operator. The following proposition summarizes these results.

Proposition 11.2 ([82, 29]). *Let $\mathcal{E}$ be a set of epistemic states, let $*$ be an AGM revision operator for $\mathcal{E}$, and let $\Psi \mapsto \leq_\Psi$ be a faithful assignment that is revision-compatible with $*$. The following statements are equivalent:*

- *The operator $*$ satisfies $(\mathrm{IR}_{\mathrm{ind}})$.*
- *The operator $*$ satisfies $(\mathrm{IR}_{\mathrm{ind}}^{\mathrm{cond}})$.*
- *The postulate $(\mathrm{IR}_{\mathrm{ind}}^{\mathrm{rel}})$ is satisfied.*

---

[2]   The subscript *ind* stands for *independence*.

Booth and Meyer point out [29] that the independence principle could be understood as a stronger version of (IR4) (given on p. 236). AGM revision operators that satisfy (IR1), (IR2) and (IR$_{ind}$) are called *admissible* revision operators [29].

Lexicographic Revision.   As last principle, we consider lexicographic revisions which are given by (IR1), (IR2) and by one of the following postulates[3] [110, 29]:

(IR$_{lex}$) If $\beta \not\models \neg\alpha$, then $\Psi * \alpha * \beta \models \alpha$.
(IR$_{lex}^{cond}$) If $\Psi * \beta \not\models \neg\alpha$, then $\Psi * \alpha \models (\alpha \mid \beta)$.
(IR$_{lex}^{rel}$) If $\omega_1 \in [\![\alpha]\!]$ and $\omega_2 \in [\![\neg\alpha]\!]$, then $\omega_1 <_{\Psi*\alpha} \omega_2$.

The postulate (IR$_{lex}$) is sometimes also called *recalcitrance* [82, 29]. Lexicographic revision was introduced by Nayak as an approach to revision which gives higher priority to beliefs compatible with new information than to other beliefs, while staying sensitive to the priorities given by the revision history [110]. Equivalence of (IR$_{lex}$) and (IR$_{lex}^{cond}$) is given by Proposition 9.15 and the equivalence between (IR$_{lex}$) and (IR$_{lex}^{rel}$) has been shown by Booth and Meyer [29].

Proposition 11.3 ([29]). *Let $\mathcal{E}$ be a set of epistemic states, let $*$ be an AGM revision operator for $\mathcal{E}$, and let $\Psi \mapsto \leq_\Psi$ be a faithful assignment that is revision-compatible with $*$. The following statements are equivalent:*

- *The operator $*$ satisfies (IR$_{lex}$).*
- *The operator $*$ satisfies (IR$_{lex}^{cond}$).*
- *The postulate (IR$_{lex}^{rel}$) is satisfied.*

Lexicographic revision, as presented here, has been identified as one of the most conservative (admissible) revision operators [29]. Note that other variations of lexicographic revision are considered, and the version we use here is also denoted as *simple* lexicographic revision [113].

---

[3]   The subscript *lex* stands for *lexicographic*.

11.2. Independence for Contraction

In this section, we discuss multiple contraction analogues to the independence principle for revision by Jin and Thielscher [82], which was introduced in the previous section. We will start by introducing the notion of dependence used by Jin and Thielscher and present then their independence principle. As the next step, we discuss the relation between acceptance of contractionals and independence in the context of AGM contraction operators for epistemic states. Afterwards, we consider different notions of independence for contraction, both based on the postulates for independent revision presented in the prior section.

Dependence and Independence for Revision and Contraction.
Jin and Thielscher based their independence principles for revision on the following notion of dependence:

Definition 11.4 (Revision-Dependence, adapted [82]). *Let $\mathcal{E}$ be a set of epistemic states and let $*$ be an AGM revision operator for $\mathcal{E}$. We say that α is* revision-dependent *on β in $\Psi \in \mathcal{E}$ (with respect to $*$) if $\Psi \models \alpha$ and $\Psi * \neg\beta \not\models \alpha$.*

Intuitively, revision-dependence of α on β states that α is revoked when β is invalidated. Based on their notion of dependence, Jin and Thielscher suggested

(IR$_{\text{ind}}$) If $\Psi * \neg\beta \not\models \neg\alpha$, then $\Psi * \alpha * \neg\beta \models \alpha$.

which is given in Section 11.1, but is presented here in a reformulated[4] way such that the correspondence to the notion of revision-dependence is highlighted. The premise of (IR$_{\text{ind}}$), $\Psi * \beta \not\models \neg\alpha$, is meant to express a weak form of "revision-independence", and the conclusion, $\Psi * \alpha * \beta \models \alpha$, expresses a stronger version of "revision-independence" [82]. Thus, (IR$_{\text{ind}}$) states (roughly) that if α is "revision-independent" of β in Ψ, then α is also "revision-independent" of β in $\Psi * \alpha$.

As we discussed in Section 9.4 (see p. 227), contractionals encode the independence with respect to a contraction operator. In particular, we argued that $\Psi \models [\beta \mid \alpha]$ expresses that believing in β is independent

---

4   Note that in the context considered here, substituting β by $\neg\beta$ in (IR$_{\text{ind}}$) has no influence on the constraint expressed by the postulate (IR$_{\text{ind}}$).

of believing in α with respect to Ψ (and with respect to an underlying AGM contraction operator for epistemic states). Based on this observation the following postulate

(ind-candidate) If $\Psi \models [\gamma \mid \beta]$, then $\Psi \div \alpha \models [\gamma \mid \beta]$.

seems to be an appropriate candidate for a notion of independence for contraction. Intuitively, the postulate (ind-candidate) expresses that whenever γ is independent of β in Ψ, then γ is also independent of β in $\Psi \div \alpha$. Unfortunately, (ind-candidate) implies the postulate $(\text{IC3}_{\text{dca}}^{\text{cond}})$, introduced in Section 10.2, where we showed that $(\text{IC3}_{\text{dca}}^{\text{cond}})$ is incompatible with AGM contraction operators for epistemic states (cf. Proposition 10.2). Consequently, (ind-candidate) is incompatible with AGM contraction operators for epistemic states as well.

Independence via Contractionals. As an alternative, we propose to consider the following postulates, which we already encountered in Section 10.4.4, as independence postulates:

$(\text{IC3}_{\text{alt}}^{\text{cond}})$ If $\neg\alpha \models \gamma$, then $\Psi \models [\gamma \mid \beta] \Rightarrow \Psi \div \alpha \models [\gamma \mid \beta]$.

$(\text{IC4}_{\text{alt}}^{\text{cond}})$ If $\alpha \models \gamma$, then $\Psi \div \alpha \models [\gamma \mid \beta] \Rightarrow \Psi \models [\gamma \mid \beta]$.

The postulates $(\text{IC3}_{\text{alt}}^{\text{cond}})$ expresses that, under the circumstances of $\neg\alpha \models \gamma$, that independence of γ from β is preserved when contracting α. Dually, $(\text{IC4}_{\text{alt}}^{\text{cond}})$ expresses that, under the circumstances of $\alpha \models \gamma$, no independence of γ from β is introduced when contracting α. In the following, we fully characterize $(\text{IC3}_{\text{alt}})$ and $(\text{IC4}_{\text{alt}})$ in the context for AGM contraction operators for epistemic states. To this end, we establish that the postulates

$(\text{IC3}_{\text{alt}}^{\text{rel}})$ If $\omega_1 \in \Omega$ and $\omega_2 \in [\![\alpha]\!]$, then $\omega_1 <_\Psi \omega_2 \Rightarrow \omega_1 <_{\Psi \div \alpha} \omega_2$.

$(\text{IC4}_{\text{alt}}^{\text{rel}})$ If $\omega_1 \in [\![\neg\alpha]\!]$ and $\omega_2 \in \Omega$, then $\omega_1 \leq_\Psi \omega_2 \Rightarrow \omega_1 \leq_{\Psi \div \alpha} \omega_2$.

capture $(\text{IC3}_{\text{alt}})$ and $(\text{IC4}_{\text{alt}})$, where $(\text{IC3}_{\text{alt}}^{\text{rel}})$ is a stronger version of $(\text{IC3}^{\text{rel}})$, and $(\text{IC4}_{\text{alt}}^{\text{rel}})$ is a stronger version of $(\text{IC4}^{\text{rel}})$.

Proposition 11.5. *Let $\mathcal{E}$ be a set of epistemic states, let $\div$ be an AGM contraction operator for $\mathcal{E}$, and let $\Psi \mapsto \leq_\Psi$ be a faithful assignment that is contraction-compatible with $\div$. The operator $\div$ satisfies (IC3$_{\mathrm{alt}}$), respectively (IC4$_{\mathrm{alt}}$), if and only if (IC3$_{\mathrm{alt}}^{\mathrm{rel}}$), respectively (IC4$_{\mathrm{alt}}^{\mathrm{rel}}$), is satisfied.*

Proof. The proof is similar to the proof of Proposition 10.22. We consider both direction of the claim independently.

At first, we show that (IC3$_{\mathrm{alt}}^{\mathrm{rel}}$) is satisfied when (IC3$_{\mathrm{alt}}$) is satisfied, and we show satisfaction of (IC4$_{\mathrm{alt}}^{\mathrm{rel}}$) when (IC4$_{\mathrm{alt}}$) is satisfied, respectively.

(IC3$_{\mathrm{alt}}^{\mathrm{rel}}$) Suppose $\omega_1 \in \Omega$, $\omega_2 \in [\![\alpha]\!]$ and $\omega_1 <_\Psi \omega_2$. We will show $\omega_1 <_{\Psi \div \alpha} \omega_2$. In the following let β be a formula such that $[\![\neg\beta]\!] = \{\omega_1, \omega_2\}$. Since $\Psi \mapsto \leq_\Psi$ is a faithful assignment, we obtain $\omega_2 \notin [\![\Psi]\!]$ from (FA2). By using the contraction-compatibility of $\div$ with $\Psi \mapsto \leq_\Psi$, we obtain $\omega_2 \notin [\![\Psi \div \beta]\!]$ and $\omega_1 \in [\![\Psi \div \beta]\!]$ from $\omega_1 <_\Psi \omega_2$. Now let $\gamma = \gamma' \vee \neg\alpha$, where γ' is a formula with $[\![\Psi \div \beta]\!] = [\![\gamma']\!]$. In summary, we have $\omega_1 \in [\![\gamma']\!]$ and $\neg\alpha \models \gamma$ and $\omega_1 \models \gamma$ and $\omega_2 \not\models \gamma$. From (IC3$_{\mathrm{alt}}$) we conclude $\Psi \div \alpha \div \beta \models \gamma$. The latter observation implies $\omega_2 \notin [\![\Psi \div \alpha \div \beta]\!]$. Note that $[\![\neg\beta]\!] = \{\omega_1, \omega_2\}$ and thus, the contraction-compatibility of $\div$ with $\Psi \mapsto \leq_\Psi$ yields $\omega_1 \in [\![\Psi \div \alpha \div \beta]\!]$ or $\omega_2 \in [\![\Psi \div \alpha \div \beta]\!]$. Since the latter leads to a contradiction, $\omega_1 \in [\![\Psi \div \alpha \div \beta]\!]$ remains as the only possible case. We obtain $\omega_1 <_{\Psi \div \alpha} \omega_2$.

(IC4$_{\mathrm{alt}}^{\mathrm{rel}}$) We show that the contraposition of (IC4$_{\mathrm{alt}}^{\mathrm{rel}}$) holds. Suppose $\omega_1 \in [\![\neg\alpha]\!]$, $\omega_2 \in \Omega$ and $\omega_2 <_{\Psi \div \alpha} \omega_1$. We will show $\omega_2 <_\Psi \omega_1$. Since $\Psi \mapsto \leq_\Psi$ is a faithful assignment, we obtain $\omega_1 \notin [\![\Psi \div \alpha]\!]$ from (FA2) and $\omega_2 <_{\Psi \div \alpha} \omega_1$. In the following let β be a formula such that $[\![\neg\beta]\!] = \{\omega_1, \omega_2\}$. Because $\div$ is contraction-compatible with $\Psi \mapsto \leq_\Psi$, we have $[\![\Psi \div \alpha \div \beta]\!] = [\![\Psi \div \alpha]\!] \cup \min([\![\neg\beta]\!], \leq_{\Psi \div \alpha})$. Consequently, $\omega_2 <_{\Psi \div \alpha} \omega_1$ implies $[\![\Psi \div \alpha \div \beta]\!] = [\![\Psi \div \alpha]\!] \cup \{\omega_2\}$. Now let $\gamma = \gamma' \vee \alpha$, where γ' is a formula with $[\![\gamma']\!] = [\![\Psi \div \alpha]\!] \cup \{\omega_2\}$. By definition of γ it is the case that $\Psi \div \alpha \div \beta \models \gamma$. Furthermore, by definition and $\omega_1 \notin [\![\Psi \div \alpha]\!]$, we have $\alpha \models \gamma$ and $\omega_1 \not\models \gamma$ and $\omega_2 \models \gamma$. Because of these observations, we obtain $\Psi \div \beta \models \gamma$ from application of (IC4$_{\mathrm{alt}}$). Recall that $\div$ is contraction-compatible with $\Psi \mapsto \leq_\Psi$, and therefore, at least one of $\omega_1 \in [\![\Psi \div \beta]\!]$ or $\omega_2 \in [\![\Psi \div \beta]\!]$ holds. Since we have

$\Psi \div \beta \models \gamma$, the former case of $\omega_1 \in [\![\Psi \div \beta]\!]$ is not possible. From $\omega_2 \in [\![\Psi \div \beta]\!]$ and (FA2) we obtain $\omega_2 <_\Psi \omega_1$.

Next, we show that (IC3$_{\text{alt}}$) is satisfied when (IC3$_{\text{alt}}^{\text{rel}}$) is given, and we show that (IC4$_{\text{alt}}$) is satisfied when (IC4$_{\text{alt}}^{\text{rel}}$) is given, respectively.

(IC3$_{\text{alt}}$) Suppose that $\neg\alpha \models \gamma$ and $\Psi \div \beta \models \gamma$ holds. From the contraction-compatibility of $\div$ with $\Psi \mapsto \leq_\Psi$ we obtain the following two equations:

$$[\![\Psi \div \beta]\!] = [\![\Psi]\!] \cup \min([\![\neg\beta]\!], \leq_\Psi) \subseteq [\![\gamma]\!] \tag{11.1}$$

$$[\![\Psi \div \alpha \div \beta]\!] = [\![\Psi]\!] \cup \min([\![\neg\alpha]\!], \leq_\Psi) \cup \min([\![\neg\beta]\!], \leq_{\Psi \div \alpha}). \tag{11.2}$$

To show satisfaction of (IC3$_{\text{alt}}$), we show that every $\omega \in [\![\Psi \div \alpha \div \beta]\!]$ is a model of γ. By Equation (11.2), we have that either $\omega \in [\![\Psi]\!]$, $\omega \in \min([\![\neg\alpha]\!], \leq_\Psi)$ or $\omega \in \min([\![\neg\beta]\!], \leq_{\Psi \div \alpha})$ holds. In the following we consider these three cases:

$\omega \in [\![\Psi]\!]$. For this case, we obtain $\omega \models \gamma$ from Equation (11.1).

$\omega \in \min([\![\neg\alpha]\!], \leq_\Psi)$. We obtain $\omega \in [\![\neg\alpha]\!]$ from $\omega \in \min([\![\neg\alpha]\!], \leq_\Psi)$. Consequently, the assumption $\neg\alpha \models \gamma$ implies $\omega \models \gamma$.

$\omega \in \min([\![\neg\beta]\!], \leq_{\Psi \div \alpha})$. As shown before, we have that $\omega \models \neg\alpha$ implies $\omega \models \gamma$. For the remaining case of $\omega \models \alpha$, we show $\omega \models \gamma$ by contradiction, i.e., we assume $\omega \models \neg\gamma$ in the following. Since $\min([\![\neg\beta]\!], \leq_\Psi)$ is non-empty and $\min([\![\neg\beta]\!], \leq_\Psi) \subseteq [\![\gamma]\!]$ holds, there must be an interpretation $\omega_1 \in \min([\![\neg\beta]\!], \leq_\Psi)$ with $\omega_1 <_\Psi \omega$. By using (IC3$_{\text{alt}}^{\text{rel}}$), we conclude $\omega_1 <_{\Psi \div \alpha} \omega$ from $\omega \in [\![\alpha]\!]$. We have shown $\omega_1 <_{\Psi \div \alpha} \omega$ for all cases, which is a contradiction to the minimality of ω with respect to $\leq_{\Psi \div \alpha}$.

In summary, we obtain $\omega \models \gamma$, which implies $\Psi \div \alpha \div \beta \models \gamma$.

(IC4$_{\text{alt}}$) Suppose $\alpha \models \gamma$ and $\Psi \div \alpha \div \beta \models \gamma$. The contraction-compatibility of $\div$ with $\Psi \mapsto \leq_\Psi$ yields $[\![\Psi]\!] \subseteq [\![\gamma]\!]$ and $\min([\![\neg\beta]\!], \leq_{\Psi \div \alpha}) \subseteq [\![\gamma]\!]$. Let $\omega_1 \in [\![\neg\beta]\!]$ such that $\omega_1 \notin \min([\![\neg\beta]\!], \leq_{\Psi \div \alpha})$. We show that either $\omega_1 \notin \min([\![\neg\beta]\!], \leq_\Psi)$ or $\omega_1 \models \gamma$ holds, which is equivalent to showing that $\div$ satisfies (IC4$_{\text{alt}}$). Let $\omega_2 \in \min([\![\neg\beta]\!], \leq_{\Psi \div \alpha})$ and thus, $\omega_2 <_{\Psi \div \alpha} \omega_1$. We consider two cases. If $\omega_1 \in [\![\alpha]\!]$, then $\alpha \models \gamma$ yields $\omega \models \gamma$. If $\omega_1 \in [\![\neg\alpha]\!]$, then, by using the contraposition of (IC4$_{\text{alt}}^{\text{rel}}$), we obtain $\omega_2 <_\Psi \omega_1$ from $\omega_2 <_{\Psi \div \alpha} \omega_1$. This shows that either $\omega_2 <_\Psi \omega_1$ or $\omega_1 \models \gamma$. The first case implies

$\omega_1 \notin \min(\llbracket\neg\beta\rrbracket, \leq_\Psi)$, and thus yields $\min(\llbracket\neg\beta\rrbracket, \leq_\Psi) \subseteq \llbracket\gamma\rrbracket$. In summary, we have $\llbracket\Psi \div \beta\rrbracket = \llbracket\Psi\rrbracket \cup \min(\llbracket\neg\beta\rrbracket, \leq_\Psi) \subseteq \llbracket\gamma\rrbracket$. $\square$

Next, we establish that (IC3$_{\text{alt}}$) and (IC4$_{\text{alt}}$) are satisfied by linear AGM contraction operators for epistemic states and by full meet AGM contraction operators for epistemic states.

Proposition 11.6. *Let $\mathcal{E}$ be a set of epistemic states, let $\div$ be an AGM contraction operator for $\mathcal{E}$. If $\div$ is linear or full meet, then (IC3$_{\text{alt}}$) and (IC4$_{\text{alt}}$) are satisfied.*

Proof. Observe that by Definition 9.7 and Proposition 9.6 we have $\omega_1 \leq_\Psi \omega_2$ if and only if $\omega_1 \leq_{\Psi\div\alpha} \omega_2$ for all $\omega_1, \omega_2 \notin \llbracket\Psi \div \alpha\rrbracket$. This, together with Proposition 11.5 and the contraction-compatibility of $\div$ with $\Psi \mapsto \leq_\Psi$ yields the claim. $\square$

A consequence of Proposition 11.6, together with Proposition 10.14 (see p. 253), is that (IC3$_{\text{alt}}$) and (IC4$_{\text{alt}}$) are compatible with the postulates (IC1)–(IC4).

Intuitively, (IC3$_{\text{alt}}$) and (IC4$_{\text{alt}}$) prevent revocation of existing independencies, and the introduction of independencies, respectively. However, the semantic characterization of (IC3$_{\text{alt}}$) and (IC4$_{\text{alt}}$) by Proposition 11.5 reveals that these postulates are not as strong as (IR$_{\text{ind}}$) for revision. In the following, we undertake a semantic approach to independence for contraction.

Semantic Independence Principle. We apply again the idea of obtaining a postulate for contraction by adapting the semantic postulate (IR$_{\text{ind}}^{\text{rel}}$) for revision, as we did in the Chapter 10, where we, e.g, considered (IC1)–(IC4), the analogues to (IR1^{rel})–(IR4^{rel}). More specifically, we adapt (IR$_{\text{ind}}^{\text{rel}}$), i.e., the postulate

If $\omega_1 \in \llbracket\alpha\rrbracket$ and $\omega_2 \in \llbracket\neg\alpha\rrbracket$, then $\omega_1 \leq_\Psi \omega_2 \Rightarrow \omega_1 <_{\Psi*\alpha} \omega_2$. ,

which is the semantic analogue to (IR$_{\text{ind}}$), to the following semantic postulate:

(IC$_{\text{ind}}^{\text{rel}}$) If $\omega_1 \in \llbracket\neg\alpha\rrbracket$ and $\omega_2 \in \llbracket\alpha\rrbracket\backslash\llbracket\Psi\rrbracket$, then $\omega_1 \leq_\Psi \omega_2 \Rightarrow \omega_1 <_{\Psi\div\alpha} \omega_2$.

Analogously to $(\text{IR}_{\text{ind}}^{\text{rel}})$ for revision, postulate $(\text{IC}_{\text{ind}}^{\text{rel}})$ demands strict improvement of counter-models of α over models of α when contracting by α. But to deal with the inclusion postulate of contraction (C1), which semantically expressed demands $[\![\Psi]\!] \subseteq [\![\Psi \div \alpha]\!]$, strict improvement has to be restricted to non-models of Ψ. A contractional counter-part to $(\text{IC}_{\text{ind}}^{\text{rel}})$ is the following postulate:

(IC_{ind}) If $\neg\alpha \models \gamma$ and $\Psi \div \beta \not\models \neg\alpha \to \beta$, then $\Psi \div \alpha \models \gamma \Rightarrow \Psi \div \alpha \div \beta \models \gamma$.

> *Explanation:* If contraction by β ensures that $\neg\alpha$ does not imply β, then every consequence γ of $\neg\alpha$, which is considered to be true after contraction with α, is not discarded by a subsequent contraction with β.

As before, we obtain an equivalent postulate to $(\text{IC}_{\text{ind}}^{\text{rel}})$ for contractionals by employing Proposition 9.18:

$(\text{IC}_{\text{ind}}^{\text{cond}})$ If $\neg\alpha \models \gamma$ and $\Psi \not\models [\neg\alpha \to \beta \,|\, \beta]$, then $\Psi \models [\gamma \,|\, \alpha] \Rightarrow \Psi \div \alpha \models [\gamma \,|\, \beta]$.

In the following, we will show that $(\text{IC}_{\text{ind}}^{\text{rel}})$ is equivalent to $(\text{IC}_{\text{ind}}^{\text{rel}})$ for AGM contraction operators for epistemic states.

Proposition 11.7. *Let $\mathcal{E}$ be a set of epistemic states, let $\div$ be an AGM contraction operator for $\mathcal{E}$, and let $\Psi \mapsto \leq_\Psi$ be a faithful assignment that is contraction-compatible with $\div$. The operator $\div$ satisfies the postulate $(\text{IC}_{\text{ind}}^{\text{rel}})$ if and only if (IC_{ind}) is satisfied.*

Proof. We show the direction from $(\text{IC}_{\text{ind}}^{\text{rel}})$ to (IC_{ind}) and the direction from (IC_{ind}) to $(\text{IC}_{\text{ind}}^{\text{rel}})$ independently.

From $(\text{IC}_{\text{ind}}^{\text{rel}})$ to (IC_{ind}). Let $\neg\alpha \models \gamma$ and $\Psi \div \alpha \models \gamma$ and $\Psi \div \beta \not\models \neg\alpha \to \beta$. Towards a contradiction, assume that $\Psi \div \alpha \div \beta \not\models \gamma$ holds. From this assumption and Proposition 9.3 we obtain that there exists some $\omega_2 \in \Omega$ such that $\omega_2 \not\models \gamma$ and

$$\omega_2 \in [\![\Psi \div \alpha \div \beta]\!] = [\![\Psi \div \alpha]\!] \cup \min([\![\neg\beta]\!], \leq_{\Psi \div \alpha}) \tag{11.3}$$

holds. From (11.3) and $\Psi \div \alpha \models \gamma$, we obtain $\omega_2 \in \min([\![\neg\beta]\!], \leq_{\Psi \div \alpha})$. Because we have $\omega_2 \not\models \gamma$, and we have $\neg\alpha \models \gamma$, we directly obtain $\omega_2 \models \neg\beta \wedge \alpha$.

From $\Psi \div \beta \not\models \neg\alpha \to \beta$ we obtain that there exists some $\omega_1 \in \Omega$ such that $\omega_1 \in [\![\Psi \div \beta]\!]$ and $\omega_1 \models \neg\alpha \wedge \neg\beta$ holds. From the observation that $\neg\beta$ is consistent, we obtain, by using Proposition 9.3 again, that $\omega_1 \in \min([\![\neg\beta]\!], \leq_\Psi) \subseteq [\![\Psi \div \beta]\!]$ holds.

In summary, we have $\omega_1 \in \min([\![\neg\beta]\!], \leq_\Psi) \cap [\![\neg\alpha]\!]$ and $\omega_2 \in \min([\![\neg\beta]\!], \leq_{\Psi \div \alpha}) \cap [\![\alpha]\!]$. The latter yields, together with $\omega_2 \not\models \gamma$ and $\Psi \div \alpha \models \gamma$, that $\omega_2 \notin [\![\Psi]\!]$ holds. From the first we obtain $\omega_1 \leq_\Psi \omega_2$, and thus by $(\mathrm{IC}_{\mathrm{ind}}^{\mathrm{rel}})$, we obtain $\omega_1 <_{\Psi \div \alpha} \omega_2$. This last observation contradicts the minimality of ω_2.

From $(\mathrm{IR}_{\mathrm{ind}}^{\mathrm{rel}})$ *to* $(\mathrm{IC}_{\mathrm{ind}}^{\mathrm{rel}})$. Let $\omega_1 \in [\![\neg\alpha]\!]$ and $\omega_2 \in [\![\alpha]\!] \setminus [\![\Psi]\!]$ and $\omega_1 \leq_\Psi \omega_2$. We show that $\omega_1 <_{\Psi \div \alpha} \omega_2$ holds.

Choose $\beta, \gamma \in \mathcal{L}$ such that $[\![\gamma]\!] = \Omega \setminus \{\omega_2\}$ and $[\![\neg\beta]\!] = \{\omega_1, \omega_2\}$. By definition, we obtain $\neg\alpha \models \gamma$. Because of $\omega_2 \notin [\![\Psi]\!]$ and $\omega_2 \models \alpha$ and contraction-compatibility of $\Psi \mapsto \leq_\Psi$ with $\div$ from Proposition 9.3, we have $\Psi \div \alpha \models \gamma$. Using contraction-compatibility again together with $\omega_1 \leq_\Psi \omega_2$ yields $\omega_1 \in [\![\Psi \div \beta]\!]$ and thus $\Psi \div \beta \not\models \neg\alpha \to \beta$, as $\omega_1 \not\models \neg\alpha \to \beta$. Since all preconditions are satisfied, we can apply $(\mathrm{IC}_{\mathrm{ind}})$ and obtain $\Psi \div \alpha \div \beta \models \gamma$. Because of $\omega_2 \not\models \gamma$, we obtain $\omega_2 \notin \Psi \div \alpha \div \beta$, implying $\omega_2 \notin \min([\![\neg\beta]\!], \leq_{\Psi \div \alpha})$. Because $\neg\beta$ has only two models, we obtain that $\omega_1 \in \min([\![\neg\beta]\!], \leq_{\Psi \div \alpha})$ holds. Consequently, we obtain the desired result $\omega_1 <_{\Psi \div \alpha} \omega_2$. □

Next, we consider the relation of $(\mathrm{IC}_{\mathrm{ind}})$ to linear AGM contraction operators for epistemic states and to full meet AGM contraction operators for epistemic states. At first, we establish that $(\mathrm{IC}_{\mathrm{ind}})$ are satisfied by linear AGM contraction operators for epistemic states.

Proposition 11.8. *Let $\mathcal{E}$ be a set of epistemic states, let $\div$ be an AGM contraction operator for $\mathcal{E}$. If $\div$ is linear, then $(\mathrm{IC}_{\mathrm{ind}})$ is satisfied.*

Proof. Observe that by Definition 9.7 we have $\omega_1 \leq_\Psi \omega_2$ if and only if $\omega_1 \leq_{\Psi \div \alpha} \omega_2$ for all $\omega_1, \omega_2 \notin [\![\Psi \div \alpha]\!]$. In particular, note that we have $\omega_1 <_\Psi \omega_2$ or $\omega_2 <_\Psi \omega_1$ for each $\omega_1, \omega_2 \notin [\![\Psi]\!]$ and $\Psi \in \mathcal{E}$. Having both observations, together with Proposition 11.7 and the contraction-compatibility of $\div$ with $\Psi \mapsto \leq_\Psi$, yields the claim. □

A consequence of Proposition 11.6, together with Proposition 10.14 (see p. 253), is that $(\mathrm{IC}_{\mathrm{ind}})$ is compatible with the postulates (IC1)–(IC4).

For full meet AGM contraction operators for epistemic states, we obtain that these operators, in general, do not satisfy (IC_{ind}). The following proposition considers sets of epistemic states $\mathcal{E}$ where at least one epistemic state $\Psi_{\mathcal{H}} \in \mathcal{E}$ exists and two interpretations that are not models of $Bel(\Psi_{\mathcal{H}})$, for instance, this is the case when $\mathcal{E}$ is unbiased.

Proposition 11.9. *Suppose $|\Sigma| \geq 2$. Let $\mathcal{E}$ be a set of epistemic states such that there is at least one epistemic state $\Psi_{\mathcal{H}} \in \mathcal{E}$ with $|\Omega \setminus [\![\Psi_{\mathcal{H}}]\!]| \geq 2$. Every full meet AGM contraction operators for $\mathcal{E}$ violates (IC_{ind}).*

Proof. Let $\div$ be a full meet AGM contraction operator for $\mathcal{E}$. Furthermore, let $\omega_1, \omega_2 \in \Omega$ such that $\omega_1, \omega_2 \notin [\![\Psi_{\mathcal{H}}]\!]$. From existence of $\div$, and existence of $\Psi_{\mathcal{H}}$, and $|\Sigma| \geq 2$, and Proposition 9.12 we obtain that there exists an epistemic state $\Phi \in \mathcal{E}$ with $\omega_1, \omega_2 \notin [\![\Phi]\!]$ and $[\![\Phi]\!] \neq \emptyset$. Let $\omega \in [\![\Phi]\!]$ and let α be a formula such that $[\![\neg\alpha]\!] = \{\omega, \omega_1\}$. By Proposition 9.6, we obtain that $\div$ is contraction-compatible with the flat faithful assignment $\Psi \mapsto \leq_\Psi^{flat}$ for $\mathcal{E}$ (see p. 220). From this, we obtain that $[\![\Phi \div \alpha]\!] = [\![\Phi]\!]$ and $\omega_1 \leq_\Psi^{flat} \omega_2$ and $\omega_2 \leq_{\Psi \div \alpha}^{flat} \omega_1$, i.e., $\omega_1 \not<_{\Psi \div \alpha}^{flat} \omega_2$. This provides a violation of (IC_{ind}) by $\div$. $\qquad\square$

From Proposition 11.9 and Proposition 11.6 we immediately obtain that (IC_{ind}) describes an iteration principle which is different from $(IC3_{alt})$ and $(IC4_{alt})$, as full meet AGM contraction operators for epistemic states satisfy $(IC3_{alt})$ and $(IC4_{alt})$ (see Proposition 11.6).

11.3. Natural and Moderate Contraction

A fundamental investigation of strategies for iterated contraction is due to Nayak, Orgun et al. [112, 111, 123]. In particular, they consider different types of iterated contraction approaches, defined from a semantic viewpoint. We consider natural contraction and moderate contraction:

- *Natural Contraction*: Shift the relation between worlds as little as possible when contracting. This is also known as *conservative contraction*.

- *Moderate Contraction*: After contraction of α, strictly prefer counter models of α over models of α (whenever possible). This is also known as *priority contraction*.

Characterizations in syntactic terms of these contraction operations are given in the literature [112, 111, 123]. In the following, we will present elegant alternative characterizations in terms of change of belief in contractionals.

Natural Contraction. Following Ramachandran et al. [123], we define natural contraction as operators keeping as much as possible of the prior total preorder when changing.

Definition 11.10 (Natural Contraction, Adapted, [123]). *Let $\mathcal{E}$ be a set of epistemic states, let $\div$ be an AGM contraction operator for $\mathcal{E}$, and let $\Psi \mapsto \leq_\Psi$ be a faithful assignment that is contraction-compatible with $\div$. The operator $\div$ is said to be a* natural contraction *if the following holds[5]:*

$(\mathrm{IC}_{\mathrm{nc}}^{\mathrm{rel}})$ *If $\omega_1, \omega_2 \notin [\![\Psi \div \alpha]\!]$, then $\omega_1 \leq_\Psi \omega_2 \Leftrightarrow \omega_1 \leq_{\Psi \div \alpha} \omega_2$.*

Briefly explained, natural contraction describes such AGM contraction operators for epistemic states where preferences between worlds changes minimally, i.e., $(\mathrm{IC}_{\mathrm{nc}}^{\mathrm{rel}})$ demands to change the total preorder $\leq_\Psi$ as minimally as possible. As shown in Proposition 9.18, the total preorder $\leq_\Psi$ determines the contractionals accepted by Ψ, and vice versa, respectively. Thus, $(\mathrm{IC}_{\mathrm{nc}}^{\mathrm{rel}})$ also expresses that believing in contractionals is affected minimally when changing Ψ to $\Psi \div \alpha$. It has been shown that natural contraction is characterized by the following postulate [111, 123]:

(Insertion) If $\beta \in \mathrm{Bel}(\Psi \div \alpha)$, then $\mathrm{Bel}(\Psi \div \alpha \div \beta) = \mathrm{Bel}(\Psi \div \alpha) \cap \mathrm{Bel}(\Psi \div \beta)$.

However, (Insertion) provides only a limited overview of the impact on conditional beliefs. In the following, we provide a postulate which highlights how natural contraction alters conditional beliefs. We provide a succinct characterization by α-equivalence in the following proposition.

---

[5] The subscript *nc* stands for *natural contraction*.

Proposition 11.11. *Let $\mathcal{E}$ be a set of epistemic states and let $\div$ be an AGM contraction operator for $\mathcal{E}$. Then $\div$ is a natural contraction if and only if the following is satisfied:*

(IC$_{\mathrm{nc}}^{\mathrm{cond}}$) *If $\Psi \div \alpha \models \beta$, then $\Psi \div \alpha \models [\neg\beta \to \gamma \,|\, \beta]$ if and only if $\Psi \models [\neg\beta \to \gamma \,|\, \beta]$.*

Proof. Let $\Psi \mapsto \leq_\Psi$ be a faithful assignment that is contraction-compatible with $\div$. First, note that due to Proposition 9.24 the postulate (IC$_{\mathrm{nc}}^{\mathrm{cond}}$) is equivalent to:

(IC$_{\mathrm{nc}}$) *If $\Psi \div \alpha \models \beta$, then $\mathrm{Bel}(\Psi \div \alpha \div \beta) \equiv_{\neg\beta} \mathrm{Bel}(\Psi \div \beta)$.*

We show equivalence of (IC$_{\mathrm{nc}}$) and (IC$_{\mathrm{nc}}^{\mathrm{rel}}$) by considering both directions of the claim independently.

From (IC$_{\mathrm{nc}}$) *to* (IC$_{\mathrm{nc}}^{\mathrm{rel}}$). Suppose that $\omega_1, \omega_2 \notin [\![\Psi \div \alpha]\!]$ holds. We show equivalence of $\omega_1 <_\Psi \omega_2$ and $\omega_1 <_{\Psi \div \alpha} \omega_2$ in two steps.

First, assume that $\omega_1 <_\Psi \omega_2$ holds. We show that $\omega_1 <_{\Psi \div \alpha} \omega_2$ holds. Let β such that $[\![\beta]\!] = \Omega \setminus \{\omega_1, \omega_2\}$ holds. By Proposition 9.3, we obtain $\Psi \div \alpha \models \beta$, i.e. $[\![\Psi \div \alpha]\!] \cap [\![\neg\beta]\!] = \emptyset$. Moreover, because of $\omega_1 <_\Psi \omega_2$ and Proposition 9.3 we obtain $[\![\Psi \div \beta]\!] \cap [\![\neg\beta]\!] = \{\omega_1\}$. Employing (IC$_{\mathrm{nc}}$) yields $[\![\Psi \div \alpha \div \beta]\!] \cap [\![\neg\beta]\!] = \{\omega_1\}$. In summary, together with Proposition 9.3, we obtain $\omega_1 <_{\Psi \div \alpha} \omega_2$.

Second, assume that $\omega_1 <_{\Psi \div \alpha} \omega_2$ holds. We show that $\omega_1 <_\Psi \omega_2$ holds. Let β such that $[\![\beta]\!] = \Omega \setminus \{\omega_1, \omega_2\}$ holds. We obtain $[\![\Psi \div \alpha \div \beta]\!] \cap [\![\neg\beta]\!] = \{\omega_1\}$. Because of (IC$_{\mathrm{nc}}$), we also have $[\![\Psi \div \beta]\!] \cap [\![\neg\beta]\!] = \{\omega_1\}$. This implies $\omega_1 <_\Psi \omega_2$.

From (IC$_{\mathrm{nc}}^{\mathrm{rel}}$) *to* (IC$_{\mathrm{nc}}$). From $\Psi \div \alpha \models \beta$ and Proposition 9.3 conclude $[\![\Psi]\!] \cap [\![\neg\beta]\!] = \emptyset$ and $\min([\![\neg\alpha]\!], \leq_\Psi) \cap [\![\neg\beta]\!] = \emptyset$. Consequently, we obtain from Proposition 9.3 that $\mathrm{Bel}(\Psi \div \alpha \div \beta) \equiv_{\neg\beta} \mathrm{Bel}(\Psi \div \beta)$ holds if and only if $\min([\![\neg\beta]\!], \leq_\Psi) = \min([\![\neg\beta]\!], \leq_{\Psi \div \alpha})$ holds. Towards a contradiction we suppose $\min([\![\neg\beta]\!], \leq_\Psi) \neq \min([\![\neg\beta]\!], \leq_{\Psi \div \alpha})$. Then there are two interpretations $\omega_1, \omega_2 \in [\![\neg\beta]\!]$ such that $\omega_1 \leq_\Psi \omega_2$ if and only if $\omega_2 <_{\Psi \div \alpha} \omega_1$. Note that $\omega_1, \omega_2 \notin [\![\Psi \div \alpha]\!]$. We obtain a direct contradiction to (IC$_{\mathrm{nc}}^{\mathrm{rel}}$). $\qquad\square$

Proposition 11.11 shows that natural contraction leads to minimal change on the level of contractionals, as the total preorder changes only minimally. We want to emphasize that in particular (IC_{nc}), i.e.,

(IC_{nc}) If $\Psi \div \alpha \models \beta$, then $\mathrm{Bel}(\Psi \div \alpha \div \beta) \equiv_{\neg\beta} \mathrm{Bel}(\Psi \div \beta)$.

used in the proof of Proposition 11.11 shows the conceptual similarity to Boutilier's proposal [32] to minimize changes of conditional beliefs in the process of iterated revision (see (IR_{min}) in Section 11.1).

Before considering moderate contraction in the next step, we show compatibility of (IC_{nc}) with linear and full meet AGM contraction operators for epistemic states.

Proposition 11.12. *Let $\mathcal{E}$ be a set of epistemic states, let $\div$ be an AGM contraction operator for $\mathcal{E}$. If $\div$ is linear or full meet, then (IC_{nc}) is satisfied.*

Proof. Let $\Psi \mapsto \leq_\Psi$ be a faithful assignment that is contraction-compatible with $\div$. Recall that by Proposition 11.11, the belief change operator $\div$ satisfies (IC_{nc}) if and only if (IC_{nc}^{rel}) is satisfied. In the following, we show that (IC_{nc}^{rel}) is satisfied, i.e., that for each $\omega_1, \omega_2 \notin [\![\Psi]\!]$ we have that $\omega_1 \leq_\Psi \omega_2$ holds if and only if $\omega_1 \leq_{\Psi \div \alpha} \omega_2$ holds.

For the case that $\div$ is linear, observe that by Definition 9.7 and Proposition 9.8 we immediately obtain the desired result that $\omega_1 \leq_\Psi \omega_2$ holds if and only if $\omega_1 \leq_{\Psi \div \alpha} \omega_2$ holds for all $\omega_1, \omega_2 \notin [\![\Psi \div \alpha]\!]$.

For the case that $\div$ is full meet, recall that by Proposition 9.6, the flat faithful assignment for $\mathcal{E}$ is contraction-compatible with $\div$. By this assignment, we obtain that $\omega_1, \omega_2 \notin [\![\Psi]\!]$ implies $\omega_1 \leq_\Psi \omega_2$ if and only if $\omega_2 <_\Psi \omega_1$ for each $\Psi \in \mathcal{E}$. Both observations, together with the contraction-compatibility of $\div$ with $\Psi \mapsto \leq_\Psi$, yield the desired result. $\qquad\square$

Note that Proposition 11.12 implicitly shows that (IC_{nc}) does not imply (IC_{ind}). Moreover, in Section 11.5 we will consider an AGM contraction operator for epistemic states that satisfies (IC_{ind}), yet violating (IC_{nc}), which shows that (IC_{nc}) and (IC_{ind}) give rise to distinct classes of AGM contraction operators for epistemic states.

Moderate Contraction. We define moderate contraction as an AGM contraction operator for epistemic states which gives precedence to counter-models of α when contracting by α.

Definition 11.13 (Moderate Contraction, adapted [123]). *Let $\mathcal{E}$ be a set of epistemic states, let $\div$ be an AGM contraction operator for $\mathcal{E}$, and let $\Psi \mapsto \leq_\Psi$ be a faithful assignment that is contraction-compatible with $\div$. Then $\div$ is called a* moderate contraction *if* (IC1^{rel}), (IC2^{rel}) *and the following holds[6]:*

(IC$_{mc}^{rel}$) *If $\omega_1 \in [\![\neg\alpha]\!]$, $\omega_2 \in [\![\alpha]\!]$ and $\omega_2 \notin [\![\Psi \div \alpha]\!]$, then $\omega_1 <_{\Psi \div \alpha} \omega_2$.*

As (IC$_{mc}^{rel}$) highlights, moderate contraction might behave very drastically when considering the changes between $\leq_\Psi$ and $\leq_{\Psi \div \alpha}$. In particular, (IC$_{mc}^{rel}$) does not take the prior structure of $\leq_\Psi$ into account regrading the relation of models of α and $\neg\alpha$. However, in moderate contraction, (IC$_{mc}^{rel}$) is accompanied by (IC1^{rel}) and (IC2^{rel}), and thus the relationship between models of α, and models of $\neg\alpha$, respectively, is preserved. We characterize moderate contraction in the following proposition. The main contribution of this proposition is the syntactic characterization of (IC$_{mc}^{rel}$), because (IC1^{rel}) and (IC2^{rel}) have been characterized before.

Proposition 11.14. *Let $\mathcal{E}$ be a set of epistemic states and let $\div$ be an AGM contraction operator for $\mathcal{E}$. The operator $\div$ is a moderate contraction if and only if* (IC1), (IC2) *and the following is satisfied:*

(IC$_{mc}^{cond}$) *If $\neg\alpha \models \gamma$ and $\alpha \vee \beta \not\equiv \top$, then $\Psi \models [\gamma \mid \alpha]$ implies $\Psi \div \alpha \models [\gamma \mid \beta]$.*

Proof. Let $\Psi \mapsto \leq_\Psi$ be a faithful assignment that is contraction-compatible with $\div$. The correspondence between (IC1^{rel}), (IC2^{rel}) and (IC1), (IC2) is given in Proposition 10.16 (see p. 256). Thus, it suffices to show the correspondence between (IC$_{mc}^{cond}$) and (IC$_{mc}^{rel}$). Note that (IC$_{mc}^{cond}$) is equivalent to the following postulate due to Proposition 9.18:

(IC$_{mc}$) *If $\neg\alpha \models \gamma$ and $\alpha \vee \beta \not\equiv \top$, then $\Psi \div \alpha \models \gamma$ implies $\Psi \div \alpha \div \beta \models \gamma$.*

---

[6]   The subscript *mc* stands for *moderate contraction*.

We show equivalence of $(\mathrm{IC_{mc}})$ and $(\mathrm{IC_{mc}^{rel}})$ by considering both directions of the claim independently.

From $(\mathrm{IC_{mc}})$ *to* $(\mathrm{IC_{mc}^{rel}})$. Let $\omega_1 \in [\![\neg\alpha]\!]$ and $\omega_2 \in [\![\alpha]\!] \setminus [\![\Psi \div \alpha]\!]$. Towards a contradiction assume $\omega_2 \leq_{\Psi \div \alpha} \omega_1$. Choose $\beta, \gamma \in \mathcal{L}$ such that $[\![\beta]\!] = \Omega \setminus \{\omega_1, \omega_2\}$ and $[\![\gamma]\!] = [\![\Psi \div \alpha]\!] \cup [\![\neg\alpha]\!]$. We obtain that $[\![\neg\beta]\!] = \{\omega_1, \omega_2\}$. Moreover, we have $\neg\alpha \models \gamma$, $\gamma \in \mathrm{Bel}(\Psi \div \alpha)$ and $\alpha \vee \beta \not\equiv \top$. Therefore, by $(\mathrm{IC_{mc}})$ we obtain $\gamma \in \mathrm{Bel}(\Psi \div \alpha \div \beta)$. This implies that $\omega_2 \notin [\![\Psi \div \alpha \div \beta]\!]$. However, by Proposition 9.3 we obtain the contradiction $\omega_2 \in [\![\Psi \div \alpha \div \beta]\!]$, because $\omega_2 \in \min([\![\neg\beta]\!], \leq_{\Psi \div \alpha})$. Therefore, it is the case that $\omega_1 <_{\Psi \div \alpha} \omega_2$ and thus the postulate $(\mathrm{IC_{mc}^{rel}})$ is satisfied.

From $(\mathrm{IC_{mc}^{rel}})$ *to* $(\mathrm{IC_{mc}})$. Suppose that $\neg\alpha \models \gamma$, $\beta \vee \alpha \not\equiv \top$ and $\Psi \div \alpha \models \gamma$. Towards a contraction assume that $\Psi \div \alpha \div \beta \not\models \gamma$. This implies that there is some $\omega_2 \in [\![\Psi \div \alpha \div \beta]\!]$ with $\omega_2 \not\models \gamma$. By Proposition 9.3, we obtain that $\omega_2 \in \min([\![\neg\beta]\!], \leq_{\Psi \div \alpha})$. Consequently, we obtain that $\omega_2 \models \alpha$. Moreover, because $\beta \vee \alpha \not\equiv \top$, there is some $\omega_1 \in \Omega$ with $\omega_1 \models \neg\beta \wedge \neg\alpha$. Therefore, we have $\omega_1 \models \gamma$. In summary, we obtain that $\omega_2 \leq_{\Psi \div \alpha} \omega_1$, which is a contradiction to $(\mathrm{IC_{mc}^{rel}})$. $\square$

The proof of Proposition 11.14 shows additionally that $(\mathrm{IC_{mc}^{rel}})$ is equivalent to

$(\mathrm{IC_{mc}})$ If $\neg\alpha \models \gamma$ and $\alpha \vee \beta \not\equiv \top$, then $\Psi \div \alpha \models \gamma$ implies $\Psi \div \alpha \div \beta \models \gamma$.

, when considering AGM contraction operators for epistemic states. We obtain the following proposition on the relationship between moderate contraction and $(\mathrm{IC_{ind}})$.

Proposition 11.15. *Let $\mathcal{E}$ be a set of epistemic states and let $\div$ be an AGM contraction operator for $\mathcal{E}$. If $\div$ satisfies $(\mathrm{IC_{mc}})$, then $\div$ satisfies $(\mathrm{IC_{ind}})$.*

Proof. Let $\div$ is an AGM contraction operator and let $\Psi \mapsto \leq_\Psi$ be a faithful assignment that is contraction-compatible with $\div$. We obtain that satisfaction of $(\mathrm{IC_{mc}^{rel}})$ implies satisfaction of $(\mathrm{IC_{ind}^{rel}})$. By using Proposition 11.7, we obtain that $\div$ satisfies $(\mathrm{IC_{ind}})$ from the satisfaction of $(\mathrm{IC_{ind}^{rel}})$. Moreover, from the proof of Proposition 11.14 we obtain that satisfaction of $(\mathrm{IC_{mc}^{rel}})$ implies satisfaction of $(\mathrm{IC_{mc}})$.

We obtain that the satisfaction of $(\mathrm{IC_{mc}})$ by $\div$ implies the satisfaction of $(\mathrm{IC_{ind}})$ by $\div$.   □

Proposition 11.15 yields the following statement.

Corollary 11.16. *Let $\mathcal{E}$ be a set of epistemic states. Every moderate AGM contraction operator for $\mathcal{E}$ satisfies $(\mathrm{IC_{ind}})$.*

In the following, we show that linear AGM contraction operators for epistemic state and full meet AGM contraction operators for epistemic states violate $(\mathrm{IC_{mc}})$. Note that $(\mathrm{IC_{mc}})$ is the only principle for AGM contraction operators for epistemic states with this property that we have encountered so far.

Proposition 11.17. *Suppose $|\Sigma| \geq 2$. Let $\mathcal{E}$ be a set of epistemic states such that there is at least one epistemic state $\Psi_{\mathcal{H}} \in \mathcal{E}$ with $|\Omega \setminus [\![\Psi_{\mathcal{H}}]\!]| \geq 3$. The following statements hold:*

- *Every full meet AGM contraction operator for $\mathcal{E}$ violates $(\mathrm{IC_{mc}})$.*
- *Every linear AGM contraction operator for $\mathcal{E}$ violates $(\mathrm{IC_{mc}})$.*

Proof. If no AGM contraction operator for $\mathcal{E}$ exists, then both statements are trivially true. In the following, suppose that there exists an AGM contraction operator $\div$ for $\mathcal{E}$ and let $\Psi \mapsto \leq_\Psi$ be a faithful assignment that is contraction-compatible with $\div$. We consider both statements independently.

Full Meet Contraction. Suppose $\div$ is a full meet AGM contraction operator for $\mathcal{E}$ that satisfies $(\mathrm{IC_{mc}})$. Then, due to Proposition 11.15, we obtain that $\div$ satisfies $(\mathrm{IC_{ind}})$. We obtain, because $\div$ satisfies $(\mathrm{IC_{ind}})$, from Proposition 11.9 the contradiction that $\div$ is not a full meet AGM contraction operator for $\mathcal{E}$.

Linear Contraction. Suppose $\div$ is a linear AGM contraction operator for $\mathcal{E}$ that satisfies $(\mathrm{IC_{mc}})$. In the following let $\omega_1, \omega_2, \omega_3 \in \Omega$ such that $\omega_1, \omega_2, \omega_3 \notin [\![\Psi_{\mathcal{H}}]\!]$. Because $\div$ is a linear AGM contraction operator for $\mathcal{E}$, we have that $\omega_1, \omega_2, \omega_3$ are linear ordered by $\leq_{\Psi_{\mathcal{H}}}$. Without loss of generality, we assume $\omega_1 <_{\Psi_{\mathcal{H}}} \omega_2 <_{\Psi_{\mathcal{H}}} \omega_3$ in the following. Now let α be a formula such that $[\![\neg\alpha]\!] = \{\omega_1, \omega_3\}$. From the contraction-compatibility of $\Psi \mapsto \leq_\Psi$ with $\div$, we obtain $\omega_1 \in [\![\Psi_{\mathcal{H}} \div \alpha]\!]$ Moreover, because $\div$ is a linear AGM contraction operator for $\mathcal{E}$, we obtain $\omega_2 <_{\Psi_{\mathcal{H}} \div \alpha} \omega_3$.

Note that we have $\omega_3 \in [\![\neg\alpha]\!]$ and $\omega_2 \in [\![\alpha]\!]$, thus $\omega_2 <_{\Psi_{\mu\pi}} \omega_3$ shows a contradiction to $(\mathrm{IC}_{\mathrm{mc}}^{\mathrm{rel}})$. Due to Proposition 11.14, the violation of $(\mathrm{IC}_{\mathrm{mc}}^{\mathrm{rel}})$ implies violation of $(\mathrm{IC}_{\mathrm{mc}})$, which yields a contradiction. □

We close with a remark: one might wonder about the term moderate contraction, because the strategy of moderate contraction seems to be analogue to the idea of (simple) lexicographic revision [113] (see Section 11.1). Note that there is a notion of lexicographic contraction, which is different from moderate contraction [110]. Moreover, lexicographic revision [110] only coincides with simplex lexicographic revision in certain cases [113, p. 214].

11.4. Gentle Contraction Strategies

Natural contraction, moderate contraction and $(\mathrm{IC_{ind}})$ are very drastic kinds of AGM contraction operators for epistemic states, when it comes to change the change strategy itself. As the change strategy is (partially) encoded in the total preorder $\leq_\Psi$ for each epistemic state $\Psi \in \mathcal{E}$, the drastic behaviour becomes visible when considering the change from $\leq_\Psi$ to $\leq_{\Psi \div \alpha}$:

Natural Contraction. This kind of change is, like natural revision, very restrictive, as it enforces minimal changes of conditional beliefs. A consequence is that all parts of $\leq_{\Psi \div \alpha}$, except for $\min(\Omega, \leq_{\Psi \div \alpha})$, are determined by $\leq_\Psi$ without considering α at all. For revision, such a behaviour was criticized by Darwiche and Pearl [41].

Moderate Contraction. When changing $\leq_\Psi$ to $\leq_{\Psi \div \alpha}$, this kind of change reorganizes $\leq_\Psi$ such that all models of $\neg\alpha$ are preferred over model of α. Thus, all previously existing dependencies between models of $\neg\alpha$ and models of α that may be given in $\leq_\Psi$ are ignored. This happens in particular in cases where the set of beliefs is not changed at all when contracting a belief α.

Independence Principle. The postulate $(\mathrm{IC_{ind}})$ enforces to improve the preference of models of $\neg\alpha$. Unlike moderate contraction, previously existing dependencies between models of $\neg\alpha$ and models of α that may be given in $\leq_\Psi$ are respected by $(\mathrm{IC_{ind}})$. However, the requirement of improving the preference of models of $\neg\alpha$ applies also in cases where the set of prior beliefs is not changed at all when contracting a belief α.

In this section, we gently restrict these principles to specific cases. The restrictions we consider in the following treat the change of the change strategy, for which we take guidance from the following policies:

- When no change is necessary on the beliefs, then do not (drastically) change the change strategy.
- When a change is necessary on the beliefs, then also change of the change strategy itself should be possible.

The principles (IC1)–(IC4) respect these policies. However, as argued at the beginning of this chapter, (IC1)–(IC4) may be too liberal in certain cases. Accompanying (IC1)–(IC4) with the new principles we present in the course of this section, might be a reasonable compromise. We start with natural contraction.

Gentle Natural Contraction. For natural contraction, we propose to limit "naturalness" to such cases where α is not believed anyway previously, i.e., having minimal change of conditional beliefs in such cases. Formally, we propose to change

(IC$_{\text{nc}}^{\text{rel}}$) If $\omega_1, \omega_2 \notin [\![\Psi \div \alpha]\!]$, then $\omega_1 \leq_\Psi \omega_2 \Leftrightarrow \omega_1 \leq_{\Psi \div \alpha} \omega_2.$,

given in Section 11.3 (see p. 285), to[7]:

(IC$_{\text{gnc}}^{\text{rel}}$) If $[\![\Psi]\!] \not\subseteq [\![\alpha]\!]$, then $\omega_1 \leq_\Psi \omega_2 \Leftrightarrow \omega_1 \leq_{\Psi \div \alpha} \omega_2.$

The difference between (IC$_{\text{nc}}^{\text{rel}}$) and (IC$_{\text{gnc}}^{\text{rel}}$) is that $\omega_1, \omega_2 \notin [\![\Psi \div \alpha]\!]$ is replaced by $[\![\Psi]\!] \not\subseteq [\![\alpha]\!]$. Note that for AGM contraction operators for epistemic states, we assume satisfaction for (C1) and (C2), stating together that whenever $[\![\Psi]\!] \not\subseteq [\![\alpha]\!]$ holds, then we have $[\![\Psi]\!] = [\![\Psi \div \alpha]\!]$. Consequently, putting condition $\omega_1, \omega_2 \notin [\![\Psi \div \alpha]\!]$ into (IC$_{\text{gnc}}^{\text{rel}}$) is superfluous. We will see that (IC$_{\text{gnc}}^{\text{rel}}$) is equivalent to

(IC$_{\text{gnc}}$) If $\alpha \notin \mathrm{Bel}(\Psi)$, then $\Psi \div \beta \models \gamma \Leftrightarrow \Psi \div \alpha \div \beta \models \gamma.$,

which is, due to Proposition 9.18, equivalent to:

(IC$_{\text{gnc}}^{\text{cond}}$) If $\alpha \notin \mathrm{Bel}(\Psi)$, then $\Psi \models [\gamma \,|\, \beta] \Leftrightarrow \Psi \div \alpha \models [\gamma \,|\, \beta].$

The following proposition proves the correspondence between (IC$_{\text{gnc}}$) and (IC$_{\text{gnc}}^{\text{rel}}$).

Proposition 11.18 (Gentle Natural Contraction). *Let $\mathcal{E}$ be a set of epistemic states, let $\div$ be an AGM contraction operator for $\mathcal{E}$, and let $\Psi \mapsto \leq_\Psi$ be a faithful assignment that is contraction-compatible with $\div$. The postulate (IC$_{\text{gnc}}$) is satisfied by $\div$ if and only if (IC$_{\text{gnc}}^{\text{rel}}$) is satisfied.*

Proof. We consider both directions of the claim independently.

---

[7]   The subscript *gnc* stands for *gentle natural contraction.*

From $(\mathrm{IC_{gnc}})$ *to* $(\mathrm{IC^{rel}_{gnc}})$. Suppose we have $[\![\Psi]\!] \not\subseteq [\![\alpha]\!]$, i.e., there exists $\omega \in [\![\neg\alpha]\!]$ such that $\omega \in [\![\Psi]\!]$. Because $\div$ satisfies (C1) and (C2), we obtain $[\![\Psi]\!] = [\![\Psi \div \alpha]\!]$ from $[\![\Psi]\!] \not\subseteq [\![\alpha]\!]$. In the following let $\omega_1, \omega_2 \in \Omega$. Furthermore, let β, γ be formulas such that $[\![\neg\beta]\!] = \{\omega_1, \omega_2\}$ and $[\![\gamma]\!] = [\![\Psi]\!] \cup \{\omega_2\}$.

Towards a contradiction, suppose $\omega_1 \leq_\Psi \omega_2$ and $\omega_2 <_{\Psi \div \alpha} \omega_1$. We obtain $\Psi \div \alpha \div \beta \models \gamma$ from $\omega_2 <_{\Psi \div \alpha} \omega_1$ and the contraction-compatibility of $\div$ with $\Psi \mapsto \leq_\Psi$. This yields $\Psi \div \alpha \div \beta \models \gamma$, because $\div$ satisfies $(\mathrm{IC_{gmc}})$. From (C1) and $\omega_2 <_{\Psi \div \alpha} \omega_1$, we obtain $\omega_1 \notin [\![\Psi]\!]$. Using the contraction-compatibility of $\div$ with $\Psi \mapsto \leq_\Psi$ again, we obtain $\omega_1 \notin \min([\![\neg\beta]\!], \leq_\Psi)$ from $\omega_1 \notin [\![\Psi]\!]$ and $\Psi \div \alpha \div \beta \models \gamma$. The observation $\omega_1 \notin \min([\![\neg\beta]\!], \leq_\Psi)$ contradicts $\omega_1 \leq_\Psi \omega_2$.

The proof for $\omega_1 \leq_{\Psi \div \alpha} \omega_2$ and $\omega_2 <_\Psi \omega_1$ is analogue to the prior case.

From $(\mathrm{IC^{rel}_{gnc}})$ *to* $(\mathrm{IC_{gnc}})$. Suppose we have $[\![\Psi]\!] \not\subseteq [\![\alpha]\!]$. Because $\div$ satisfies (C1) and (C2), we obtain $[\![\Psi]\!] = [\![\Psi \div \alpha]\!]$ from $[\![\Psi]\!] \not\subseteq [\![\alpha]\!]$. Moreover, $[\![\Psi]\!] \not\subseteq [\![\alpha]\!]$ implies that $[\![\Psi]\!] \neq \emptyset$, i.e, $\omega_1 \in [\![\Psi]\!]$. We show equivalence in two steps.

From $\Psi \div \beta \models \gamma$ *to* $\Psi \div \alpha \div \beta \models \gamma$. Towards a contradiction we assume $\Psi \div \beta \models \gamma$ and $\Psi \div \alpha \div \beta \not\models \gamma$. From this, we obtain $\omega_2 \in [\![\Psi \div \alpha \div \beta]\!] \setminus [\![\Psi \div \beta]\!]$ such that $\omega_2 \notin [\![\gamma]\!]$. Because $\div$ is contraction-compatible with $\Psi \mapsto \leq_\Psi$, we obtain $\omega_2 \in [\![\Psi \div \alpha]\!]$ or $\omega_2 \in \min([\![\neg\beta]\!], \leq_{\Psi \div \alpha})$.

For the case of $\omega_2 \in [\![\Psi \div \alpha]\!]$, we obtain $\omega_2 \in [\![\Psi]\!]$ from $[\![\Psi]\!] = [\![\Psi \div \alpha]\!]$. From (C1), we obtain $\omega_2 \in [\![\Psi \div \beta]\!]$, yielding the contradiction $\Psi \div \beta \not\models \gamma$.

For the case of $\omega_2 \in \min([\![\neg\beta]\!], \leq_{\Psi \div \alpha})$ and $\omega_2 \notin [\![\Psi \div \alpha]\!]$. We obtain $\omega_2 \notin [\![\Psi]\!]$ from $[\![\Psi]\!] = [\![\Psi \div \alpha]\!]$. Because $\div$ is contraction-compatible with $\Psi \mapsto \leq_\Psi$, we have that $\omega_2 \notin [\![\Psi]\!]$ implies $\omega_3 \in \min([\![\neg\beta]\!], \leq_\Psi)$. From $\Psi \div \beta \models \gamma$ and $\omega_2 \notin [\![\gamma]\!]$, we obtain $\omega_3 <_\Psi \omega_2$. Then, the last observation, together with (C1), implies $\omega_3 <_{\Psi \div \alpha} \omega_2$. Clearly, because of $\omega_3 \in [\![\neg\beta]\!]$, this is a contradiction to $\omega_2 \in \min([\![\neg\beta]\!], \leq_{\Psi \div \alpha})$.

From $\Psi \div \alpha \div \beta \models \gamma$ *to* $\Psi \div \beta \models \gamma$. Towards a contradiction we assume $\Psi \div \alpha \div \beta \models \gamma$ and $\Psi \div \beta \not\models \gamma$. From this, we obtain $\omega_2 \in [\![\Psi \div \beta]\!] \setminus [\![\Psi \div \alpha \div \beta]\!]$ such that $\omega_2 \notin [\![\gamma]\!]$. Because $\div$ is contraction-compatible with $\Psi \mapsto \leq_\Psi$, we obtain $\omega_2 \in [\![\Psi]\!]$ or $\omega_2 \in \min([\![\neg\beta]\!], \leq_\Psi)$.

For the case of $w_2 \in [\![\Psi]\!]$, we obtain $w_2 \in [\![\Psi \div \alpha \div \beta]\!]$ from (C1), yielding the contradiction $\Psi \div \beta \not\models \gamma$.

For the case of $w_2 \in \min([\![\neg\beta]\!], \leq_\Psi)$ and $w_2 \notin [\![\Psi]\!]$. We obtain $w_2 \notin [\![\Psi \div \alpha]\!]$ from $[\![\Psi]\!] = [\![\Psi \div \alpha]\!]$. Because $\div$ is contraction-compatible with $\Psi \mapsto \leq_\Psi$, we have that $w_2 \notin [\![\Psi]\!]$ implies $w_3 \in \min([\![\neg\beta]\!], \leq_\Psi)$. From $\Psi \div \beta \models \gamma$ and $w_2 \notin [\![\gamma]\!]$, we obtain $w_3 <_{\Psi \div \alpha} w_2$. Then, the last observation, together with (C1), implies $w_3 <_\Psi w_2$. Clearly, because of $w_3 \in [\![\neg\beta]\!]$, this is a contradiction to $w_2 \in \min([\![\neg\beta]\!], \leq_\Psi)$. □

Gentle Moderate Contraction.

For moderate contraction, we propose to limit "moderateness" to cases where α is believed previously, i.e., reorganization of $\leq_\Psi$ according to $(\mathrm{IC}^{\mathrm{rel}}_{\mathrm{mc}})$ is only enforced in this case. Formally, we propose to change

$(\mathrm{IC}^{\mathrm{rel}}_{\mathrm{mc}})$ If $w_1 \in [\![\neg\alpha]\!]$, $w_2 \in [\![\alpha]\!]$ and $w_2 \notin [\![\Psi \div \alpha]\!]$, then $w_1 <_{\Psi \div \alpha} w_2$. ,

given in Section 11.3 (see p. 288), to[8]

$(\mathrm{IC}^{\mathrm{rel}}_{\mathrm{gmc}})$ If $w_1 \in [\![\neg\alpha]\!]$, $w_2 \in [\![\alpha]\!] \setminus [\![\Psi]\!]$ and $[\![\Psi]\!] \subseteq [\![\alpha]\!]$, then $w_1 <_{\Psi \div \alpha} w_2$.

The difference between $(\mathrm{IC}^{\mathrm{rel}}_{\mathrm{mc}})$ and $(\mathrm{IC}^{\mathrm{rel}}_{\mathrm{gmc}})$ is the additional condition $[\![\Psi]\!] \subseteq [\![\alpha]\!]$. Note that $[\![\Psi]\!] \subseteq [\![\alpha]\!]$ is equivalent to having $\alpha \in \mathrm{Bel}(\Psi)$. Thus, whenever $\div$ is an AGM contraction operator for epistemic states (and $\alpha \not\equiv \top$), we will obtain $\alpha \notin \mathrm{Bel}(\Psi \div \alpha)$. Due to this new condition, the drastic reorganization of $\leq_\Psi$ to $\leq_{\Psi \div \alpha}$ such that all models of $\neg\alpha$ are preferred over models of α is only enforced whenever $\alpha \in \mathrm{Bel}(\Psi)$. We will see that $(\mathrm{IC}^{\mathrm{rel}}_{\mathrm{gmc}})$ is equivalent to

$(\mathrm{IC}_{\mathrm{gmc}})$ If $\neg\alpha \not\models \beta$, then $\Psi \models \alpha \wedge \beta \Rightarrow \Psi \div \alpha \div \beta \models \alpha \to \beta$. ,

which is, due to Proposition 9.18, equivalent to

$(\mathrm{IC}^{\mathrm{cond}}_{\mathrm{gmc}})$ If $\neg\alpha \not\models \beta$, then $\Psi \models \alpha \wedge \beta \Rightarrow \Psi \div \alpha \models [\alpha \to \beta \,|\, \beta]$.

The following proposition proves the correspondence between $(\mathrm{IC}^{\mathrm{rel}}_{\mathrm{gmc}})$ and $(\mathrm{IC}_{\mathrm{gmc}})$.

---

[8]   The subscript *gmc* stands for *gentle moderate contraction*.

Proposition 11.19 (Gentle Moderate Contraction). *Let $\mathcal{E}$ be a set of epistemic states, let $\div$ be an AGM contraction operator for $\mathcal{E}$, and let $\Psi \mapsto \leq_\Psi$ be a faithful assignment that is contraction-compatible with $\div$. The postulate $(\mathrm{IC_{gmc}})$ is satisfied by $\div$ if and only if $(\mathrm{IC_{gmc}^{rel}})$ is satisfied.*

Proof. We consider both directions of the claim independently.

- *From* $(\mathrm{IC_{gmc}})$ *to* $(\mathrm{IC_{gmc}^{rel}})$. Suppose we have $\omega_1 \in [\![\neg\alpha]\!]$ and $\omega_2 \in [\![\alpha]\!] \setminus [\![\Psi]\!]$ and $[\![\Psi]\!] \subseteq [\![\alpha]\!]$. Towards a contradiction, assume that $\omega_2 \leq_{\Psi \div \alpha} \omega_1$ holds. Let β be a formula with $[\![\neg\beta]\!] = \{\omega_1, \omega_2\}$, and thus we have $\neg\alpha \not\models \beta$. We obtain $\omega_1, \omega_2 \notin [\![\Psi]\!]$ from $[\![\Psi]\!] \subseteq [\![\alpha]\!]$, $\omega_1 \in [\![\neg\alpha]\!]$ and $\omega_2 \in [\![\alpha]\!] \setminus [\![\Psi]\!]$. Because $\div$ is contraction-compatible with $\Psi \mapsto \leq_\Psi$, we obtain $\Psi \div \alpha \div \beta \not\models \alpha \to \beta$ from $\omega_2 \leq_{\Psi \div \alpha} \omega_1$. Consequently, because $\div$ satisfies $(\mathrm{IC_{gmc}})$, we have $\Psi \not\models \alpha \wedge \beta$. This is a contradiction to $[\![\Psi]\!] \subseteq [\![\alpha]\!]$ and $\omega_1, \omega_2 \notin [\![\Psi]\!]$.

- *From* $(\mathrm{IC_{gmc}^{rel}})$ *to* $(\mathrm{IC_{gmc}})$. Suppose that $\neg\alpha \not\models \beta$ and $\Psi \models \alpha \wedge \beta$ and $[\![\Psi]\!] \subseteq [\![\alpha]\!]$ holds. We show $\Psi \div \alpha \div \beta \models \alpha \to \beta$ by contradiction, i.e., from $\Psi \div \alpha \div \beta \not\models \alpha \to \beta$ we conclude a contradiction. By using our assumptions, we obtain an interpretation ω with $\omega \in [\![\alpha \wedge \neg\beta]\!]$ and $\omega \in [\![\Psi \div \alpha \div \beta]\!]$. Because $\div$ is contraction-compatible with $\Psi \mapsto \leq_\Psi$, we obtain from $\omega \in [\![\Psi \div \alpha \div \beta]\!]$ that either $\omega \in [\![\Psi]\!]$ or $\omega \in \min([\![\neg\alpha]\!], \leq_\Psi)$ or $\omega \in \min([\![\neg\beta]\!], \leq_{\Psi \div \alpha})$ holds. Clearly, $\omega \in [\![\alpha \wedge \neg\beta]\!]$ and $[\![\Psi]\!] \subseteq [\![\alpha]\!]$ imply that $\omega \notin [\![\Psi]\!]$ and $\omega \notin \min([\![\neg\alpha]\!], \leq_\Psi)$ holds. This renders $\omega \in \min([\![\neg\beta]\!], \leq_{\Psi \div \alpha})$ as the only possible case. Note that we have $\neg\alpha \not\models \beta$, which implies $\neg\beta \not\models \alpha$. Consequently, there exists some interpretation ω' with $\omega' \in [\![\neg\alpha \wedge \neg\beta]\!]$. We obtain $\omega \leq_{\Psi \div \alpha} \omega'$ from $\omega \in \min([\![\neg\beta]\!], \leq_{\Psi \div \alpha})$. As $\div$ satisfies $(\mathrm{IC_{gmc}^{rel}})$, we obtain $\omega \in [\![\Psi]\!]$ from $\omega_1 \in [\![\neg\alpha]\!]$, $\omega_2 \in [\![\alpha]\!]$, $[\![\Psi]\!] \subseteq [\![\alpha]\!]$ and $\omega_2 \leq_{\Psi \div \alpha} \omega'$. Recall that we have $\omega \in [\![\alpha \wedge \neg\beta]\!]$, and thus, $\omega \in [\![\Psi]\!]$ and $\Psi \models \alpha \wedge \beta$, yielding a contradiction. $\square$

Gentle Semantic Independences. For the semantic independence principle $(\mathrm{IC_{ind}^{rel}})$, which is equivalent to $(\mathrm{IC_{ind}})$ due to Proposition 11.7, we propose a limitation of $(\mathrm{IC_{ind}^{rel}})$ to such cases where α is believed previously, i.e., the reorganization of $\leq_\Psi$ demanded in $(\mathrm{IC_{ind}^{rel}})$ is only enforced in such cases. Formally, we propose to change $(\mathrm{IC_{ind}^{rel}})$ from

(IC_{ind}^{rel}) If $\omega_1 \in [\![\neg\alpha]\!]$ and $\omega_2 \in [\![\alpha]\!] \setminus [\![\Psi]\!]$, then $\omega_1 \leq_\Psi \omega_2 \Rightarrow \omega_1 <_{\Psi\div\alpha} \omega_2$. ,

as given in Section 11.3 (see p. 281), to the following postulate[9]:

(IC_{gic}^{rel}) If $\omega_1 \in [\![\neg\alpha]\!]$, $\omega_2 \in [\![\alpha]\!] \setminus [\![\Psi]\!]$ and $[\![\Psi]\!] \subseteq [\![\alpha]\!]$, then $\omega_1 \leq_\Psi \omega_2 \Rightarrow \omega_1 <_{\Psi\div\alpha} \omega_2$.

The difference between (IC_{ind}^{rel}) and (IC_{gic}^{rel}) is the additional condition $[\![\Psi]\!] \subseteq [\![\alpha]\!]$. Note that, $[\![\Psi]\!] \subseteq [\![\alpha]\!]$ is equivalent to having $\alpha \in Bel(\Psi)$. Thus, the new condition (IC_{gic}^{rel}) demands reorganization of $\leq_\Psi$ to $\leq_{\Psi\div\alpha}$ such that the preference of models of $\neg\alpha$ is improved with respect to models of α only if $\alpha \in Bel(\Psi)$ holds. We will see that (IC_{gic}^{rel}) is equivalent to

(IC_{gic}) If $\Psi \models \alpha$ and $\Psi\div\alpha \models \alpha \to \beta$, then $\Psi\div\beta \not\models \alpha \Rightarrow \Psi\div\alpha\div\beta \models \alpha \to \beta$.

which is, due to Proposition 9.18, equivalent to

(IC_{gic}^{cond}) If $\Psi \models \alpha$ and $\Psi \models [\alpha{\to}\beta \,|\, \alpha]$, then $\Psi \not\models [\alpha\,|\,\beta] \Rightarrow \Psi\div\alpha \models [\alpha{\to}\beta\,|\,\beta]$.

The following proposition proves the correspondence between (IC_{gic}^{rel}) and (IC_{gic}).

Proposition 11.20 (Gentle Semantic Independence). *Let $\mathcal{E}$ be a set of epistemic states, let $\div$ be an AGM contraction operator for $\mathcal{E}$, and let $\Psi \mapsto \leq_\Psi$ be a faithful assignment that is contraction-compatible with $\div$. The postulate (IC_{gic}) is satisfied by $\div$ if and only if (IC_{gic}^{rel}) is satisfied.*

Proof. We consider both directions of the claim independently.

From (IC_{gmc}) to (IC_{gmc}^{rel}). Suppose that $[\![\Psi]\!] \subseteq [\![\alpha]\!]$ and $\omega_1 \in [\![\neg\alpha]\!]$ and $\omega_2 \in [\![\alpha]\!] \setminus [\![\Psi]\!]$ holds. Moreover, let $\omega_1 \leq_\Psi \omega_2$. We show $\omega_1 <_{\Psi\div\alpha} \omega_2$ by contradiction, i.e., from $\omega_2 \leq_{\Psi\div\alpha} \omega_1$ we obtain a

---

9   The subscript *gic* stands for *gentle independence* principle for *contraction*.

contradiction. Let β be a formula with $[\![\neg\beta]\!] = \{\omega_1, \omega_2\}$. Now observe that the following is equivalent to $(\mathrm{IC_{gmc}})$:

if $\Psi \models \alpha$ and $\Psi \div \alpha \div \beta \not\models \alpha \to \beta$,

then $\Psi \div \beta \not\models \alpha \Rightarrow \Psi \div \alpha \not\models \alpha \to \beta$ (★)

Because $\div$ is contraction-compatible with $\Psi \mapsto \leq_\Psi$, we obtain $\Psi \div \alpha \div \beta \not\models \alpha \to \beta$ from $\omega_2 \leq_{\Psi \div \alpha} \omega_1$ and $\omega_2 \in [\![\alpha \wedge \neg\beta]\!]$. Using contraction-compatibility again, we obtain $\Psi \div \beta \not\models \alpha$ from $\omega_1 \leq_\Psi \omega_2$. These observations, together with $[\![\Psi]\!] \subseteq [\![\alpha]\!]$ and (★), yield $\Psi \div \alpha \not\models \alpha \to \beta$. Note that ω_2 is the only interpretation with $\omega_2 \in [\![\alpha \wedge \neg\beta]\!]$. Consequently, we have $\omega_2 \in [\![\Psi \div \alpha]\!]$. Thus, the contraction-compatibility of $\div$ with $\Psi \mapsto \leq_\Psi$ implies that we have $\omega_2 \in [\![\Psi]\!]$. This is a contradiction to our initial assumption of $\omega_2 \in [\![\alpha]\!] \setminus [\![\Psi]\!]$.

From $(\mathrm{IC_{gic}^{rel}})$ *to* $(\mathrm{IC_{gic}})$. Suppose we have $[\![\Psi]\!] \subseteq [\![\alpha]\!]$, and $\Psi \div \alpha \models \beta$, and $\Psi \div \beta \not\models \alpha$. Towards a contradiction, assume that $\Psi \div \alpha \div \beta \not\models \alpha \to \beta$ holds.

We obtain $\omega_1 \in [\![\neg\alpha]\!]$ with $\omega_1 \in [\![\Psi \div \beta]\!]$ from $\Psi \div \beta \not\models \alpha$. Because of $[\![\Psi]\!] \subseteq [\![\alpha]\!]$, we obtain $\omega_1 \notin [\![\Psi]\!]$ and $\omega_1 \in \min(\neg\beta, \leq_\Psi)$ from the contraction-compatibility of $\div$ with $\Psi \mapsto \leq_\Psi$.

By using $\Psi \div \alpha \div \beta \not\models \alpha \to \beta$, we obtain an interpretation $\omega_2 \in [\![\Psi \div \alpha \div \beta]\!]$ with $\omega_2 \in [\![\alpha \wedge \neg\beta]\!]$. The contraction-compatibility of $\div$ with $\Psi \mapsto \leq_\Psi$, together with $\Psi \div \alpha \models \alpha \to \beta$, yields $\omega_2 \notin [\![\Psi \div \alpha]\!]$ and $\omega_2 \in \min(\neg\beta, \leq_{\Psi \div \alpha})$. Consequently, because $\div$ satisfies (C1), we have $\omega_2 \notin [\![\Psi]\!]$. From $\omega_1 \in \min(\neg\beta, \leq_\Psi)$ and $\omega_2 \in [\![\alpha \wedge \neg\beta]\!]$ we obtain $\omega_1 \leq_\Psi \omega_2$. By using $(\mathrm{IC_{gic}^{rel}})$, we obtain $\omega_1 <_{\Psi \div \alpha} \omega_2$ from $\omega_1 \in [\![\neg\alpha]\!]$, $\omega_2 \in [\![\alpha]\!] \setminus [\![\Psi]\!]$, $[\![\Psi]\!] \subseteq [\![\alpha]\!]$ and $\omega_1 \leq_\Psi \omega_2$. This last observation yields a contradiction to $\omega_2 \in \min(\neg\beta, \leq_{\Psi \div \alpha})$. □

11.5. Relationships among Postulates and Example

In this section, we briefly consider the relationships among postulates presented in this part. Furthermore, we present an extensive example that revisits the different principles for AGM contraction operators for epistemic states that we encountered in the course of this chapter.

Relationships among Postulates   Table 10.1 (see p. 234) lists most of the principles considered in Chapter 10. Besides the principles addressed in Chapter 10, in this chapter we considered natural contraction (IC_{nc}), moderate contraction (IC_{mc}) and independence of contraction (IC_{ind}). Many of the principles considered in this part are interconnected and their connection is not obvious given their formulation as postulates for the change of beliefs or as postulates for the change of conditional beliefs. However, their corresponding characterization by postulates of change of relations gives insight into their interconnections. Table 11.1 (see p. 300) presents an overview of relational formulations of many iteration principles considered in this part. Figure 11.1 (see p. 301) presents several relations among postulates, which can be obtained from Table 11.1.

Example   The example provides four belief change operators, illustrating how to realize operators having properties discussed in this chapter. These operators also separate some principles from each other.

Example 11.21. *Let $\Sigma = \{a, b\}$ and thus $\Omega = \{ab, \overline{a}b, a\overline{b}, \overline{a}\overline{b}\}$. Moreover, let $\mathcal{E}_{TPO}$ denote the set of all total preorders over Ω. In the following, we consider $\mathcal{E}_{TPO}$ as a set of epistemic states, where for each $\leqslant \in \mathcal{E}$ we have $[\![\leqslant]\!] = [\![Bel(\leqslant)]\!] = \min(\Omega, \leqslant)$. Note that there is no epistemic state $\leqslant \in \mathcal{E}$ with $[\![\leqslant]\!] = \emptyset$. In the following let $\Psi \mapsto \leq_\Psi$ be the function with $\leq_\Psi = \leqslant$ for each $\Psi = \leqslant \in \mathcal{E}_{TPO}$. Clearly, $\Psi \mapsto \leq_\Psi$ is a faithful assignment and we have that $\leq_\leqslant = \leq_\Psi = \leqslant = \Psi$ holds for each $\Psi = \leqslant \in \mathcal{E}_{TPO}$. Because of this property, we identify $\leq_\Psi$ and Ψ in the following. Furthermore, let $\ll$ be the linear order on Ω with*

$$ab \ll \overline{a}b \ll a\overline{b} \ll \overline{a}\overline{b}.$$

Next, we define a series of different belief change operators for $\mathcal{E}_{TPO}$.

Natural contraction operator.
We start with the operator $\dot{-}_{nco}$ which is given by

$$\leq_\Psi \dot{-}_{nco} \alpha = (\leq_\Psi \setminus (\Omega \times \min([\![\neg\alpha]\!], \leq_\Psi))) \cup (\min([\![\neg\alpha]\!], \leq_\Psi) \times \Omega).$$

*The operator $\dot{-}_{nco}$ realizes **natural contraction** (IC_{nc}), i.e., the belief change operator $\dot{-}_{nco}$ changes the total predoreder $\leq_\Psi$ minimally, i.e, everything of $\leq_{\Psi \dot{-}_{nco}\alpha}$ is the same as $\leq_\Psi$, except for the minimal models of $\neg\alpha$, which are added to the lowermost layer of $\leq_{\Psi \dot{-}_{nco}\alpha}$.*

Abbreviation		Proposition	Relational Postulate
Syn.	Sem.		
(IC1)	(IC1^{rel})	Prop. 10.16	if $\omega_1, \omega_2 \in [\alpha]$, then $\omega_1 \leq_\psi \omega_2 \Leftrightarrow \omega_1 \leq_{\psi \dot{-} \alpha} \omega_2$
(IC2)	(IC2^{rel})	Prop. 10.16	if $\omega_1, \omega_2 \in [\neg\alpha]$, then $\omega_1 \leq_\psi \omega_2 \Leftrightarrow \omega_1 \leq_{\psi \dot{-} \alpha} \omega_2$
(IC3)	(IC3^{rel})	Prop. 10.20	if $\omega_1 \in [\neg\alpha]$ and $\omega_2 \in [\alpha]$, then $\omega_1 <_\psi \omega_2 \Rightarrow \omega_1 <_{\psi \dot{-} \alpha} \omega_2$
(IC4)	(IC4^{rel})	Prop. 10.20	if $\omega_1 \in [\neg\alpha]$ and $\omega_2 \in [\alpha]$, then $\omega_1 \leq_\psi \omega_2 \Rightarrow \omega_1 \leq_{\psi \dot{-} \alpha} \omega_2$
(IC1cond)	(IC1$^{rel}_{\Rightarrow}$)	Prop. 10.6	if $\omega_1, \omega_2 \in [\alpha]$, then $\omega_1 \leq_\psi \omega_2 \Rightarrow \omega_1 \leq_{\psi \dot{-} \alpha} \omega_2$
(IC2cond)	(IC2$^{rel}_{\Rightarrow}$)	Prop. 10.7	if $\omega_1, \omega_2 \in [\neg\alpha]$, then $\omega_1 \leq_\psi \omega_2 \Rightarrow \omega_1 \leq_{\psi \dot{-} \alpha} \omega_2$
(IC3ca)	(IC3$^{rel}_{ca}$)	Prop. 10.11	if $\omega_1 \in [\neg\alpha]$, $\omega_2 \in [\alpha]$, $[\Psi] \subseteq [\neg\alpha]$, then $\omega_1 <_\psi \omega_2 \Rightarrow \omega_1 <_{\psi \dot{-} \alpha} \omega_2$
(IC4weak)	(IC4$^{rel}_{weak}$)	Prop. 10.13	if $\omega_1 \in [\neg\alpha]$, $\omega_2 \in [\alpha]$, $[\Psi] \subseteq [\neg\alpha]$, then $\omega_1 \leq_\psi \omega_2 \Rightarrow \omega_1 \leq_{\psi \dot{-} \alpha} \omega_2$
(IC4dca)	(IC4$^{rel}_{dca}$)	Prop. 10.3	if $\omega_1 \in [\neg\alpha]$, $\omega_2 \in [\alpha]$, $[\Psi] \subseteq [\neg\alpha]$, then $\omega_2 \leq_\psi \omega_1 \Rightarrow \omega_2 \leq_{\psi \dot{-} \alpha} \omega_1$
(IC3alt)	(IC3$^{rel}_{alt}$)	Prop. 11.5	if $\omega_1 \in \Omega$ and $\omega_2 \in [\alpha]$, then $\omega_1 <_\psi \omega_2 \Rightarrow \omega_1 <_{\psi \dot{-} \alpha} \omega_2$
(IC4alt)	(IC4$^{rel}_{alt}$)	Prop. 11.5	if $\omega_1 \in [\neg\alpha]$ and $\omega_2 \in \Omega$, then $\omega_1 \leq_\psi \omega_2 \Rightarrow \omega_1 \leq_{\psi \dot{-} \alpha} \omega_2$
(IC$_{ind}$)	(IC$^{rel}_{ind}$)	Prop. 11.7	if $\omega_1 \in [\neg\alpha]$ and $\omega_2 \in [\alpha] \setminus [\Psi]$, then $\omega_1 \leq_\psi \omega_2 \Rightarrow \omega_1 <_{\psi \dot{-} \alpha} \omega_2$
(IC$_{nc}$)	(IC$^{rel}_{nc}$)	Prop. 11.11	if $\omega_1, \omega_2 \notin [\Psi \dot{-} \alpha]$, then $\omega_1 \leq_\psi \omega_2 \Leftrightarrow \omega_1 \leq_{\psi \dot{-} \alpha} \omega_2$
(IC$_{mc}$)	(IC$^{rel}_{mc}$)	Prop. 11.14	if $\omega_1 \in [\neg\alpha]$ and $\omega_2 \notin [\Psi \dot{-} \alpha]$, then $\omega_1 <_{\psi \dot{-} \alpha} \omega_2$
(IC$_{gnc}$)	(IC$^{rel}_{gnc}$)	Prop. 11.18	if $[\Psi] \not\subseteq [\alpha]$, then $\omega_1 \leq_\psi \omega_2 \Leftrightarrow \omega_1 \leq_{\psi \dot{-} \alpha} \omega_2$
(IC$_{gmc}$)	(IC$^{rel}_{gmc}$)	Prop. 11.19	if $\omega_1 \in [\neg\alpha]$, $\omega_2 \in [\alpha] \setminus [\Psi]$, $[\Psi] \subseteq [\alpha]$, then $\omega_1 <_{\psi \dot{-} \alpha} \omega_2$
(IC$_{gic}$)	(IC$^{rel}_{gic}$)	Prop. 11.20	if $\omega_1 \in [\neg\alpha]$, $\omega_2 \in [\alpha] \setminus [\Psi]$, $[\Psi] \subseteq [\alpha]$, then $\omega_1 \leq_\psi \omega_2 \Rightarrow \omega_1 <_{\psi \dot{-} \alpha} \omega_2$

Table 11.1: Overview of the equivalent syntactic and semantic postulates, with reference to the corresponding characterization theorems, given in Chapter 10 and Chapter 11. For comparison, the table contains the relational formulation of these principles.

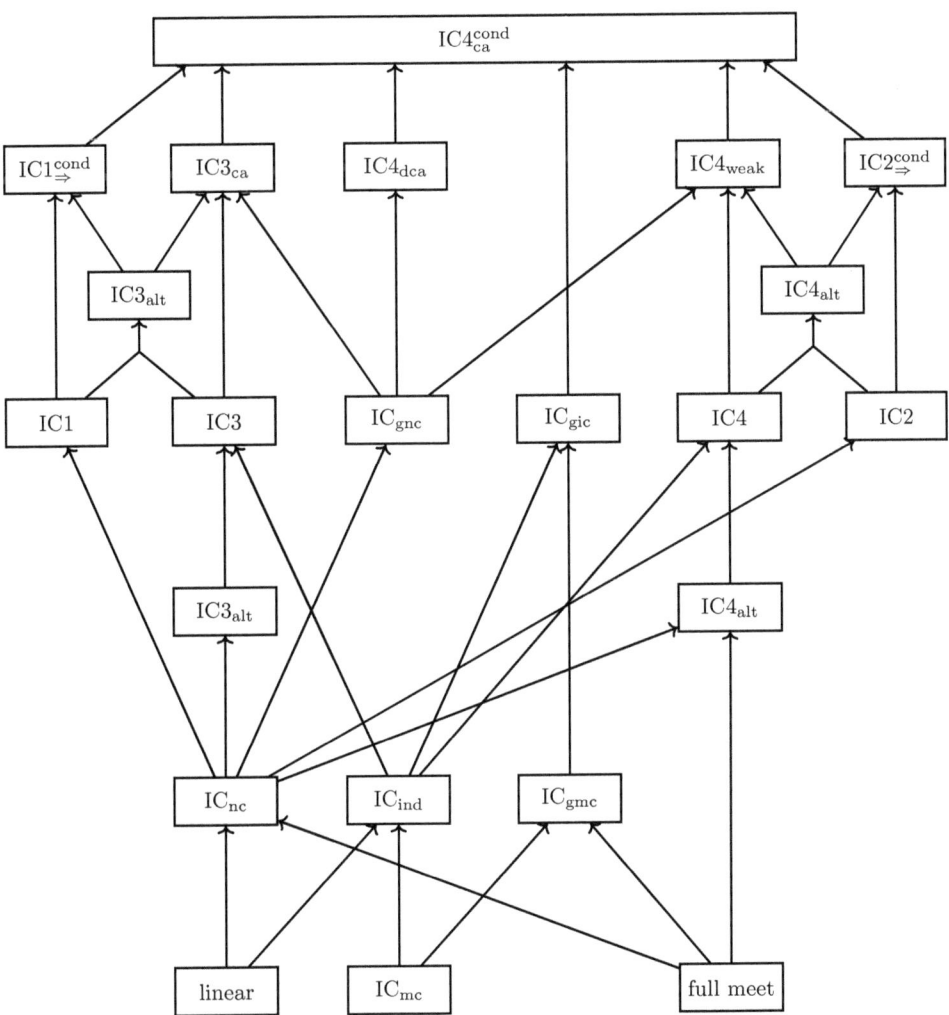

Figure 11.1: Overview of relationships among different postulates for iterated contraction considered in this part. An arrow from a postulate P to another postulate Q denotes that for every set of epistemic states $\mathcal{E}$ the following holds: If an AGM contraction operator $\div$ for $\mathcal{E}$ satisfies P then $\div$ satisfies also Q. Note that this is a transitive relation among postulates. If an arrow has two origins P_1 and P_2, then both postulates P_1 and P_2 together imply the postulate Q at the destination of the arrow, i.e., for every set of epistemic states $\mathcal{E}$ the following holds: If an AGM contraction operator $\div$ for $\mathcal{E}$ satisfies P_1 and P_2, then $\div$ satisfies also Q.

Natural Contraction with Fusion of Layers.

Second, the belief change operator $\dot{-}_{\text{fus}}$, given by

$$\leq_{\Psi} \dot{-}_{\text{fus}} \alpha = \quad \{(\omega_1, \omega_2) \mid \omega_1 \in [\![\Psi]\!] \cup \min([\![\neg\alpha]\!], \leq_{\Psi})\} \qquad \text{(Fus1)}$$

$$\cup \{(\omega_1, \omega_2) \mid \omega_1 \in [\![\neg\alpha]\!] \ \textit{and} \ \omega_2 \in [\![\alpha]\!] \setminus [\![\Psi]\!]\} \qquad \text{(Fus2)}$$

$$\cup \{(\omega_1, \omega_2) \mid \omega_1, \omega_2 \in [\![\alpha]\!] \setminus [\![\Psi]\!]\} \qquad \text{(Fus3)}$$

$$\cup \{(\omega_1, \omega_2) \mid \omega_1, \omega_2 \in [\![\neg\alpha]\!] \ \textit{and} \ \omega_1 \leq_{\Psi} \omega_2\} \ , \qquad \text{(Fus4)}$$

takes the prior preorder $\leq_{\Psi}$ and reorganizes this preorder as follows:

(Fus1) *To obtain compliance with AGM contraction, the minimal models of $\neg\alpha$ are added to the lowermost layer of the prior order, i.e., in the end we will have:*

$$[\![\leq_{\Psi}\dot{-}_{\text{fus}}\alpha]\!] = [\![\Psi]\!] \cup \min([\![\neg\alpha]\!], \leq_{\Psi}) = \min(\Omega, \leq_{\Psi}) \cup \min([\![\neg\alpha]\!], \leq_{\Psi})$$

(Fus2) *All models of α (except for those which are in $[\![\leq_{\Psi} \dot{-}_{\text{fus}} \alpha]\!]$) are shifted above all counter-models of α, i.e., in the end we will have:*

if $\omega_1 \in [\![\neg\alpha]\!]$, $\omega_2 \in [\![\alpha]\!]$ and $\omega_2 \notin [\![\leq_{\Psi}\dot{-}_{\text{fus}}\alpha]\!]$, then $\omega_1 <_{\Psi\dot{-}_{\text{fus}}\alpha} \omega_2$

(Fus3) *All models of α (except for those which are in $[\![\leq_{\Psi} \dot{-}_{\text{fus}} \alpha]\!]$) are **fused** into one layer, i.e., in the end we will have:*

if $\omega_1, \omega_2 \in [\![\alpha]\!]$ and $\omega_2 \notin [\![\leq_{\Psi} \dot{-}_{\text{fus}} \alpha]\!]$, then $\omega_1 \leq_{\Psi\dot{-}_{\text{fus}}\alpha} \omega_2$

(Fus4) *The relationship among elements of $\neg\alpha$ by $\leq_{\Psi\dot{-}_{\text{fus}}\alpha}$ is the same as before by $\leq_{\Psi}$, i.e., in the end we will have:*

if $\omega_1, \omega_2 \in [\![\neg\alpha]\!]$, then $\omega_1 \leq_{\Psi} \omega_2 \Leftrightarrow \omega_1 \leq_{\Psi\dot{-}_{\text{fus}}\alpha} \omega_2$

Natural Contraction with Reordering of Layers.

Next, the belief change operator $\dot{-}_{\text{ord}}$, given by

$$\leq_{\Psi} \dot{-}_{\text{ord}} \alpha = \quad \{(\omega_1, \omega_2) \mid \omega_1 \in [\![\Psi]\!] \cup \min([\![\neg\alpha]\!], \leq_{\Psi})\} \qquad \text{(Ord1)}$$

$$\cup \{(\omega_1, \omega_2) \mid \omega_1 \in [\![\neg\alpha]\!] \ \textit{and} \ \omega_2 \in [\![\alpha]\!] \setminus [\![\Psi]\!]\} \qquad \text{(Ord2)}$$

$$\cup \{(\omega_1, \omega_2) \mid \omega_1, \omega_2 \in [\![\alpha]\!] \setminus [\![\Psi]\!] \ \textit{and} \ \omega_1 \leq_{\Psi} \omega_2\}$$
$$\qquad \text{(Ord3)}$$

$$\cup \{(\omega_1, \omega_2) \mid \omega_1, \omega_2 \in [\![\neg\alpha]\!], \ \omega_1 \ll \omega_2$$
$$\textit{and} \ \omega_2 \notin [\![\Psi]\!] \cup \min([\![\neg\alpha]\!], \leq_{\Psi})\} \ ,$$
$$\qquad \text{(Ord4)}$$

takes the prior preorder $\leq_{\Psi}$ and reorganizes this preorder as follows:

(Ord1) *To obtain compliance with AGM contraction, the minimal models of $\neg\alpha$ are added to the lowermost layer of the prior order, i.e., in the end we will have:*

$$[\![\leq_\Psi \div_{\mathrm{ord}} \alpha]\!] = [\![\Psi]\!] \cup \min([\![\neg\alpha]\!], \leq_\Psi) = \min(\Omega, \leq_\Psi) \cup \min([\![\neg\alpha]\!], \leq_\Psi)$$

(Ord2) *All models of α (except for those which are in $[\![\leq_\Psi \div_{\mathrm{ord}} \alpha]\!]$) are shifted above all counter-models of α, i.e., in the end we will have:*

$$\text{if } \omega_1 \in [\![\neg\alpha]\!], \ \omega_2 \in [\![\alpha]\!] \text{ and } \omega_2 \notin [\![\leq_\Psi \div_{\mathrm{ord}} \alpha]\!], \text{ then } \omega_1 <_{\Psi \div_{\mathrm{fus}} \alpha} \omega_2$$

(Ord3) *The relationship among elements of α by $\leq_{\Psi \div_{\mathrm{ord}} \alpha}$ is the same as before by $\leq_\Psi$, i.e., in the end we will have:*

$$\text{if } \omega_1, \omega_2 \in [\![\alpha]\!], \text{ then } \omega_1 \leq_\Psi \omega_2 \Leftrightarrow \omega_1 \leq_{\Psi \div_{\mathrm{ord}} \alpha} \omega_2$$

(Ord4) *The elements of $\neg\alpha$ are re-**ordered** according to $\ll$ (except for those which are in $[\![\leq_\Psi \div_{\mathrm{ord}} \alpha]\!]$), i.e., in the end we will have:*

$$\text{if } \omega_1, \omega_2 \in [\![\neg\alpha]\!] \setminus [\![\leq_\Psi \div_{\mathrm{ord}} \alpha]\!], \text{ then } \omega_1 \ll \omega_2 \Rightarrow \omega_1 <_{\Psi \div_{\mathrm{ord}} \alpha} \omega_2$$

Gentle Natural Moderate Contraction.
Last, the belief change operator $\div_{\mathrm{gnm}}$, given by

$$
\begin{aligned}
\leq_\Psi \div_{\mathrm{gnm}} \alpha = \ & \{(\omega_1, \omega_2) \mid \omega_1 \in [\![\Psi]\!] \cup \min([\![\neg\alpha]\!], \leq_\Psi)\} && \text{(Gnm1)} \\
& \cup \{(\omega_1, \omega_2) \mid [\![\Psi]\!] \nsubseteq [\![\alpha]\!] \text{ and } \omega_1 \leq_\Psi \omega_2\} && \text{(Gnm2)} \\
& \cup \{(\omega_1, \omega_2) \mid [\![\Psi]\!] \subseteq [\![\alpha]\!], \ \omega_1 \in [\![\neg\alpha]\!] \text{ and } \omega_2 \in [\![\alpha]\!] \setminus [\![\Psi]\!]\} && \\
& && \text{(Gnm3)} \\
& \cup \{(\omega_1, \omega_2) \mid [\![\Psi]\!] \subseteq [\![\alpha]\!] \ \omega_1, \omega_2 \in [\![\alpha]\!] \setminus [\![\Psi]\!] \text{ and } \omega_1 \leq_\Psi \omega_2\} && \\
& && \text{(Gnm4)} \\
& \cup \{(\omega_1, \omega_2) \mid [\![\Psi]\!] \subseteq [\![\alpha]\!] \ \omega_1, \omega_2 \in [\![\neg\alpha]\!] \text{ and } \omega_1 \leq_\Psi \omega_2\}, && \\
& && \text{(Gnm5)}
\end{aligned}
$$

takes the prior preorder $\leq_\Psi$ and reorganizes this preorder as follows:

(Gnm1) *If $\alpha \notin \mathrm{Bel}(\leq)$, then everything is kept as before, i.e., we have $\leq_\Psi \div_{\mathrm{gnm}} \alpha = \leq_\Psi$.*

(Gnm2) *If $\alpha \in \mathrm{Bel}(\leq)$, then, to obtain compliance with AGM contraction, the minimal models of $\neg\alpha$ are added to the lowermost layer of the prior order, i.e., in the end we will have:*

$$[\![\leq_\Psi \div_{\mathrm{gnm}} \alpha]\!] = [\![\Psi]\!] \cup \min([\![\neg\alpha]\!], \leq_\Psi) = \min(\Omega, \leq_\Psi) \cup \min([\![\neg\alpha]\!], \leq_\Psi)$$

Operator	Postulates								
	(IC1)	(IC2)	(IC3)	(IC4)	(IC1$^{\text{cond}}_{\Rightarrow}$)	(IC2$^{\text{cond}}_{\Rightarrow}$)	(IC3$_{\text{ca}}$)	(IC4$_{\text{weak}}$)	(IC4$_{\text{dca}}$)
$\dot{-}_{\text{nco}}$	✓	✓	✓	✓	✓	✓	✓	✓	✓
$\dot{-}_{\text{fus}}$	-	✓	✓	✓	✓	✓	✓	✓	-
$\dot{-}_{\text{ord}}$	✓	-	✓	✓	✓	-	✓	✓	-
$\dot{-}_{\text{gnm}}$	✓	✓	✓	✓	✓	✓	✓	✓	-

Table 11.2: Overview of satisfaction of the postulates considered in Chapter 10 by the operators given in Example 11.21. A ✓ denotes satisfaction of this postulate, while a - means that the postulate is violated.

(Gnm3) *Moreover, if $\alpha \in \text{Bel}(\leq)$, then all models of α (except for those which are in $[\![\leq_{\Psi} \dot{-}_{\text{gnm}} \alpha]\!]$) are shifted above all counter-models of α, i.e., in the end we will have:*

$$\text{if } \omega_1 \in [\![\neg\alpha]\!], \ \omega_2 \in [\![\alpha]\!] \text{ and } \omega_2 \notin [\![\leq_{\Psi} \dot{-}_{\text{gnm}} \alpha]\!],$$
$$\text{then } \omega_1 <_{\Psi \dot{-}_{\text{gnm}}\alpha} \omega_2$$

(Gnm4) *Moreover, if $\alpha \in \text{Bel}(\leq)$, then all models of α are keeping their relationship, i.e., in the end we will have:*

$$\text{if } \omega_1, \omega_2 \in [\![\alpha]\!], \text{ then } \omega_1 \leq_{\Psi} \omega_2 \Leftrightarrow \omega_1 \leq_{\Psi \dot{-}_{\text{gnm}}\alpha} \omega_2$$

(Gnm5) *If $\alpha \in \text{Bel}(\leq)$, then the elements of $\neg\alpha$ are ordered by $\leq_{\Psi \dot{-}_{\text{gnm}}\alpha}$ as before by $\leq_{\Psi}$, i.e., in the end we will have:*

$$\text{if } \omega_1, \omega_2 \in [\![\neg\alpha]\!], \text{ then } \omega_1 \leq_{\Psi} \omega_2 \Leftrightarrow \omega_1 \leq_{\Psi \dot{-}_{\text{gnm}}\alpha} \omega_2$$

Table 11.3 and Table 11.2 present satisfactions and violations, respectively, of principles, we encountered in this part, by the AGM contraction operators for $\mathcal{E}_{\text{TPO}}$ considered in this example. In the following, we make use of Figure 11.1 (from p. 301) which describes the relationship among various postulates considered in this part. Note that the properties given for $\dot{-}_{\text{nco}}$, $\dot{-}_{\text{fus}}$, $\dot{-}_{\text{ord}}$ and $\dot{-}_{\text{gnm}}$ imply satisfaction of the properties given in Table 11.3 and Table 11.2. We will see in the following examples for the violations of principles given in Table 11.3 and Table 11.2 by these operators. We make use of the following *total preorder $\trianglelefteq$ given by:*

$$\omega_1 \trianglelefteq \omega_2 \qquad \omega_2 \trianglelefteq \omega_3 \qquad \omega_3 \trianglelefteq \omega_2$$

$$\omega_1 \trianglelefteq \omega_3 \qquad \omega_2 \trianglelefteq \omega_4 \qquad \omega_3 \trianglelefteq \omega_4$$

$$\omega_1 \trianglelefteq \omega_4$$

For easy reading, we write $\trianglelefteq$, and other total preorders, vertically as follows:

$$\omega_4$$
$$\omega_2 \ \omega_3$$
$$\omega_1$$

We also use the total preorders $\trianglelefteq_1$ to $\trianglelefteq_6$ given by:

		ω_4			
$\omega_2 \ \omega_4$	ω_2	ω_4	ω_2		ω_3
ω_3	ω_3	ω_2	ω_4	$\omega_2 \ \omega_3$	ω_2
ω_1	ω_1	$\omega_1 \ \omega_3$	$\omega_1 \ \omega_3$	$\omega_1 \ \omega_4$	$\omega_1 \ \omega_4$
$\trianglelefteq_1$	$\trianglelefteq_2$	$\trianglelefteq_3$	$\trianglelefteq_4$	$\trianglelefteq_5$	$\trianglelefteq_6$

We consider the operators independently:

The operator $\dot{\div}_{\mathrm{nco}}$. *Consider the following changes*

$$\trianglelefteq \dot{\div}_{\mathrm{nco}} \varphi_{\omega_2,\omega_4} = \trianglelefteq \qquad \trianglelefteq \dot{\div}_{\mathrm{nco}} \varphi_{\omega_1,\omega_2} = \trianglelefteq_3 \qquad \trianglelefteq_2 \dot{\div}_{\mathrm{nco}} \varphi_{\omega_1,\omega_2,\omega_3} = \trianglelefteq_3$$

These changes demonstrates the typical behaviour of natural contraction, except for the beliefs in $\mathrm{Bel}(\Psi)$, the remaining order is not changed. This is in particular true for $\trianglelefteq \dot{\div}_{\mathrm{nco}} \varphi_{\omega_1,\omega_2} = \trianglelefteq_3$, by which the order is not changed, except for the minimal elements of $[\![\varphi_{\omega_1,\omega_2}]\!]$, as the interpretation ω_3 is added to the lowermost layer. This proves that $(\mathrm{IC}_{\mathrm{gic}})$ is violated by $\dot{\div}_{\mathrm{nco}}$. Consequently, $\dot{\div}_{\mathrm{nco}}$ violates also $(\mathrm{IC}_{\mathrm{ind}})$, $(\mathrm{IC}_{\mathrm{gmc}})$, and $(\mathrm{IC}_{\mathrm{mc}})$. From the change $\trianglelefteq_2 \dot{\div}_{\mathrm{nco}} \varphi_{\omega_1,\omega_2,\omega_3} = \trianglelefteq_3$ we obtain that $(\mathrm{IC}_{\mathrm{gic}})$ is violated by $\dot{\div}_{\mathrm{nco}}$. Consequently, $\dot{\div}_{\mathrm{nco}}$ violates also $(\mathrm{IC}_{\mathrm{ind}})$, $(\mathrm{IC}_{\mathrm{gmc}})$, $(\mathrm{IC}_{\mathrm{mc}})$. Clearly, $\dot{\div}_{\mathrm{nco}}$ satisfies $(\mathrm{IC}_{\mathrm{nc}})$, and thus, according to Figure 11.1, we obtain all entries for $\dot{\div}_{\mathrm{nco}}$ in Table 11.2. Moreover, satisfaction of $\dot{\div}_{\mathrm{nco}}$ implies satisfaction of $(\mathrm{IC3}_{\mathrm{alt}})$ and $(\mathrm{IC4}_{\mathrm{alt}})$ by $\dot{\div}_{\mathrm{nco}}$.

Operator	Postulates							
	$(IC3_{alt})$	$(IC4_{alt})$	(IC_{ind})	(IC_{nc})	(IC_{mc})	(IC_{gnc})	(IC_{gmc})	(IC_{gic})
$\dot{-}_{nco}$	✓	✓	-	✓	-	✓	-	-
$\dot{-}_{fus}$	-	✓	✓	-	✓	-	✓	✓
$\dot{-}_{ord}$	✓	-	✓	-	✓	-	✓	✓
$\dot{-}_{gnm}$	✓	✓	-	-	-	✓	✓	✓

Table 11.3: Overview of satisfaction of the postulates considered in this chapter by the operators given in Example 11.21. A ✓ denotes satisfaction of this postulate, while a - means that the postulate is violated.

The operator $\dot{-}_{fus}$. *Consider the following changes*

$$\trianglelefteq \dot{-}_{fus} \varphi_{\omega_1,\omega_2,\omega_4} = \trianglelefteq_5$$

The change $\trianglelefteq \dot{-}_{fus} \varphi_{\omega_2,\omega_4} = \trianglelefteq_5$ demonstrates (Fus2). All interpretations of $[\![\varphi_{\omega_2,\omega_4}]\!]$, the interpretations ω_2, ω_4, are ordered equally in $\trianglelefteq \dot{-}_{fus} \varphi_{\omega_2,\omega_4}$, as given by (Fus2). This proves that (IC_{gnc}), (IC1) and $(IC3_{alt})$ are violated by $\dot{-}_{fus}$. Consequently, $\dot{-}_{fus}$ violates also (IC_{nc}).

The operator $\dot{-}_{ord}$. *Consider the following changes*

$$\trianglelefteq_1 \dot{-}_{ord} \varphi_{\omega_1} = \trianglelefteq_3 \qquad\qquad \trianglelefteq \dot{-}_{ord} \varphi_{\omega_4} = \trianglelefteq_2$$

The change $\trianglelefteq \dot{-}_{ord} \varphi_{\omega_4} = \trianglelefteq_2$ demonstrates (Ord3). All interpretations of $[\![\neg\varphi_{\omega_4}]\!] = \{\omega_1, \omega_2, \omega_3\}$, and especially the interpretations ω_2, ω_3, are structured according to $\ll$. The change $\trianglelefteq_1 \dot{-}_{ord} \varphi_{\omega_1} = \trianglelefteq_3$ shows a violation of $(IC2_{\Rightarrow}^{cond})$. Consequently, $\dot{-}_{ord}$ violates also (IC_{nc}), $(IC4_{alt})$, and (IC1).

The operator $\dot{-}_{gnm}$. *Consider the following changes*

$$\trianglelefteq \dot{-}_{gnm} \varphi_{\omega_1,\omega_4} = \trianglelefteq_4 \qquad\qquad \trianglelefteq \dot{-}_{gnm} \varphi_{\omega_2,\omega_4} = \trianglelefteq$$

Compare this last change to the change $\trianglelefteq \dot{-}_{gnm} \varphi_{\omega_1,\omega_2} = \trianglelefteq_4$, which demonstrates that, as described by (Gnm3), all models of $[\![\neg\varphi_{\omega_1,\omega_2}]\!]$ are prioritized over the interpretations in $[\![\varphi_{\omega_1,\omega_2}]\!] \setminus [\![\trianglelefteq\dot{-}_{gnm}]\!]$. This change also shows violation of (IC_{nc}) by $\dot{-}_{gnm}$. Moreover, the change $\trianglelefteq \dot{-}_{ord} \varphi_{\omega_2,\omega_4} = \trianglelefteq$ shows violation of (IR_{ind}) by $\dot{-}_{gnm}$. Consequently, (IC_{mc}) is violated by $\dot{-}_{gnm}$.

11.6. Summary

In this part, we considered several iteration principles for contractions that are inspired by the various existing iteration principles for revision. We have seen that there are three forms of representations of the principles by Darwiche and Pearl: postulates that restrict the change of belief, postulates that restrict the change of conditional beliefs, and postulates that restrict the change of relations of interpretations. For most iteration principles for contraction given in this part we considered likewise three kinds of postulates: postulates that restrict the change of belief, postulates that restrict the change of conditional beliefs, and postulates that restrict the change of relations over interpretations.

For revision, an appropriated semantics for conditionals is given by the Ramsey-test. Analogously, we proposed to use contractionals as specific conditionals for contraction. The observations on conditionals in Chapter 9 (see Section 9.3 and see Section 9.4) may give the impression that the differentiation between the viewpoint of changing of beliefs and the viewpoint of changing of conditional beliefs is just a matter of syntactic different representation. However, for investigations of principles and formulation of novel postulates, the consideration of conditionals yields a different perspective on contraction than the perspective of change of mere beliefs. Our investigations of independence for contraction in Section 11.2 is attesting this impression, as the mere existence of contractions, made it easier to come up with appropriate postulates. Moreover, contractionals are connected to α-equivalence, which we introduced as a form of equivalence between epistemic states with respect to a sentence α in Section 9.5. We showed the usefulness of this relation, in particular for the formulation of succinct postulates, and how it allows us to provide insights about invariants in belief change.

The iteration principles presented in Chapter 10 are postulates that correspond to the principles for iterated revision by Darwiche and Pearl. Chapter 10 describes multiple attempts of obtaining postulates:

- We started in Section 10.2 with evaluating the unmodified syntactic Darwiche-Pearl postulates (IR1)–(IR4) as contraction postulates (IC1_{dca})–(IC4_{dca}). However, as shown in this section,

$(IC1_{dca})$–$(IC3_{dca})$ are not compatible with AGM contraction operators for epistemic states (see Proposition 10.2), and the remaining postulate $(IC4_{dca})$ is counter-intuitive for contraction.

- As next attempt, we modified $(IR1^{cond})$–$(IR4^{cond})$ in Section 10.3 slightly to $(IC1_{ca}^{cond})$–$(IC4_{ca}^{cond})$, such that they fit better to the overall intention of contraction, with the intention to overcome the impossibility results obtained for $(IC1_{dca})$–$(IC3_{dca})$. However, also $(IC1_{ca}^{cond})$ and $(IC2_{ca}^{cond})$ are not compatible with AGM contraction operators for epistemic states (see Proposition 10.5 and Proposition 10.8). We observed that one half of each of the postulates $(IC1_{ca}^{cond})$ and $(IC2_{ca}^{cond})$ is compatible with AGM contraction operators for epistemic states. This yields the postulates $(IC1_{\Rightarrow}^{cond})$ and $(IC2_{\Rightarrow}^{cond})$. The remaining postulates $(IC3_{ca}^{cond})$ and $(IC4_{ca}^{cond})$ can be considered as not fully satisfactory contraction postulates, as they only apply when the to be contracted belief is not believed anyway.

- In Section 10.3.3, we considered the semantic postulates $(IC1^{rel})$–$(IC4^{rel})$ for iterated contraction, which are contraction analogous to the postulates $(IR1^{rel})$–$(IR4^{rel})$. We provided a set of syntactic postulates $(IC1)$–$(IC4)$ which are equivalent to $(IC1^{rel})$–$(IC4^{rel})$ and more succinct than $(IC1_{KPP})$ to $(IC4_{KPP})$ proposed by Konieczny and Pino Pérez [98]. Moreover, without $(IC1)$ to $(IC4)$ it would be difficult to obtain $(IC1^{cond})$ to $(IC4^{cond})$. We proved an extended characterization theorem for iterated contraction, showing that all these different sets of postulates describe the same set of operators.

In Chapter 11, we considered mainly three approaches to contraction:

- In Section 11.2, we considered an analogue to the independence principle (IR_{ind}) of revision by Jin and Thielscher [82]. Following the argumentation of Section 9.3, we used contractionals as a representation of independencies and argued that an independence principle would keep as many conditional beliefs as possible in the course of change. The natural (and very strong) principle of preserving all prior conditional beliefs as an independence postulate for contraction, was shown to be incompatible with AGM contraction operators for epistemic states. We considered two alternatives. At first, we considered the two principles $(IC3_{alt})$ and $(IC4_{alt})$ which conserve certain conditional beliefs and prevent the introduction of new conditional beliefs. The second approach proposes (IC_{ind}^{rel}), which we obtained from (IR_{ind}^{rel}), the semantic analogue to (IR_{ind}).

- Section 11.3 considered natural contraction and moderated contraction. For both types of AGM contraction operators for epistemic sates, we contributed elegant novel postulates that highlight how conditional beliefs are affected by natural contraction and by moderated contraction. We showed that linear and full meet AGM contraction operators for epistemic states are natural contraction operators, but they are not moderate contraction operators. Moreover, we provided the relationship between natural contraction and moderated contraction, and (IR_{ind}).

- In Section 11.4, we proposed to restrict natural contraction, moderated contraction and (IR_{ind}) to specific cases. The restrictions were chosen according to two guiding principles: whenever the beliefs are not altered, then the change strategy should not change; and whenever the belief is altered, then the change of the strategy should be generally possible. For natural contraction, moderated contraction and (IR_{ind}) we considered corresponding characterization theorems.

- Finally, in Section 11.5, we considered the relationship among many principles considered in this part. Furthermore, we developed an extensive example making use of the new principles introduced in this chapter.

In summary, this part closes several gaps on the logic of iterated contraction. In particular, we have seen that, analogously to iterated revision, for iterated contraction there exists a similar rich landscape of iteration principles. Some principles considered here are novel for contraction, but corresponding principles for iterated revision have been known before. Moreover, for those iteration principles for contractions that were known before, our investigations add new perspectives by novel postulates which show how conditional beliefs are affected. Furthermore, the restrictions to "gentle" versions in Section 11.4 have not been considered before for iterated revision so far.

Chapter 12

Conclusions and Future Work

Since its establishment in the mid-1980s, the approach by Alchourrón, Gärdenfors, and Makinson (AGM) to belief change is the predominating base of the area of belief change. However, to make this approach applicable in areas like intentional forgetting or cognitive logics, extensions of the AGM approach in various directions are desirable. In particular, it is very likely that research in intentional forgetting [129] or cognitive logic challenges the state-of-the-art of the theory of belief change, either by having the demand for belief change operators with a specific behaviour or by having the demand for complex logics. The results given in this thesis provide foundational insights on this matter, regarding three aspects.

We identified the limits for the existence of belief change operators; our investigations considered the question:

> *What are the requirements for a set of epistemic states $\mathcal{E}$ such that a belief change operator for $\mathcal{E}$ of a certain type exists?*

We gave a precise answer to this question for propositional logic for AGM revision and AGM contraction. For revision, we extended this question to a question on the realizability of belief change operators with a certain acceptance behaviour. We choose credibility-limited revision as starting point for further investigations, and considered the question of

> *Which generalization of credibility-limited revision operators is*
> *able to reproduce arbitrary patterns of the acceptance for revision*
> *for arbitrary sets of epistemic states, while keeping the original*
> *spirit of credibility-limited revision?*

The solution presented in this thesis are dynamic-limited revision operators. However, while dynamic-limited revision operators allow realization of many acceptance descriptions, they do not realize arbitrary ones.

Second, we identified limits where AGM revision behaves as "expected". Representing belief change operators by total preorders (or richer representations) is a standard approach today, especially for the area of iterated belief change [57]. The characterization result given in Theorem 5.4 solves the question

> *In which Tarskian logics is every AGM revision operator total-*
> *preorder-representable?*

by showing that the absence of *critical loops* (also introduced here) is the sufficient and necessary criterion for ensuring that every AGM revision operator is total-preorder-representable. This result will help to choose the right logical setting for applications of belief revision.

Third, we provide insights on principles where AGM contraction follows certain behaviour for an iterative application. In particular, we considered the question:

> *What are natural analogues for contraction to iteration principles*
> *for revision?*

Our investigations in this thesis provide a large body of different principles that are inspired by principles for iterated revision. We showed for several natural postulates that they are incompatible with AGM contractions. For the remaining principles, only further investigations will show to which extent they are useful properties for iterated contraction.

We already mentioned several open questions in the course of this thesis. In the following, we consider (possible) connections to other research activities and topics for future investigations.

Sets of Epistemic States in the Darwiche-Pearl Framework.
The Darwiche-Pearl framework, presented in Section 6.1, explicitly
models sets of epistemic states on which the belief change takes place.
This specificity of the Darwiche-Pearl framework should be further
investigated regarding various aspects, for which we discuss examples
in the following.

Existence of Belief Change Operators. In this thesis, we tackled the
question of the existence of AGM revision and AGM contraction
operators in arbitrary sets of epistemic states. Such investigations
should be extended to other families of belief change operators, in
particular the role of iteration principles should be investigated. We
want to note that the existence of belief change operators has been
considered regarding the underlying logic. Ribeiro, Wassermann,
Flouris, and Antoniou characterized those Tarskian logics for which
AGM contraction operators exist[1], a property which is called *AGM-
compliance*[2] [125, 61]. It is an open task to explore how the results on
the existence of AGM revision operators and the existence of AGM
contraction operators given in this thesis are related to the notion of
AGM-compliance.

Change in different Logics. Similarly, it is very likely that certain
instantiations of the sets of epistemic states correspond to having
belief change in fragments of propositional logic. For instance, one
could choose the set of epistemic states such that every belief set is
in the Horn-fragment of propositional logic. Generally, belief change
in non-classical logics [124] should be linked with the choice of the
set of epistemic states. This includes investigations on the connection
between the notion of base logics from Part I (see Section 5.6) in this
thesis and the Darwiche-Pearl framework.

Modelling of Attitudes and Capabilities. Different sets of epistemic
states could act as a model for different attitudes and capabilities of
agents. While there are no works that explicitly employ sets of epistemic states in the Darwiche-Pearl framework for this, consideration
of different attitudes of agents regarding beliefs is a recent topic in
belief change [79]. The research on hyperintensional belief change by

---

[1]   Thanks to Özgür Özçep for pointing to the work by Flouris et al.
[2]   More specifically: AGM-compliance is a property of a logic that demands
       existence of a belief change operator that satisfies the basic AGM contraction
       postulates.

Souza and Wassermann [145] might be related to such considerations. Hyperintensionallity is modelled by considering an additional logic $\mathcal{L}_C$, which is a "sublogic" of the underlying logic $\mathcal{L}$. Hyperintensional belief change considers belief change operators over $\mathcal{L}$ but assumes that the result of a belief change is closed with respect to $\mathcal{L}_C$ [145]. Another research that considers alternative attitudes is due to Raidl, which considers belief change operators that allow the reintroduction of previously neglected beliefs [121]. The relationship between trust and belief revision is also a recent topic [28, 3].

Iterated (Non-Prioritized) Belief Change. Successive application of belief changes is vivid area of research. This field holds many interesting research questions yet to explore. In the following, we discuss some aspects to explore.

Principles for Iteration of Belief Change. Investigations of further principles for iterated belief change is an ongoing important topic in the area of (iterated) belief change. However, there are only few works on iteration principles for non-prioritized change. Examples are the investigations for the iteration of credibility-limited revision [27] and for improvement operators by Konieczny and Pino Pérez [97, 96], and combination of credibility-limited revision and improvement operators [26]. Besides of identification of novel principles, research should also focus on the critical evaluation of iteration principles. Non-prioritized change operators are highly flexible, and thus might be the right realm for such investigations [138].

Interrelationship Among Belief Change Operators. Another topic with many open questions is the question of interrelationships among different kinds of belief change operators. One problem to address is the interdefinability of belief change operators by other types of belief change operators. Prominent examples are the well-known connections between AGM revision and AGM contraction by the Levi-identity and Harper-identity (see Section 3.1 and the discussion at the end of Section 9.2), which has been addressed in the iterative context by, e.g., Booth and Chandler [25] and Konieczny and Pino Pérez [98]. Interdefinablility has also been discussed by Schwind and Konieczny with respect to improvement operators [139]. Another related topic is the question of how different kinds of belief changes should influence one another. One rare example for such research is given by Chopra,

Ghose, Meyer, and Wong, which considers iteration principles describing how revisions influence subsequent contractions [40]. Related to this topic is also the question of how to change the change strategy [30, 15] (which is an implicit theme of all iteration principles). Liberatore [104] discusses the change between iteration strategies for iterated revision. This is also connected to the revision of condition beliefs, which has been, for instance, investigated by Chandler and Booth [39], and has been explored broadly by Kern-Isberner [89, 86, 87, 88].

We close with a final remark on semantic perspectives on belief change. All semantic approaches considered in this thesis are rooted in the approach by Katsuno and Mendelzon [84] (see Chapter 3). This semantic approach on belief change is highly intuitive and a powerful means for deep theoretical investigations on the subject of belief change, especially because semantic investigations bring things to the point. For instance, this semantic viewpoint clearly captures the nature of different kinds of belief changes and unveils the impact of iteration postulates. The Darwiche-Pearl framework [41] and the framework of belief change over base logics are very expressive successors of the approach by Katsuno and Mendelzon. As discussed in this thesis, further adjustments or generalizations of the approach are likely to support dealing with more kinds of belief change operators. The propositions and theorems presented in this thesis, as well as the discussed further opportunities and extensions, underpin that the Katsuno and Mendelzon approach is and will be a valuable means for the theory of belief change.

Bibliography

[1] Marc Aiguier, Jamal Atif, Isabelle Bloch, and Céline Hudelot. "Belief revision, minimal change and relaxation: A general framework based on satisfaction systems, and applications to description logics". In: *Artificial Intelligence* 256 (2018), pp. 160–180.

[2] Carlos E. Alchourrón, Peter Gärdenfors, and David Makinson. "On the Logic of Theory Change: Partial Meet Contraction and Revision Functions". In: *The Journal of Symbolic Logic* 50.2 (1985), pp. 510–530.

[3] Yasser Ammar and Haythem O. Ismail. "On the Joint Revision of Belief and Trust". In: *Proceedings of the 6th Workshop on Formal and Cognitive Reasoning (FCR 2020) co-located with the 43rd German Conference on Artificial Intelligence (KI 2020)*. Ed. by Christoph Beierle, Marco Ragni, Frieder Stolzenburg, and Matthias Thimm. Vol. 2680. CEUR Workshop Proceedings. CEUR-WS.org, 2020, pp. 55–68.

[4] John R. Anderson, Michael D. Byrne, Scott Douglass, Christian Lebiere, and Yulin Qin. "An Integrated Theory of the Mind". In: *Psychological Review* 111.4 (2004), pp. 1036–1050.

[5] Theofanis Aravanis, Pavlos Peppas, and Mary-Anne Williams. "Observations on Darwiche and Pearl's Approach for Iterated Belief Revision". In: *Proceedings of the 28th International Joint Conference on Artificial Intelligence (IJCAI 2019)*. Ed. by Sarit Kraus. ijcai.org, 2019, pp. 1509–1515.

[6] Theofanis I. Aravanis, Pavlos Peppas, and Mary-Anne Williams. "Full Characterization of Parikh's Relevance-Sensitive Axiom for Belief Revision". In: *Journal of Artificial Intelligence Research* 66 (2019), pp. 765–792.

[7]   Carlos Areces and Verónica Becher. "Iterable AGM Func-
       tions". In: *Frontiers in Belief Revision*. Ed. by H. Rott and
       M. Williams. Vol. 22. Applied Logic Series. Kluwer Academic
       Publishers, 2001, pp. 261–277.

[8]   Alexander Becker, Gabriele Kern-Isberner, Kai Sauerwald, and
       Christoph Beierle. "Forgetting Formulas and Signature Ele-
       ments in Epistemic States". In: *Proceedings of the 19th Inter-
       national Workshop on Non-Monotonic Reasoning (NMR 2021)*.
       Ed. by Leila Amgoud and Richard Booth. 2021, pp. 233–242.

[9]   Christoph Beierle, Tanja Bock, Gabriele Kern-Isberner, Marco
       Ragni, and Kai Sauerwald. "Kinds and Aspects of Forgetting
       in Common-Sense Knowledge and Belief Management". In:
       *Proceedings of the 41st German Conference on Artificial Intel-
       ligence (KI 2018)*. Ed. by Frank Trollmann and Anni-Yasmin
       Turhan. 2018, pp. 366–373.

[10]   Christoph Beierle, Christian Eichhorn, and Gabriele Kern-
       Isberner. "Skeptical Inference Based on C-representations and
       its Characterization as a Constraint Satisfaction Problem".
       In: *Foundations of Information and Knowledge Systems - 9th
       International Symposium (FoIKS 2016)*. Ed. by Marc Gyssens
       and Guillermo Ricardo Simari. Vol. 9616. Lecture Notes in
       Computer Science. Springer, 2016, pp. 65–82.

[11]   Christoph Beierle, Christian Eichhorn, Gabriele Kern-Isberner,
       and Steven Kutsch. "Properties and Interrelationships of Skep-
       tical, Weakly Skeptical, and Credulous Inference Induced by
       Classes of Minimal Models". In: *Artificial Intelligence* 297
       (2021).

[12]   Christoph Beierle, Christian Eichhorn, Gabriele Kern-Isberner,
       and Steven Kutsch. "Properties of skeptical c-inference for
       conditional knowledge bases and its realization as a constraint
       satisfaction problem". In: *Annals of Mathematics and Artificial
       Intelligence* 83.3-4 (2018), pp. 247–275.

[13]   Christoph Beierle, Christian Eichhorn, Gabriele Kern-Isberner,
       and Steven Kutsch. "Skeptical, Weakly Skeptical, and Cred-
       ulous Inference Based on Preferred Ranking Functions". In:
       *Proceedings of the 22nd European Conference on Artificial In-
       telligence (ECAI-2016)*. Ed. by Gal A. Kaminka, Maria Fox,
       Paolo Bouquet, Eyke Hüllermeier, Virginia Dignum, Frank
       Dignum, and Frank van Harmelen. Vol. 285. Frontiers in Arti-

ficial Intelligence and Applications. IOS Press, 2016, pp. 1149–1157.

[14] Christoph Beierle, Marc Finthammer, Nico Potyka, Julian Varghese, and Gabriele Kern-Isberner. "A Framework for Versatile Knowledge and Belief Management Operations in a Probabilistic Conditional Logic". In: *IfCoLog Journal of Logics and Their Applications* 4.7 (2017), pp. 2063–2095.

[15] Christoph Beierle and Gabriele Kern-Isberner. "Selection Strategies for Inductive Reasoning From Conditional Belief Bases and for Belief Change Respecting the Principle of Conditional Preservation". In: *Proceedings of the 34th International Florida Artificial Intelligence Research Society Conference (FLAIRS-34)*. Ed. by E. Bell and F. Keshtkar. 2021.

[16] Christoph Beierle, Gabriele Kern-Isberner, Kai Sauerwald, Tanja Bock, and Marco Ragni. "Towards a General Framework for Kinds of Forgetting in Common-Sense Belief Management". In: *Künstliche Intelligenz* 33.1 (2019), pp. 57–68.

[17] Christoph Beierle, Steven Kutsch, and Henning Breuers. "On Rational Monotony and Weak Rational Monotony for Inference Relations Induced by Sets of Minimal C-Representations". In: *Proceedings of the 32nd International Florida Artificial Intelligence Research Society Conference (FLAIRS-32*. Ed. by Roman Barták and Keith W. Brawner. AAAI Press, 2019.

[18] Christoph Beierle, Steven Kutsch, and Andreas Obergrusberger. "On the Interrelationships Among C-Inference Relations Based on Preferred Models for Sets of Default Rules". In: *Proceedings of the 30th International Florida Artificial Intelligence Research Society Conference (FLAIRS-30)*. Ed. by Vasile Rus and Zdravko Markov. AAAI Press, 2017, pp. 724–729.

[19] Christoph Beierle, Steven Kutsch, and Kai Sauerwald. "Compilation of Conditional Knowledge Bases for Computing C-Inference Relations". In: *Foundations of Information and Knowledge Systems - 10th International Symposium (FoIKS 2018)*. Ed. by Flavio Ferrarotti and Stefan Woltran. Vol. 10833. Lecture Notes in Computer Science. Springer, 2018, pp. 34–54.

[20] Christoph Beierle, Steven Kutsch, and Kai Sauerwald. "Compilation of static and evolving conditional knowledge bases for computing induced nonmonotonic inference relations". In:

Annals of Mathematics and Artificial Intelligence 87.1-2 (2019), pp. 5–41.

[21] Christoph Beierle and Ingo J. Timm. "Intentional Forgetting: An Emerging Field in AI and Beyond". In: *KI – Künstliche Intelligenz* 33.1 (2019), pp. 5–8.

[22] Salem Benferhat, Sébastien Konieczny, Odile Papini, and Ramón Pino Pérez. "Iterated Revision by Epistemic States: Axioms, Semantics and Syntax". In: *Proceedings of the 14th European Conference on Artificial Intelligence (ECAI 2000)*. Ed. by Werner Horn. IOS Press, 2000, pp. 13–17.

[23] Salem Benferhat, Sylvain Lagrue, and Odile Papini. "Revision of Partially Ordered Information: Axiomatization, Semantics and Iteration". In: *Proceedings of the 19th International Joint Conference on Artificial Intelligence (IJCAI 2005)*. Ed. by Leslie Pack Kaelbling and Alessandro Saffiotti. Professional Book Center, 2005, pp. 376–381.

[24] Alexander Bochman. *A logical theory of nonmonotonic inference and belief change - numerical methods*. Springer, 2001.

[25] Richard Booth and Jake Chandler. "From iterated revision to iterated contraction: Extending the Harper Identity". In: *Artificial Intelligence* 277 (2019).

[26] Richard Booth, Eduardo L. Fermé, Sébastien Konieczny, and Ramón Pino Pérez. "Credibility-Limited Improvement Operators". In: *Proceedings of the 21st European Conference on Artificial Intelligence (ECAI 2014)*. Ed. by Torsten Schaub, Gerhard Friedrich, and Barry O'Sullivan. Vol. 263. Frontiers in Artificial Intelligence and Applications. IOS Press, 2014, pp. 123–128.

[27] Richard Booth, Eduardo L. Fermé, Sébastien Konieczny, and Ramón Pino Pérez. "Credibility-Limited Revision Operators in Propositional Logic". In: *Proceedings of the 30th International Conference on Principles of Knowledge Representation and Reasoning (KR 2012)*. Ed. by Gerhard Brewka, Thomas Eiter, and Sheila A. McIlraith. AAAI Press, 2012, pp. 116–125.

[28] Richard Booth and Aaron Hunter. "Trust as a Precursor to Belief Revision". In: *Journal of Artificial Intelligence Research* 61 (2018), pp. 699–722.

[29] Richard Booth and Thomas Andreas Meyer. "Admissible and Restrained Revision". In: *Journal of Artificial Intelligence Research* 26 (2006), pp. 127–151.

[30] Richard Booth and Thomas Andreas Meyer. "How to Revise a Total Preorder". In: *Journal of Philosophical Logic* 40.2 (2011), pp. 193–238.

[31] Richard Booth and Thomas Andreas Meyer. "On the Dynamics of Total Preorders: Revising Abstract Interval Orders". In: *Proceedings of the 9th European Conference Symbolic and Quantitative Approaches to Reasoning with Uncertainty (ECSQARU 2007)*. Ed. by Khaled Mellouli. Vol. 4724. Lecture Notes in Computer Science. Springer, 2007, pp. 42–53.

[32] Craig Boutilier. "Iterated revision and minimal change of conditional beliefs". In: *Journal of Philosophical Logic* 25.3 (1996), pp. 263–305.

[33] Craig Boutilier. "On the Revision of Probabilistic Belief States". In: *Notre Dame Journal of Formal Logic* 36.1 (1995), pp. 158–183.

[34] Ronald J. Brachman and Hector J. Levesque. *Knowledge Representation and Reasoning*. Elsevier, 2004.

[35] Michael E. Bratman. *Intention, plans, and practical reason*. Cambridge, MA: Harvard University Press, 1987.

[36] John Cantwell. "Logics of Belief Change without Linearity". In: *The Journal of Symbolic Logic* 65.4 (2000), pp. 1556–1575.

[37] Thomas Caridroit, Sébastien Konieczny, and Pierre Marquis. "Contraction in Propositional Logic". In: *Proceedings of the 13th European Conference Symbolic and Quantitative Approaches to Reasoning with Uncertainty (ECSQARU 2015)*. Ed. by Sébastien Destercke and Thierry Denoeux. Vol. 9161. Lecture Notes in Computer Science. Springer, 2015, pp. 186–196.

[38] Thomas Caridroit, Sébastien Konieczny, and Pierre Marquis. "Contraction in propositional logic". In: *International Journal of Approximate Reasoning* 80 (2017), pp. 428–442.

[39] Jake Chandler and Richard Booth. "Revision by Conditionals: From Hook to Arrow". In: *Proceedings of the 17th International Conference on Principles of Knowledge Representation and Reasoning*. 2020, pp. 233–242.

[40] Samir Chopra, Aditya Ghose, Thomas Andreas Meyer, and Ka-Shu Wong. "Iterated Belief Change and the Recovery Axiom". In: *Journal of Philosophical Logic* 37.5 (2008), pp. 501–520.

[41] Adnan Darwiche and Judea Pearl. "On the logic of iterated belief revision". In: *Artificial Intelligence* 89 (1997), pp. 1–29.

[42] Randall Davis, Howard E. Shrobe, and Peter Szolovits. "What Is a Knowledge Representation?" In: *AI Magazine* 14.1 (1993), pp. 17–33.

[43] James Delgrande and Yi Jin. "Parallel belief revision: Revising by sets of formulas". In: *Artificial Intelligence* 176.1 (2012), pp. 2223–2245.

[44] James P. Delgrande. "A Knowledge Level Account of Forgetting". In: *Journal of Artificial Intelligence Research* 60 (2017), pp. 1165–1213.

[45] James P. Delgrande and Pavlos Peppas. "Belief revision in Horn theories". In: *Artificial Intelligence* 218 (2015), pp. 1–22.

[46] James P. Delgrande, Pavlos Peppas, and Stefan Woltran. "General Belief Revision". In: *Journal of the ACM* 65.5 (2018), 29:1–29:34.

[47] Jon Doyle. "A Truth Maintenance System". In: *Artificial Intelligence* 12.3 (1979), pp. 231–272.

[48] Didier Dubois and Henri Prade. "Focusing vs. belief revision: A fundamental distinction when dealing with generic knowledge". In: *Qualitative and Quantitative Practical Reasoning*. Ed. by Dov M. Gabbay, Rudolf Kruse, Andreas Nonnengart, and Hans Jürgen Ohlbach. Berlin, Heidelberg: Springer Berlin Heidelberg, 1997, pp. 96–107.

[49] Didier Dubois and Henri Prade. *Possibility Theory - An Approach to Computerized Processing of Uncertainty*. Springer, 1988.

[50] Thomas Eiter and Gabriele Kern-Isberner. "A Brief Survey on Forgetting from a Knowledge Representation and Reasoning Perspective". In: *KI – Künstliche Intelligenz* 33.1 (2019), pp. 9–33.

[51] Ronald Fagin, Gabriel M. Kuper, Jeffrey D. Ullman, and Moshe Y. Vardi. "Updating Logical Databases". In: *Advances in Computing Research* 3 (1986), pp. 1–18.

[52] Ronald Fagin, Jeffrey D. Ullman, and Moshe Y. Vardi. "On the Semantics of Updates in Databases". In: *Proceedings of*

the 2nd ACM SIGACT-SIGMOD Symposium on Principles of Database Systems (PODS 1983). Ed. by Ronald Fagin and Philip A. Bernstein. ACM, 1983, pp. 352–365.

[53] Faiq Miftakhul Falakh, Sebastian Rudolph, and Kai Sauerwald. "A Katsuno-Mendelzon-Style Characterization of AGM Belief Base Revision for Arbitrary Monotonic Logics (Preliminary Report)". In: *Proceedings of the 7th Workshop on Formal and Cognitive Reasoning (FCR 2021) co-located with the 44th German Conference on Artificial Intelligence (KI 2021)*. Ed. by Christoph Beierle, Marco Ragni, Frieder Stolzenburg, and Matthias Thimm. Vol. 2961. CEUR Workshop Proceedings. CEUR-WS.org, 2021, pp. 48–59.

[54] Faiq Miftakhul Falakh, Sebastian Rudolph, and Kai Sauerwald. *Semantic Characterizations of General Belief Base Revision*. A preprint is available, 62 pp., arXiv: 2104.14512. Submitted for publication (2021).

[55] Marcelo A. Falappa, Gabriele Kern-Isberner, Maurício D. Luís Reis, and Guillermo Ricardo Simari. "Prioritized and Non-prioritized Multiple Change on Belief Bases". In: *Journal of Philosophical Logic* 41.1 (2012), pp. 77–113.

[56] Eduardo L. Fermé and Sven Ove Hansson. "AGM 25 Years - Twenty-Five Years of Research in Belief Change". In: *Journal of Philosophical Logic* 40.2 (2011), pp. 295–331.

[57] Eduardo L. Fermé and Sven Ove Hansson. *Belief Change - Introduction and Overview*. Springer Briefs in Intelligent Systems. Springer, 2018.

[58] Eduardo L. Fermé and Sven Ove Hansson. "Selective Revision". In: *Studia Logica* 63.3 (1999), pp. 331–342.

[59] Eduardo L. Fermé and Renata Wassermann. "On the logic of theory change: iteration of expansion". In: *Journal of the Brazilian Computer Society* 24.1 (2018), 8:1–8:9.

[60] M. Finthammer, C. Beierle, B. Berger, and G. Kern-Isberner. "An Implementation of Belief Change Operations Based on Probabilistic Conditional Logic". In: *Procdeedings of the 10th International Conference Conference on Logic Programming and Nonmonotonic Reasoning*. Ed. by Esra Erdem, Fangzhen Lin, and Torsten Schaub. Vol. 5753. LNCS. Springer, 2009, pp. 496–501.

[61] Giorgos Flouris, Dimitris Plexousakis, and Grigoris Antoniou. "Generalizing the AGM postulates: preliminary results and applications". In: *Proceedings of the 10th International Workshop on Non-Monotonic Reasoning (NMR 2004)*. Ed. by James P. Delgrande and Torsten Schaub. 2004, pp. 171–179.

[62] Nir Friedman and Joseph Y. Halpern. "Belief Revision: A Critique". In: *Proceedings of the 5th International Conference on Principles of Knowledge Representation and Reasoning (KR 1996)*. Ed. by Luigia Carlucci Aiello, Jon Doyle, and Stuart C. Shapiro. Morgan Kaufmann, 1996, pp. 421–431.

[63] Peter Gärdenfors. *Knowledge in flux : modeling the dynamics of epistemic states*. MIT Press Cambridge, 1988.

[64] Peter Gärdenfors and Hans Rott. "Belief Revision". In: *Handbook of Logic in Artificial Intelligence and Logic Programming (Vol. 4)*. Ed. by Dov M. Gabbay, C. J. Hogger, and J. A. Robinson. Oxford, UK: Oxford University Press, 1995, pp. 35–132.

[65] Patrick Girard and Hans Rott. "Belief Revision and Dynamic Logic". In: *Johan van Benthem on Logic and Information Dynamics*. Ed. by Alexandru Baltag and Sonja Smets. Springer, 2014, pp. 203–233.

[66] Moisés Goldszmidt and Judea Pearl. "Qualitative probabilities for default reasoning, belief revision, and causal modeling". In: *Artificial Intelligence* 84 (1996), pp. 57–112.

[67] Adam Grove. "Two modellings for theory change". In: *Journal of Philosophical Logic* 17.2 (1988), pp. 157–170.

[68] Joans Haldimann, Kai Sauerwald, Martin von Berg, Gabriele Kern-Isberner, and Christoph Beierle. "Towards a Framework of Hansson's Descriptor Revision for Conditionals". In: *Proceedings of the 36th ACM/SIGAPP Symposium on Applied Computing (SAC 2021)*. Ed. by Chih-Cheng Hung, Jiman Hong, Alessio Bechini, and Eunjee Song. New York, NY, USA: ACM, 2021, pp. 889–891.

[69] Jonas Haldimann, Kai Sauerwald, Martin von Berg, Gabriele Kern-Isberner, and Christoph Beierle. "Conditional Descriptor Revision and Its Modelling by a CSP". In: *Proceedings of the 17th European Conference on Logics in Artificial Intelligence (JELIA 2021)*. Ed. by Wolfgang Faber, Gerhard Friedrich,

Martin Gebser, and Michael Morak. Vol. 12678. Lecture Notes in Computer Science. Springer, 2021, pp. 35–49.

[70] Jonas Philipp Haldimann, Gabriele Kern-Isberner, and Christoph Beierle. "Syntax Splitting for Iterated Contractions". In: *Proceedings of the 17th International Conference on Principles of Knowledge Representation and Reasoning (KR 2020)*. Ed. by Diego Calvanese, Esra Erdem, and Michael Thielscher. 2020, pp. 465–475.

[71] Bengt Hansson. "Choice Structures and Preference Relations". In: *Synthese* 18.4 (1968), pp. 443–458.

[72] Sven Ove Hansson. "A Survey of non-Prioritized Belief Revision". In: *Erkenntnis* 50.2 (1999), pp. 413–427.

[73] Sven Ove Hansson. *A Textbook of Belief Dynamics: Theory Change and Database Updating*. Springer, 1999.

[74] Sven Ove Hansson. "Descriptor Revision". In: *Studia Logica* 102.5 (2014), pp. 955–980.

[75] Sven Ove Hansson. "Kernel Contraction". In: *The Journal of Symbolic Logic* 59.3 (1994), pp. 845–859.

[76] Sven Ove Hansson. "Revision of Belief Sets and Belief Bases". In: *Belief Change*. Ed. by Didier Dubois and Henri Prade. Dordrecht: Springer Netherlands, 1998, pp. 17–75.

[77] Sven Ove Hansson, Eduardo L. Fermé, John Cantwell, and Marcelo A. Falappa. "Credibility Limited Revision". In: *The Journal of Symbolic Logic* 66.4 (2001), pp. 1581–1596.

[78] Sven-Ove Hansson. *Descriptor Revision*. Springer International Publishing, 2017.

[79] Adrian Haret and Stefan Woltran. "Belief Revision Operators with Varying Attitudes Towards Initial Beliefs". In: *Proceedings of the 28th International Joint Conference on Artificial Intelligence (IJCAI 2019)*. Ed. by Sarit Kraus. ijcai.org, 2019, pp. 1726–1733.

[80] William L. Harper. "Rational Conceptual Change". In: *PSA: Proceedings of the Biennial Meeting of the Philosophy of Science Association* 1976 (1976), pp. 462–494.

[81] Matthias Hild and Wolfgang Spohn. "The measurement of ranks and the laws of iterated contraction". In: *Artificial Intelligence* 172.10 (2008), pp. 1195–1218.

[82] Yi Jin and Michael Thielscher. "Iterated belief revision, revised". In: *Artificial Intelligence* 171.1 (2007), pp. 1–18.

[83] Hirofumi Katsuno and Alberto O. Mendelzon. "On the Difference between Updating a Knowledge Base and Revising It". In: *Proceedings of the 2nd International Conference on Principles of Knowledge Representation and Reasoning (KR 1991)*. Ed. by James F. Allen, Richard Fikes, and Erik Sandewall. Morgan Kaufmann, 1991, pp. 387–394.

[84] Hirofumi Katsuno and Alberto O. Mendelzon. "Propositional Knowledge Base Revision and Minimal Change". In: *Artificial Intelligence* 52.3 (1992), pp. 263–294.

[85] Ken-ichi Kawarabayashi and Bojan Mohar. "Some Recent Progress and Applications in Graph Minor Theory". In: *Graphs and Combinatorics* 23.1 (2007), pp. 1–46.

[86] Gabriele Kern-Isberner. "A thorough axiomatization of a principle of conditional preservation in belief revision". In: *Annals of Mathematics and Artificial Intelligence* 40(1-2) (2004), pp. 127–164.

[87] Gabriele Kern-Isberner. *Conditionals in Nonmonotonic Reasoning and Belief Revision - Considering Conditionals as Agents*. Vol. 2087. Lecture Notes in Computer Science. Springer, 2001.

[88] Gabriele Kern-Isberner. "Linking Iterated Belief Change Operations to Nonmonotonic Reasoning". In: *Proceedings of the 11th International Conference of Principles of Knowledge Representation and Reasoning (KR 2008)*. Ed. by Gerhard Brewka and Jérôme Lang. AAAI Press, 2008, pp. 166–176.

[89] Gabriele Kern-Isberner. "Postulates for Conditional Belief Revision". In: *Proceedings of the 16th International Joint Conference on Artificial Intelligence (IJCAI 1999)*. Ed. by Thomas Dean. 1999, pp. 186–191.

[90] Gabriele Kern-Isberner, Tanja Bock, Christoph Beierle, and Kai Sauerwald. "Axiomatic Evaluation of Epistemic Forgetting Operators". In: *Proceedings of the 32nd International Florida Artificial Intelligence Research Society Conference (FLAIRS-32)*. Ed. by Roman Barták and Keith W. Brawner. 2019, pp. 470–475.

[91] Gabriele Kern-Isberner, Tanja Bock, Kai Sauerwald, and Christoph Beierle. "Belief Change Properties of Forgetting Operations over Ranking Functions". In: *Proceedings of the 16th Pacific Rim International Conference on Artificial Intel-*

ligence (PRICAI 2019). Ed. by Abhaya C. Nayak and Alok Sharma. 2019, pp. 459–472.

[92]   Gabriele Kern-Isberner, Tanja Bock, Kai Sauerwald, and Christoph Beierle. "Iterated contraction of propositions and conditionals under the principle of conditional preservation". In: *Proceedings of the 3rd Global Conference on Artificial Intelligence (GCAI 2017)*. Ed. by Christoph Benzmüller, Christine Lisetti, and Martin Theobald. Vol. 50. EPiC Series in Computing. EasyChair, 2017, pp. 78–92.

[93]   Gabriele Kern-Isberner and Gerhard Brewka. "Strong Syntax Splitting for Iterated Belief Revision". In: *Proceedings of the Twenty-Sixth International Joint Conference on Artificial Intelligence (IJCAI-17)*. 2017, pp. 1131–1137.

[94]   Gabriele Kern-Isberner and Daniela Huvermann. "What kind of independence do we need for multiple iterated belief change?" In: *Journal of Applied Logic* 22 (2017), pp. 91–119.

[95]   Stephen Cole Kleene. "On the interpretation of intuitionistic number theory". In: *Journal of Symbolic Logic* 10.4 (1945), pp. 109–124.

[96]   Sébastien Konieczny, Mattia Medina Grespan, and Ramón Pino Pérez. "Taxonomy of Improvement Operators and the Problem of Minimal Change". In: *Proceedings of the 12th International Conference on Principles of Knowledge Representation and Reasoning (KR 2010)*. Ed. by Fangzhen Lin, Ulrike Sattler, and Miroslaw Truszczynski. AAAI Press, 2010.

[97]   Sébastien Konieczny and Ramón Pino Pérez. "Improvement Operators". In: *Proceedings of the 11th International Conference on Principles of Knowledge Representation and Reasoning (KR 2008)*. Ed. by Gerhard Brewka and Jérôme Lang. AAAI Press, 2008, pp. 177–187.

[98]   Sébastien Konieczny and Ramón Pino Pérez. "On Iterated Contraction: syntactic characterization, representation theorem and limitations of the Levi identity". In: *Proceedings of the 11th International Conference on Scalable Uncertainty Management (SUM 2017)*. Ed. by Serafín Moral, Olivier Pivert, Daniel Sánchez, and Nicolás Marín. Vol. 10564. Lecture Notes in Artificial Intelligence. Springer, 2017.

[99] Sarit Kraus, Daniel Lehmann, and Menachem Magidor. "Non-monotonic Reasoning, Preferential Models and Cumulative Logics". In: *Artificial Intelligence* 44.1-2 (1990), pp. 167–207.

[100] Steven Kutsch and Christoph Beierle. "InfOCF-Web: An Online Tool for Nonmonotonic Reasoning with Conditionals and Ranking Functions". In: *Proceedings of the 30th International Joint Conference on Artificial Intelligence (IJCAI 2021)*. Ed. by Zhi-Hua Zhou. ijcai.org, 2021, pp. 4996–4999.

[101] John E. Laird. *The Soar Cognitive Architecture*. MIT Press, 2012.

[102] Isaac Levi. "Subjunctives, dispositions and chances". In: *Synthese* 34.4 (1977), pp. 423–455.

[103] David K. Lewis. *Counterfactuals*. Cambridge, Massachusetts: Harvard University Press, 1973.

[104] Paolo Liberatore. "On Mixed Iterated Revisions". In: *CoRR* abs/2104.03571 (2021). arXiv: 2104.03571.

[105] Paolo Liberatore. "The Complexity of Iterated Belief Revision". In: *Proceedings of the 6th International Conference on Database Theory (ICDT 1997)*. Ed. by Foto N. Afrati and Phokion G. Kolaitis. Vol. 1186. Lecture Notes in Computer Science. Springer, 1997, pp. 276–290.

[106] Fangzhen Lin and Ray Reiter. "Forget It!" In: *Proceedings of the AAAI Fall Symposium on Relevance*. AAAI Press, Menlo Park, CA, 1994, pp. 154–159.

[107] Sten Lindström and Wlodzimierz Rabinowicz. "Epistemic entrenchment with incomparabilities and relational belief revision". In: *The Logic of Theory Change, Workshop, Konstanz, FRG, October 13-15, 1989, Proceedings*. Ed. by André Fuhrmann and Michael Morreau. Vol. 465. Lecture Notes in Computer Science. Springer, 1989, pp. 93–126.

[108] David C. Makinson. "Completeness Theorems, Representation Theorems: What's the Difference?" In: *Hommage À Wlodek: Philosophical Papers Dedicated to Wlodek Rabinowicz*. Ed. by Toni Rønnow-Rasmussen, Björn Petersson, Jonas Josefsson, and Dan Egonsson. Department of Philosophy, Lund University, 2007.

[109] Edward Marczewski. "Sur l'extension de l'ordre partiel". In: *Fundamenta Mathematicae* 16 (1930), pp. 386–389.

[110]   Abhaya C. Nayak. "Iterated belief change based on epistemic entrenchment". In: *Erkenntnis* 41.3 (1994), pp. 353–390.

[111]   Abhaya C. Nayak, Randy Goebel, and Mehmet A. Orgun. "Iterated Belief Contraction from First Principles". In: *Proceedings of the 20th International Joint Conference on Artificial Intelligence (IJCAI 2007)*. Ed. by Manuela M. Veloso. 2007, pp. 2568–2573.

[112]   Abhaya C. Nayak, Randy Goebel, Mehmet A. Orgun, and Tam Pham. "Taking Levi Identity Seriously: A Plea for Iterated Belief Contraction". In: *Proceedings of the 1st International Conference on Knowledge Science, Engineering and Management (KSEM 2006)*. Ed. by Jérôme Lang, Fangzhen Lin, and Ju Wang. Vol. 4092. Lecture Notes in Computer Science. Springer, 2006, pp. 305–317.

[113]   Abhaya C. Nayak, Maurice Pagnucco, and Pavlos Peppas. "Dynamic belief revision operators". In: *Artificial Intelligence* 146.2 (2003), pp. 193–228.

[114]   Pavlos Peppas. "The Limit Assumption and Multiple Revision". In: *Journal of Logic and Computation* 14.3 (2004), pp. 355–371.

[115]   Pavlos Peppas and Mary-Anne Williams. "Belief Change and Semiorders". In: *Proceedings of the 14th International Conference on Principles of Knowledge Representation and Reasoning (KR 2014)*. Ed. by Chitta Baral, Giuseppe De Giacomo, and Thomas Eiter. AAAI Press, 2014.

[116]   Pavlos Peppas and Mary-Anne Williams. "Parametrised Difference Revision". In: *Proceedings of the 16th International ConferencePrinciples of Knowledge Representation and Reasoning (KR 2018)*. Ed. by Michael Thielscher, Francesca Toni, and Frank Wolter. AAAI Press, 2018, pp. 277–286.

[117]   Elise Perrotin and Fernando R. Velázquez-Quesada. "A Semantic Approach to Non-prioritized Belief Revision". In: *Logic Journal of the IGPL* 29.4 (2021), pp. 644–671.

[118]   Guilin Qi, Weiru Liu, and David A. Bell. "Knowledge Base Revision in Description Logics". In: *Proceedings of the 10th European Conference of Logics in Artificial Intelligence (JELIA 2006)*. Ed. by Michael Fisher, Wiebe van der Hoek, Boris Konev, and Alexei Lisitsa. Vol. 4160. Lecture Notes in Computer Science. Springer, 2006, pp. 386–398.

[119]   Marco Ragni, Gabriele Kern-Isberner, Christoph Beierle, and
        Kai Sauerwald. "Cognitive Logics - Features, Formalisms, and
        Challenges". In: *Proceedings of the 24nd European Conference
        on Artificial Intelligence (ECAI 2020)*. Ed. by Giuseppe De
        Giacomo, Alejandro Catalá, Bistra Dilkina, Michela Milano,
        Senén Barro, Alberto Bugarín, and Jérôme Lang. Vol. 325.
        Frontiers in Artificial Intelligence and Applications. IOS Press,
        2020, pp. 2931–2932.

[120]   Marco Ragni, Kai Sauerwald, Tanja Bock, Gabriele Kern-
        Isberner, Paulina Friemann, and Christoph Beierle. "Towards a
        Formal Foundation of Cognitive Architectures". In: *Proceedings
        of the 40th Annual Meeting of the Cognitive Science Society
        (CogSci 2018)*. Ed. by Chuck Kalish, Martina A. Rau, Xiaojin
        (Jerry) Zhu, and Timothy T. Rogers. 2018.

[121]   Eric Raidl. "Open-Minded Orthodox Bayesianism by Epsilon-
        Conditionalization". In: *The British Journal for the Philosophy
        of Science* 71.1 (2020), pp. 139–176.

[122]   Eric Raidl and Hand Rott. *Revising threshold-based belief:
        the view from ranking theory*. pp. 51. 2021. Submitted for
        publication.

[123]   Raghav Ramachandran, Abhaya Nayak, and Mehmet Orgun.
        "Three Approaches to Iterated Belief Contraction". In: *Journal
        of Philosophical Logic* 41.1 (2012), pp. 115–142.

[124]   Márcio Moretto Ribeiro. *Belief Revision in Non-Classical
        Logics*. Springer Briefs in Computer Science. Springer, 2013.

[125]   Márcio Moretto Ribeiro, Renata Wassermann, Giorgos Flouris,
        and Grigoris Antoniou. "Minimal change: Relevance and re-
        covery revisited". In: *Artificial Intelligence* 201 (2013), pp. 59–
        80.

[126]   Hans Rott. "Coherence and Conservatism in the Dynamics
        of Belief II: Iterated Belief Change without Dispositional Co-
        herence". In: *Journal of Logic and Computation* 13.1 (2003),
        pp. 111–145.

[127]   Hans Rott. "Shifting Priorities: Simple Representations
        for Twenty-Seven Iterated Theory Change Operators". In:
        *Towards Mathematical Philosophy: Papers from the Studia Log-
        ica conference Trends in Logic IV*. Ed. by David Makinson,
        Jacek Malinowski, and Heinrich Wansing. Dordrecht: Springer
        Netherlands, 2009, pp. 269–296.

[128] Stuart Russell and Peter Norvig. *Artificial Intelligence: A Modern Approach*. 3rd ed. Prentice Hall, 2010.

[129] Kai Sauerwald. "Modelling the dynamics of forgetting and remembering by a system of belief changes: student research abstract". In: *Proceedings of the 34th ACM/SIGAPP Symposium on Applied Computing (SAC 2019)*. Ed. by Chih-Cheng Hung and George A. Papadopoulos. ACM, 2019, pp. 1168–1171.

[130] Kai Sauerwald and Christoph Beierle. "Decrement Operators in Belief Change". In: *Proceedings of the 15th European Conference Symbolic and Quantitative Approaches to Reasoning with Uncertainty (ECSQARU 2019)*. Ed. by Gabriele Kern-Isberner and Zoran Ognjanovic. Vol. 11726. Lecture Notes in Computer Science. Springer, 2019, pp. 251–262.

[131] Kai Sauerwald and Christoph Beierle. "Iterated Belief Change, Computationally". In: *Proceedings of the 19th International Conference on Principles of Knowledge Representation and Reasoning (KR 2022)*. Ed. by Gabriele Kern-Isberner and Thomas Meyer. 2022. To appear.

[132] Kai Sauerwald and Jonas Haldimann. "WHIWAP: Checking Iterative Belief Changes". In: *Proceedings of the 8th Workshop on Dynamics of Knowledge and Belief (DKB-2019) and the 7th Workshop KI & Kognition (KIK-2019) co-located with the 42rd German Conference on Artificial Intelligence (KI 2019)*. Ed. by Christoph Beierle, Marco Ragni, Frieder Stolzenburg, and Matthias Thimm. Vol. 2445. CEUR Workshop Proceedings. CEUR-WS.org, 2019, pp. 14–23.

[133] Kai Sauerwald, Jonas Haldimann, Martin von Berg, and Christoph Beierle. "Descriptor Revision for Conditionals: Literal Descriptors and Conditional Preservation". In: *Proceedings of the 43rd German Conference on Artificial Intelligence (KI 2020)*. Ed. by Ute Schmid, Franziska Klügl, and Diedrich Wolter. Vol. 12325. Lecture Notes in Computer Science. Springer, 2020, pp. 204–218.

[134] Kai Sauerwald and Philip Heltweg. "On Using Model Checking for the Certification of Iterated Belief Changes". In: *Proceedings of the 7th Workshop on Formal and Cognitive Reasoning (FCR 2021) co-located with the 44th German Conference on Artificial Intelligence (KI 2021)*. Ed. by Christoph Beierle, Marco Ragni,

Frieder Stolzenburg, and Matthias Thimm. Vol. 2961. CEUR Workshop Proceedings. CEUR-WS.org, 2021, pp. 23–33.

[135] Kai Sauerwald, Philip Heltweg, and Christoph Beierle. "Certification of Iterated Belief Changes via Model Checking and its Implementation". In: *Proceedings of the 19th International Workshop on Non-Monotonic Reasoning (NMR 2021)*. Ed. by Leila Amgoud and Richard Booth. 2021, pp. 250–253.

[136] Kai Sauerwald, Gabriele Kern-Isberner, and Christoph Beierle. "A Conditional Perspective for Iterated Belief Contraction". In: *Proceedings of the 24nd European Conference on Artificial Intelligence (ECAI 2020)*. Ed. by Giuseppe De Giacomo, Alejandro Catalá, Bistra Dilkina, Michela Milano, Senén Barro, Alberto Bugarín, and Jérôme Lang. IOS Press, 2020, pp. 889–896.

[137] Kai Sauerwald, Gabriele Kern-Isberner, and Christoph Beierle. *A Conditional Perspective on the Logic of Iterated Belief Contraction*. A preprint is available, 37 pp., arXiv: 2202.03196. Submitted for publication (2022).

[138] Kai Sauerwald, Gabriele Kern-Isberner, and Christoph Beierle. "On Limited Non-Prioritised Belief Revision Operators with Dynamic Scope". In: *CoRR* abs/2108.07769 (2021). arXiv: 2108.07769.

[139] Nicolas Schwind and Sébastien Konieczny. "Non-Prioritized Iterated Revision: Improvement via Incremental Belief Merging". In: *Proceedings of the 17th International Conference on Principles of Knowledge Representation and Reasoning (KR 2020)*. Ed. by Diego Calvanese, Esra Erdem, and Michael Thielscher. 2020, pp. 738–747.

[140] Nicolas Schwind, Sébastien Konieczny, Jean-Marie Lagniez, and Pierre Marquis. "On Computational Aspects of Iterated Belief Change". In: *Proceedings of the 29th International Joint Conference on Artificial Intelligence (IJCAI 2020)*. Ed. by Christian Bessiere. 2020, pp. 1770–1776.

[141] Krister Segerberg. "Irrevocable Belief Revision in Dynamic Doxastic Logic". In: *Notre Dame Journal of Formal Logic* 39.3 (1998), pp. 287–306.

[142] Krister Segerberg. "The basic dynamic doxastic logic of AGM". In: *Frontiers in Belief Revision*. Ed. by H. Rott and M. Williams. Vol. 22. Applied Logic Series. Kluwer Academic Publishers, 2001, pp. 57–84.

[143]   Amílcar Sernadas, Cristina Sernadas, and Carlos Caleiro. "Synchronization of Logics". In: *Studia Logica* 59.1 (1997), pp. 217–247.

[144]   Raymond M. Smullyan. "Logicians Who Reason About Themselves". In: *Proceedings of the 1st Conference on Theoretical Aspects of Reasoning about Knowledge (TARK 1986)*. Ed. by Joseph Y. Halpern. Morgan Kaufmann, 1986, pp. 341–352.

[145]   Marlo Souza and Renata Wassermann. "Belief Contraction in Non-classical logics as Hyperintensional Belief Change". In: *Proceedings of the 18th International Conference on Principles of Knowledge Representation and Reasoning (KR 2021)*. Ed. by Meghyn Bienvenu, Gerhard Lakemeyer, and Esra Erdem. 2021, pp. 588–598.

[146]   Wolfgang Spohn. "Ordinal conditional functions: a dynamic theory of epistemic states". In: *Causation in Decision, Belief Change, and Statistics, II*. Ed. by W.L. Harper and B. Skyrms. Kluwer Academic Publishers, 1988, pp. 105–134.

[147]   Wolfgang Spohn. *The Laws of Belief: Ranking Theory and Its Philosophical Applications*. Oxford University Press, 2012.

[148]   Robert Stalnaker. "A Theory of Conditionals". In: *Studies in Logical Theory (American Philosophical Quarterly Monographs 2)*. Ed. by Nicholas Rescher. Oxford: Blackwell, 1968, pp. 98–112.

[149]   Robert Stalnaker. "The Problem of Logical Omniscience, I". In: *Synthese* 89.3 (1991), pp. 425–440.

[150]   Alfred Tarski. *Logic Semantics, Metamathematics: Papers From 1923 to 1938*. Translated by J.H. Woodger. Clarendon Press, 1956.

[151]   Ingo J. Timm, Steffen Staab, Michael Siebers, Claudia Schon, Ute Schmid, Kai Sauerwald, Lukas Reuter, Marco Ragni, Claudia Niederée, Heiko Maus, Gabriele Kern-Isberner, Christian Jilek, Paulina Friemann, Thomas Eiter, Andreas Dengel, Hannah Dames, Tanja Bock, Jan Ole Berndt, and Christoph Beierle. "Intentional Forgetting in Artificial Intelligence Systems: Perspectives and Challenges". In: *Proceedings of the 41st German Conference on Artificial Intelligence (KI 2018)*. Ed. by Frank Trollmann and Anni-Yasmin Turhan. 2018, pp. 357–365.

[152]   Moshe Y. Vardi. "An Automata-Theoretic Approach to Fair Realizability and Synthesis". In: *Proceedings of the 7th Inter-

national Conference on Computer Aided Verification. Ed. by Pierre Wolper. Vol. 939. Lecture Notes in Computer Science. Springer, 1995, pp. 267–278.

[153] Marco Wilhelm, Diana Howey, Gabriele Kern-Isberner, Kai Sauerwald, and Christoph Beierle. "A Brief Introduction Into Activation-Based Conditional Inference". In: *Proceedings of the 7th Workshop on Formal and Cognitive Reasoning (FCR 2021) co-located with the 44th German Conference on Artificial Intelligence (KI 2021)*. Ed. by Christoph Beierle, Marco Ragni, Frieder Stolzenburg, and Matthias Thimm. Vol. 2961. CEUR Workshop Proceedings. CEUR-WS.org, 2021, pp. 4–8.

[154] Marco Wilhelm, Diana Howey, Gabriele Kern-Isberner, Kai Sauerwald, and Christoph Beierle. "Integrating Cognitive Principles From ACT-R Into Probabilistic Conditional Reasoning by Taking the Example of Maximum Entropy Reasoning". In: *Proceedings of the 35th International Florida Artificial Intelligence Research Society Conference (FLAIRS-35)*. 2022. To appear.

[155] Marco Wilhelm and Gabriele Kern-Isberner. "Focused Inference and System P". In: *Proceedings of the 35th AAAI Conference on Artificial Intelligence (AAAI 2021)*. AAAI Press, 2021, pp. 6522–6529.

[156] Ernst Zermelo. "Beweis, daß jede Menge wohlgeordnet werden kann. (Aus einem an Herrn Hilbert gerichteten Briefe)". In: *Mathematische Annalen* 59 (1904), pp. 514–516.

[157] Dongmo Zhang. "Belief revision by sets of sentences". In: *Journal of Computer Science and Technology* 11.2 (1996), pp. 108–125.

[158] Zhiqiang Zhuang, Zhe Wang, Kewen Wang, and James P. Delgrande. "A Generalisation of AGM Contraction and Revision to Fragments of First-Order Logic". In: *Journal of Artificial Intelligence Research* 64 (2019), pp. 147–179.

List of Postulates

Postulates for Revision and Non-Prioritized Revision

	AGM revision postulates (see p. 27)
(AGM∗1)	$\alpha \in K * \alpha$,
(AGM∗2)	$K * \alpha \subseteq K + \alpha$,
(AGM∗3)	If $K + \alpha$ is consistent, then $K * \alpha = K + \alpha$,
(AGM∗4)	If α is consistent, then $K * \alpha$ is consistent,
(AGM∗5)	If $\alpha \equiv \beta$, then $K * \alpha = K * \beta$,
(AGM∗6)	$K * (\alpha \wedge \beta) \subseteq (K * \alpha) + \beta$,
(AGM∗7)	If $\neg \beta \notin K * \alpha$, then $(K * \alpha) + \beta \subseteq K * (\alpha \wedge \beta)$,

	Revision postulates propositional logic (see p. 30)
(KM1)	$\varphi \circ \alpha \models \alpha$.
(KM2)	If $\varphi \wedge \alpha$ is consistent, then $\varphi \circ \alpha \equiv \varphi \wedge \alpha$.
(KM3)	If α is consistent, then $\varphi \circ \alpha$ is consistent.
(KM4)	If $\varphi_1 \equiv \varphi_2$ and $\alpha \equiv \beta$, then $\varphi_1 \circ \alpha \equiv \varphi_2 \circ \beta$.
(KM5)	$(\varphi \circ \alpha) \wedge \beta \models \varphi \circ (\alpha \wedge \beta)$.
(KM6)	If $(\varphi \circ \alpha) \wedge \beta$ is consistent, then $\varphi \circ (\alpha \wedge \beta) \models (\varphi \circ \alpha) \wedge \beta$.

	Revision postulates for base logics (see p. 51)
(G1)	$\mathcal{K} \circ \Gamma \models \Gamma$.
(G2)	If $[\![\mathcal{K} \uplus \Gamma]\!] \neq \emptyset$ then $\mathcal{K} \circ \Gamma \equiv \mathcal{K} \uplus \Gamma$.
(G3)	If $[\![\Gamma]\!] \neq \emptyset$ then $[\![\mathcal{K} \circ \Gamma]\!] \neq \emptyset$.
(G4)	If $\mathcal{K}_1 \equiv \mathcal{K}_2$ and $\Gamma_1 \equiv \Gamma_2$ then $\mathcal{K}_1 \circ \Gamma_1 \equiv \mathcal{K}_2 \circ \Gamma_2$.
(G5)	$(\mathcal{K} \circ \Gamma_1) \uplus \Gamma_2 \models \mathcal{K} \circ (\Gamma_1 \uplus \Gamma_2)$.
(G6)	If $[\![(\mathcal{K} \circ \Gamma_1) \uplus \Gamma_2]\!] \neq \emptyset$ then $\mathcal{K} \circ (\Gamma_1 \uplus \Gamma_2) \models (\mathcal{K} \circ \Gamma_1) \uplus \Gamma_2$.
(G4w)	If $\Gamma_1 \equiv \Gamma_2$, then $\mathcal{K} \circ \Gamma_1 \equiv \mathcal{K} \circ \Gamma_2$. (p. 71)

	Revision postulates for epistemic states (see p. 121)
(R1)	$\alpha \in \mathrm{Bel}(\Psi * \alpha)$.
(R2)	If $\mathrm{Bel}(\Psi) + \alpha$ consistent, then $\mathrm{Bel}(\Psi * \alpha) = \mathrm{Bel}(\Psi) + \alpha$.
(R3)	If α is consistent, then $\mathrm{Bel}(\Psi * \alpha)$ is consistent.
(R4)	If $\alpha \equiv \beta$, then $\mathrm{Bel}(\Psi * \alpha) = \mathrm{Bel}(\Psi * \beta)$.
(R5)	$\mathrm{Bel}(\Psi * (\alpha \wedge \beta)) \subseteq \mathrm{Bel}(\Psi * \alpha) + \beta$.
(R6)	If $\mathrm{Bel}(\Psi * \alpha) + \beta$ is consistent, then $\mathrm{Bel}(\Psi * \alpha) + \beta \subseteq \mathrm{Bel}(\Psi * (\alpha \wedge \beta))$.

	Credibility-limited revision (see p. 138 and p. 142f)
(CL1)	$\alpha \in \mathrm{Bel}(\Psi \circledast \alpha)$ or $\mathrm{Bel}(\Psi \circledast \alpha) = \mathrm{Bel}(\Psi)$.
(CL2)	If $\mathrm{Bel}(\Psi) + \alpha$ is consistent, then $\mathrm{Bel}(\Psi \circledast \alpha) = \mathrm{Bel}(\Psi) + \alpha$.
(CL3)	$\mathrm{Bel}(\Psi \circledast \alpha)$ is consistent.
(CL4)	If $\alpha \equiv \beta$, then $\mathrm{Bel}(\Psi \circledast \alpha) = \mathrm{Bel}(\Psi \circledast \beta)$.
(CL5)	If $\alpha \in \mathrm{Bel}(\Psi \circledast \alpha)$ and $\alpha \models \beta$, then $\beta \in \mathrm{Bel}(\Psi \circledast \beta)$.
(CL6)	$\mathrm{Bel}(\Psi \circledast (\alpha \vee \beta)) = \begin{cases} \mathrm{Bel}(\Psi \circledast \alpha) \text{ or} \\ \mathrm{Bel}(\Psi \circledast \beta) \text{ or} \\ \mathrm{Bel}(\Psi \circledast \alpha) \cap \mathrm{Bel}(\Psi \circledast \beta) \end{cases}$.
(CL3wcp)	If $\mathrm{Bel}(\Psi \circledast \alpha)$ is inconsistent, then $\mathrm{Bel}(\Psi)$ or α is inconsistent.
(WCP)	If $\mathrm{Bel}(\Psi)$ and α are consistent, then $\mathrm{Bel}(\Psi \circledast \alpha)$ is consistent.
(CL3u)	If $\mathrm{Bel}(\Psi \circledast \alpha)$ is consistent and $\alpha \models \beta$, then $\mathrm{Bel}(\Psi \circledast \beta)$ is consistent.

	Generalized credibility-limited revision (see p. 143)
(GCL1)	$\alpha \in \mathrm{Bel}(\Psi \circledast \alpha)$ or $\mathrm{Bel}(\Psi \circledast \alpha) = \mathrm{Bel}(\Psi)$.
(GCL2)	If $\mathrm{Bel}(\Psi) + \alpha$ is consistent, then $\mathrm{Bel}(\Psi \circledast \alpha) = \mathrm{Bel}(\Psi) + \alpha$.
(GCL3)	If $\mathrm{Bel}(\Psi \circledast \alpha)$ is inconsistent, then $\mathrm{Bel}(\Psi)$ or α is inconsistent.
(GCL4)	If $\mathrm{Bel}(\Psi \circledast \alpha)$ is consistent and $\alpha \models \beta$, then $\mathrm{Bel}(\Psi \circledast \beta)$ is consistent.

(GCL5)	If $\alpha \equiv \beta$, then $\mathrm{Bel}(\Psi \circledast \alpha) = \mathrm{Bel}(\Psi \circledast \beta)$.
(GCL6)	If $\alpha \in \mathrm{Bel}(\Psi \circledast \alpha)$ and $\alpha \models \beta$, then $\beta \in \mathrm{Bel}(\Psi \circledast \beta)$.

$$(\mathrm{GCL7}) \quad \mathrm{Bel}(\Psi \circledast (\alpha \vee \beta)) = \begin{cases} \mathrm{Bel}(\Psi \circledast \alpha) \text{ or} \\ \mathrm{Bel}(\Psi \circledast \beta) \text{ or} \\ \mathrm{Bel}(\Psi \circledast \alpha) \cap \mathrm{Bel}(\Psi \circledast \beta) \end{cases}.$$

(GCL2$_{\mathrm{sem}}$)	If $[\![\Psi]\!] \cap [\![\alpha]\!] \neq \emptyset$, then $[\![\Psi \circ \alpha]\!] = [\![\Psi]\!] \cap [\![\alpha]\!]$. (p. 164)

Dynamic-limited revision (see p. 167)

(DL0)	$\mathrm{Bel}(\Psi \star \alpha) = \mathrm{Bel}(\Psi)$ or $\alpha \in \mathrm{Bel}(\Psi \star \alpha)$.
(DL1)	If $\mathrm{Bel}(\Psi) \cup \mathrm{Bel}(\Psi \star \alpha)$ is consistent, then $\mathrm{Bel}(\Psi) \subseteq \mathrm{Bel}(\Psi \star \alpha)$.
(DL2)	If $\mathrm{Bel}(\Psi) \cup \mathrm{Bel}(\Psi \star (\alpha \wedge \beta))$ is consistent and $\mathrm{Bel}(\Psi) \neq \mathrm{Bel}(\Psi \star (\alpha \wedge \beta))$, then $\mathrm{Bel}(\Psi \star \alpha) \cup \mathrm{Bel}(\Psi \star \beta)$ is consistent.
(DL3)	If $\mathrm{Bel}(\Psi) \cup \mathrm{Bel}(\Psi \star \alpha)$ and $\mathrm{Bel}(\Psi) + \alpha$ are consistent, and $\alpha \models \gamma$ and $\mathrm{Bel}(\Psi \star \gamma) \not\subseteq \mathrm{Cn}(\alpha)$ holds, then consistency of β and inconsistency of $\mathrm{Bel}(\Psi) \cup \mathrm{Bel}(\Psi \star \beta)$ together imply that $\mathrm{Bel}(\Psi) \cup \mathrm{Bel}(\Psi \star (\alpha \vee \beta))$ is inconsistent.
(DL4)	If $\mathrm{Bel}(\Psi)$ and α are consistent, then $\mathrm{Bel}(\Psi \star \alpha)$ is consistent.
(DL5)	If $\mathrm{Bel}(\Psi \star \alpha)$ is consistent and $\alpha \models \beta$, then $\mathrm{Bel}(\Psi \star \beta)$ is consistent.
(DL6)	If $\alpha \equiv \beta$, then $\mathrm{Bel}(\Psi \star \alpha) = \mathrm{Bel}(\Psi \star \beta)$.
(DL7)	If α is consistent and $\alpha \in \mathrm{Bel}(\Psi \star \alpha)$, then $\alpha \models \beta$ implies $\beta \in \mathrm{Bel}(\Psi \star \beta)$.
(DL8)	If α, β are consistent and $\mathrm{Bel}(\Psi \star \alpha) \neq \mathrm{Bel}(\Psi)$ and $\mathrm{Bel}(\Psi \star \beta) = \mathrm{Bel}(\Psi)$, then $\beta \notin \mathrm{Bel}(\Psi)$ implies $\mathrm{Bel}(\Psi \star (\alpha \vee \beta)) + \beta$ is inconsistent.

$$(\mathrm{DL9}) \quad \mathrm{Bel}(\Psi \star (\alpha \vee \beta)) = \begin{cases} \mathrm{Bel}(\Psi \star \alpha) \text{ or} \\ \mathrm{Bel}(\Psi \star \beta) \text{ or} \\ \mathrm{Bel}(\Psi \star \alpha) \cap \mathrm{Bel}(\Psi \star \beta) \end{cases}.$$

Iteration Postulates for Revision

	Darwiche-Pearl postulates (see p. 236f)
(IR1)	If $\beta \models \alpha$, then $\mathrm{Bel}(\Psi * \alpha * \beta) = \mathrm{Bel}(\Psi * \beta)$.
(IR2)	If $\beta \models \neg\alpha$, then $\mathrm{Bel}(\Psi * \alpha * \beta) = \mathrm{Bel}(\Psi * \beta)$.
(IR3)	If $\Psi * \beta \models \alpha$, then $\Psi * \alpha * \beta \models \alpha$.
(IR4)	If $\Psi * \beta \not\models \neg\alpha$, then $\Psi * \alpha * \beta \not\models \neg\alpha$.
(IR1^{cond})	If $\beta \models \alpha$, then $\Psi \models (\gamma \mid \beta) \Leftrightarrow \Psi * \alpha \models (\gamma \mid \beta)$.
(IR2^{cond})	If $\beta \models \neg\alpha$, then $\Psi \models (\gamma \mid \beta) \Leftrightarrow \Psi * \alpha \models (\gamma \mid \beta)$.
(IR3^{cond})	If $\Psi \models (\alpha \mid \beta)$, then $\Psi * \alpha \models (\alpha \mid \beta)$.
(IR4^{cond})	If $\Psi \not\models (\neg\alpha \mid \beta)$, then $\Psi * \alpha \not\models (\neg\alpha \mid \beta)$.
(IR1^{rel})	If $\omega_1, \omega_2 \in [\![\alpha]\!]$, then $\omega_1 \leq_\Psi \omega_2 \Leftrightarrow \omega_1 \leq_{\Psi * \alpha} \omega_2$.
(IR2^{rel})	If $\omega_1, \omega_2 \in [\![\neg\alpha]\!]$, then $\omega_1 \leq_\Psi \omega_2 \Leftrightarrow \omega_1 \leq_{\Psi * \alpha} \omega_2$.
(IR3^{rel})	If $\omega_1 \in [\![\alpha]\!]$ and $\omega_2 \in [\![\neg\alpha]\!]$, then $\omega_1 <_\Psi \omega_2 \Rightarrow \omega_1 <_{\Psi * \alpha} \omega_2$.
(IR4^{rel})	If $\omega_1 \in [\![\alpha]\!]$ and $\omega_2 \in [\![\neg\alpha]\!]$, then $\omega_1 \leq_\Psi \omega_2 \Rightarrow \omega_1 \leq_{\Psi * \alpha} \omega_2$.
	Revision strategies (see p. 274f)
(IR$_{\mathrm{min}}^{\mathrm{cond}}$)	If $\Psi * \alpha \models \neg\beta$, then $\Psi * \alpha \models (\gamma \mid \beta) \Leftrightarrow \Psi \models (\gamma \mid \beta)$.
(IR$_{\mathrm{min}}$)	If $\Psi * \alpha \models \neg\beta$, then $\mathrm{Bel}(\Psi * \alpha * \beta) = \mathrm{Bel}(\Psi * \beta)$.
(IR$_{\mathrm{min}}^{\mathrm{rel}}$))	If $\omega_1, \omega_2 \notin [\![\Psi * \alpha]\!]$, then $\omega_1 \leq_\Psi \omega_2 \Leftrightarrow \omega_1 \leq_{\Psi * \alpha} \omega_2$.
(IR$_{\mathrm{ind}}$)	If $\Psi * \beta \not\models \neg\alpha$, then $\Psi * \alpha * \beta \models \alpha$.
(IR$_{\mathrm{ind}}^{\mathrm{cond}}$)	If $\Psi * \beta \not\models \neg\alpha$, then $\Psi * \alpha \models (\alpha \mid \beta)$.
(IR$_{\mathrm{ind}}^{\mathrm{rel}}$)	If $\omega_1 \in [\![\alpha]\!]$ and $\omega_2 \in [\![\neg\alpha]\!]$, then $\omega_1 \leq_\Psi \omega_2 \Rightarrow \omega_1 <_{\Psi * \alpha} \omega_2$.
(IR$_{\mathrm{lex}}$)	If $\beta \not\models \neg\alpha$, then $\Psi * \alpha * \beta \models \alpha$.
(IR$_{\mathrm{lex}}^{\mathrm{cond}}$)	If $\Psi * \beta \not\models \neg\alpha$, then $\Psi * \alpha \models (\alpha \mid \beta)$.
(IR$_{\mathrm{lex}}^{\mathrm{rel}}$)	If $\omega_1 \in [\![\alpha]\!]$ and $\omega_2 \in [\![\neg\alpha]\!]$, then $\omega_1 <_{\Psi * \alpha} \omega_2$.

Postulates for Contraction

AGM contraction postulates (see p. 28)

(AGM÷1)	$K \div \alpha \subseteq K$.
(AGM÷2)	$\alpha \notin K \div \alpha$.
(AGM÷3)	If $\alpha \notin K$, then $K \div \alpha = K$.
(AGM÷4)	If $\alpha \equiv \beta$, then $K \div \alpha = K \div \beta$.
(AGM÷5)	$K \subseteq (K \div \alpha) + \alpha$.
(AGM÷6)	$(K \div \alpha) \cap (K \div \beta) \subseteq K \div (\alpha \wedge \beta)$.
(AGM÷7)	If $\alpha \notin K \div (\alpha \wedge \beta)$, then $K \div (\alpha \wedge \beta) \subseteq K \div \alpha$.

Contraction postulates for propositional logic (see p. 31)

(CKM1)	$\varphi \models \varphi \div \alpha$.
(CKM2)	If $\varphi \not\models \alpha$, then $\varphi \div \alpha \models \varphi$.
(CKM3)	If $\varphi \div \alpha \models \alpha$, then $\alpha \equiv \top$.
(CKM4)	$(\varphi \div \alpha) \wedge \alpha \models \varphi$.
(CKM5)	If $\varphi \equiv \psi$ and $\alpha \equiv \beta$, then $\varphi \div \alpha \equiv \psi \div \beta$.
(CKM6)	$\varphi \div (\alpha \wedge \beta) \models (\varphi \div \alpha) \vee (\varphi \div \beta)$.
(CKM7)	If $\varphi \div (\alpha \wedge \beta) \not\models \alpha$, then $\varphi \div \alpha \models \varphi \div (\alpha \wedge \beta)$.

Contraction postulates for epistemic states (see p. 217)

(C1)	$\mathrm{Bel}(\Psi \div \alpha) \subseteq \mathrm{Bel}(\Psi)$.
(C2)	If $\alpha \notin \mathrm{Bel}(\Psi)$, then $\mathrm{Bel}(\Psi) \subseteq \mathrm{Bel}(\Psi \div \alpha)$.
(C3)	If $\alpha \not\equiv \top$, then $\alpha \notin \mathrm{Bel}(\Psi \div \alpha)$.
(C4)	$\mathrm{Bel}(\Psi) \subseteq \mathrm{Bel}(\Psi \div \alpha) + \alpha$.
(C5)	If $\alpha \equiv \beta$, then $\mathrm{Bel}(\Psi \div \alpha) = \mathrm{Bel}(\Psi \div \beta)$.
(C6)	$\mathrm{Bel}(\Psi \div \alpha) \cap \mathrm{Bel}(\Psi \div \beta) \subseteq \mathrm{Bel}(\Psi \div (\alpha \wedge \beta))$.
(C7)	If $\beta \notin \mathrm{Bel}(\Psi \div (\alpha \wedge \beta))$, then $\mathrm{Bel}(\Psi \div (\alpha \wedge \beta)) \subseteq \mathrm{Bel}(\Psi \div \beta)$.
(Invariance)	If $\neg \alpha \wedge \beta \equiv \bot$, then $\mathrm{Bel}(\Psi) =_\beta \mathrm{Bel}(\Psi \div \alpha)$. (p. 230)

Iteration Postulates for Contraction

Syntactic Darwiche-Pearl postulates as contraction postulates (see p. 236f)

(IC1$_{\mathrm{dca}}$)	If $\beta \models \alpha$, then $\Psi \div \alpha \div \beta \models \gamma \Leftrightarrow \Psi \div \beta \models \gamma$.
(IC2$_{\mathrm{dca}}$)	If $\beta \models \neg\alpha$, then $\Psi \div \alpha \div \beta \models \gamma \Leftrightarrow \Psi \div \beta \models \gamma$.
(IC3$_{\mathrm{dca}}$)	If $\Psi \div \beta \models \alpha$, then $\Psi \div \alpha \div \beta \models \alpha$.
(IC4$_{\mathrm{dca}}$)	If $\Psi \div \alpha \div \beta \models \neg\alpha$, then $\Psi \div \beta \models \neg\alpha$.
(IC1$_{\mathrm{dca}}^{\mathrm{cond}}$)	If $\beta \models \alpha$, then $\Psi \div \alpha \models [\gamma\,|\,\beta] \Leftrightarrow \Psi \models [\gamma\,|\,\beta]$.
(IC2$_{\mathrm{dca}}^{\mathrm{cond}}$)	If $\beta \models \neg\alpha$, then $\Psi \div \alpha \models [\gamma\,|\,\beta] \Leftrightarrow \Psi \models [\gamma\,|\,\beta]$.
(IC3$_{\mathrm{dca}}^{\mathrm{cond}}$)	If $\Psi \models [\alpha\,|\,\beta]$, then $\Psi \div \alpha \models [\alpha\,|\,\beta]$.
(IC4$_{\mathrm{dca}}^{\mathrm{cond}}$)	If $\Psi \div \alpha \models [\neg\alpha\,|\,\beta]$, then $\Psi \models [\neg\alpha\,|\,\beta]$.
(IC4$_{\mathrm{dca}}^{\mathrm{rel}}$)	If $\omega_1 \in [\![\neg\alpha]\!]$, $\omega_2 \in [\![\alpha]\!]$ and $[\![\Psi]\!] \subseteq [\![\neg\alpha]\!]$, then $\omega_2 \leq_\Psi \omega_1 \Rightarrow \omega_2 \leq_{\Psi \div \alpha} \omega_1$

Contraction analogues to (IR1)–(IR4) (see p. 242ff)

(IC1$_{\mathrm{ca}}^{\mathrm{cond}}$)	If $\neg\alpha \models \beta$, then $\Psi \div \alpha \models [\gamma\,|\,\beta] \Leftrightarrow \Psi \models [\gamma\,|\,\beta]$.
(IC2$_{\mathrm{ca}}^{\mathrm{cond}}$)	If $\alpha \models \beta$, then $\Psi \div \alpha \models [\gamma\,|\,\beta] \Leftrightarrow \Psi \models [\gamma\,|\,\beta]$.
(IC3$_{\mathrm{ca}}^{\mathrm{cond}}$)	If $\Psi \models [\neg\alpha\,|\,\beta]$, then $\Psi \div \alpha \models [\neg\alpha\,|\,\beta]$
(IC4$_{\mathrm{ca}}^{\mathrm{cond}}$)	If $\Psi \div \alpha \models [\alpha\,|\,\beta]$, then $\Psi \models [\alpha\,|\,\beta]$
(IC1$_{\Leftarrow}^{\mathrm{cond}}$)	If $\neg\alpha \models \beta$, then $\Psi \div \alpha \models [\gamma\,|\,\beta] \Leftarrow \Psi \models [\gamma\,|\,\beta]$.
(IC2$_{\Leftarrow}^{\mathrm{cond}}$)	If $\alpha \models \beta$, then $\Psi \div \alpha \models [\gamma\,|\,\beta] \Leftarrow \Psi \models [\gamma\,|\,\beta]$.
(IC1$_{\Rightarrow}^{\mathrm{cond}}$)	If $\neg\alpha \models \beta$, then $\Psi \div \alpha \models [\gamma\,|\,\beta] \Rightarrow \Psi \models [\gamma\,|\,\beta]$
(IC1$_{\Rightarrow}^{\mathrm{rel}}$)	If $\omega_1, \omega_2 \in [\![\alpha]\!]$, then $\omega_1 \leq_\Psi \omega_2 \Rightarrow \omega_1 \leq_{\Psi \div \alpha} \omega_2$
(IC2$_{\Rightarrow}^{\mathrm{cond}}$)	If $\alpha \models \beta$, then $\Psi \div \alpha \models [\gamma\,|\,\beta] \Rightarrow \Psi \models [\gamma\,|\,\beta]$
(IC2$_{\Rightarrow}^{\mathrm{rel}}$)	If $\omega_1, \omega_2 \in [\![\neg\alpha]\!]$, then $\omega_1 \leq_\Psi \omega_2 \Rightarrow \omega_1 \leq_{\Psi \div \alpha} \omega_2$
(IC3$_{\mathrm{ca}}$)	If $\Psi \div \beta \models \neg\alpha$, then $\Psi \div \alpha \div \beta \models \neg\alpha$.
(IC3$_{\mathrm{ca}}^{\mathrm{rel}}$)	If $\omega_1 \in [\![\neg\alpha]\!]$, $\omega_2 \in [\![\alpha]\!]$ and $[\![\Psi]\!] \subseteq [\![\neg\alpha]\!]$, then $\omega_1 <_\Psi \omega_2 \Rightarrow \omega_1 <_{\Psi \div \alpha} \omega_2$.
(IC4$_{\mathrm{dca\text{-}c}}^{\mathrm{rel}}$)	If $\omega_1 \in [\![\neg\alpha]\!]$, $\omega_2 \in [\![\alpha]\!]$ and $[\![\Psi]\!] \subseteq [\![\neg\alpha]\!]$, then $\omega_1 <_{\Psi \div \alpha} \omega_2 \Rightarrow \omega_1 <_\Psi \omega_2$.
(IC4$_{\mathrm{weak}}$)	If $\Psi \models \neg\alpha$ and $\Psi \div \beta \not\models \neg\alpha \to \beta$, then $\Psi \div \alpha \div \beta \not\models \neg\alpha \to \beta$.
(IC4$_{\mathrm{weak}}^{\mathrm{rel}}$)	If $\omega_1 \in [\![\neg\alpha]\!]$, $\omega_2 \in [\![\alpha]\!]$ and $[\![\Psi]\!] \subseteq [\![\neg\alpha]\!]$, then $\omega_1 \leq_\Psi \omega_2 \Rightarrow \omega_1 \leq_{\Psi \div \alpha} \omega_2$.
(IC4$_{\mathrm{weak}}^{\mathrm{cond}}$)	If $\Psi \models \neg\alpha$ and $\Psi \not\models [\neg\alpha{\to}\beta\,|\,\beta]$, then $\Psi \div \alpha \not\models [\neg\alpha{\to}\beta\,|\,\beta]$.

	Contraction analogues to $(\text{IR1}^{\text{rel}})$–$(\text{IR4}^{\text{rel}})$ (see p. 253ff)
$(\text{IC1}^{\text{rel}})$	If $\omega_1, \omega_2 \in [\![\alpha]\!]$, then $\omega_1 \leq_\Psi \omega_2 \Leftrightarrow \omega_1 \leq_{\Psi \div \alpha} \omega_2$.
$(\text{IC2}^{\text{rel}})$	If $\omega_1, \omega_2 \in [\![\neg\alpha]\!]$, then $\omega_1 \leq_\Psi \omega_2 \Leftrightarrow \omega_1 \leq_{\Psi \div \alpha} \omega_2$.
$(\text{IC3}^{\text{rel}})$	If $\omega_1 \in [\![\neg\alpha]\!]$ and $\omega_2 \in [\![\alpha]\!]$, then $\omega_1 <_\Psi \omega_2 \Rightarrow$ $\omega_1 <_{\Psi \div \alpha} \omega_2$.
$(\text{IC4}^{\text{rel}})$	If $\omega_1 \in [\![\neg\alpha]\!]$ and $\omega_2 \in [\![\alpha]\!]$, then $\omega_1 \leq_\Psi \omega_2 \Rightarrow$ $\omega_1 \leq_{\Psi \div \alpha} \omega_2$.
$(\text{IC1}_{\text{KPP}})$	If $\neg\alpha \models \gamma$, then $\text{Bel}(\Psi \div \alpha) \subseteq \text{Bel}(\Psi \div (\alpha \vee \beta)) \Leftrightarrow \text{Bel}(\Psi \div \gamma \div \alpha) \subseteq \text{Bel}(\Psi \div \gamma \div (\alpha \vee \beta))$.
$(\text{IC2}_{\text{KPP}})$	If $\gamma \models \alpha$, then $\text{Bel}(\Psi \div \alpha) \subseteq \text{Bel}(\Psi \div (\alpha \vee \beta)) \Leftrightarrow \text{Bel}(\Psi \div \gamma \div \alpha) \subseteq \text{Bel}(\Psi \div \gamma \div (\alpha \vee \beta))$.
$(\text{IC3}_{\text{KPP}})$	If $\neg\beta \models \gamma$, then $\text{Bel}(\Psi \div \gamma \div \alpha) \subseteq \text{Bel}(\Psi \div \gamma \div (\alpha \vee \beta)) \Rightarrow \text{Bel}(\Psi \div \alpha) \subseteq \text{Bel}(\Psi \div (\alpha \vee \beta))$.
$(\text{IC4}_{\text{KPP}})$	If $\gamma \models \beta$, then $\text{Bel}(\Psi \div \gamma \div \alpha) \subseteq \text{Bel}(\Psi \div \gamma \div (\alpha \vee \beta)) \Rightarrow \text{Bel}(\Psi \div \alpha) \subseteq \text{Bel}(\Psi \div (\alpha \vee \beta))$.
(IC1)	If $\neg\alpha \models \beta$, then $\text{Bel}(\Psi \div \alpha \div \beta) =_\alpha \text{Bel}(\Psi \div \beta)$.
$(\text{IC1}^{\text{cond}})$	If $\neg\alpha \models \beta$, then $\Psi \div \alpha \models [\alpha \to \gamma \,|\, \beta] \Leftrightarrow \Psi \models [\alpha \to \gamma \,|\, \beta]$.
(IC2)	If $\alpha \models \beta$, then $\text{Bel}(\Psi \div \alpha \div \beta) =_{\neg\beta} \text{Bel}(\Psi \div \beta)$.
$(\text{IC2}^{\text{cond}})$	If $\alpha \models \beta$, then $\Psi \div \alpha \models [\neg\beta \to \gamma \,|\, \beta] \Leftrightarrow \Psi \models [\neg\beta \to \gamma \,|\, \beta]$.
$(\text{IC2}')$	If $\alpha \models \beta$, then $\text{Bel}(\Psi \div \alpha \div \beta) =_{\neg\alpha} \text{Bel}(\Psi \div \beta)$.
(IC3)	If $\gamma \models \beta$, then $\Psi \div \beta \models \alpha \to \gamma \Rightarrow \Psi \div \alpha \div \beta \models \alpha \to \gamma$.
$(\text{IC3}^{\text{cond}})$	If $\gamma \models \beta$, then $\Psi \models [\alpha \to \gamma \,|\, \beta] \Rightarrow \Psi \div \alpha \models [\alpha \to \gamma \,|\, \beta]$.
(IC4)	If $\gamma \models \beta$, then $\Psi \div \alpha \div \beta \models \neg\alpha \to \gamma \Rightarrow \Psi \div \beta \models \neg\alpha \to \gamma$.
$(\text{IC4}^{\text{cond}})$	If $\gamma \models \beta$, then $\Psi \div \alpha \models [\neg\alpha \to \gamma \,|\, \beta] \Rightarrow \Psi \models [\neg\alpha \to \gamma \,|\, \beta]$.
$(\text{IC3}_{\text{alt}})$	If $\neg\alpha \models \gamma$, then $\Psi \div \beta \models \gamma$ implies $\Psi \div \alpha \div \beta \models \gamma$.
$(\text{IC3}^{\text{cond}}_{\text{alt}})$	If $\neg\alpha \models \gamma$, then $\Psi \models [\gamma \,|\, \beta]$ implies $\Psi \div \alpha \models [\gamma \,|\, \beta]$.
$(\text{IC3}^{\text{rel}}_{\text{alt}})$	If $\omega_1 \in \Omega$ and $\omega_2 \in [\![\alpha]\!]$, then $\omega_1 <_\Psi \omega_2 \Rightarrow \omega_1 <_{\Psi \div \alpha} \omega_2$. (p. 278)
$(\text{IC4}_{\text{alt}})$	If $\alpha \models \gamma$, then $\Psi \div \alpha \div \beta \models \gamma$ implies $\Psi \div \beta \models \gamma$.
$(\text{IC4}^{\text{cond}}_{\text{alt}})$	If $\alpha \models \gamma$, then $\Psi \div \alpha \models [\gamma \,|\, \beta]$ implies $\Psi \models [\gamma \,|\, \beta]$.
$(\text{IC4}^{\text{rel}}_{\text{alt}})$	If $\omega_1 \in [\![\neg\alpha]\!]$ and $\omega_2 \in \Omega$, then $\omega_1 \leq_\Psi \omega_2 \Rightarrow \omega_1 \leq_{\Psi \div \alpha} \omega_2$. (p. 278)

	Contraction strategies (see p. 281ff)
$(\mathrm{IC_{ind}})$	If $\neg\alpha \models \gamma$ and $\Psi \div \beta \not\models \neg\alpha \to \beta$, then $\Psi \div \alpha \models \gamma \Rightarrow$ $\Psi \div \alpha \div \beta \models \gamma$.
$(\mathrm{IC_{ind}^{cond}})$	If $\neg\alpha \models \gamma$ and $\Psi \not\models [\neg\alpha \to \beta \,|\, \beta]$, then $\Psi \models [\gamma \,|\, \alpha] \Rightarrow \Psi \div \alpha \models [\gamma \,|\, \beta]$.
$(\mathrm{IC_{ind}^{rel}})$	If $\omega_1 \in [\![\neg\alpha]\!]$ and $\omega_2 \in [\![\alpha]\!] \setminus [\![\Psi]\!]$, then $\omega_1 \leq_\Psi \omega_2 \Rightarrow$ $\omega_1 <_{\Psi\div\alpha} \omega_2$.
$(\mathrm{IC_{nc}})$	If $\Psi \div \alpha \models \beta$, then $\mathrm{Bel}(\Psi \div \alpha \div \beta) \equiv_{\neg\beta} \mathrm{Bel}(\Psi \div \beta)$.
$(\mathrm{IC_{nc}^{cond}})$	If $\Psi \div \alpha \models \beta$, then $\Psi \div \alpha \models [\neg\beta \to \gamma \,|\, \beta]$ if and only if $\Psi \models [\neg\beta \to \gamma \,|\, \beta]$.
$(\mathrm{IC_{nc}^{rel}})$	If $\omega_1, \omega_2 \notin [\![\Psi \div \alpha]\!]$, then $\omega_1 \leq_\Psi \omega_2 \Leftrightarrow \omega_1 \leq_{\Psi\div\alpha} \omega_2$.
(Insertion)	If $\beta \in \mathrm{Bel}(\Psi \div \alpha)$, then $\mathrm{Bel}(\Psi \div \alpha \div \beta) = \mathrm{Bel}(\Psi \div \alpha) \cap \mathrm{Bel}(\Psi \div \beta)$.
$(\mathrm{IC_{mc}})$	If $\neg\alpha \models \gamma$ and $\alpha \vee \beta \not\equiv \top$, then $\Psi \div \alpha \models \gamma$ implies $\Psi \div \alpha \div \beta \models \gamma$.
$(\mathrm{IC_{mc}^{cond}})$	If $\neg\alpha \models \gamma$ and $\alpha \vee \beta \not\equiv \top$, then $\Psi \models [\gamma \,|\, \alpha]$ implies $\Psi \div \alpha \models [\gamma \,|\, \beta]$.
$(\mathrm{IC_{mc}^{rel}})$	If $\omega_1 \in [\![\neg\alpha]\!]$, $\omega_2 \in [\![\alpha]\!]$ and $\omega_2 \notin [\![\Psi \div \alpha]\!]$, then $\omega_1 <_{\Psi\div\alpha} \omega_2$.
$(\mathrm{IC_{gnc}})$	If $\alpha \notin \mathrm{Bel}(\Psi)$, then $\Psi \div \beta \models \gamma \Leftrightarrow \Psi \div \alpha \div \beta \models \gamma$.
$(\mathrm{IC_{gnc}^{cond}})$	If $\alpha \notin \mathrm{Bel}(\Psi)$, then $\Psi \models [\gamma \,|\, \beta] \Leftrightarrow \Psi \div \alpha \models [\gamma \,|\, \beta]$.
$(\mathrm{IC_{gnc}^{rel}})$	If $[\![\Psi]\!] \not\subseteq [\![\alpha]\!]$, then $\omega_1 \leq_\Psi \omega_2 \Leftrightarrow \omega_1 \leq_{\Psi\div\alpha} \omega_2$.
$(\mathrm{IC_{gmc}})$	If $\neg\alpha \not\models \beta$, then $\Psi \models \alpha \wedge \beta \Rightarrow \Psi \div \alpha \div \beta \models \alpha \to \beta$.
$(\mathrm{IC_{gmc}^{cond}})$	If $\neg\alpha \not\models \beta$, then $\Psi \models \alpha \wedge \beta \Rightarrow \Psi \div \alpha \models [\alpha \to \beta \,|\, \beta]$.
$(\mathrm{IC_{gmc}^{rel}})$	If $\omega_1 \in [\![\neg\alpha]\!]$, $\omega_2 \in [\![\alpha]\!] \setminus [\![\Psi]\!]$ and $[\![\Psi]\!] \subseteq [\![\alpha]\!]$, then $\omega_1 <_{\Psi\div\alpha} \omega_2$.
$(\mathrm{IC_{gic}})$	If $\Psi \models \alpha$ and $\Psi \div \alpha \models \alpha \to \beta$, then $\Psi \div \beta \not\models \alpha \Rightarrow$ $\Psi \div \alpha \div \beta \models \alpha \to \beta$.
$(\mathrm{IC_{gic}^{cond}})$	If $\Psi \models \alpha$ and $\Psi \models [\alpha \to \beta \,|\, \alpha]$, then $\Psi \not\models [\alpha \,|\, \beta] \Rightarrow \Psi \div \alpha \models [\alpha \to \beta \,|\, \beta]$.
$(\mathrm{IC_{gic}^{rel}})$	If $\omega_1 \in [\![\neg\alpha]\!]$, $\omega_2 \in [\![\alpha]\!] \setminus [\![\Psi]\!]$ and $[\![\Psi]\!] \subseteq [\![\alpha]\!]$, then $\omega_1 \leq_\Psi \omega_2 \Rightarrow \omega_1 <_{\Psi\div\alpha} \omega_2$.

Information on abbreviations for postulates

AGM	Alchourrón, Gärdenfors, and Makinson
alt	*alternative*
ca	*contraction analogue*
C	*contraction* (for epistemic states)
CKM	Caridroit, Konieczny, and Marquis
CL	*credibility-limited* revision
cond	*conditional*
dca	*direct contraction analogue*
DL	*dynamic-limited* revision
G	*generalized* revision postulate (to base logics)
GCL	*generalized credibility-limited* revision
gic	*gentle independence* principle for *contraction*
gmc	*gentle moderate contraction*
gnc	*gentle natural contraction*
IC	*iterated contraction*
ind	*independence* principle
IR	*iterated revision*
KM	Katsuno and Mendelzon
KPP	Konieczny and Pino Pérez
lex	*lexicographic* revision/contraction
mc	*moderate contraction*
min	*minimal*
nc	*natural contraction*
R	*revision* (for epistemic states)
rel	*relational*
weak	*weakening* of another postulate

Index